MERCEDES-BENZ C 111
THE DEFINITIVE HISTORY OF THE MYSTERIOUS SUPERCAR THAT NEVER WAS

Gerhard Heidbrink • Joachim Hack

4880 Lower Valley Road • Atglen, PA 19310

Other Schiffer Books on Related Subjects:

Mercedes-Benz Supercars: From 1901 to Today, Thomas Wirth,
    ISBN 978-0-7643-4090-1
The Mercedes-Benz G-Class: The Complete History of an Off-Road Classic, Jörg Sand,
    ISBN 978-0-7643-6263-7
McLaren: The Road Cars, 2010–2024, Kyle Fortune,
    ISBN 978-0-7643-6731-1

Copyright ©2025 by Schiffer Publishing Ltd.

Originally published as *Mercedes-Benz C 111: Design-Ikone, Traumsportswagen und Rekordjäger* by Motorbuch Verlag, Stuttgart, ©2023
Translated from the German.

Library of Congress Control Number: 2024941568

All rights reserved. No part of this work may be reproduced or used in any form or by any means—graphic, electronic, or mechanical, including photocopying or information storage and retrieval systems—without written permission from the publisher.

The scanning, uploading, and distribution of this book or any part thereof via the Internet or any other means without the permission of the publisher is illegal and punishable by law. Please purchase only authorized editions and do not participate in or encourage the electronic piracy of copyrighted materials.

"Schiffer," "Schiffer Publishing, Ltd.," and the pen and inkwell logo are registered trademarks of Schiffer Publishing, Ltd.

Cover design by Jack Chappell
Design by Lukas Kretzschmar
Type set in Vitesse / Roboto
ISBN: 978-0-7643-6900-1
Printed in China

Published by Schiffer Publishing, Ltd.
4880 Lower Valley Road
Atglen, PA 19310
Phone: (610) 593-1777; Fax: (610) 593-2002
Email: Info@schifferbooks.com
Web: www.schifferbooks.com

For our complete selection of fine books on this and related subjects, please visit our website at www.schifferbooks.com. You may also write for a free catalog.

Schiffer Publishing's titles are available at special discounts for bulk purchases for sales promotions or premiums. Special editions, including personalized covers, corporate imprints, and excerpts, can be created in large quantities for special needs. For more information, contact the publisher.

We are always looking for people to write books on new and related subjects. If you have an idea for a book, please contact us at proposals@schifferbooks.com.

Contents

New Promise:
The Wankel Engine 10

Much Light and Much Shadow:
The Development History 14

Cardinal Question:
What to Do with the Wankel Engine? 25

The Final Chord:
Changed Framework 27

Dream Sports Car and Laboratory on Wheels: The C 111 32

Business Exercises:
The Roots of the C 111 33

Renewed Departure:
The C 101 Project 44

Concretization:
Concept Definition of the C 101 49

Sportiness and Fascination:
The Design Development 57

Innovative Methods:
Computer-Aided Development 72

Odd Testing Platform:
The Sledge 76

Metamorphosis:
From Sledge to Super Sports Car 87

From the Stock Exchange to the Media:
The C 101 in Public 111

New Generation:
The C 111-II 153

Protracted Decision:
The Question of Series Production 200

New Technologies: The C 111
with Plastic Floor Assembly 246

Aiming for Maximum Performance:
The C 111 as a Record-Setting Car 270

From Mobile Laboratory to Record Hunter:
The C 111-II D 271

With Aerodynamics to Success:
The C 111-III 294

New Power Unit, Optimized Aerodynamics:
The C 111-IV 365

Unfinished Vision:
The C 111-V 386

Lifelines:
Biographies of All C 111s Ever Built 402

Unbroken Fascination:
The C 111 Today 424

Future and Tradition:
The Vision One-Eleven 474

The Exterior:
One-Bow Design in Its Most Athletic Form 482

The Interior Design:
First Sports Car Interior with a Lounge Concept ... 490

Fusion of Analog and Digital:
UI/UX with Retro-Futuristic Pixel Look 501

Exclusive Products from the Mercedes-Benz Collection:
The "LIMITED EDITION 1 OF 111" 504

Innovative Electric Power Train:
High-Performance Axial-Flux Motor and All-New
Battery Technology 507

In the Spotlight:
World Premiere in Carlsbad, California 510

Appendix:
Data, Codes, and Sources 512

Dedication

The authors and project instigator dedicate this book to
- all those who conceived and implemented the extraordinary C 101 and Vision One-Eleven projects in all their facets and documented the results;
- the Classic Division of Mercedes-Benz, which keeps the historic vehicles covered in this book alive and preserves information, reports, photos, and films for posterity; and
- their wives, Constanze Heidbrink, Regina Kraus, and Dina Kalbhenn, who have shown a great deal of patience and understanding over a long period of time while this book was being written.

The Authors and Project Instigator

Gerhard Heidbrink

held various positions at Mercedes-Benz Classic from 1991 to 2020. He has been fascinated by the C 111 since his childhood, when he found the motorized Schuco model of this vehicle under the Christmas tree.

Joachim Hack

understood early on how to combine his passion for books and for cars. He has always had a special love for those brands and models that have left a special mark on automotive chronicle through their unique history and tradition—a criterion that the C 111 without a doubt effortlessly fulfills.

Photo Credits

All illustrations © **Mercedes-Benz AG**, with the following exceptions:
© **MOTORWORLD Group:** p. 9 left
© **Audi AG:** p. 11 top
© **Gretel, Dirk, and Jörg Bensinger family:** p. 12
© **Wolfgang Kalbhenn:** p. 21 bottom right
© **Revs Institute:** pp. 85 bottom, 93 top, 101 bottom, 126 bottom, 127 top, 189 top (Kurt Wörner Archive @ Revs Institute); pp. 96, 108 right, 125 right, 126 top, 127 bottom, 128, 130, 131 (Karl Ludvigsen Archive @ Revs Institute)
© **BASF Corporate History, Ludwigshafen am Rhein:** p. 91 bottom left
© **Archive Peter Kurze/Paul Botzenhardt:** pp. 95, 102, 108 left, 109 top, 121
© **Autocar:** p. 109 bottom
© **Axel Springer Syndication/Peter J. Glodschey:** pp. 113, 212
© **Auto Zeitung:** pp. 114, 239 top, 354 top, 357 top
© **Motor Presse Stuttgart:** pp. 115, 117 top, 118 top, 222, 229, 308, 356 top, 380 bottom
© **Spiegel-Verlag:** p. 116
© **hobby/Ehapa Verlag:** pp. 117 center and bottom, 178, 239 center and bottom
© **Abendzeitung München:** p. 118 bottom
© **Karl Lemberger:** p. 198 top
© **Playboy Germany:** p. 240
© **Shell Historical Heritage & Archive, The Hague:** p. 242 top
© **Bayer AG, Corporate History & Archives:** p. 246 bottom
© **Opel Automobile GmbH:** p. 271
© **Auto & Traktor Museum Uhldingen:** p. 275
© **NASA:** p. 276
© **Deutsche Lufthansa AG:** p. 292 bottom
© **Jörg Maschke:** p. 354 bottom
© **Rüdiger Faul:** pp. 373, 379, 382
© **Michelin:** p. 380 top
© **He&Me:** p. 427
© **Régis Krol:** p. 430 top
© **Royce Rumsey:** pp. 439, 440
© **Christof Vieweg:** p. 443
© **Philipp Deppe:** pp. 444, 445 top
© **Philipp Rupprecht:** pp. 446–447
© **Petersen Automotive Museum:** pp. 454 bottom, 455, 456 top

Foreword by Chief Design Officer Gorden Wagener

Dear Design Lovers

Every designer strives to create something new and unique and, in so doing, make a statement that resonates long into the future. But whether or not a designer's work actually becomes an icon becomes apparent only with the passage of time. However, it's icons that count. They define luxury and embody specific characteristics. They are original and unmistakable, pursue a clear aim, are based on a powerful idea, and, therefore, can also be polarizing. Products, brands, people, or also a style can be iconic.

An icon must, by definition, be beautiful and, moreover, timeless. It doesn't just capture and surpass the current trends or zeitgeist, it sets them—and it's not a fashion or fad. It would literally go out of fashion before it had a chance to achieve icon status.

Our goal at Mercedes-Benz is not to do styling—our goal is to create icons. To me, that makes the difference between mainstream design and luxury. Design icons such as the 300 SL and C 111 models—both with gullwing doors—are part of our DNA.

These legendary vehicles were major inspirations for the iconic design of the Mercedes-Benz Vision One-Eleven. This is beauty and the extraordinary united in one vision of the future. Our all-electric vision show car is the modern-day interpretation of the C 111, which was avant-garde at the time. Much like its historic predecessor, the Vision One-Eleven combines stunning design with groundbreaking powertrain technology that explores new avenues for the future of sporting performance.

The show car's element of surprise comes from its exceptionally clean, purist and, at the same time, extremely muscular proportions. This iconic clarity is also reflected in the interior. The equally sensual but minimalist design language stands for ICONIC LUXURY by Mercedes-Benz.

Immerse yourself in the fascinating world of Mercedes-Benz design and gain an impression of our work, which aims to continually realize the vision of the world's most desirable automobiles.

Prof Dr. h.c. Gorden Wagener

Chief Design Officer
Mercedes-Benz Group AG

Preface by the Editor

Dear Readers

When Mercedes-Benz Classic put a C 111 back on the road in July 2014 for the first time in many years, the reaction from the media and the public was overwhelming. The dream sports car presented forty-five years earlier was once again talked about everywhere and omnipresent in the automotive trade publications.

The comprehensive special exhibition that the Mercedes-Benz Museum dedicated to the C 111 from April to November 2015 also helped keep the fascination of this brand icon alive. These activities prompted former employees of the company to take the initiative of documenting the development history of the C 111 in all its facets and thus preserving it for posterity.

Mercedes-Benz Classic offered the most favorable conditions for this project, not only with its rich archive holdings, but also with its extensive vehicle collection, which preserves all C 111s that still exist today, and its workshop, which has been providing technical support for the vehicles for many years.

This is how, after extensive research and analysis, this book came into being, which traces the origins and development of the fascinating sports car in a way that is as rich in detail as it is vivid. The Mercedes-Benz Vision One-Eleven, a progressive interpretation of the brand icon presented in June 2023, impressively demonstrates just how much the C 111 is still present in people's minds today. This became evident once again in August 2024, when Mercedes-Benz Heritage presented a roadworthy C 111 with an original four-cylinder Wankel engine from 1970 to the public and the media for the first time after a break of over 21 years.

Let us take you on a trip into the future and back to the 1960s and 1970s. With the help of authentic archival sources and numerous original quotes, experience the history of a unique sports car whose charisma remains unbroken to this day.

I hope you'll enjoy a stimulating read.

Alexandra Süß
Head of Mercedes-Benz Classic

Introduction

When rumors of a Mercedes-Benz Wankel sports car hit the press in March 1969, the public and experts were equally electrified. With the press presentation and the trade fair premiere in September 1969, the C 111 became the object of desire and remained the focus of interest in the period that followed. Prospective buyers sent blank checks, and in Untertürkheim, the question of a possible series production was controversially discussed by the decision-makers. The dream sports car is still regarded as an outstanding icon of the Mercedes-Benz brand like hardly any other model. It is all the more astonishing that the development of the C 111 has not yet been comprehensively documented in any book publication, whereas several dozen books have been published on the 300 SL, for example, another important brand icon.

This statement is in no way intended to diminish the merits of the existing publications on the C 111. First and foremost, there is the very good account by Karl E. Ludvigsen, originally published in *Automobile Quarterly* in spring 1970 and later integrated with additions into the standard work *Mercedes-Benz Racing and Sports Cars*. The book, published by Paul Frère and Julius Weitmann in 1981, is well worth reading and richly illustrated and also describes the development from the beginning but focuses on the history of the record car variants of the C 111.

The continuing media interest in the C 111 to this day and the limited availability of detailed and comprehensive information ultimately led to this book. From the outset, the aim of this publication was to produce a comprehensive documentation in which the documents available in the Mercedes-Benz Classic archives are linked with the memories and explanations of those involved in the project at the time and in this combination reveal the proverbial common thread.

With its depth of detail, the documentation follows only one goal: to meticulously trace the development of the C 111 and present the overall picture on this basis. It would have been easy to include numerous other details, especially from construction, testing, engine development, and aerodynamics—but in the interests of a consumable presentation, these were left out, as were footnotes and more detailed source attributions. For reasons of comprehensibility and transparency, however, a very large proportion of the original sources cited are specifically named. The numerous quotations from the archived minutes and reports as well as the relevant press articles are intended to bring the story to life and to transport you, dear readers, to that time.

We have deliberately refrained from evaluating the development described, even if this is reflected to some extent in the summary introduction to the development of the Wankel engine. From today's perspective, it may seem difficult to understand why a company like Daimler-Benz, with its traditionally very results-oriented, stringent, and successful approach, struggled for a long time to make a clear decision on the question of a series production of the C 111. This was undoubtedly due to the complex constraints: on the one hand, the question of how much effort the further development of the Wankel engine would require with regard to the stability to be achieved—the fuel consumption and the exhaust emissions remained open until the end, but on the other hand, the strongly increasing legal requirements with regard to safety and environmental issues at that time, which had to be taken into account especially for the important US market.

The work on this book has not only demanded a lot from the authors but has also given them a great deal of pleasure. If we can convey even a part of this to you, dear readers, then we see that an important goal of this book has been achieved.

As a sign of the great interest in our book, we consider the surprising fact that the first edition was already sold out four weeks after it was published by the publishing company.

We are also pleased and proud to be able to present the Mercedes-Benz Vision One-Eleven in this book—an extraordinary sports car study inspired by the C 111. We have dedicated a richly illustrated chapter to it.

Have fun browsing and reading.
    —Gerhard Heidbrink
    —Joachim Hack

Acknowledgments

A book such as this can only achieve its stated goal of comprehensive documentation if all available sources are taken into account. Numerous people and institutions have contributed to this, and the authors would like to thank them—starting with the management and staff of Mercedes-Benz Classic and Mercedes-Benz Design for the extensive support they have provided.

Dr.-Ing. Fritz Naumann, a test engineer from the very beginning of the development of the C 111, was kind enough to provide the Corporate Archives with a short documentation and a number of his own photos as early as 2009.

The designers Holger Hutzenlaub, Hans-Harald Hanson, and Jörn Petersen are to be thanked for repeatedly making valuable documents and information on the Mercedes-Benz design history, from which this book benefits greatly, available to the Corporate Archives and thus preserving them for posterity.

Important background information, which supplemented the documented files and facilitated their assessment, was provided by conversations with the protagonists and contemporary witnesses of the time. Many thanks to Dr.-Ing. h.c. Bruno Sacco, Prof. Peter Pfeiffer, Prof. Stefan Heiliger, Dipl.-Ing. Arno Jambor, Dipl.-Ing. Joachim Kaden, and Dipl.-Ing. Rüdiger Faul for their kind help and clarifying explanations.

This also applies in particular to Prof. Klaus Matthias, who tirelessly and with utmost commitment made a particularly complex facet of the C 111 history understandable in numerous long discussions: the development of the exotic-looking variant with plastic floor assembly largely unknown to the public, which is comprehensively presented in this book for the first time.

The authors owe further important information and impressions to Karl Lemberger, Manfred Dierks, Hans-Peter Hiller, Rolf Kreß, and Robert Münzmay, who were involved in the project at the time and to whom we would also like to express our sincere thanks.

Prof. Gorden Wagener, Steffen Köhl, Stefan Lamm, Hartmut Sinkwitz, Belinda Günther, and Benjamin Kuhn have kindly made their considerations transparent in the conception and design of the spectacular Vision One-Eleven.

With the provision and kind permission to reprint press articles and advertisements, Dr. Isabella Blank-Elsbree from BASF Corporate History, Ludwigshafen am Rhein; Mark Tisshaw from *Autocar;* Jan-Philipp Bahr from Axel Springer Syndication; Willi Kock from the archives of *Auto Bild;* Nils Koshofer from *Auto Zeitung,* Motor Presse Stuttgart; Jörg Rehder from Spiegel-Verlag; Astrid Götz from *Abendzeitung München*; Michael Brunnbauer from *Playboy Germany;* Rosalie van Egmond from Shell Historical Heritage & Archive, The Hague; and Anna Magdalena Pasternak from Michelin provided valuable support.

Special thanks go to Mark Vargas, Director Library and Archives, and Scott George, Curator and Vice President of the Revs Institute, for their kind, efficient, and generous provision of photographs from the Revs Library's extensive archives to enrich the visual aspect of this book. With photos by automotive journalist Karl E. Ludvigsen and photographer Kurt Wörner, which were taken at the press presentation of the C 111 at the Hockenheimring in September 1969, the Revs Library was able to close a serious documentation gap.

Additional photos were kindly provided by Liganova Horizon GmbH as well as Frederic Seemann, Erik Degen, Mario Simon, Andreas Fischer, Dominic Baumann, and Maxim Kimmerle from Mercedes-Benz Design in Sindelfingen. The same applies to Sigrid Oelze from the Bayer AG Archive, Leif Rohwedder from Opel Automobile GmbH, Silvia Georgi from the Auto & Traktor Museum Uhldingen, Luisa Schürmann from Deutsche Lufthansa AG, Horst-Dieter Görg, Uta Möller, Hilmar Giese, Igor Panitz, He&Me, and Oliver Roggenbuck.

The Gretel, Dirk, and Jörg Bensinger family as well as Peter Kurze, Karl Lemberger, Jörg Maschke, Rüdiger Faul, Régis Krol, Royce Rumsey, Christof Vieweg, Philipp Deppe, Philipp Rupprecht, and the Petersen Automotive Museum also very generously supported the project with artistic photographs that enrich the book.

Valuable advice after reviewing the manuscript was provided by Dr.-Ing. Detlef Schulze-Fehrenbach, Heinrich Heller, Matthias Knebel, Frank Mühling, Manuel König, René Olma, Ulrike Glöckler, and Philipp Zürn. With their constructive comments and suggestions, they all made a decisive contribution to ensuring that the tunnel effect familiar to many authors remained limited.

Graphic designer Lukas Kretzschmar, who is responsible for the design of the German edition, deserves credit for having cast the manuscript with its almost unmanageable flood of text and hundreds of pictures into an extremely clear and also very appealing layout. Ro Shillingford adapted it skilfully to the American version. Many thanks to both of them, and equally to Jack Chappell, who is responsible for the attractive exterior of this version of the book.

Last but not least, the authors would also like to thank Motorbuch Verlag and in particular the responsible program manager Joachim Kuch, who has shown the utmost patience in accompanying the elaborate project. The same applies to Carey Massimini and Karla Rosenbusch of Schiffer Publishing, to whom the authors also extend their sincere thanks.

We would also like to thank you, dear readers, for having received the book so kindly despite the sometimes long waiting period after its publication.

Awards

The German edition of this work received special recognition when it was awarded two coveted prizes: an honorary prize in the brand book category as part of the MOTORWORLD Book Prize 2022, as well as the Nicolas-Joseph Cugnot Award, Language Other Than English, which has been awarded annually by the renowned Society of Automotive Historians in Hershey, Pennsylvania, since 2000.

The authors, editors, graphic designers, and publishers greatly appreciate the recognition associated with these awards and take them as a sign that their work is being honored and that this book has been able to fill a long-standing gap.

Presentation of the MOTORWORLD Book Prize Munich on May 24, 2022. *From left to right*, **Jürgen Lewandowski**, initiator of the book prize and chairman of the eight-member jury; the project instigator **Wolfgang Kalbhenn**; authors **Gerhard Heidbrink** and **Joachim Hack**; and graphic designer **Lukas Kretzschmar.**

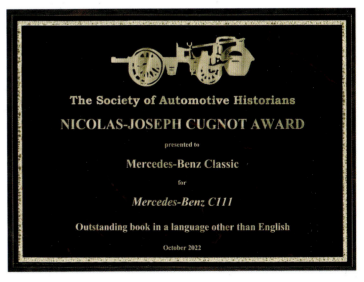

New Promise:
The Wankel Engine

Starting in the late 1950s, the invention and further development of the rotary engine with the aim of achieving production maturity became increasingly relevant in the development departments of large parts of the European, US, and Asian automotive industries. The novel, at-first-glance-ingenious functional principle that Felix Wankel devised in 1954 left behind the system of pistons moving back and forth in the cylinder, which had been in use since the invention of the internal combustion engine, and replaced it with a complex rotary motion of a so-called rotor, the rotary piston. It had a triangular basic shape, the sides of which were a slightly convex curve. The surrounding housing, along whose wall the rotary piston ran, had a basic shape similar to an "8"—but with only a very slightly constricted waist. Within this geometric figure, known as an (epi)trochoid, the rotary piston rotated around its central axis, which can be described as tumbling due to its eccentric bearing. The interaction of this rotational movement with the geometry of the sliding surface of the housing continuously opens and closes three chambers, which are sealed from each other by the rotor. Their size changes with the rotational movement. The familiar four-stroke process takes place in these chambers at staggered intervals, whereby one ignition process takes place per revolution of the eccentric shaft—which in a sense could also be regarded as the counterpart to the crankshaft of a reciprocating engine. In contrast, a reciprocating engine requires two revolutions for one application of energy in the power stroke.

Wankel's endeavor to realize a functional principle of an internal combustion engine based solely on rotational movements, which was basically simpler and required fewer components, led to a technical concept that ultimately remained contradictory. Although in the end it essentially fulfilled some of the postulates that were supposed to make it theoretically superior to the reciprocating

The man and his work: Felix Wankel's invention—shown here in an early version as a rotary engine with a stationary centershaft—occupied large parts of the automotive industry for around two decades.

engine, the road to this point proved to be exceedingly long and rocky. Even experienced development engineers were often unfamiliar with the complex physical processes in such an engine compared to the familiar reciprocating engine that had been established for many decades with its easily comprehensible mechanical processes. The rotary engine, commonly referred to as the Wankel engine, demanded much more abstract thinking from

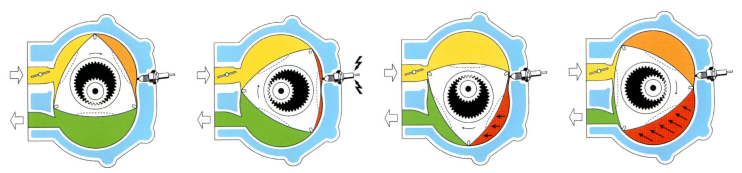

Ingenious, but complex and harder to manage than expected: the operating principle of a rotary piston engine. The colors indicate the current phase of the respective chamber: yellow for intake, orange for compression, red for ignition and combustion, green for exhaust.

New Promise: The Wankel Engine

constructors accustomed to tangible parameters such as bore, stroke, and compression. While the reciprocating engine was an object that was considered to have a soul of some sort after decades of technical evolution, the Wankel engine seemed to be a rather brittle academic construct that some development engineers had difficulty to really come to grips with.

Moreover, even in the early stages of the Wankel engine's development, it became clear that, despite their apparent simplicity, such engines required an unexpectedly great deal of basic research. The developers quickly realized that the devil was in the details of the Wankel engine, and it took a lot of time and material resources to gain a reasonable understanding of the rotary engine itself and its specific characteristics and requirements, and to get a better handle on it step by step.

Revolution on the Way?

At Mercedes-Benz, where it has always been part of the credo to pursue technical advancement in a highly serious and competent manner and—if necessary—with a great deal of staying power, the emergence of the new, potentially groundbreaking engine technology caused more commotion than elsewhere: within the company, there was a staunch advocate for the new type of drive in the person of Wolf-Dieter Bensinger, head of engine development. Bensinger, who was Felix Wankel's companion at work for a time during the Second World War and also had close personal ties to the inventor, was fascinated by the numerous—at least theoretical—advantages of the functional principle and made the subject of rotary engines an important part of his agenda at Daimler-Benz early on. At the end of the 1950s and beginning of the 1960s, neither he nor his senior staff nor engine developers from other car manufacturers working in a similar capacity could credibly predict whether or not the Wankel engine would ever be able to revolutionize vehicle powertrains.

Given this background, it was not surprising that Daimler-Benz was one of the very early interested parties in this technology, the rights to which were held equally by Felix Wankel or Wankel GmbH and NSU-Werke AG. In 1957, the Neckarsulm-based company, under the leadership of Dr. Walter Froede, head of the research department, had modified the functional principle of the engine in such a way that its use as a vehicle engine became practicable in the first place. While NSU, in spite of limited financial resources, then virtually pounced on the realization and, from 1964 onward, on the series production of the rotary engine with the Wankel Spider while holding all the trump cards with regard to licensing,

Wolf-Dieter Bensinger and Felix Wankel—two friends on a boat trip together on Lake Constance

everyone directly involved in the development in Neckarsulm and elsewhere probably underestimated the immense development efforts that would ultimately be required to actually make the Wankel engine suitable for series production on a large scale.

In retrospect, it seems astonishing that apparently the developers initially did not become more aware of the fundamental physics problems arising from the Wankel functional principle—in particular that of the combustion process with a rotating piston that keeps the combustion chamber in constant motion. The perceived advantages of the innovative engine concept—superior smooth running, few moving parts, compact design, low weight, comparatively low production costs—seemed perhaps too tempting. However, this was by no means only true for the engine developers at Daimler-Benz, who started out with a healthy pioneering spirit: the fact that Wankel's idea captivated no fewer than twenty-eight licensees by 1973 can be seen as evidence of the widespread belief in progress and technology during that era. The gradually growing Wankel surge was accompanied by a press landscape that initially reacted enthusiastically to the innovative technology. Quite a few representatives of the trade press and the daily press, as well as some entertainment newspapers and magazines, already saw the dawning of a paradigm shift in vehicle powertrains. Occasional reservations expressed by competent parties with regard to the unconditional suitability of the Wankel engine as a passenger car engine were lost in the chorus of euphoric, speculative headlines.

The Wankel engine also enjoyed media attention during the second half of the 1960s—but now often of the opposite kind: NSU, as the pioneer in Wankel technology, had to pay more dearly than was good for the company for using a rotary piston engine in the sensational Ro 80 sedan, which had been in series production since 1967. Nevertheless, important players in the global automotive industry continued to appear on the scene in Wankel engine matters; General Motors and Ford, the two US giants, acquired appropriate licenses in 1970 and the following year. The question was still being asked not only at Daimler-Benz, where they had already been dealing with the Wankel engine in practice for almost a decade at this point, but also in the development departments of other major car manufacturers, whether they could afford not to push the new technology with all their might when even the very big players had come on board—the basic problems of the Wankel engine that had become apparent in the meantime would eventually be solved.

Development Activities with Sound Judgment

With the sustained support of engine design chief Wolf-Dieter Bensinger as the most important protagonist in the company, Daimler-Benz had already turned to Wankel technology starting in 1960. Individual positive test results achieved with a small-capacity single-rotor test engine provided by NSU prompted the Daimler-Benz Board of Management—which overall was quite hesitant—to acquire an appropriate license from the consortium consisting of NSU-Werke AG and Wankel GmbH at the end of 1961. As if to demonstrate the correctness of the decision taken, the first positive news came of a Daimler-Benz test engine with the designation M 70 F just over two months later, at the end of February 1962. It had apparently already been under development behind the scenes. The two-rotor engine with 700 cc chamber volume had successfully completed a twenty-hour endurance run on the engine test bench. In March, Bensinger also presented individual components of the in-house-developed engine to the Supervisory Board of Daimler-Benz AG. As a result, the Wankel project, which was ultimately classified as strategically important, officially picked up speed in the company—admittedly due to limited resources with less personnel and budgetary momentum from the outset than the chief engine designer had imagined, who thought all the pros were on his side.

The reasons for this were manifold: on the one hand, the decision-making and supervisory bodies of Daimler-Benz AG, with all due respect for the demonstrated innovative spirit, continued to adopt a wait-and-see attitude and did not allow themselves to be put under pressure in view of the unclear overall situation regarding Wankel engine development. The company always remained aware of the problems, and therefore, at no time were brand-specific quality standards or fundamental business maxims of the company even remotely up for discussion. On the other hand, it became clear that at the operational level of engine development, certain pro- and contra-Wankel engine factions emerged, which at times was not conducive to development progress. The advocates for conventional combustion engine technology, who still saw considerable development potential in reciprocating engines, may also have had the uneasy feeling that by pushing the Wankel engine they were giving up a constitutive element of their own technological identity—after all, in the extreme case, they would have to act as a licensee in the core competence of engine construction in future.

Much Light and Much Shadow:
The Development History

The fact that the development of Wankel engines with a view to an eventual series production turned out to be much more demanding because it was more complex than was assumed, considering the simplicity of the functional principle, already became clear when the engineers started to delve into the fundamentals of Wankel technology in detail at the beginning. The typical problem areas of a rotary engine came to light equally quickly and clearly.

Essentially, the following areas were initially identified as in urgent need of experimentation: the cooling of the rotor and housing, the sealing of the three chambers created during the rotation process against each other and from the housing, and the selection of suitable metals and coatings for the housing, rotor, and sliding surfaces. In addition, because of the different combustion process, new solutions had to be found for ignition and mixture preparation.

In addition, the special functionality of a Wankel engine raised the question of the most suitable gas exchange system. Although a rotary engine does not have a valve control system, the developers had to make the fundamental decision as to whether the gas exchange should take place at the housing shell—that is, the actual engine housing (peripheral intake ports/PI), or at the side housing (side intake ports/SI)—a decision that had to be made at the beginning of the development process, but whose far-reaching effects not only on the engine characteristics could by no means be foreseen at that time.

Under Bensinger's leadership, engine development at Daimler-Benz opted for the peripheral intake ports option. NSU

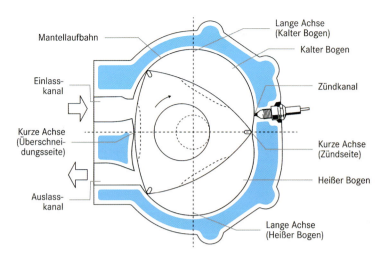

New type of combustion engine, new type of terminology: the rotary piston engine challenged the developers in more ways than one.

also relied on this solution for the KKM 612 two-rotor Wankel engine with which the NSU Ro 80 was equipped at the start of series production in the summer of 1967. The main reason for this decision was the conceptually high potential power output of a PI engine combined with the prospect of realizing an engine kit with many common parts that could be produced efficiently and cost-effectively thanks to an unsplit eccentric shaft. The fact that—as quickly became apparent—the theoretically high power output was always accompanied by a pronounced lack of torque in the lower rev range had to be acknowledged but was considered manageable in the context of further development.

The wear phenomenon of what is known as "chatter marks," which unexpectedly appeared in the early development and testing phase of the Wankel engine during the first half of the 1960s, proved to be extremely persistent. The wave-shaped damage

Analysis of extensive tests on material combinations of housing jacket and apex seal. Compilation of Daimler-Benz engine design of March 1970.

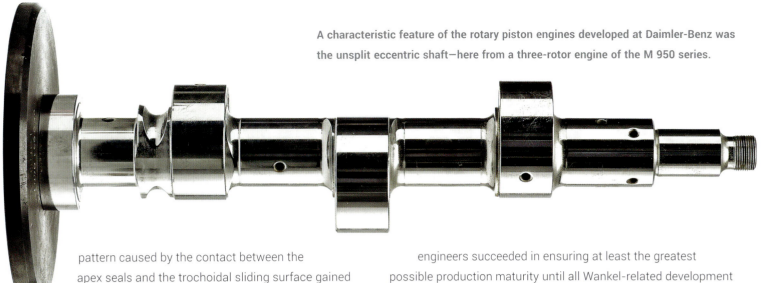

A characteristic feature of the rotary piston engines developed at Daimler-Benz was the unsplit eccentric shaft—here from a three-rotor engine of the M 950 series.

pattern caused by the contact between the apex seals and the trochoidal sliding surface gained dubious fame everywhere as a typical Wankel engine phenomenon—mainly because, despite significant inventions such as the Nikasil sliding surface coating invented by Mahle in 1965, none of the worldwide Wankel development teams could eliminate it for good until the late 1960s.

The situation was similar with another key Wankel theme: the creation of absolute gas tightness at the rotor. Here, the notorious apex seals—especially those that were supposed to seal the three chambers against each other—were the subject of elaborate test series in terms of design and material from the start of development until at least 1973. In the process, Daimler-Benz engineers succeeded in ensuring at least the greatest possible production maturity until all Wankel-related development activities came to a halt.

The development of optimal rotors with regard to suitable material, combustion chamber shape, lubricant supply, and radial oil sealing also proved to be anything but simple and could only be brought to the high production maturity level required by Daimler-Benz after more than ten years of Wankel development. However, the development of the engine housings proved to be an even more challenging task. Significant progress was made here, particularly in the choice of materials with regard to the thermal sensitivity of the Wankel engine, the dimensional accuracy of sealing surfaces, and the durability of sliding surface coatings,

This is what the "chatter marks" looked like on the trochoidal sliding surface. At the time, they became a permanent problem for the developers—and not only at Daimler-Benz.

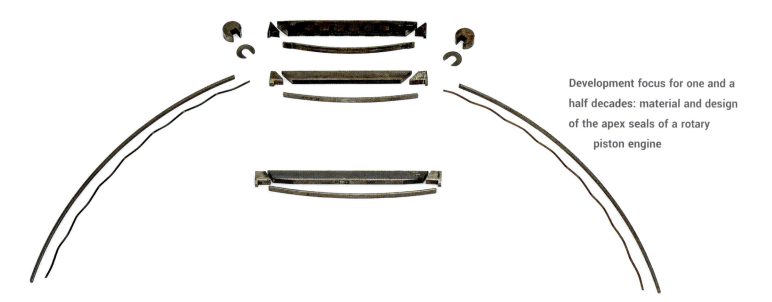

Development focus for one and a half decades: material and design of the apex seals of a rotary piston engine

from the start of development work until it was finally halted at the beginning of 1976, but no technical standard was achieved that would have allowed the Wankel engine to be adopted in series production in accordance with the quality specifications of Mercedes-Benz.

By contrast, however, mature solutions had been found by this time for the ignition system and—since the advent of the mechanical Bosch K-Jetronic injection system in the first half of the 1970s—the mixture preparation system. The main reason for the tentative progress in development was, in addition to the limited human and material resources made available, a complexity of mutual physical dependencies in a Wankel engine unknown from the reciprocating engine. From the perspective of those directly involved, the development efforts turned out to be a bottomless pit over time. If promising solutions were found in one problem area, new difficulties arose in one or more others.

The question of material determined the development of the rotors just as much as the optimal shape of the combustion chamber. *On the left*, **a rotor made of malleable cast iron (M 950);** *on the right*, **an example made of cast aluminum (M 951).**

In times without high computing power, without sophisticated simulation software, and without advanced electronic control components, the Wankel engine development, if its results were to meet the standards of Daimler-Benz, turned into a true Herculean task with numerous unknowns and ultimately an uncertain outcome.

Rising Learning Curve: The Research Engines

The series of Daimler-Benz Wankel research engines began, as mentioned, with the M 70 F prototype sample, which was subjected to its first bench test in the spring of 1961. The engine—one- and two-rotor versions were built—had a jacket width of 70 mm and immediately fulfilled the expectation of a high power output. The extremely compact engine with 700 cc chamber volume soon delivered an astonishing 170 hp/125 kW in a two-rotor version but showed no prospects of durability due to permanent temperature-related apex seal problems and the formation of chatter marks. Only in a modified version, reduced to 145 hp/107 kW, could the first endurance tests be completed with any prospect of success. It took a good two years for a specimen of this first generation of engines to survive a 400-hour stress bench test without major damage. At this point, the Wankel project at Daimler-Benz, which was hardly making any progress, was already under a certain amount of pressure, and an early halt to all development work could not be ruled out.

Two-rotor test engine of the M 70 F generation—the example with the designation KP 4 is shown.

Spurred on by the success of the test bench, the second generation of Wankel research engines followed at the end of 1963 in the form of the M 45 F. It had—technically improved in

The fundamentally compact design—especially, as here, in a two-rotor version—was one of the undeniable strengths of the Wankel engine.

many respects—a jacket width of 60 mm, and one of these engines with a chamber volume of 450 cc survived a 140-hour endurance test without failure. With a view to possible subsequent road tests, an installable version of this was also produced, which came up with up to 210 hp/184 kW in three-rotor specification. In fact, a power unit of this evolutionary stage, throttled down to 141 hp/104 kW for consumption reasons, was implanted in a W 111 sedan in the summer of 1965 but stood out negatively there due to the emission of larger bluish-white clouds of smoke and had an oil consumption of 4 liters/1,000 km.

In May 1966, the third, further-improved engine generation followed in the form of the M 50 F. Equipped with intermediate and side housings made of aluminum as well as a jacket width of 70 mm and a chamber volume of 560 cc, the three-rotor version with initially 180 hp/132 kW and later 170 hp/125 kW delivered pleasing endurance tests under test bench conditions. Up to 100 hours could be completed without serious defects. However, test drives carried out from September onward with a W 108 sedan equipped with such an M 50 F engine showed alarmingly high fuel consumption in real road traffic conditions. Further development work aimed at optimizing the combustion process promised improvement here. The latent problem of excessively high housing temperatures seemed to be under control to some extent at this point.

According to the assessment of those responsible at the time, the level of development achieved now offered the prospect of series production, and the engine generation was subsequently given the designation M 170 F. Some of the preparatory

With its chamber volume of 560 cc, the 121 kg M 50 F three-rotor engine produced impressive power and torque figures.

organizational and infrastructural measures required in the run-up to series production planning were taken, and the issue of production costs now also came under greater scrutiny. In addition, the first scenarios for the concrete use of engines of this Wankel engine generation in two- and three-rotor design—for example, a use in the Unimog S—were drafted, still based on a small series. Although this did not happen in the end, more than forty units of these engines were built for further development work and various testing purposes. The latter culminated in further road tests as early as 1966, which were conducted with W 108 sedans and SL roadsters of the W 113 "Pagoda" series.

Premiere: the technically improved M 45 F engine generation also represented the first realization of a three-rotor power unit.

Nomenclature of the Mercedes-Benz Wankel Engines

As early as the beginning of the 1960s, a designation principle was created at Daimler-Benz that took into account the innovative character of the new power unit and stood out from the company's established nomenclature system for reciprocating engines.

In the early phase of development, the designation consisted of the letter combination "KM," which stood for "Kreiskolbenmotor" or rotary piston engine in English, followed by a two- or three-digit number, which—after multiplication by 10—indicated the rounded chamber volume. The KM 70 was therefore a Wankel engine with 700 cc chamber volume per rotor or jacket.

The closer the Wankel engines came to possible series production, the more important it became to adapt the designation to the usual nomenclature and documentation systems. This can be seen in the designations of the Mercedes-Benz Wankel engine generations: M 70 F, M 45 F, and M 50 F basically followed the original system or were derived from it. The M 50 F was renamed M 170 F and had thus arrived in the established engine nomenclature system.

In the first engine generations, the "F" apparently stood for "Forschungsmotor" or research engine. In the last series, M 950 and M 951, the "F" was only used sporadically, and in addition, with the 950 numbers, a separate new number range had also been introduced for the Wankel engines. Because the engine series from the M 45 F onward were built in several variants with different numbers of jackets and rotors, the number of jackets was simply added to the series code with a slash: M 50/2 F accordingly designates a two-rotor variant of the M 50 F, M 950/3 a three-rotor engine of the M 950 series.

In development and testing, the technicians and engineers at Mercedes-Benz have always attached importance to being able to name even individual vehicles and engines clearly and efficiently at the same time. For this purpose, a nomenclature system was developed in which the engine series was designated only by a capital letter appended to the "K" (for rotary piston engine), dispensing with the two- or three-digit series code. The following list compares these letter combinations with the corresponding series codes:

```
KP – M 70 F
KA – M 45 F
KC – M 50 F or M 170 F
KE – M 950
KF – M 951
```

The background to the decision to begin with P and skip the letters B and D is unfortunately not documented. In principle, however, the designation of individual engines was easily possible in conjunction with these letter combinations, whereby two different systems were also used here. As long as there was only one variant per series with regard to the number of rotors, the combination of letter code and consecutive number was unambiguous and meaningful. Engine KP 7 was accordingly the M 70 F with the serial number 7. When the development of the Wankel engine series from the M 45 F onward took place in different variants, the number of rotors was initially appended to the consecutive number with a slash—KA 9/3 designated the M 45 F with the serial number 9, which was designed as a three-rotor engine.

As the number of test engines increased, this system was adapted again. The consecutive number was now always three digits long, with the first digit designating the number of rotors and the following two digits the actual consecutive number. Thus, the KC 317 was the seventeenth three-rotor engine of the M 50 F or M 170 F series, the KE 406 the sixth four-rotor engine of the M 950 series, and the KF 402 the second four-rotor engine of the M 951 model series. Within this system, the build version of the individual engine could be marked with a slash: In this context, KC 315/6 stood for the fifteenth three-rotor engine of the M 170 F series, which had been assembled for the sixth time.

Desire and Reality: Unclear Series Production Prospects

Against the background of considerations to use the Wankel engine in Mercedes-Benz production passenger cars at least in the medium term, it was decided to design an optimized engine generation taking into account prior experience. In this case, the fundamental issues of durability and fuel consumption were to continue to be the most important development goals. The first engine of the new evolutionary stage, which bore the designation M 950 and had a chamber volume of 600 cc with a 75 mm jacket width, made its debut on the engine test bench in September 1968 in a two-rotor version. At the beginning of the following year, the first three-rotor engine was completed. In a second, further-developed build version, a four-rotor engine was realized for the first time. Last but not least, this reflected the thrust of the M 950 power units, which, in addition to further improving and validating the basic engine qualities, aimed in particular at a high power

As part of the test fleet, this "Stroke Eight" sedan housed a two-rotor engine of the M 950 generation. This configuration did not lack installation space.

To the surprise of the developers, the three-rotor version of the M 950 proved to be less stable and made hopes of a series production seem illusory for the time being.

Depressing reading for the Wankel developers at Daimler-Benz: test log of the long-distance testing with engines of the generation M 950, 1973

output—after all, the first regular use of this generation of engines was to be in the new C 101 mid-engined sports car project. Mainly thanks to higher revs, the M 950 could be brought up to a power level of over 350 hp/257 kW in the four-rotor version by late summer 1969.

Endurance tests with the new high-performance engines, however, brought an unexpected setback for Wankel engine development at Daimler-Benz: Thermal and mechanical problems on the test engines, which were thought to have been largely overcome, resulted in a large number of early and major defects, which, along with other factors, rendered the cautious considerations regarding a production start of the high-performance sports car in 1971 obsolete. In order to have at least a certain number of test and demonstration vehicles of the fascinating coupe ready for use, the individual three- and four-rotor versions had to be extensively and expensively modified. Subsequently, the developers turned again more toward the technically less complex two-rotor versions of the M 950. The focus here was once again on reducing fuel consumption and optimizing the performance characteristics, the dominant feature of which was still a pronounced lack of pulling power in the lower rev range. To alleviate the latter in the long term, developments such as an innovative variable-length intake manifold and, after extensive testing, a specially configured single pipe exhaust system were used.

Until around mid-1971, the engine developers at Daimler-Benz worked on a total of four build versions of the M 950, each of which featured various improvements, but ultimately did not lead to a breakthrough in terms of series production prospects, mainly due to persistent thermal problems. With a few exceptions, only power units from the first two build versions were implanted in the C 111.

Eccentric shaft of an M 950 three-rotor engine with center rotor and split bearing shells

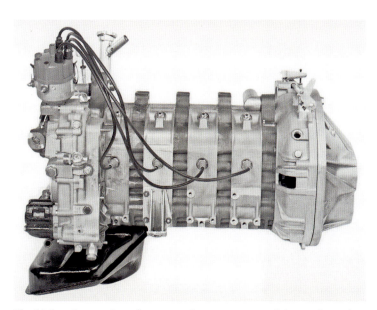

The higher the number of rotors and power output of the engines, the greater the problems with reliability and durability. The four-rotor versions of the M 950 were the best example.

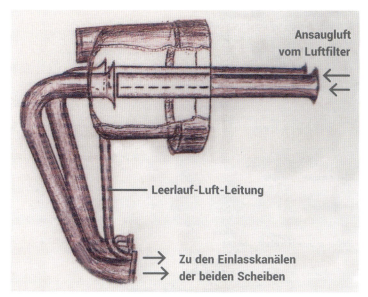

The variable-length intake manifold—shown here in an x-ray drawing by its inventor, Wolfgang Kalbhenn—proved to be an efficient solution to overcome the Wankel engine's lack of torque in the lower rev range.

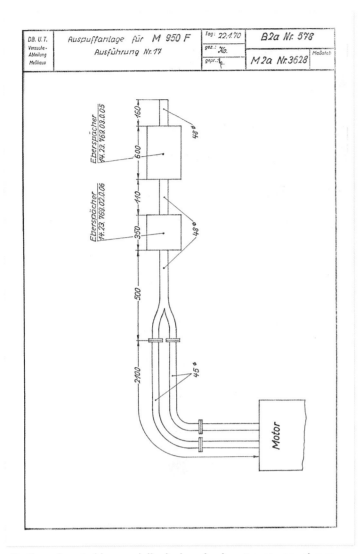

On the exhaust side, specially designed exhaust systems—shown here in a single exhaust version for the M 950—supported the generation of fuller torque curves.

The Highest Stage of Development: Engine Generation M 951

At the beginning of the 1970s, the development of Wankel engines at Daimler-Benz, which had been going on with varying intensity for about ten years, came under increasing pressure to synchronize with the development of potentially Wankel-powered vehicles in the future passenger car range. After all, the different installation conditions for Wankel and reciprocating engines had to be taken into account in the body design in advance. This was specifically the case for the SL model series 107, the S-Class model series 116,

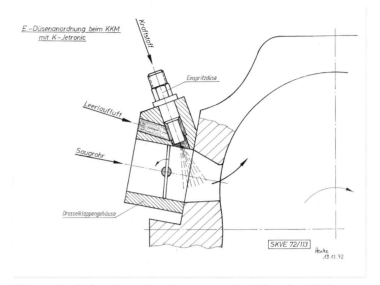

The result of a lengthy series of tests was the oblique installation position of the K-Jetronic injector nozzle near the intake port.

and the mid-range model series 123. Due to the unexpected difficulties with the M 950 engine generation, however, a comprehensively revised version of the Wankel engine became imperative at the same time. The objectives of the relevant development work had been defined since February 1971. This included taking into account the installation conditions especially in the future 123 model series vehicles, eliminating the housing leaks identified as a major cause of the problem and introducing side housings made of hypereutectic aluminum alloy, a metallurgical innovation that General Motors had advanced and introduced in parts of its own engine production. Against this background, the time horizon for a possible series launch of the Wankel engine at Daimler-Benz was initially set for 1973 but was soon extended to 1976 due to continued unsuitability for series production.

The power units of the new M 951 engine generation completed in 1972 presented themselves in fact more as completely new than as a comprehensive further development. Significant progress was now being made in terms of thermal stability and wear reduction, in particular through the hypereutectic side housings, significantly improved lubrication of the sealing elements, a more robust design of the jackets, new aluminum rotors, and a significantly more efficient cooling circuit. Among other things, these were accompanied by the first use of the Bosch K-Jetronic mechanical intake manifold injection system, which was being tested at Daimler-Benz at the time and proved to be by far the most efficient mixture preparation system

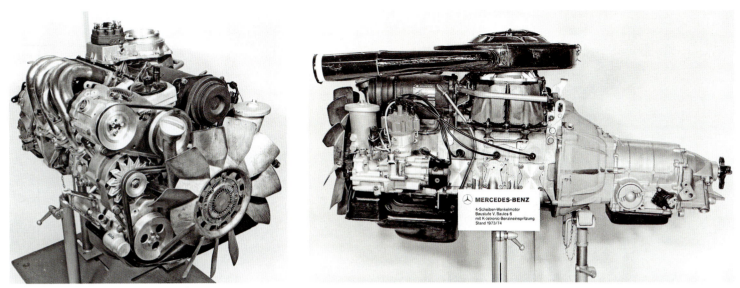

In this final form, the four-rotor version of the M 951 was to be used in a limited number of SL/SLC vehicles of the R/C 107 model series in mid-1975. At times, production of 250 units per month was envisaged, which were to be delivered to hand-picked customers with a view to testing in everyday conditions.

Culmination of Wankel engine development at Daimler-Benz: jacket, aluminum rotor, and hypereutectic side housings of an M 951

to date in terms of both power output and fuel consumption. In conjunction with the variable-length intake manifold, the K-Jetronic also provided a fuller torque curve and thus a more harmonious power characteristic.

Valuable Helpers: External Development Services Providers

To be able to carry out the basic research on the Wankel engine despite limited personnel resources, research that became increasingly urgent and extensive over the course of the many years of development, Daimler-Benz chief engine designer Wolf-Dieter Bensinger often made use of external help. In the period from the mid-1960s to around 1973, a large number of research contracts were awarded to scientific institutions under his lead, the most important of which were linked to Daimler-Benz in one way or another. The Technical Development Center (TES), based in Lindau and founded by Felix Wankel at the beginning of the 1960s, as well as the Institut für Motorenbau Prof. Huber GmbH (IMH) in Munich, financially supported by Daimler-Benz, were contracted most often in this regard. These institutes dealt with questions on the topics of apex seals, oil cooling of the rotors, and optimization potentials of the combustion processes, for example. With the massive curtailment of Wankel development ordered by the Daimler-Benz Board of Management at the end of 1973, the commissioning of these external research institutes also came to an end, and their budgets shrank massively as a result.

Intimate Connection: C 111 and Wankel Engine

The development of Wankel engines at Daimler-Benz, which lasted around fifteen years, remained largely unknown to the general public and even to those interested in cars. The media landscape of the 1960s and 1970s also took little notice of the many efforts made in engine development at Untertürkheim to give the Wankel engine series production prospects in passenger car construction that met Daimler-Benz's specific quality standards. Various reasons for this generally reserved treatment of the topic may have played a role here. The Wankel technology had undoubtedly lost its appeal in view of the problems that NSU had to overcome with the Ro 80 for everyone to see from 1967 onward, and Daimler-Benz also kept a very low profile on the subject in terms of communication policy in view of some technical difficulties in the development of its own Wankel engines and in view of the generally dynamic development in the field of passenger car powertrains.

The fact is that the Wankel engine only appears once at Mercedes-Benz in the collective perception of the brand's history—in connection with the sensational high-performance C 111 Coupe, which ultimately emerged as an experimental vehicle and, after months of speculation, made its debut at the International Motor Show (IAA) in Frankfurt/Main in September 1969 and was rightly perceived as a sensation.

It can be seen as a kind of ironic footnote in automotive history that, given the very high overall technical level of Wankel engine development at Daimler-Benz, the complex and powerful three- and four-rotor power units of the M 950 engine generation used in the various C 111s, of all things, came into historical focus as exponents of this drive technology. The numerous problems with these engines caused the progress of the further development process at Daimler-Benz to stagnate to a certain extent and cast a shadow—quite undeservedly—over the technical level that had been achieved in the meantime, which was also impressive in the details.

The fact that the C 111 became the undisputed star of the 1969 IAA was surely only partly due to the functional principle of its power unit—the majority of the interested public were certainly aware of the difficulties with the Wankel engine of the Ro 80, which were eagerly picked up by the media—but at least as much due to its fascinating appearance, the ultramodern vehicle concept with mid-engine and plastic body, as well as the performance data communicated at the time. With the mid-engined sports car, Daimler-Benz showed that twelve years after production of the legendary 300 SL "Gullwing" Coupe had been discontinued, the company had courage again and intended to shake off the certain conventionality that had found its way into the Mercedes-Benz passenger car model range over the years. After a number of controversial discussions within the Board of Management in the run-up to the IAA appearance, the C 111 perfectly played its intended role as an "image booster," albeit explicitly only as an experimental vehicle, for good reasons. The motor show star thus also gave the new generation of modern V8 engines from the M 116 series, which were also celebrating their premiere at the 1969 IAA, enough room to launch their successful career in the Mercedes-Benz passenger car range.

Cardinal Question:
What to Do with the Wankel Engine?

Despite the overwhelming worldwide response to the C 111, the question of what the prospects for Wankel engine development actually were at Daimler-Benz remained without a concrete answer on the part of the company. Speculation in the media and sometimes probing questions at the general meetings of Daimler-Benz AG were, as had been the case for many years, also warded off repeatedly at the beginning of the 1970s, and always with reference to the development process not yet being completed. That was factually completely correct and reflected nothing other than reality. After all, the signals pointing in the direction of for or against remained ambivalent. On the one hand, there were the still very mixed experiences with the protracted in-house Wankel engine development and the perception of what NSU or, since 1969, the newly founded Audi NSU Auto Union AG experienced with the Ro 80. But on the other hand, there was the success of Toyo Kogyo with their Wankel-powered Mazda cars, especially in North America, as well as the clear commitment of General Motors and Ford in the matter of rotary piston engines.

Daimler-Benz thus had to continue to perform a difficult balancing act as far as the strategic orientation of its passenger car activities was concerned. Not least because the continuous planning of the passenger car range with its long-term, fixed development cycles demanded concrete fundamental decisions in this question, despite all the uncertainty about an in-house series use of the Wankel engine and the relevant events in the global competition—after all, specific characteristics and dimensions and different installation conditions of the Wankel power units had to be taken into account in good time in the vehicle development. This situation was flanked by increasingly dynamic legislation in terms of exhaust emissions reduction and passive accident safety, which in turn also influenced the development process on both the drive system and vehicle side.

Unchanged Focus: Key Technical Problems

No other car manufacturer put up higher hurdles before introducing new developments into series production than Daimler-Benz. The uncompromising quality standard has always served as a guideline for action during the development phase of the Wankel engines, which spanned around one and a half decades, and was never diluted at any time. The dominant theme was and remained the achievement of a level of durability comparable to that of reciprocating engines. Despite extensive basic research and numerous innovative technical solutions, the criteria for production maturity—500 hours of trouble-free running on the test bench under full load and 100,000 road kilometers—which had already been regarded as the benchmark in the company at the beginning of the 1960s, could not be represented in a statistically reproducible manner by the time all development activities for the Wankel engine designs were halted. Although individual engines of the respective technical evolutionary stage repeatedly succeeded in achieving one or the other of these goals over the years, in the perception of the developers directly involved at the time, these also seemed to be successes that were based more on the principle of chance and could not always be explained. Although some of the fundamental problems of the Wankel engines, including those inherent in the principle, could be completely eliminated constructionally, others proved not to be satisfactorily manageable despite all efforts.

Thousands and thousands of hours on engine test benches and several million test kilometers on the road ultimately did not result in a technical reliability of the rotary engines that was suitable for series production according to Daimler-Benz standards. Countless endurance tests of the various engine generations had a depressing outcome. Sometimes it helped to reduce the output level, but even this measure was not always

A look at the competition: in a fuel consumption comparison with an NSU Ro 80, the advantages for a "Stroke Eight" sedan conventionally powered by the M 110 six-cylinder remained unchanged.

expedient. Other constant side effects of the tests were frequent spark plug changes, clouds of blue smoke coming out of the exhaust systems, and jerking in overrun mode and under light load that could not be cured entirely.

Beyond these primary problems, the issues of fuel and oil consumption and the resulting questions about the Wankel engine's pollutant emissions rapidly gained relevance from the second half of the 1960s onward. The necessary system comparison with the reciprocating engine and, in particular, what was known as the "oil crisis" that unfolded in 1973 considerably increased the pressure on the project. It had long since become clear that the Wankel engine, due to its specific functionality, had fundamental disadvantages in terms of petrol and oil consumption compared to conventional petrol engines. The underlying sealing problems and the less favorable conditions during the combustion process increasingly put the Wankel engine on the defensive at Daimler-Benz—and not only there. Its propagated qualities, which it could only demonstrate to a limited extent under the given conditions anyway, shrank to almost zero in the scenario that had arisen in the meantime: From the beginning of the 1970s at the latest, it was no longer possible to speak of the inherent superiority of the Wankel engine over the classic reciprocating engine.

In the run-up to the mandatory use of catalytic converters, which came into force in the USA in 1974, engines of the M 950 generation were already equipped with emission control components such as a thermoreactor and air pump.

As far as fuel and lubricant consumption were concerned, the development from this point on was only concerned with keeping the disadvantages of the Wankel engine within tolerable limits that could still be communicated to potential customers. Over the years, the Daimler-Benz developers made enormous progress, especially with regard to petrol consumption: The initially determined additional consumption in the range of 50% could be reduced to about 10%. However, a stable parity with reciprocating engines in all driving conditions remained unattainable in the end—and not only for the Stuttgart engineers. The situation with oil consumption was much more critical. In those days, Mercedes-Benz drivers were used to having the petrol station attendant top off a liter of engine oil once between service appointments at most. Wankel engines required far more attention in this respect: Until the test drives in regular operation on the road were discontinued, astronomical consumption values of around 5 l/1,000 km were repeatedly recorded for individual engines, for which clear technical reasons could not be identified in all cases.

Against this background, the increasingly urgent demands for a reduction of pollutant emissions in road traffic, first in the USA in the 1970s, became highly topical. Initial euphoria about the exhaust gas composition of a Wankel engine was soon followed by the sobering realization that it would not be possible to get by without additional exhaust gas aftertreatment—a technology that was still in its infancy at the time. After all, the nitrogen oxide emissions, which were initially regarded as advantageously low, were offset by particularly large quantities of unburned hydrocarbons and carbon monoxide, which the reciprocating petrol engine did not produce.

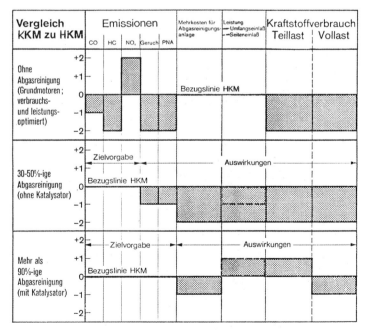

In addition to fuel consumption, the exhaust emissions of the Wankel engine also became a central issue in the mid-1970s. This graph shows that only with the use of a catalytic converter could overall parity with a reciprocating engine be achieved.

The Final Chord:
Changed Framework

The oil crisis that unfolded in late autumn 1973, with artificial shortages of petroleum and Sunday driving bans on German motorways, had a shocking effect on the economy and society alike. Large parts of the automotive industry were particularly affected, which—greatly unsettled—questioned its product policy, especially in the passenger car sector. The main focus of the examination was on more-powerful and larger-capacity petrol engines, whose higher fuel consumption no longer seemed hardly acceptable under the given circumstances. At Daimler-Benz, with its range of vehicles exclusively in the upper mid-size and luxury segments, the Wankel engine, which was known to be less economical, also very quickly came under scrutiny.

Immediate analyses of the development status by the head of passenger car development, Friedrich van Winsen, confirmed that the technical status of the Wankel engine was still unsatisfactory in some areas—it was not yet possible to foresee whether the engine would reach production maturity. In view of this situation, it was no wonder that the Board of Management of Daimler-Benz AG decreed at the end of 1973 to reduce the relevant development activities by 75%. This was true both in terms of personnel and budget. All Wankel research contracts on which external cooperation partners were still working were also stopped, and the components provided were scrapped under supervision. Almost all available resources were subsequently concentrated on the further development of the existing and planned range of reciprocating engines and vehicles. From then on, special attention was paid to further reductions in consumption and emissions. The issue of the Wankel engine at Daimler-Benz was thus effectively dead, at least at Board of Management level.

Two aspects of the rotary piston intermezzo at Daimler-Benz, which lasted around one and a half decades, deserve special attention in the overall context: on the one hand, production planning and, on the other hand, the costing side. Both of these factors seemed to speak strongly in favor of introducing the new engine design at the beginning of development. The lower number of components compared to conventional four-stroke combustion engines and the possibility of establishing cost-efficient production processes thanks to a manageable modular system presented themselves at first glance as tangible advantages of the new drive technology. But here, too, the initial enthusiasm proved premature—as in many other fields of development of the Wankel engine. The production of key components such as the apex seals, the eccentric bearings, the rotors, and the jacket housings, or questions such as the optimal sliding surface coating, demanded increasingly complex and precise processes the more intensively basic research was pursued. In order to master them, appropriate know-how often had to be acquired first. Last but not least, engine assembly itself was a great challenge in the capacity dimensions that were envisaged for a while at Daimler-Benz in the early 1970s. In order to be able to produce 6,000 Wankel engines per month in the required quality, considerable investment in the production facilities would have been imperative.

Although the Wankel engine was by no means ready for series production according to Daimler-Benz standards at the beginning of the 1970s, concrete production planning was already well advanced. Here is an excerpt of the production steps required for the manufacture of rotors and housing jackets.

Over the years, various scenarios for the introduction of the Wankel engine in series production at Mercedes-Benz were put forward but always had to be abandoned due to the consistently inadequate development status. The first of these was the SL roadster of the R 107 model series, launched in 1971. Since this was already designed accordingly on the installation side, it was to be offered alternatively with a three-rotor engine based on the M 950 generation. The S-Class sedan of the 116 series and the new mid-range models of the 123 model series, which did not make their debut until January 1976, were also considered for the use of a Wankel engine. These vehicles were to be equipped with power units from the envisaged Wankel engine modular system of the then-current M 951 generation. According to a view expressed by engine boss Bensinger in 1971, three basic models, a two-rotor, a three-rotor, and a four-rotor engine, and power outputs between 120 hp/88 kW and 280 hp/206 kW, would have been sufficient to cover the wide range of power outputs of these vehicles. In the end, the oil crisis and what developed from it finally killed all Wankel visions at Daimler-Benz.

Corresponding to the production planning, the cost side of a Wankel engine introduction had also been under latent pressure since the early 1970s. Just as on the technical and production side, there were no known parameters in terms of costing that those responsible could have used as a guide. Since the Wankel engines were not intended to replace the existing range of proven reciprocating engines—that much was clear by now—but to supplement them in parts, they had to be on a par with them in terms of cost. This in turn led to discussions about the benchmark to be used, especially for the two-rotor engines: Should four-cylinder or, rather, six-cylinder engines of a similar output class be compared here? In addition, there was the question of whether and to what extent the special installation requirements of the Wankel engines should be included in the costing.

How high the manufacturing costs of such engines would actually turn out to be remained controversial until the end. The large number of sample calculations presented at Daimler-Benz over the years led to less clarity rather than greater clarity, since their bases and assumptions only ever reflected the current perspective and therefore mostly differed. Whereas in the second half of the 1960s, according to the first more concrete calculations, the production costs of Wankel engines were in some cases significantly lower than those of comparable reciprocating engines, the picture changed in the early years of the 1970s. With a sharpened view thanks to the further progress in development,

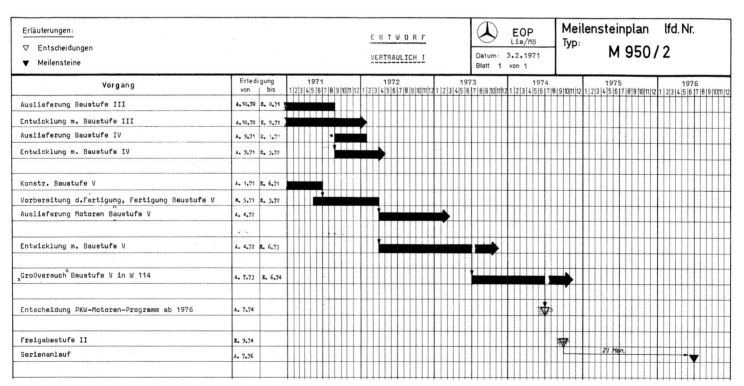

Five years lead time: as early as February 1971, this "milestone plan" was fixed for the operational steps up to the start of series production of the M 950. The two-rotor version was to be integrated into the engine range in mid-1976.

28 New Promise: The Wankel Engine

the costing seemed to suggest that Wankel engines could only be realized in a production mix of two-, three-, and four-rotor units, which ensured a sufficiently high total production quantity. However, the exact quantitative distribution of this mix was not defined in more detail at the time, since even at this stage there was no clear planning perspective for a series launch. Incidentally, in these calculation models, as in all those that continued to be drawn up at Daimler-Benz until the final Wankel discontinuation, economic risk factors such as increased warranty requirements—like the ones that had ultimately driven NSU into the arms of Audi—or potential burdens due to service problems in connection with the new types of power units were completely ignored.

The Hour of the Undaunted: New Perspectives?

With Wolf-Dieter Bensinger's retirement at the beginning of 1973, Wankel engine development at Daimler-Benz lost its leading protagonist, but it was above all one of his comrades-in-arms, Helmut Dobler, who had been operationally in charge of the design of rotary piston engines since the 1960s, who carried on Bensinger's legacy. It was due to Dobler's commitment that the Wankel engine did not disappear for the time being, even after the drastic reduction in development activities imposed at the end of the year. Although only certain scopes were to be pursued in connection with the Wankel engines, which were by then no longer quite so new, Dobler immediately started thinking about a more cost-effective overall design concept for the Wankel engine against the background of the critical costing questions. These led to the construction of a further fifteen two- and four-rotor engines of the most modern generation, the M 951, on which attempts were made again and again into the year 1975 to achieve progress in the known problem areas.

Although under the given circumstances any prospects of series production for the Wankel engine at Daimler-Benz had evaporated, the crucial question of "peripheral intake ports or side intake ports," which had already been answered ten years earlier, became once again the focus of engineers dealing with the topic. To a certain extent, they took note of the fact that the side-intake concept, which had in the meantime also been pursued by Audi NSU, Toyo Kogyo/Mazda, and even by General Motors, had proven to be easier to master developmentally—even if this meant having to say goodbye to the creation of cost-reducing modularity of a

Motor-bezeichnung	Hubraum (Ltr.)	Scheibenzahl	Gemischaufbereitung	Motor-*) gewicht (kg)
KKM 2 V 20	2,0	2	SE/V	142
KKM 2 V 23	2,3	2	SE/V	145
KKM 2 V 26	2,6	2	SE/V	148
KKM 2 V 29	2,9	2	SE/V	151
KKM 3 E 32	3,2	3	UE/K-Jet.	173
KKM 3 E 39	3,9	3	UE/K-Jet.	182
KKM 4 E 52	5,2	4	UE/K-Jet.	205

*) Motorgewichte ohne Getriebe, Öl, Wasser und SA-Teile aber mit therm. Reaktor und Luftpumpe

SE = Seiteneinlaß
UE = Umfangseinlaß
V = Vergaser
K-Jet.= Benzineinspritzung mit K-Jetronic

In 1975, the company envisioned a Wankel engine range consisting of side and peripheral intake engines that covered the entire output spectrum.

Wankel engine family, which had been the aim for over a decade. Willi Springer, responsible for fundamental issues in Wankel engine design at Daimler-Benz, undertook to draw up a detailed concept for a two-rotor engine with side intake ports, risking a glance at the two-rotor test engine with development code EA 871 that had been created at Audi NSU in the meantime, but whose adoption in large-scale production also remained an unfulfilled dream of its designers.

In retrospect, it is astonishing that Daimler-Benz's preoccupation with the Wankel engine went on another loop—albeit a severely limited one—lasting a good two years, even with concrete proposals for the restructuring of a corresponding range of engines. A well-founded prospect of remedying the still-existing weaknesses of these engines in a convincing way no longer existed in all these mental games. Especially since the inherent consumption disadvantage compared to reciprocating engines was now also acknowledged, which was diametrically opposed to the discussion at the time about reducing consumption and emissions.

The continuous development of the reciprocating engine range at Daimler-Benz also had to be taken into account. Here, new potential was tapped to a considerable extent, such as the V8 engines of the M 116 series, which were presented in 1969 in parallel to the C 111 and were still equipped with a gray cast iron block, as well as the ultramodern DOHC inline six-cylinder engines

These competitors of the Daimler-Benz Wankel engines, some of which were developed in parallel, set the bar high. The 3.5-liter V8 with the internal designation M 116 (*top*) was introduced in 1969 in the sedans of the W 109 series and the coupes and cabriolets of the W 111 model series. The straight-six M 110 with two overhead camshafts and 2.8-liter displacement (*center*) made its debut in the "Stroke Eight" models of the W 114 series in 1972. And the four-cylinder M 102 (*bottom*) launched its impressive career in the mid-range 123 model series in 1980.

of the M 110 series, introduced in 1972, or later the four-cylinder engines of the M 102 model series, presented in 1980.

In the end, the ideas put forward on the subject of the Wankel engine were not substantiated further, and when Friedrich van Winsen, head of passenger car development, finally and irrevocably put an end to some sixteen years of checkered development work in mid-February 1976, he knew that he was in agreement with Joachim-Hubertus Sorsche, head of passenger car construction at the time; Kurt Obländer, the head of engine development; and other senior employees from the development department. The decision was by no means taken lightly—after more than a decade and a half of dealing with a high-profile innovation topic, the company was not willing and able to draw this conclusion so easily—especially because the high development effort had no visible effects on the passenger car range in the end. Thus, in the general perception, the experimental vehicle C 111 remained the only exponent of the Wankel era at Daimler-Benz.

During a visit to the editorial office of *auto, motor und sport,* Hans Scherenberg, member of the Board of Management for Development, formulated a short and concise summary of the background, which could be read in the issue of July 21, 1976: "We have stopped advanced development work on the Wankel engine. For the following reasons: It needs too much petrol, cannot be operated as a diesel variant or converted to fuel stratified injection. In addition, it is very difficult in terms of production technology to produce Wankel engines with different numbers of rotors based on an efficient modular system. Moreover, a two-rotor engine is more expensive to produce than a six-cylinder engine."

The basis of the company's, when viewed soberly, long overdue decision was not only the multitude of technical and costing factors mentioned by Scherenberg, but also strategic considerations; the latter, above all, with regard to urgently needed resources in the development area, since the construction of a new generation of modern, consumption- and emissions-optimized four-cylinder petrol engines (which then appeared in 1980 in the form of the M 102 model series) was at the top of the agenda. Also, by the mid-1970s the competitive situation in the most important automotive markets had changed.

Not only at Daimler-Benz, but also at other manufacturers, realism had set in with regard to the Wankel engine: The Ro 80 had reached the home stretch of its life cycle, and under the new aegis of Audi NSU or Volkswagen, a Wankel-engined successor was not to be expected. The US giant General Motors had also shelved the already well-advanced development of a two-rotor Wankel engine in 1974–75, never to be seen again, while Ford had limited itself to pertinent research activities anyway. Only the persistent Japanese company Toyo Kogyo remained loyal to the rotary engine and undauntedly and successfully continued to develop it as a higher-quality engine alternative for certain segments of their Mazda passenger car range.

Wankel-motor zu Hubkolben-motor	KKM 2 V 20 Al M 101 V 20 GG	KKM 2 V 26 Al M 106 V 26 Al	KKM 3 V30/E32 Al M 106 V29/E32 Al	KKM 3 E 39 Al M 116 E 38 Al	KKM 4 E 52 Al M 117 E 50 Al	Scheibenzahl Gemischaufb./Hubvol. Gehäusewerkstoff Motortyp Gemischaufb./Hubvol. Kurbelgeh.-Werkstoff
Vergleich von:						Bemerkung:
1 Herstellkosten	−	+	−	+	+	einschl. Mehrkosten für KKM-Wageneinbauteile
2 Motoreinbaugewicht	○	○	○	○	○	einschl. Mehrgewicht für KKM-Wageneinbauteile
3 Baulänge	+	+	○	+	+	H'kante Schwungrad - V'kante Lüfter
4 mechan. Geräusch	+	○	+	○	○	Ventiltrieb V-Motoren mit hydr. Spielausgleich
5 Saug-u. Auspuffgeräusch	○	○	○	○	○	
6 Laufruhe	+	○	+	○	+	fehlende freie Massenkräfte und -momente
7 Drehmom.-Verlauf	−	−	−	−	−	niederes M_D unter n= 2000
8 Wartung	+	○	○	○	○	keine Ventilspieleinstellung kein Ölwechsel

+ = KKM günstiger   − = KKM ungünstiger   ○ = kein Unterschied

Vorausgesetzt wird, daß zwischen HKM u. KKM kein Unterschied im Kraftstoffverbrauch, Schadstoffemission u. Ruckelverhalten besteht.

Vor- und Nachteile des Wankelmotors

Bild 1

At the beginning of 1976, this simple grid drawn up at Daimler-Benz—which compared the Wankel and reciprocating engine developments planned at the time but left out some important aspects—got to the heart of the matter. Looking at the full picture, the Wankel engine option could be considered obsolete.

Positive Despite Everything: The Result of Wankel Engine Development at Daimler-Benz

The bottom line was that the development costs incurred by Daimler-Benz over the entire duration of the Wankel engine adventure added up to about 100 million deutsch marks. This investment did not result in an engine family that Daimler-Benz considered ready for series production, which would have made it possible to amortize the funds spent, but only in an estimated 300 test engines that were largely scrapped after the end of all development activities. But the invested funds could not be considered completely lost, either, since on closer examination they certainly had a value for the company—namely, on a more intangible level. The basic research that went into the Wankel engine for a good decade and a half produced numerous new insights that were also of considerable importance for the further development of reciprocating engines at Daimler-Benz. These include, first and foremost, the use and handling of hypereutectic (i.e., silicon-rich) aluminum alloys for engine parts, which has led to a significantly increased wear resistance of various components, a much better understanding of the combustion process in the four-stroke principle, and—not to be forgotten— early experience with innovative sliding surface coatings. The benefit of the variable-length intake manifold principle for the torque characteristics of petrol-powered reciprocating engines was also recognized at an early stage thanks to Wankel engine development. From Daimler-Benz's point of view, there was de facto no alternative to researching fundamentally new technologies with regard to their suitability for future use in series production.

To be able to assess Daimler-Benz's use of resources appropriately from the perspective of the time, it is also worth taking a look at the proportions in terms of the development budget: Of the total research and development money spent by the Group in the decade and a half of the Wankel engine era, less than 3% was spent on the innovative power units—an almost negligible proportion when one takes into account the lasting worldwide image boost that the Wankel-engined C 111 in particular provided the Mercedes-Benz brand. This assessment was apparently shared by Daimler-Benz members of the Board of Management, Joachim Zahn and Heinz Schmidt, who attested to the C 111's "still extraordinary advertising effect" as well as its "outstanding positive impact on our range."

Dream Sports Car and Laboratory on Wheels: The C 111

Since its creation, the Mercedes-Benz C 111 has represented an exceptional car in every respect and is often regarded as the crowning achievement of the Wankel development. It was not only the first officially presented Mercedes-Benz model with a rotary engine, but also the world's first car with the three-rotor variant of the innovative drive unit. To this day, the C 111 is regarded as a spectacular icon of the Mercedes-Benz brand and is one of the most prominent vehicles in automotive history. The extensive documentation in the Mercedes-Benz Classic Archives brings to life the history of this dream sports car, which is still fascinating today, and makes it possible to trace its creation and development from the very beginning along its sometimes winding paths.

Business Exercises:
The Roots of the C 111

Since the second half of the 1950s, Daimler-Benz had been repeatedly considering a successor to the legendary 300 SL sports car. Initially, the idea was to use the M 100 V8 engine for this purpose, which—originally with 5 liters of displacement—was just in the early stages of development and was intended for the W 100 luxury-class sedan. Unlike this vehicle, which finally debuted in 1963 as the 600 model, the sports car project known internally as the W 102 was not pursued in the end due to a lack of development capacity.

Instead, from mid-1961 on, the focus was on an additional variant of the W 113, which was currently being developed and was to appear in 1963 as the 230 SL. As early as the spring of 1960, the idea had been floated of including not only the performance-enhanced engine of the 220 SE for the W 113, but also the light-alloy version of the M 198 3-liter engine intended for the 300 SL (and introduced in March 1962).

From March 1962 on, the Wankel engine also came into play in these deliberations, when head of development Fritz Nallinger commissioned passenger car development to conduct the 500-hour endurance run of an F-engine, as the Wankel engine was initially called internally. However, the objective pursued in this way, to get an idea of the current development status, seemed to recede into the distant future after the testing department considered it unrealistic at that time to achieve the required durability of the engine.

At the end of October 1962, Nallinger became more specific and suggested using the Wankel engine initially in a sports car in order to be able to gain practical and production experience in small series. At the same time, he pointed out that a possible failure to fulfill the expectations placed in the Wankel engine would inevitably lead to the development of new series of the reciprocating engine. In December 1962, Nallinger appealed to the sales department to dispense with the 3-liter engine in the W 113 because of the high development costs involved. However, a connection between a more powerful sports car above the W 113 and a Wankel engine was again being considered—at least if it could be "brought to really advanced production maturity." The V8 engine was again mentioned as a possible alternative, which at that time was about to go into series production as the M 100. Also in December 1962, the Board of Management made the statement that the W 113 itself "would, however, also be suitable for the introduction of the Wankel engine."

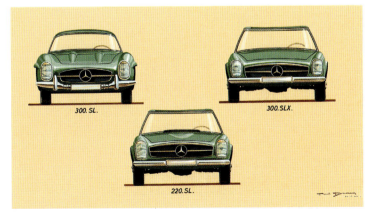 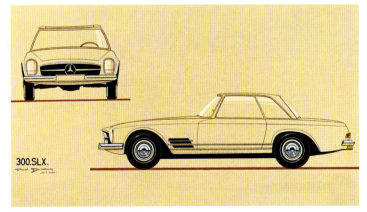

The drawings by designer Paul Bracq, which date from May 1962, visualize the considerations to complement the future "Pagoda SL" with a high-performance sports car, here dubbed the 300 SLX.

New Products: Inexpensive Two-Seater and Rally Cars

At the end of March 1963—the 230 SL had just celebrated its world premiere at the Geneva Motor Show—Nallinger addressed Rudolf Uhlenhaut, Josef Müller, Wolf-Dieter Bensinger, and Karl Wilfert in a memo with the subject "New small, inexpensive two-seater sports car" and encouraged his senior staff to begin conceptual deliberations on an "inexpensive sports car for young people." For the engine, he suggested a more powerful version of the 1.7-liter four-cylinder M 118, which was being developed in Untertürkheim for future models of the then subsidiary Auto Union, and also immediately thought of an alternative: "Of course, if we were ready with the Wankel engine by then, we could provide for a Wankel engine for this vehicle."

At that time, the novel engine was thus being discussed as a possible drive unit for three different sports cars: for the W 113, for a high-performance sports car above the SL of the time, and for a small, inexpensive sports car below the "Pagoda SL." From March 1964 on, thoughts of developing new sports car models came back

In March 1963, after the 230 SL made its debut at the Geneva Motor Show, Paul Bracq drew two variants with a hatchback, one of them for motor racing use.

Design drawings by Paul Bracq presenting different variants of the sports car study also known as the W 113 b

The 1:5 model of the W 113 b sports car study being measured in the model wind tunnel in Sindelfingen in February 1964

into focus when Fritz Nallinger asked head of passenger car development Rudolf Uhlenhaut, and Karl Wilfert, head of passenger car body development, in an internal memo to think about developing rally cars with a chance of success. Nallinger saw the future 250 SL as the basis and emphasized the possible weight savings through the use of a plastic body and improved aerodynamics. On the engine side, such a car could be "equipped with a 3-liter engine with increased performance and then, as a prototype, with a Wankel engine as early as possible." At the time of Nallinger's communication, the design department in Sindelfingen (then called Stylistics) was already busy designing 1:5 models of a more streamlined sports car and was also investigating these models in the wind tunnel. Under the designation W 113 b or W 113 X, these vehicles were developed in different variants and in individual cases even built as 1:1 design models.

Against the background of a possible future use of plastic bodies or body components, a delegation of Daimler-Benz employees from the process development, passenger car development, and testing departments visited Ernst Heinkel Flugzeugbau GmbH in Speyer in August 1964, where the bodies of the Porsche Carrera GTS (904) were made of fiberglass reinforced polyester resin (FRP). The travel report summarizes findings and potentials: "The production of the FRP parts is still very improvised and did not show anything significantly new. . . . On the other hand, a body divided into load-bearing frame structure and clad plastic body provides simpler and clearer load conditions. Furthermore, it is easier and quicker to change the shape of the body, as the base frame can usually retain its shape."

The W 113 b as a 1:1 design model in April 1964, photographed in the styling department in Sindelfingen

 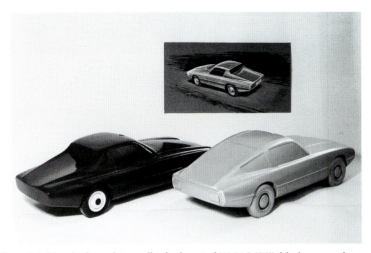

Two further variants of a sports car study designed by Paul Bracq in a 1:5 model. The designs, internally designated W 113 X III (*dark car on the left*) and W 113 X I, were created in May 1964.

The design drawing by Paul Bracq, dated May 11, 1964, shows a variant of the W 113 X III sports car study.

Change of Position: First Mid-Engine Concepts

In August 1964, the first design drawings by designer Paul Bracq showing a mid-engined sports car were also produced in the styling department. The underlying concept, including the dimensional concept, came from the later head of design, Bruno Sacco, who at the time was working in the body advance design department headed by Béla Barényi. In October, this concept was also implemented as a 1:5 design model in different variants under the designation W 113 X and tested in the wind tunnel.

The further development in February–March 1965 was fueled by discussions on the Board of Management about the future participation of Daimler-Benz AG in rallies. Nallinger stated on February 11 that "we would simply have to build a sports racing car," and the Board of Management decided at its meeting on March 3 to "set up a commission consisting of Messrs. Nallinger, Scherenberg, Langheck, and Staelin to work on this problem." Achieving this goal must have appeared to be a problem because, on the one hand, even Dr. Joachim Zahn, the financial director, who always acted with restraint, saw "a continuation of our rallying activities as a means of preserving our brand," while, on the other hand, Fritz Nallinger, a committed motorsport advocate, emphasized that "this class [of sports racing cars] will face competition with 7–7½-liter engines."

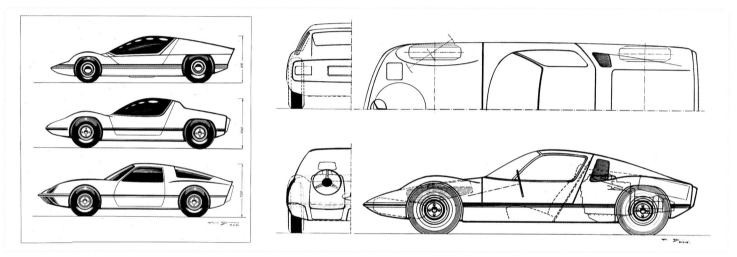

In August 1964, Paul Bracq drew several variants of a mid-engined sports car. The image on the right visualizes the basic layout.

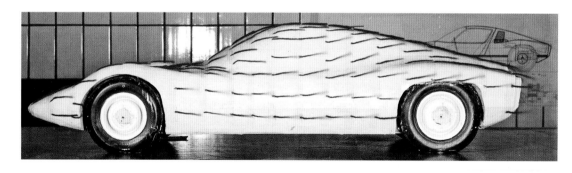

In October 1964, a 1:5 model of the sports car designated as the S II (*top*) was measured in the wind tunnel. A revised model with a more pronounced rear end followed in January 1965.

38 Dream Sports Car and Laboratory on Wheels: The C 111

The design drafts by Paul Bracq, dating from mid-January to early February 1965, show different variants of a sports car study with a longitudinally or transversely mounted mid-engine. The design was further developed on the basis of the version shown below on the left.

In February–March 1965, a further developed design of the sports car study, called the "sports car with central rear engine" or W 113 X, was presented in a 1:5 model. Paul Bracq (*on the right*) and his colleague Giorgio Battistella were responsible for the design.

39

At the same time, detailed designs and design models on a scale of 1:5 were created by Paul Bracq and Giorgio Battistella, some of which were in the style of racing prototypes of the time. The development of the sports car continued on the technical side, too. In a memorandum from March 1965, dedicated to the braking performance and brake temperature of the vehicle in comparison to the 600 Pullman model, a top speed of 300 km/h and a weight of 1,200 kg are mentioned for the "X model."

Only a few days later, at the beginning of April 1965, Friedrich van Winsen, head of passenger car advance design engineering, and his colleague Arthur Mähler presented the construction drawing of the chassis of the vehicle W 101 mentioned here, which was "designed as a racing sports car with minimal seat or maximal dimensions," during a visit to the styling department in Sindelfingen. On the basis of Karl Wilfert's statement that he envisioned a "touring sports car version" that "could be sold to a certain clientele," van Winsen agreed to develop a corresponding chassis variant. The 6.3-liter M 100 engine was intended as the power unit, as van Winsen was of the opinion that "there would be no perfected Wankel engine in the foreseeable future."

At the board meeting on September 3, 1965, under the agenda item "Designs for racing sports cars and the so-called small sports car," Nallinger presented the concepts that had emerged in the advance stylistics department. At the beginning of November, Dr. Hans Scherenberg, who was to take over from Prof. Fritz Nallinger as head of development, asked the stylistics department to

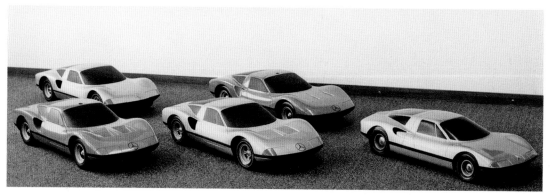

Different variants of the mid-engined sports car in 1:5 scale, now dubbed the 700 SL, taken in June 1965 in front of a 1:1 drawing in the presentation room of the styling department (*top*) **and in November 1965 in Paul Bracq's office**

The two drawings by Giorgio Battistella, dated May 1965, indicate that the high-performance sports car was also intended for competition use. The designation 630 SL suggests that the 6.3-liter V8 M 100 was to be used as the power unit.

In April 1966, the 1:1 design model of the sports car designated as the W 113 X was measured in the large wind tunnel of the FKFS (Forschungsinstitut für Kraftfahrwesen und Fahrzeugmotoren Stuttgart).

complete the model of the "large sports car" currently in the works as agreed, but "not to carry out any further work on this model for the time being until an internal discussion could be held." He referred to a 1:1 design model of the vehicle, which was called the "Model X," "X-Wagen," "SLX," "W 113 X," "W 101," or "Großer Sportwagen" (large sports car). In April 1966, this 1:1 model was examined in the large wind tunnel in Untertürkheim. The drag coefficient c_d was determined to be 0.356.

With regard to a possible motorsport commitment, the Board of Management had determined on March 29, 1966, on the occasion of the seventy-fifth birthday of the legendary racing director Alfred Neubauer, that "we must not allow ourselves to be drawn into the still very lively public discussion about the participation of German automotive companies in the races readily. DBAG will continue to maintain its involvement in rallies; there are currently no further plans within the company to resume racing operations and racing car construction per se."

In July 1966, future sports car projects were the subject of discussion at two consecutive board meetings. In his function as spokesman of the board, Dr. Joachim Zahn asked chief development officer Scherenberg to "think about a faster sports car" as an addition to the passenger car sales range.

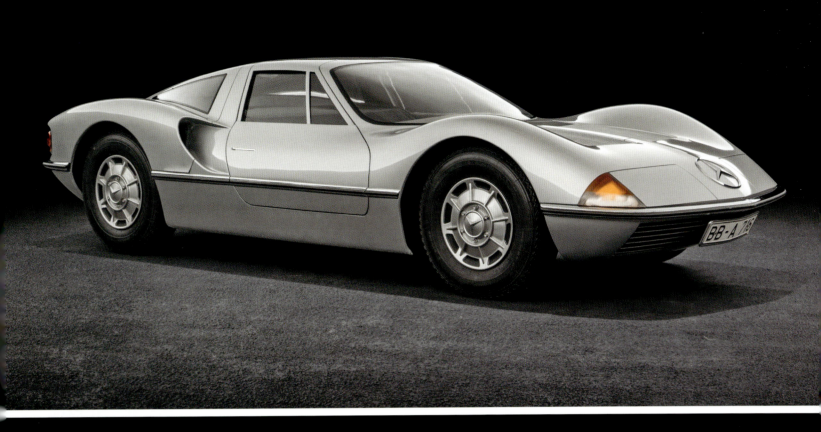
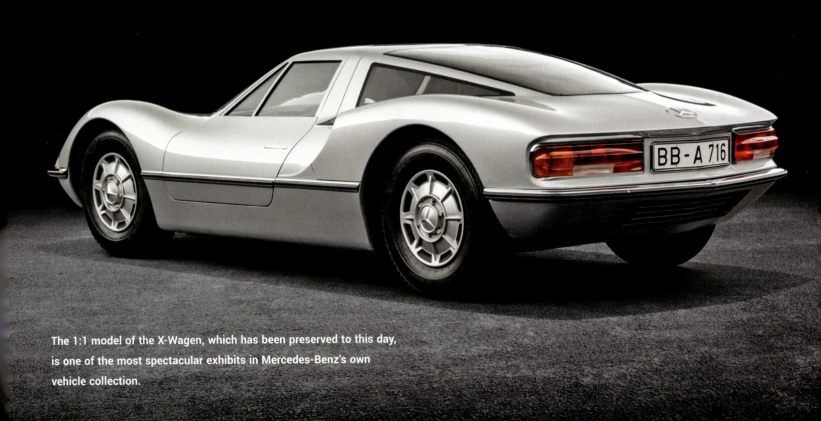

The 1:1 model of the X-Wagen, which has been preserved to this day, is one of the most spectacular exhibits in Mercedes-Benz's own vehicle collection.

Renewed Departure:
The C 101 Project

After the intensive discussions in July 1966, the sports car projects took a back seat again and were not pursued further for the time being. This only changed a good two years later. During a joint visit to the Turin Motor Show, which opened on October 30, 1968, head of development Scherenberg instructed the directors of passenger car development to examine the concept of a sporty vehicle with a Wankel engine, whereby the "high revs and low weight" made the new type of engine seem particularly suitable.

In the "Passenger Car Technical Meeting," which Scherenberg held at least once a week in Sindelfingen with the senior staff of the passenger car development department, the future sports car became a topic starting in late November 1968. Under the agenda item "New Projects," the meeting on November 25 put forward three different concepts for discussion and suggested considerations in this regard: first a "vehicle for racing events," for which a W 114 Coupe with 4.5-liter V8 engine M 117 was considered, then a "small sporty vehicle . . . for rallying, possibly a mid-engined car with two- or three-rotor Wankel engine for younger people, perhaps as a successor to the 190 SL, devoid of comfort" and finally a "sports car with M 100 . . . as a successor to the 300 SL." The meeting noted that the development department in Untertürkheim had begun work on a "platform for the small sporty vehicle" that Scherenberg had proposed.

At this time, the design engineers in the advance engineering department at Untertürkheim, led by Dr. Kurt Enke, were already working on the dimensional concept of the new sports car as well as on the design of the floor assembly and the chassis components. In principle, there were two alternatives to choose from: an all-steel body of conventional design or the tubular frame with light-alloy or GRP body panels that was often used in competition vehicles. An interim solution was eventually realized: a sheet steel floor pan with bonded GRP bodywork, which also met certain comfort requirements and represented the best compromise in terms of weight, rigidity requirements, deadline situation, and manufacturing costs as well as appealing passenger compartment design and extensive use of the existing production capacity. A frame construction made of aluminum, which would have provided weight advantages over the steel version while offering the same rigidity, would only have been appropriate for an all-out competition vehicle because of the higher material and production costs. The decision as to whether the body should be made of light alloy or GRP remained open at first and was finally made at the end of April.

In a sense, the vehicle was designed from scratch on a blank sheet of paper, from the inside out. The dimensional concept of the interior and the exterior dimensions resulted from the interaction of a few factors: the now-defined mid-engine concept, the required ground clearance, the distance between the driver's seat and the pedals, and the space requirements of the roll bar and the engine/transmission combination. For the wheelbase, this resulted in a value of 2,500 mm—100 mm more than in the SL sports cars of the 1950s and 1960s. As a result of the fuel tanks being positioned in the side sills, the car was built similarly tall in the entry area as the classic 300 SL, and thus the characteristic gullwing doors were almost a matter of course, which—not without intention—evoked memories of the legendary sports car of 1954.

The new sports car project was discussed in detail at the technical meeting on December 2, 1968. The engine radiator was

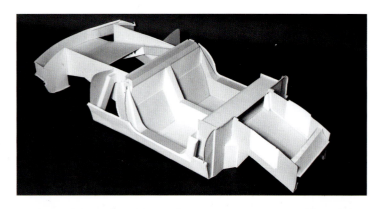

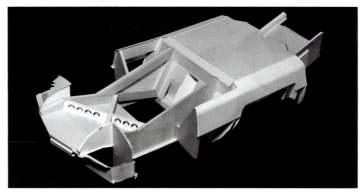

The 1:5 scale model of the frame floor system made from cardboard for a mid-engined sports car initially called "Sport X 2" is considered the constructive basis from which the "substructure for the small sporty vehicle" emerged as the starting point for the development of the C 111. Views from above and below.

located at the front, and the mid-engine arrangement required an opening for the air intake at the side in front of the rear wheel arch. The minutes also stated that the headlights must not be covered and that a roll bar with a wide base must be taken into account. For the wind tunnel investigation of front and rear axle lift and drag coefficients, the creation of models was required as soon as possible. In particular, the front-end design was to be developed in detail in the wind tunnel.

The plans called for using the M 950 engine in the new sports car, which was then currently being developed as a three-rotor engine. In a note from the passenger car advance engineering department dated December 6, 1968, the design engineers defined the changes that a mid-engine installation would require. This included a redesigned oil pan for an increased oil volume of 7 liters and the engine installed slanted by 7° to the rear. The ignition distributor needed to be rotated and the water and oil filler necks moved to the rear so that they no longer protruded forward beyond the distributor housing. The flywheel had to be adapted to the intended clutch, and of the peripherals, the vacuum pump, the power steering pump, and the air conditioning compressor were to be omitted. By dispensing with brake booster, power steering, and air conditioning, the decision to forgo comfort, as formulated in the conceptual considerations, had apparently been taken very literally, which was to change in the further course of the project, at least in parts. The examination of fundamental details was also addressed—such as the questions of whether the water pump was sufficient for the expected increased resistance in the cooling system, whether the necessary silencer volume had already been

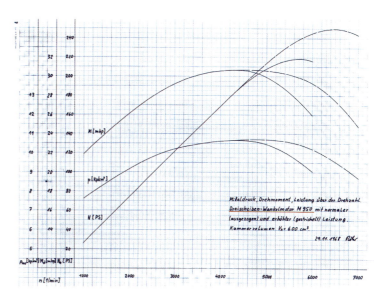

This diagram, dated November 29, 1968, presents the calculated engine speed curve of mean pressure, torque, and power for the three-rotor Wankel engine M 950/3 with "normal" and "increased" output. The maximum outputs of 219 hp/161 kW and 245 hp/180 kW assumed here could be significantly increased in the course of the project.

defined, and whether dry sump lubrication was possible. However, this note is of historical interest primarily because in its subject line, a proper name for the new sports car was documented for the first time: The designation C 101 W 36 stood for a coupe of the 101 model series with a Wankel engine and a displacement equivalent of 3.6 liters.

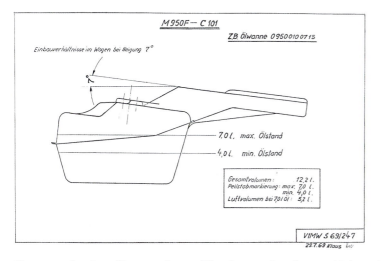
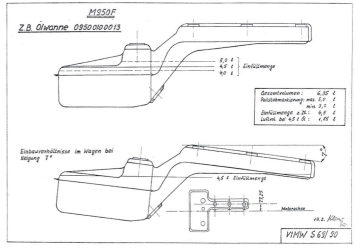

These two drawings illustrate the modifications to the oil pan, which made the required oil capacity of 7 liters and a 7° rearward slanted engine installation possible.

Form Finding: First Design Drafts of the C 101

Because of the concept worked out in the advance engineering phase, stylists Joseph Gallitzendörfer, Andreas Langenbeck, Ferdinand Hellhake, and Gérard Cardiet developed the first design drafts at the beginning of December 1968, which were presented at the technical meeting on December 9 and dealt with together with questions of the dimensional concept. The weight according to the concept so far was given as approximately 900 kg—a value that was later to prove illusory. The chassis designed by the passenger car advance engineering department in Untertürkheim in November 1968 had already been modified in detail on December 12. The pedals, steering wheel, and seat were moved back by 15 mm, and the seat backrest was now 30 mm thinner in order to be able to retain the wheelbase of 2,500 mm. On the basis of the updated chassis drawing provided on December 12, Sindelfingen immediately began with the body development, and at the beginning of January 1969, chief stylist Friedrich Geiger sent two first drawings—a detailed side elevation and a rather sketch-like cross section—to Friedrich van Winsen, by then head of passenger car construction in Untertürkheim.

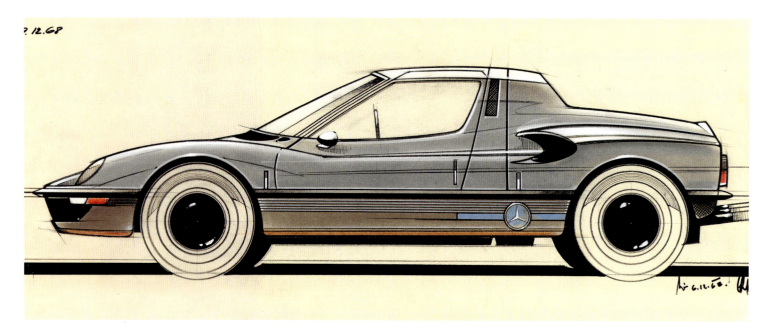

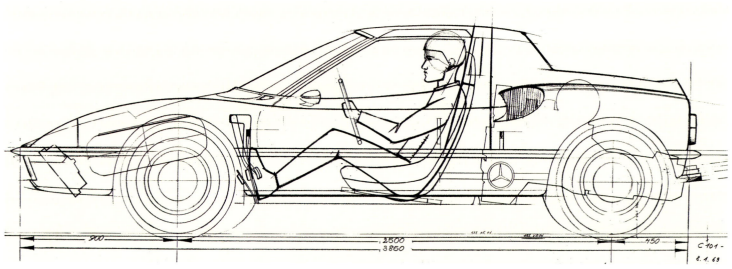

This longitudinal section, dated January 8, 1969, and worked out in detail in the styling department, was the first drawing to show the C 101 as a complete vehicle with interior and power unit position.

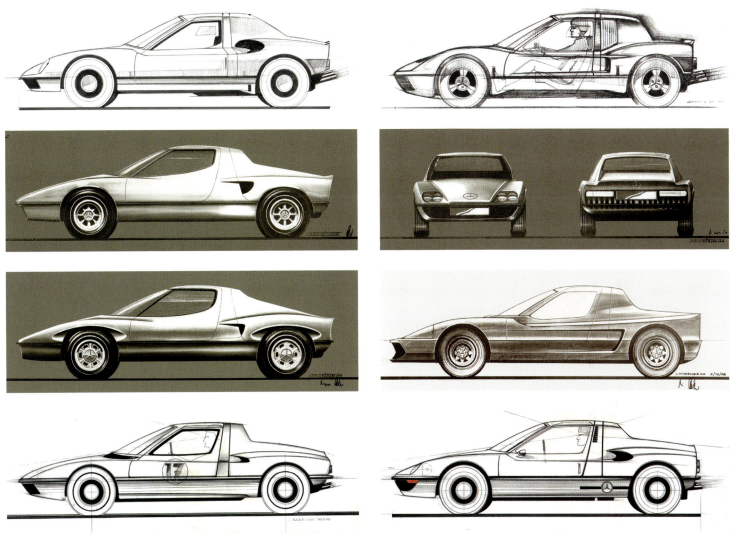

The first design drawings of the C 101, dated from November–December 1968, created by stylists Joseph Gallitzendörfer (*opposite page and first row*), Gérard Cardiet (*second row and third row left*), Andreas Langenbeck (*third row right*), and Ferdinand Hellhake (*fourth row*)

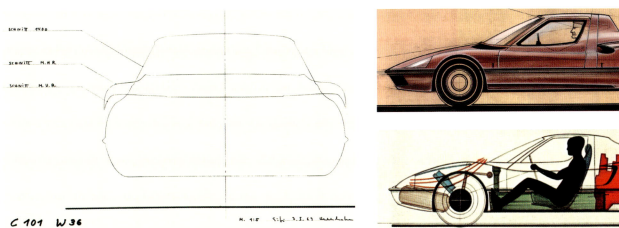

Body cross-sections of the C 101, drawn by Ferdinand Hellhake in early January 1969

Design drawing by Ferdinand Hellhake from December 1968 (*top*) and longitudinal section by Joseph Gallitzendörfer from January 1969 (*bottom*)

On December 17, 1968, the new sports car was also discussed for the first time in a board meeting. Regarding the considerations to equip the vehicle with a Wankel engine, head of development Dr. Hans Scherenberg pointed out that a test engine had recently reached a mileage of 85,000 km for the first time. The discussion immediately turned to the question of possible motorsport applications. In response to the comment that the installation of the Wankel engine in a sporty vehicle in particular might not be uncritical, Scherenberg replied that "the use of the Wankel engine in a vehicle intended for sporting competition is safe, since the engine is only ever stressed for a relatively short time here." Scherenberg answered Dr. Joachim Zahn's question in the affirmative as to whether a reciprocating engine could be envisaged as a replacement for the Wankel engine—albeit with the restriction that "the studies for this have not yet been completed and the installation of these large-capacity engines will pose considerably greater difficulties."

In accordance with the current status of the concept, Scherenberg gave the following key data in the board meeting:

Engine output	219 or 245 hp
Total weight	825–870 kg
Kerb weight	750–800 kg
Frontal area	1.55 m²
C_d value	0.36
Wheelbase	2.50 m
Center-of-gravity height	approximately 0.40 m
Overall length	approximately 3.85 m
Overall height	approximately 1.13 m
Overall width	approximately 1.64 m

Based on these key data and the power and torque diagram of the M 950/3 three-rotor engine dated November 29, 1968, the advance engineering department in Untertürkheim had calculated performance diagrams on December 6 and 12.

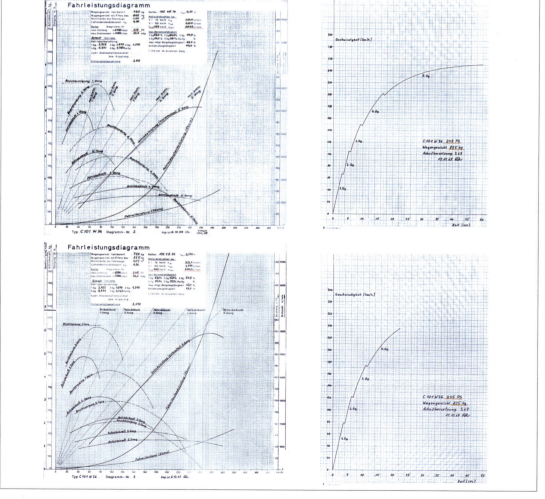

At the beginning of December 1968, performance and acceleration diagrams for the C 101 were calculated for engine variants with 219 hp/ 161 kW and 245 hp/180 kW, assuming a car weight of 825 kg. Although there was a significant increase in weight in the course of development, the calculated values for top speed and acceleration were essentially achieved in the end.

48   Dream Sports Car and Laboratory on Wheels: The C 111

Concretization:
Concept Definition of the C 101

The C 101 played a leading role in the passenger car technical meeting on January 20, 1969. The minutes document, in unusually clear terms, the need for action in all fundamental aspects of the project development: "Deadline situation is unclear. The quantity is unclear. Equipment (compared to the R 107) is unclear. C 101 is to be dealt with urgently in the next meeting. To this end, a catalog of arguments is to be prepared by Dr. Enke and Mr. Andres, which is to be discussed before the next meeting." The addressed staff took immediate action, and by January 24 a comprehensive paper had been produced under the title "C 101 W 36—Unanswered Questions," which, in addition to a seven-page questionnaire, also contained a four-page list of comparison vehicles of motorsport groups 3 (GT) and 4 (sports cars), subdivided by class and very broad in scope. The questionnaire is reproduced here in unabridged form:

I. **Intended use** yes / no
  A. **Competition only** (see explanations below)
    When 1st competition: 1969
    1970
    1971?
  B. **Racing and sports car* in small numbers**
    (see explanations below)
    When 1st test car: 1970
    1971
    1972?
  C. **Sports car* with great comfort (not competition)**
    (see explanations below)
    When 1st test car: 1970
    1971
    1972?
  *Sports car along the lines of 280 SL and 300 SL
  D. **Show car in the shape** A.
    B.
    C.
  for IAA Frankfurt 1969 (similar to Opel GT in Frankfurt 1965 and Rover [P 6 BS, the author] in Brussels 1969)

Explanations for A.
1. **Engine**
   Available: three-rotor Wankel with about 270 hp (3.6 l); unfavorable, as class size for competition 3 l to 5 l!
   Available in 9 months: three-rotor Wankel with about 360 hp (3.6 l) (racing use)
   Available in approximately 9 months: four-rotor Wankel with approximately 480 hp (4.8 l) (2 units for racing)

2. **Racing axles** need to be developed.

3. **General**
   Car should have victories before exhibition. Later, A. could then be developed into the car B.
   But B. can only come after the R 107!
   Some vehicles can be made quickly by "tinkering."
   More general safety regulations are not taken into account.
   No comfort (without heating, but with ventilation).

Explanations for B.
This car is probably also to be exported.
Since the points listed below must then be taken into account, development cannot be completed quickly.
Time-consuming points include:
1. Steering wheel displacement;
2. 30-mile test; [limitation of steering wheel displacement in an impact at 30 mph]
3. Windshield defroster;
4. Size of windshield wiper swept area;
5. Position, dimensions and approval of the lights;
6. Sight angles;
7. Instrument panel padding;
8. Exhaust gas purification!;
9. Side tank arrangement (impact regulations).

Explanations for C.
Car would have to stand out from R 107 with futuristic body shape and powerful engine, otherwise competition for R 107.

II. **Should car be a GT or sports car?**
   Required: as GT 500 units/year (from 1971: 1,000 units/year)
   as a sports car 25 units/year
   as a sports prototype

III. **Design for victory in class or overall classification?**

IV. Which engine:	a. Wankel 3 rotors (3.6 l)
	b. Wankel 4 rotors (4.8 l)
	c. Reciprocating piston?
		2. Flaps	a. front flap bolted
			b. door hinge on roof
			   door hinge on firewall pillar
			   door hinge on roof and fire wall pillar

V. Which axles:	a. Racing axles b. Production component axles?	**3. Protection profiles**	a. front/rear bumper b. protective rail front/rear c. protective rail on the side of the side rail (tank)
VI. Export to which countries:	a. USA b. Sweden?	**4. Trunk**	a. according to sports car regulations b. according to DB W 113 luggage set
VII. Manufacture in which quantity:	a. 50 units b. 500 units c. 5,000 units	**5. Air conditioning**	a. no heating, good ventilation b. heating and good ventilation c. installation of air conditioning system possible
VIII. Design for which price range:	a. DM 14,000–20,000 b. DM 20,000–25,000 c. DM 25,000–30,000**?**	**6. Seats**	a. simple bucket seat b. comfortable bucket seat c. Spring core bucket seat d. seat bolted down e. bolted seat with 70 mm adjustment f. seat rails with arrestor g. backrest adjustment.
IX. When should vehicle be shown:	a. 1969 b. 1970 c. 1971?		

Detailed Questions

Chassis:
1. Are parts to be made of titanium and beryllium as far as possible?
2. Pedals and steering wheel adjustable?
3. Anti-lock device?
4. Brake booster?
5. Does track width have to be the same for competition and customer vehicle?
6. Must wider tires be covered at the rear?
7. Are production components to be used for
   a. Steering
   b. Pedals?
8. Is right-hand drive required?

7. Side windows
a. rigid
b. ventilation plate
c. split and sliding
d. to crank down partially or completely
e. glass
f. plexiglass.

Body:
1. Coachwork
   a. of aluminum
   b. of magnesium
   c. of plastic
   d. of steel
   e. mixed construction
   f. partially riveted
   g. welding spots visible

8. Lights
   Headlights
   a. recessed with removable cover
   b. recessed, covered with plexiglass
   c. recessed and rotating
   d. top-mounted.

9. Radio

10. Windshield wiper	a. one wiper blade
	b. two wiper blades in parallel
	c. two wiper blades counter-moving
11. Ashtray	
12. Cigar lighter	
13. Door locks and handles	a. production handle
	b. handle recessed
	c. without handle
14. Floor trim	a. carpet
	b. rubber mat
	c. none

15. Spare wheel at the front outside, folding down?

16. What angle of approach must be taken into account?

On February 3, this questionnaire was the subject of an extensive discussion in the technical meeting, the results of which are recorded in detail:

A 1. Intended use:
Competition and sports cars in small numbers; five cars (preferably for IAA, Frankfurt) will be entered.

A 2. Consideration of certain regulations:
(The number indicates urgency level)
a) Steering wheel displacement (1)
b) Lights, individual approval if necessary (1)
c) Sight angles for road use (1)
d) Instrument panel padding (1)
e) Exhaust gas purification (idle) (1)
f) Fuel tank arrangement (side) (1)
g) 30-mile test (2)
h) Windshield defroster (2)
i) Windshield wiper swept area (2)

A 3. Version sports car
(25 cars per year)

A 4. Engine
Wankel engine for 3 and 4 rotors
Reciprocating piston engine probably not

A 5. Axles
Production components (1)
Racing axles (2)

A 6. Export
USA, Sweden (2)

A 7. Quantity
500 units

A 8. Price range
up to DM 20,000

A 9. Weight
According to Mr. van Winsen for competition vehicle with minimum equipment and 100-liter fuel tank 912 kp; of which frame and body 223 kp.

A 10. Chassis
a) Special metals — no
b) Adjustable pedals and steering wheel — no
c) Anti-lock device — no
d) Brake booster — no
e) Track width: may be different for competition and customer vehicle
f) wider rear tire cover necessary
g) steering and pedals production components
h) right-hand drive — yes

A 11. Coachwork
Material: Aluminum or plastic or mixed construction. Welding spots and rivets may be visible.

A 12. Protective profiles
Protective rail front and rear yes, lateral — no

A 13. Trunk
according to sports car regulations

A 14. Air conditioning
Heating and good ventilation — yes
Installation of air conditioning system — no

A 15. Seats
a) Simple bucket seat
b) Seat bolted down with screw-type adjustment
c) Backrest adjustment — no

A 16. Side windows a) split and sliding
b) Material: glass
c) for competition vehicles plexiglass

A 17. Headlights
top-mounted

A 18. Installation option for radio — no

A 19. Ashtray — yes
Cigar lighter — no

A 20. Lockable doors
Recessed exterior door handles, basically like 300 SL

A 21. Floor trim, door trim
a) Rubber mat
b) Interior door trim as a simple cover

A 22. Spare wheel
Removable from the front if possible

A 23. Angle of approach/departure
Aerodynamics have priority for the size of the angle of approach/departure.

On the organizational side, it was noted that the so-called enrollment (i.e., the Board of Management's concrete commissioning of the vehicles to be built) must now take place and that a special clearing office, separate from the other accounts, must be set up for the project. With regard to the required capacities, it was determined that the C 101 project should not be at the expense of the ongoing projects. However, the sober assessment "How this will be solved is completely open" is also documented. This meant that the ambitious sports car project was subject to capacity restrictions right from the start, which had been an issue in the Mercedes-Benz development division for years.

Open Questions: Motorsport Use and Series Production

As early as January 15, Rainer Schick, an employee of the development organization and planning department, had summarized the current ideas with regard to possible motor racing applications in a note to his manager, Karl-Wilhelm Müller. Referring to a communication from Dr. Kurt Enke, Schick stated that two versions of the C 101 were being considered, and also commented on the design of the body. Schick's remarks are quoted verbatim below:

    1.) Road vehicle with three-rotor Wankel engine (VD = 3.6 ltr.),
    output approximately 300 hp,
    Interior dimensions like passenger car,
    homologation limit as vehicle for rally events   500 units

    2.) Racing car with four-rotor Wankel engine (VD = 4.8 ltr.),
    output > 400 hp,
    thanks to 4th rotor of the Wankel engine. Interior dimensions only for small drivers,
    homologation threshold as a racing vehicle
    for e.g. Le Mans, Sebring, Nürburgring   50 units

The body is to be made of plastic. For the 1st version, we are possibly also considering an aluminum design. Sifi [Sindelfingen] is currently working on the 3rd model (scale 1:5), Ut [Untertürkheim]. (Mr. Nadolny) has one model ready.
It would be urgent to clarify in a board meeting whether DB is actually able to produce plastic bodywork.

Karl-Wilhelm Müller doubted that a racing car "only for small drivers" was the right solution, noting on Schick's memo, "The installation of the four-rotor Wankel engine should be provided for from the outset. Mr. Uhlenhaut did say that this could be done by simply lengthening the wheelbase; the only question here is whether this wheelbase should not be provided for in general."

The advance design engineering department dealt in detail with the opportunities of a possible motorsport engagement and the conceptual aspects to be considered in this context. On January 24, Dr. Kurt Enke summarized his initial findings in this regard in a paper titled "Possibilities for the use of the C 101 for sports purposes and the consequences for design and number of units." In his analysis, he disregarded Group 1 (production touring cars) and Group 2 (touring cars) and concentrated instead on the framework conditions and conceivable competitors in Group 3 (GT vehicles with a homologation quantity of 500 units/year), Group 4 (sports cars with a homologation quantity of 25 units/year), and Group 6 (sports prototypes without a quantity requirement with extensive freedom in design). Uncertainty arose from expected but not yet finally defined future changes regarding the group classifications of the sports cars, as well as their impact on the manufacturer championship. If this were to be competed for with sports prototypes, Enke feared major challenges in achieving the power density of 150 hp required to be competitive in this category.

Enke's colleague Erwin Löffler continued the considerations in great detail and documented the results in the paper "Design of the C 101 W 36 if it is to be used for competitions," dated January 29, 1969. For the engine configuration of a competition variant, it was assumed in this study that a three-rotor engine with the displacement equivalent of 3.6 liters could achieve approximately 360 hp/265 kW and a four-rotor engine with a displacement equivalent of 4.8 liters, which is more appropriate according to the new FIA guidelines, could achieve approximately 480 hp/353 kW—however, it was noted that the engine would have to be redesigned to allow for a presumed 100 hp/liter output in the process. Because of the 500 vehicles required in Group 3 within twelve months, Löffler ruled out the use of titanium or beryllium but considered an aluminum floor pan with a plastic body conceivable. In order to be able to compete in Group 4, Löffler considered it necessary to develop axles specially suited for racing tires; in addition, the weight would have to be kept extremely low and a four-rotor engine would have to be used to exploit the displacement limits. Even for a use in Group 6, the challenges seemed almost insurmountable: The weight had to be "lowered extremely by using titanium and beryllium, and should not exceed 600 kg. . . . Wide 15-inch racing tires must be used at the front and rear (this means the development of racing car axles)." The result of Löffler's analysis was accordingly sobering: with the construction status at the time (three-rotor engine and production axles [from the W 114/115]), the C 101 could not be used in motor racing, and even extremely costly development measures on the engine, chassis, and axles could not be considered a guarantee for competitiveness in the sport.

Irrespective of this assessment (and also not exclusively related to the C 101), head of development Scherenberg pointed out in the board meeting on February 4, 1969, that the 1969 development budget did not yet include any expenditure for sports purposes, so that additional funds might have to be made available for this as part of a special budget. In response to a question from Dr. Hanns Martin Schleyer, responsible for the central planning and central administration department, he reported in this context that "the Wankel engine for the sporty vehicle (C 101) currently in the works is to be approved shortly." It could be expected that "the chassis and engine of the first test specimen would be ready by the beginning of April 1969." The advance engineering department in Sindelfingen is currently examining "whether an aluminum or plastic body should be used." If possible, four to five vehicles should be available by the 1969 IAA. Scherenberg's colleagues acknowledged the report with approval but noted that the final use of the vehicle model—and any associated investments—"should not be decided until later."

One day later, on February 5, the new sports car was discussed for the first time in the passenger car commission. The commission consisted of high-ranking representatives from development, product planning, the technical plant management of the Untertürkheim and Sindelfingen plants, and the finance and accounting departments, as well as various sales departments, and back then met on average once a month. It had the task of ensuring a continuous flow of information between the specialist departments, advancing cross-divisional issues by commissioning the specialist departments involved, and drawing up recommendations for the Board of Management.

As the meeting minutes document, the project was discussed extensively and in detail: "Uhlenhaut reports on the C 101 to the commission and explains that the Board of Management has repeatedly requested vehicles for sporting activities from the development department. The C 101 was now presented in response . . . a mid-engine car with two seats (engine between the seats and the rear axle), with sporty equipment designed as a very low-profile coupe. If possible, it should weigh less than 1,000 kg and be equipped with a three-rotor Wankel engine of approximately 300–350 hp. In principle, the axles should be adopted from our series production. The transmission integral with the differential is to be supplied by ZF [Zahnradfabrik Friedrichshafen]. In response to corresponding inquiries, Uhlenhaut explains that the C 101 is not suitable for events such as Sebring and Le Mans etc. but is intended as a sporty image vehicle. The development department envisages that the C 101 could make its debut at the 1969 IAA with one exhibition vehicle and four demonstration vehicles . . . and that around 100 vehicles could be produced in 1970. Uhlenhaut mentions DM 20,000 to 25,000 as the target price." That notion turned out to be anything but realistic.

Uhlenhaut's commission colleagues pointed out that such a low production quantity could also result in a much-higher price, and noted that investments for a series production of the C 101

Rudolf Uhlenhaut, head of passenger car development, photographed in October 1969 with the M 950/3 three-rotor Wankel engine

sports car could only be approved if the facts required as part of the usual planning processes were available. For this purpose, development dates would have to be presented in milestone plans, especially by the development division. The commission members stated for the record that if this sports car were to be shown at the 1969 IAA, it would have to be known from when this model would be produced and in what numbers. They were in favor of the C 101 for image reasons but pointed out that this should in no way affect the deadlines for the W 116 or the R 107. In addition, they made it clear that the durability of the Wankel engine must be guaranteed in this model in particular. The price, they stated, did not play a decisive role for this vehicle. Also discussed was the aspect that if the C 101 were to debut at the IAA at the same time, two different high-performance engines would be presented to the public for the first time: the 3.5-liter V8 engine M 116 and the three-rotor Wankel engine. The resulting consequences would have to be carefully reviewed. Finally, the passenger car commission instructed the development division in a formal resolution to announce the development dates for the C 101 sports car in detail, in order to be able to check the dates and expenses for a later series production on this basis.

Four weeks after the commission meeting, on March 4, 1969, the project was also discussed again by the Board of Management. As part of the preparations for the Supervisory Board meeting on March 12, Schleyer "asked whether the investments of DM 2.5 million that would become necessary in connection with the production of a larger number of the experimental model C 101 should already be applied for now." Scherenberg explained that "the vehicle was to be presented at the IAA 1969 and that six vehicles were to be produced by that time. In order to then be able to produce twenty-five to fifty vehicles of this model in the spring of 1970, the investment of DM 2.5 million would have to be made." If the vehicle were not built, only "DM 0.6 million, which is accounted for by model-related operating resources, would be lost . . . , since the remaining DM 1.9 million is investment in machinery that can also be used for other purposes."

After a short discussion, the Board of Management decided to "first wait for the success of the six prototypes, for which the enrolment is now approved, in order to then make a decision on the investment of DM 2.5 million necessary for a series of twenty-five to fifty vehicles." On the same day, the development organization and planning department informed the central planning department in a message:

Based on today's Board of Management resolution (according to Mr. Schroeder, secr. Dr. Scherenberg, as per Management Resolution No. 5757 <u>6 mid-engined C 101 vehicles</u> are to be produced.

Production:	DBAG W 19 testing department, UT
	DBAG W 50 testing department, Sifi
Account assignment	64116 12114
Project:	135 000

In addition, <u>50 mid-engined C 101 vehicles</u> are to be enrolled as a small series (W 10 and W 50).

Account assignment: Series

Compared to the recorded Board of Management resolution, which had made the enrolment of the small series dependent on the "success of the six prototypes," the communication to the central planning division went one step further on two points: on the one hand, a quantity of fifty vehicles was defined and, on the other hand, the enrollment of the small series was not linked to any prerequisites.

On March 5, one day after the decision by the Board of Management, development management and the development organization and planning department summarized the key data and defined the approval stages for the main major assemblies in accordance with the usual procedure for series production vehicles.

Wheelbase	2,500 mm
Front track	1,380 mm
Rear track	1,370 mm
Engine	three-rotor Wankel
	3.6 ltr. displacement 270 hp / 7,000
Transmission	ZF 5 DS—25-1
Front axle	W 116 lb.
Rear axle	Parallel axle ("racing axle")

In contrast to the originally favored use of production axles, a complex rear-axle design in the style of a racing car was now surmised—a change of direction, whose usefulness was to become apparent during the first test drives.

On April 3, 1969, an official "approval notice" provided information about the newly defined model variant: The

C 101 W 36 was given the model code 101.020, the three-rotor Wankel engine M 950/3 the engine code 950.930. This meant that nothing stood in the way of a series production, at least on the part of product documentation.

In a letter to Rolf Staelin, the member of the Board of Management responsible for domestic sales, Helmut Schmidt, the director in charge of sales promotion, market research, and sales planning, had addressed the issue of a future motorsport participation by Daimler-Benz on March 14, which was increasingly being discussed in public and would undoubtedly attract further attention with the C 101. Against this background, Schmidt demanded that "engineering must clearly present the conception and task of this new model" and posed two key questions:

1). Is the C 101 intended to be a truly sporty vehicle? We would like to point out that the 350 SL and 450 SL models will be available from the end of 1970.
2). In which area of motor racing would a C 101 really stand a chance?

When assessing success, Schmidt referred to the Porsche 917 and Ford GT 40 racing sports cars and concluded, "If the C 101 cannot become a real sports car, there is no chance of using it to revitalize our image in the direction of sportiness and youthfulness. It must also be feared that the closer the C 101 is to the performance of our conventional engines, the more likely it is that there are expectations that this engine will be adopted for production vehicles. Our sales situation could possibly be upset."

Four days later, on March 18, Hans Scherenberg summarized the background and the objective of the C 101 project in a memo to his fellow board members. In it he wrote,

"We were clear from the outset that we wanted to create a kind of prototype that was to be light and fast but, on the other hand, also offer the possibility of driving on normal roads, similar to the old 300 SL with gullwing doors. This means a certain level of comfort, e.g., with regard to the seating position.

"Apart from that, the vehicle should not become too large in dimensions and too "harsh" of a vehicle, however, in which one consciously forgoes certain comforts and equipment. The vehicle must therefore be quite deliberately differentiated from the touring sports cars under development, such as today's 280 SL and its successor, the R 107. Of course, compared to earlier times, these vehicles, especially when the R 107 is equipped with the 4.5-ltr. engine, are also already quite sporty and will reach speeds of over 200 km/h.

"On the other hand, the sports cars comparable to the C 101 have also become much faster, as the latest developments of the Porsche 917 or the Ford GT 40 show. The latter, however, are specialist competition cars, whereas we are thinking of offering our C 101 for more normal use to sporty gentlemen in a deliberately limited scope.

"We believe that the program of this C 101 should achieve some essential things:

1). Raise our reputation in terms of sporting and technical tendency.
2). Possibility of supplying such vehicles to special customers who are public figures . . .
3). Introduction and testing of the Wankel engine without clashing with current production models. In the process, valuable opportunities for our model series can arise from the experience and pressure to bring the Wankel engine to a higher level of maturity here. . . .
4). The favorable possibility of a modular design of the Wankel engine would also allow various vehicle models to be provided with two, 3 or 4 rotors in special sporty versions. Although we start with the three-rotor version in the C 101, we have designed the vehicle so that the four-rotor version also fits. . .

"In line with the purpose of the vehicle, we should be clear that this is a low-volume special vehicle that needs to be adaptable at all times. We must be able to use this vehicle to modify it with regard to the axle to be more like a sports car in order to use it ourselves potentially or to have it used by fitting customers. We also need to be able to use different body styles not only in terms of shape but also in terms of body material, e.g. plastic or light alloy. Only in this way will we also have the corresponding gain for our development.

"As has already happened on several occasions, I would like to stress here once again that we should not wait too long to approve 50 more vehicles. We have to leave some leeway here, otherwise the interval between the prototype exhibited in Frankfurt and the possible delivery to customers, as described above, will be too long. Apart from that, if you think of sporting use, 25 or 50 cars would have to be built before approval is granted."

With regard to the controversially discussed and not conclusively assessed question of possible motor racing applications for the C 101, Georg von Bismarck—responsible in the development organization and planning division for the technical market observation field of work—prepared a detailed analysis, which he summarized on April 21, 1969, under the title "Considerations on the program of sporty DB passenger cars with regard to motor racing participation." In conclusion, von Bismarck stated, "For DB, only overall victories can be considered as desired successes. Since these cannot be achieved with sufficient certainty in the 'sports prototype' or 'sports car' groups, the European Rally Championship remains as the goal. It can be realized first and foremost with a successful 'Grand Touring Car,' especially through a 'Special Grand Touring Car.'"

This summary was based on very detailed research that looked at the C 101 in the relevant motor racing categories in comparison with the respective competitor vehicles. In Group 4 (sports cars), the C 101 with a four-rotor engine was not considered to have any chance of success against the competition due to insufficient power density. Von Bismarck saw certain prospects in Group 3 (Grand Tourisme cars) and especially in Group 4, which was redefined in 1970 (now for special Grand Tourisme cars) but noted a risk from competitors with powerful reciprocating engines and increased power densities. Moreover, participation in both groups would have required a production of 500 vehicles within twelve months. As a possible alternative, von Bismarck presented the option of foregoing motorsport ambitions and aiming not for motorsport success with sporty cars such as the C 101, but exclusively for sales success.

Regardless of the sobering overall results of this analysis, possible motor racing applications were still not explicitly ruled out. The advance engineering department in Untertürkheim even designed a C 101 with a four-rotor Wankel engine as a Group 4 racing sports car in August 1969, but the project was not pursued further. Unfortunately, the reasons for this are not documented. The decisive factor here was probably, above all, the competitive situation in the racing scene, as explained in detail by von Bismarck, and the production quantity of 500 vehicles required by the regulations.

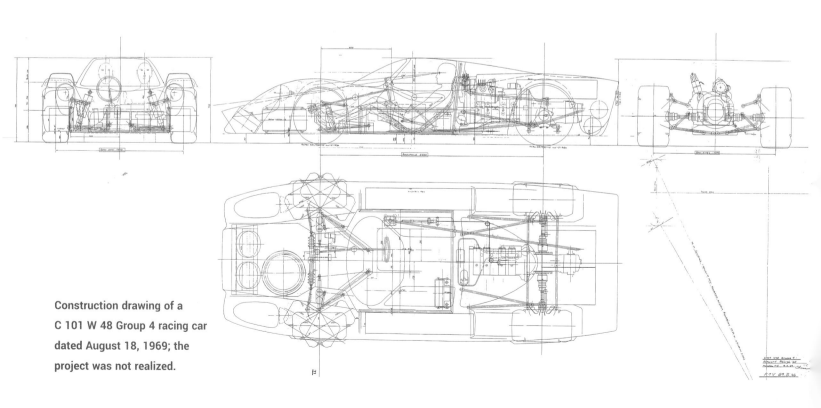

Construction drawing of a C 101 W 48 Group 4 racing car dated August 18, 1969; the project was not realized.

Dream Sports Car and Laboratory on Wheels: The C 111

Sportiness and Fascination:
The Design Development

Based on the chassis drawings from Untertürkheim, design development of the C 101 had already begun in early December 1968. Based on the first drafts and the drawings produced at the beginning of January 1969, the first design models were produced in 1:5 scale before the end of January. What was unusual was the fact that in addition to the full-time stylists from Sindelfingen, the advance engineering department in Untertürkheim had also developed design ambitions and created a design model.

This design was the work of Stefan Heiliger, who had worked as a stylist in the advance engineering department in Untertürkheim since 1964. As part of this activity, Heiliger also designed the first light-alloy rims for Mercedes-Benz vehicles; both the five-spoke wheels with which the Wankel sports car debuted at the IAA and the fifteen-hole rims of the test cars were based on his designs. A 14-inch version of the fifteen-hole rim was then also available from August 1970 as special equipment for the 108/109, 111, and 113 passenger car model series. Today, enthusiasts like to affectionately and irreverently refer to this classic rim forged by the Fuchs company in Meinerzhagen as the "baroque rim." Incidentally, Heiliger's attention to detail is also evident in the fact that the 1:5 scale models of his design were equipped with true-to-scale replicas of the light-alloy wheels he designed.

Five 1:5 models in all were created in Sindelfingen in the first phase of the design development as variations of two different basic shapes, plus there was the model from Untertürkheim.

In order to coordinate the work of the various involved parties from design and testing in Untertürkheim and design and stylistics in Sindelfingen, chief designer Geiger suggested in a memo dated February 11, 1969, that "Bruno Sacco from the stylistics department should take the lead on this model." Italian-born Bruno Sacco, who had been active in the design division since the beginning of 1958, had moved to the advance body engineering department headed by Béla Barényi in 1963, where he had developed the dimensional concept for the SLX sports car study in 1965, among other things. On January 1, 1969, he had returned to Friedrich Geiger in the styling

The drawing produced by the advance engineering department presents the chassis of the C 101 in all its details. The version shown reflects the updated status of March 3, 1969. Although the position of the radiator and the spare wheel no longer correspond to the original design status, it is noted on the drawing as "not yet final."

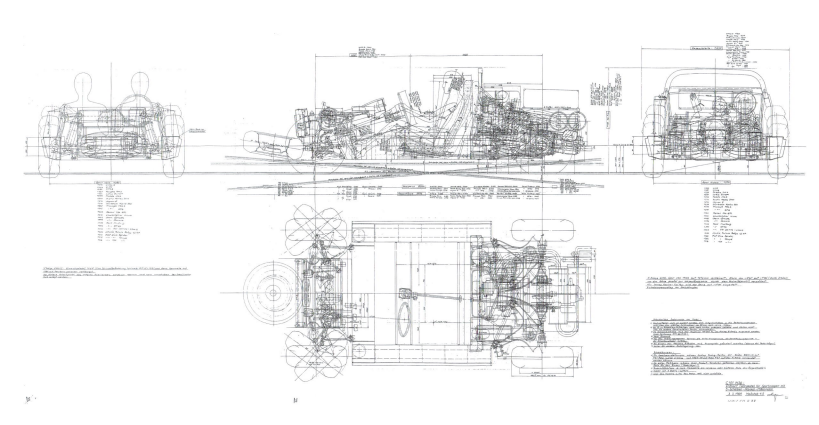

department and since then had been mainly concerned with the design of interiors. The machine required to create a 1:1 design model started up in Sindelfingen on February 12, 1969. Coordinated by project manager Sacco, two carpenters, a metal worker, and four stylists delved into completing a clay model in 1:1 scale in three weeks, by the desired deadline. The so-called clay model was actually a plasticine model. The C 101 was the first vehicle for which Mercedes-Benz used the new plasticine, also known as clay, in the form-finding process. The designer (and later head of design) Peter Pfeiffer, who had moved from Ford to Daimler-Benz on April 1, 1968, introduced the then-innovative material in Sindelfingen and thus revolutionized the design process at Daimler-Benz. In particular, the possibility of further developing the design very quickly directly on the model held unimagined potential for faster and more efficient form development. Invented as early as 1890 by the Munich pharmacist Frank Kolb, plasticine had been used by American manufacturers in automotive design since the 1950s and offered a whole range of compelling advantages: it is easy to shape, does not require long drying times, is dimensionally stable—in contrast to mineral clay—and is easy to work with afterward.

The first wind tunnel tests on the 1:5 models were already discussed at the technical meeting on February 24. The Untertürkheim design had resulted in a c_d value of 0.38 without

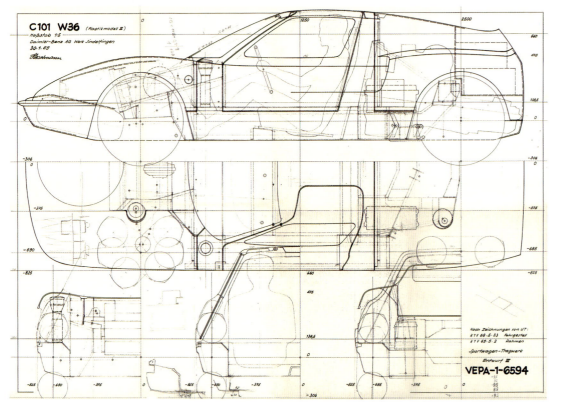

Design drawing by Joseph Gallitzendörfer dated January 10, 1969, and the construction drawing derived from this design by Heinrich Haselmann, an employee in the advance engineering department for passenger car bodies headed by Béla Barényi, dated January 30, 1969

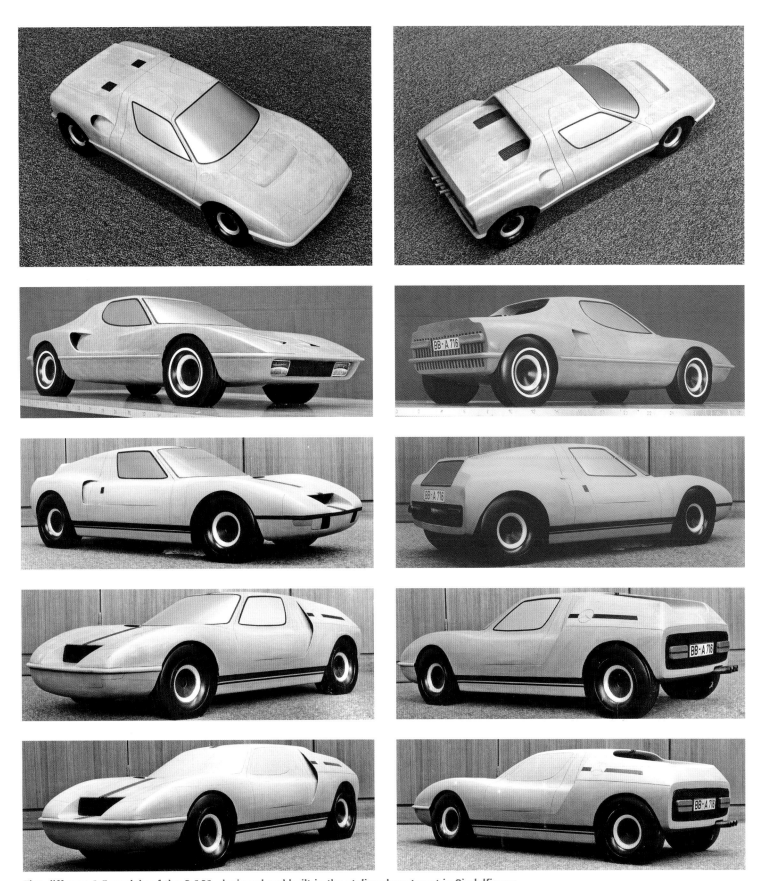

Five different 1:5 models of the C 101, designed and built in the styling department in Sindelfingen

 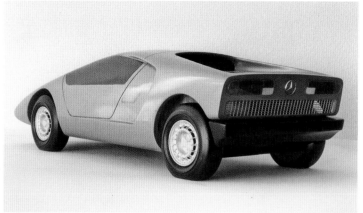

The competitor's design from Untertürkheim, developed by Stefan Heiliger in January 1969. Clearly visible are the light-alloy rims, reproduced in detail, as they were also available for the Mercedes-Benz production passenger cars from August 1970 onward.

and 0.36 with cooling air flow. The Sindelfingen design recorded 0.34 without flow, whereby the measurement with air flow was still pending. On March 3, it was announced that a 200 mm extension and a taper of the rear end would improve the c_d value, and it was decided to continue working on the basis of the Sindelfingen model. Apparently, however, the discussion about which variant should be given preference continued. Head of development Scherenberg informed his fellow board members in the

The 1:5 model from Untertürkheim during aerodynamic measurement in the model wind tunnel in Sindelfingen

aforementioned note of March 18 of his assessment that although the Sindelfingen model had a very low c_d value, the model from advance engineering in Untertürkheim "looks more attractive."

This prompted Karl Wilfert to present Scherenberg with a detailed and unusually clear statement in a memo dated March 24. In it, he described the Untertürkheim design as a "copy of a pretty Bertone model with a low utility value, and unsuitable for sale even in small numbers." The elegant lines had been achieved "by a large windshield curved in both directions and steeply raked" and A-pillars that "practically ran in a straight line from the front bumper." As disadvantages, he named "unbearable" heat radiation, US regulations regarding wiper field and de-icing that could not be met, and severely restricted sight lines. In addition, the "optics are unacceptable because of the expected ghost images, especially for a fast vehicle."

Wilfert also criticized the door construction: The Untertürkheim team had planned to hinge the doors at an angle at the front, while the Sindelfingen model was deliberately to use the classic solution with gullwing doors familiar from the 300 SL, "which was generally well received and gave the vehicle [the 300 SL] a special touch." In addition, the Sindelfingen model was designed from the outset for a low c_d value and downforce instead of lift. Due to corrections to the Untertürkheim model, which were "necessary to improve the c_d value and to reduce lift and to install the headlights correctly," the model had "lost a considerable portion of 'sleekness'."

Finally, Wilfert went into detail about the competition that went on here between Untertürkheim and Sindelfingen. The establishment of a design department in Sindelfingen in 1956 had ended a duplication of work at the time, which had had a negative effect in every respect. In this regard, Wilfert saw the danger of a step backward and pointed out that due to the insufficient capacity of the Sindelfingen wind tunnel, the measurements and optimizations carried out on the C 101 models from Sindelfingen and Untertürkheim so far had already affected the necessary work on the W 116 and C 107 production vehicle projects. Scherenberg's answer is not documented, but ultimately the emerging and actually already decided preference for the Sindelfingen design remained in place.

At the technical meeting on March 17, 1969, it was decided to increase the vehicle length and wheelbase by 120 mm, and this was formally confirmed on March 24; 110 mm was necessary to accommodate a four-rotor engine, and another 10 mm because of the reinforced clutch this required. On March 24, the Sindelfingen

The modified design from Untertürkheim in a 1:5 model, photographed in February 1969 on the premises of the "Einfahrbahn," as the test track at the Untertürkheim plant was known internally

stylists had also completed the 1:1 plasticine model and could now start refining it in order to—as the minutes of the technical meeting stated—"be stylistically prepared for small-scale production." The Untertürkheim 1:5 model was also examined

The C 101 is gradually taking shape: The 1:5 model above still shows a close relationship to the original Sindelfingen designs, while the model below already features the extended wheelbase decided on March 17, 1969, and represents a milestone in the development to the final form.

The first 1:1 model of the C 101 with a work status of March 21, 1969, is based on the 1:5 model shown above and already corresponds in its basic features to the form actually realized.

62 Dream Sports Car and Laboratory on Wheels: The C 111

The design drawings by Joseph Gallitzendörfer from the spring of 1969 still reveal a certain amount of design imagination compared to the final form. The two sketches in the first and second row on the right were already published in the press in April 1969.

On April 16, the 1:1 model of the C 101 presents itself with two differently designed halves. The driver's side features a very striking rear design, while the passenger side has a less bulky rear end and front and rear bumper horns. The further development of the design was based on the status shown on the passenger's side.

Using the 1:1 plasticine model of the C 101, which is given a perfect finish by applying a white paint film, executives from the body development and styling departments, including Karl Wilfert and Friedrich Geiger, get an idea of how to work with the newly introduced material.

again with the optimizations that had been made in the meantime. At the end of April, the revision of the plasticine model with white car film in a perfect finish was completed, and the inspection by the Board of Management took place in Sindelfingen on April 30. The model already had the basic shape and numerous design details of the vehicle that was actually realized in the end. The light-alloy wheels designed by Stefan Heiliger were also shown in two versions—on the left side of the vehicle with racing tires and on the passenger side with street tires. Not all aspects of the new sports car were appreciated. During the inspection, Dr. Zahn, spokesman of the Board of Management, had expressed that "he personally liked the front and sides of the C 101 model, but not the rear end. . . . On the other hand, it should not be overlooked that the task set for the development department was to present a 'harsh,' sporty vehicle in order to dispel the generally publicized notion of a 'granny version of the DB vehicles' and to have a model in the range again that could compete in the sporty vehicle sector. Furthermore, it seems urgent to refresh the image of the 300 SL model, which is still very strong after fifteen years, with an appropriate successor model."

As the minutes record, deputy member of the board responsible for sales and marketing Rolf Staelin "largely agreed with Zahn's remarks and expressed his doubts as to whether this sports car could already be presented at the 1969 IAA. He himself

The clay model of the C 101 with white wrap, presented during the inspection by the Board of Management on April 30, 1969. The 300 SL, the W 113, the R 107, which was still in development, and even a Lotus 47, the racing version of the Lotus Europa, were available for comparison. Daimler-Benz had already acquired the Lotus in 1967 for study purposes via its British distributor. The 300 SL was no ordinary example of the super sports car either. Apart from the gullwing doors and the white paintwork, it had another thing in common with the C 101—a plastic body. On the large blackboards in the background, dimensional comparison drawings illustrated the external and interior dimensions of the C 101 and the relevant comparison vehicles.

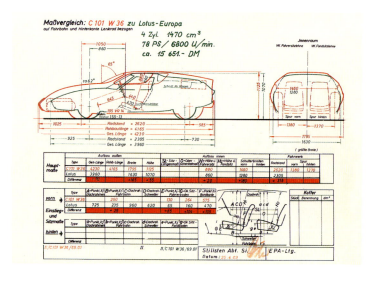
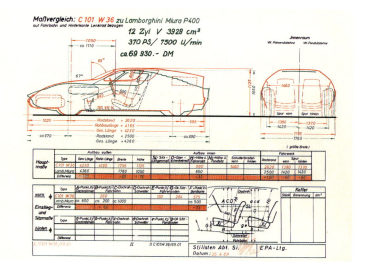
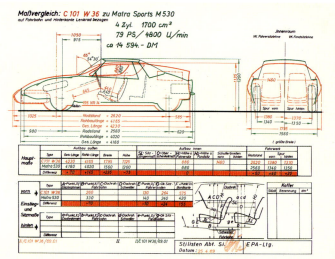
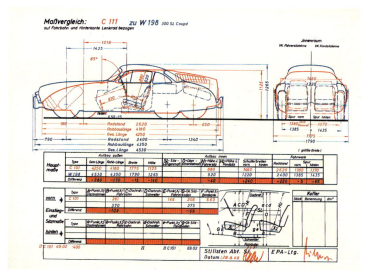

Dimensional comparison drawings comparing the dimensions and interior dimensions of the C 101 with selected sports car models from the competition as well as the legendary 300 SL "Gullwing"

was also very "shocked" by the lines of the rear end of this vehicle, while the other parts were appealing. An attempt should be made to make the rear end a little less "brutal" (according to Mr. Uhlenhaut, this was hardly feasible, since the vehicle would then no longer serve its purpose and would appear "sugary," apart from the fact that then it also would no longer be possible to meet the technical requirements).

Head of development Scherenberg reported that the bodies for the first six prototype vehicles were going to be made of plastic and manufactured quickly by Waggonfabrik Rastatt, which had also produced the plastic bodies for various Porsche vehicles. The plastic vehicle body was chosen for these first vehicles because it could be produced as quickly as possible and at relatively low cost. In addition, the design in plastic would allow a greater variation of the outer skin and would also provide the opportunity to test this material more thoroughly on the road and to gain valuable experience for future developments.

The decision to use fiberglass-reinforced plastic (GRP) instead of aluminum for the bodywork had been made only a short time before. On April 19, project manager Bruno Sacco was still on the phone researching coachbuilders in Italy that could be entrusted with the production of the bodywork. Two days later, a delegation of Daimler-Benz employees from the areas of body construction, body testing, preproduction, and procurement visited

Busy activity in the styling department, taken in March (*above*) and May 1969 (*below*). Design development on the plasticine models in 1:1 and 1:5 is proceeding at full speed. In the picture above, on the left in the background is Joseph Gallitzendörfer, and in the picture below is Peter Pfeiffer (on the 1:1 model, in the white shirt), who was instrumental in developing the shape of the C 101 on the plasticine model.

the Waggonfabrik Rastatt (WFR) to gain an impression of the production facilities there. The company had relevant experience and had already produced the GRP bodies for the Porsche Carrera 6 (906) racing cars. The visit report stated that WFR needed a painted and sanded positive mold of the vehicle with a flawless surface from which to mold the negative models needed to produce the body components. Using this procedure, the company would be able to produce one vehicle a day. Three months were allotted for the production of the tool and die set, then another month for the assembly of the first body.

During another visit on April 28 (two days before the board visit), which was also attended by Karl Wilfert, Werner Breitschwerdt, and Friedrich Geiger on the part of Daimler-Benz, WFR presented a complete body of the Porsche 908 Spider as well as some skin panels, including the negative models required for them. In contrast to the Porsche racing cars, with wall thicknesses of 0.8 to 1.2 mm, 2.0 to 2.5 mm was to be planned for the C 101 for the benefit of the surface quality. Issues of passive safety, painting, and repair options were also discussed. Compared to the statements made a week earlier, the outlook was more encouraging in terms of deadlines, certainly also because the focus was no longer on a possible series production, but explicitly on the production of a few prototypes. In this case, about four weeks were estimated for the production of the molds and another two to three weeks for the delivery of the individual body components for the first car.

With the provision of the master model by May 9, the car factory held out the prospect of completing the tools and dies by June 7 and delivery of the first finished body on June 30. On this basis, the completion of five bodies by mid-August seemed realistic. The summary of the visit report made unreservedly positive reading: "The car factory has valuable experience in the field of GRP bodywork production, is flexible, knows how to improvise, and can make changes independently because it has patternmakers. The possibility of molding negative shells from the clay model saves valuable time that would be needed to make the mallets or stretch forming dies. The cost for these wooden models can likewise be saved." After the commissioning, which was highly logical in the light of this assessment, employees of the body construction department and a representative of BASF visited Waggonfabrik Rastatt on May 6 to clarify detailed questions of design and production technology. The bodywork material was specified as 70% Palatal P 6 by weight and 30% Palatal P 35 by weight, and the body was to consist of two 300 g/m² fiberglass mats and one 450 g/m² layer of twill fabric. The wall thickness was specified as 2.5 mm and the specific gravity as 1.5 to 1.6. The short-term heat resistance was to be 200°C–250°C (390°F–480°F), and the paint baking temperature was not to exceed 60°C (140°F).

In order to be able to produce the most perfect surface quality possible for the body, with good transitions between the individual parts, the specialists at WFR suggested not to use the negative mold taken from the plasticine model for the production of the body parts immediately, but first to create an intermediate positive. This could then be given a finish of the required surface quality and used to make an impression of the negative mold needed for the production process. This approach avoided the disadvantage that the desired perfect surface quality could not be achieved in every respect on the 1:1 design model made of the recently introduced plasticine.

The 1:1 plasticine model in the work status of May 14, 1969, equipped with racing tires (*left*) and street tires (*right*)

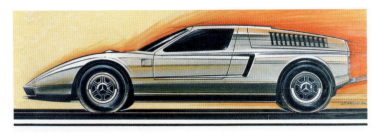

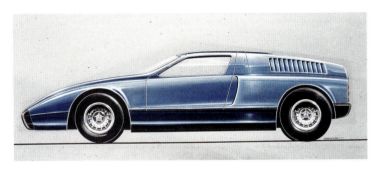
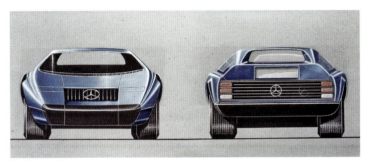

Stylists Joseph Gallitzendörfer (*top and second row*) and Gérard Cardiet (*bottom*) captured the final shape of the C 101 in appealing design drawings. The reason Cardiet chose the blue color scheme is not documented.

After the board inspection of the C 101, which was marked by controversial discussions, Friedrich Geiger had summarized the result in a memo on May 2: "In comparison, the C 101 [in contrast to the 350 SLC presented at the same time] was less appealing. The extremely sporty touch was perceived to be too rustic. Above all, the rear end was not liked. . . . We will revise the shape of the C 101 again." In a communication dated May 7, Friedrich Geiger compiled a series of changes to constructive details that were to go hand in hand with the design optimizations. The revision was tackled immediately, and the result, completed on May 14, was transported to Rastatt the same day, where it arrived at 10:15 p.m. For impression taking, the plasticine model was coated with

The plasticine model of the C 101 was molded at Waggonfabrik Rastatt. The negative mold created in this process was used to produce the plastic body after a further molding step.

The plasticine model of the C 101 was badly damaged during demolding. The photos taken in the styling department on June 3, 1969, document the condition upon delivery in Sindelfingen.

 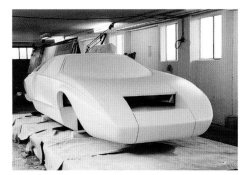 

The negative molds created from the plasticine model were used to make the intermediate positive of the C 101 at Waggonfabrik Rastatt, from which a final negative mold was then cast as the basis for body production.

several layers of polyester resin and covered with fiberglass mats. In order to be able to lift the mold better later, wooden spacer strips had been attached before applying the plastic. After the application of polyester resin and fiberglass mats, the negative shell completed on May 23 was reinforced by a wooden framework so that the shape did not change during drying and curing. In order to be able to separate the negative mold from the original plasticine model after it had hardened, small tubes had been cast in, through which compressed air could now be blown in; in addition, the shell was sawn open at certain contours.

Despite these precautions, the plasticine model was badly damaged on May 28 when the negative mold was lifted off—a circumstance that was probably also due to the fact that the people in Rastatt did not yet have any experience with handling plasticine models. After the production and surface smoothing of the intermediate positive and the creation of the final negative mold, the first body parts were created at the end of June.

The design department in Sindelfingen had begun creating an interior mockup on May 16, which in addition to the floor and wraparound for the occupant space was to include preparations for the dashboard, seat, door trim, flooring and headliner, and rear

Production of the hatch of the C 101, which serves as the engine hood, at Waggonfabrik Rastatt

The intermediate positive from the molding process was perfectly prepared in Rastatt for the assessment and final acceptance with silver paintwork and detachable parts such as windshield wipers, taillights, and license plates. On the driver's side, the model is equipped with impressive racing tires, on the passenger's side with street tires.

wall trim. As a result of the extensive design changes, the original production schedule could no longer be met, as the production planning department announced on May 21 and substantiated with a new "schedule for test builds." The latter now envisaged completion of vehicles 3 to 6 in the period from August 1 to 28.

The instrumentation of the C 101 was specified at the end of June and communicated to the project participants in a memo from Werner Breitschwerdt and Karl Wilfert dated July 3. Seven instruments were listed: rev counter, speedometer, oil pressure gauge, oil temperature and coolant temperature gauge, fuel gauge, and clock. Indicator lamps for the left turn signal, right turn signal, and main beam were to be positioned between rev counter and speedometer. Additional indicator lamps for parking brake and "vacuum for brakes" were intended in the rev counter, a charging indicator lamp in the oil pressure gauge, and a fuel reserve lamp in the fuel gauge.

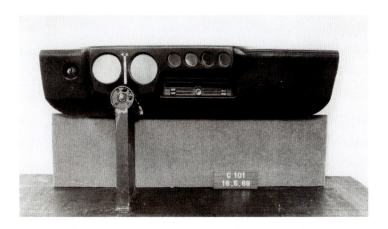

Start of the interior design: 1:1 model of the cockpit as of May 16, 1969

Innovative Methods:
Computer-Aided Development

The extremely ambitious time schedule of the project from the very beginning, which would not have been realizable with the classic development processes of the automotive industry that were common at the time, was made possible in the first place by the use of state-of-the-art design methods. With the elasto-static element method ESEM, a special variant of the finite element method (FEM) developed at Daimler-Benz and used for the first time from the beginning, the rigidity of the frame floor assembly designed on the drawing board was calculated, using a mainframe computer from IBM. To do this, the design drawing first had to be digitized, using a process that is hardly comprehensible today, and then transferred to the computer via punched cards. In addition to the statics, even dynamic load situations of the design could be simulated with the software used. The basic principle of ESEM was to model the object to be calculated in a structure of finite beam, surface, and spatial elements that are connected to each other via nodes. The material data relevant for the elastic behavior for each individual element were stored in the structural model. The smaller the elements and the more detailed the structure, the more accurate the calculation result, but the higher the computational effort.

Dr. Alfred Zimmer, calculation engineer in passenger car advance engineering at Daimler-Benz, had already started developing a calculation program for frames in 1963, which he called RB (Rahmen-Berechnung or frame calculation). Together with his colleague Peter Groth, he steadily advanced the program and, after ten hours of calculating the frame floor assembly of the Mercedes-Benz 600, was able to determine such precise comparative values that colleagues in the testing department initially suspected a case of internal espionage and data theft. To obtain further comparative figures between calculation and measurement, the body of the 230 SL was also recalculated, using the RB method. At that time, no external memory other than punched cards was available, and so around 120,000 punched cards were needed as intermediate storage for the calculation of the 230 SL, for example. From the RB program, Zimmer and Groth developed the ESEM method—the world's first FEM program developed by an industrial company. Its first important use was assisting in the body development of the W 114/115 mid-range series. The body model had 319 nodes, 443 elements, and 1,684 degrees of freedom—from the point of view of the time, a complex structure that was almost impossible to control mathematically, whereas today, a good fifty years later, calculations with several million elements are carried out. One of the biggest challenges was error-free data entry, since input errors were often only discovered after days of calculation. That is why Zimmer and Groth supplemented the program with a powerful input check, which they called "numerical data diagnostics."

Due to the tight schedule of the C 101 project, the individual phases in the construction of the frame floor assembly—design overall concept, structural analysis, frame design 1:5, rigidity calculation, optimization, and construction 1:1—were constantly subjected to computational assessment on the computer. For example, the consistent use of ESEM and the virtual testing of the frame floor assembly on the computer made it possible to dispense with the construction of a prototype for the C 101 that

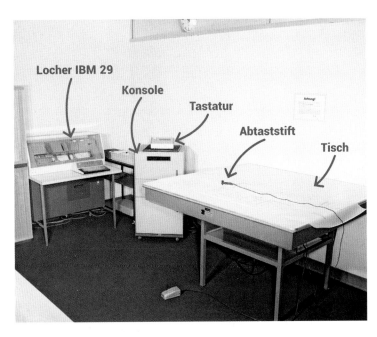

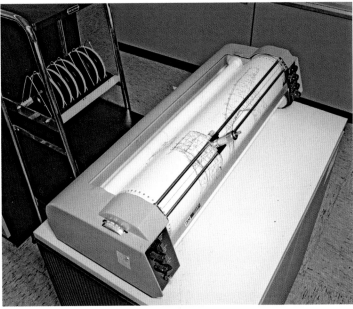

The IBM hardware used for the ESEM process was comprised of, in addition to the mainframe computer (not shown here)—what back then was considered a high-performance computer—the punch card puncher, the control console with keyboard, and the digitizing device with drawing table and scanning stylus, as well as the plotter and the screen with light pen.

was only used for load tests, and this alone saved four months of development time. The C 101 was thus the world's first car to be designed from scratch on the computer—an innovation that was also highlighted in communications. Daimler-Benz used the specially produced development film *The Car that Came Out of the Computer* for this purpose, which even won an award in November 1970—first prize in the "Technical Films" category at the International Motor Film Festival in Karlovy Vary, in what was the ČSSR (Czechoslovak Socialist Republic) back then. The revolutionary nature of the ESEM method developed by Daimler-Benz at the time is also evident in the fact that IBM presented this method at the Hanover Fair in April 1972, using a real C 111 as an eye-catcher on its stand. Incidentally, the first series-production vehicle to be designed entirely with the aid of ESEM was the Mercedes-Benz S-Class of the 116 series, introduced in 1972. Designing the C 101 also for four-rotor Wankel engines, a decision

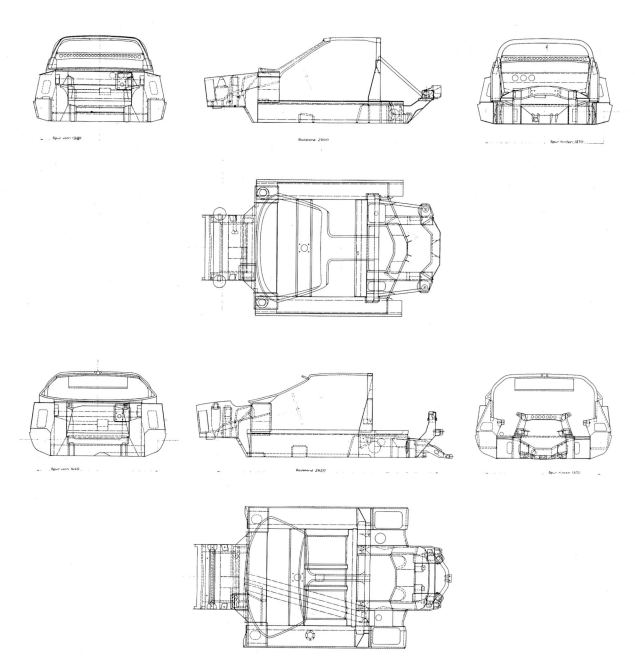

Construction drawing of the frame floor system of the C 101, designed by constructor Hans-Helmut Jülicher with the aid of ESEM. Above is the original version; below is the version with a 2,620 mm wheelbase tuned to the "racing rear axle."

Dream Sports Car and Laboratory on Wheels: The C 111

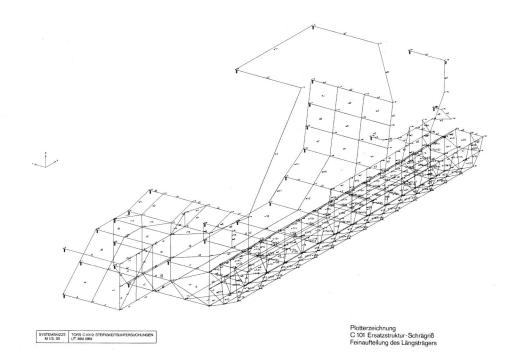

Oblique section of the C 101 floor assembly with fine division of the side rail as an example of a plotter drawing from the ESEM process

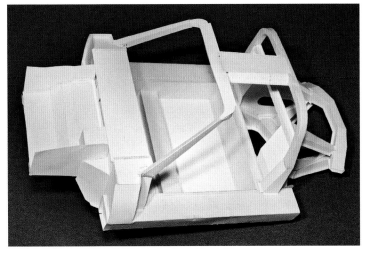
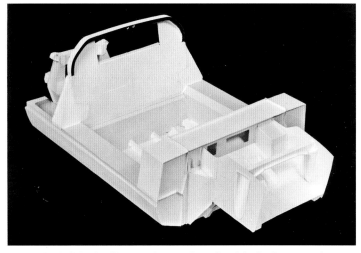

1:5 models of the C 101 floor assembly constructed using the ESEM method: on the left is the first version, and on the right is the second version for the racing rear axle and 2,620 mm wheelbase.

made on March 24, 1969, made it necessary to stretch the wheelbase by 120 mm to 2,620 mm. The first frame floor assembly of this specification, which was also designed for the so-called "racing rear axle," weighed 153 kg in the body shell. The original version with a 2,500 mm wheelbase, which was still designed for the semi-trailing arm rear axle, was 25 kg lighter and also had a calculated 40% higher torsional rigidity.

The original roof design, which as in the first version had provided for the windshield frame, roof, and roll-over bar to be part of the sheet steel outer skin, could not be adopted due to the requirement for uniform surface finish of the body. The windshield frame and roof braces made of tubular steel with GRP outer skin replaced the sheet metal parts. The resulting loss of torsional strength was exacerbated by the wheelbase extension as well as by changed installation conditions that the new rear axle design, the air filter system, and accessibility to the fuel delivery system required. Even the use of thicker sheet metal for the rear section of the frame floor assembly could not fundamentally improve this situation, and so the not very satisfactory torsional rigidity in the rear section remained a permanent point of criticism.

Odd Testing Platform:
The Sledge

In order to be able to start testing the chassis, suspension, and engine in view of the tight schedule and to be independent of the design development and body production, the first vehicle to be built as part of the C 101 project was a hand-built prototype with a very provisional-looking makeshift body, which quickly received the nickname Sledge internally due to its angular exterior. In contrast to the following vehicles, it had a floor assembly of the first version with the original wheelbase of 2,500 mm.

The frame floor assembly of this first prototype of the C 101 was built in March 1969 in the advance engineering department in Untertürkheim and weighed 128 kg. With coolant hoses, covers, and baffle plates, the weight increased by 15 kg to 143 kg. In order to save weight and still achieve the desired rigidity, sheets of different thicknesses (0.75/0.88/1.00 and 1.25 mm) were used for the floor assembly. A measurement of the rigidity carried out in

The frame floor system of the first C 101, still designed with a 2,500 mm wheelbase, was manufactured in the test department in Untertürkheim. The photos document the completion in March 1969.

Assembly of the first C 101 test car in the test department in Untertürkheim, taken at the end of March 1969. The semi-trailing arm rear axle, which was still used on car 1, is clearly visible.

Sindelfingen in March 1969 showed that the twist between the axles was 12% higher than on the SL of the R 107 model series currently under development. In the passenger compartment, the situation was reversed: Because of the closed body of the C 101, the twist was 22% less than in the R 107. Overall, the developers considered the measured values to be satisfactory.

With the aim of reducing the dependence of the C 101 project on the development progress of the M 950 three-rotor engine, the

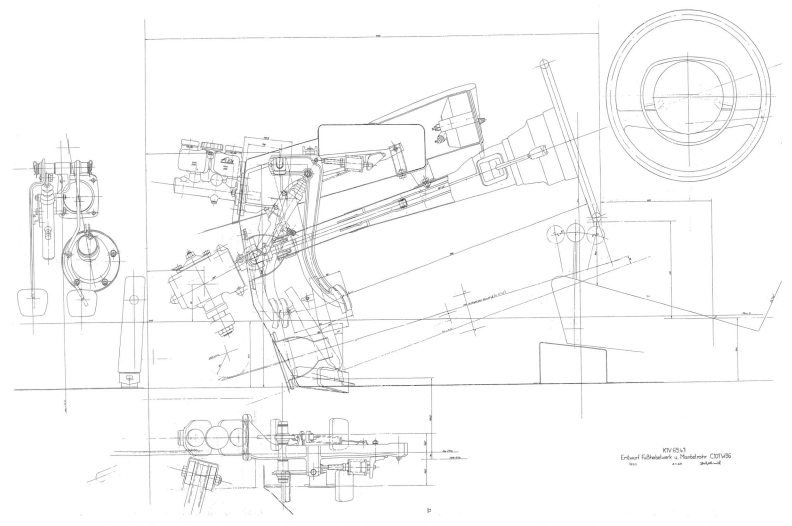

The construction drawing of the pedal system and the steering column tube, dated January 2, 1969, illustrates how the C 101 was designed in every detail from the very beginning.

Internally dubbed the Sledge because of its strange appearance, the first C 101 was completed on April 1, 1969. The photos show the vehicle already equipped with roof and side walls.

Dream Sports Car and Laboratory on Wheels: The C 111

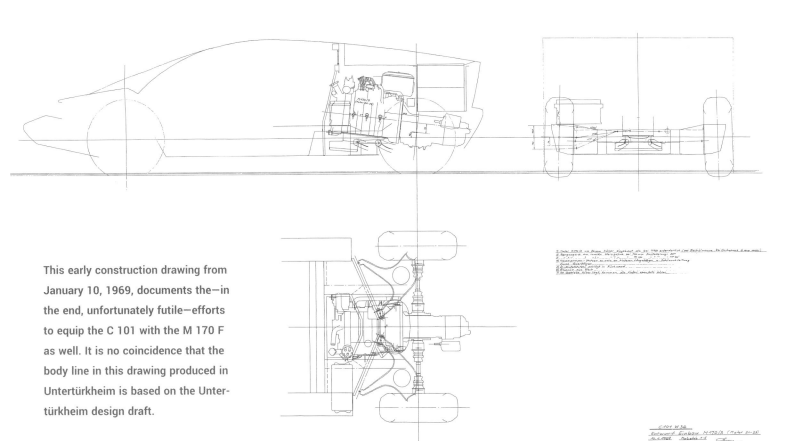

This early construction drawing from January 10, 1969, documents the—in the end, unfortunately futile—efforts to equip the C 101 with the M 170 F as well. It is no coincidence that the body line in this drawing produced in Untertürkheim is based on the Untertürkheim design draft.

question had already been raised in January 1969 as to whether the existing M 170/3 three-rotor engine could also be used for testing. However, this turned out to be practically infeasible, since the different shape of the trochoidal housing would have required an engine installation higher by 26 mm and would have resulted in a reduction of the rebound travel of the rear wheels from 90 mm to 70 mm. In view of the maxim of soft springing and firm damping pursued in Untertürkheim, this was seen as a serious obstacle.

This meant that the M 950 had to be used exclusively, which proved to be a limiting factor throughout the project due to the still-unsatisfactory degree of maturity. A note on the engine test of February 4, 1969, reports a ten-hour full load endurance run of the KE 301/2, which achieved only 191 hp/140 kW at 7,000 rpm in the process, however. After this run and a total operating time of fifty-one hours, the examination of the engine revealed the following findings: an oil feed bearing that received no oil on the front half, cracks in all

The M 950/3 three-rotor Wankel engine in combination with ZF five-speed transmission and integrated axle drive as used in the C 101

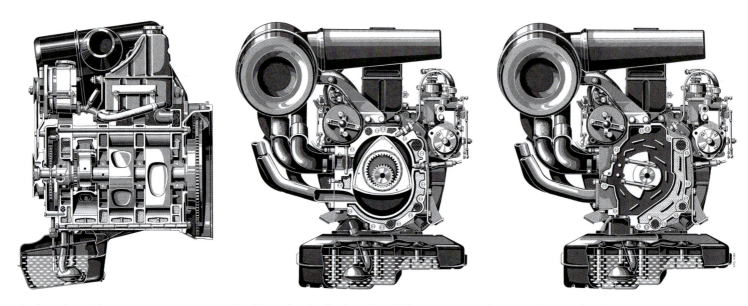

Technical graphics of the M 950/3 used in the C 101: longitudinal section (*left*) **and cross section through trochoidal housing** (*center*) **and intermediate housing** (*right*)

three rotors, and a broken bearing on one of them. The KE 303/1 fared even worse, as evidenced by a memo dated February 10. After eight hours of full-load endurance testing at 190 hp/140 kW and 7,000 rpm, the second main bearing seized and the bearing shell broke. In the end, the KE 308 was installed in the first test cars with a makeshift body after it had completed a 17.5-hour endurance run on the test bench. This first M 950 in three-rotor design ready for installation provided an output of 258 hp/199 kW at 7,000 rpm and weighed 152.7 kg without the clutch.

The 5 DS-25/1 five-speed transmission, weighing 58.6 kg, was manufactured by Zahnradfabrik Friedrichshafen in Schwäbisch-Gmünd and was used as standard in the Italian De Tomaso

Assembly (*left*) **and test bench run** (*right*) **of a three-rotor M 950 engine**

Dream Sports Car and Laboratory on Wheels: The C 111

Mangusta small-series sports car. Due to time constraints, the company not only abstained from developing its own transmission but also had to make do with the unchanged gear ratios of 2.42/1.47/1.09/0.958/0.846, with a final drive ratio of 4.22. This resulted in final speeds of 83/137/184/210/240 km/h. Numerous modifications were made before installation or planned for the subsequent vehicles based on the experience with the first test car. One of the most profound changes was the redesign of the shift linkage with multiple deflections, which in the original design resulted in sluggish, poorly defined, and imprecise gear shifts, and was fitted with direct actuation in the cars that followed.

The realization of the fuel system was more complex than expected. Initially planned plastic tanks could not be installed because they were not leak-proof in the first version and also had a tendency toward strong diffusion through the tank wall. Two aluminum side tanks, each with a capacity of 58 liters, were therefore made in the testing department for the first car and installed in the frame side rails with vulcanized rubber bearings. The fuel was taken from the middle of the five compartments, which were connected to a central collector pot with a capacity of approximately 3 liters, located on the right side behind the baffle plate. The fuel pump delivered the fuel from the collector pot to the injection pump and back again. Although both tanks were connected to each other via the collector pot, they each had to be refueled separately via their filler necks. During testing, there were no problems at first, but on the big circuit in Hockenheim, the fuel supply was interrupted at times with approximately 25 liters of fuel left in the tank.

An ultimately successful solution to this problem was suggested by test department employee Fritz Naumann in July 1969, when he envisaged a fluidics element to control the fuel return to the two tanks. This was to regulate the return flow depending on the tank fill level so that no single tank is ever empty. The process engineering department provided such a component in December 1969, and the testing that finally took place in car 9 confirmed the effectiveness of the system.

The first test drive of the still-open-top prototype with a Plexiglas windshield and camouflage only at the front and rear took place on April 1, 1969, on the "Einfahrbahn," the test track at the Untertürkheim plant. On April 16, Rudolf Uhlenhaut and project leader Dr. Hans Liebold drove on public roads for the first time after the test department workshop had completed the body with fixed side panels and a roof with gullwing doors.

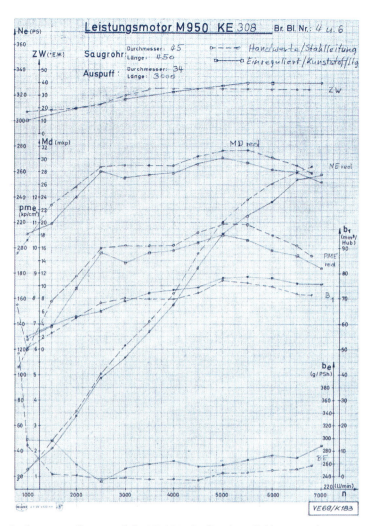

Performance diagram of the KE 308, the first installable M 950 in three-rotor design, which was used in the Sledge during its first test drives

On its first run (still without roof and side panels), the makeshift vehicle with full tanks weighed only 990 kg, of which the floor assembly accounted for 143 kg and the body for 115 kg; the weight distribution was 43.5% front to 56.5% rear. The relatively low weight—which was still about 190 kg above the first estimates, however—and the quite satisfactory output of 258 hp/190 kW of the first three-rotor engine ensured decent driving performance with sufficient ride comfort running on 195 VR 14 street tires, as the test report of April 29 stated. On April 24, Guido Moch, head of the operational testing department, carried out the first driving performance measurements on the test track. Acceleration from 0 to 100 km/h was measured at 5.2 seconds, which meant that the C 101 was 0.2 seconds faster than the W 108, with a 318 hp/234 kW, 6.9-liter, high-performance V8 used

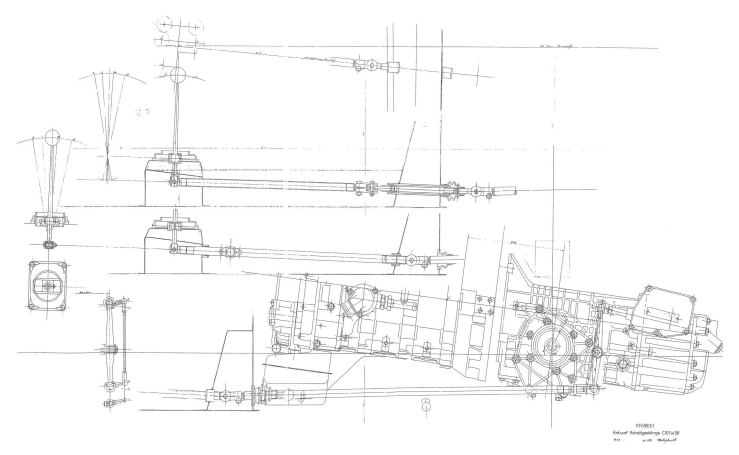

The construction drawing from January 21, 1969, illustrates the complicated design of the shift linkage.

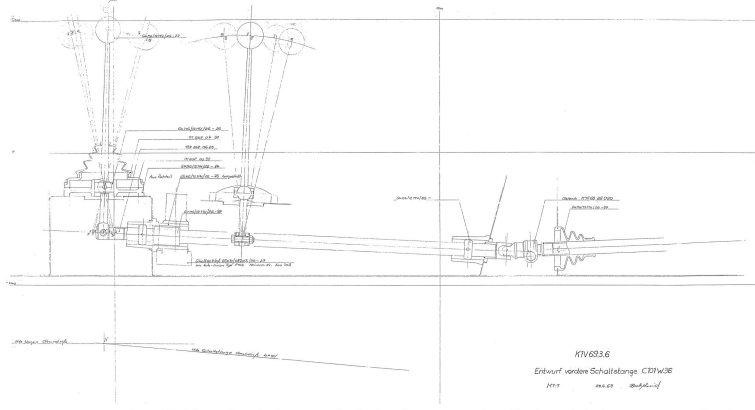

The further-developed front shift linkage, shown in the construction drawing of June 23, together with other optimization measures, contributed to a more precise and less sluggish gear shift.

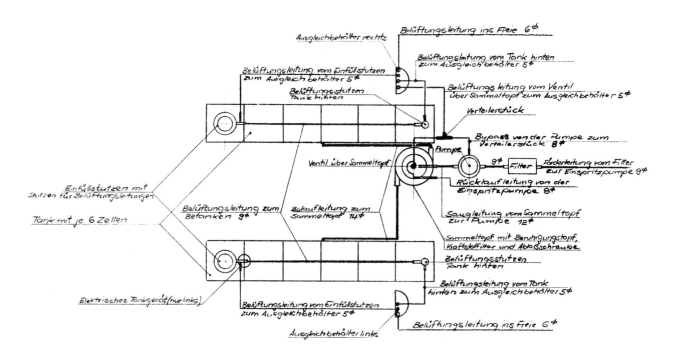

Schematic representation of the fuel system of the C 101, as of February 27, 1969

for comparison, although it did weigh in at 1,730 kg. The top speed of the Wankel prototype was 230 km/h, and the fuel consumption was about 29 l/100 km. Dr. Liebold attributed the "relatively high consumption" and the low top speed to the very high aerodynamic drag with the makeshift body. However, hopes were not only pinned on better aerodynamics in the future, but also on a weight reduction thanks to the GRP body, for which Hans Liebold estimated a savings of about 50 kg. However, this proved to be a miscalculation—not least because of the much more elaborate equipment: All the subsequent vehicles were significantly heavier than the Sledge. The main points of criticism during the first test drives were the gear shift, which Liebold classified in the test report as "extraordinarily imprecise and sluggish," the clutch, which was initially still a little too heavy, and the seats with excessively curved backrests. After the brakes without power assistance initially required very high pedal pressures, a brake booster was fitted. Together with harder brake pads, this resulted in acceptable operating forces. With non-vented wheels and brake discs, the pads were subjected to a lot of stress, so the cars that followed were built with modified wheels and vented brake discs.

On May 2, the first test took place at the Hockenheimring track, but the lap times achieved were disappointing. Moreover, the top speed measured at the fastest point of the big circuit was just 214 km/h (at 7,200 rpm in fourth gear). Liebold attributed these less-than-satisfactory values primarily to the unsatisfactory aerodynamics of the makeshift body.

A modified front with a lower and more streamlined hood, with which the Sledge was tested for the first time in Hockenheim on May 13, 1969, increased the top speed to 221.5 km/h (at 6,500 rpm in fifth gear).

In terms of driving characteristics, however, there were disadvantages with the new body. With street tires and despite a high tire pressure, the car rolled around the vertical axis so much that, as Liebold stated in his test report of May 16, "it could only be kept on course with extreme concentration." The project manager suspected aerodynamic instability caused by irregular vortex shedding due to the "still very unfavorable design of the rear end and side walls."

The cooling air supply was also worsened by the body modification. With the fan running most of the time, the cooling was still sufficient at first, but later, with air temperatures above 30°C (85°F), the water temperature rose to 95°C (200°F) and the oil temperature to just under 150°C (300°F). An enlargement of the cooling air outlet gap brought a slight improvement.

Schematic representation of the fluidic element proposed by Fritz Naumann and tested from August 1970 onward, which made it possible to empty the two side tanks evenly at all

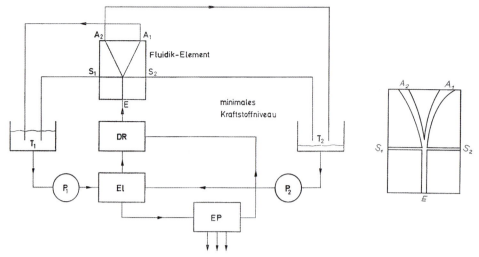

In May 1969, the Sledge received a new front end with a lower and more streamlined hood, which, however, worsened the overall aerodynamics. The cooling air ducting also proved to be unsatisfactory.

Dream Sports Car and Laboratory on Wheels: The C 111

After the first KE 308 engine had failed on May 20 after about 2,000 km due to separation of the molybdenum layer on a side housing, the 259 hp/190 kW KE 301 was installed, and the bodywork was optimized by reducing the taper of the body sides. This made the car a little faster, and it also reached 230 km/h at 7,000 rpm in fifth gear with the racing tires. With street tires, however, it still had a tendency to roll around the vertical axis, and even at speeds of around 100 km/h, steering movements could cause it to roll. With Michelin X 205 VR 14 tires, the car had largely stable handling, but exceptionally poor straight-line stability on bumpy roads, with highly unsteady steering.

At the beginning of June, the Sledge received a further optimized front end. In this form, the car was "also relatively good to drive in Hockenheim" with the Michelin tires, as Liebold put it. The lap times for the small circuit were 1:23.4 minutes, for the large circuit 2:25.3 minutes, and the speeds achieved were 232.5 km/h and 238 km/h, respectively. However, the driving characteristics showed an unexpectedly strong dependence on the tires: with Continental 195 VR 14, the car with optimized bodywork was "slightly better but still tended to roll around the vertical axis," and with Dunlop SP 195 VR 14 tires, "it appeared catastrophically unstable and required almost the entire width of

At the beginning of June 1969, the Sledge was equipped with a front that had been optimized once again. The test drives took place on the test track in Untertürkheim, on the Hockenheimring, and on the Nürburgring.

the road on the undulating section before the Ostkurve bend." With the previous racing tires, the Sledge, even after changing the axle and suspension setup several times, was "still very unsteady on the aforementioned section of the track, with the yawing movements clearly initiated by the changes in toe of the rear axle."

The mesh-covered air intake of the new body front also affected cooling, causing periodic temperature fluctuations between 80°C and 110°C (175°F and 230°F) at outside temperatures of 25°C to 30°C (77°F to 85°F). When stationary, the water temperature rose to 120°C (248°F) within thirty seconds despite the electric fans. The second KE 301 engine was already removed after 1,000 kilometers on the road and 500 km on the roller dynamometer because of its "very high oil consumption (most recently approximately 10 l/1,000 km)" and on June 23, the KE 308, which had been repaired in the meantime, was reinstalled. The output was stated as 292 hp/215 kW, but the oil consumption was 4.5 liters for 680 km. Fuel consumption was uniformly around 33 l/100 km with all three engines when driving hard. During further tests, a coolant hose was damaged after a crack in the right engine mount, which was subject to particular thermal stress. After failing to vent the coolant circuit of the hot engine sufficiently, brief overheating led to a failure. Afterward, the KE 315 engine was installed. It was actually intended for car 3 but had slightly less output and only reached 245 km/h on July 15 in Hockenheim, whereas 252 km/h had been measured several times with the previous engine, and even 256 km/h in one measurement.

The chassis of the Sledge relied on proven components from the current or future series production, because a near-series

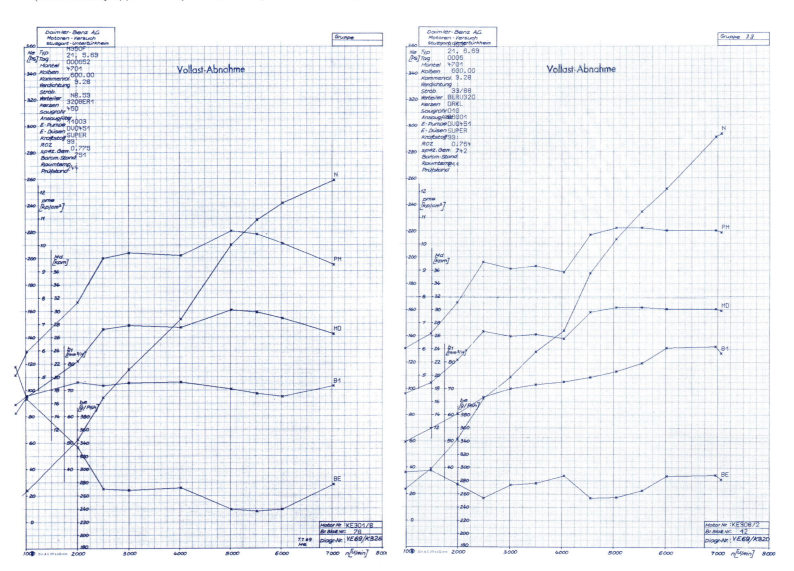

Power diagrams of the KE 301 (*left*) **and KE 308** (*right*) **motors used in the Sledge**

solution had originally been favored. At the front, a double wishbone axle was used, similar to the one that later debuted in the S-Class sedans of the 116 series. In the C 101, however, it was designed as a variant with struts. The rear axle was initially a semi-trailing arm axle from the mid-range W 114/115 model series. However, with the intended wide tires, especially with racing tires, this could not guarantee a level contact patch, so that practical testing of the chassis revealed the already described need for optimization.

A remedy was promised by the new, typically low-camber rear suspension in the style of a racing car with five links each—three transverse links and two trailing arms—which the design engineers in the advance engineering department under Dr. Kurt Enke and Erwin Löffler had designed and perfected by computer, using the ESEM process. The computer helped determine the length and position of the five links as well as the pivot points on the frame and the wheel carrier, and 350 variants were calculated. The new "miracle axle" was then used for the first time in the second test car, the first "real" C 101 with a GRP body. Incidentally, the kinematics of the front axle had also been optimized beforehand with the aid of a computer.

Metamorphosis:
From Sledge to Super Sports Car

While the first test car was thoroughly put through its paces, the development and construction of the following vehicles of the first production batch proceeded at full speed in all areas. In a note dated May 29, 1969, Dr. Hans Liebold noted that "there is frighteningly little time left for testing the car in the intended form before the Frankfurt exhibition" and went on to say, "Mr. Uhlenhaut is therefore demanding that all departments concerned work at breakneck speed. This means that in particular, the departments whose work in each case determines deadlines must work in at least two shifts a day." Three and a half weeks later, at the technical meeting on June 23, Karl Wilfert took up the tiresome issue of capacity and deadlines. He stated that working evenings and Saturdays was already required as part of the production vehicle development, and pointed out, "The C 101 has required working regularly until 8 p.m. and to a considerable extent on Sundays. This is a condition that can only be tolerated for very short periods of time."

Prototype manufacturing began with the production of the floor assembly in the body testing department in Sindelfingen. The frame floor assembly with an extended wheelbase, used from car 2 on, was made in different sheet thicknesses like the first version—floor panel, pedal floor, and front end in 0.88 mm; the outer sills in 1.0 mm; and the rear end in 1.25 mm. From car 3 on, the rear section was reinforced and made of 1.75 mm thick sheet metal, which increased the weight of the frame floor assembly by 12 kg to 165 kg. For the installation of the engine and transmission, the floor assembly

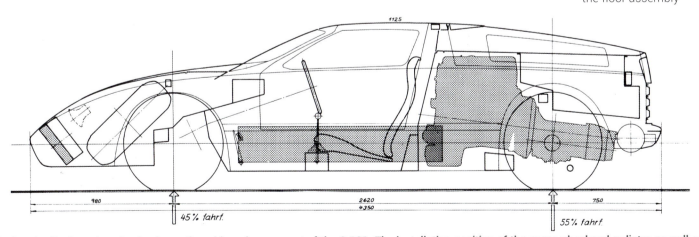

The longitudinal section clearly shows the mid-engine concept of the C 101. The installation position of the spare wheel and radiator as well as the fuel tanks housed in the side sills are also clearly visible.

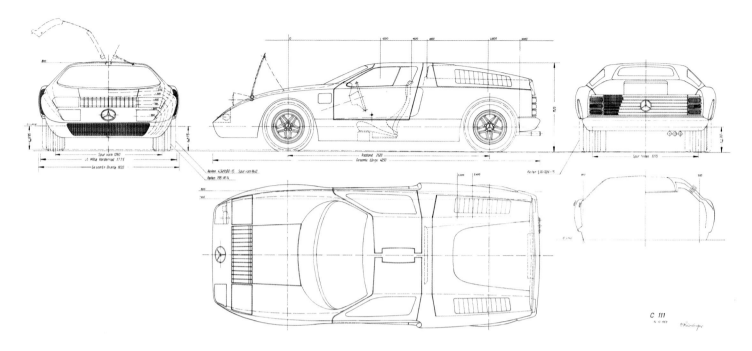

The C 101 with light-alloy wheels and street tires in four-sided view with additional sectional views. The drawing was made by body design engineer Erich Rühringer.

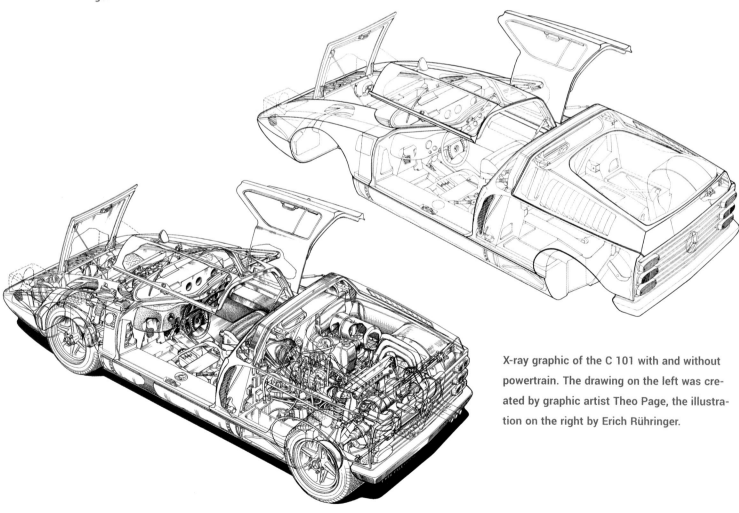

X-ray graphic of the C 101 with and without powertrain. The drawing on the left was created by graphic artist Theo Page, the illustration on the right by Erich Rühringer.

In June 1969, the first C 101 floor assembly of the second variant was produced in Sindelfingen—with a 2,620 mm wheelbase and designed for the "racing rear axle." The windshield frame and roof struts are now made of steel tubes (20 x 2 mm).

The chassis completed in the Untertürkheim test department was delivered to Rastatt on June 25, 1969. The radiator is still relatively far back, as in the Sledge, at about the level of the front wheels.

Front axle (*left*) and rear axle (*center and right*) of the C 101. The rear suspension shown is the five-link "racing rear axle" as used from car 2 on.

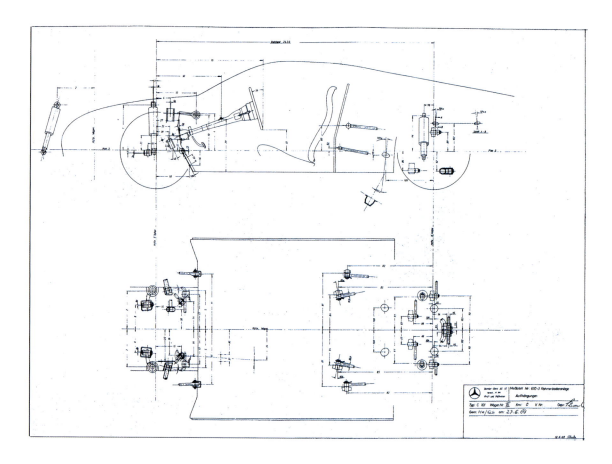

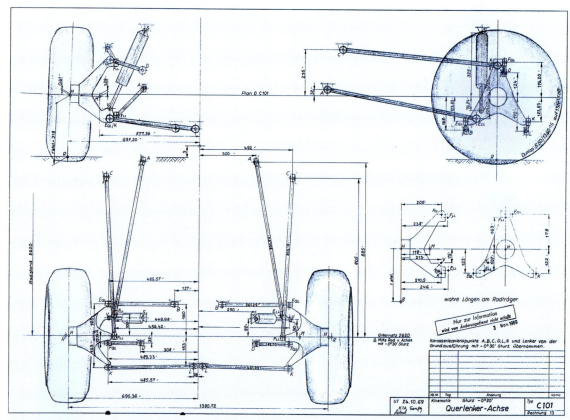

The two technical drawings show the frame reference dimensions that had to be observed for the correct positioning and installation of the wheel suspension.

went to the testing department in Untertürkheim, and from there to the Waggonfabrik Rastatt, where the production and assembly of the GRP body took place. Body design engineer Theodor Reinhard in Sindelfingen was in charge on the part of Daimler-Benz. The plastic used was the standard polyester resins Palatal P 6 and P 35 from BASF. The laminate thickness of 3 mm was initially higher than the originally envisaged 2 to 2.5 mm but was reduced to 1.5 mm from the second body onward.

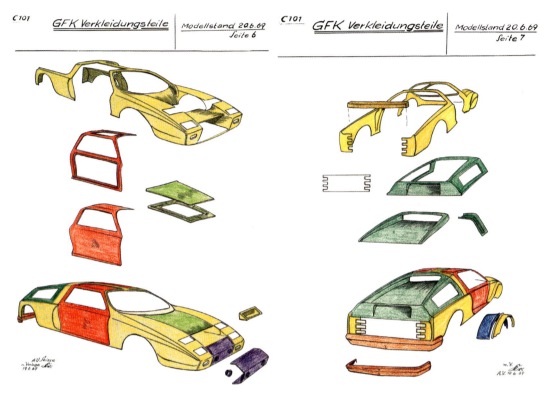

The drawings, dated June 19, 1969, and prepared by the pre-production shop, illustrate the compostion of the GRP body.

BASF and Gevetex, manufacturers of the materials used for the GRP body, used the spectacular sports car in their advertising.

Car 2—the first "real" C 101—during the assembly of the body at Waggonfabrik Rastatt

After completion, the plastic skin was riveted and glued to the frame floor assembly, and the windows were glued in. The engine compartment was lined with several layers of aluminum fleece to counteract the enormous heat build-up when the engine was running—especially when stationary without the cooling air supply—and to prevent discoloration of the paintwork or even the bodywork catching fire. After the production and assembly of the body, the painting and finally the interior installation were carried out in Sindelfingen, and the finished vehicle was then transported to Untertürkheim, where the first driving tests were carried out by the advance engineering department.

Birthday Present: The First "Real" C 101

After the Sledge, with original floor assembly, semi-trailing arm rear axle, and makeshift body, car 2—the first "real" C 101—was built in June–July 1969. On June 10, the testing department in Untertürkheim had received the floor assembly from Sindelfingen, and after it was completed with axles, transmission, and a dummy engine, it was delivered to Rastatt on June 25. After painting and interior finishing in Sindelfingen, the car returned to Untertürkheim on July 14, where it was prepared for testing in Hockenheim—just in time for the sixty-third birthday of Rudolf Uhlenhaut on July 15, 1969. The head of passenger car development, known to be a gifted driver, did not miss the opportunity to drop by Hockenheim and fine-tune his "birthday present" in person. As Theodor Reinhard later recalled, you "couldn't get him out of the car," and he even drank his birthday coffee in the driver's seat. Uhlenhaut and Reinhard drove lap after lap with coffee and cake. "In the Ostkurve," as Reinhard reported, "you could have put a handkerchief down on the racing line; he would always have hit it going 200 km/h. In the car, you didn't notice anything about the speed. It was like riding on a bus."

But July 15, 1969, was also an important date for the C 101 project in organizational terms. On this day, Karl-Wilhelm Müller,

The first "real" C 101 in July 1969 on the test track at the Untertürkheim plant. The position of the grille in the front and the design of the door suspension in the roof, which differ from the later vehicles, are clearly visible.

Car 2—on the top together with car 1—during testing at the Hockenheimring

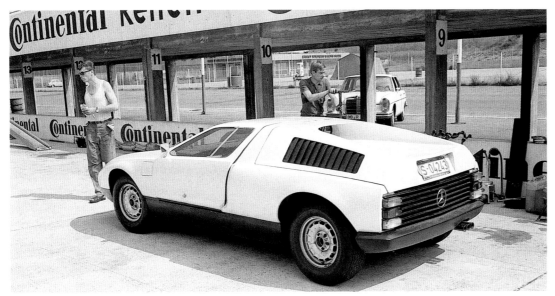

head of development organization and planning, informed the senior managers in the passenger car development department of the account numbers to which "all testing measures that cause labor and material costs" were to be posted. For the Untertürkheim scopes, this was no. 64116 12114, already defined on March 4, 1969, and for Sindelfingen no. 64517 50975. Although the numbers mentioned have only company-internal significance, they can be found in the chassis numbers and body numbers of the first series of the C 101.

Car 2, with its GRP body, seemed much more solid than the first test car, with a makeshift body, which was reflected in the noise behavior, among other things. Unfortunately, it had also become considerably heavier. With street tires, the fully fueled car weighed 1,218 kg and with racing tires 1,256 kg, while car 1, with racing tires, had last weighed 1,059 kg. In the overall weight, the GRP body accounted for 370 kg; this only changed on the next vehicle, with a significantly reduced laminate thickness. Numerous body details proved to need optimization, which was hardly surprising considering the very short development period. Complaints were made about "the excessively high and heavy seats with unsatisfactory head and shoulder support, . . . the doors that were difficult to open and did not open wide enough and did not close properly, the inadequate insulation of the trunk lid, the insufficiently heat-resistant design of the luggage compartment, the front wheel housings that were too low, the windshield wipers parked in the field of vision, the uneven floor, the design of the instrument panel that tended to reflect light and the initially inadequate ventilation."

Due to the high weight, greater gear ratios, and aerodynamically disturbing air intake from the engine compartment, the driving performance was initially disappointing. Although the installed KE 309 three-rotor engine with 297 hp/ 218 kW was well above the official rated output, car 2 only reached 236 km/h, and its lap times were 7.5 seconds slower than those of car 1. As expected, these were not the only points of criticism. Due to leaks in the tanks, the side sills had to be removed and riveted back on twice—certainly not a suitable permanent solution with 180 rivets per side. Instead of the originally used GRP-covered aluminum tanks, each with a capacity of 60 liters, new fuel tanks made of 1.5 mm thick soft aluminum with rounded walls on all sides were installed. A foam filling was to prevent the fuel from sloshing.

Cooling and visibility were also rated to need improvement. Even on the first run at Hockenheim, the engine cooling seemed, as Hans Liebold put it, "only just adequate." Wind tunnel measurements carried out shortly afterward showed that the flow through the radiator was even worse than in the Sledge. It was then decided to provide only one spare wheel with street tires instead of the previous racing tires for the other test cars, and to place it at an angle in front of the front upper crossbar. This allowed the radiator to be moved all the way to the front, and the cooling air intake and outlet to be positioned in the most favorable

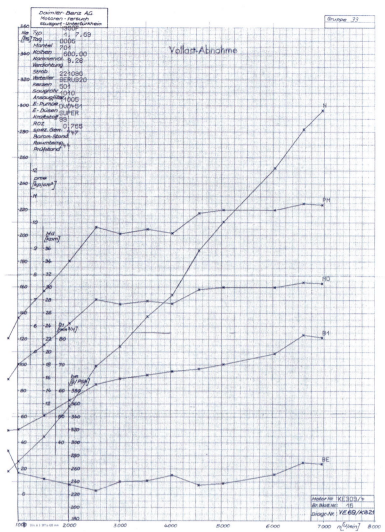

The full throttle acceptance test carried out on July 1, 1969, of the KE 309 three-rotor engine then fitted in car 2 shows an impressive output of 297 hp/218 kW at just under 7,000 rpm.

The C 101 during high-speed testing at the Hockenheimring—with racing tires (left) and street tires (right)

Car 2 during testing on the Hockenheimring, captured in the photos by well-known automotive photographer Paul Botzenhardt

The driver's workplace in the C 101 of the first series. The additional pedal to the left of the accelerator pedal, suggested by Uhlenhaut, for double clutching, which was tested from mid-August, is clearly visible. The push button on the gear lever knob was used to release the lock that prevented unintentional engagement of first gear and the reverse gear. The photo was taken in September 1969 and shows car 3.

zone. This was also intended to reduce the flow of hot air around the windshield and side windows, which apparently played a central role in heating up the car's interior. Another concern was the oil temperature, which had reached 150°C (300°F) after three laps on the large circuit and was to be curtailed by installing a second oil cooler.

After testing in Hockenheim, the KE 309 engine was replaced due to pronounced fluctuations in idle speed and severe compression loss. Due to a lack of available alternatives, KE 312 from car 1 had to be used as a replacement. Test drives were carried out with it again in Hockenheim on July 29, whereby cooling at oil temperatures of 145°C (295°F) and water temperatures of over 100°C (212°F) proved to be a major challenge. Only the installation of a second oil cooler on the right side of the vehicle brought the desired success and led to oil temperatures of around 110°C (230°F) and water temperatures of around 90°C (194°F).

The ZF five-speed transmission with multidisc, limited-slip differential used in the C 101 showed another peculiarity in addition to the already described need for optimization in terms of shifting precision, which Fritz Naumann later put in a nutshell: "If you wanted to shift quickly, you either had to apply great shifting forces to get the synchronizers to work quickly, or you had to double-clutch. Metering this correctly was difficult. Most of the time, the engine without load revved too high." A protrusion at the lower left end of the originally designed accelerator pedal allowed the heel of the right foot to double-clutch while the front of the foot operated the brake pedal. Instead, Uhlenhaut suggested an additional, differently geared accelerator pedal for double clutching, which was provisionally installed in car 3 and turned out to the complete satisfaction of the master. Like Liebold, Fritz Naumann initially regarded the shift throws as a kind of gamble. As part of the aforementioned redesign of the gear shift linkage, an innovative solution was also tested here from August onward, which proved to be very successful. The gate for first and reverse gears could only be accessed by pressing a push-button on the shift knob, which released the locking of the corresponding shift shaft at the transmission by means of a solenoid switch.

 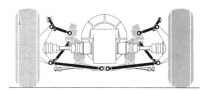  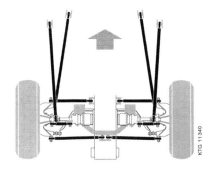

The five-link "racing rear axle" of the C 101 with street tires in detail view and overview

The newly designed racing rear axle with five push-pull rods on each side gave the C 101, as Fritz Naumann later put it, "stable handling as docile as a lamb" and made it possible "to steer with your knee at 200 km/h on the motorway and peel an orange with both hands." Daimler-Benz was thus unquestionably ahead of its time. A similar design in principle, likewise a five-link axle, made its debut at the end of 1982 under the name "multilink axle" in the compact W 201 passenger car model series—a wheel suspension that has been the benchmark for safety and comfort in production passenger cars ever since.

Naumann also described the cornering behavior as "sensational." However, it was necessary to adjust the camber on the rear axle according to the tires. The Continental 195 VR 14 or Michelin 205 VR 14 used as street tires required 3° at the rear axle, a significantly higher negative camber than the Dunlop racing tires (4.30/11.60-15 at the front and 5.30/13.60-15 at the rear), where the camber was set to just twenty minutes of arc due to their wide contact patch. If necessary, a sway bar on the rear axle was also part of the racing setup. Because the switch from one type of tire to the other was carried out quite often in testing, two sets of upper wishbones of different lengths were kept ready for each car, which then enabled a very quick conversion. The decisive factor was that with a spring travel of 100 mm, the rear wheel camber only changed by 2 to 3 minutes of arc. The axle load distribution for all vehicles was 45.5% front to 54.5% rear.

The two aluminum wheel carriers for the rear axle were not designed as castings, because casting alloys with the required ductility and fracture strength were not yet available at the beginning. Instead, they were milled from a solid piece, using the AlCuMg1 wrought alloy. At the instigation of Fritz Naumann, the company nevertheless ventured into the experimental production of cast work pieces in June 1971, after Aluminumhütte Rheinfelden GmbH had proposed the Alufont-47 [AlCu4TiMg] alloy with a silver content of 1% and a tensile strength of 48 kg/mm², which was exceptionally high for light-metal alloys.

Construction drawing of the five-link "racing rear axle" with racing tires

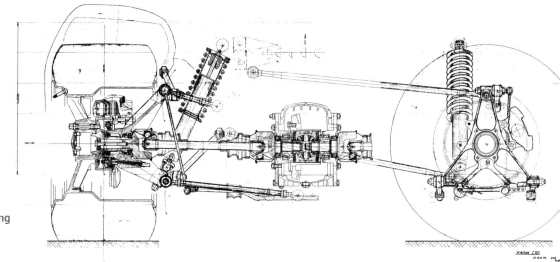

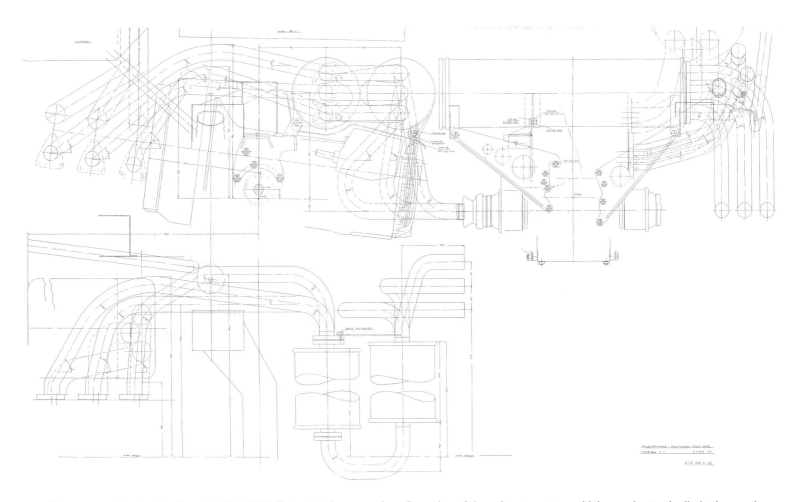

The construction drawing from April 3, 1969, illustrates the unusual configuration of the exhaust system, which was due to the limited space in the rear of the car.

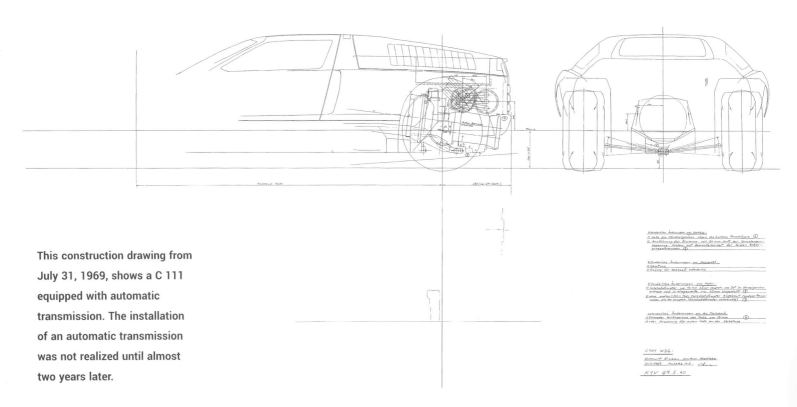

This construction drawing from July 31, 1969, shows a C 111 equipped with automatic transmission. The installation of an automatic transmission was not realized until almost two years later.

In the Wind Tunnel: The Aerodynamics Development

Starting in February 1969, 1:5 models of the C 101 had been measured in the wind tunnel and aerodynamically optimized at various stages of the project. In June, the first test car with the makeshift body (in its third and final version) was then also examined in the wind tunnel to obtain results in relation to the model figures—including with regard to the expected top speed. In the initial state, with lateral tail fins extending to the upper edge of the roof and an upper rear end sloping toward the rear, the result was a c_d value of 0.390, with a frontal area of 1.754 m². At 250 km/h, a downforce of 96 kp was measured at the front axle and a lift of 119 kp at the rear axle—values that, in combination, can initiate instability at higher driving speeds. A much more favorable lift distribution was achieved by a slightly positive angle of attack of the body by a mere 25 minutes of arc. The front-axle lift was thus still 20 kp, and the rear-axle lift was reduced to 35 kp. The c_d value was reduced to 0.365 by the omission of the tail fins and a horizontal of the upper rear end. Accordingly, the shape of the rear end was slightly changed as a result of the examination. The top was made completely level and practically horizontal with a 15 mm high spoiler edge as the rear end.

Immediately after the first tests at the Hockenheimring, the first "real" C 101, car 2, was measured in the large wind tunnel on the Untertürkheim factory premises on July 16 and 17, 1969. With street tires, it achieved a remarkable c_d value of 0.340, with a frontal area of 1.6647 m². To achieve the development goal of enabling good downforce figures even without spoilers and wing, the underbody was completely smooth and only provided with a small service opening. At 250 km/h, a downforce of 26 kp at the front and a lift of 34 kp at the rear were ascertained.

A 1:5 model of the C 101 being measured in the model wind tunnel in Sindelfingen

The last version of the Sledge during the measurement in the wind tunnel of the FKFS in June 1969. The tailfins on the hood, which extend to the top edge of the roof, are clearly visible and were removed as a result of the wind tunnel test.

On July 16 and 17, 1969, car 2, still with its original body, was measured in the wind tunnel of the FKFS in Untertürkheim.

The wind tunnel tests were also informative in another respect: Investigations into the cooling air flow showed that the air velocity in front of the radiator surface was very uneven. In the upper area, it was one sixth; in the lower area, partially covered by the spare wheel, it was only one fourteenth of the driving speed. Two cooling fans increased the air flow rate by approximately 28%. The cause was determined to be the unfavorable setup of the radiator intake and outlet openings in terms of pressure. In particular, the entire area of the cooling air outlet in front of the windshield was in a positive pressure zone. Based on these findings, the following changes were proposed: The cooling air intake was to be relocated to the high positive area of the almost vertical front end surface, and the previous air intake on the top of the front end was to be used as the cooling air outlet but moved about 150 mm to the rear. The radiator itself was to be placed at an angle between the intake and outlet openings.

Light and Shadow: New Test Cars, Few Engines

Just in time for another test scheduled for August 4 in Hockenheim, another vehicle was available in the form of car 3. It was only at the last minute that it had been possible to provide the 270 hp/199 kW KE 315 three-rotor engine, after two initially planned engines had failed during the test bench run. To improve the heat management of the car, the cooling air ducting was modified according to the findings of the wind tunnel measurements of car 2. The air intake was now at the bottom of the car's front end, and the outlet at the level of the hidden headlights. Accordingly, the radiator had also been moved farther forward, and the oil cooler was installed behind it. Nevertheless, the hoped-for improvements failed to materialize. At 35°C (95°F) outside temperature, the temperature level could not be reduced compared to car 2 (in the initial version with only one oil cooler). In this respect, neither the removal of the fans located in front of the radiator nor the installation of an oil-water heat exchanger helped. Only by connecting the heat exchanger in series with an additional lateral oil cooler could the water temperature be reduced to approximately 90°C (194°F) and the oil temperature to a maximum of 125°C (257°F). Based on these results, changes were planned after discussion with Behr, the radiator supplier: A radiator with an increased block depth of 68 mm and an oil cooler with an approximately 50% larger frontal area were to be tested. In this configuration, the fans had to be arranged behind the radiator.

Car 3, with street tires on steel rims, had a kerb weight of 1,190 kg. Since the bodywork had an average laminate thickness of 1.5 mm instead of the previous 3 mm, the small difference in weight compared to car 2 was initially perceived as disappointing. In view of the second oil cooler with the additional pipes, the steering lock, the steel wheels, and the greater sheet thickness at the rear of the frame—points that added up to 30 kg—there was nevertheless a weight reduction of the body of 60 kg.

On August 13, car 2 (with street tires) and car 3 (with racing tires) were tested and fine-tuned at the Nürburgring. In the meantime, as planned, car 3 had received an oil cooler with a 50% larger cooling surface, which was installed in front of the radiator.

Despite the dynamics, the driving shots of car 2 (*left*) and car 3 (*right*) show the changed front design with the modified headlights and the relocated grille. Originally intended as an air intake opening, the grille was moved about 100 mm to the rear as a result of the wind tunnel measurement and converted into an outlet opening.

Car 3 was completed in early August 1969 and, still in its original white livery, was photographed on the test track in Untertürkheim together with the classic 300 SL. The "Gullwing" from the 1950s was a unique piece with a plastic body, as was the case at the board's inspection on April 30. The cognac-colored interior of the C 101 met not only with approval, as press chief Artur Keser expressed to Friedrich Geiger on August 8, suggesting a change in the interior color. On August 4, 1969, the first driving test took place in Hockenheim.

Car 2 (*in front*) and car 3 (*in the background*) **during testing at the Hockenheimring on August 4, 1969**

These photos of car 3 were taken by Paul Botzenhardt at the beginning of August 1969, immediately after the vehicle was completed on the grounds of the test track at the Mercedes-Benz plant in Untertürkheim.

After returning from its first tests in Hockenheim, car 3 was given a coat of signal orange paint on the initiative of Sindelfingen styling department—a color that was particularly noticeable even in adverse visibility conditions. The picture on the left shows the car during the test drive at the Nürburgring on August 13.

The latter had been fitted with fans on the back that sucked the air through the radiator. Even when driving hard, the oil temperature did not now rise above 95°C (200°F), while the water temperature was 90°C (194°F). Since the fans were apparently running constantly, but this could not be reliably determined under the conditions of the test due to the lack of an indicator lamp, further improvement of the water cooling was deemed necessary. For this purpose, a narrower oil cooler with a width of 127 instead of 150 mm was to be used to

View from behind into the engine compartment of car 3

The view from above illustrates the installation conditions of the engine and transmission with axle drive.

103

The four-spoke safety steering wheel with large-area impact plate and impact absorber—here two photos of the first model from June 1969—was used for the first time in the C 101. In the spring of 1971, it was introduced in slightly modified form for production cars with the 350 SL (R 107). In the C 101, the steering wheel diameter was 380 mm, 50 mm less than in the 350 SL.

Attractive workplace: the cockpit of the C 101, photographed at the beginning of August 1969 in car 3. Accelerator pedal (without additional pedal for double clutching) and gear lever (without push button for electromagnetic lock) still correspond to the original design status.

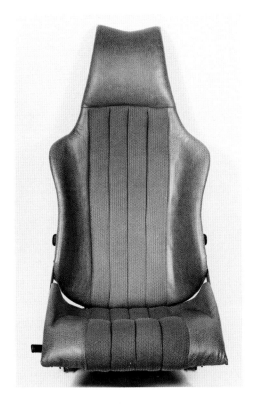

The seats specially designed for the C 101 initially met with criticism and were extensively revised after being tested in the Sledge.

The seats of the C 101 in their revised version—in removed and installed condition (in car 4). Including the seat rails, a seat weighed only 9.5 kg—only about half as much as the seats used in Mercedes-Benz production cars at the time.

The light-alloy wheels designed by Stefan Heiliger made their debut on the C 101. Starting in August 1970, the 14-inch version was available as special equipment for Mercedes-Benz passenger cars in the 108/109, 111, and 113 model series. The spare wheel (here the version on a steel rim) was located under the front hood behind the front-mounted radiator—not too favorable a position for the engine's heat balance.

allow "better air flow through the radiator with probably still sufficient oil cooling." In addition, an enlargement of the cooling air intake opening was provided for cars 5 and 6. Fuel consumption during testing at the Nürburgring was 30.7 l/100 km over 385 km for car 2 and 33.6 l/100 km over 566 km for car 3. Both cars consumed approximately 3 liters of oil per 1,000 km.

A few days later, car 4 was added to the test fleet. Delivered from Sindelfingen on August 15, the third "real" C 101 was fitted with street tires in the test department in Untertürkheim and tested together with car 3 in Hockenheim on August 19. In addition to numerous technical optimization potentials, the test drives in July and August also revealed shortcomings of the bodywork that affected the daily practicality. Visibility to the front, especially for shorter people, was limited by the high wing line in front of the A-pillars; more serious, however, was the inadequate visibility to the rear, which made it difficult to enter the motorway and made reverse parking virtually impossible without outside help.

In the last week of August, cars 3 and 4 were individually inspected by TÜV Stuttgart as part of their registration process. The expert disapproved of three points that had to be taken into account for further development—especially with regard to a possible future series production. On the one hand, the indicator lamps were to be modified to ensure visibility from the side as well. In addition, the C 101 had a total of six headlights due to the lamps for the headlight flasher system, two more than stipulated by the Road Traffic Licensing Regulations (StVZO). To make it possible to get the necessary exemption, the Sindelfingen body developers proposed to implement a clear separation of headlight flasher and main beam by changing the contacts on the steering column switch, so that simultaneous operation would be impossible. The third complaint was that due to their angular shape, the popped-up headlights were classified as vehicle parts that pose a hazard for traffic within the meaning of the StVZO. Since no quick fix could be found, the directive was issued to present the vehicle at exhibitions only with the headlights folded away.

Maturation Process: First Evolutions of the C 101

The latest findings from testing were always incorporated into new detailed solutions during the development of the C 101. After the test run at the Nürburgring on August 13, car 2 immediately went to Rastatt, where it received a lightened and visually modernized body with a revised front. The modifications also included the retractable headlights, which were now operated by a modified mechanism, as was already the case with car 3. Originally, the concealed main headlights on this vehicle popped up like drawers—a sight that took some getting used to and is unfortunately not documented by photograph.

Also modified was the design of the door hinges and the trunk, which was enlarged to 224 liters and made accessible from the outside via a separate flap without opening the hood. Due to the confined space in the rear, this required a modification of the exhaust system. Instead of the two round silencers arranged in sequence above the transmission, the main silencer was now moved down behind the transmission, and the front silencer, which had been reduced in size by 30%, was positioned above the rear right wheel well. The triple tailpipe thus moved from the right

The main headlights of the C 101 were under spring tension and popped up by operating a pull knob. A foot pedal was used to bring them back into the rest position.

to the left side of the vehicle. To make these changes possible, the body aft of the rear axle had to be extended by 65 mm (instead of the 60 mm initially specified by the design). However, the smaller front silencer resulted in a noticeable deterioration in driving performance.

In addition to the enlarged luggage compartment, car 2 also received an additional option for luggage storage "in the English variant," where a light-alloy suitcase could be strapped to the trunk lid with two tensioning straps. Suggested by Rudolf Uhlenhaut, the "butter test" was also introduced: A packet of butter placed in the trunk was not allowed to melt, even when driving hard. For this purpose, the luggage compartment was shielded from the engine heat by insulating it with aluminum-fleece sandwich material. As part of the aforementioned modifications, the shape of the hatch was also changed somewhat to improve the insufficient visibility to the rear corners.

The photo of car 3 with open hatch shows the cramped space, which in the original version only allowed for a very small trunk capacity, which at 105 liters just barely met the requirements of the FIA.

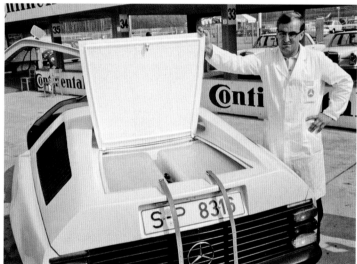

After the modification, car 2 had a trunk enlarged to 224 liters, which could be accessed without opening the trunk hatch and could accommodate three pieces of tailor-made luggage—at the very bottom, a medium-sized case lying crosswise, and, above it lengthwise, two smaller ones.

In the area immediately behind the rear window, the side panels of the hood on the left and right were fitted with windows, and the angle of the louvers of the engine bay ventilation was changed. These measures enabled the driver to see the area to the right of the vehicle through the louvers when looking over their shoulder. Similarly, the passenger was given a corresponding view through the louvres on the left side. A second exterior mirror mounted on the right also served to improve visibility, which in addition to car 2 was also fitted to all the other cars completed at this time. The measures made both reversing and merging into traffic much easier.

The test drives with the first C 101s were generally overshadowed by frequent engine changes due to high oil consumption and performance losses after only a few thousand kilometers. In the prevailing tough test conditions, the three-rotor engines of the M 950 series did not even reach 6,000 km—the average was 3,700 km. During the test drives, all defects were meticulously recorded, and the cars were subsequently checked at the factory. Development engineer Fritz Naumann later summed up this phase: "But no matter what we did ourselves, we could neither bring the always unsatisfactory performance nor the durability of the Wankel engines to an acceptable level."

A fourth, larger suitcase could be strapped to the outside of the trunk if required.

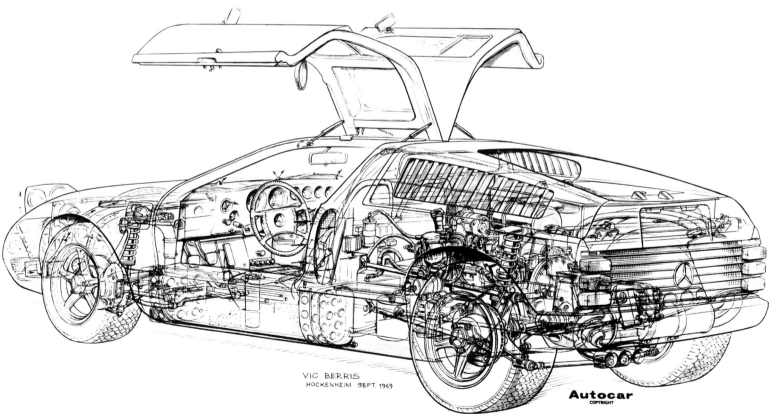

Graphic artist Vic Berris created an x-ray drawing of car 2 after the conversion for British magazine *The Autocar*. The viewing windows in the engine compartment hatch and the modified exhaust system with the tailpipes relocated to the left side are clearly visible.

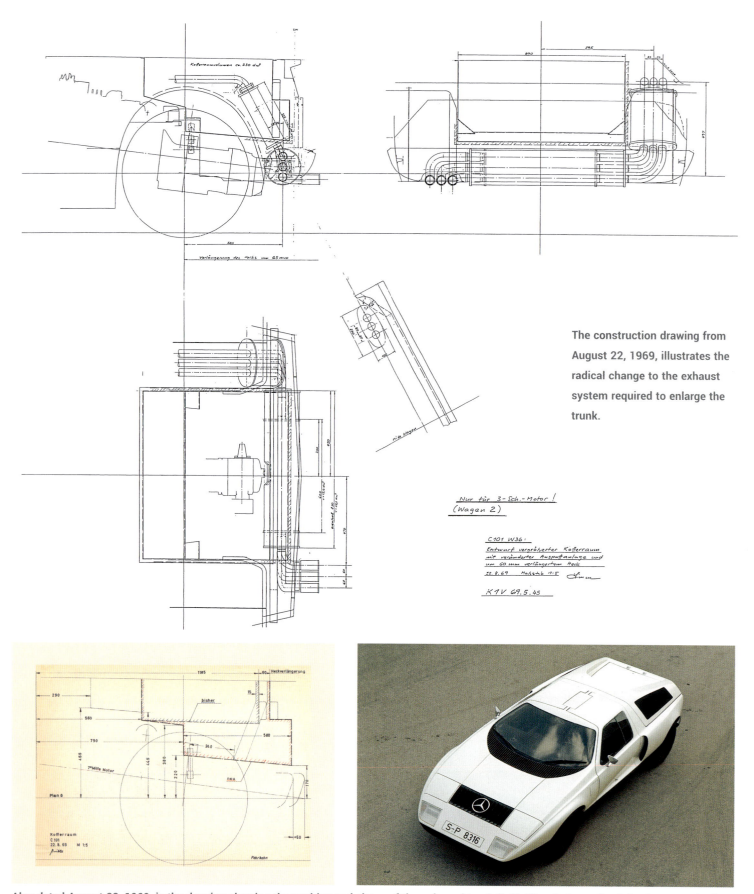

The construction drawing from August 22, 1969, illustrates the radical change to the exhaust system required to enlarge the trunk.

Also dated August 22, 1969, is the drawing showing the position and shape of the enlarged trunk (*left*). The photo on the right shows car 2 after conversion. The two eyelets at the rear are used to attach the tensioning straps for the externally mounted trunk.

From the Stock Exchange to the Media:
The C 101 in Public

The C 101 had already been present in public since spring 1969, although not initially under this designation. In connection with speculations about profit-sharing certificates, which were supposed to make the approval of the planned merger with the VW subsidiary Audi palatable to NSU shareholders, a rumor was spread—apparently from within NSU circles—that caused a sensation: Daimler-Benz is building a Wankel sports car. The first mention of this rumor was in the *Frankfurter Börsenbrief* of March 10, 1969. Under the headline "NSU-Genußscheine auf die Wankel-Erfindung" (NSU profit-sharing certificates for the Wankel invention), it said, "Every announcement of a new Wankel car in the world will stimulate the share price of the share of NSU AG as licensor for the Wankel engine]. As an exclusive in this regard: The first Mercedes sports car with a Wankel engine is to be presented in autumn."

On the same day, however, the Daimler-Benz Board of Management had still controversially discussed the C 101 and its impact on image and publicity. Dr. Hanns Martin Schleyer considered it imperative "to reconsider the question of the Wankel engine thoroughly, not least because if the C 101 were to be presented at the 1969 IAA, comments in the press could be expected to the effect that DB had now decided in principle in favor of the Wankel engine." In his response, head of development Scherenberg summarized that "the question now is no longer whether the Wankel engine should be used in principle, but only in which area." Arnold Wychodil, responsible for international sales, did not consider "the inclusion of the Wankel engine in the passenger car range to be unproblematic" and pointed out "the presentation of the C 101 would have to be linked to a targeted press campaign, emphasizing that the C 101 was a special model with no consequences for the rest of the passenger car range."

Speculation Topic: Wankel Sports Cars and Corporate Mergers

Interestingly, the next press release on the rumors published by *Börsenbrief* appeared only fourteen days later. On March 24, *Stuttgarter Zeitung* reported on a Mercedes sports car with a Wankel engine in a short article on page 1 under the headline "Wankel car from Daimler expected." "In the discussion about the . . . NSU profit-sharing certificates, there is talk in Frankfurt banking and stock exchange circles that Daimler-Benz AG Stuttgart is working on the development of a three-rotor Wankel engine. The development work is to result in the presentation of a passenger car with a Wankel engine as early as this year's International Motor Show in Frankfurt." This was followed in the business section by a story with the headline "Daimler-Benz/BMW as an alternative for NSU? Mercedes-Benz sports coupe with three-rotor Wankel engine expected." The story not only delved deeper into the subject but also made a statement with even-higher sensational potential. "In industry circles it is expected that Daimler-Benz AG will choose the same path for its first Wankel car as NSU did at the time with the Wankel Spider and will launch a sports coupe with a Wankel engine that is likely to be below the current Mercedes-Benz sports car range in terms of size and price. Similar to NSU, this sports car would appeal to motorists and sports fans interested in technical innovations, who may not be able to afford a large Mercedes-Benz sports car for their hobby, but are prepared to accept the unpredictability possible with the first series of technologically new cars." Even more attention-grabbing than this news item, which was surprising in itself, was the article's conclusion, which picked up on its spectacular headline: "It is pointed out that, in terms of the developmental strength of the German automotive companies, an alliance of BMW-NSU-Daimler-Benz would even be more favorable than the merger of NSU with Auto Union. So, if the NSU shareholders . . . reject a merger of NSU and Auto Union, there would still be the possibility of finding an alliance together with BMW and Daimler-Benz AG."

The explosive power of this report prompted Daimler-Benz to make an immediate statement, which was picked up by *Stuttgarter Nachrichten* on March 25: "The progress of the work on the Wankel principle has been reported on regularly for years. In the course of this development work, several sports cars equipped with Wankel engines are being tested for experimental and demonstration purposes. This does not imply a decision on the question of a possible later series introduction. Speculations about industrial alliances between Daimler-Benz and other German car manufacturers have no basis." The issue of *Stuttgarter Zeitung* on the same day commented accordingly but, interestingly, also quoted statements by NSU and BMW: "A spokesman for NSU Motorenwerke said in contrast that in his company the possibility of an alliance of NSU–Daimler-Benz–BMW had been given much consideration. From circles close to BMW it is confirmed that an alliance of NSU–Daimler-Benz–BMW would be more favorable in terms of development potential than the alliance NSU–Auto Union."

At the board meeting on March 25, the C 101 was again the subject of controversial discussions. The minutes state, "In connection with Scherenberg's comment that the details of the vehicle were already known to a whole series of trade journalists anyway, Schleyer points out that in this case in particular every effort must be made to reveal the sources of the indiscretions. He finds it remarkable that the publications on the C 101 followed shortly after the last board meeting, where a resolution was tabled in view of the concerns he had raised. Moreover, in his opinion, the abundance of disclosed details proves that the indiscretions did not originate from individual low-level clerks." Board spokesman Joachim Zahn drew attention to the fact that "certain negative consequences must also be taken into consideration if there is no presentation of the C 101 with a Wankel engine at the 1969 IAA. In view of the publications since then, the impression could possibly arise that our Wankel development has remained unsuccessful—although the NSU Ro 80 has in the meantime proven the applicability of the Wankel principle. Conversely, such a decision could also cause unwelcome speculation that we had postponed the presentation of the C 101 in order to prepare for a forthcoming introduction of the Wankel engine for the range of volume produced vehicles."

Rolf Staelin raised the question of whether it might not be "expedient to limit oneself to a less spectacular presentation—such as a demonstration at the Hockenheimring" but considered it crucial "first to clarify for what purpose the vehicle is to be built," in particular "whether the C 101 is to be sold or merely made available to a limited group as a test vehicle." He expressed the view that "by the C 101 becoming known—no matter how this has happened—a situation has been created that we now have to account for with concrete measures" and considered "the clear announcement of this model with the simultaneous explanation that it is a special vehicle with no impact on the volume produced vehicles to be the most appropriate solution as things stand."

Incidentally, the passenger car commission had also advocated at its meeting on March 21 that "the C 101 model should be presented at the 1969 IAA." According to the commission members, "equipping the vehicle with a Wankel engine . . . would not have any detrimental effect on sales of volume produced vehicles and special vehicles with reciprocating engines. Too strong a trend toward the Wankel engine in the technical areas of the company" was not feared either.

Rolf Staelin's suggestion to proactively announce the C 101 was not pursued further, but the Mercedes-Benz Wankel sports car nevertheless caused a sensation a short time later and was covered by the entire press within a few days. *Der Motorist, Presse- und Nachrichtendienst für das deutsche Kraftfahrwesen* (*The Motorist, Press and News Service for German Automotive Engineering*) speculated on April 8 under the headline "Super sports car from Mercedes" about "a highly interesting project being prepared at Daimler-Benz and possibly to be presented to the public as early as the IAA." A new sports car is being built in Stuttgart, uncompromising in its design and certainly as trendsetting as the 300 SLR back then. For the first time in the tradition-steeped history of the company, Mercedes engineers use a Wankel engine as the power unit . . . . And anyone who knows the Mercedes engineers knows that they will build a sports car that will also be trendsetting in terms of body and chassis and will give new momentum to sports car construction as a whole. Daimler-Benz, by the way, does not intend to put merely a 'show object' together."

Media Star: The C 101 in the Tabloid Press and in Trade Magazines

On the same day, *Bild-Zeitung* ran the headline "Car Sensation 69. Mercedes is building new Wankel car," dropping a bombshell: "Will the car sensation of the year come from Daimler-Benz? Is the Wankel engine starting its victory march at Mercedes? . . . The rotary piston SL from Stuttgart gets a three-rotor Wankel engine. . . . Contrary to Mercedes tradition, the super two-seater . . . will dispense with superfluous equipment: a tough car for tough men. Apparently, Mercedes wants to be back at rallies and airfield races with a real sports car. Full of pride, the young engineers say, 'We may be an old company, but we don't build grandpa cars.' More importantly: From 1970 onward, every better Mercedes was to have the option of a Wankel engine. The very fussy Mercedes test engineers are quite satisfied after the Wankel test drives through southern France: Even in the lower rev range, the Mercedes three-rotor Wankel accelerates first-class. . . . Minorities are still trying to put the brakes on this technical progress, but you don't have to be a clairvoyant to predict that the Wankel engine has a bright future. Provided that Germany's car businessmen are no dumber than Germany's car engineers." With all these assessments, *Bild-Zeitung* had overshot reality by far, but at least a sensation had been caused. Individual board members urged a clear denial, but board spokesperson Zahn recommended refraining from doing so in order to "avoid consolidating false reports as a result."

However, one day later, on April 9, 1969, *Frankfurter Allgemeine Zeitung* published a report from UPI news agency under the headline "No series Wankel at Mercedes": "Daimler-Benz AG, Stuttgart. No vehicle with a Wankel engine will go into series production at the company. As a spokesperson for the company has now stated, there are also no plans to equip a production passenger car with an optional Wankel engine. He emphasized that Daimler-Benz was intensively continuing the ongoing tests with a Wankel sports car. . . . It is also not yet certain whether this sports car will already be shown at the International Motor Show in Frankfurt." On the same day, *FAZ* reported on its page *Der Motor* under the headline "Mercedes-Wankel at the IAA?: "In the last few days there have been increasing reports that Daimler-Benz will bring some prototypes with a Wankel engine to the International Motor Show in Frankfurt (September 11 to 21). . . . Opinions differ about the shape of the body. There are some indications that it will be a sporty version. . . . When asked, Daimler-Benz only confirmed that they had been working on such an engine for years and that test runs on the bench had been satisfactory. However, a series production was still out of the question."

On the same day, *Bild-Zeitung* again put it plainly. On page 1, the article headline proclaimed, "A great fellow, the Wankel Mercedes." Pictured was a rather free design sketch from the pen of Joseph Gallitzendörfer, whose origin, however, was not mentioned. The text read, "This is what the first Wankel Mercedes looks like, which . . . is being built in Stuttgart and will be presented at the Frankfurt Motor Show in September. It is an ultra-low sports two-seater, just under 1.10 m high, independent suspension, five-speed transmission, mid-mounted engine, three-rotor Wankel with a total of 1,800 cc chamber volume (the tax office multiplies that by two: so 3.6 liters are taxable), 260 hp at 7,000 rpm, top speed: over 250 km/h." This meant the cat was out of the bag. The continuation followed on page 2 under the headline "No Wankel Mercedes yet for the family." "Daimler-Benz confirmed yesterday that this Mercedes Wankel will be built in a small series. However, the factory has officially denied that it intends to offer Wankel engines as an option for its production models from 1970. BILD has learned that there is still some disagreement about the future of the Wankel engine at Mercedes. The Daimler-Benz test engineers are very satisfied with the performance and service life of their rotary piston engines. But sales strategists concerned about the Mercedes reputation think: We don't just need test results; we need the Wankel engine to prove itself in everyday life. Now the Wankel sports car has to prove whether it runs and runs and runs. Only then will Daimler-Benz decide whether or not to build Wankel engines in large-scale production." In the days that followed, the automotive trade press gratefully took up the topic of the "Mercedes-Benz Wankel sports car" and reported on the new sports car in great detail, but to varying degrees. Swiss *Automobil Revue* and *Deutsche Auto Zeitung* were the first on April 10. The tradition-steeped Swiss magazine, known for its integrity, read, "The chances of another car model with NSU/Wankel rotary engine are increasing. This time they concern a vehicle of the sporty top class. Daimler-Benz AG, which has been carrying out extensive design and test work on this type of engine for several years, has developed a two-seater sports coupe of very high performance, fitted with a three-rotor Wankel engine in front of the rear axle. Currently, the decision is being debated in Stuttgart as to whether this car

An April 9, 1969, article in *Bild-Zeitung* **showed a design sketch made by Joseph Gallitzendörfer, admittedly without citing the source, and gave realistic technical data.**

should be presented to the public at the Frankfurt Motor Show next September. The intention is to build a small test series of this special vehicle; interested parties who are particularly keen on innovations and have the appropriate funds could then gain some good and possibly also some not-so-good practical experience that must be available before a renowned factory can decide to embark on the path of the rotary engine, which is still posted with many a question mark today. . . . There are still few authentic details known about the planned Daimler-Benz sports car, which is the starting point for this description of the situation. The sketch published on this page, however, reveals that the coupe under discussion does not have much in common with the brand's previous stylistic tradition but will have decidedly futuristic, unconventional features. The front design is also likely to differ significantly from the previous bearers of the brand star. . . . Nevertheless, the eventual debut of a Wankel mid-engine sports coupe in the autumn would be one of the significant events in automotive engineering." Incidentally, the article was illustrated with a sketch-like but still halfway realistic drawing, also from the pen of Joseph Gallitzendörfer, which was dubbed a "professional sketch" but—like the drawing published the day before by *Bild-Zeitung*—did not give a source reference.

Deutsche Auto Zeitung magazine, just launched and still in daily newspaper format, devoted the front page of its first issue to the C 101 with the sensational headline "Mercedes shocked the whole car world. Soon Silver Arrows with rotary engines?" In keeping with the sub-headline, DAZ highlighted motorsport competitions and also quoted racing legend Hermann Lang, who had celebrated his sixtieth birthday a few days earlier, "Flick and even Quandt, they are already old people for this. They no longer have the energy to get into racing!" Three days after ex-racing driver Hermann Lang had thoughtfully pondered this, rumors and reports about a new Mercedes racing sports car with a Wankel engine fascinated car fans all over the world. The Daimler-Benz press department also had its say and put the statements of *Bild-Zeitung* in perspective: "There is practically only one drawing of the whole car. There's not a single one of them yet, but people are acting like the dream car will be on sale next week," Mercedes press spokesman Reinert wondered and went on full frontal attack against *Bild*. "What they wrote is outright fake news. The projected sports car and our production models with reciprocating engines are two different things. The 280 SL will not be replaced and no one is thinking of installing optional Wankel engines in our normal sedans from 1970 onward."

With regard to the conception, *DAZ* showed itself to be very well informed and not only speculated on the sales price, but also went into detail about the importance of motor racing: "Although no prototype of the imaginary car is yet driving on Untertürkheim's test tracks, the three-rotor Wankel engines of the equivalent of 1,800 cc have undergone tough tests on the test bench and on the road. It is also true that the Daimler Board of Management has made no decision on participating in sports car races, but the design of the planned model with the engine between the axles, aluminum body, gullwing doors, 120-liter tank, and a functional wedge shape is so purpose-built that the thought of a sports application must have played a significant role in the design, especially since the performance data of the rotary engine, estimated at between 240 and 260 hp, are hardly in the civilian range, nor is the price, which is likely to be unaffordable for normal people and close to the 100,000-mark limit. . . . It may be that Daimler-Benz, the brand that has become world famous for its sporting successes, feels the time has come to present a sporting masterpiece as demonstrative proof of unchanged technical superiority. But the engineers in Untertürkheim will also know that the image of a genuine sports car and its advertising value for the company ultimately arise solely from the battle on the racetrack. Irrespective of such considerations, the almost unbelievable response to the news from Stuttgart proves what passionate sympathy car fans on all continents feel when sporty engine noise is heard in Untertürkheim."

"Mercedes shocked the whole car world." In its first issue on April 10, 1969, *Deutsche Auto Zeitung* devoted the front-page headline to the new Wankel sports car from Mercedes-Benz.

114   Dream Sports Car and Laboratory on Wheels: The C 111

With this illustrated article, *auto, motor und sport* reported on the Wankel sports car from Mercedes-Benz for the first time in its issue of April 12, 1969. The design sketch prepared by Joseph Gallitzendörfer had already appeared in the Viennese *Kurier* on April 9, in *Automobil Revue* on April 10, and in *Welt am Sonntag* on April 13—also without citation of the source in these cases.

Two days later, the Stuttgart-based trade journal *auto, motor und sport* devoted a two-page article to the Mercedes-Benz Wankel sports car in its April 12 issue. Illustrated with the side view already known from *Automobil Revue*, the article reported in great detail and in almost all points accurately about the C 101 and its technical concept. About the presentation date, it said, "The C 101, as it is known internally, is scheduled for presentation in the autumn. It will most likely be exhibited at the International Motor Show in Frankfurt but will certainly be available to drive as a demonstration car."

On the same day, the Viennese daily newspaper *Kurier*, which had already reported on the Wankel sports car on April 9, published an article under the headline "Mercedes with Wankel!," a short news item that contained a spectacular claim right at the beginning: "So Mercedes will go back to sport. That's already been decided." This did not correspond to the facts, but the article not only showed the sketch known from *Bild-Zeitung* but also announced interesting details: "The Mercedes Wankel sports car should be a bombshell. It has been designed in such a way that it is possible to use not only the three-rotor Wankel that is under development (this engine will produce 260 hp at 7,000 rpm), but also a four-rotor Wankel, which would produce 350 hp. The top speed of the 260-horsepower model will be 280 km/h, while the 350-horsepower model will reach more than 300 km/h!" Even if the latter figures were a little high, the engines and their performance data were accurately represented.

A short article in *Welt am Sonntag* on April 13 had a rather speculative character, as the headline "New 'Silver Arrow' with Wankel engine?" revealed, "At this news, both motorists and car industries around the world pricked up their ears: They are trying their hand at a "Silver Arrow" with a Wankel engine in Untertürkheim. The competition fears that Mercedes wants to build on old racing successes with a new super racing car." The article named a "three-chamber rotary piston engine" as the engine configuration and speculated that this could "hardly be true, if only because the presumed chamber volume of 1,800 cc would correspond to a conventional 3.6-liter engine. However, since the racing formula for 1970 allowed vehicles of 3.5 to 5 liters, the guys from Untertürkheim would have no chance with a 3.6-liter car against the larger-volume competitors." Finally, the article referred to statements by "Mercedes": "We are working on a sports car with a Wankel engine. Such cars are now being tested. The body shape has not yet been finalized. . . . Should the tests prove positive, small numbers of the new sports car will be produced. But under no circumstances will the Wankel engine be going into series production."

Under the headline "Lovely rotors," even renowned news magazine *Der Spiegel* reported on the future dream sports car in its April 14 issue, "Wings it has. Fly it cannot. But its three power rotors should finally bring home international victory laurels to Germany's oldest motor racing team again." The article essentially referred to the report in *auto, motor und sport* and even included an illustration of the vehicle, which, however, had been created with a high degree of imagination and had little in common with the actual design apart from the basic principle. About the design, it said, "With the ultra-low streamlined shape (height: 1.10 meters) and the front end without a radiator grille, the Daimler-Benz designers ventured for the first time to make the leap away from the traditional Mercedes look to a more functional and aerodynamically sophisticated body shape." The article also addressed possible motor racing applications and the future of the Wankel engine: "The managers in Untertürkheim are still divided as to whether they want to set up their own racing team again or prefer to sell the C 101 only to private racing and sports drivers. In any case, the test with the Wankel sprinters is intended to show whether this first rotary piston engine from the

"Lovely rotors." In April 1969, the spectacular sports car project, including imaginative illustrations, even made it into *Der Spiegel* news magazine.

Daimler workshop is potentially suitable for other Mercedes cars. . . . However, Daimler's market strategists do not want to hear anything about speculations that the rotary piston engine will replace the traditional reciprocating engine still in this generation. Press spokesman Reinert: 'Absolutely inaccurate rumors.'" *Stern* magazine also took up the topic and presented the "Jet-set sports car against international competition" in its April 20 issue with an imaginative illustration that bore astonishing resemblance to the depiction in *Der Spiegel* magazine.

Item for Discussion: The C 101 on the Board Of Management and at the General Meeting

The Daimler-Benz Board of Management was less than amused: The publications in the press and their backgrounds were discussed in detail at the Board of Management meeting on April 15 under the agenda item "Press and publicity issues at DBAG." In the meeting, the board considered the possibility that "a certain degree of influence on the NSU transactions was sought by interested parties," but also an "influence on Board of Management decisions" through targeted indiscretions. In the course of the discussion, it was agreed that the "overall complex . . . must be the subject of careful further consideration." The Board of Management member responsible for public relations, Heinz Schmidt, was instructed to prepare documents for a discussion to be held with head of development Scherenberg on the "handling of questions concerning the development department in terms of publicity."

Five weeks later, at its meeting on May 20, 1969, the Board of Management also discussed the question of the presentation to the public under the agenda item "Further procedure regarding C 101." Heinz Schmidt advocated for using the presentation of the C 101 to improve the image in the passenger car sector but also pointed out that "the familiar publications have created corresponding expectations that should not be disappointed." Against this background, he considered it "expedient and necessary to exhibit the C 101 at the 1969 IAA and, if possible, also to have at least a few examples available for test drives." Rolf Staelin agreed with Schmidt's assessment of the "situation that has arisen as a result of the various newspaper reports" and expressed the view that "while we are taking a risk with regard to our image if we do not present the C 101, on the other hand we are running an even-greater risk if we do so before a final assessment of the Wankel engine is possible." Schmidt explained that "no expectations of a series introduction of the Wankel engine were attached to the presentation of the C 101 to the public at the IAA" and considered "critical effects on our production range" to be out of the question under these circumstances.

At the end of the discussion, the Board of Management confirmed its agreement that, if possible, "the car should be presented as a 'dream car' at the time of the IAA" and added, "The determination of the further details (in particular occasion, time and place) is deferred, as is the decision on the final use of the vehicle."

In the meantime, the press had already devoted further reports to the fascinating sports car. *auto, motor und sport* again carried a two-page article in its May 10 issue that contained a very imaginative large drawing in addition to the already published design sketch. More detailed depictions from different perspectives, which also demonstrated a high degree of creativity, also appeared on June 11 in *hobby* magazine, which even featured their interpretation of the C 101 on the cover of this issue. The ever-active spy photographers had also been successful but had only been able to catch the Sledge in its various versions, since the actual vehicle with plastic bodywork had not even been completed yet. Automotive magazine *mot* had already published a somewhat blurred picture on May 3, apparently showing the first version of the Sledge on the test track in Untertürkheim. On June 7, *auto, motor und sport* presented three somewhat blurry photos of the second variant taken during testing at Hockenheim. And pictures of the third version, also

In its issue of May 10, 1969, *auto, motor und sport* continued its coverage. In addition to the already published design sketch by Joseph Gallitzendörfer, an imaginative drawing by the magazine's own graphic designer was also shown.

shot by photographer Kurt Wörner during test drives in Hockenheim, appeared simultaneously in *Stuttgarter Nachrichten* and *Automobil Revue* on June 19. Subsequently, they were also published in the German automotive trade journals.

On June 12, the Wankel sports car from Mercedes-Benz had even made it onto television. The *Abendschau* (Evening Show) of *Süddeutscher Rundfunk* and *Südwestfunk* broadcast a report with film footage of the testing of the C 101 in Hockenheim. The anchor said, "This footage shows more of the vehicle than sparse photographic reports have been able to do before. But although the final body is still unknown, interested parties are already jostling, especially from jet-set circles. They will probably also be the buyers of the future sports coupe, because the price will make sure of that. Asked about the identity of the vehicle, board spokesman Dr. Zahn now admits: 'I would like to say to your question, is that it or is that not it, it is indeed. Perhaps it is a little overrated in its topicality and importance. We have indeed been

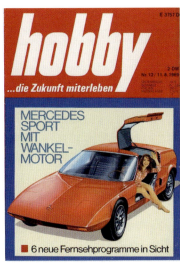

More detailed, but no less imaginative, were the drawings published in *hobby* magazine on June 11, 1969.

Automotive trade magazines *mot* (*left*) and *auto, motor und sport* had already published photos of the first test car in its different variants from the beginning of May to the beginning of July 1969. The first photos of the Sledge in its final version appeared on June 19 in *Stuttgarter Nachrichten* and *Automobil Revue*.

very active in Wankel development for years and have done a lot of work and spent a lot of time and also money on it. . . . Now, in a few months, we also want to show such a vehicle with a Wankel engine to the public, which for us—and I would like to make this quite clear once again—will primarily be a test vehicle, a vehicle that should also convince us when and under what conditions a Wankel vehicle and a Wankel engine would be suitable to be used as a drive unit for parts of our production range.'"

At its meeting on July 18, three days after the first drive of the now-completed first "real" C 101, the Daimler-Benz Board of Management discussed "the experience gained from the reaction of the public." In the opinion of Dr. Hanns Martin Schleyer, the press response showed once more that "it was questionable to be guided predominantly by publicity considerations when deciding on the presentation of a vehicle of this kind that was not ready in terms of development." In contrast, Dr. Scherenberg pointed to the great success in the public eye and emphasized that, in his opinion, "we succeeded in fully achieving our actual goal—to have a vehicle available that is suitable for road testing of the Wankel engine." He also emphasized that "the further development of the C 101 is of course not influenced by any expressions of opinion in publications," so that any related interference with the normal development of the series would be ruled out.

As expected, the C 101 was also a topic at the general meeting of Daimler-Benz AG on July 24. The day before, Hans Scherenberg had specified how all inquiries regarding the C 101 should be answered: "The purpose of the experimental vehicle [C 101] is to push the testing of the Wankel engine on the road and to test this type of drive in a vehicle specially designed for it. There shall be no mention of any possibility of sales or a series production in any way. It is to remain open whether the car will be exhibited and taken on press tours. There is a likelihood, but a decision on this has not yet been taken by the management of our company. I ask you not to mention anywhere that the Wankel engine's status of development has reached the point where production—even if in small numbers—seems reasonable."

As in previous years, shareholders at the general meeting asked about the status of Wankel engine development, this time supplemented by specific questions about the sports car that had

During the test drives at the Hockenheimring, project manager Hans Liebold was encouraged by test staff to mobilize all his reserves. Photographer Kurt Wörner, who was present, captured this in a picture, and *Münchner Abendzeitung* ran the headline in its issue of July 16, 1969: "Flat out for the boss."

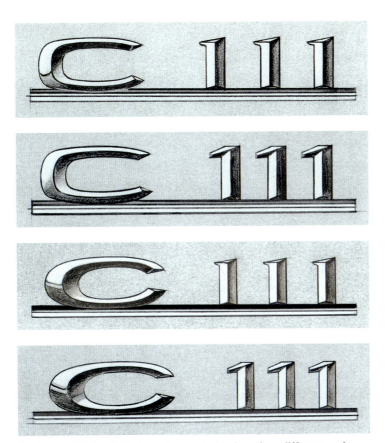

On August 18, 1969, Andreas Langenbeck drew four different variants of a nameplate with the new designation C 111. None of the variants were used—the vehicle was so distinctive right away that it didn't need a nameplate.

been the subject of press coverage. In his reply, Hans Scherenberg stated that "our main work is in the field of normal reciprocating engines, because these have still made considerable progress in recent years, both in the car and truck sectors. We are absolutely dependent on that for the near future as well." After talking about exhaust gas detoxification, diesel engines, and gas turbine development, the head of development went on to talk about the Wankel engine "because this type of drive is always the focus of particular interest" and continued, "The development of this type of drive made progress again last year. We therefore felt compelled to design a special vehicle with which we can take this type of drive further in hard testing, especially on the road. This is how the experimental car C 101, as it is internally called, came into being. It has also already been shown that we can advance the development with this, and apart from that, we have also given our test department team, which is always sporty-minded, a bit of a boost. It is still not clear when the Wankel engine will go into series production. Our studies and intensive work are primarily concerned with making progress on durability, clarifying the consumption issue, and, as I said at the beginning, bringing about clarification on the issue of exhaust gas detoxification. One of the gentlemen asked the question, Why show such a vehicle at all? It is not yet decided whether we will show this vehicle in Frankfurt, but the possibility exists. And it is precisely today's interest in these things that has shown that one should show and say something."

At the Board of Management meeting on August 5, 1969, a lively discussion arose about the model designation of the vehicle. The reason for this was the realization that Peugeot's industrial property rights were affected by three-digit numbers with a zero in the middle, which meant that the internal designation C 101 used up to now was out of the question for external communication. After a "short debate" on the proposals C 100 and SLX—the latter had also been favored by Karl Wilfert—the Board of Management passed the resolution that "the Coupe C 101 will be presented with the model designation 'C 111.'" This

The nameplate with the originally intended designation SLX was already finished when the decision for C 111 was made. SL X3 apparently stands for the version of the sports car equipped with a three-rotor Wankel engine.

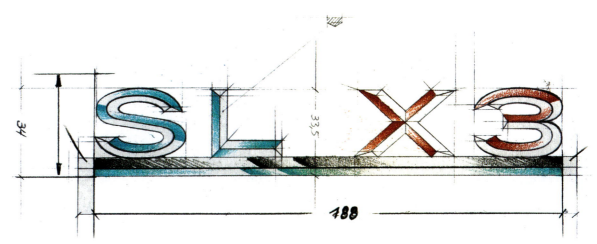

choice sparked debates not least because C 111 was also used as the internal model series code for the 280 SE Coupe (and the future 280 SE 3.5 Coupe). Accordingly, a distinction had to be made between the designation C 101, which continued to be used internally, and the external vehicle designation or product name "C 111." In communication with the public, this differentiation was consistently followed, while in internal communications and minutes both designations were used. Against this background, both C 111 and C 101 will also be used in the following, depending on the context.

On one point, the Board of Management's decision had come too late. As chief stylist Friedrich Geiger noted in an internal memo dated August 7, 1969, the design of the SLX model plates had already begun. A draft for the designation SL X3, in which the 3 was presumably intended to refer to the three-rotor Wankel engine, is documented in the Mercedes-Benz Archives.

Secret Revealed: Press Launch in Stuttgart and Hockenheim

Four weeks before the IAA, Daimler-Benz lifted the veil on the Wankel sports car. On August 15, the press department sent a short information text, technical data, and photos to editorial offices all over the world, after the press agencies dpa and UPI had already provided two pictures a few days earlier. In his letter, chief press officer Artur Keser referred directly to the rampant speculations and clarified: "You have probably heard a good many rumors or half-truths over the past few months about the Mercedes-Benz research and development car with three-chamber rotary Wankel engine. The information on the C 111— this is the final name we gave it—sent to you today will clarify all conjectures."

The worldwide press response was overwhelming. There was hardly a newspaper or magazine that did not feature the C 111 at least in a short report. Even the venerable *Times* and the *International Herald Tribune* reported on the Wankel sports car from Untertürkheim.

Deutsche Auto Zeitung wrote in its August 22 issue under the headline "Mercedes C 111—the car that takes your breath away." "Anyone who has the old Mercedes 300 SL sports coupe from 1954 in their garage can count themselves among the owners of the most costly used car. Enthusiasts still shell out up to 30,000

The first photos of the C 111 were officially published by the Daimler-Benz press department in August. Pictured is car 3, which was photographed immediately after its completion at the beginning of August 1969 on the test track in Untertürkheim.

marks for this car, of which half the series was built as a gullwing version. After this car, Daimler-Benz preferred the conservative corporate image to the sporty one. This era seems to be coming to an end soon. For the ultra-low Mercedes racer 'C 111,' which has now been presented and for the time being is described as a test car, and of which *DAZ* has published the first color photographs, opens the floodgates to speculation. Even if potential sports car buyers shelved their purchase intentions when the first rumors about this car surfaced—Mercedes does not plan to offer this car for sale. A series of only fifty vehicles is to be built for testing purposes. Nevertheless, this unprecedented, consistently built 'wedge' will make the blood rush to the head of any car enthusiast."

Although the new Mercedes-Benz sports car presented itself in a rather unspectacular white, there had been intensive advance discussions about the color scheme of the vehicles. The

The new Mercedes-Benz passenger cars presented at the 1969 International Motor Show in Frankfurt, photographed by Paul Botzenhardt on the grounds of the test track of the Untertürkheim plant: C 111, 300 SEL 3.5, 280 SE 3.5 Coupe, 280 SE 3.5 Cabriolet

Experimental car 3 in its new signal orange livery, photographed in August 1969 on the test track in Untertürkheim

suggestions, some of which seemed quite bizarre, ranged from colors such as vermilion to the use of rally stripes, which were often common on motorsport vehicles. At the beginning of July, the traditional German racing color of white had been chosen, but in special effect paint reserved for the C 111. But for the test run on the Nürburgring on August 13, 1969, car 3, which was the second "real" C 111 to be completed, was painted in fluorescent orange at short notice at the request of the Sindelfingen body development department, after tests had shown that the visibility of this color was five times higher than that of white.

For the stand car at the IAA, the decision was made on August 28 to use the eye-catching "weissherbst" acrylic effect paint instead of white—an orange metallic shade that was to become the hallmark color of the C 111. The color scheme, named after a popular rosé wine variant of similar coloring, was first documented in July 1969. As late as July 18, Friedrich Geiger had noted in a memo that the "effect paint white, acrylic quality, . . . will be used for the other C 101 VS cars [Versuchswagen or test cars] and supplied by Glasurit on demand," and added: "The . . . paint material for the C 101 in the color shade weissherbst (vin gris), acrylic quality, made to [order] of 9.7.69, is probably no longer needed for this purpose. The manufactured delivery quantity remains at the disposal of Glasurit for possible call-off." Instead, Glasurit was to produce this color shade "in modified quality as a stoving paint top coat material for two test cars and one sample door." The unusual color scheme was now apparently intended for other experimental cars with classic sheet steel bodies but was ultimately used on the C 111 and remained reserved for this model.

The interior of the show car was to be finished in black man-made leather and combined with the "pepita cognac" fabric design for the center section of the bucket seats. The remaining four vehicles of the first generation, which were used as demonstration cars retained their white appearance—the car painted in fluorescent orange had been repainted accordingly—and each received slightly different interior appointments. Later, the paintwork of the demonstration cars was also gradually changed to weissherbst as soon as they were on-site in Sindelfingen for major modifications.

The photographs taken during testing at the Hockenheimring show car 3 in its new livery in signal orange.

Car 5, the exhibition car for the IAA 1969, was the first C 111 to be painted in the new, extremely eye-catching color "weissherbst (vin gris)."

From September 1 to 5, 1969, cars 2, 3, and 4—the three road-worthy C 111s available at the time—were presented to the international press and Mercedes-Benz sales managers at the Hockenheimring, together with the other new Mercedes-Benz models for the IAA. In his address to the press representatives, Board of Management member Scherenberg went into detail about the new models, dedicating particular attention to the C 111.

"I know that you are particularly interested in our C 111 experimental vehicle. We see this C 111 first and foremost as a test vehicle for Wankel engines, for whose development we have spared no expense and development capacity in construction and test bench runs over many years of work. The time therefore seemed right to test this engine design in a fitting vehicle in extreme conditions on the road. As the Wankel engine is particularly attractive as a mid-engine in a sports car due to its compact form, low weight, and fast revving, we created the C 111 at short notice for the purpose of experimental testing.

"The three-rotor version we developed with petrol injection and transistor ignition produces around 280 hp. Further increases in performance are possible, but we see our tasks in development primarily in the further improvement of durability, in the reduction of fuel consumption, and in the question of exhaust gas composition (i.e., the testing of special exhaust systems like the Wankel engine needs).

"However, it is not only the Wankel engine that gave rise to such an experimental vehicle as the C 111. We also intended to tackle the investigation of wheel suspension variants, the use of plastic for the bodywork, and the clarification of aerodynamic problems. As is well known, the use of plastic bodywork makes it possible to produce variants at short notice, to get by with inexpensive tools for small series, etc. We had already produced a

Dream Sports Car and Laboratory on Wheels: The C 111

plastic body for the 300 SL on a trial basis. However, we still lack broader experience. . . .

"Incidentally, we only started the initial work on this vehicle—excluding the engine—in November last year. It is only thanks to the tireless commitment and enthusiasm of all those involved in the development that, in addition to the main tasks for the series development of our production program, the C 111 was created and today 3 vehicles are available ready to drive. This enthusiasm for sporty vehicles, especially among the younger engineers in design and testing, confirms that the concept of the C 111 is also practical in this respect and will radiate to our production models. I believe that here and now is the right moment to express special thanks to all those involved, at the top to Mr. Uhlenhaut and Mr. Wilfert and their staff, for this achievement.

"The first rumors and reports about the C 111 have in many cases led the public to conclusions that go far beyond the current status quo. Decisions on the production and sale of this car are not up for debate in our company because, as I said, these are purely test vehicles. Rather, within the scope of our advance engineering department we will build a number of vehicles, depending on the needs of the test program, in order to carry out the basic tests with them. But we will of course carefully note the reactions here in Hockenheim and at the International Motor Show in Frankfurt, where the vehicle will also be on display, with a view to future considerations.

"Although the idea of creating this test vehicle is less than a year old, concrete test results are already emerging today, even if only with regard to the studied engines or other concepts. You will have the opportunity to experience the unusual driving experience in the C 111 later."

In contrast to the usual procedure, journalists were not given the opportunity to drive the C 111 themselves for once—the prototypes were too valuable and the risk of damage too great. Instead, they were chauffeured by Rudolf Uhlenhaut and other experienced test drivers from the advance engineering department over one big and one small lap each at racing speed. Only the automotive journalist and former racing driver Paul Frère was allowed a test drive at the wheel of a C 111 at the end and, as expected, returned car 4 entrusted to him undamaged.

During the demonstration runs at the Hockenheimring, each of the three cars covered between 1,450 and 1,815 km. Fuel consumption was between 37.7 and 38.2 l/100 km and oil

Rudolf Uhlenhaut in the C 111, taken in September 1969 at the press demonstration in Hockenheim. *On the left*, **the head of passenger car development, who was on the job practically non-stop, replenishes his energy with coffee and cake. The photo** *on the right* **was taken by journalist and author Karl E. Ludvigsen immediately before taking the passenger seat for a demonstration lap.**

Car 2 with street tires on steel rims at the press demonstration of the C 111 at the Hockenheimring in September 1969

Cars 4 (*front*), 2 (*center*), and 3 (*right*) at the same event. Car 4 is now equipped with street tires on steel rims, car 2 with street tires on light-alloy rims, and car 3 with racing tires on light-alloy rims.

Cars 2 (*right*), 4 (*center*), and 3 (*left*) start behind a camera car for the demonstration lap.

This photo, which was taken by automotive journalist Karl E. Ludvigsen as Rudolf Uhlenhaut's passenger through the windshield of car 3, shows car 2 (*in front*) and car 4 (*in the background*) equipped with street tires at the press driving demonstration at the Hockenheimring.

consumption between 2.75 l and 6.25 l/1,000 km. Car 2 and car 4 were equipped with street tires, car 3 with racing tires. The three-rotor engines, trimmed for high performance, started readily when cold and warm and idled smoothly at 1,000 rpm. Below 2,000 rpm, however, they bucked noticeably and offered hardly any pulling power due to their lack of torque in the lower rev range. None of the cars needed any work during the demonstrations; the doors on car 3 and car 4 were readjusted between the demonstration runs, and the exhaust as well as the front brake discs on car 4 were replaced. After the event, heavy wear was found on all clutches; the front brake discs were also replaced on car 2, and the engine had to be changed on car 3 after one rotor showed a sharp loss of compression.

The press trial drive of the C 111 and the Mercedes-Benz range of new models once again attracted considerable press coverage worldwide—especially from the trade journals, but also from the daily press and general-interest magazines. Even *Bild-Zeitung* had something to say—on September 3 under the headline "Trial run in the 'White Giant'": "Mercedes head of development Rudolf Uhlenhaut 'flew' around the Hockenheimring (near Darmstadt) with me. The

Technical inspection and maintenance of car 3 (*front*), car 2 (*rear left*), and car 4 (*rear right*) after their grueling service at the press demonstration at the Hockenheimring

'White Giant,' as the engineers call it, is far too valuable to leave it in the hands of strangers even for minutes. Result of the test from the passenger seat: a super fast chassis with an exotic engine. . . . The 'C 111' shoos away the hairiest curves as if they were only slightly curved straights. Driver Uhlenhaut laconically: 'It's a normal car, just with extra good grip!' I can only agree. . . . Daimler-Benz declares: 'We will still do some things differently.' However, the 'C 111' still has quite a bit of road ahead of it before it is ready for everyday use." On September 9, the paper reported under the headline "No malfunction": "The demonstration of the experimental car on five days last week for dealers, journalists, and guests at the Hockenheimring proved to be the biggest stress test for the 'C 111' Wankel-Mercedes so far. Each of the three vehicles covered between 3,000 and 5,000 km—trouble-free."

After his test drive with car 4, which he conducted on the motorway between Hockenheim and Frankfurt, Paul Frère included his impressions in an article in *auto, motor und sport*, which editor-in-chief Heinz-Ulrich Wieselmann published in the issue of September 27, 1969: "It's a shock when you see the Wankel Mercedes for the first time: an ungainly monstrosity with small side windows and a rear end brutally cut off immediately after the rear wheels, as functional as a transformer and with just as much restrained charm. When you drive the Wankel Mercedes for the first time, it warms your heart and makes your back wet: there has never been a car like this. The perfectionists at Daimler-Benz succeeded in creating a vehicle with unusual characteristics with the hitherto unrealized combination of Wankel system, mid-engine, and racing car suspension. . .

"The most unusual feature is undoubtedly the C 111's smooth running. The engine noise of the rotary engine, that largely revs without vibrations, is so well muffled that one is initially disappointed when accelerating sharply in the lower gears; there is no roaring engine to give one the feeling of extraordinary acceleration. It is only when you look at the rev counter that you are startled to have already exceeded the 7,000 rpm limit again. . . .

"Another unusual feature of the C 111 is its handling. What it builds up in terms of cornering forces in fast turns, thanks to the low center of gravity, and the balanced weight distribution, thanks to the mid-engine on the one hand, and the racing car-like wheel suspension and wide tires on the other, seems absolutely incredible to anyone who is not familiar with the handling of modern racing sports cars. . . .

"You keep entering the corner faster and faster, and every time you notice that the limit is far from being reached. Later, the Mercedes test engineers confirmed the personal experience. The notoriously fast drivers among them admitted that, despite many test laps at Hockenheim and the Nürburgring, they still had to get a feel for the limits set by the chassis. It can be said that this safety built into the design and the resulting experience for production car construction alone give the bold C 111 project the right to live."

Critical comments by Wieselmann were directed at the unclear purpose of the vehicle, the partly insufficient daily practicality, especially with regard to the visibility, the trunk, and the aesthetics: "Thus not a racing sports car, but a fast sports car for the road, a modern, unconventional successor to the famous 300 SL? . . . Mercedes-Benz bodies are among the most timelessly beautiful in international automotive engineering. The Wankel-Mercedes C 111 had the chance to shake the generally accepted primacy of the Italians in building classically beautiful high-performance sports cars. But it didn't seize it."

Incidentally, a good month after his first drive, Frère was again given the opportunity to drive a C 111, this time car 2. In a conversation with Hans Liebold, he was very positive about the handling and ride quality, which he rated better than the comparable Lamborghini Miura. The latter, however, had "(with much-stronger engine noise) a much better torque at low revs," as Liebold commented in a note to Hans Scherenberg on October 9, and continued, "For the C 101, even now—especially on the motorway—he would wish for an automatic transmission. He also praised the brakes and steering. Until now, he would have considered rack-and-pinion steering to be absolutely necessary for such vehicles. He found the cornering stability with standard tires remarkable." Without the rear torsion bar, however, the car seemed to him "to have a little too much understeer, although he added that he was not aware of any powerful car that with the same setup behaved equally well in fast and tight corners."

The assessment by Fritz B. Busch, published by *Stern* in its September 21 issue, reads quite differently: "Mercedes entices and shocks the public with its C 111 Wankel rocket, of which no one knows whether it is supposed to be a road-going sports car or a racing car. This latest car from Daimler-Benz is merely a Christmas cracker, because for now no one can buy it. The real sensation is the three-rotor Wankel engine with its boundless power. . . . The C 111 experimental car does not seem the right launch vehicle for this promising engine. Because the C 111 is 1. much too heavy as a competition vehicle (with a kerb weight of 1,100 kg, as heavy as a sedan), [and] 2. hardly justifiable as a road vehicle for Mr. X with his fat wallet. This is because visibility from the cockpit is poor (even catastrophic to the rear), and getting in and out is extremely problematic. Besides, I don't see the slightest reason to develop a vehicle for millions of marks for playboys who can use it to disturb the traffic... We don't need motorway racing cars, but compact cars appropriate for traffic that finally represent something new after more than eight decades of automotive history." In contrast to this very critical assessment, however, most press reviews conveyed an extremely positive impression.

The C 111's "biggest stress test to date" at its press trial drive was continued after a short breather on the occasion of the traditional test day organized by the Motor Presse Club (MPC), also at the Hockenheimring, on September 10. *Deutsche Auto Zeitung* wrote about this in its September 19 issue: "At the Motodrom in Hockenheim, the German car manufacturers had brought a considerable fleet of new passenger cars to make them available to journalists for initial test drives . . . and so car characters with final speeds between 110 km/h and 260 km/h cavorted around the high-speed track. The fact that this mix of vehicles harbors some problems became clear already in the first hours of this day. There were two accidents with considerable injury and vehicle damage, which led to most of the participants on the test day adopting a more moderate driving style. Mercedes took precautions ahead and did not even allow its C 111 test car to be driven by external people, not even at the official presentation of the new range two weeks earlier. The much-admired car, which the Stuttgart-based company constantly emphasizes is not intended for sale as a production vehicle, put on an impressive show at Hockenheim. With noise levels approaching those of a two-stroke engine, it accelerates like a rocket to 100 km/h in about five seconds. . . . To make chassis comparisons with this consistently well-thought-out car, it would have to compete on the race track. After all, there is hardly a car in the standard vehicle range that would be able to follow the

Car 6, equipped with a four-rotor engine and racing tires, on its first outing, the MPC test day at the Hockenheimring on September 10, 1969. The first C 111 with four-rotor Wankel had newly designed exterior mirrors with painted streamlined housings.

C 111 around a fast bend. But race tracks are not being considered at all, says Daimler-Benz."

Top Performer: The C 111 with a Four-Rotor Wankel Engine

For the MPC test day, Daimler-Benz had added a fourth C 111 to the test fleet: car 6, which was completed just in time and—unnoticed by the journalists—was the first test car ever to be equipped with a four-rotor engine. For camouflage purposes, the exhaust system on this vehicle was also fitted with the usual three tailpipes. However, the hot exhaust gases destroyed the sound insulation in the silencers, which could be clearly heard in the throaty sound—a considerable 84 phons were measured on-site when driving past.

Car 6, which was the last of the first production batch, had a lightened body with a thinner outer skin, lighter doors with Plexiglas windows without twist-locks, a corresponding rear window, and lightened fittings that saved a total of 35 kg. With the four-rotor KE 402/2 engine, which delivered a hefty 367 hp/ 270 kW and weighed a total of 265 kg, including transmission, driveshafts, and oil but without vacuum pump, the car's kerb weight was 1,217 kg, with an unchanged weight distribution of 45%:55%.

This made the C 111 number 6 look much livelier in the whole driving range than cars 2 to 4, equipped with the three-rotor version. However, due to leaking O-rings, the engine suffered water penetration after only one day and a driving distance of 675 km.

As Dr. Hans Liebold reported in a test report dated February 11, 1970, only the sixth newly built four-rotor engine survived the test bench trials and was ready for installation in the car. This engine also performed very well, and the car immediately achieved a lap time of 2:10 minutes on the big circuit in Hockenheim, with light barriers in front of the east bend, measuring 273 km/h, still in the acceleration phase. With cars 2 to 4, the best times had been eleven seconds worse, and even

Car 3, also equipped with racing tires, at the same event. Just like cars 2 and 4, it was equipped with chrome-plated exterior mirrors similar to the versions used for Mercedes-Benz production cars.

with the lighter Sledge they had not managed under 2:16 minutes. However, the cooling capacity again proved to be insufficient due to the increased heat generation of the four-rotor engine. After just two or three sharp laps, the oil temperature rose to over 140°C (285°F), making a cool-down lap necessary. The water temperature was a constant 105°C (220°F).

After the driving event in Hockenheim, the bodywork of car 6 was modified at the front and rear. A more efficient flow to the radiator was realized at the front, and the rear end was lengthened by 100 mm. As on car 2, this created space for the larger luggage compartment initiated by Rudolf Uhlenhaut, as well as for an improved and enlarged rear silencer.

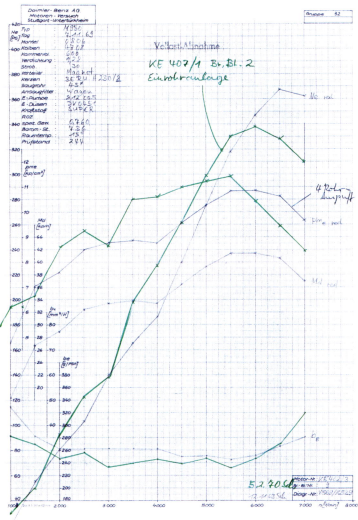

The four-rotor version of the M 950 was used for the first time in car 6.

The full-throttle acceptance test of the KE 402 four-rotor engine used in car 6, carried out on November 7, 1969, shows an output of an impressive 367 hp/270 kW at just over 7,000 rpm. The first installable four-rotor engine had been removed in September 1969 after water penetrated the trochoidal housing and was repaired and reinstalled in November. The measurement graphs drawn in green show the result of a measurement taken on February 5, 1970, when the engine was equipped with a single-pipe exhaust system.

132   Dream Sports Car and Laboratory on Wheels: The C 111

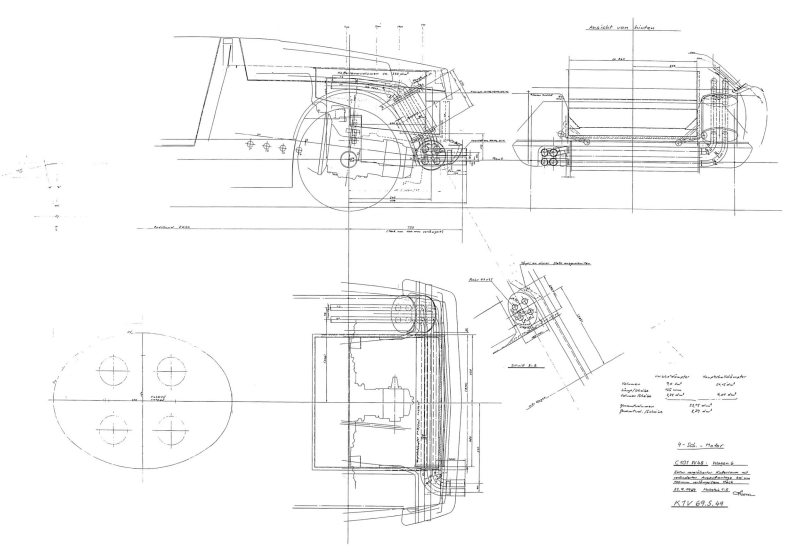

The construction drawing dated September 25, 1969, shows the changes to the body and exhaust system that were necessary on car 6 to realize a larger trunk, as was already the case with car 2. Because of the longer four-rotor engine, these were even more profound and required an extension of the rear section by 100 mm.

In the Spotlight: The C 111 at Trade Fairs and Events

Despite all the challenges, there was no question: The IAA in Frankfurt, which opened on September 11, and the media had their star. Car 5, the exhibition vehicle painted in weissherbst, was equipped with a mockup of the three-rotor engine and was presented to the public on a pedestal in a slightly inclined position in order to highlight it and make it look particularly dynamic. The racing tires of the show car were mounted on newly designed five-spoke, light-alloy rims made of cast magnesium, perfectly matching the sporty appearance. In contrast, demonstration cars 2 to 4, which were placed in the outdoor area and gleamed in white effect paint, had fifteen-hole, light-alloy wheels. Both rims were based on designs drawn up by Stefan Heiliger in the advance engineering department in Untertürkheim.

After the spectacular first trade fair appearance in Frankfurt, the C 111 caused a sensation at further trade fairs and exhibitions all over the world in quick succession: in October 1969 at the Paris

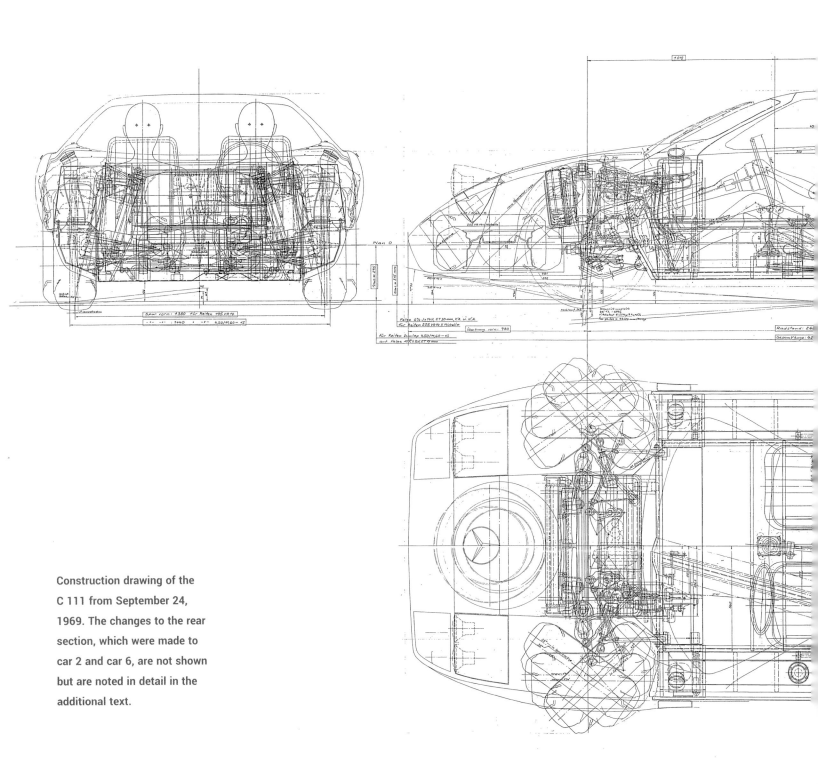

Construction drawing of the C 111 from September 24, 1969. The changes to the rear section, which were made to car 2 and car 6, are not shown but are noted in detail in the additional text.

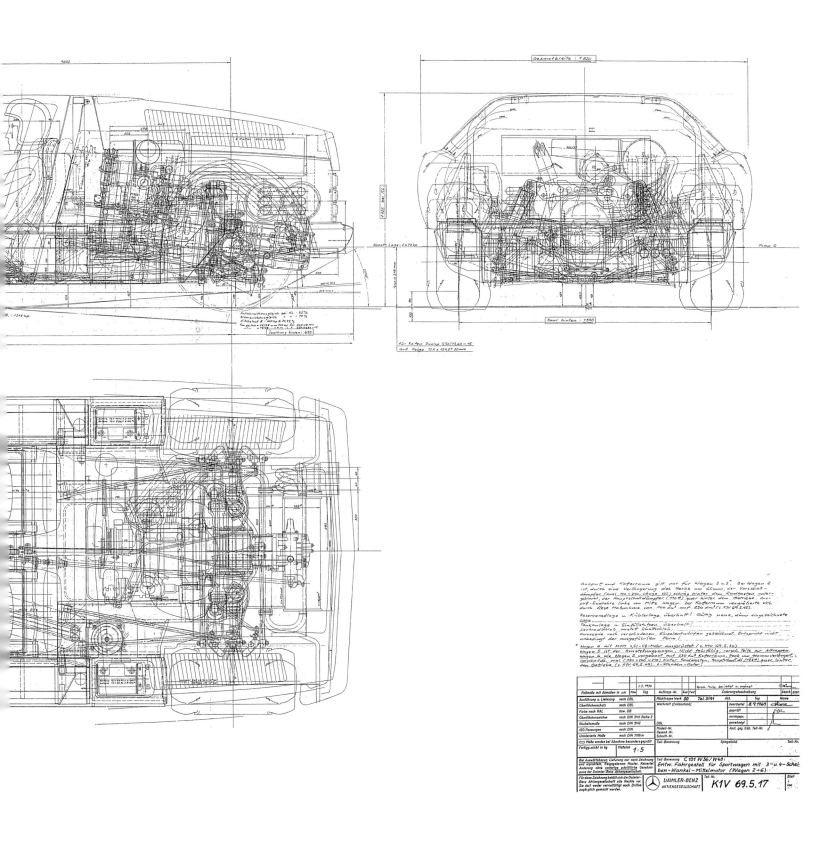

Motor Show and the London Motor Show, in October–November at the Turin Motor Show, in November at the Jochen Rindt Show in Vienna and in December at the event of the same name in Essen and Munich, in January 1970 at the Brussels Motor Show, in February 1970 at the "Motor-Sport-Freizeit" (Motor-Sport-Leisure) trade fair in Stuttgart, and finally at the Chicago Auto Show. Not only was the spectacular sports car a public attraction, but it also attracted serious potential buyers.

At the Motor Show in London, British enthusiasts pulled out their checkbooks and offered up to 20,000 pounds sterling— around DM 180,000 at the time. One Briton even handed over a blank check, with the remark that he would instruct his bank to cash it up to half a million DM. This unusual procedure was even

The future of the automobile is on display at the IAA in Frankfurt; the C 111 conveyed this message from Mercedes-Benz. With its striking appearance, the dream sports car was one of the stars of the exhibition.

At the IAA, car 2 was the showpiece among the three demonstration vehicles. Thanks to the enlarged trunk, four specially designed aluminum suitcases could be accommodated: three of them in the trunk itself and one lashed to the top of the hatch.

worth a press release from Daimler-Benz AG on November 3, 1969, in which it was again emphasized that the C 111 was not for sale and would continue to serve as a mobile test laboratory. Nevertheless, the interest continued unabated, and inquiries continued to arrive in Untertürkheim from people wanting to buy.

The C 111 was also used at sporting events with great public appeal. At the opening of the Salzburgring on September 20 and 21, 1969, the Wankel sports car was presented to the Austrian press, and test department employee Fritz Naumann drove the attending journalists around the circuit in car 2 for one lap each. Three weeks later, on October 11, 1969, the C 111 was presented to the public together with the entire Mercedes-Benz passenger car range during the half-time interval of the Bundesliga match between VfB Stuttgart and Hannover 96 in what was then the Neckar Stadium (today the Mercedes-Benz Arena). The Wankel sports car seems to have brought VfB luck. The traditional Stuttgart club won the match against the guests from Hanover.

Car 2 with board spokesman Dr. Joachim Zahn in the outdoor area in Frankfurt

On October 11, 1969, the C 111 was presented to the public together with the Mercedes-Benz passenger car model range during half-time at the Bundesliga match between VfB Stuttgart and Hannover 96. A 200 model—the entry-level model in the Mercedes-Benz passenger car range at the time—was also raffled off. The venue, which was a track-and-field stadium at the time and was known as the Neckar Stadium, is today called the Mercedes-Benz Arena.

Immediately after the end of the show, the IAA exhibition car repeated its star appearance at numerous international motor shows: in Paris, Turin, Vienna, Munich, Brussels, Leiden, Stuttgart, and Chicago (*from top left to bottom right*). At the Jochen Rindt Show in Vienna, the spectacular sports car met the no less spectacular jet-powered record car "The Green Monster."

At the London Motor Show in October 1969, British enthusiasts offered big money for the car—even though it wasn't for sale. One of them even handed over a blank check.

Mercedes-Benz advertised in the local press for the Stuttgart "Motor-Sport-Freizeit" trade fair in January–February 1970: "Now you have the opportunity to see the car that no one can buy yet."

Calculated and Measured: The Driving Performance of the C 101

The press release published at the beginning of September for the press demonstration of the C 111 at the Hockenheimring and subsequently for the IAA had mentioned an engine output of 280 hp/206 kW at 7,000 rpm and a top speed of 260 km/h in the technical data. On September 23, 1969—the IAA had just closed its doors—the proof followed when the driving performance of the C 111 was measured on the Karlsruhe-Basel motorway with car 3 on racing tires. The three-rotor KE 312 engine mobilized a peak output of 285 hp/210 kW; the kerb weight had been brought down to 1,150 kg by removing the spare wheel and an almost empty tank. During the top speed measurement, which was carried out at 6 a.m. due to the expected traffic conditions, the C 111 with Guido Moch at the wheel reached a top speed of 263 km/h. The acceleration behavior was found to be insufficient, which is why the test report of October 3, 1969, recommended using a four-rotor engine in the future. Moch described the starting behavior from a standstill as very problematic with the then-current gear ratios. Maximum acceleration was only possible with prolonged clutch feathering, and after a total of four hard starting attempts, the clutch was, as Moch put it, "practically destroyed."

Even before this practical measurement, the design engineering department had calculated driving performance diagrams for the C 111 with a three-rotor and a four-rotor engine and summarized them on September 15 together with comparative values in a memo to head of development Scherenberg. Assuming engine outputs of 280 hp/206 kW and 375 hp/276 kW, respectively, this resulted in top speeds of 275 and 300 km/h and acceleration times of 6 and 5.1 seconds, respectively. The comparative calculations with twelve sports cars from Mercedes-Benz and other brands showed that, over a distance of 1,000 meters, only the Lamborghini Miura, with 370 hp/272 kW and a kerb weight of 1,075 kg, was faster than the C 111 with a four-rotor engine.

On September 18, 1969, a good two weeks before Guido Moch recommended in his test report that the C 111 should in the future be equipped with the four-rotor engine, Hans Scherenberg had already decided that the C 111 should be further developed exclusively in the more powerful variant. In addition, the four-rotor engine was to be used in the future 107 and 116 passenger car model series. As a design drawing dated October 1, 1969, shows, a variant of the C 111 with two two-rotor engines and a central fuel tank had also been designed and the expected performance calculated, but this variant was not pursued further.

Also in September, the testing department in Untertürkheim had examined the starting behavior of the C 111, which had previously been the subject of repeated complaints, and summarized the results in a memo dated September 26, 1969. Car 2, which had a normal clutch disc with clutch spring and torsion damper, and car 3, with simplified disc without clutch spring and without torsion damper, were examined. This showed that a fast start from a standstill with car 2 was only possible if

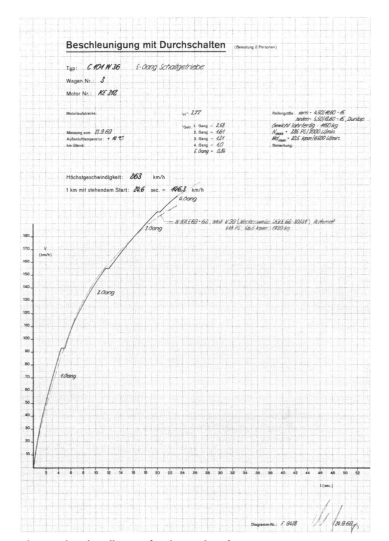

The acceleration diagram for the road performance measurements dated September 23, 1969, shows a value of 5.5 seconds for the 0 to 100 km/h sprint. The W 108 test car—with a 318 hp/234 kW 6.9-liter engine—used as a comparison vehicle was initially almost as fast but fell behind past 180 km/h.

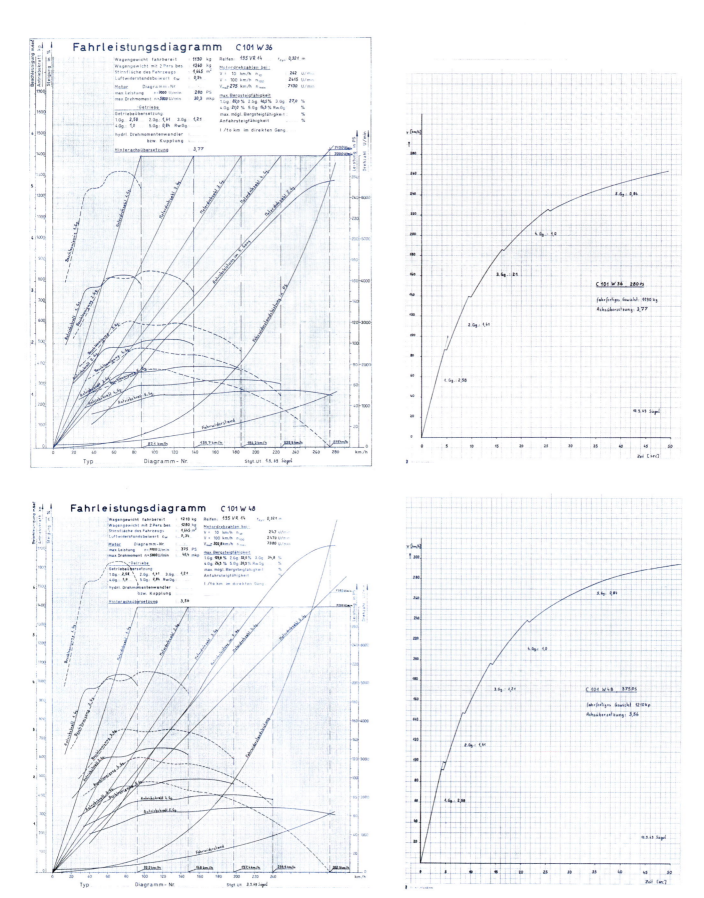

Performance and acceleration diagrams of the C 111 with a three-rotor engine and four-rotor engine, calculated on September 3 and September 10, 1969, respectively

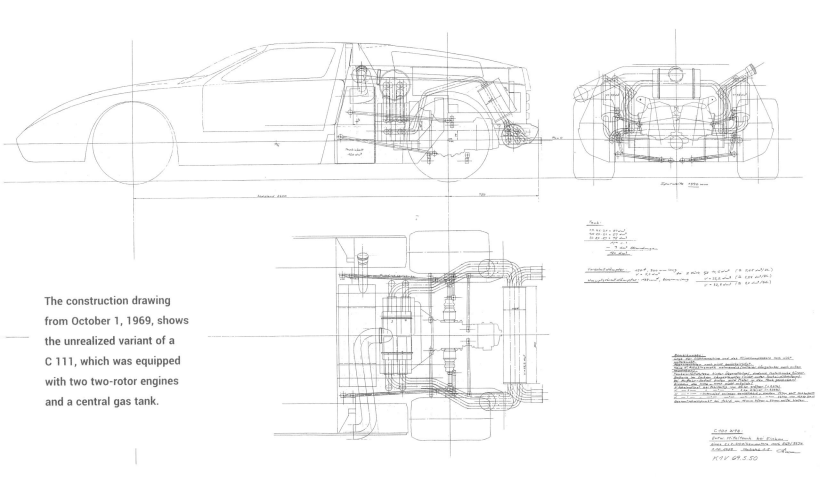

The construction drawing from October 1, 1969, shows the unrealized variant of a C 111, which was equipped with two two-rotor engines and a central gas tank.

the clutch was allowed to feather at 3,000 to 4,000 rpm, which of course the lining could not withstand. During normal start-up, the engine stalled. On car 3, with the unsprung disc, the starting off proved to be even more difficult. On the 20% hill, "one could only get going with a smelly clutch as an experienced driver after prior practice," as the test report put it. As a remedy, a shorter ratio was proposed for first gear (e.g., 3.00 instead of 2.58), and this was also mathematically underpinned. The work done, which is converted into heat during the starting process, was calculated to be 373 mkp for a 300 SEL 3.5, but 3,420 mkp for the C 111. The proposed change in gear ratio reduced the calculated value to a still very high 1,130 mkp.

Despite a number of challenges, the C 111 was overall a resounding success. The fact that stylistic revisions seemed necessary and, above all, that visibility and cooling had to be improved did not detract from this, especially as the necessary modifications had already been commissioned by the responsible parties.

Not a Foregone Conclusion: The Development Status in Autumn 1969

On October 24, a month after the IAA with the star appearance of the C 111 had ended, the advance engineering testing department documented the status achieved and the most important test results in a detailed test report. This report summarizes the development status very well and is quoted here in excerpts:

"The start of the press demonstrations on 1.9. and the partly intensive use for demonstration purposes even beforehand did not allow for systematic development on the usual scale, even if the remaining time was optimally utilized. Inevitably, however, an overview of the problems of a sporty mid-engined car was gained, especially in connection with the Wankel engine, a plastic body and modern racing tires. . . .

"The concept of the C 101 as a mid-engine car enabled an extremely low design with a low center of gravity and small frontal area. The lateral arrangement of the tanks contributes significantly to keeping the moment of inertia around the vertical axis and differences in the axle load distribution low. The expected favorable effects on the handling—especially in curves—were confirmed in the course of the tests.

"The bodywork was generally pleasing in terms of form initially, even if it was heavily criticized in isolated cases. Visibility, on the other hand, was insufficient from the outset. . . . The stylistic changes planned for further prototypes (lowering of the beltline) were intended to improve visibility to the front and sides, and to largely eliminate the psychological constriction caused by the instrument panel, which is very high by today's standards. . . . Entry through the gullwing doors is convenient with the low car. A trunk of 220 dm³ could be realized subsequently; further stowage possibilities still have to be created.

"Aerodynamically, the body produced very satisfactory values right from the start (c_d 0.355, at 250 km/h, 15 kp downforce at the front, 50 kp lift at the rear). In contrast to the first attempt with the makeshift body, the aerodynamic directional stability is also flawless. Difficulties were caused by the cooling air ducting, which had to be changed several times in the course of the tests and to which much attention still has to be paid in the envisaged, improved form.

"The body itself, made of fiberglass-reinforced polyester plastic, has so far proved its worth in terms of strength and undoubtedly contributes to the relatively good insulation of the passenger compartment from road and powertrain noise. The great agility in making changes and improvisations helped a lot in conducting the tests quickly. . . . Unfortunately, the weight of the structurally non-supporting body is still somewhat high at around 240 to 280 kp (fully equipped) and contributes not insignificantly to the total weight of a good 1,200 kp—kerb weight with 120 l of fuel and street tires. (For comparison: Lamborghini Miura, with 4-liter V12 and 90 l fuel 1,075 kp).

"The floor assembly made of sheet steel is also not light at just over 150 kp. In terms of rigidity and durability, it has been satisfactory so far after adding some reinforcements. Changes are still necessary, especially in the rear section.

"The Wankel engine largely determines the character of the car. The low noise level, the lack of vibrations, and the elasticity are generally noted positively, while the lack of torque from low revs is disadvantageous and, more than the little pronounced bucking in overrun mode, gave rise to the occasional wish for an automatic transmission.

Car 3 in its original white livery in August 1969, photographed on the test track in Untertürkheim

The two side gas tanks were each filled via an opening behind the front wheels.

A view into the engine compartment equipped with the three-rotor engine

The C 111 with camera car in front during filming on the high-banked curve of the test track in Untertürkheim

"In general, the car seems underpowered with the M 950 in the three-rotor version, despite the average 280 hp at 7,000 rpm and the speed of 260 km/h that can be achieved with it. Only with the four-rotor engine of initially 370 hp, which had only been driven for a short time so far, did it acquire the expected temperament throughout the range and became comparable with corresponding cars in terms of driving performance. . . .

"The service life of the three-rotor engines has so far been a maximum of just under 6,000 km—albeit under partly racing-like stress. The main causes of failure were jammed apex seals and difficulties with the cooling circuit and oil flow. An effective remedy should be expected in the near future.

"The power transmission has so far been exclusively via a single-disc dry clutch and a ZF five-speed transmission with two-shaft design with integral differential and limited slip, as used as standard by de Tomaso, for example. Due to the low starting torque and the lack of transmissions with a long first gear, the clutch has been hopelessly overstressed with a correspondingly short service life. Even with the envisaged modified gear ratio, it will not be possible to avoid using the two-disc clutch that has been prepared in the meantime. (In addition, the planned testing of an automatic transmission should be interesting.) The gear shift is reasonably satisfactory after several changes. Among other things, an electrical interlock was improvised for the gate of first and reverse gear. . . .

"The axles were initially taken from production developments. While the slightly modified W 116 front axle enables precise handling when adjusted accordingly, it was not possible to achieve really perfect straight-line running on undulating roads with the semi-trailing arm rear axle in the first car. . . . The double wishbone rear axle used on cars 2 to 6 in racing car design with very little toe and camber changes during spring travel proved to be substantially superior in every respect.

"The springing and damping had to be designed relatively stiff, as high vertical accelerations occur even with small bumps at the possible speeds. In the course of the tests, it was possible to find settings that were sufficiently stiff for sporty driving without being uncomfortable on the road. This normally avoided the need to replace the springs and dampers when changing between street and racing tires, which was made more difficult by the suspension strut design. However, changing a stabilizer torsion bar and the wheel alignment (toe and camber) remains necessary and can be carried out relatively quickly. . . .

"The tires have a decisive influence on the handling. Due to the small polar moment of inertia around the vertical axis and the wide track relative to the wheelbase, the car reacts very sensitively even to small disturbing forces. . . . Compared to conventionally designed vehicles, much higher cornering speeds are possible in any case. This applies to a greater extent to the racing tires . . . , which still show favorable wear behavior even with a relatively soft rubber compound. However, these tires are not suitable for road use because of their low ride comfort, high steering forces, poor straight-line stability at slow speeds, and tendency toward hydroplaning.

"The steering corresponds to the W 115 model series. With a spindle pitch of 11.5 mm, a compromise could be made between the demands for a sufficiently direct ratio and not excessively high steering forces. Compared to the rack-and-pinion steering systems used in comparable vehicles, no noticeable disadvantage was found. The steering wheel diameter of 380 mm was generally accepted. Power steering is not being considered for the time being.

"The brakes required ventilated wheels and brake discs, considering the weight of the car and the possible driving speed. A brake booster also proved necessary for road use, while an unboosted version was preferred for sporty driving. At present, brake calipers made of gray cast iron are still in use. Despite a 45%/55% axle load distribution and a low center of gravity, the front axle has to handle the majority of the braking forces (calipers with 57 Ø at the front, 38 Ø at the rear). Therefore, additional quenching is planned for them.

"After initial tests with plastic and plastic-coated, flat light sheet metal, the side tanks are now made of soft aluminum in a rounded shape without intermediate bulkheads and foamed. As they are undoubtedly more prone to accidents, investigations on rubber tanks are still planned. After numerous tests . . . a satisfactory fuel supply and refueling possibility under all circumstances was achieved. Attempts at simplification are still ongoing.

"Among other things, exhaust gas detoxification and the installation of an air conditioning system have not yet been tested. Also, endurance testing is partially still pending at the moment."

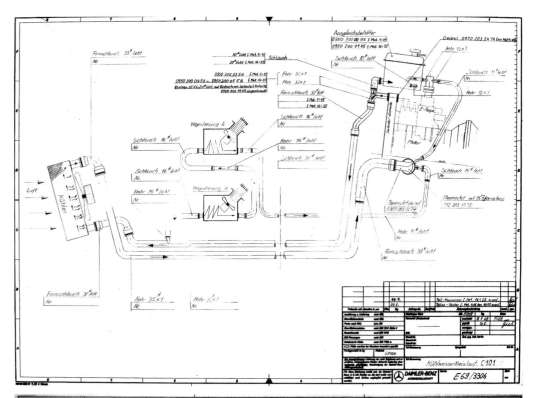

This schematic drawing from August 18, 1969, shows the coolant circuit of the C 111. The thermal problems observed during the test runs repeatedly gave rise to modifications.

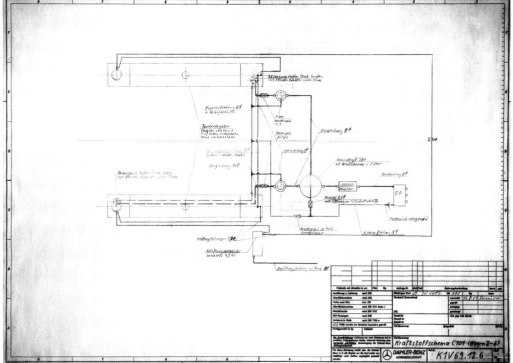

The schematic drawing of June 12, 1969, shows the fuel system of the C 101 as it was realized on cars 2 to 6.

Ambitious Goals: The Further Development of the C 111

In summary, the report stated that "further development definitely seems worthwhile." However, availability of the test vehicles needed for this was very limited. Car 3 was handed over to Sindelfingen in autumn 1969 for bodywork tests. In addition to the IAA exhibition car, which was only equipped with a dummy engine, there were thus only three vehicles left for systematic road testing. The lack of availability of ready-to-install Wankel engines, whether in three-rotor or four-rotor versions, also proved to be a major challenge.

Against this background, a more powerful 4.5-liter V8 from the as-yet-unlaunched M 117 engine model series was prepared at the end of 1969. Thanks to the use of eight individual air

Car 5 (car 25 according to the new nomenclature), the former car on the IAA stand, received a 4.5-liter V8 engine from the as-yet-unintroduced M 117 model series in June 1970, as Wankel engines were still considered a scarce commodity. The modified cooling air ducting and the modified hatch due to the taller V8 engine are clearly visible.

The 4.5-liter V8 engine installed in car 25 filled the engine compartment very well—so well that the hatch had to be modified.

Performance diagram of the 4.5-liter V8 engine U 18 used in car 25. The eight-cylinder engine, equipped with eight individual intake manifolds, mobilized an impressive 330 hp/242 kW at 6,100 rpm.

intakes, the reciprocating engine with the individual engine number U 18 produced an impressive 330 hp/242 kW at 6,100 rpm. A largely identical V8 had already been installed in car 4 in October 1969, but it was converted back to a three-rotor Wankel after just three months. So this very special M 117 was finally used in car 25 after it returned from its exhibition world tour.

During testing, the C 111 with a V8 engine "stood out particularly for its substantial fuel consumption figures over the first 1,500 km: Fuel 46.7 l/100 km, oil 10.5 l/1,000 km"—this is how Dr. Hans Liebold put it on October 30, 1970, in a note to Dr. Kurt Obländer, responsible for injection engines in the passenger car engine test department. The engine also seemed rougher and less refined than the Wankel engines installed in the sister vehicles. These were bolted directly to the rear beam of the frame floor system, but their running characteristics gave the feeling of actually being softly and elastically suspended. *sport auto* magazine quoted Hans Liebold on this in September 1986: "When we first installed our famously refined running eight-cylinder without noise-insulating elastic mounts for testing purposes, we sat in the front of the cockpit afterward, dreading the rattling grinding mill in the engine compartment." However, the car was still very pleasant to drive in everyday traffic and served Fritz Naumann as a "company car" for a while, with which the test engineer undertook numerous test drives.

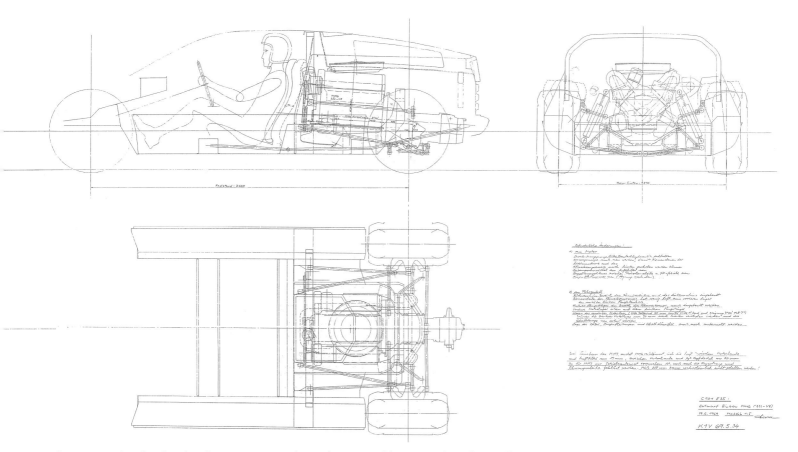

The construction drawing dated June 18, 1969, shows the C 111 with a V8 engine. The 3.5-liter M 116 engine is shown, but the slightly taller 4.5-liter M 117 variant, which was then installed in car 5, is also noted with its spatial implications.

In autumn 1969, a new internal nomenclature had been introduced for the C 111 experimental cars. This no longer relied on consecutive numbering of all built examples but differentiated between the two series—thus, the five cars of the first series were now designated with the numbers 22 to 26, and the cars of the second series, presented in March 1970, started with number 31. As comprehensible as this system may be in principle, the classification of the Sledge as car 21 does not appear to be very stringent. It would have been easier to understand the number 11, whereby the first "real" C 111 would then have continued the sequence with 21. One of the numbers was assigned twice—a new vehicle was built in April 1970 to replace the crashed car 24, which was given the internal number 24 a.

Cars 22 and 23 (originally designated as car 2 and car 3) were also converted to the four-rotor engine in July and June 1970, respectively, and were ready for endurance testing along with car 26 and the gradually completed second-generation vehicles. Although the second version, presented in March 1970 and optimized in many respects, now embodied the latest development status, the vehicles of the first generation were urgently needed as test cars for the further testing of all components and repeatedly led to findings that were incorporated into the development.

During the endurance testing of car 22, the tentative relocation of the pre-silencer under the trunk, especially in combination with the four-rotor engine, proved to be extremely unfavorable for temperature reasons. For example, the right camber strut joint on the frame was scorched despite being shielded with aluminum and asbestos. Despite an approximately 10 mm thick glass wool mat and additional aluminum sheet, the trunk floor became so hot in the area of the pre-silencer that it deformed and the carpet mat laid inside was singed yellow. In addition, the frame rail around the exhaust had warped and corroded. Rudolf Uhlenhaut thereupon agreed to the relocation back above the right wheel arch, as Fritz Naumann recorded in a memo dated August 28, 1970. A contact protection was to prevent injuries from the hot exhaust pipe. With the KE 406 four-rotor engine installed in August 1970, car 22 eventually reached a

The exhaust pipe and pre-silencer were moved next to the transmission below the trunk on a trial basis, as shown in the photos of car 32 (*left*, taken on February 26, 1970) and car 24 a (*right*, taken on May 8, 1970). This change, which was also implemented on car 22, proved to be less practical due to temperature development and was reversed in favor of the original position above the right wheel arch. The shielding plate visible in the picture on the right had only been able to fulfill its intended function to a limited extent.

respectable 62,810 km in road endurance testing without damage, although the top speed was limited to 220 km/h and the maximum revs to 6,000 rpm. After a total loss accident in April 1972, the endurance testing of this test car came to an end. It had consumed an average of 26.9 liters of fuel per 100 kilometers and 2.5 liters of oil per 1,000 kilometers.

With car 23, a first attempt with air conditioning was made in April 1970 even before fitting a four-rotor engine, after installing the system without drawings and with a high degree of improvisation. This was possible mainly because the three-rotor engine left enough installation space for mounting the air conditioning compressor and the other components. The conclusion of the tests was that the cold air outlets at the side and in the middle were positioned too low and too far away from the driver, the amount of air delivered was insufficient, the air inlet for the condenser was too small and the condenser itself was not powerful enough, and the alternator output was too low for three additional fans. After all, when measured in the climate chamber at an ambient temperature of 30°C (85°F) and an engine speed of 1,000 rpm, an interior cooling by 11.8°C (53.2°F) was measured after ten minutes and 14.1°C (57.4°F) after twenty minutes. After thirty minutes, the engine speed was increased to 3,000 rpm, and the interior cooling settled at a little over 15°C (59°F). The stationary test was stopped in the fifty-third minute after the coolant temperature had reached 120°C (248°F). As a result of the high exhaust temperature, the paint on the air outlet gills of the outer skin was burnt.

In early summer of 1971, car 23 was also used in investigations into exhaust gas detoxification by means of exhaust gas afterburning. Since the pollutants (mainly

Car 23 was the first C 111 to be equipped with air conditioning on a trial basis. The photos show the cold air outlet in the dashboard (*left*) and in the center console (*center*) and the air conditioning compressor in the engine compartment (*right*).

hydrocarbons) in the exhaust gas of a Wankel engine can inherently be reduced much less effectively by design changes to the engine than is possible with reciprocating engines by changing the compression ratio, combustion chamber design, stroke, and bore, exhaust gas afterburning was the obvious method for reducing pollutants. Compared to catalytic aftertreatment, this had the advantages of low performance losses, long service life, and a smaller space requirement.

The KE 403 engine used in car 23 was initially mounted on the test bench for the tests, and the already developed single-pipe exhaust system was fitted with a pipe to supply the secondary air for afterburning. Shortly before the collector pipe entered the pre-silencer, a spark plug powered by buzz ignition was fitted to support afterburning. The collector pipe after the pipe joint and the pre-silencer behind it worked as a reactor, and the secondary air was drawn in by the outflowing exhaust gases themselves via a check valve. The engine was adjusted to the most favorable emission values on the test bench, then re-installed in car 23 and tested on the roller dynamometer.

As the development report of August 11, 1971, stated, the output of 336 hp/247 kW and the maximum torque of 39 kpm were maintained without losses despite the afterburning system. The report was also optimistic in other respects: "The measured emission values, which should be able to be improved considerably by the installation of a flame start system, show that by saving an air pump and combining a pre-silencer/reactor, a relatively inexpensive exhaust gas detoxification system can be realized on the four-rotor Wankel engine."

Car 24 after its collision with the north gate of the Hockenheimring in January 1970. The car was provisionally repaired and then used in two crash tests to research the crashworthiness of the fuel tanks.

Car 4 or 24, which had been in use since August 1969, was no longer available after an accident in Hockenheim in January 1970. A test driver had collided with the north gate of the circuit, ripping the heavy gate wing off its hinges. While the driver luckily escaped with a scare, the car was severely damaged in the front area. The development department in Sindelfingen, which was to have received the vehicle in exchange for car 3 as a body test car, received a new vehicle as a replacement in July 1970, which had been built with a body from the second version presented in March 1970. It was given the car number 24 a, although from the outside it could be assigned to the second series and was registered with number plate BB–K 390. As there were not enough four-rotor engines available, the three-rotor KE 308 engine was installed. The crashed car, whose body had been largely repaired in the meantime, was used for two crash tests at the Sindelfingen test site in June 1970. The main focus was on the accident safety of the fuel tanks mounted in the side rails.

Also in June 1970, the C 111 of the first version could once again show what it was made of. Car 6, now called car 26, was used for top speed measurements on the motorway between Lahr and Riegel on June 2. A good eight months earlier, car 3, with a three-rotor engine, had reached 263 km/h on the same route. Due to the expected traffic conditions, the measurement drive was started at 4 a.m. Car 26 was equipped with the four-rotor KE 405 engine, in which four 800 mm long individual exhaust pipes had been routed to a collector fitting and then connected to the previous exhaust silencers. On the intake side, four 500 mm long pipes were routed in pairs to a double intake filter. With these tweaks, KE 405 achieved 400 hp/294 kW at 6,700 rpm on the dyno, and car 6 right away averaged 295 km/h from both directions. However, the oil temperature rising above 140°C (284°F) forced the measurement to be aborted after every 4 to 5 km of full throttle driving. Further tests with the rear tires of dimension 5.50/13.60-15, which were slightly larger in rolling circumference, and slightly richer engine settings, showed an average of 297 km/h from both directions, and after removing the two exterior mirrors, the top speed was 299 km/h. Afterward, acceleration tests were carried out, during which the dual-disc clutch, which had been installed in the meantime, proved to be excellently stable; 5.3 seconds for 0–100 km/h and 15.1 seconds for 0–200 km/h were measured. For 1 kilometer with a standing start, car 26 needed only 22.9 seconds and achieved a final speed of 237 km/h.

New Generation: The C 111-II

The test car, which had achieved spectacular results in the driving performance measurements in June 1970, no longer represented the latest development status at that time. A year earlier, the course had already been set for a fundamental overhaul of the mid-engined sports car. The background to these measures was the fact that the outer form did not meet with undivided approval in all points and repeatedly provoked criticism of individual design features. A visit by Daimler-Benz Supervisory Board members Friedrich-Karl Flick and Eberhard von Brauchitsch on July 23, 1969, also contributed to this. The day after, Friedrich Geiger remarked in a note about the visit that he liked the shape of the model very much. However, the purpose of the vehicle was probably not yet clearly defined, which is why "even greater emphasis should be placed on the exterior." He commissioned his employees Bruno Sacco and Joseph Gallitzendörfer to "revise the existing [shape] again to enhance the appearance." For capacity reasons, this could, as Geiger wrote, "only be done as buffer work in the design office" but was to be "pushed ahead in such a way that we soon come to a result." A week later, on August 1, the chief stylist commissioned the existing interior mockup to be completed into a second 1:1 plasticine model "in the shortest possible time (fourteen days)." The position of the windshield and the "windshield supports" (A-pillars) were also to be changed—above all for the benefit of driver visibility, which was often criticized in the completed car 2. In the end, there was not enough time to create a complete mockup model, but they improvised with a 1:1 body model with window openings and doors, which made it possible to assess the visibility.

The shape changes on the C 111 were first examined for their aerodynamic effect by measuring the 1:5 model. Wing extensions were also tested, as shown on the model in the picture at the top right.

There was no time to complete the interior mockup into the 1:1 clay model commissioned by Geiger. The improvised 1:1 mockup model allowed the visibility to be assessed in relation to the changes in shape at the front of the car.

Detailed Work with Great Effect: The Design Development for the C 111-II

The new form began to manifest itself in its basic features as early as the end of August 1969. After a visit by Rudolf Uhlenhaut on August 21, Friedrich Geiger, in a note, summarized the progress already made and the points still to be worked on. For a better view to the side at the front, the windshield had been widened, moved back by 35 mm, and run into the wing area at the bottom; furthermore, the A-pillar had been raked farther back, and the lower edge of the side windows had been lowered by about 40 mm. To improve the view to the rear right, the striking louver in the rear area was to be modified to allow a view to the rear. The rear window was to use the entire width of the center wall, and the trunk lid was to be cut out so that the visibility past the center of the rear wheel was possible. The intention was to improve the visibility to the rear left by extending the side window to the center wall, which made it necessary to extend the doors. The stylists had arranged the dashboard lower "for a better sense of space," but Uhlenhaut complained that the right-hand instrument cluster could not be seen and had to be moved. He also wanted to provide for two externally mounted trunks in addition to a practical luggage compartment under the hood.

Five days later, Uhlenhaut examined the proposed measures to improve visibility based on drawings and immediately made further requests, which the chief stylist documented in a note to Karl Wilfert on August 26: "1.) The rear window is to be made larger" and "the lower edge is to be slanted toward the hood. 2.) Provisions for an air conditioning system are to be made. 3.) The air intake at the bottom of the front is to be given special consideration in the redesign, [and] 4.) . . . the new door locks will be installed as soon as possible." With regard to the rear-end design, Geiger noted that "the four-rotor Wankel engine must be taken into account; above all, the accommodation of the exhaust system behind the transmission, so that . . . the car must be lengthened not by 60 mm, but by 100 mm."

In September, experiments were still being carried out with curvatures on the front hood, reminiscent of power domes, which, like the flared wing extensions, were tested on 1:5 models in the wind tunnel. Three weeks later, the design development was almost complete, and on October 21, 1969, the 1:1 clay model largely showed the final lines. In the technical meeting on October

27, the provisional mockup interior and visibility model, created at short notice, were examined. However, in a project meeting of the body development department the following day, a number of design- and function-related detail changes were still defined.

Once again, the priority was to improve visibility. For this purpose, the upper edge of the front wings was to be lowered, taking into account the maximum deflection of the front wheels by 90 mm in height. The roof section was to be raised by 15 mm in the head

The plasticine model in 1:1 presented the state of shape development on August 22, 1969. The eye-catching taillights wrapping around the corner were not realized, nor was the C 111 lettering placed on the left of the trunk lid.

On September 29, 1969, the 1:1 model also featured two elements reminiscent of power domes in addition to the pronounced openings for the cooling air intake and outlet on the front hood.

Three weeks later, on October 21, the supposed power domes were history and the shape development was almost complete. The rectangular but stylistically very coherent taillights, which were now no longer wrapping around, were not realized in the end for cost reasons.

area "to at least partially eradicate the oppressive feeling caused by the current position of the upper windshield cross rail." It was also decided to lower the center section of the trunk lid area by 40 mm to improve visibility to the rear. Another design adjustment concerned the taillights, which in their proposed form would "entail prohibitive tooling costs." With this in mind, it was decided to "use Hella's circular truck lights with a diameter of 180 mm."

In order to meet the tight schedule, the clay model had to be ready as early as November 8, 1969, in order to be available for wind tunnel tests two days later. On November 13, it was to be scanned to produce a digital data set, and on November 17,

To optimize the aerodynamics, various aids such as this "aerofoil over the rear hatch" were developed and tested in the wind tunnel.

Final touch: For the air outlet on the front hood, experiments were carried out with different cover grilles (*left*), and variants with louvers were also investigated for the hatch. The photos in the Sindelfingen styling studio were taken in early November 1969.

The rear-end design with the standard taillights from the accessories range used at the end was shown in two different variants on the 1:1 plasticine model. In the end, the design shown in the picture on the left was pursued further.

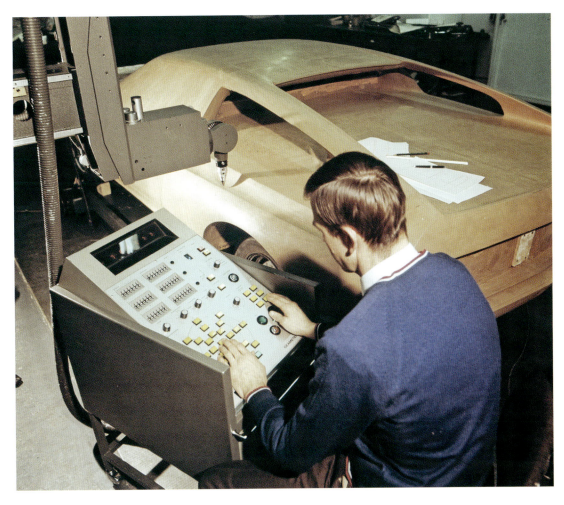

By scanning the plasticine model, a digital data set of the body of the C 111-II was generated.

Critical examination of the original model of the C 111-II with its immaculate finish. This is the intermediate positive made of plastic in Rastatt from which the final tools for body production were molded.

delivery had to be made in Rastatt to ensure the presentation scheduled for the Geneva Motor Show in early March 1970. Assembly and interior fitting of the first two vehicles were scheduled for mid-February and early March, respectively, followed by road tests.

Extensive Fine-Tuning: Optimization of the Aerodynamics

Already at the end of October, even before the final shape changes were decided, the 1:1 model had been extensively examined in the wind tunnel. This resulted in a drag coefficient c_d of 0.325 with racing tires and 0.307 with standard tires. Taking into account the smaller frontal area of 1,631 m² (1,711 m² with racing tires) compared to the first version and a slightly higher c_d value for the roadworthy version, this suggested a reduction in drag by 8.5% compared to the drivable cars of the first series. The previously small front-axle lift had become a slight downforce of 5 kp (at 250 km/h), while the rear-axle lift of 34 kp was the same as that of the previous cars. A significant improvement was noted in the cooling air ducting. The air flow rate increased by 50%, and the velocity distribution over the radiator face was very uniform. The preferential outflow was via the center of the windshield and the roof surface; edge flows swept the lateral window surfaces.

In mid-November, the 1:1 model, which had been improved in the meantime and served as a sample for body production, was measured again in the wind tunnel. The most important changes compared to the previous status were the roof, which was more curved in the longitudinal direction and 15 mm higher at head height, and the rear tub, which was 40 mm lower. The c_d value, determined with racing tires, had remained virtually the same at 0.326, and in view of the minimally larger frontal area of 1.722 m² compared with the previous status, as well as a slightly higher c_d value for the roadworthy version, this resulted in an 8% reduction in aerodynamic drag compared to the first version of the C 111. The aerodynamic lift was also changed: at 250 km/h, the front-axle lift was now 8 kp and rear-axle lift was 45 kp. As the measurement of different configurations showed, downforce could be achieved on the front axle (23 kp) by means of a small spoiler on the front wing side and on the rear axle (20 kp) with the help of an air foil placed above the rear tub. However, the c_d value increased significantly by 3% and 19%, respectively. The installation of louvers or a glass panel in the open visibility cutouts of the upper rear side surfaces increased rear-axle lift by 9 kp and 12 kp, respectively, without significantly worsening the c_d value.

In April 1970, a month after its presentation, the finished vehicle was also examined in the large wind tunnel. A c_d value of 0.333 was determined with street tires and a value of 0.350 with racing tires. The frontal areas were 1.680 and 1.722 m², respectively. With an enclosure below the front axle, the c_d values improved to 0.320 and 0.337, respectively. The c_d value, measured at 0.403 with the headlights popped up, was strikingly high. The lift at 250 km/h with street tires was 3 kp at the front axle and 43 kp at the rear axle, minimally below the favorable values determined on the 1:1 model. With racing tires, the tire-induced negative angle of attack of the body resulted in a downforce of 37 kp at the front axle, with an unchanged rear-axle lift of 43 kp.

Great care during the loading of the still-louvered 1:1 model of the C 111-II. The complex aerodynamic measurement was carried out in the wind tunnel of the FKFS in Untertürkheim.

Stylists' studio in Sindelfingen in December 1969; in the top photo, *on the right in the foreground*, **Peter Pfeiffer and interior stylist Gitta Scholl**, *far rear left*, **Gérard Cardiet**; and, *seated in the back on the right*, **Joseph Gallitzendörfer with Ferdinand Hellhake, Manfred Schneider, and Andreas Langenbeck. In the bottom photo, Joseph Gallitzendörfer** (*center*) **and Ferdinand Hellhake** (*right*).

Development Outcome: Stylistic and Technical Improvements

By revising the body design, decisive improvements were achieved as intended: Not only did the C 111 of the second version offer better visibility and was aerodynamically even more efficient than its predecessor, but it had also become more elegant. The most striking differences compared with the first version were the slightly lower beltline, the larger window areas, and the lower rear section with sight-line openings at the sides—changes that made the car appear lighter overall. The design modifications also included details such as the front turn signals, which had been relocated to the upper edge of the wings and were now also clearly visible from the side.

The interior of the sports car was significantly revised as well, with a modern design that inspired future generations of Mercedes-Benz vehicles. In particular, the dashboard was less dominant than in the first version and thus very clearly reduced the previously criticized psychologically impairing constriction of driver and passenger. The shortcoming that test drivers complained about—namely, that they came into conflict with the center console when shifting gears—was eliminated with the new interior design, as was the lack of a facility for hanging up jackets, which Uhlenhaut had previously complained about. Functional

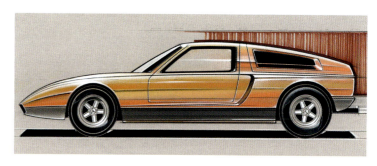

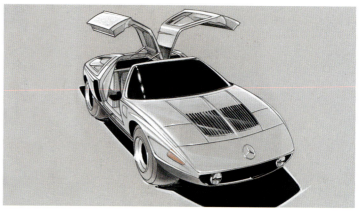

The design drawings by Gérard Cardiet (second row on the left) and Joseph Gallitzendörfer (all others) reflect the final form very accurately for the most part, but still show deviations in some details.

Dream Sports Car and Laboratory on Wheels: The C 111

 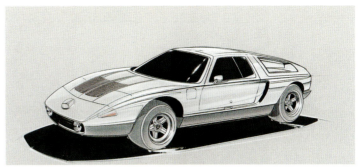

These four drawings by Joseph Gallitzendörfer correspond to the final state of the new variant in every detail.

In a direct comparison, the differences between the two generations of the C 111 become clearly visible. The series of photos was taken on the grounds of the test track of the Untertürkheim plant in late February 1970.

subtleties were also taken into account and controls were optimized during the redesign of the interior. One of these improvements concerned the headlights. For the second version of the C 111, the previous mechanical pop-up mechanism was replaced by an electric one that was automatically activated when the driving lights were switched on. This freed up space to the left of the clutch pedal, which could now be used as a place to rest the left foot and a wiper-washer foot pump. However, the old wisdom that additional systems can also bring additional problems was confirmed—a test drive with car 31, for example, which went from Stuttgart to the Turin Motor Show at the end of October 1970, had to be interrupted because the headlights could no longer be popped up after refueling in Zurich. The jamming of the right headlight had triggered an electrical defect. The alternative solution of popping up the headlights mechanically from the spare wheel compartment by means of a crank in future cases was not feasible because the headlights could not be deployed when the hood was raised.

The trunk was also further developed. The luggage compartment of the first version, which originally only complied

The interior mockup was an important tool for the development of the interior—shown here is the work status of January 15, 1970.

The interior of the C 111-II presented itself in a fundamentally evolved form.

One of the characteristic design elements of the mid-engined coupe was the upper end of the hood, now without side louvers.

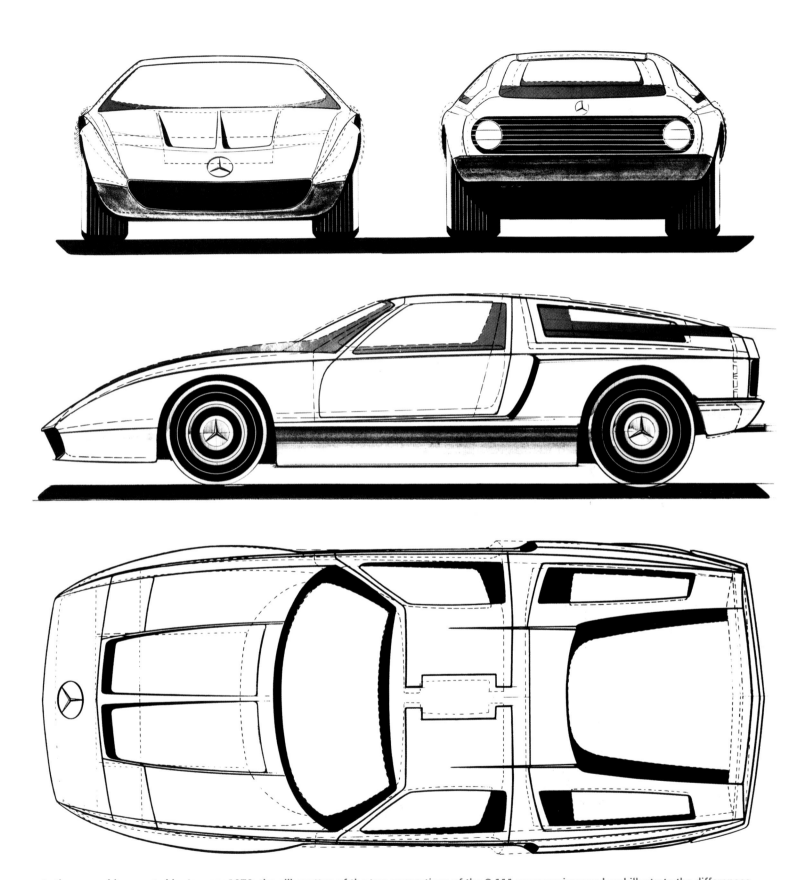

In these graphics created in January 1970, the silhouettes of the two generations of the C 111 are superimposed and illustrate the differences in the side, front, and rear views as well as the top view.

For the photo series taken at the end of February 1970 on the test track in Untertürkheim, the Sledge also received an orange paint finish.

Even before the presentation in Geneva, the first C 111-II was photographed on the test track of the Mercedes-Benz Untertürkheim plant.

with the FIA regulations and had first been enlarged on cars 2 and 6 and then also on cars 3 and 4, could accommodate up to three pieces of luggage in the second version from the outset and was designed in such a way that two medium-sized and one large suitcase of the classic Mercedes-Benz luggage set could be used. This came at the cost of the unusual installation position of the pre-silencer, already familiar from cars 2 and 6, which meant that the exhaust manifold could not be dismantled in the finished vehicle and could only be installed and removed together with the engine. The only remedy in this respect was to make substantial changes to the rear-axle strut turrets and the cross rail, for which the chassis design department in Untertürkheim submitted an elaborate proposal on May 21, 1970, which was to be implemented in the next frame to be delivered. However, the planned relocation of the exhaust lower down was later abandoned.

Apart from the striking design changes, the most spectacular innovation concerned the engine. The C 111 of the second version was now equipped with the four-rotor version of the M 950. This had already been used on the last car of the first version but had not been communicated and had therefore gone unnoticed by experts and the public. Compared to the three-rotor engine, which was always perceived as somewhat weak, the new power unit marked real progress. The nominal peak power was 350 hp/257 kW at 7,000 rpm, but the torque maximum of over 40 mkg/392 Nm, which was decent in principle, was only available at 5,000 rpm.

At a meeting on November 12, 1969, to which Rudolf Uhlenhaut had invited his senior staff and those involved in the project from the design and advance engineering departments, the technical changes to be made to the C 111 had been defined in detail. By changing the twin headlights into single headlights, space was to be created to accommodate the oil cooler next to the coolant radiator—a decision that was withdrawn at the passenger car technical meeting five days later in view of the very tight deadline situation, as the schedule now no longer permitted any bodywork modifications. This meant that other solutions had to be found at a critical point—the cooling system had proved to be a problem child in the development of the C 111 from the very beginning and now had to meet increased requirements due to the performance level of the four-rotor engine. As recommended after the wind tunnel measurements in July 1969 and already realized on car 6, the cooling air also entered the C 111 of the second series at the bottom of the car's front and exited again just in front of the center of the hood. This cooling air flow was supported by the negative pressure on the upper side of the hood, created at high speeds. However, as was soon to become apparent, this still did not solve the cooling problem: The

In the trunk of the C 111-II, there was now room for three suitcases of the familiar Mercedes-Benz luggage set.

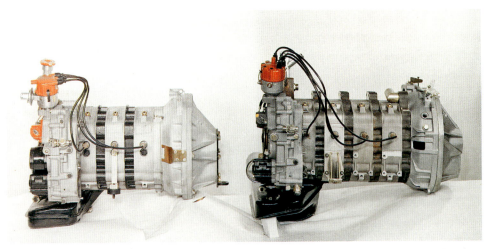

The four-rotor version of the M 950 in direct comparison with the three-rotor version. The picture on the right shows the high-performance engine with the injection system and air filter installed.

The four-rotor engine M 950/4, right side, with intake and exhaust ports without and with air filter

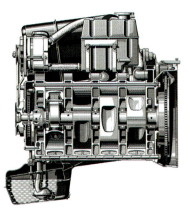

Technical graphics of the four-rotor engine M 950/4: longitudinal section (*left*) and cross-section through trochoidal housing (*center*) and intermediate housing (*right*)

View into the engine compartment with the four-rotor M 950 engine. The injection pump, the alternator, and the filler openings for engine oil (*left*) and coolant (*right*) are clearly visible.

The underbody paneling of the C 111 had only a small cutout for the oil pan.

From this rather unusual angle, the grilled air vents in the front hood of the C 111 are clearly visible.

increased power led to water temperatures of around 110°C (230°F) and oil temperatures of more than 140°C (284°F) during full-load measurements on the motorway and on the big circuit of the Hockenheimring—clearly too high in the opinion of the engine developers. Subsequently, the cooling system was optimized again and again through constant modifications.

Further changes were discussed regarding the chassis design. Here, a tubular frame construction for the rear section was considered as an alternative, but this was only to be realized if a significant weight savings was possible with sufficient frame rigidity. It was decided to build five new cars, three of which were intended for the Geneva Motor Show. The first two vehicles were to be designed with the previous frame-rear end construction. However, this design was also used

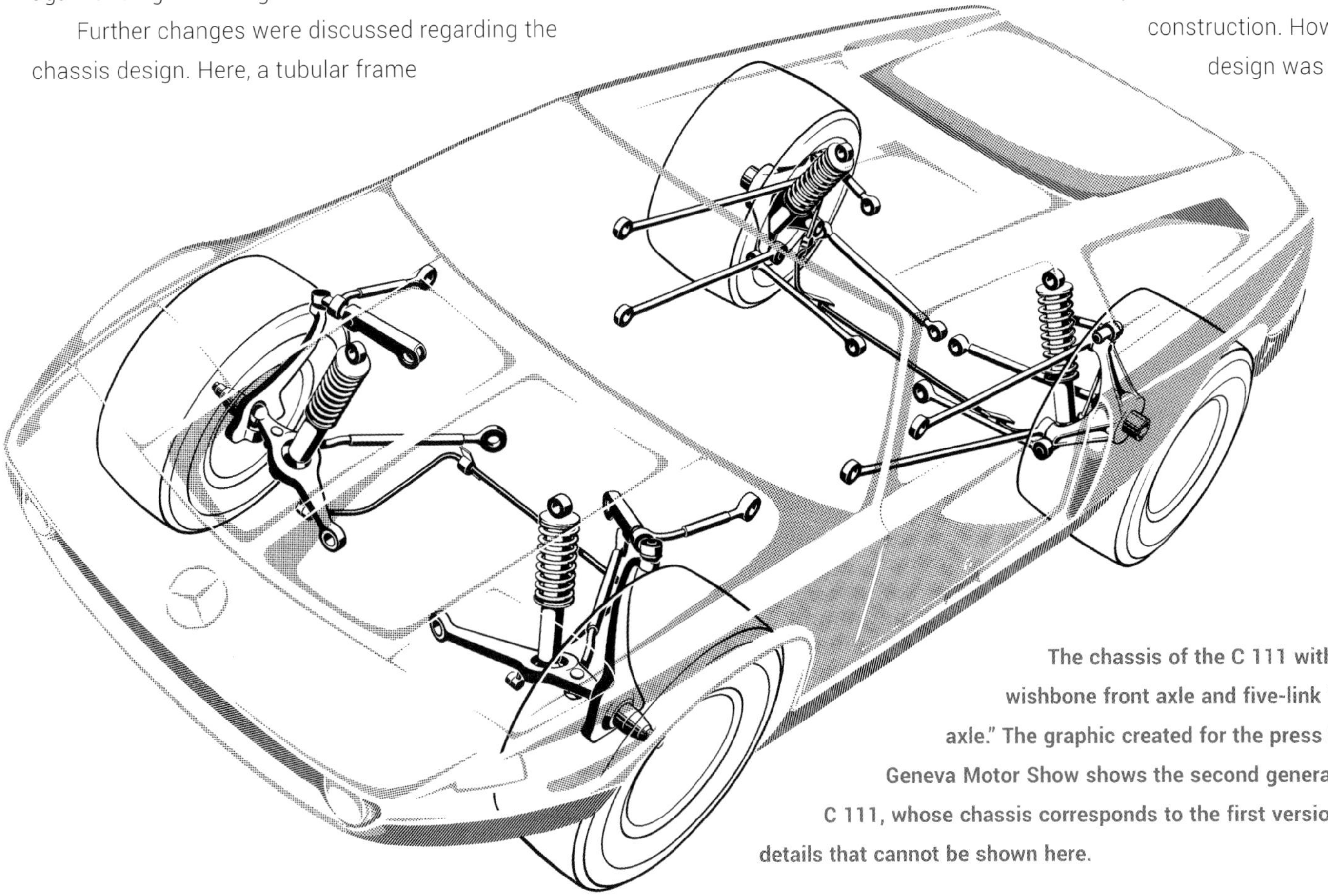

The chassis of the C 111 with double wishbone front axle and five-link "racing rear axle." The graphic created for the press kit for the Geneva Motor Show shows the second generation of the C 111, whose chassis corresponds to the first version except for details that cannot be shown here.

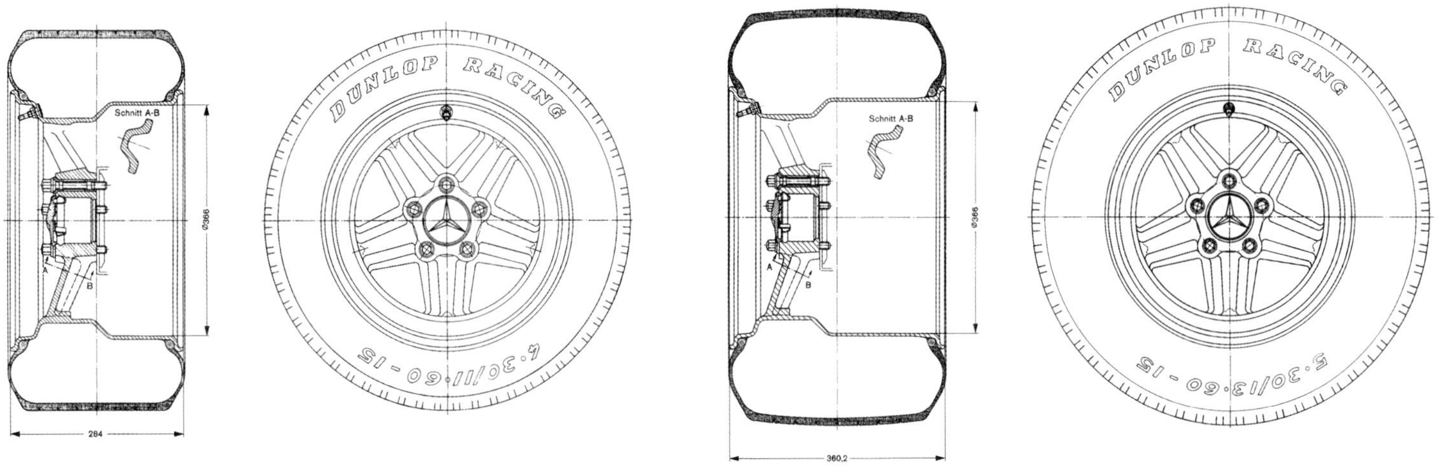

Front wheel and rear wheel of the C 111 in the version with racing tires

for the remaining vehicles, and the tubular frame version was not used.

Modifications to the drivetrain were not only to account for the realities of the four-rotor engine, but also to eliminate previously identified weaknesses. Optimization of the transmission had already been discussed in detail on November 6, 1969, during the visit of a delegation from ZF. The further development of the transmission was to include a reinforcement of the clutch actuation, a new gearshift, the electric release of the reverse gear stop, modified gear ratios, and a number of other points. In order to facilitate starting off with the engine, which was relatively low in torque in the lower speed range—a point that had already been demanded again and again in the first version of the C 111—a hydraulically operated dual-disc clutch from Fichtel & Sachs was installed, which was also to be fitted to the last car of the first series at the same time.

For the oval silencer, as it was envisaged regarding the planned trunk, it was demanded in the meeting on November 12 that it should retain its shape even when hot. For exhaust gas purification at low speeds, an afterburning system was deemed necessary, as it was then tested in 1971.

Detailed improvements were also made to the chassis. Thanks to new ball joints with plastic shells, it was possible to significantly reduce the rolling noise at the rear axle compared

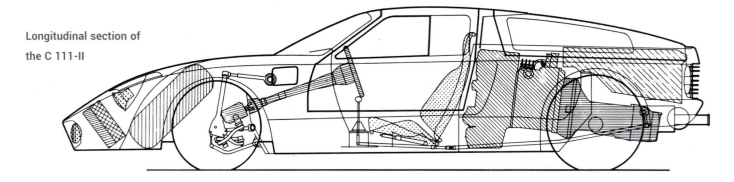

Longitudinal section of the C 111-II

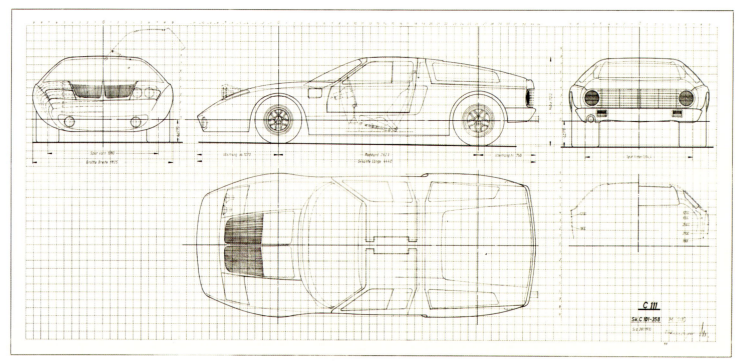

The C 111-II with light-alloy wheels and racing tires in four-sided view with additional sectional views. The drawing was made by body designer Erich Rühringer.

Mercedes-Benz C-111 1970

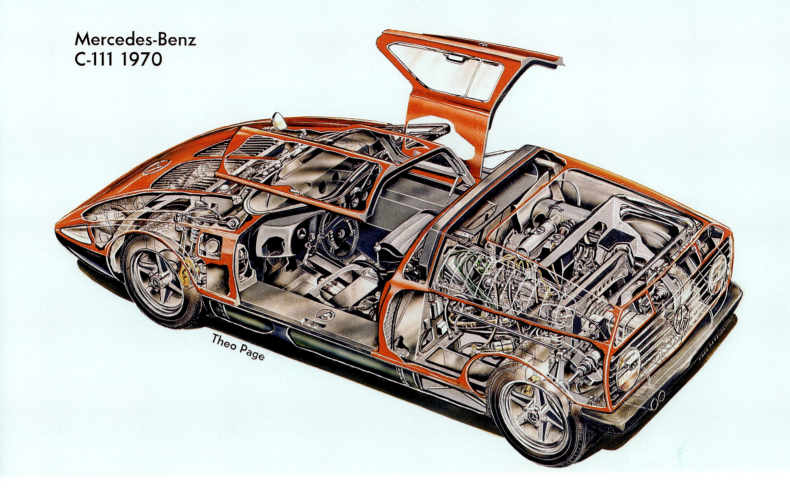

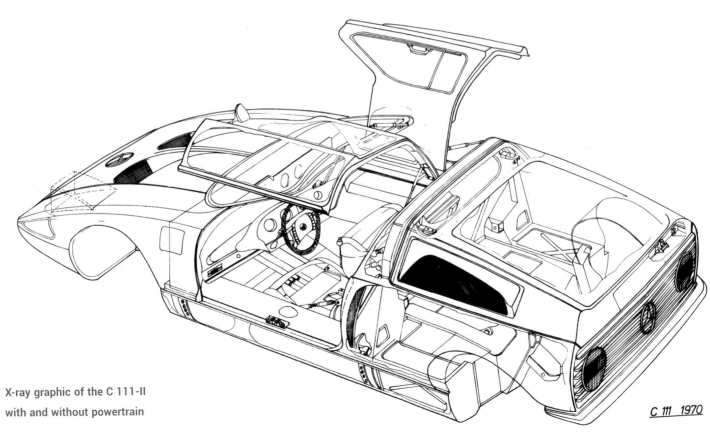

X-ray graphic of the C 111-II with and without powertrain

with the vehicles of the first series. In contrast to the first version, which required re-lubrication, the new joints also had the advantage of being maintenance-free. The fastening was also simplified: Instead of the previously used welded-in threaded sleeves, only through holes and additional mounting holes on the frame base were required. The front axle and steering were also modified, and the brake system was optimized in detail. The brake calipers on the rear wheels, which were located at the front of the wheel carrier in the vehicles of the first version, were now mounted at the rear in the second version—as was intended from the outset in terms of design—which significantly reduced the forces acting on the wheel bearings during braking.

A technical detail change that eventually led to further modifications was replacing the two-arm windshield wiper system with a version with only one arm. This made a larger wiped area possible and disappeared from the airflow in the rest position. Not only was it simpler in design, which was to benefit reliability, but it was also significantly lighter than the previous design and met the relevant requirements of the US authorities. One disadvantage of the single-arm wiper, however, was the installation geometry, which required further modifications—a good example of the consequences that supposedly minor design changes can have. The use of the originally planned brake booster in 8-inch single diaphragm design, defined in the meeting on November 12, was now no longer possible due to a lack of space, so that the development of a new control element for shorter response time with the 6-inch twin-diaphragm unit used until now became inevitable. Due to the development time of about six months, the first two vehicles of the second version had to be equipped with the existing 6-inch units. On February 5, 1970, the body design department in Sindelfingen announced that the installation of a 9-inch Mastervac brake booster was possible from car 9 onward with the following body modifications: bolt-fitted design of the crossrail between the suspension struts, indentation on the floor at the front (accepting a reduced air supply), windshield wiper linkage turned at the link point, and forward shifted position of the spare wheel.

The question of the fuel tanks, in particular the safety conditions of a foam-lined design, was also addressed at the meeting on November 12. In addition to corresponding tests on this issue, the development of a rubber fuel tank was also commissioned. The expansion possibilities of the tank in the body side rail were also to be investigated.

Major Attraction: Presentation in Geneva

Five test cars of the new version of the C 111 were to be built, as decided on November 12 and formally confirmed by a management decision on December 1, 1969. Due to scheduling restrictions, two of these—and not three as originally planned—were scheduled for the presentation at the Geneva Motor Show in March 1970: one show car and one demonstration car. Internally, they were consequently on the books as cars 7 and 8, but were also given the numbers 31 and 32, which followed the new system.

On January 20, 1970, Karl Wilfert decided on a weissherbst color scheme for the demonstration car with the number 31 and the show car with the number 32—the same color as the exhibition car at the IAA. Friedrich Geiger and his team chose different colors for the interiors of the two vehicles. Seat center sections and door panels were to be executed in the fabric pattern "houndstooth gray/white" for car 31 and in "houndstooth cognac light" for car 32. All other interior parts were designed in black man-made leather or black foam sheeting.

The bodywork of the first two cars of the second series was made of Palatal epoxy resin supplied by BASF, as was the case with cars 22 to 26. As early as August 1969, at the instigation of Farbenfabriken Bayer, the use of a material produced by Bayer had also been considered, and approval had been given in principle on condition that the material properties were essentially the same as before, that paintability with the Glasurit color weissherbst was guaranteed, and that the delivery dates of the finished car bodies were not postponed under any circumstances.

Following the formal approval by the management of passenger car body development in mid-November, the details were clarified on November 24 at a meeting at Waggonfabrik Rastatt. It was decided—not least for scheduling reasons—that the bodies of cars 31 and 32 would be made from the BASF material used up to now. Two further cars were to receive bodies made of epoxy resin from Bayer AG. In addition to the requirements already formulated in August, it was also specified that the resin would have to be equally suitable for laminating and bonding. Likewise, the crisscross pattern of the fiberglass, the surface finish, and the paintability would have to be at least as good as before. Preliminary tests with the materials in question would have to be completed by the time the new molds were ready. These tests were to be carried out with a door die of the old mold.

The frame floor system of the first C 111 of the second generation. Views from the rear (*right*), from the front (*center*), and diagonally in front were taken in Sindelfingen in January 1970.

According to the original plan, the body of another vehicle was to be made with epoxy resin from Borden Chemicals. However, the material delivered to Rastatt required such unfavorable production temperatures that use was out of the question. The production of a car body could, as the memo of November 27 stated, "only take place if work can be carried out at room temperatures and if there are no delays for WFR [Waggonfabrik Rastatt]."

The complex production process remained largely unchanged compared to the vehicles of the first version. The frame floor system of car 31, the first car of the second series, was built in Sindelfingen between December 10, 1969, and January 14, 1970, and was delivered to the Untertürkheim test department on January 14. There, the 171.8 kg frame floor system was completed with a dummy engine, the remaining major assemblies, and the drivetrain and delivered to Rastatt nine days later. The chassis, fitted with racing tires on cast light-alloy rims, weighed 724 kg and was fitted at Waggonfabrik Rastatt with a body of the new shape. On February 9, it went to Sindelfingen for painting and interior finishing, and exactly seven days later the completed vehicle was transferred to the test department in Untertürkheim for final assembly and fine-tuning.

In view of the tight schedule and the short time interval remaining for testing the new car before the press demonstration on March 10, head of passenger car testing Karl-Heinz Göschel addressed the engine test team on February 11 with an urgent request to deliver four-rotor engines in time. He reminded them that due to the failure of the first four-rotor engine after only 2,200 km, testing had no longer been possible. For Geneva, at least one backup engine would have to be planned in addition to two suitably equipped demonstration cars, and "there is no point in engines with 300 hp for demonstrations." These clear words once again pointed to one of the greatest challenges of development—and apparently had an effect, because the four-rotor KE 408 engine was available for installation on February 17.

During the final assembly of the vehicle in the advance engineering test department, a whole series of detail problems still had to be solved, which resulted from deviations between the

The frame floor system was fitted with the body (*left*) at Waggonfabrik Rastatt. The two pictures in the middle and on the right show the first vehicle of the second series in the Sindelfingen plant, where painting and interior finishing were carried out.

The interior of the first C 111-II. The steering wheel, still fitted here in classic Mercedes-Benz style, was eventually replaced by the four-spoke safety steering wheel with which the first version of the C 111 had already been equipped.

design drawings and the real installation conditions and are listed in the assembly report of February 18, 1970, written by Fritz Naumann. This concerned the installation of the engine, insufficient distances between major assembly components and the water pipes of the cooling system, filler necks of the coolant radiator (which did not fit and prevented installation), the oversized air filter, the exhaust system (which did not fit into the available space), the incorrectly positioned retaining ring of the steering shaft (which prevented the steering wheel lock from engaging), shift tubes that were too short, insufficient securing of the shift lever knob, headlights for parking and passing lights that were positioned too far inboard, and tank filler necks that were too small and didn't allow filling with a full stream from a canister.

There was also a lot to criticize about the bodywork and equipment, as Fritz Naumann noted in the aforementioned assembly report: "The seat side bolsters and the trim of the hand brake and the wiring running up to the rear window impede shifting into 1st, 3rd, and 5th gear. The trim also sits right on the shift tube and does not take into account the routing of the accelerator cable. It weighs 2.8 kp! It also obstructs the only space for hanging up a jacket or the like, as requested by Mr. Uhlenhaut. The console with the radio and heater is too far back. The distance to the gear lever in positions R, 2nd, and 4th gear is too small. When shifting, the ashtray is half closed. The so-called regulation suitcases do not fit into the suitcase box. Contrary to our mutual agreements, the fresh air hose strongly impedes the removal of the front suspension struts. The subsequently bolted-on body support at the rear was in the way of the exhaust and no longer allowed the nuts of the axle struts to be loosened or tightened. It was modified. The aluminum wheel arch on the right is still missing. Part of the footwell trim is in the way of the footrest with the windshield washer pump. The trim parts are for the most part incredibly heavy. We urge you not to lose sight of the standards of a sporty car. The Mercedes star on the front also doesn't have to weigh half a pound." The kerb weight of the car with Michelin tires 205 VR 14 on 7½-inch steel rims was 1,287 kp.

In light of this very extensive list of necessary modifications, it is almost a miracle that car 31 was nevertheless completed on time—this also in view of the fact that extensive testing was necessary before the demonstration in Geneva and that a total of five days also had to be planned for press photos.

On February 5, 1970, even before the completion of car 31, the member of the board responsible for foreign sales, Arnold Wychodil, had suggested that in addition to the vehicles planned for the Geneva Motor Show, two further examples should be produced by March to enable them to be used at further exhibitions abroad and to satisfy the high demand in this respect. The range planning department in Sindelfingen had to reject this request and stated in its reply that even a provision at the earliest possible date of April 1970 would result in a postponement of the test car range of the R/C 107 and W 116 model series by two to three weeks, which would also affect the start of series production of these models. In view of this, these two vehicles should not be scheduled before January–February 1971.

The two test cars scheduled for the press demonstration, no. 26 and no. 31—the last car of the first series and the first car of the second series—were extensively tested in advance on the small circuit in Hockenheim. Dr. Hans Liebold summarized the results in a report dated March 18, 1970. On car 26, registration number S–P 2288, the oil temperature reached an alarming 150°C (302°F) after three laps at 0°C (32°F) outside temperature. By installing a second oil cooler at the rear left, the oil temperature was reduced to 110°C (230°F) and remained below 130°C (266°F) even during a later performance measurement on the motorway. Car 31, with the registration number S–U 21, caught fire several times from the exhaust due to the limited space in the rear. The remedy was sheathing the front exhaust parts, modified insulation, and additional shielding. The oil temperature, which was 110°C (230°F) at Hockenheim, was more pleasing.

The press demonstration at the Geneva Motor Show took place on March 10 and 11 at the Circuit de Monthoux near Geneva. The circuit, which was only a little over a kilometer long and had a very good grip, consisted mainly of a succession of right and left turns driven flat out, which resulted in very high stress for both vehicles during the demonstration runs. On car 31, this led to a break of the left rear wheel hub, and on car 26, with Rudolf Uhlenhaut at the wheel, to a break of one of the lateral

Car 31, the first C 111 of the second version, photographed in Sindelfingen immediately after its completion on February 16, 1970. The position of the trademark mounted in the air intake was not only unfortunate with regard to the cooling air supply but also prompted Friedrich Geiger to write a memorandum in which he demanded that the star be placed "on the front end, in the middle between the front end opening and the air outlet, as it was always shown on the sketches." The position of the headlights for the headlight flasher and parking light was also changed; these interfered with the installation of the oil cooler and were therefore moved farther out.

Car 31 after detail optimization and correct positioning of the Mercedes star (at the very top), photographed on the test track of the Sindelfingen plant in March 1970, immediately before delivery to Untertürkheim and dispatch to Geneva.

The interior of the C 111-II in its final version, now with the four-spoke safety steering wheel already familiar from the first series. The seats had also been modified compared with the first version and equipped with molded head restraints.

The media interest in the press presentation of the C 111-II at the Geneva Motor Show was enormous. In addition to car 32, which was placed in the exhibition following the press conference, two demonstration cars—car 26 and car 31—were also on-site.

links of the rear axle. Because three test employees posed in front of the stranded vehicle in a relaxed pose, the mishap went undetected by the attending media representatives. Both damages could be repaired quickly by installing prepared spare parts.

Car 32, which differed in external details from demonstration car no. 31 and was equipped with a mockup of the four-rotor engine, was used as the show car for the Geneva Motor Show. The floor assembly was built in Sindelfingen between January 15 and 27, and the drivetrain was fitted in Untertürkheim by February 5. Waggonfabrik Rastatt then installed the body and delivered the vehicle on February 23, initially to the test department in Untertürkheim, which transferred the vehicle to Sindelfingen three days later after optimizing the details. Painting and interior finishing were carried out there by March 7, and the finished vehicle was delivered to Untertürkheim on March 9—just in time for the premiere at the Geneva Show. For the presentation at the exhibition, an elevated and forward-tilted placement of the vehicle on a pedestal was again chosen, as already realized in a similar form at the IAA. In contrast to demonstration car no. 31, the stationary car lacked the black cover grilles on the cooling air outlets in the hood.

The presentation of the second version of the C 111 in Geneva could be considered a complete success—just like the debut of the first version at the IAA six months earlier. The media response to the new design and the spectacular, significantly increased driving performance was extremely positive, and the

Car 31, the first C 111 of the second version, during testing at the Hockenheimring (*left*), and during the press demonstration at the Circuit de Monthoux near Geneva (*right*)

public's interest was unbroken. However, there were also dissenting voices to be heard about the design of the mid-engined coupe—including one, as usual, that was clear-cut: Luigi Colani, enfant terrible among industrial designers, expressed his opinion that the C 111 was a "lousy cucumber" for which the Untertürkheim company had borrowed the body style elements from Italy and the Ford GT 40 "with an unsurpassable lack of ideas." With this provocation and similarly pompous assessments of numerous other design objects—from cars to consumer electronics to porcelain items—Colani even made it into renowned news magazine *Der Spiegel* in March 1970. In an article published in *hobby* magazine in September 1970 and dedicated to the Colani GT, a plastic coupe on a VW chassis announced for the spring of 1971, the industry shocker went one step further in September 1970 and provided a photo of the C 111 with his usual provocative assessments: "Overall rating mediocre. Lots of stylistic elements thrown together by a design team that somewhat lost its edge." He also presented a sketch of an avant-garde alternative study. According to *hobby*, Daimler-Benz press spokesman Reinert "was not amused by the designer's attack and the offer to take Colani's paper car apart" and is quoted as saying, "We are still of the opinion that comments on a vehicle that one cannot know in all details are surely very dubious."

The press release published by the company under the headline "C 111—Now faster, stronger and more interesting" for the Geneva Motor Show also conveyed the overall extremely positive public perception, in contrast to Colani's assessment: "At the 1969 IAA Frankfurt, Daimler-Benz caused amazement and speculations with the presentation of the C 111 experimental vehicle. We had dared to take a step into the future and combined the two 'wunderkinds' of car construction, the Wankel engine and the plastic body, into a new concept. Despite the elegant, aerodynamically sophisticated shape and impressive driving results, it proved quite clear that the C 111 is a test vehicle, a kind of mobile laboratory that is being further developed under the eyes of the public into a car that is impressive in terms of technology and design. With it, Daimler-Benz gives everyone interested in cars the opportunity to take a look at its testing and development work. In the meantime, half a year has passed. In the fields of aerodynamics, stability, plastics processing, and, last but not least, the rotary engine, new experience and knowledge have been gained which will be presented in Geneva in the form of a further evolutionary stage of the C 111."

While the question of a possible series production was discussed by the Board of Management and other company committees and examined from a wide range of perspectives, the development continued unabated with the testing of the available vehicles and the construction of further test cars. In addition to endurance testing of the body, the engine, and a wide variety of components, new focal points were also pursued, such as equipping the C 111 with air conditioning, automatic transmission, and the ABS anti-lock braking system, which was then under development. The cooling system and the fuel system, especially the tanks, were also the subject of further investigations.

An article about the Colani GT in the September 2, 1970, edition of *hobby* **magazine was used by the designer to once again gain publicity with provocative statements. In addition to a review of the C 111, he presented a sketch of an alternative sports car study.**

Car 32, the second completed C 111-II, was used as the show car at the Geneva Motor Show after the press conference.

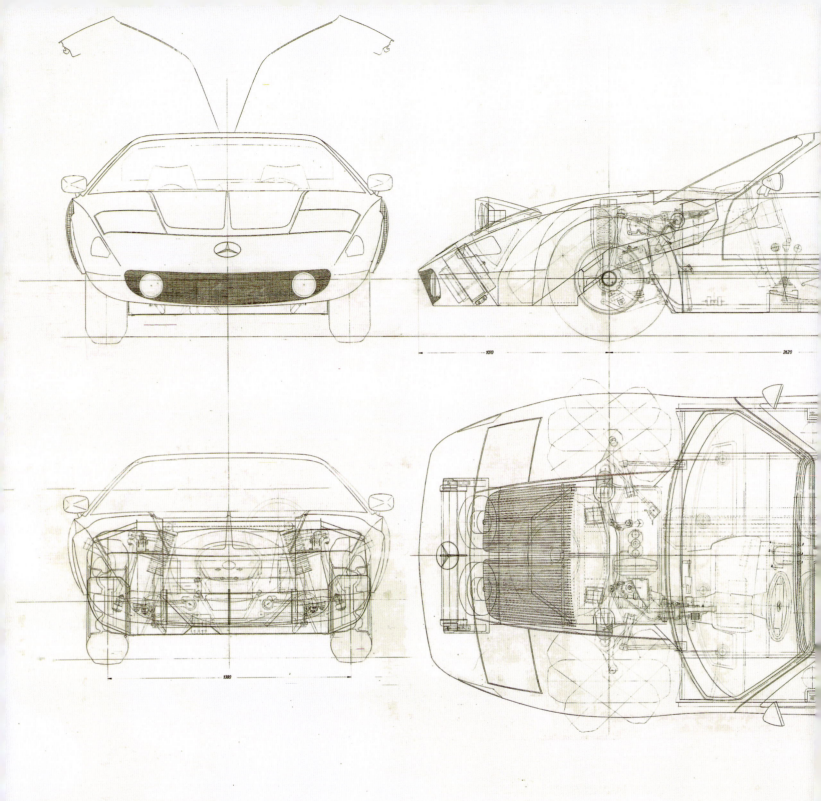

Construction drawing of the C 111-II dated April 17, 1970

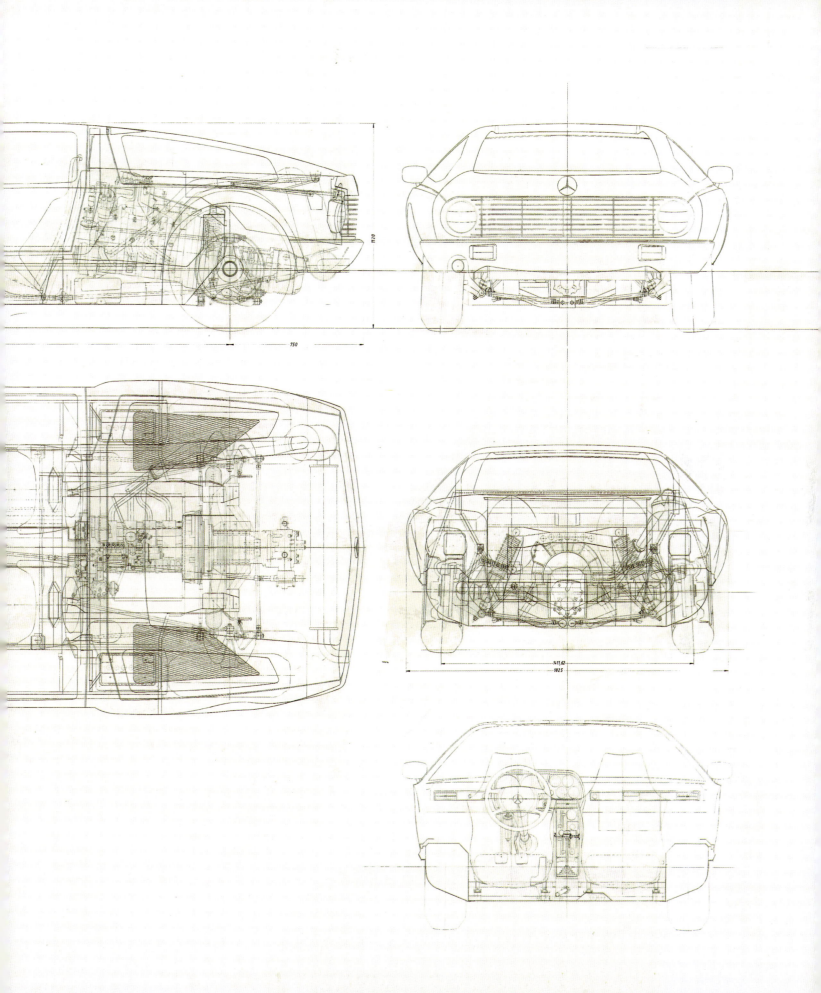

Gradual Progress: The Development Status in the Summer of 1970

Dr. Liebold summarized the current status in a test report dated August 18, 1970. The four-rotor engines, as he stated in this report, seemed more durable since the beginning of the year. During further testing, however, the KE 405 (with sticking apex seals) and the KE 404 and KE 406 (due to mechanical rattling, presumably as a result of damage to the spur gear bearing liner) failed. All three engines were to be rebuilt, while according to Liebold, two of the KE 401, KE 403, and KE 407 engines that failed on the test bench were irreparably damaged. In addition to the KE 408 endurance testing engine equipped with Ferro-TiC apex seals and cast-iron pistons, originally installed in car 31 and since July 1970 in car 22, only KE 402 (with 335 hp/246 kW at 6,400 rpm) was available at that time. Against this background, building engines of the next development stage—stage III, with stiffer intermediate housing sections and rearranged peripherals—appeared to be a matter of urgency.

In terms of performance, the four-rotor engines were subjectively satisfactory, as Liebold noted, even though only 280 km/h had been achieved in the performance measurement of car 31 (with KE 408) on June 2, 1970. Their output ranged from 335 hp/246 kW to 400 hp/294 kW, depending on the intake and exhaust systems fitted and on their technical condition. The spectacular maximum value had been achieved by the KE 405 engine, with four 500 mm long intake pipes as well as four 800 mm long individual exhaust pipes, enabling car 26, the last car of the first series, to approach the magic 300 km/h barrier when measured on June 2. The acceleration time of 15.1 seconds for the sprint from 0 to 200 km/h achieved with this car was also simply phenomenal—especially for the time. During the top speed measurements on the Karlsruhe–Basel motorway, the tread of one front tire and one rear tire separated at a speed of 280 km/h. Investigations by Dunlop in Birmingham revealed that the damage to the front tire was apparently due to high load with insufficient air pressure.

Dr. Liebold rated the intake and exhaust noises as in need of improvement and noted that "the engine's social acceptance still suffers somewhat from the heavy smoke development when starting and the pungent exhaust smell." Fuel consumption was 25-30 l/100 km on the road over longer distances with mostly hard driving, and oil consumption was 4 l/1,000 km. During the aforementioned drive to Turin, a petrol consumption of 22.3 l/100 km and an oil consumption of just under 2 l/1,000 km were measured over 1,865 km with a very brisk driving style. The values compiled in April 1971 at the request of the engine test department were at the level mentioned by Liebold. Cars 26, 31, and 33 had an average petrol consumption of 24 to 25.5 l/100 km and an oil consumption of 1.5 to 4 l/1,000 km with mileages between 8,000 and 24,000 km. Car 34 was a little out of the ordinary, with 35 l/100 km, but the value was based on a mileage of just 1,895 km.

Liebold described the cooling—with the exception of the top speed measurement—as sufficient even in motorway operation. During the road tests carried out in June 1970 on the big circuit in Hockenheim, the oil temperature had caused difficulties. In the summery outside temperatures, a cool-down lap had to follow each fast lap, as the oil temperature had risen above 140°C (284°F). Liebold saw a possible connection with the new spray oil cooling system of the pistons. Better cooling air sealing and a harder spring in the oil cooler bypass valve improved cooling at 110°C (230°F) water temperature to such an extent that 140°C (284°F) was only reached after three hot laps in Hockenheim. Further improvements resulted from the installation of an aluminum coolant radiator instead of the previous brass design, and the fitting of an oil cooler with a 12.5% larger frontal area.

In spite of these improvements, Hans Liebold stated in his report of August 18 that unacceptably high water and oil temperatures were still reached when the engine was used for racing purposes from an outside temperature of approximately 27°C (80°F). In the next test car, changes to the radiator inlet and a constant flow through the heat exchangers were to provide a remedy, as well as, "as a last resort," as Liebold put it, the installation of an additional oil cooler at the rear left.

When outside temperatures were high, the ventilation caused grief even with the new bodywork, as Dr. Liebold had communicated in his report of June 25. Improved sealing of the feed channels and the installation of an additional water shut-off valve for the heating water circuit remedied the heating up of the fresh air, but a greater air flow rate could only be achieved by removing the additional headlights located exactly in front of the air intake openings and by improving the air exhaust by opening the rear side windows. The heating of the interior was particularly caused by the large, strongly raked windshield, which was also strongly heated by the hot radiator exhaust air. For a possible series production, Liebold therefore suggested the installation of crank windows, since the hinged windows also required a certain effort in terms of controls and, in addition, were pushed shut by the air flow when driving fast. In his report of August 18, he described the ventilation "in terms of bodywork... still the most in need of improvement." He hoped to make progress with the modified air intake and outlet in car 33 and a windshield made of heat-insulating, double-pane laminated glass.

The power transmission had improved thanks to the dual-disc clutch, which made starting off much easier with lower pedal forces. The new transmission ratios implemented by ZF in the meantime (first gear 2.857, second gear 1.72, third gear 1.21, fourth gear 0.92, fifth gear 0.705, reverse gear 2.86) proved to be beneficial. However, the service life of the synchromesh, especially of second and third gear, was unsatisfactory on all ZF transmissions supplied.

On the chassis side, it turned out that the long-awaited first samples of Dunlop 245/60 VR 15 tires were not satisfactory in any way, while a short test with the new Michelin 205/70 VR 15 tires was positive. Initial test bench runs also gave rise to hopes that the Michelin tires would be suitable for higher speeds, so that a replacement of the 205 VR 14 tires used until then seemed possible. This was also desirable because the announced 8-inch-wide, 15-inch light-alloy wheels could then replace the previously exclusively available unventilated 14-inch steel wheels, which had repeatedly led to impairments with regard to the brakes.

After the light-alloy cast rims were finally finished, some comparative tests between the previously used Michelin X 205 VR 14 and the alternative sizes 205/70 VR 15 as well as 215/70 VR 15 were carried out, which Dr. Liebold summarized in a note dated November 12. Neither 15-inch variant reached the qualities of the 14-inch tire. As on the steel rims, the 205/70 VR 15 seemed a little less precise in control but was only marginally worse in straight-line running, while the 215/70 VR 15 confirmed the impression of very poor straight-line running. On the small circuit in Hockenheim, both tires were "otherwise quite good" to drive but resulted in lap times that were consistently two- to three-tenths below those of the 14-inch tires. Against this background, Liebold also urgently requested that the development of a forged 7.5-inch-wide, 14-inch light-alloy rim or, if necessary, an 8-inch-wide cast version now be pushed, after Rudolf Uhlenhaut had already demanded this for some time.

Further tire tests, the results of which Dr. Liebold reported in a note to the tire development department on February 10, 1971, did not yield any significant progress either. The new Dunlop 245/60 VR 15s "again seemed quite disappointing," while the new Michelin 225/70 VR 15s, tested for the first time, "made a decent impression right away but did not allow for higher lateral forces than the 205/70 VR 15s with the same tread wear and air pressure."

Summing up, Liebold stated, "Best street tire is still the 205 VR 14, for which we are still urgently waiting for suitable light-alloy wheels. As the rolling out of the Fuchs wheels has obviously

Thanks to the dismantled hatch, the photos of car 33 show not only the shape and size of the trunk, but also the somewhat adventurous-looking routing of the exhaust system. As the picture on the right shows, other solutions would not have made it possible to have a trunk that was even remotely practical.

not led to any success, we now ask you again to have 14-inch magnesium wheels cast in 7½- or 8-inch width."

A few days before the second version of the C 111 celebrated its world premiere in Geneva, production of the three remaining test cars had restarted on March 4, 1970. By the end of the month, the floor assembly of car 33 (car 9 according to the old designation), the third car of the second series, was built in Sindelfingen and fitted with the drivetrain in Untertürkheim in April. The body was installed in Rastatt from the end of April to mid-May, and on May 25 it was delivered to Sindelfingen, where painting and interior finishing were carried out in June. Since operational four-rotor Wankel engines were still only available to a limited extent, the car, which was given registration number S—Y 6200, could not be completed with an engine until August 1970. The rebuilt KE 404 was used for this. The fluidic element for uniform tank emptying provided by the process engineering department in Untertürkheim in December 1969 was tested for the first time in this vehicle. Due to the tight test program to be completed with the few available vehicles and the tight schedule for the construction of car 31, neither a conversion of a vehicle of the first series nor an installation in the first car of the second version had been possible before. During the tests, the tank contents of both side tanks (a total of around 116 liters) could be withdrawn down to a minimal rest before the engine stopped, as Fritz Naumann commented in a note on September 30, 1970.

In accordance with the decision taken at the project meeting on November 12, extensive efforts were also devoted to the development of the tanks themselves, which were the focus of particular attention due to their exposed position in the side sills. On the one hand, unusual solutions were discussed, such as the combination of rigid tanks with a protective artificial gas bubble, but on the other hand, the use of flexible tanks was also discussed. A particular challenge was to comply with the diffusion limits required by the US authorities in the so-called shed test. In April 1970, different tank variants were tested for their accident safety during sledge tests at the Sindelfingen plant. The tank to be tested, filled with water and resting against a rigid barrier, was subjected to an impact force of 100 kp at about 10 m/s by a small skid. Aluminum tanks with and without rubber sheathing were examined, whereby the sheathing had a thickness of 2 or 3 mm and was glued to the tank or not. As a result, it was found that the aluminum body already cracked at the welding seam at comparatively low impact energy. However, due to the rubber coating, the tank remained tight, even when the aluminum body was torn open to a relatively large extent. The recommendation resulting from the tests was to use rubber-encased tanks with a layer thickness of 3 mm in a bonded design. Based on these results, all C 111s in the test fleet were converted to encased tanks from May 1970 on. For weight reasons, a coating of 2 mm thickness applied with an elastic adhesive was chosen.

In June 1970, side impact tests were also carried out with the tanks realistically installed in the vehicle. To obtain findings on the accident safety of the fuel tanks mounted in the side rails, the soft aluminum tanks used so far were compared with nylon fuel tanks from Pirelli. The question of the suitability of flexible tanks was also relevant because, according to the FIA decision of May 1970, elastic tanks integrated into a solid shell structure were mandatory for racing cars and racing sports cars in the future.

Sledge tests conducted in Sindelfingen in April 1970 served to investigate different tank variants. As a result of the test series, all vehicles in the C 111 test fleet were converted to fuel tanks with bonded rubber casing.

In June 1970, the provisionally repaired car 4 was used in side impact tests in Sindelfingen. The 1.4-ton moving barrier was first directed at the left side (*top pictures*) and then, in a later test, at the right side (*bottom pictures*) of the C 111.

Rudolf Uhlenhaut had then suggested that such tanks be considered in the development of the C 111.

The accident tests were carried out with the provisionally repaired car 24, the car from the first series that had been involved in the accident at Hockenheim. A 1.4-ton, non-deformable mobile barrier with its edge aimed at the front door gap collided with the test car from the front at a 45° angle. The impact at about 35 km/h was equivalent to the impact of a car travelling at about 50–55 km/h. In both tests, the permanent deformation depth in the center of the door was approximately 300 mm, with the fuel tanks being squeezed almost flat. The remaining survival space for the driver in the event of such a collision was classified as "still sufficient"—an assessment that must be evaluated against the background of the state of the art at the time and would probably be different today. The tests did not reveal a clear preference for one of the two tank designs: The nylon tank also cracked, and to a much greater extent than the aluminum tank. Since the diffusion test did not produce any promising results, it was decided to continue using the encased tanks made of soft aluminum for the time being.

At the beginning of 1972, there was once again movement in the tank development. In January, the test department contacted Autodelta in Milan; the motorsport subsidiary of Alfa Romeo had developed safety tanks in a patented honeycomb design that promised protection against fire in the first twenty to thirty seconds after destruction. In its reply, Autodelta stated that it normally only grants licenses for competition vehicles. In view of the experimental nature of the C 111, however, an exception could be conceivable that permitted the construction and use of such tanks against payment of a symbolic license fee of 100 lira. In the end, the cooperation did not materialize—mainly because the further development of the C 111 was by then no longer one of the priority goals.

A Firm Eye on Production Maturity: The Further Development of the C 111

On October 14, 1970, Dr. Liebold summarized the status of the further development of the C 111 since August in a test report—the last documented comprehensive report. At the same time, the last two test cars of the second series, cars 34 and 35, were nearing completion. One focus of development was the still not conclusively solved questions regarding ventilation and cooling. Tests with a new hood, in which only a small part of the cooling air was discharged upward and the rest laterally through the wheel arches, reduced the heating of the windshield but resulted in less efficient cooling of the engine. While the temperature in front of the center windshield was only 20°C–25°C (68°F–75°F) instead of 45°C–55°C (113°F–131°F) before, the radiator exhaust air with the new hood now had a temperature of 65°C–84°C (149°F–183°F) instead of 55°C–70°C (131°F–158°F) before. This poorer outflow prevented the use of the new hood, as on the second lap of the big circuit at Hockenheim the oil temperature already rose to 140°C (284°F), with the water temperature ranging between 90°C and 93°C (194°F and 200°F). A remedy was hoped for in the form of an increased fresh air outlet along the lower edge of the windshield, which was to be investigated in car 34. For this purpose, the newest vehicle, as well as car 35, had been given an additional opening in front of the headlights for ram-air intake. In other respects, car 34 was unique. It was the only car in the second series to have a trunk that was accessible from the outside via a separate flap without opening the hood. A similar solution had already been implemented in car 22 at the end of August 1969.

In the aforementioned test report, Hans Liebold also rated the engine cooling system itself as still in need of major improvement, despite the numerous measures already implemented, and noted that the heat emission of the individual engines apparently showed a wide variation: Car 31, for example, still reached 140°C (284°F) oil temperature with the KE 402 engine at water temperatures of 86°C–89°C (186°F–192°F) despite damp and cool outside air, while the same car had "just about" managed with the KE 406 at 27°C (81°F) outside temperature and dry air at the beginning of July 1970. A slight improvement (not for the driver, as Liebold noted) was provided by the fully switched-on heater, which achieved an oil temperature of 139°C and water temperatures of 84°C–85°C (183°F–185°F). The enlarged heat exchangers with constant flow planned for car 34 thus suggested a slight but not yet sufficient improvement. As a conclusion, Dr. Liebold saw it as inevitable to change the cooling air intake (if possible together with the fresh air intake), for which he considered a widening of the front of the car necessary.

However, the test report of October 14 also contained good news: "More favorable results could be achieved with regard to the intake noise that used to be dominant some cars." With the help of a snorkel tube placed at the lower end of the air intake behind the driver's door, the intake noise could be almost completely suppressed throughout the entire rev range without any loss of power. In contrast, the exhaust noise—which was subjectively satisfying as long as the silencers were "not yet blown out"—was rated as still slightly too loud based on the measured values of up to 89 phons.

Further advances concerned the fueling and the accelerator pedal. The fueling, which was initially perceived as very awkward with the new body, could be improved by slanted filler necks, so that fueling could be carried out at normal speed again. The double-clutching pedal initiated by Uhlenhaut, which in its original hanging version to the left of the main pedal had not been entirely satisfactory, was further developed and integrated into the main accelerator pedal. This was made possible by a solution developed by Fritz Naumann, in which the standing accelerator pedal was articulated on its transverse center axis, so that one could accelerate as usual with the front foot over the upper half of the pedal, while double clutching was carried out with the heel of the shoe over the lower half of the pedal.

On October 14, 1970, the same day that Dr. Liebold had written his summary test report, Fritz Naumann asked his colleagues from the engine test department to "pick an M 116 from series production and bring it up to the status of the U 18 in the endurance test vehicle C 101 E 45-25 with regard to the water pump, oil circuit, flywheel, and engine speed sensor." This was the second time that a C 111 was to be equipped with a V8 engine, "since we are currently unable to obtain a Wankel engine for the C 101-35 bodywork test car," as Naumann put it. On October 30, he received the reply that the engine was in the works and that delivery was scheduled for November 10.

Cultivation of a Super Sports Car: ABS, Air Conditioning, and Automatic Transmission

On October 1, Rudolf Uhlenhaut had determined to "equip the C 101 with the Teldix anti-skid brake control system" (i.e., the first version of the anti-lock braking system, developed together with the eponymous Heidelberg-based electronics company). The first C 111 to receive the brand-new system was car 34, which was then being built. The hydraulic unit was to be arranged to the right of the master brake cylinder, whereby the container for the windshield wiper fluid positioned there had to be relocated. The electronic control unit was to be installed in the front of the car, where the spare wheel had previously been housed, which did not necessarily have to be carried along for road tests.

Also at the beginning of October 1970, Rudolf Uhlenhaut suggested that the "C 101 with automatic transmission, ABS, and air conditioning" be demonstrated in Geneva "in order to continue to justify the 'mobile laboratory' designation." This provided another reason to push the construction of four-rotor engines of construction stage III. For installation tests, a corresponding dummy with refrigerant compressor and second alternator was delivered on October 14. In mid-November, Uhlenhaut also expressed a number of wishes regarding the bodywork, which Dr. Liebold recorded in a note dated November 17. For example, all cars were to receive the easier-to-open doors with optimized gas-filled dampers as well as the improved ventilation. The air conditioning system should at least be prepared for all vehicles so that it can be installed "to the extent that construction stage III engines are available."

For longer journeys, "provision for a strap-on suitcase should also be made that matches the shape and color of the car. The fact that this cuts off the direct view to the rear must be accepted. . . . In addition, great importance is once again attached to maximum thermal insulation of the trunk." Uhlenhaut had already demanded to make provisions for two externally mounted trunks—as well as air conditioning—for the second version of the C 111 in August 1969. But his wishes went even further, as Liebold

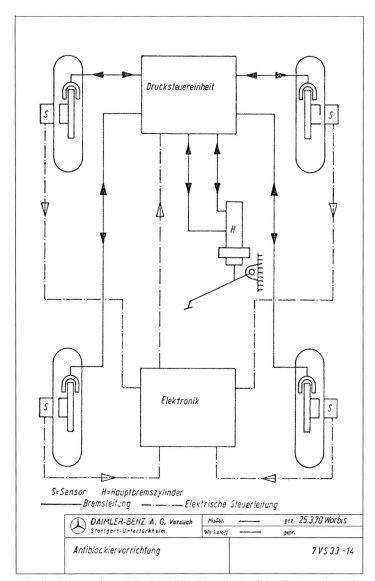

Principal illustration of the "anti-blocking device," the first version of the anti-lock braking system developed together with Teldix

reported: "Mr. Huber has promised to deliver suitable ski racks within the next eight days. Provision must therefore be made for the strap-on trunk and ski racks to be used together." Unfortunately, no further information about the ski rack is documented, but there is a series of pictures of the "strap-on trunk" dated January 26, 1971, with the Sindelfingen bodywork test car 24 a, which shows two externally mounted trunks of different sizes. The larger of the two made the best possible use of the space available on the hatch between the two side panels.

The subject of trunk temperature, repeatedly addressed by Uhlenhaut, was also examined in detail in December 1970. The measurement program carried out with car 33 included the motorway drive to Hockenheim and three laps of the big circuit, both without additional ventilation, as well as two further cycles: three laps on the big circuit with extraction through the engine air filter and two laps at Hockenheim with extraction through an electric fan. During all test cycles, the temperature in the trunk was recorded at four different measuring points. Interestingly, the trunk heated up only marginally during the tests without ventilation and only briefly exceeded the 20°C (68°F) limit. It was similar with extraction through the engine air filter: The trunk only heated up by a few degrees and always remained below 19°C (66°F) over the course. With extraction by the electric fan, starting at a temperature of 19°C (66°F), there was initially a drop to 15°C (59°F), but then a heating up to 28°C (82°F) and a renewed drop to 20°C (68°F). This meant that the trunk had passed its thermal test—at least in the conditions prevailing during the measurements—and heating up due to engine waste heat was no longer relevant.

Uhlenhaut's requests for improvement also partly concerned points that Karl Wilfert had criticized in August–September 1970 and that Friedrich Geiger had documented in two notes. For example, Wilfert had noticed that the car was getting too hot and that there was not enough visibility to the side and down at the rear. When looking back, "there is an effect that makes you believe that an overtaking car is approaching." This "malaise is to be

The Sindelfingen designers found a solution that was as unusual as it was attractive for the "strap-on trunk" demanded by Rudolf Uhlenhaut.

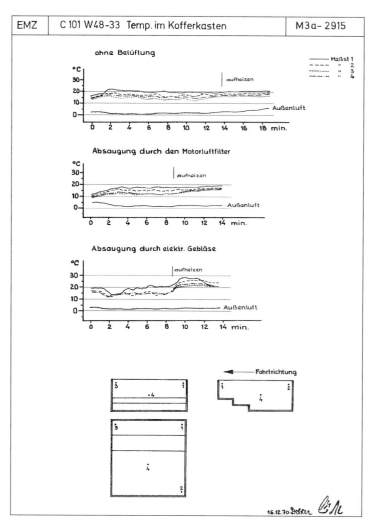

The series of tests carried out on car 33 in December 1970 to measure the trunk temperature was vividly presented by Albert Dobler, a member of staff at the measurement center of the development division in Untertürkheim.

Car 33 on the test track in Untertürkheim

remedied by a black or an identification color." What was obviously meant here was the painting of the hatch with matte black paint, as was then done from January 1971 on, starting with car 24 a.

To better assess the temperature balance and its dependencies, cooling performance measurements were carried out on car 31 in the large wind tunnel in Untertürkheim from October 26 to November 4. This confirmed the assumption that the electric radiator fans, which were absolutely necessary for low speeds, considerably obstructed the air flow at higher speeds from about 120 km/h. As a solution, Dr. Liebold suggested freewheeling fan blades or blades with an adjustable angle of attack right after the start of the investigation.

Further measurements from November 23 to December 4, 1970, yielded findings that were as detailed as they were interesting. With the aluminum coolant radiator used, which had a block depth of 68 mm and a frontal area of 23.4 dm², the following extractable heat quantities were measured at a permissible temperature difference of 75°C (167°F):

Car 24 a, the "bodywork test car" stationed in Sindelfingen, received a partial matte black paint job for the top of the hatch and the air outlet ducts of the hood in January 1971.

v [km/h]	Extractable coolant heat [kcal/h]	Coolant heat of the engine [kcal/h)]
150	83.000	63.000
200	104.200	80.000
250	115.000	95.000
300	123.000	105.000

This led to the realization that the coolant radiator alone was quite sufficient. The oil cooler mounted in front of the water cooler reduced the amount of heat that could be dissipated by 26% at 150 km/h and by 19% at 240 km/h. The test report stated, "The coolant temperatures are made unacceptably worse by the upstream oil cooler." In addition, it was shown that the oil cooler, with a width of 200 mm and a frontal area of 14.6 dm², was only able to dissipate a heat quantity of 45,800 kcal/h at a permissible engine oil temperature difference of 100°C and a speed of 300 km/h, while the target value of 75,500 kcal/h was 65% higher. The test report got to the heart of the matter: "The oil cooling system is thus completely inadequate in its current state. This results in engine oil temperature differences of over 150°C. It does not make sense to increase the size of the oil cooler in front of the coolant radiator, as this further worsens the water temperature. . . . In order to get into a useful operating range of the oil cooler, approximately four times the oil quantity is necessary. To achieve healthy conditions, a revision of the oil circuit is inevitable."

Another result of the tests was an increase in the amount of heat that can be dissipated by 10% if both heat exchangers were also used for heat dissipation. This corresponded to an improvement in the coolant temperature difference of approximately 7°C (45°F). To achieve a satisfactory cooling situation, the following measures were recommended as necessary in the test report:

1. Accommodation of the water and oil cooler side by side in the front end
2. Coolant radiator frontal area 19 dm²
3. Oil cooler frontal area 17 dm²
4. Oil flow rate approximately 200 kg/min at 7,000 rpm
5. Adaptation of the oil line cross-sections to the larger quantity

By arranging the water and oil coolers next to each other, a reduction in the windshield heating by half was additionally promised. The test report recommended that in connection with the investigation of how to realize a larger radiator frontal area, it should also be examined whether all the cooling air could be discharged downward. Other conceivable solutions already proved infeasible during the investigation—a forced-air oil cooler in the rear failed due to the amount of heat that could be dissipated, and dissipating the oil heat via the coolant would have required too much construction work for an oil-water heat exchanger.

In January 1971, Dr. Liebold summarized the results of a meeting in which the findings of the cooling performance measurements and the possibilities for improvement derived from them were discussed. Design investigations showed that the required radiator frontal area of approximately 35 dm² could be realized by widening the front of the car by approximately 70 mm to each side. For this purpose, the course of the outer edge of the body between the front of the vehicle and the A-pillar had to be changed. Apart from the improved cooling performance, this change promised further advantages: reduced heating of the windshield, more effective heating and ventilation, and, finally, a hood that can be opened even when the headlights are popped up. Against this background, it was not surprising that it was decided to implement this change, even if the bridges between the headlights and the hood resulting from the widening incurred the displeasure of the stylists for design reasons. A 1:5 model of the new variant with a widened front end was inspected at the passenger car technical meeting on March 10, 1971, and approved by this body on April 7, 1971. However, the implementation had to be put on hold for the time being, as the completion of the ESF experimental safety vehicle had absolute priority.

At the beginning of February 1971, the first rear axle for the C 111 designed for use with an automatic transmission was built. The four-speed automatic with hydraulic clutch had been developed from the production transmission of the Mercedes-Benz 600 (W 100), with each shift point specially adapted and the transmission housing completely redesigned for the integral axle drive. However, the installation in car 34 could not be realized immediately, as the planned engine was not yet available. On January 28, Liebold had already urgently requested in a memo to the engine test department that only the stage III four-rotor engine KE 412 be made available on time, as car 34, planned for the demonstration in Geneva, could now no longer be equipped with a stage II engine (due to the differently arranged additional assemblies). On the test bench it then becomes apparent, as the engine test stated in a note dated

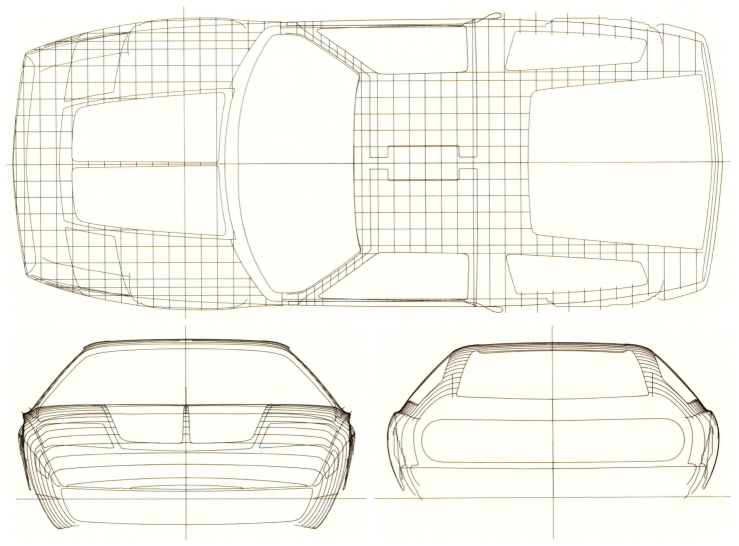

Scanning plan of the C 111 with widened front end. The plan was created by scanning the 1:5 model and accordingly still shows certain inaccuracies—especially in the area of the rear wheel arches. Clearly visible are the bridges between the front flap and the headlights created by the widening.

The four-speed automatic transmission adapted for use in the C 111 consisted of a completely newly developed transmission housing with integrated rear axle drive and differential.

February 10, that the KE 412 could not be operated with more than 5 liters of oil in the oil pan due to oil entrainment in the blow-by. Since 5 liters was considered too low as the maximum oil filling in car operation, the engine was converted to dry sump lubrication. On the test bench, it could be driven perfectly with 7 liters of oil up to 7,000 rpm, but the oil outlet temperature was over 150°C at the above-mentioned speed. For car operation, the engine test department recommended that the function of the dry sump lubrication be checked again with regard to filling quantity and oil entrainment.

Further challenges arose regarding a possible demonstration in Geneva. Test runs with car 26, which was equipped with ABS, had shown that the front brakes could not withstand the stresses when ABS was used. Against this background, a demonstration of the C 111 with ABS at the Geneva Motor Show was considered a risk, especially "if journalists are allowed to drive it at will." The problems and delays meant that the planned presentation of the further developed C 111 at the 1971 Geneva Motor Show did not materialize in the end.

Progress and Stagnation: The Development Status in May 1971

On May 11, Dr. Liebold documented the development status in a note to head of development Scherenberg, who had commissioned an analysis of the scope of work required for possible small-scale production of the C 111 in a letter dated April 29, 1971. The project manager pointed out that no more mechanical or thermal damage had recently occurred on the engines of construction stage II and that an engine with IKA apex seals had already completed 20,000 test kilometers. The first stage III engine intended for testing with automatic transmission and air conditioning, on the other hand, had "so far only run briefly with great difficulty (throwing oil with and without dry sump lubrication, unsatisfactory water circuit, extreme exhaust heat)." The production of further engines is progressing slowly, so that endurance run results for this construction stage are not available. It is also feared that the output of the four-rotor engines complying with future emissions regulations and equipped with standard silencing will be reduced from 350 hp/257 kW to 280 to 300 hp (206 to 220 kW). With a pre-silencer as an afterburner, the stricter USA regulations would be met by 1975 without regard to exhaust noise.

As far as the floor assembly is concerned, Liebold stated that in the opinion of the design engineering department in Sindelfingen, "primarily the plastic floor assembly in sandwich construction" can be considered for series production. The first floor assembly was to be delivered in mid-August 1971. A total of nine test cars would be needed for tests in Sindelfingen and Untertürkheim and for testing the plastic floor assembly.

As for the body, Liebold thought it would be possible to test the widening of the front end, which he hoped would have positive effects, in car 31 from August on. Regarding the drivetrain, he stated that ZF required a lead time of twelve months for series production of the five-speed transmission with the desired ratios. The dual-disc clutch from Fichtel & Sachs still had to be fully developed but would then be available on short notice. So far, only a four-speed clutch transmission had been used briefly as an automatic; testing of the planned four-speed torque converter transmission was expected to begin in a few months.

Liebold also presented detailed figures on the development effort: "For the production of the first six test platforms, the UT test department (without engine departments, but with mechanical production and chipless forming) required an average of 9,300 hours per car, for the next six cars 3,800. An average of 2,250 hours was spent testing each vehicle. Considering the somewhat changed situation, we reckon on about 4000 h of production and 3,000 h of testing for the proposed nine cars per vehicle; i.e., a total of about 60,000 to 65,000 hours (excluding engine development and Sindelfingen scope)."

With regard to the current and future performance of the four-rotor engines, the engine development department had its say on May 6, 1971. To achieve the prescribed noise level with the same silencer size, the output would have to be reduced from 350 to about 300 hp (257 to 220 kW). Taking into account the exhaust gas detoxification regulations foreseen (e.g., in California from 1972 on), the output would drop by a further 5% because a reactor (5-liter capacity) would have to be installed in the exhaust system. The extent to which performance will be further reduced by the California 1975 emission standards is not yet known. In January 1972, the developers did give corresponding forecasts on the performance values with exhaust gas detoxification: for 1974, in Europe 300 hp/ 220 kW and in the USA 260 hp/191 kW; then for 1976, 280 hp/ 206 kW and 240 hp/177 kW, respectively. For the maximum torque, they gave a value of 40 mkp, which could be in a speed range between 3,000 and 5,000 rpm, depending on the design.

Car 34, with registration number S–Z 4170, whose first test with automatic transmission, air conditioning, and ABS had taken place in February–March 1971, could be used again since July 1971, as Dr. Liebold recorded in a note to the head of development on August 2. The stage III engine, installed for the first time, would lack more than 50 hp/37 kW compared with the previous engines. The clutch transmission still shifted very harshly, but it was not worth investing further development work, as a four-speed torque converter transmission should be available from autumn. The spring setup also had to be corrected after the higher weight on the rear axle had made stiffer springs necessary.

A few days later, on August 6, Rudolf Uhlenhaut determined that all C 111s should be equipped with ABS, especially cars 31 and 33, as well as the Sindelfingen test car 24 a.

On August 13, Liebold took up the perennial topic of oil temperature again after the testing of car 31 with the now-widened front had begun. The body modification enabled not only a larger air intake, but also sufficiently large water and oil coolers, which could now be arranged next to each other instead of one behind the other as before. In a note to engine boss Bensinger, Liebold noted that although the water temperature was perfect under all circumstances, the oil still reached "the previously always respected limit of 140°C [284°F]" when driven in extreme conditions ("small circuit in Hockenheim, racing style") from an outside temperature of about 28°C (82°F). Liebold described the flow rate of 43 liters per minute, measured at an oil temperature of 125°C (257°F) and 7,000 rpm, as far too low and considered it essential to beef up the oil circuit through the cooler (e.g., by increasing the size of the oil pump or by increasing the drive speed). In their response, the engine designers pointed out a number of possible measures that could remedy the situation in the future, but first referred to a heat balance measurement they had carried out at the IMH research institute of Prof. Huber in Munich.

At the beginning of 1972, a presentation of the further-developed C 111, equipped with automatic transmission, air conditioning, and ABS, was again envisaged in Geneva. On January 25, Dr. Liebold approached his colleagues from the engine test department and asked for the accelerated construction of a stage III engine, as the KE 412 installed in car 34 was very unsatisfactory in terms of performance. Three weeks later, on February 17, Liebold took up the issue again. The KE 416 engine, under construction in the further-developed stage IV version, was now to be provided for car 35, which was then being prepared for tests with rear tanks and torque converter transmission. KE 416 was therefore equipped with a cast oil pan and air-conditioning compressor, as well as a flywheel driver for torque converter transmissions.

On February 29, 1972, Dr. Liebold again stated that car 34, which had been running "since this week with a torque converter transmission," should receive an engine with higher output as soon as possible. Since the KE 416 originally planned for the now-canceled demonstration in Geneva was then being fitted into car 35, Liebold asked for another four-rotor engine with a stage IV housing, dry sump lubrication, air conditioning compressor, and flywheel for automatic transmission to be built from the existing parts.

Car 34 had already delivered important results a year and a half earlier. In June 1970, it had completed rigidity measurements in the body test department in Sindelfingen. Body constructor Klaus Matthias, who was to play an important role in the further

The automatic transmission, modified for use in the C 111, was tested in car 34 in the spring of 1971.

Car 31 after the widening of the front section, during which additional air intake openings and rectangular additional headlights were realized at the same time. The photo was taken in July 1972 on the test track in Untertürkheim.

development of the C 111, had already suggested in January 1970 that the floor system of car 9 be planned for rigidity measurements, after this had not been possible with cars 2 to 6 (and then again with cars 7 and 8) for reasons of time. Finally, car 10 (in the new designation car 34) was used. On the one hand, the load-bearing sheet steel floor assembly was measured, and, on the other hand, the "ready-to-fit body" (i.e., the combination of the floor assembly with the riveted and glued plastic body). Contrary

The frame floor system of car 34 during rigidity measurements in the body development department in Sindelfingen

to expectations, the measurement showed that the body accounted for a high proportion of the overall rigidity of the assembled bodywork: The torsional rigidity between the axles and the specific torsional rigidity of the passenger compartment increased by 30% due to the bodywork, and the deflection was reduced by as much as 22%. Interestingly, the rigidity values were improved compared to the floor assembly of the Sledge, although a deterioration by 40% had been calculated due to the longer wheelbase, the modified rear axle, and the installation geometry in the rear area. The torsional rigidity between the axles was 30% higher, the specific torsional rigidity in the passenger compartment was 8% higher than in the Sledge, and the deflection at the side rails was 14% lower.

Car 35, registration number S–AN 6611, had initially been fitted with a 3.5-liter V8 engine in December 1970, since no Wankel engine had been available, and was used for bodywork testing. In the spring of 1972, it was fitted with two rear tanks—cuboid fuel tanks of 35 liters each, mounted on the left and right of the bulkhead in the engine compartment. In May 1972 it finally received the KE 416 four-rotor engine, which had a number of improvements over its predecessors. The core of these measures was the so-called variable-length intake manifold, which Wolfgang Kalbhenn—the project instigator of this book—had devised and developed. This innovative design had already been tested in the two-rotor engine, and a patent application was filed by Daimler-Benz AG on August 3, 1972. Patent specification DE 2238238 C2, titled "Suction line of a reciprocating internal combustion engine," identifies Wolfgang Kalbhenn and his boss at the time, Karl-Walter Schmidt, as the inventors. Thanks to the variable-length intake manifold, the engine already provided noticeably improved torque in the lower and middle rev range, which was 10% to 20% higher than before. Already from 2,000 rpm, the four-rotor powerplant heaved a tremendous 38 mkg/ 357 Nm onto the eccentric shaft. In addition, this significantly optimized torque curve was supported by a resonance exhaust with a pipe cross-section of only 25 mm, which transitioned to a larger cross-section required for exhaust gas aftertreatment about 70 cm aft of the manifold. This special exhaust configuration also resulted in a misfire-free, stable idle speed of only 635 rpm and significantly reduced the tendency to jerk in overrun mode. The engine was specified according to the emission regulations valid in Europe at the time and was also designed for optimal intake and exhaust noise silencing. Exhaust

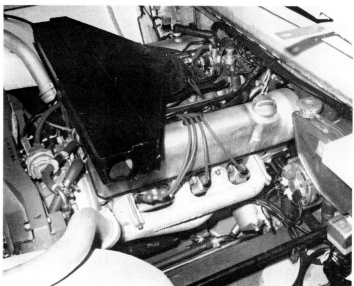

Car 35 was fitted with a 3.5-liter V8 engine from the M 116 series in December 1970, as a four-rotor Wankel engine was not available.

ducts with blow-down enabled slow exhaust port opening and thus contributed to noise optimization. All this progress, however, had to be bought with reduced peak power, which was "only" 304 hp/224 kW at 6,000 rpm. Despite this loss, the power delivery of this four-rotor power unit evoked the almost incredulous amazement of project manager Dr. Liebold during the first test drive, as lazy gear changing was now finally possible. For example, the improvement in lap time on the small circuit at

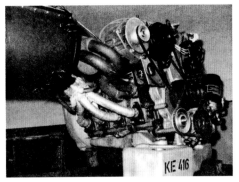  

In this configuration, the KE 416 four-rotor engine, equipped with a variable-length intake manifold, provided noticeably improved torque in the lower and medium speed range.

Hockenheim by shifting gears 2 to 4 compared to operating only in fourth gear was less than one second. Over time, car 34 also received an engine with a variable-length intake manifold.

From the very beginning, the development of the C 111 and all its components had been carried out in the design engineering and test departments with the utmost meticulousness and, despite massive time pressure, with the

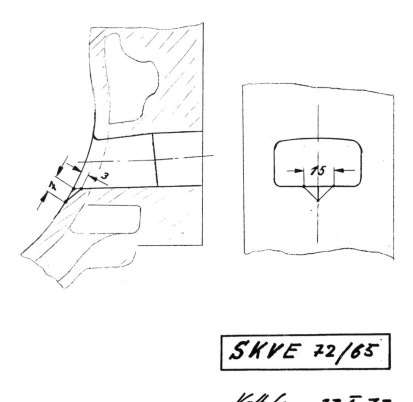

The exhaust duct with blowdown shown in the drawing by Wolfgang Kalbhenn enabled slow outlet opening and thus contributed to noise optimization.

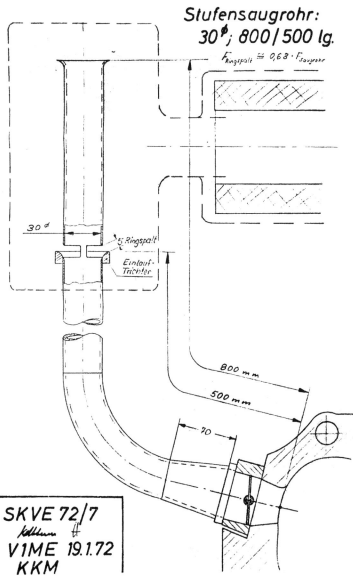

The variable-length intake manifold was first developed for the two-rotor version of the M 951 engine and presented by Wolfgang Kalbhenn in this design drawing.

attention to detail typical of Daimler-Benz. Even though in the context of this account it is the common theme that takes center stage, and not every facet of the development could be included, the variety of considerations and investigations is nevertheless comprehensively documented by countless test reports and memos in the company's archives.

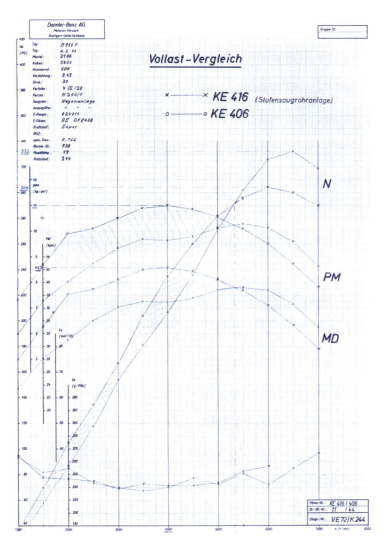

The full-throttle comparison contrasts the KE 416 with variable-length intake manifold system with the KE 406, which is basically identical in construction and has a conventional intake manifold: Although the variable-length intake manifold reduces the maximum power from 332 hp/ 244 kW to 304 hp/224 kW, the torque increases from 31 mkp to 38.2 mkp already at 2,000 rpm, and with 42.3 mkp at 4,000 rpm is also clearly above the 37.0 mkp without variable-length intake manifold.

Test and Demonstration Drives with the C 111

Only appropriately instructed drivers were given the opportunity to drive a C 111—also because the clutch burned out very quickly if left "feathered" for too long; for example, when starting uphill. First of all, the enthusiastic test drivers from the advance engineering department, such as Dr. Liebold, Fritz Naumann, and Joachim Kaden, and, on suitable occasions, grand seigneur Rudolf Uhlenhaut, got behind the wheel, of course.

During VIP visits to Sindelfingen or Untertürkheim, one of the dream sports cars was gladly made available and demonstrated. Such demonstrations are documented, for example, for the star conductor and car enthusiast Herbert von Karajan (in April 1971), for pop star Udo Jürgens (in September 1969), for the French chansonnier Gilbert Bécaud, also known as "Monsieur 100,000 Volt" (in April 1970), and for the amateur racing driver King Hussein of Jordan (in December 1970). Also the Apollo 14

Rudolf Uhlenhaut and Dr. Hans Liebold with a C 111 of the first series, taken in Hockenheim in August 1969

The C 111 test fleet in August 1971 during a family photo at the Hockenheimring: Car 31 (fitted with a widened front shortly before), car 34, car 33, and car 25, still fitted with a V8 engine (*from left to right*)

astronauts Alan Shepard and Edgar Mitchell, who completed geological field training in the Nördlinger Ries impact crater in August 1970 in preparation for their flight to the moon, were given the opportunity to take a ride on the test track as part of their visit program, together with their backup crew Eugene Cernan and Joe Engle as well as geologists Mike McEwen and Fred Hörz. During the visit of German President Walter Scheel in October 1974, as recommended by then chairman of the board Zahn, "a certain restraint should be exercised in demonstrating the C 111 . . . and the focus should be on DB's activities in the field of noise and emission absorption, and on the electric bus." Nevertheless, Walter Scheel also had the pleasure of riding along on a test drive with the then latest example of the C 111 and head of development Hans Scherenberg at the wheel.

Stars among themselves: the C 111 with Udo Jürgens (in September 1969), Gilbert Bécaud (in April 1970), and Herbert von Karajan (in April 1971)

Apollo 14 astronauts (*right to left*) **Alan Shepard** and **Edgar Mitchell** with their backup crew **Eugene Cernan** and **Joe Engle** at a demonstration of the C 111 on the test track in August 1970

Daimler-Benz Board Member for Development Dr. Hans Scherenberg had the rare pleasure of chauffeuring a German President in October 1974 at a demonstration of the C 111 on the test track in Untertürkheim.

Protracted Decision:
The Question of Series Production

Protracted and controversial discussions about a possible series production had characterized the C 101 project from the very beginning. In a memo to Hans Scherenberg, the member of the board responsible for development, and Rolf Staelin, the member of the board responsible for sales and marketing, Arnold Wychodil, the member of the board responsible for exports, and his employee Heinrich Will had stated on March 5, 1969, after talks in the USA, "We expect this model to have good sales potential in the USA, but provisions should be made for the USA also to equip this vehicle with air conditioning and possibly a radio." At the board meeting on March 10, 1969, Scherenberg advocated for the production of about fifty vehicles. When asked by Staelin, he let the board know that "the asking price . . . was DM 20,000 to 25,000"; that is, in the ballpark of a Porsche 911 at the time. His colleague Wilhelm Langheck, who was responsible for passenger car production, also pointed out at this meeting that if the Wankel engine was presented "at the 1969 IAA, it would have to be built in series production by 1971 at the latest." In order to build the C 111 in a small series of fifty units, Scherenberg explained, "It is now absolutely necessary to approve the investments of 2.5 million already mentioned in the last board meeting." Staelin pointed out that "such a small number as fifty vehicles for sale—domestic and export together—was unrealistic." Finally, the board "agreed to carry out a study of the possible number of C 101 cars to be produced (alternative, e.g., 50–500 units) with regard to sales

New guiding star of the model range? The C 111 in August 1969 with Mercedes-Benz production sedans during test and demonstration drives at the Hockenheimring.

potential, investments, costs, price, and general effects on the passenger car range."

The aspects of the C 101 associated with the presentation and possible series production were also discussed controversially at the passenger car commission meeting on March 21, 1969. It was critically noted that "a presentation of this car at the 1969 IAA would mean a certain commitment of Daimler-Benz AG to the Wankel engine." We must therefore "ask what will happen with the Wankel engine at Daimler-Benz AG after the possible presentation of the C 101 with a Wankel engine at the 1969 IAA: Will the Wankel engine go into series production in other cars? If so, in which cars? Is it conceivable that Daimler-Benz AG will one day replace all its petrol reciprocating engines with Wankel engines?"

Uhlenhaut stated that "the development division is working on the installation of the Wankel engine in our various passenger car models; as is well known, decisions have not yet been made as to in which production models the Wankel engine will be installed as an alternative or later solely." He referred to "the development of new cylinder heads with two overhead camshafts and to the V-engine development. This work proved the importance the development division attaches to the reciprocating engine." In his opinion, "the C 101 with a Wankel engine does not interfere with our other passenger car range. At the IAA it will be demonstrated that we are coming onto the market with a new V8 engine. From the point of view of the development division, the purpose of the C 101 is to enhance our sporting image, as requested by the Board of Management, even though the C 101 as a customer car is not at the same time suitable for competitions at Le Mans, Daytona, or Sebring." Uhlenhaut also stated that even in the extreme case, he could not imagine that "the entire petrol reciprocating engine production at DB will be replaced by Wankel engine production in the foreseeable future."

The members of the commission agreed that the C 101 "must also be sold in larger quantities" if it is shown at the IAA. The majority of the commission members feared "that the C 101 would then really have to be fully developed as a vehicle for sale" and would inevitably impact the work on the W 116. It was decided to compile a technical description, the schedule situation as well as the investments, operating resources, and prime costs for a total run of 250, 500, and 1,000 cars at a production of 1-2 cars per day as a "basis for the final decisions of the Board of Management on the entire C 101 with Wankel engine issue."

Zigzag Course: Test Series with Fifty Units?

At the board meeting of March 25, 1969, Scherenberg again advocated for "enrolling 50 more C 101 cars now," also pointing out that the C 101's approval for competition depended on a minimum series of fifty cars being built. Schleyer pointed out that in his opinion, "a presentation of the C 101 with a Wankel engine at the 1969 IAA must inevitably lead to the impression in the public mind that we have now decided in principle in favor of the Wankel engine." This could have "extremely critical consequences for our entire range of volume-produced vehicles." In his opinion, therefore, "the decision on such a course of action should be postponed until we finally have a full picture of the question of the further use of the Wankel engine." This also applied to the requested enrollment of fifty vehicles. He went on to say "the launch of an initial series of fifty vehicles would inevitably have the consequence of a larger production run and thus have corresponding repercussions on the evaluation of our volume-produced vehicles (with conventional engines) by the clientele." Langheck shared Schleyer's view but considered it "indispensable to provide for the Wankel engine as soon as possible for volume-produced vehicles as well, with the consequence that during a transition period, reciprocating and Wankel engines would have to be produced and offered simultaneously." Scherenberg underlined in this context that "it does not seem justifiable to him to oppose the foreseeable future development" and continued, "The problems that have existed up to now with regard to the Wankel engine now seem to be largely solvable. This also applies to the question of exhaust gas detoxification. It therefore looks as if the familiar advantages of the Wankel engine—including lower manufacturing costs and facilitation of the modular design principle—may come to fruition in the foreseeable future." However, he saw "the possibility of sufficient testing in special vehicles" as a prerequisite for the use of Wankel engines in large-scale production, for which he considered the C 101 to be "exceptionally suitable." Moreover, "starting with the R/C 107, all vehicle models under development are being prepared for the optional installation of Wankel engines." Against the background described above, Scherenberg once again recommended that the enrolment of fifty vehicles be approved.

Board spokesman Joachim Zahn concluded by explaining that "for the production of the fifty requested vehicles, relatively minor capital expenditures . . . in the amount of approximately DM 2.7 million . . . are necessary and "in view of the importance of the entire Wankel development for the future development of our company . . . considered it justifiable to spend these funds even if it should turn out later that it is expedient to dispense with the presentation and sale of the C 101." Accordingly, he proposed to approve the requested enrollment "with the proviso that a final decision on the use of the vehicle—including any presentation date—be deferred until the statement announced by Scherenberg on the possibility of a future use of the Wankel engine in the volume-produced passenger cars is available."

The minutes of the meeting document "agreement that the final decision on the use and presentation of the C 101 with a Wankel engine is dependent on the presentation of a concept for the future use of the Wankel engine within the range of volume-produced passenger cars by the development division." Ulrich Raue, responsible for the commercial vehicles production division, suggested that in the run-up to a final decision, it should be examined "to what extent it is possible and expedient to launch the C 101 not only with the Wankel engine but potentially also with a V8 reciprocating engine at the same time." This could "weaken the impression of the superiority of the Wankel engine over the reciprocating engine for series production when DBAG presents a vehicle with a Wankel engine for the first time."

Based on the preceding discussion, the board passed the resolution to approve the enrollment of fifty vehicles of the C 101 with a three-rotor Wankel engine—at Zahn's suggestion, however, subject to Schleyer, who had left the meeting in the meantime—subsequently giving his consent. At the board meeting on April 15, however, it was then stated—in the absence of Hans Scherenberg—that "the planned enrollment of fifty C 101 vehicles has been postponed for the time being." The minutes went on to say, "Since the planning of the development division does not permit the production of the vehicles until the first half of 1970 anyway, it would seem possible to reconsider the entire complex of questions—especially the quantity to be enrolled and the expected production costs—in detail before a final decision is taken. This will not affect the production of the first 5-6 vehicles."

Despite all internal considerations and discussions, series production of the C 101 was apparently out of the question for the trade press. *auto, motor und sport* wrote in its issue of April 12, 1969, "Of course, as interesting and attractive as such a sports car will be for a large number of customers, especially in the USA, it will never be able to meet the comfort requirements placed on a 280 SL, for example. It would therefore be absurd to assume that the C 101 (it will be given a different name by the time it is presented) could replace the current model series of sporty provenance at Mercedes-Benz. Rather, the Wankel sports car from Untertürkheim—of which, if it is to be considered for the Gran Turismo category, at least 1,000 units will have to be built from 1970 onward—will remain something very unusual, lovable, and unique in the car range of the Daimler-Benz."

Four weeks later, in the May 10 issue, the trade journal was even more specific: "With the C 101, of which *auto motor und sport* published the first realistic sketch in issue 8 . . . , the Mercedes stylists have thrown all the traditions associated with the Mercedes radiator and star overboard. . . . The 110 cm low C 101 (as it is provisionally called) is far more than an experiment. It is to be built in small series and brought to market at a price of about 25,000 marks. The sales prospects are excellent: Interest in exclusive sports cars is growing all the time. The Italian luxury sports cars, most of which are considerably more expensive, are being ripped out of their manufacturers' hands. . . . Daimler-Benz will probably build Wankel engines and reciprocating engines side by side for many years. The C 101 is thus the beginning of a development planned over the long term. It marks an important turning point in the company history of Daimler-Benz: In addition to the sense of tradition, there is a future orientation; technically and stylistically, new ground is being broken.

In Figures: The Cost Estimates for the C 101

On April 9, 1969, the advance manufacturing planning department in Sindelfingen had already prepared a cost estimate for the production of the C 101. The expenditure of DM 77,200 per vehicle calculated in the report—for labor and operating costs of the Sindelfingen scopes alone and excluding material costs—did not seem "justifiable for a production run of fifty vehicles." The recommendation of the advance manufacturing planning department was, accordingly, "Based on our rough estimate, at least 500 to 1,000 cars should be built." In any case, the sales price originally quoted by Scherenberg must have seemed completely illusory under the circumstances.

In a meeting on April 17, attended by Werner Breitschwerdt (head of body testing), August Knapp (head of advance manufacturing planning, preproduction shop Sindelfingen), Dr. Kurt Enke and Erwin Löffler (advance design engineering), and Rainer Schick (development organization and planning), the question was discussed to what extent a production quantity of 1,000 vehicles would result in "postponements for the C 101 and the W 116, R and C 107 projects." The discussion led to the realization that, on the one hand, no further design effort would probably be required, but on the other hand, the mid-October deadline for the approval of the body could only be met if the American, Swedish, and right-hand-drive versions did not have to be available right from the start. Within this framework, it was assumed that the preproduction shop vehicle would be built in mid-March 1970 and that series production would begin four months later. In this scenario, series production of the initially postponed variants was to start at the beginning of March 1971. Since the decision for the body material had not yet been made, 0.8 mm thick steel sheet or 1.5 mm thick aluminum sheet was favored for manufacturing reasons—with the comment that "Mr. Wilfert and Mr. Breitschwerdt would like to study the use of plastic for the floor and body despite the longer development time." The opportunity to do so was to arise quickly. Still in April, the choice fell on a plastic body, and this is also where the roots for the development of a variant with a plastic floor assembly lie. On April 17, a sheet steel body was still favored for the exhibition car at the IAA—on the one hand, because of the surface quality, which was considered better than plastic, and, on the other hand, because it

Against the background of a possible series production, detailed documentations were created in the responsible specialist departments. The beginning was made by the "Description C 101," drawn up on June 13, 1969, by Theodor Reinhard, Construction Passenger Car Bodies.

was less susceptible to dents caused by overly intensive contact with trade fair visitors than aluminum.

In a very detailed note to Dr. Scherenberg, Karl-Wilhelm Müller, head of development organization and planning, shed light on all the important aspects of series production. He first stated that the fifty vehicles in the board's decision could only be a preproduction series and not a test series, as no more than the six test vehicles already enrolled would be needed for the development of this model. This differentiation seemed particularly important because the development capacity of the test department in Untertürkheim and Sindelfingen was not able to produce "fifty cars of the C 101 without suffering a significant setback in the R 107, C 107, and W 116 development work." Müller's conclusion was that the fifty vehicles should be built "with the cooperation of the test departments in the production plants, if necessary." An additional design effort, initially considered for the revision of the concept as a basis for the production of 1,000 vehicles, was deemed unnecessary, as discussed in the previous day's meeting. In a rough calculation, Müller estimated the cost of the test production of fifty cars in Sindelfingen at about DM 73,000 (of which DM 5,000 for materials) and in Untertürkheim (for engine, axles, transmission, labor, and materials) at about DM 25,000, resulting in an estimated total production cost of DM 100,000. For a quantity of 1,000 vehicles, Müller assumed a reduction to about DM 73,000, taking into account the necessary operating resources. However, he clarified, "The aforementioned figures must be treated with

Preliminary equipment description C 101, drawn up on June 15, 1969, by Advance Manufacturing Planning of the Preproduction Shop

great caution as they are based on a very rough estimate. In any case, this consideration shows that more than fifty vehicles will have to be built if a fairly reasonable price is to be realized." He concluded by suggesting that "this whole complex of issues [be] dealt with as soon as possible, since nothing will be done on the part of production until there is a board decision on the production of the fifty preproduction vehicles."

On April 21, the technical meeting in Sindelfingen dealt not only with the cost situation, but also with aspects of production. According to the calculation of the preproduction shop, fifty vehicles would cost about DM 8 million, so that "according to Mr. Wilfert, at least 1,000 vehicles, better 1,500 to 2,000 vehicles, should be built." The previous enrollment of fifty vehicles as a test series would [as stated by Karl-Wilhelm Müller] mean that the factories do not carry out any production engineering. "Several combinations of steel, aluminum, and plastic" were discussed as possible materials. Reports were given on investigations of a body production in Sindelfingen, on negotiations with Bayer Leverkusen, and on a visit to the Waggonfabrik Rastatt, whose plastic parts production is working for Porsche.

At the board meeting the following day, Wilhelm Langheck, member of the board responsible for production, mentioned that "there are already some preliminary calculations for the C 101, which show that costs of about DM 70,000 for the body and about DM 50,000 for the chassis and engine are to be expected for the first 5 vehicles. For the planned 50 additional vehicles of the C 101 model, costs of approximately DM 40,000–50,000 per unit should be expected." He pointed out that "in contrast to the 300 SEL [presumably the V8 model 300 SEL 6.3 was meant, the author], we cannot not fall back on existing production parts for the C 101" and that "obviously the completion of the W 116 would be affected by the development work on the C 101." Rolf Staelin commented on the expected costs mentioned by Langheck that "due to the resulting pricing, this model will only be of interest to a very narrow group of buyers." Board spokesman Joachim Zahn added that "however, if the quantity is small (e.g., 300 units in total), it would be justifiable to refrain from passing on the full cost in the price and apply the difference to the budgets for development and advertising."

In mid-May, the central pricing department sprang into action and, with a view to the board meeting on May 20, prepared a paper dated May 14, 1969, on technical equipment, competing vehicles, and the crucial issue of "costs and price," which was outlined:

"Recently, widely varying cost valuations of DM 25,000 to DM 70,000 have been quoted for the C 101. This is due to the fact that the technical scope of delivery is still subject to continual changes. For example, it was unknown until recently whether the vehicle would receive a very expensive aluminum body or the supposedly much cheaper plastic body.

Even today, there is still uncertainty about the production quantities with their impact on the cost level. The board initially agreed to an enrollment of five vehicles.

C 111—Form, report of the stylists' department of August 28, 1969

"The aforementioned results in a completely uncertain cost situation, so that costs are currently ruled out as a guide for pricing. It would be desirable that the development division provides the departments estimating costs with sufficient documentation for initial project calculations as soon as possible.

"In this situation, it seems right to us to primarily use the market or competitive situation for the C 101 as a basis for pricing considerations. The competitive comparison [with nineteen sports car models] shows that the C 101 is comparable with vehicles costing DM 60,000 and more in terms of new equipment features and its performance. We are of the opinion that at the present time, an asking price in the range of DM 50,000 to DM 60,000 is right. It is unfortunate that one could already read the completely inadequate asking price of approximately DM 25,000 mentioned in-house in a trade journal. We will give further consideration to the pricing of the C 101 once costing documents are available."

The latter were not long in coming. On May 19, probably also as a basis for the board meeting the following day, the business administration department prepared a first detailed cost estimate for the C 101 based on the reported estimated values of the Sindelfingen and Untertürkheim plants and communicated the result to the board.

The estimated prime cost per vehicle was DM 76,200 for a total of 50 vehicles, DM 51,700 for 500 vehicles, and DM 46,500 for 1,000 vehicles. For "racing tires with the corresponding aluminum

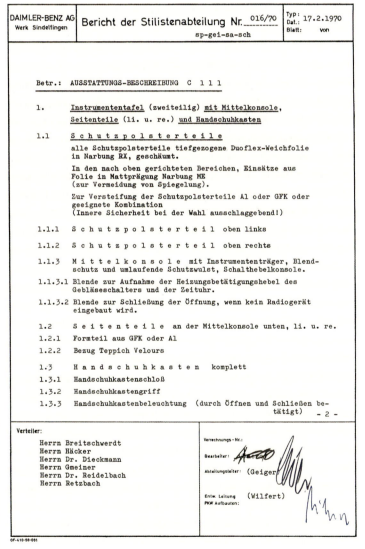

Equipment description C 111, report of the stylists' department of February 17, 1970

rims," additional costs of DM 2100 were estimated in this scope. In view of these figures, the concluding statement seems very cautiously formulated: "The present cost estimate confirms our previous view that the asking price of DM 25,000/vehicle quoted by others does not ensure cost recovery."

Ongoing Discussion: Costs, Dates, and Capacities

At the board meeting on May 20, the production of the C 101 was discussed again, among other aspects. In the event that the car should only be produced in small numbers, Rolf Staelin raised the question of "in what way sufficient service possibilities should be ensured, especially since limiting sales to individual countries does not seem feasible in practice." As had been the case four weeks earlier, Wilhelm Langheck was again skeptical, noting that "considerable development capacity is now being used for the C 101." The start-up of a significant series does not seem "possible in any case before the end of the year." Moreover, "under the given circumstances, it is not yet possible to assess whether the presentation of the C 101 will lead to success or failure." Based on the cost estimate from the previous day, he pointed out that "the preliminary costing of the C 101 with a production of fifty units came up with prime costs of approximately DM 76,000, and, with a production of 1,000 units, a prime cost of approximately

```
Stil.Ber. 016/70       - 3 -

4.2      H a u p t l i c h t s c h a l t e r
         und angeschlossene Ausfahrvorrichtung für Scheinwerfer, mit
4.2.1    Standlicht
4.2.2    Abblend- und Fernlicht
4.2.3    Parklicht re. u. li.
4.2.4    Nebelscheinwerferschalter
4.3      Warnblinkanlage
4.4      Lenkschloß mit Zündschloßschalter
4.5      Zigarrenanzünder
4.6      Betätigung für Scheibenwaschanlage
4.7      Frontklappenentriegelung
         (auf Vorderwandsäule links unten)
4.8      Heckklappenentriegelung
         (im Mittelteil auf d. Rückwand)
4.9      Schalthebel
4.10     Handbremshebel
4.11     Sicherungskasten
         (in der Instrumententafel unten rechts, hinter dem
         Handschuhkasten)

5.       H e i z u n g  -  L ü f t u n g  -  K ü h l u n g
5.1      B e t ä t i g u n g s h e b e l  (4 Stück) für Heizung
         und Lüftung (auf Blende)
5.2      G e b l ä s e s c h a l t e r  (auf Blende)
5.3      K l i m a - S c h a l t e r  (nur bei Kühl-Anlage)
5.4      L u f t d ü s e n  rund (4 Stück)
         auf der Instrumententafel, nach oben gerichtet, durch
         Drehung des Einsatzes verschließbar.
5.5      L u f t d ü s e n  rechteckig (3 Stück)
         auf der Instrumententafel, nach dem Fahrer gerichtet,
         durch Hebel verschließbar.

6.       S i t z e
6.1.     S c h a l e n s i t z :
6.1.1    Sitzkissenschale mit eingespannten Zugfedern
6.1.2    Polsterung Gummihaarmatte mit Watteauflage
6.1.3    Bezug:
         Kunstleder Narbung WV, Mittelteil Polsterstoff,
         querlaufende Absteppungen

                                                    - 4 -
```

```
Stil.Ber. 016/70       - 4 -

6.3      Sitzführungsschienen mit Feststeller
6.4      Rückenlehnenverstellung
         (auf der Innenseite, daher linke und rechte Sitze!)

7.       S i t z - S e i t e n t e i l e  u n d
         Z w i s c h e n t e i l
7.1      S e i t e n t e i l  (li. und re.)
7.1.1    Formteil aus GFK oder Al mit offener Ablage
         (für sperrige Güter, z.B. Rolleiflex u.ä.)
7.1.2    Bezug:
         Kunstleder Narbung WV
7.2      Z w i s c h e n t e i l  (in der Mitte, von der Schalthebel-
         konsole nach hinten)
7.2.1    Formteil aus GFK oder Al mit offener Ablage,
         Befestigungsmöglichkeit für die Heckklappenentriegelung und
         Schlitz für den Handbremshebel.
7.2.2    Bezug:
         Kunstleder Narbung WV.

8.       T ü r e n
8.1      V e r k l e i d u n g s t e i l e
8.1.1    Türinnenteil und Rahmen mit Kunstleder Narbung WV ausgeschlagen
8.1.2    Einsatz im Türinnenteil aus GFK oder Al mit Bezugstoff versehen
8.1.3    Einsatz am Türoberteil (Himmel mit Bezugstoff versehen
8.1.4    Verkleidungsteil für Befestigungspunkt der Gasfeder
8.2      Türzuziehgriff (lange Schlaufe) mit Halterung
8.3      Griff zum Öffnen der Türe
         (beide Grifffunktionen können nicht vereinheitlicht werden)
8.4      Türöffner
8.5      Schloß
8.6      Drehfenster-Schnellbetätigungsgriff
8.7      Lautsprecherblende
8.8      Verstellhebel für Außen-Rückspiegel

                                                    - 5 -
```

DM 46,000." Dr. Hanns Martin Schleyer believed "an enrollment of fifty vehicles only seems to make sense if a series of at least 1,000 units is subsequently brought to market" and asked "whether Scherenberg is prepared to take on the associated responsibility given the current state of Wankel development." The head of development took the view that "it will not be possible to avoid a decision on the Wankel question anyway. However, such a decision cannot be based purely on test bench results but must be underpinned by practical experience on the road. . . . From this point of view alone, the 50 vehicles of the C 101 under discussion are necessary, even if they are ultimately not sold but only available for testing purposes." Rolf Staelin considered "the handing over of not yet fully developed vehicles to a group of persons, however defined . . . to be questionable in any case as long as it was to be a real sale." On the other hand, it seemed to him "fundamentally problematic to produce a vehicle from the outset in such small numbers that it can only be sold to a small proportion of the potentially interested parties."

Joachim Zahn pointed out that "as a result of what has been published in the meantime, we are already largely committed with regard to our further course of action" and shared Scherenberg's view that "in principle, it does not appear reasonable to approve a Wankel engine for installation in production vehicles without the corresponding practical road experience being available." All in all, he considered it "urgent, given the state of affairs, to first do everything possible to make at least a few examples of the C 101 ready to demonstrate and drive by the 1969 IAA." In contrast, the determination of a possible group of customers could still be deferred. Ulrich Raue, member of the Board of Management responsible for commercial vehicles, was of the opinion that "a possible departure from the previous decision-making process would have a detrimental effect in the public eye, and, on the other hand, sufficient support for a small series of fifty units would in any case be much easier than for a series of, for example, 1,000 units." With regard to the cost situation, board spokesman Zahn explained that, "based on the cost estimates mentioned by Langheck, the construction of an initial fifty vehicles would not cost more than approximately DM 3.5 million." He considered "such an expense acceptable in view of the importance of the whole matter even if the amount in question were to be fully at our expense." With regard to the future pricing, he expressed his regret that "due to obvious renewed indiscretions in our company, information had appeared in a specialist publication in which a price of approximately DM 25,000 is mentioned." On the other hand, "the preliminary cost estimates and price comparisons made in the meantime suggest to consider prices of DM 50,000–60,000, whereby the decision on this question could be "deferred" for the time being. In summary, Zahn saw "the production approval of a Wankel vehicle as a matter of fundamental importance within the meaning of the standing rules."

In conclusion, Scherenberg made the motion "to confirm the decision taken on March 25 and to approve fifty vehicles of the C 101 model for registration under the conditions set out in this decision." This would leave it to him to "apply for the actual production of the vehicles depending on the progress of the development work—if necessary also in individual lots." A resolution on the approval of further quantities could be postponed. Scherenberg's application and the resolution of March 25 were ultimately unanimously confirmed by the board, and the enrollment of fifty vehicles was approved with the proviso that "production be carried out via parts list with requirements reporting." With the decision for this standard process, the production plants were in charge and the testing departments were relieved of the responsibility for the production of the planned preproduction series.

In a memo dated June 20, 1969, the program planning department in Sindelfingen took up the board's decision and defined the following dates for the start of series production of the C 101, which essentially corresponded to the scenario for the production of 1,000 units discussed on April 17:

Construction	
(only assembly drawings)	1.10.69–31.3.70
Preproduction shop	
specification vehicles	2.1.70–29.5.70
Workshop equipment production	1.12.69–30.4.70
Tools and dies—	
mallets and Cerrotru parts	3.11.69–30.4.70
Process engineering—	
plastic body by	4.5.70
Series—body shell work from	1.4.70
Series start-up, June 1970	2 cars
Quantities, July–Dec. 1970	8 cars each

As prerequisites for meeting the design engineering deadlines, it was specified that the chassis documents be provided by Untertürkheim by September 30, 1969, and that the design group be increased to twenty constructors if drawings of individual parts were necessary. This schedule does not seem very realistic from today's perspective, even if one bases it on ideal conditions and disregards all the challenges that were to arise during development and testing.

On August 26, 1969, this scenario changed fundamentally, as the advance manufacturing planning department of the preproduction shop summarized in a memo to the technical plant management in Untertürkheim: "The planned number of fifty vehicles spread over the months of June–December 1970 is reduced to ten. These vehicles are all different from each other (stylistics, axles, frames, etc.). The production is being taken over by the test department. A decision on the quantity and specification of the C 101 to go into series production is scheduled for October 1970. If there is strong interest in having the C 101 at the IAA Frankfurt, it is planned to move the decision on a series production to spring/summer 1970. Conclusion: All plans for the preparation of the C 101 for series production are to be discontinued on the part of Plant 10."

In contrast to these in-house business exercises, the press release prepared for the premiere in Hockenheim and at the IAA was unambiguous. "With the C 111 test vehicle, Daimler-Benz AG presents a sports car with a three-rotor Wankel engine that is one of the most advanced and interesting technical development projects in international automotive engineering. This car—only built in a few units—is not for sale. Rather, it is a piece of the future that gives the general public the rare opportunity to take a look behind the scenes of the Mercedes-Benz testing and development departments."

Mobile Laboratory, Test Series, or Series Production: The Future of the C 111

At the board meeting on October 22—four weeks after the IAA had closed its doors—Hans Scherenberg announced that he would prepare a concept for one of the next meetings on the future use of the Wankel engine within the range of volume-produced passenger cars and on further considerations regarding the C 111. In this context, he outlined the following possible uses of the C 111 in advance:

1. Continuation as an experimental vehicle
2. Production of fifty vehicles, some of which will be handed over to suitable customers
3. Launch of a small series corresponding to the earlier 300 SL sports car model with gullwing doors

On the same day, he asked the directors of passenger car development in Untertürkheim and Sindelfingen "whether we have any capacity at all, in addition to the work on the new models in testing and design engineering, to complete the vehicle by about the second half of next year in such a way that one can think of a point 2.) or 3.)" and "what facilities, e.g., for 3.) would have to be created, what they cost, and what the vehicles themselves then cost." He also tasked Karl-Wilhelm Müller to

One of the key questions for the future of the C 111: Will the Wankel engine be able to meet the high demands of the Mercedes-Benz developers in terms of its reliability and stability? The photo was taken at the Hockenheimring in August 1969.

"clarify things in cooperation with the departments concerned in advance so that the decision paper can be prepared shortly," adding: "In this, I ask you to work without the so-called 'enthusiasm factor.'" Regardless of the enthusiasm of the people involved, however, the decision paper for the Board of Management was to be quite awhile in coming.

One month later, on November 23, 1969, Scherenberg had his say in Bild am Sonntag. Under the attention-grabbing headline "Rather not for playboys!," the article addressed the future of the C 111 and the Wankel engine at Daimler-Benz and began with the statement "The success of the Mercedes C 111 experimental coupe with a Wankel engine is by no means a victory for the rotary engine at Germany's most renowned car manufacturer!" According to a quote from the head of development, "The work on the Wankel and on conventional new engines is running absolutely in parallel at our company!" The article went into the current status of Wankel engine development: "Neither in terms of durability nor consumption has the Wankel engine fully satisfied the engineers in Stuttgart-Untertürkheim so far. The literally hottest problem of Wankel engines, effective exhaust detoxification, is apparently closer to a solution at Mercedes than at other Wankel licensees." Then he quoted Hans Scherenberg again: "We don't yet know for sure for which area of application the Wankel is best."

With regard to the C 111, facts and half-truths were garnished with speculations: "The C 111 test car has already brought new insights. Four of the five prototypes built so far are currently being dismantled and modified. Some of the things happening with this coupe indicate that despite all the fundamental reservations about mass production of the Wankel, a small series of this sports car is now being considered after all. The wedge-shaped body is being made even more visually elegant. The beltline of the sports car will slide down considerably. With it, the rather high instrument panel. The side windows will be larger and the rear window (in front of the mid-engine) will also be enlarged."

Production and sales of the dream sports car also came up—again with a combination of facts and interpretations: "The concerns of the technicians are not the concerns of the C-111 fans. There are enough of them around the globe to build a significant series. The very first bidder to be registered was Karim Aga Khan. He wanted to order right away when there was not even a picture of the car. Since then, Mercedes has been besieged to build this car. At the London Motor Show in October, an interested party came forward to write a blank cheque for up to half a million for the C 111. The millionaires' enthusiasm for the supercar has perturbed some clever market strategists at Daimler-Benz. The C 111 was intended to polish the brand's sporting reputation. The jet-set's run on the dream car could renew in the general public the very psychological effect they seek to mitigate: Mercedes, the rich man's car. A group of market researchers groans: Don't sell the car just to playboys. Give it to great sports drivers instead. Mercedes is still on the Wankel fence . . ."

Eight days after the article appeared, on December 1, 1969, Scherenberg addressed the C 111 in a memo to his fellow board members: "As you know, we are exhibiting the C 111 with improved bodywork and four-rotor engine in Geneva. We should now be clear about what is to become of this vehicle. According to the ideas of the development division, it would be expedient to build the fifty vehicles starting in the second half of 1970 and to give it to interested parties to be selected. The main purpose of the vehicle is still to test the Wankel engine. Since we cannot start series production, even in small numbers—e.g., on special request in the R 107—without customer pre-production testing, I think it is necessary not to wait too long with this. We need broader experience with the Wankel engine here in the near future. This also applies to the exhaust system, which now delivers good values but is still unclear in continuous operation. I may have to take advantage of this opportunity for our USA export as well. After the customer trial of the 30 or so cars (out of the 50), either an increase (e.g., to 60) would have to take place or a small series for sale would have to be started, which in my opinion would not be possible in 1971–72. I propose to specify the procedure in principle. After that, there would have to be a program elaboration from which the timing etc. could become clear."

In January 1970, the question of series production was again taken up in the press. In an article that even had the headline "No standstill in the development of the Mercedes Coupe C 111" on the front page, *Stuttgarter Nachrichten* quoted an unspecified voice "from Untertürkheim" on January 22 under the headline "Mercedes Coupe C 111 not only exhibition object." "Should the interest of buyers in the C 111 continue to increase, Mercedes will of course act accordingly and include the C 111 in its sales program. This C 111 should then have a brilliant future ahead of it." Immediately afterward, however, came the more easily comprehensible statement, "Whether the Mercedes C 111 will be built in series production is to be decided in about half a year at the earliest." The report then went into quite a lot of detail on individual development priorities such as durability, oil consumption, and emissions issues, ending with the statement, "About 40 engineers are involved in the development program of the C 111. Now they have set about improving the visibility and improving the car in a few other ways as well. A series of 45 more models is still to serve even more in-depth research and development work." Here, the author of the article had apparently taken the preproduction series of fifty vehicles, which had been controversially discussed from the beginning, at face value.

"Rather not for playboys!" was the headline under which *Bild am Sonntag* reported on the development status of the C 111 in its issue of November 26, 1969, quoting Dr. Hans Scherenberg, head of development.

On January 29, another report appeared in *Stuttgarter Nachrichten* under the headline "C 111 does not go into series production," exposing the earlier article as a classic press hoax: "Mercedes reconfirmed its decision not to mass-produce the C 111 model with a three-chamber Wankel engine and not to put it on sale. Daimler-Benz knows very well from the orders still coming in that there are a lot of people interested in buying this supercar. Nevertheless, Mercedes will not sell a single C 111. The Untertürkheim plant believes it owes it to its customers to bring only cars of the highest perfection to the market. But the C 111 is an experimental vehicle."

Influencing Variables: Wankel Engine and C 111 as Image Factors

A little later, an article in *auto, motor und sport* of January 31 reignited the in-house discussion about the Wankel engine. Deputy editor-in-chief Reinhard Seiffert wrote in his test report on the NSU Ro 80: "Pessimistic news leaked out from the strong anti-Wankel camp at Daimler-Benz: The exhaust problems could not be solved, the exhaust gases were too hot, the exhaust systems too heavy. . . . W. D. Bensinger, engine development director at Daimler-Benz, recently gave a lecture in Stuttgart in an overflowing auditorium in which he hinted at possible solutions to all existing problems . . . It is also due to Bensinger's highly advanced development work that a spectacular Wankel development platform, the C 111, was put together." In connection not only with this article, board member Heinz Schmidt addressed his colleague Hans Scherenberg in a note dated February 4: "I am aware that a technical discussion, which is unavoidable especially in this area, must also be held here, but I believe that in the overall interest of our company we should avoid letting controversial points of view leak. In my opinion, there is only <u>one</u> position of our company on this issue, and that is the one you are presenting." In his reply, the head of development wrote, "Of course, this whole Wankel issue is difficult and is therefore an interesting topic for the press, but it often degenerates into sensationalism. . . . Of course, there are optimists and pessimists among us, but on the whole, the attitude is clear and points to us having to continue the tests and there being certain prospects of realization. It seems expedient to curtail further presentations, which I have arranged." In fact, on February 23, Scherenberg had informed the directors of development that "the response of the various presentations . . . was not always pleasant for our company," referring to the article in *auto, motor und sport,* "which talks about different camps." Accordingly, the head of development asked that "no presentations of any kind be given on the Wankel engine problem in the near future."

On March 5, Scherenberg again received a note from his fellow board member Heinz Schmidt, this time regarding the use of the C 111 in public relations. Schmidt was referring to a paper by his colleague Horst Wendt, head of advertising, who had summarized his thoughts on the future handling of the C 111: "The C 111 . . . is not suitable for lending to customers or other interested parties. The car is not manageable without a driver or without driver training. We have to reckon on accidents, but above all with annoying many people who want to buy this car but do not want to borrow it and find that we are lending a larger quantity of it. . . .

"My suggestion is this: We build 50–60 vehicles after they are largely mature. We keep about 15 units of these vehicles in the factory for exhibitions, press receptions, demonstration drives, film making, and tests. The remainder of 35–45 units are loaned on the basis of careful selection. . . . Because the figures who drive this vehicle determine the opinion about this car and thus also about our company. If the C 111 falls into the wrong hands, the entire benefit for the image development of our company is lost. We should leave the image of this car tough.

"Therefore, I propose to lend the car to an elite group of racing and sports car drivers for the duration of one year. This group could be joined by a second group of opinion-forming personalities who should be recruited from the field of modern technology. . . . This group of people should receive the C 111 as a test vehicle with a booklet in which they must make certain

Even if they are only orange cones instead of curbs, the reminders of a racetrack are certainly no coincidence. The picture shows the first C 111 of the second generation, taken in March 1970 on the test track at the Untertürkheim plant.

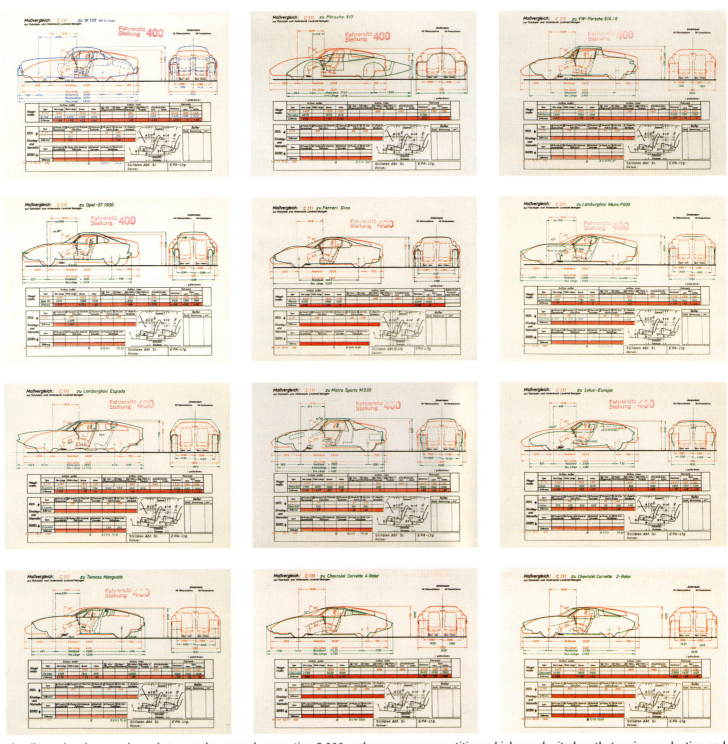

The dimensional comparisons between the second-generation C 111 and numerous competitive vehicles make it clear that series production and market launch of the C 111 were seriously considered.

entries. These entries and driving impressions will be evaluated at the end of the year and presented to the public in a big campaign."

Regardless of the company's controversial deliberations on the future of the C 111, the press release published on March 6, 1970, for the forthcoming presentation of the second version in Geneva maintained the status quo. In doing so, it once again dampened the high expectations of experts, the media, and the public with regard to a possible series production. "The design of the 'Test Lab C 111' as a two-seater sports car with a mid-engine makes it possible to achieve extreme stresses on the body and major assemblies in driving. The purpose of the further intensive work on the C 111 at the moment is neither series production nor sports use, but to answer many unanswered technical questions. Development on this piece of the future is continuing."

In an interview with the Austrian Broadcasting Corporation given at the Geneva Motor Show, head of development Scherenberg commented on the development status and future of the Wankel engine at Daimler-Benz and reiterated the position described in the press release: "We have been developing our Mercedes-Benz Wankel engine for nine years now, and we are in the process of putting it through even more stringent testing, and the result will one day lead to decisions having to be taken. However, these decisions have not yet been taken today . . . The possibility of testing the Wankel engine in an accelerated manner is essentially given, of course, if you use a sports car for it. But this is not the only reason why we built this sports car as a 'mobile laboratory'; namely as a test car. Not only was our Wankel engine to be tested with all its many advantages in tough conditions on the road—the disadvantages were to be improved and reduced as far as possible in the process—but there were also other questions that interested us in connection with the C 111." Scherenberg mentioned the plastic body, the mid-engine, as well as axle designs as focal points and concluded with the sentence "So, as I said, we have created a mobile laboratory for our testing department to study a number of urgent development issues." When asked by the reporter, the head of development confirmed that the car is not available for purchase "because we wouldn't sell a mobile laboratory," and the inevitable question about racing participation also received an unequivocal answer: "No, there is no thought of, say, racing."

Former racing driver Paul Frère—one of the few journalists to whom Daimler-Benz entrusted the wheel of a C 111—was given the opportunity to drive the new version of the dream sports car at racing speed for the March 1970 press demonstration, having already driven the first version in September and October 1969. In his test report published in *auto, motor und sport* on April 11, 1970, he stated, "When I got out of the latest version of the Mercedes-Benz C 111, which I drove for 12 to 15 fast laps around the small circuit of Monthoux near Geneva, my first thought was 'It should be called C 112 or C 222 now, because from the cockpit it has very little in common with its predecessor.' . . . The plastic body has not only been improved considerably in terms of visibility and luggage space; it is also incomparably more elegant in its lines. . . . As interesting as the first version of the C 111 was, the interesting parts could not hide some shortcomings. The parts of the car in front of the windshield was completely out of the field of vision. . . . Butter, skin cream, and similar goods soon turned into oil, milk, and other liquids in the trunk, and on the motorway you had to be bloody diligent with the gear changes if you didn't want fat gentlemen with cigars in their 6.3 sedan to pull away from you when accelerating below 160 to 180 km/h—all rather embarrassing when you came along in such a conspicuously sporty car! That has now changed—even if it is still better not to carry butter in your suitcase. But you look out of the new C 111 like out of a Porsche Targa, and for acceleration, even if you are a bit lazy changing gears, the torque is now always sufficient to accelerate at least as fast as other road users expect from such a racy-looking vehicle. . . . No decision has yet been made at Daimler-Benz about the future of this fascinating project. Fast and racy as it is, the C 111 became a luxuriously equipped and robustly built car that still weighs 1,260 kg. . . . For use in major sports car races, the C 111 would have to be completely redesigned. And even then, it could no longer be used after 1971, because engine capacity restrictions will be introduced in 1972 that would exclude it. It is much more likely that it will one day go into production as an ultra-fast GT car. Today, the four-rotor version would not only be the most comfortable and quietest, but also the fastest such car: The 300 km/h stated by the factory seems credible given today's performance. I am firmly convinced that there are thousands of customers in the world for such a car, for whom the price is of no significance at all, whereby hundreds would immediately buy the car simply because of its novelty, without giving a thought to the Daimler-Benz board that the engine might not yet have quite the same service life as an equivalent reciprocating engine. Daimler-Benz should not miss this opportunity and consider that it would be unwise to prepare a grave for the C 111 next to the never-used world record-setting car in the Daimler-Benz Museum. For such an end would look like the public confession of a misstep. And the C 111 in its current form is certainly not that."

Other journals and magazines expressed similarly positive views. *Bunte Illustrierte* magazine wrote in March 1970, "The most sensational car of the year." In his eight-page article on German cars, which appeared under the title "The Germans Are Coming" in the June issue of *Playboy* and was also devoted in detail to the C 111, author Ken W. Purdy went one step further:

"The C-111 is almost certain to be the sensation of at least the first half of the Seventies . . . As this is written, Mercedes-Benz is performing its classic publicity blitz, making an experimental prototype two-seater the most photographed, most written-about automobile of the year . . . ; the C-111 is a breakthrough vehicle of notable significance, indeed—an ultrahigh-performance automobile powered by the revolutionary Wankel engine. Even the announcement of its existence was instantly recognized all over the world as a bench mark in automobile history."

Hobby magazine concluded its detailed article on the C 111 published in the April 1970 issue with the sentences "So if the C 111 is a mobile laboratory, then Daimler-Benz is quite kind to its lab technicians. For this is 'jet-set equipment,' the likes of which are by no means better encountered in a Ferrari or Lamborghini. So should a select few be allowed to buy this car as an exception after all? We think yes; rumor has it that there will be 500 of them, but we only pass that on with all due reservations. There is even a trunk between the Wankel and the rear, an indication of 'serious intentions.' We also don't see why the Mercedes people should keep this car to themselves; the only reason would perhaps be that the Mercedes service organization is not yet geared to the Wankel. And they are fastidious about that, especially as they would have to be accommodating with a mechanic on a plane at that price.

"It is interesting that there is such a Mercedes (C 111) and that the oldest car factory in the world has taken a giant step into the future."

Despite the extremely positive assessment in the press and the appeals to the company to put the vehicle into production, the decision-making process continued to be difficult. At the board meeting of April 14, Frère's article and the photo report "New Cars 1970" published in the same issue were even the subject of controversial discussions. Rolf Staelin saw "a business-damaging event in these publications" and was of the opinion that "the underlying information could only have come directly from our company." The displeasure of the member of the board responsible for sales was probably mainly due to the fact that the preview contained a drawing of the W 116 that was at least halfway realistic, as well as information about the engines, including the 4.5-liter V8. Schmidt and Scherenberg countered that "dependence on the public's increasing need for information is also unavoidable for us," whereby Schmidt considered it remarkable that [in Frère's article] "the Board is directly addressed."

Independently of the discussions in the Board of Management, a brochure on the C 111 was published in mid-1970. This gave hope, even if the appearance did not quite seem to fit the high level of perfection and the expected price segment of the vehicle. At the Mercedes-Benz dealer, you looked in vain for this brochure, and you only discovered the catch when you took a second and very close look at pages 1 and 8. The sender was not Daimler-Benz AG, but Daimler-Benz Fahrzeug- und Motorenbau AG. This was not a subsidiary in the usual sense, but a so-called dummy company that had been founded in 1953 for the purpose of familiarizing the commercial trainees (then still called apprentices) of Daimler-Benz AG with the business processes of a public limited company through their own experience.

The employees of the dummy corporation proved to be very committed and creative. Not only were they—like many other employees of the "real" Daimler-Benz AG—fascinated by the promising dream sports car, but they also had fewer scruples than the Daimler-Benz Board of Management and included the C 111 in their production program. But much more than that, in order to be able to offer the vehicle at a price that—as the 1970 annual report announces—"is also interesting for young dummy corporation employees," a ckd version of the C 111 supplemented the range. The annual report of 1970 stated: "With this model . . . we have taken into account the wishes of those of our customers who, due to their manual skills, are able to assemble their car themselves . . . The kit, which consists of separately packaged, ready-to-install major assemblies, is completely identical to the conventional version, with the exception of some fasteners that have been modified to simplify assembly. This reduced the total assembly time for an experienced fitter to 150 man-hours."

 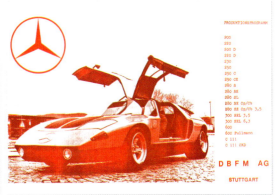

 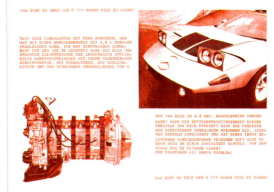

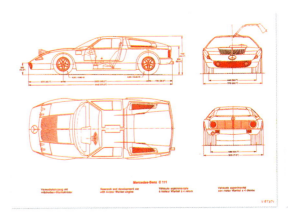 

Even if the appearance of the brochure did not quite match the positioning of the vehicle, many an interested party would certainly have been delighted if they had been allowed to fill in the order form on page 8—even if they only had enough money for the *ckd* version.

Detailed Analysis: Decision Paper on the Future of the C 101

Back to the reality of Daimler-Benz AG: In the meantime, the "concept . . . for further considerations regarding the C 111," which Scherenberg had announced at the board meeting on October 22, 1969, was gradually taking shape. Under the leadership of Karl-Wilhelm Müller, a very detailed elaboration titled "C 101—Preparation of a decision paper for the board on the further handling of the project" was produced. The paper contained a detailed technical description of the vehicle and addressed the costs, the deadline situation, the development status, the development capacity, and the response at the 1970 Geneva Motor Show, as well as sales and image issues.

With regard to the costs, the second cost estimate was included, which the business administration department had completed on the basis of the newly submitted information from the plants and addressed to the board members Zahn, Langheck, Scherenberg, and Schleyer, as well as the heads of the finance, product planning, and passenger car development departments, on March 5. The elaboration gave an estimated prime cost per vehicle of DM 103,500 for a total production run of 500 units, DM 78,000 for 1,000 units, and DM 65,600 for 2,000 vehicles. This included previously incurred as well as expected development costs totaling DM 13.2 million and tooling costs of DM 4.8 to 4.9 million.

In the summary, K.-W. Müller referred to the declared aim of the decision paper for the board: that it "compiles the criteria that are decisive for the future of the C 101 from a development perspective." The very first sentence was explosive: "Apart from market and image issues, making the C 101 ready for series production cannot be recommended because of the known overload on the development division due to the volume-produced models." The rest of the conclusion was no less sobering: "Even the production of a kind of '0-series' amounting to fifty units for partial testing in customer hands requires endurance testing on a broader basis, initially in-house.

"The development division is not in a position in the foreseeable future to create and operate the additional vehicles (+6) required to make them ready for series production, let alone commit to producing the fifty units.

"This situation contrasts, regrettably, with the public's response to the C 101, particularly at the Geneva Motor Show."

On the cover page of its 1970 annual report, Daimler-Benz Fahrzeug- und Motorenbau AG very clearly demonstrated the role of the C 111 in its model range.

In addition to the cost issue already described, the summary contained key statements on important points, which are reproduced verbatim below:

2.) Possible start of series production
Assuming sufficient development capacity, a start of series production would be possible at the earliest in the first half of 1972 (total production run 50 units February 1972, 2,000 units July 1972). An earlier start-up is also not possible for reasons of capacity for production preparation in Sifi [Sindelfingen].

3.) Development status
Overall vehicle:
There is a lack of road and rough road endurance testing on a broader basis. For a solid preparation for series production, another 6 prototype vehicles beyond the 3 vehicles of the 2nd version (Geneva) that have been completed or are in the process of being built would need to be created. Crash tests, as would have to be certified for a delivery to the USA, have not yet been carried out.

Engine:
The determining factor is the wear of the apex seal. At the earliest possible start of series production in 1972, the engine should have reached a level that would guarantee durability in road use by the customer for at least 50,000 km.

4.) Development capacity
Main bottleneck is design engineering and test department Sifi. The production of the 3 vehicles of the 2nd version for Geneva brought delays for R 107 and W 116 prototypes. In the event that the C 101 is made ready for series production, further delays for

W 116	by 3 months
W 123	by 4–6 months

would have to be expected.
Likewise, capacity bottlenecks in the preparation for series production in the areas EK1, V1A, V1EL [passenger car design engineering, major assembly test department, electrical systems test department] are to be expected. [Note: This assessment is based on development capacities still to be spent of 41,000 hours for the design engineering in Untertürkheim, 30,000 hours for the body design engineering in Sindelfingen, and 52,000 hours for the body test department Sindelfingen.]

5.) Questions of series production
  Scope Sifi—up to 500 vehicles
  Division of labor Sifi and Rastatt plants possible

Body skeleton	Sifi plant
Outer skin incl. doors, flaps, seat shells	Rastatt
Painting and final assembly	Sifi plant

  more than 500 cars

entire production incl. outer skin at	Sifi plant

  Scope Ut [Untertürkheim]
Engine can currently be produced up to a maximum of 15 engines/month (order of magnitude 500 total run). Beyond that, capacity increase required.
Transmission-axle drive (manual transmission) manufacture by ZF.
Front and rear axles in small series at Plant 10 (as far as not integral with W 116).
Steering (W 115 with modified ratio) Düsseldorf plant

6.) Response at the 1970 Geneva Motor Show
The C 101 is accepted in its present form practically without exception by the publication media, that can be considered the voice of the public. Overall impression, visibility, space, Wankel advantages, brakes, comfort, maneuverability, driving performance are all rated positively. The car is classified as a 300 SL successor and an imminent series production is taken for granted. To stop C 101 development would be to admit a mistake. A decision at DB would have to be made soon.

As K.-W. Müller formulated in a communication to Hans Scherenberg on April 17, "Mr. Uhlenhaut . . . did not agree with the recommendation formulated as a conclusion in the summary and therefore does not wish to sign it. In his view, the C 101 could be developed to production maturity by handing over a certain scope of the work to an outside company, leaving in-house development capacity untouched." Müller found this outsourcing proposal only partially expedient: "We cannot fully endorse this view, as in our opinion, even when outsourcing, the lead and thus a not insignificant commitment of capacity, particularly in the area of chassis and suspension design, is unavoidable."

The decision paper for the board did not live up to its name for the time being, as the board initially did not address the future of the C 101 any further but determined that the passenger car commission should discuss the further course of action. In its meeting 6/70, which was held in two sections on April 30 and May 5 due to a large number of agenda items, the commission engaged in a very close examination of the C 101, which is reproduced here in detail due to the controversial discussion and interesting insights. Dr. Hans Lorscheidt, head of product planning, at the beginning took the view that "the discussion of the C 101 . . . must take place completely openly and uninfluenced by . . . what has been published" and "that our company will succeed in presenting any decision on the further handling of the C 101 and the Wankel engine to the public through appropriate announcements by our company in such a way that our company suffers no damage whatsoever."

Uhlenhaut explained that "the passenger car development division must inherently deal with very fast vehicles for reasons of general research, [for] the general development of overall vehicles, and for the development and testing of future individual major components, regardless of whether the prototypes created for this purpose later go into series production or not. If the series production of a developed prototype is now proposed by the passenger car development division, . . . it can be assumed that the series version will achieve a sufficient service life."

There was agreement in the commission that "the development division must have the appropriate scope for its basic work . . .," but at the same time it was emphasized that "it can be very problematic if disclosures emanating from the development division are not coordinated with other departments." Lorscheidt expressed the opinion that "the Wankel engine was not only an interesting technical development, but also an object of speculation and publication of a high degree" and doubted that "the four-rotor Wankel engine could become a power unit that would meet DBAG's demands on quality and durability."

Uhlenhaut explained that "if the Wankel engine in the C 101 was to be sold to customers, it would have to last 100,000 km without an engine replacement. . . . Decisive improvements have been found for all major problems. The wear . . . can be reduced to 1/10 with newly developed very hard apex seals." He also saw no difficulties regarding exhaust gas purification "if the Wankel engine is equipped with afterburners, which . . . would also be required for reciprocating engines for the USA exhaust emission regulations from 1975 onward." As a result of the higher exhaust gas temperatures, the Wankel engine even has advantages here—just as with the requirements for the octane rating of the fuels. He mentioned the odor of the Wankel engine as an as-yet-unsolved problem.

Regarding the possibilities of use in motorsports, it was stated that "the C 101 is not suitable for participation in races of the racing sports car manufacturer world championship; e.g., SEBRING, LE MANS, etc." It would be conceivable to use private drivers in rallies and GT circuit races "where there are no competing cars with works drivers." The representatives of the sales division rejected "quite clearly that the C 101 is produced in the smallest quantity, total production run approximately fifty vehicles, regardless of whether these fifty vehicles are given to outsiders as amateur testers of DBAG, or are sold to exclusive customers." They stated that "the use of outsiders as 'amateur testers of DBAG' . . . would not be in keeping with the style of the company." "Selling only about fifty vehicles to the most exclusive customers would alienate thousands of other customers and have only negative consequences."

Helmut Schmidt, head of market research and sales planning, commented on the question of producing the C 101 in larger numbers, stating that "a very fast touring car with comfort . . . would of course be interesting for the sales division" and "could reach the total production run of the 300 SL (approximately 3,000 vehicles)." However, approval for series production of the C 101 would be tied to a number of requirements. These are reproduced here verbatim:

1. The C 101 must meet the usual demands that our company places on the quality and durability of our passenger cars with absolute certainty; i.e., the C 101 must be guaranteed to last 100,000 km without an engine replacement.
2. Series production of the C 101 is only a possibility if the Wankel engine is installed with absolute certainty in other vehicles in our future program.
3. The work to make the C 101 ready for series production must not cause any noticeable delay to the W/V 116 and W 123 projects.
4. Since numerous reports on the C 101 have already been published, series production would have to happen relatively quickly. If the C 101 was not sold until 1973, for example, it might already be outdated for the sales division.

Following these demands, which were understandable per se, but which in their combination set the bar very high and almost corresponded to the proverbial squaring the circle, Schmidt held out the prospect of an official statement by the sales division, coordinated with Rolf Staelin, which in his view would include the premises he had mentioned.

The representatives of the technical plant management mentioned further challenges from their areas of responsibility: Werner Fetzer, head of the preproduction shop in Sindelfingen, expected that "if a series start-up in the fourth quarter is to be achieved . . . the W 116 will be delayed by a further three months and the W 123 by four months." Hermann Haug from the plant management in Untertürkheim pointed out that "for the production of a larger number of the required engines of the C 101, neither funds nor spaces have been provided for so far." Uhlenhaut agreed with the general opinion that delays of the start-ups were out of the question, and reiterated his view, already expressed by K.-W. Müller in the minutes, that "the development work necessary to make the C 101 ready for series production in larger numbers run could be given to outside companies." Lorscheidt replied that this was then "an organizational problem of the development division regarding the handling."

Uhlenhaut was of the opinion that "DBAG should take a calculated risk by deciding immediately on a series production of the C 101 in order to achieve the earliest possible series start-up date" and pointed out that "other companies are also taking calculated risks; e.g., Boeing 747." Lorscheidt countered that "the C 101 for DB is different from the previous program and not as vital as the Jumbo Jet 747 for Boeing" and stated that he could "not imagine that the board would agree to series production unless clear deadline guarantees were given by the development division for a corresponding product program, stating at what point the four-rotor Wankel engine would reach the concurrently required mileage of 100,000 km." In this context, he quoted the longest individual distances achieved up to that time from a development division paper, which were 5,873 km for the three-rotor Wankel engine and 2,162 km for the four-rotor variant.

Finally, it was decided to continue the discussion of the topic at the next commission meeting. Helmut Schmidt was asked to "see that the statement of the sales division is available by this time." Afterward, a recommendation was then to be made to the Board of Management.

At the commission meeting on June 16, 1970, the "discussion on the further procedure regarding C 101" was continued. However, it was no longer a question of concrete substantive issues, which had previously been discussed in great detail. Rather, the determination was made that "two elaborations are necessary for the further handling of the issues C 101 and Wankel engine in the passenger car commission": the announced position paper of the sales division on the C 101 and the "statement of the development division on the durability of the variants of the Wankel engine (When does which Wankel engine reach which endurance run mileage?)." Helmut Schmidt announced that "a draft and statement from the sales division on the C 101 will be presented to the board by Mr. Staelin in the near future." The members of the commission were of the opinion that "no further disclosures should be made by our company on either the C 101 or the Wankel engine until there is clarity on how to proceed with regard to the C 101 and Wankel engine."

Image-Forming: The C 111 as Brand Ambassador

This statement subsequently caused irritation and led to discussions between the specialist units. In a communication to his colleagues on the Board of Management and the members of the commission dated July 2, Heinz Schmidt made it clear that on the question of further publications on the C 111, "the opinion of the public relations department responsible for this must probably be primarily consulted" and also announced that on the C 111, "an elaboration will also be submitted by my division." Friedrich van Winsen, who had attended the June 16 commission meeting as Rudolf Uhlenhaut's proxy, felt compelled to explain the statement criticized by Heinz Schmidt in more detail: "During the commission's discussion on this point, the focus was on the sales division's view that the Wankel engine should no longer be talked about externally as long as a series production use has not been decided. This view corresponds with the instruction that obligated the gentlemen of the development division not to give any further presentations or publish anything about the Wankel engine.

"I believe I represent the general view of the gentlemen from development when I see the C 111 primarily as a fast GT of modern character, with the focus on the overall concept rather than specifically the engine. I also expressed this view in the aforementioned commission meeting.

"The gentlemen from the sales division, however, were unanimous in their opinion that the C 111 is primarily seen as a WANKEL car by our customers. To what extent this is true, I cannot judge; but if it were true, holding back on publishing information about the C 111 would be the consequence of the Wankel order of secrecy set out at the beginning."

Independently of the activities of the passenger car commission, the statements made there, and the ensuing discussions, individual protagonists within the company had spoken out in May and June on the significance of the C 111 for the image of Daimler-Benz. On May 6, Heinz Schmidt referred in a memo to his colleagues on the board to an article by Reinhard Seiffert published in *auto, motor und sport* under the title "Der Kampf ums Image" ("The battle for the image"), which in essence presented a comparative assessment of the German car brands from an image point of view. Under the headline "Mercedes-Benz: generational problem," Seiffert wrote, "No image in the world seems as untouchable as the legend of the star. It reached its peak in the 600 model: Never before has so much solitary technical excellence been documented in a car.... But will people still be paying homage to the ideal of affluence expressed by a Mercedes in ten years' time? Daimler-Benz can only counter the danger of resting on its own glory by having the courage to try something new. And has already done so with the C 111. The C 111 is not needed for the Mercedes image of today. For the image of tomorrow, however, it is undoubtedly more important than the star and honeycomb radiator, the long-lasting but not imperishable symbols of an automotive worldview." Heinz Schmidt commented, "From this comparison follows—particularly noteworthy for us—the significant role that the C 111 plays for the image.... I would like to strongly commend this finding, made by very knowledgeable people, to your attention because I believe it is relevant to the proper evaluation of the C 111."

The assessment formulated by Karl Wilfert in a letter to Dr. Hans Scherenberg on May 25, 1970, reads quite differently. After renewed consideration of the development capacity, for which he estimated a requirement of at least 20,000 hours, Wilfert stated that the production of the fifty vehicles initially under consideration could take place on the production line of the Mercedes-Benz 600 (W 100) in agreement with the Sindelfingen plant management. Overall, however, his assessment was marked by skepticism. The C 111 had "attracted a lot of interest" but would "hardly be able to contribute to raising the sporting image and to eliminating our negative image; namely, that we are a sluggish company." In addition, he feared that "if the C 111 is sold at a high price that still covers the expenses to some extent"—in view of the expected high demands of the customers—"a great deal of capacity of the best engineers and fitters will have to be spent," "because complaints will not fail to appear."

Wilfert's conclusion left nothing to be desired in terms of clarity: "I therefore believe that this model should <u>not</u> be built in series, not even <u>in small series</u>. One could possibly announce that further development is being carried out, for example, on a special plastic substructure, and that important knowledge has been acquired thus far, but that sales are not being considered.

"The C 111 is not a racing car, and in view of the speed limit that is sure to come, its extreme handling can hardly be exploited; furthermore, it is quite uncomfortable as a road vehicle (it would then be a comparatively impractical vehicle).

In its issue of May 6, 1970, auto, motor und sport devoted an article by deputy editor-in-chief Reinhard Seiffert to the image of German car brands.

"In my opinion, the time for such vehicles is over; they should have been built a few years ago with the possibility of also installing a piston engine.

"In its conception, the C 111 is anything but a study for a safety car, but it is precisely the tendency toward a safety car . . . that stands in contrast to the propagation of such a sports car.

"Presenting a third version of the Type C 111 to the public carries the risk of negative criticism, which is already being voiced on occasion."

The "possibility of also installing a piston engine" mentioned by Wilfert had already been discussed several times. A few days before Wilfert formulated his assessment to the head of development, Joachim Zahn had commissioned the business administration department with a cost estimate for the C 111 with a 4.5-liter reciprocating engine. The result, based on the figures submitted by the Untertürkheim plant, was a unit price of DM 96,500 for 500 vehicles, DM 71,000 for 1,000 vehicles, and DM 58,600 for 2,000 vehicles. The estimated cost price was thus about DM 7,000 less than the variant with a four-rotor Wankel engine. The latter had in the meantime increased in price by DM 1,000 and was thus DM 104,500, DM 79,000, and DM 66,600, respectively.

After the assessments of the importance and future of the C 111 that Heinz Schmidt and Karl Wilfert had given at the beginning and end of May, respectively, Horst Wendt came forward with a ten-page, very detailed analysis that he addressed to his boss Heinz Schmidt on June 26. In the introduction, he outlined the objective and the questions derived from it:

"The discussion in our company about the C 111 continues. The following facts and considerations are intended to contribute to this discussion and thus also to answer the question of what benefit and future the C 111 can have.

"The contribution is divided into the three questions:
1. How well known is the C 111 to the public today?
2. What effect does the C 111 have on the Mercedes-Benz brand?
3. How can we continue the C 111?"

On the first question, Wendt stated, "It is a fact that the C 111, as a Mercedes-Benz development, is now known and familiar to several hundred million people around the world. Hundreds of press releases and articles have appeared about the C 111." He elaborated on particularly insightful statements in the articles and referred to a survey conducted by the Frankfurt advertising agency HOM (Heumann, Ogilvy and Mather) in May 1970; according to this, the C 111 was known to 78 out of 100 men interviewed.

On the second question, the head of the advertising center stated, "In the discussion, it is felt that the great interest in the C 111 would divert the public's attention and desires from the sales program to such an extent that the end effect could be negative. The attention-grabbing effect of the C 111 is undeniable and proof of obviously great pent-up demand in this field. The distraction theory, on the other hand, is unproven. It defies logic that a prospective buyer should not buy a Mercedes-Benz because we have realized new ideas in the C 111. The construction and publication of the C 111 were entrepreneurial decisions. Since these decisions have been made, the laws of psychology and the market also apply to this object, making some of the pro and con arguments pure speculation."

Concerning the facts, Wendt again quoted press reports as well as the already mentioned investigation by HOM, the results of which are reproduced here in detail:

"When asked, 'What do you think is the purpose of the C 111, why do you think Mercedes developed this car?,' 41 subjects (out of 100) mentioned the term 'test car.' Technical innovations—material—engine—shape—tests' accounted for a further 13 mentions; 'future project' only 6 mentions.

"The answers to the question 'What do you think is the significance of the C 111 for the development of Mercedes' other cars?' are also interesting. 'Developing new engines, bodies, chassis, safety, sportiness, new technical developments, and others (such as comfort etc.)' accounted for 61 mentions. 'Test Wankel engine' accounted for 36 mentions."

Wendt continued, "These and other facts tell us that the C 111 is no longer misunderstood in hardly a single case today. This observation allows us to now ask about the effective impacts of the C 111 on our "image," on the opinion about the Mercedes-Benz brand." Wendt quoted the extremely positive key statements that *Bunte Illustrierte* and *Playboy* had published in the articles already mentioned, and put them in the overall context: "Such statements should not be overrated. What is certain, however, is that our brand image is dynamized by these publications, which cannot be unwelcome to us. But even if the public sees us more active and closer to the line of progress again, we are neither alone nor first there. . . . Of course, you can't sell 270,000 Mercedes-Benz sedans with the components' 'progress' and 'technical perfection' alone. But we need these components to keep the brand reputation stable in the long run. . . . The controlled further development of our image is necessary. The question is whether the C 111 has made a contribution to this, can still make a contribution, and what is the nature of this contribution. Already proven: The C 111 has clearly reassigned the aspects of progressiveness and modernity to the Mercedes-Benz brand.

"In response to the question 'Car companies are constantly working on the further development of their models. Which cars do you consider to be the crucial developments of the recent past?,' Mercedes-Benz received 48 mentions (out of 100 respondents), NSU (Ro 80) 56, BMW only 22, and Opel 14 (multiple mentions).

"The result of the question 'In your opinion, what is the further development? What's new about this car?' is interesting as well.

"65 mentions (again out of 100 respondents) were for the Wankel engine.

"73 mentions concerned the body and the shape.

"The area of speed, acceleration, performance received 26 mentions.

"Safety and road-holding received 16 mentions.

"23 mentions concerned individual details."

Wendt then went into detail about two advertising tests that had been carried out in April and May. They were based on the

The first image advertisement featuring the C 111 (*left*) had already appeared in September 1969, to coincide with the presentation at the IAA in Frankfurt. In spring 1970, the same motif was published with the headline "We realize dreams in order to learn."

first advertisements of the new car brand campaign in Germany, which Daimler-Benz had been running in daily newspapers and magazines since mid-April 1970. Commenting on the results, the advertising director said, "Twenty-four hours after the publication of the first daily newspaper advertisement on April 15, 1970, an interview was conducted with 138 readers of *Frankfurter Allgemeine Zeitung* about advertising in the *FAZ*. 58% of the respondents could remember the Mercedes-Benz advertisement (an extraordinarily high value). 38% of the respondents remembered the image of the C 111. However, 32% could also remember a picture of a computer and even 33% a Mercedes-Benz sedan. So the C 111 dominates but certainly allows building the bridge to the sales product. The tested advertisement gives the respondents a strong impression of future-oriented attitude, of research and development, and of progress. However, many of the same respondents also say that the advertisement's claim gives them an impression of "safety, solidity, reliability, quality, and comfort." We asked ourselves whether it could really have been possible to add the aspect of technical progressiveness and agility to the solid Mercedes-Benz brand image in one and the same advertising message, by combining different elements that say progress and quality."

Commenting on the results of the subsequent second study, involving twenty-six motorists (including ten Mercedes-Benz and eight BMW drivers), Wendt wrote, "It can be considered proven for the time being that the advertisements, i.e., the concept on which they are based, communicated tradition in the sense of quality and safety. The essential elements of the Mercedes-Benz image therefore remain untouched. However, these image aspects are now expanded by the dimensions of progressiveness and modernity.

"It is clear that the image components tradition and progressiveness do not interfere with each other.... All Mercedes-Benz drivers rate the ad positively. It looks modern and progressive to them. The argumentation of the advertisement is consistent with the conviction of the Mercedes-Benz drivers.

"The BMW drivers, on the other hand, who would like to pigeon-hole the Mercedes-Benz as a 'safety car for old people,' are partly outraged by the ad. The ad highlights Mercedes-Benz arguments that BMW buyers thought they would only find in their cars. Due to the factual claims of the pictures and texts, these BMW buyers are now clearly unsettled and react nervously.... So much for the investigations. They do not claim to be strictly

Also in the spring of 1970, another ad appeared with the headline "We make dreams come true in order to learn." In autumn, "Experiment and Perfection" was published in *Motor Revue* **and** *Auto Jahr*.

A large-scale brand campaign with image advertisements, which also focused on the C 111, began on April 15, 1970. It was also the subject of market research and continued into the winter of 1970.

scientific (too-small samples), but based on all experience they come very close to the true facts.

"For all these pleasing new developments, the C 111 fulfills a kind of powertrain and evidentiary function. It facilitated the first activations in the corporate and product image. The production program is included in its aura. If we acknowledge that the C 111 is already the property of the world public today—even if only indirectly—if we further admit that the internal discussion about it has benefited us all more than it has harmed us, because we were and are forced to rethink old positions, then we can now also ask the question about the future of the C 111."

On the third question, Wendt presented "four viable concepts for dealing with the C 111":

1. Production and sales release of a series of 100 to 500 vehicles per year with a start-up by the end of 1971 at the latest

The additional advertisement with the headline "Safety," designed in the style of the 1970 image ads, appeared in the spring of 1971 in the catalog issue of *Automobil Revue*.

2. Cessation of all work on the C 111 by the beginning of 1971 at the latest and publication of a final report
3. Continuation of the work, further communication as an experimental vehicle and regular publication of reports (research bulletins, about twice a year) on the current development status
4. Production of a small series of thirty to fifty vehicles, which are given to selected drivers for testing purposes for a period of one year

Wendt's recommendation was for the fourth variant, for which the fewest disadvantages and the highest degree of credibility were seen—at least if the selected drivers, who in this scenario had to regularly fill out a test book, "correspond to the image we want (chief engineers, aircraft builders, athletes, et al.)." Wendt had already favored this group of people, in addition to racing drivers, in his communication to Heinz Schmidt at the beginning of March. In the concluding sentence of his analysis, the advertising director wrote, "However, simply making the C 111 disappear or summarily dismissing it or leaving it in its present position for a long time to come are certainly not options for our company."

The advertising campaign mentioned by Horst Wendt comprised three advertisements that were placed in the larger daily newspapers at fourteen-day intervals starting on April 15. From May 18, the series, supplemented by a fourth advertisement, also appeared in magazines such as *Der Spiegel,* and from the beginning of October, but here in a four-week cycle, in automotive magazines such as *auto, motor und sport, mot,* and *ADAC Motorwelt.* Even before this campaign, the C 111 served as an eye-catcher in image advertisements in which it addressed the theme of "automotive future." As early as September 15, to coincide with the presentation of the mid-engined coupe at the IAA, an advertisement appeared with the headline "The program of the 19 best Mercedes-Benz ideas has become a little bigger. Buy a piece of the future." The familiar motif showing the C 111 together with three Mercedes-Benz production sedans in the high-banked curve of the Untertürkheim test track served as the illustration, and the text pompously proclaimed, "The C 111 has what it takes to be a car unlike any other. Almost too fantastical. That is why it remains an experimental vehicle for the time being. It is impossible to say when its ideas will be ready for production." After the presentation of the current model range and the description of the C 111, it concluded, "So, the car future can begin. We are sure that it will be just like our present: highly promising."

In spring 1970, immediately before the premiere of the modified version in Geneva, two further advertisements appeared, showcasing the C 111 and its further development. Under the headline "We make dreams come true in order to learn," the text read, "We did not create the C 111 to fulfill the dreams of a few. It is about more. . . . It is about solving a whole series of problems for the car of tomorrow that have not yet been solved by anyone in this form. About drive units, new chassis options, brakes, new materials. . . . And that is why we are not resting on our first C 111 laurels. But keep on developing. After all, perfection has to be learned." After a description of the further developed points, the text turned to the present to conclude, "So much for the future of the car. The present is no less exciting. But mature. In eighty-four years of building cars, we have learned so much to be able to offer the most successful passenger car range in our automotive history today." Another advertisement presented an even more direct and very concrete link to a current model in autumn 1970. Under a photo showing the C 111 next to a 280 SE and the headline "Experiment and Perfection," the text proclaimed, "Two cars, one concept. Because at Mercedes-Benz, experimentation and perfection belong together. . . . And so does polishing such ideas in years of thorough development until the experiment has become a perfect, new automobile. Like the 280 S/SE, which critics have called the most balanced car in Europe."

The C 111 not only promoted the image of Mercedes-Benz in advertisements but also remained a highly sought-after exhibition and demonstration object worldwide after its presentation in Geneva. This is also how the spectacular sports car found its way to East Berlin. In early June 1970, it was the star guest at the exhibition *Das Buch vom Auto* (*The Book about the Car*), organized by the Mercedes-Benz branch in Berlin together with the German Book Trade Association. In this context, not only was the C 111 demonstrated to the public on the Berlin AVUS, but the Berlin branch also used the vehicle to step up its contacts with East Berlin. After the company had already been negotiating with the responsible authorities for several years about the delivery of commercial vehicles to the GDR, the opportunity now presented itself to fulfill the repeatedly expressed wishes of the Ministry for Foreign Trade and to present the C 111—"combined with detailed technical information"—is East Berlin.

The memo of June 30 prepared by the Berlin branch noted, "On the grounds of the Hoppegarten harness racing track, the car was shown to leading gentlemen of the vehicle industry of the GDR. . . . . On the motorway a few kilometers away, the driving characteristics of the C 111 were examined by around twenty people. Everybody was impressed. . . . A subsequent table talk gave the opportunity to learn about the experimental car right down to technical details. . . . The interest of the conversation partners was focused on an exchange of experiences about the problems of the Wankel engine." In the final evaluation, the memo noted: "To what extent the introduction of the C 111 has promoted the possibilities of supplying commercial vehicles from our company to there is difficult to judge."

At the time when the Berlin sales representative prepared his summary of the presentation of car 31 in East Berlin, car 32, the exhibition car of the Geneva Motor Show, was on tour in Great Britain. The seven-week tour began in Leeds on June 26 and continued via Manchester, Glasgow, Cardiff, Bristol, Bournemouth, Poole, London, and Hersham to Birmingham, where the spectacular vehicle could be admired on July 30 and 31. But the real highlight of the tour was still to come: On August 3, the C 111 was given a prime spot in the entrance hall of the London Science Museum for a fortnight. This was even worth a report in *Frankfurter Allgemeine Zeitung*: "The museum management decided to take this unusual step because 'we believe that this is a car of the '80s that will interest our scientifically oriented visitors.' Until now, there was a showcase with moon dust in the middle of the large entrance hall. Only once before had a motor vehicle been exhibited there: the 'Bluebird' giant with which . . . Donald Campbell had taken the speed record for himself. The C 111, a purely experimental vehicle, is insured for £60,000 (over 510,000 marks) for the duration of the exhibition." A final appearance at the Veteran Car Club Rally at London's Crystal Palace on August 16 marked the end of the almost two-month tour, and the vehicle returned to Stuttgart.

Plaything of the Engineers or Maturing Series Product: The Question behind the C 111

Exactly one month earlier, on July 16, the C 111 had again been a topic of the passenger car commission meeting, albeit only briefly. Dr. Hans Lorscheidt had confined himself to stating that "we cannot and should not talk about the C 101, since the elaboration on the C 101 announced by the sales department and the statement of the development department on the durability of the variants of the Wankel engine are not yet available." At the same time, he recommended four press articles to the commission members, the key statements of which he also documented in the minutes of the meeting. He took the main statement, "German reciprocating engine conservatives are wrong," from *Stern* magazine of June 28, the slogan "Now there is no turning back!" from *Motor-Revue* of June 1970, derived from the text passage "The car is now so far perfected that it could go readily into production...." From *Automobil Revue* of July 9, 1970 he quoted the article "VW K 70—Star of two shareholders' meetings" with the statement "The shareholders became more thoughtful when . . . the financial director of Audi/NSU described the situation . . . Neckarsulm ended with a loss of DM 17.8 million." Finally, he cited the article "Automotive report of reliability—Citroën DS 21—NSU Ro 80" in *auto, motor und sport* of July 18, 1970. As key statements, he summarized, "65% of the monitored cars [NSU Ro 80] already received a replacement engine within the first eighteen months of their life," as well as "Only 1 per cent of the cars [Citroën DS 21] ran with a replacement engine a year and a half after purchase." Even though the topic was not discussed further, the conclusions that could be derived from the quoted key statements were obvious.

At the passenger car commission meeting on September 11, 1970, the C 111 was also only briefly discussed when Helmut Schmidt explained that the announced statement by

The exhibition tour of the C 111 in Great Britain was promoted by this advertisement of the British sales organization with the headline "The car of the future is in Britain."

the sales department could only be made "when the following information requested from the development department has been provided:

1. What are the results so far regarding the durability of the Wankel engine?
2. For which other vehicles (apart from the C 101) in our future range is the Wankel engine proposed?"

This put the responsibility back on the development division. Obviously, daily issues of greater urgency prevented the clarification of the open points regarding the C 111 within the next few months.

On September 29, however, a working group consisting of representatives from body development, process engineering, materials testing, and paint engineering had met in Sindelfingen to discuss the requirements that small-series production places on the material for the body and the painting options. The hand laminating process, which can be used for up to 3,000 vehicles, allows a maximum temperature in the mold and a maximum paint baking temperature of 130°C (266°F) in the best case. However, the current possibilities at Waggonfabrik Rastatt stood in the way of this: Apart from the fact that at best only about 100 bodies could be produced with the existing provisional tools, the operating equipment only allowed working temperatures of 70°C (158°F) and mold temperatures of 100°C (212°F). The surface of the parts made from these tools was judged to be so defective that "an unjustifiable amount of effort must be expended in painting to obtain a flawless surface."

According to the meeting minutes, "the only air-drying paint system (DD, polyester, melamine acrylic resin) that ensures this finish requires 3-4 working days and can only be carried out by specialists." Another disadvantage was that "the mechanical properties of this paint . . . do not come close to meeting our requirements in driving operation" [so that the vehicles] "cannot be offered to any customer as of yet." The paint industry was apparently not in a position at the time to offer air-drying or 80° paint systems that met the requirements. The available 130° system, "the quality of which was comparable to that of our sheet metal painting" and "still achievable with a hand laminate," would require new tools made of thermosetting molding compounds.

To guarantee a consistently good surface quality over the entire production run, the new tools would have to be taken from a master model. As hand laminating required an annealing time of eight hours even at 130°C (266°F), only one car per day could be produced with one mold set.

According to the minutes, promising tests were carried out in Rastatt with doors in sandwich construction by the Bayer company. Since weight savings would be possible with the greater rigidity of the parts, it was recommended that all flaps, lids, and doors be of this design. Process engineering in Sindelfingen had also produced samples that were tested statically and for paintability and then subjected to a dynamic test. After completion of the tests, the paintability with the 130° system was to be investigated with the best laminate structure. Independently of this, tests with cold-curing synthetic resin paints were continued by the paint technology department.

Apart from the extensive development activities described in detail, it was not until the spring of 1971 that the discussion about the future of the C 111 began to pick up again. On January 16, *auto, motor und sport* had asked the question "Where is the C 111 heading?" and elaborated on this: "For one and a half years now, the fast Wankel coupe has been playing a mobile test station at Daimler-Benz. Initially operating with thick racing tires mainly on racing and test tracks . . ., the C 111 shows itself in a road-going version . . . more and more frequently in public. Senior engineers of the company are undertaking extensive journeys with the sports car, which is exciting in form and technology and whose modified bodywork has also reached a standard close to series production in terms of build quality. Plaything of the engineers or maturing series product, that is the question behind the C 111."

A good week later, there seemed to be an answer—at least in terms of tendencies and within the company: At the passenger car technical meeting in Sindelfingen on January 25, 1971, it was stated that the further development of the C 111 was "not urgent but should not be stopped." Work on the W 114 E (the first Mercedes-Benz experimental safety vehicle, presented to the public in October 1971 as the ESF 05) was unlikely to suffer as a result. It should be considered whether the necessary radiator widening addressed by Dr. Liebold should also be adopted for the "body in sandwich construction." The minutes also stated that the further development of the C 111 had to be "clarified by the Board of Management in principle." It went on to say, "As a basis for decision-making, elaborations with calculations for two possible ways are to be prepared: a) further development like in the laboratory, b) further development for a specific production quantity (e.g. 1,000)."

"Where is the C 111 headed?": *auto, motor und sport* asked this question in its issue of January 16, 1971, and summarized, "Plaything of the engineers or maturing series product, that is the question behind the C 111."

The question of sales potential in the USA also became an issue again. According to a memo dated March 8, 1971, addressed to Karl Wilfert from the US sales company Mercedes-Benz of North America, referring to a conversation with Deputy Secretary of Transportation Toms, "The law as it currently exists . . . would permit the importation of up to a maximum of 500 C-111s, even if not all safety standards could be met." Within this framework, however, the vehicles may "only be operated for demonstrations, shows, races, and sporting competitions . . ., which does not exclude leasing to interested parties." According to an amendment to the law requested by Toms in the US Senate, this regulation should in the future also allow sales "to a group of buyers chosen by the vehicle manufacturer, either by price fixing or by selection." The "selection of the group of buyers could be done," as the American distributor wrote, "by setting the price at, say, $25,000 per vehicle, which would, of course, keep the buyer pool extremely small." Disillusionment followed two months later, as Karlfried Nordmann, president of Mercedes-Benz of North America, informed Daimler-Benz board member Heinz Hoppe in a letter dated May 17, 1971: "The special rule of the '500 clause' is not applicable because Daimler-Benz's production exceeds 500. This special regulation does not apply to individual models of a manufacturer, but only to its total production of all models. Only if the vehicle complies with all existing regulations will we therefore be able to consider selling the C 111."

Management Issue: Flick and Zahn on the Series Production of the C 111

By April, the C 111 had again become an issue for the board. Earlier that month, Dr. Friedrich Karl Flick, member of the Supervisory Board and owner of a share package in Daimler-Benz AG worth billions, had been given a C 111 for test drives. He described his impressions in a letter to Hans Scherenberg and Joachim Zahn dated April 13, which is largely reproduced here verbatim, as it summarizes the relevant aspects quite well:

"The C 111 is absolutely sensational. This is also the opinion of two acquaintances of mine who have driven the fastest cars . . . . In any case, the C 111 eclipses everything that has gone before. Only small things need to be improved: For example, the ventilation, i.e., the air circulation, could be better, especially since the cabin apparently gets quite hot due to the mid-engine behind the seats. . . . Furthermore, the oil consumption is very high; perhaps it can still be reduced. Moreover, the car has quite a strong exhaust plume. In this context, the question arises whether one would be able to comply with the exhaust emission regulations with this engine, especially in the USA. . . .

"The technical design is first class (chassis, acceleration, brakes, etc.). Unlike other sports cars, the car handles very well and is easy to drive. The acceleration between 3,000 and 4,000 revs is fantastic. The gear shift is also very smooth and easy to operate. As a result of the synchromesh, it is also possible to drive without double clutching; for somewhat sportier driving, double clutching can also be used.

"On the crucial question of whether the car should be built, I would like to make the following personal comment:
"In my opinion, the car has a tremendous advertising effect. You can see this when you drive through a city like Munich and park the car in the city center. It acts like a magnet on pedestrians and motorists alike. The comments often are 'Is that actually a Mercedes?' or 'This is the new Mercedes, but it's not being built.'

"If the car were to be included in the sales program, Daimler's reputation as the world's leading car manufacturer would be enormously strengthened. We could probably also assume that the car would be featured in Hollywood and TV films. In my opinion, the publicity effect would be extraordinary. This free advertising would save us millions spent on advertising not only in the US but around the world.

"If one assumes that the production equipment for the car costs ten to fifteen million and that, assuming a maximum loss of DM 50,000 at a prime cost of approximately DM 150,000, then—with a number of, e.g., thirty vehicles per year—both the investment costs and the uncovered expenditure of 1.5 million per year are, in my opinion, well invested from the point of view of advertising. I therefore think that the question of starting production should be examined again very seriously. Selling thirty cars at a price of about DM 100,000 should not be a problem; on the contrary, one will very likely have allocation worries—as was the case when the 6.3 l went into production.

"If, on the other hand, we continue not to produce the car, we must expect a very negative effect on the public. People will then be annoyed that you show them a car as a means of advertising, but you can't buy it. This could give the impression that the car is not much good after all, so that one cannot risk producing it and putting it into the sales program.

"In this context, it is also interesting to note that for a number of years Daimler has been saving on the expense of participating in races, which used to be accepted for the sake of technical insights and also for the sake of publicity. One could take the position that one can now accept the uncovered expenses from the production of the C 111 for this.

"I assume that Daimler has carefully considered the pros and cons of producing the C 111, and I would very much appreciate it if I could receive a compilation of the respective arguments. However, I believe I can already say that in a final examination of this question, the aspects in favor of producing the car will very probably prevail.

"I think that any car factory that could develop such a vehicle would build it, especially since it would outshine anything comparable once the objectionable points have been eliminated. However, in my opinion, the decision would have to be taken very soon. The competition would certainly be uncomfortable with a positive decision—for good reasons."

On May 8, 1971, Joachim Zahn sent the influential Supervisory Board member a detailed statement, which is also reproduced here in large part:

"There is no doubt that the question of starting production must now be seriously examined again by the board. I am aware that not producing this vehicle may have negative effects on our image.

"Although there are still a number of problems to be solved—for example, the still-unsatisfactory endurance of the Wankel engine, the fulfillment of American safety regulations, especially with regard to bodywork and emissions regulations, as well as the possibility of using this vehicle in rallies—the overall development status now achieved allows a positive attitude to the question of whether the C 111 should go into production. In our considerations, the still-extraordinary advertising effect of the C 111 must be taken into account in particular. So, as soon as the fuss on the investment front has died down a bit, we will tackle this question in a very concrete way, especially since a decision on this question will have to be taken as soon as possible anyway.

"In addressing the question of starting production previously, we have assumed total production runs of 500, 1,000, and 2,000 units. According to the cost status of July 1970, the following cost prices were calculated for the total production runs mentioned:

500 units	DM 104,500
1,000 units	DM 79,000
2,000 units	DM 66,600

"The cost increases that have materialized in the meantime and various design changes make it necessary to revise this cost estimate. We will shortly receive new design documents from the development division and will then be able to get clarity on the latest cost situation. According to a rough estimate and without taking into account the design changes, the following approximate cost prices result for the individual quantity variants on today's cost basis:

with 500 units	DM 115,000
with 1,000 units	DM 87,000
with 2,000 units	DM 73,300

"As the price is likely to increase due to the design changes that have been made, these figures should only serve as a certain guide for the time being.

"The issue of production quantities poses some problems in terms of capital expenditure, the service network, and the stocking of spare parts. I tend to believe—Dr. Scherenberg and Dr. Langheck are also of this opinion—that we should limit production to about 100 vehicles per year and think of a total production run of about 250 vehicles within a period of two years. (With a production of only 250 units, however, it would still have to be reviewed whether we fulfill the quantity requirements for participation in sporting competitions such as rallies.)

"With a relatively small number of units, we would have the opportunity to sell the vehicle only to a select group of customers and give the vehicle the character of a technical test vehicle. The involvement of a relatively small group would provide the opportunity for a close exchange of technical experience, which would undoubtedly be advantageous at the current stage of development of the Wankel engine and would make it much easier to replace the engine, which will most probably be necessary after 10,000 to 20,000 km. With such individual treatment, these measures could be carried out largely inconspicuously in terms of expanding the experimental findings. Under no circumstances must we have the kind of mishaps that happened with the Ro 80.

"Another advantage of small numbers would be that we can ask almost any price for this vehicle, initially thinking of an order of magnitude of DM 150,000.

"In terms of investment, a production run of approximately fifty units would be unproblematic; i.e., we could carry out this project practically without any substantial investment.

"Meeting the demands placed on the service and parts organizations is more problematic. For relatively small quantities, for example, repairs and after-sales service could be carried out by a separate service group with so-called 'flying service.' It would be conceivable that the technical advice for this group as well as the manufacturing group could be taken over by Mr. Uhlenhaut, who will be retiring from active service in the near future anyway.

"In my opinion, the production of the vehicle should not be done in test departments, but already in small-series production. In order to gain practical production experience in the field of plastic car bodies already now, Dr. Langheck's consideration of taking over this production under our own direction is not uninteresting.

"With the above-mentioned concept, the requirements in terms of personnel and material input can be kept within reasonable limits. In addition to the possibility of a real mobile test of the Wankel engine, this concept offers above all the advantage of an extraordinary advertising effect, although it would have to be considered here whether, for example, the expense not covered by the price would be to the detriment of the advertising budget, which in my opinion is ample anyway.

"The overall attitude toward the question of starting production can be seen as positive, and I would be happy if we could talk about this complex quite soon."

Decision Paper for the Board: The Future of the C 101 from a Development Perspective

However, this rather optimistic assessment was not to last long. At the passenger car technical meeting on April 20, 1971, head of development Scherenberg had instructed the development organization and planning division (EOP) to "determine what development and production capacity is required to manufacture the C 101." A little later, he again addressed this issue and instructed the directors of passenger car development to prepare an analysis in a note dated April 29. In addition to statements about the expected effort required in design engineering and testing, this should also contain statements about the development costs, tooling costs, and investments, as well as the expected manufacturing costs of the vehicle with production runs of different quantities. Similarly, it should be investigated "to what extent such operations would create capacity bottlenecks in the priority work for W 116, W 123, etc."

Wieland Doderer, responsible for time and capacity planning at EOP, immediately began working on the new decision paper for the board, commissioned by Scherenberg in dialogue with the specialist departments.

In a memo to Friedrich Geiger dated May 27, 1971, Arno Jambor, a member of the stylistics department in Sindelfingen, estimated the total time required for a design revision of the C 111 with a view to series production at 10,000 working hours, of which 1,000 hours were to be spent on the construction, 1,500 hours on the styling, and 1,000 hours on the interior. The lion's share of 6,500 hours, however, was spent creating the 1:1 scale model, and with work starting in July 1971, Jambor reckoned it might not be completed before the end of the year.

He also pointed out that "considering this number of hours, it [is] not possible to develop a completely new outer skin," and only "a formal revision of the current C 111 can be undertaken." At the same time, he presented a seven-page list with a total of thirty-eight points where standards and regulations had to be met or had been announced specifically for the US market. Fulfillment of these regulations would have meant "that a fundamentally new outer skin would have to be developed, as the car in its current form does not fulfill the demands made on it."

In view of the exhaust gas detoxification regulations that had to be taken into account, engine development still faced a number of challenges that were difficult to assess, especially in regard to the achievable performance level and the noise limits that had to be met.

At that time, the test department also still considered many development details to be unresolved, as Dr. Liebold explained in detail in his already quoted note of May 11.

Prof. Joachim Förster, head of automatic transmission development, also expressed his skepticism in a note to K.-W. Müller on June 14, 1971. He was particularly concerned about the high performance potential of the four-rotor Wankel engine, which only harmonized to a limited extent with the three-speed automatic transmission designed for 250 hp/184 kW, and raised doubts about its stability. Furthermore, the question arose as to whether the transmission originally developed for a conventional drive configuration would meet Mercedes-Benz's high standards in terms of efficiency and comfort in combination with the mid-engine drive unit "with return driveshaft."

Karl-Heinz Göschel, head of passenger car testing, recommended in a memo of June 30 that "the following points should be considered in a redesign.

1. The suspension travel has been quite short so far. The vehicle was not unpleasant to drive, but it was definitely a bit too hard.

	Docket-Nr. US-Norm	Gesetz	ausgearb. Vorschlag	Ankündigung
Stoßfänger Durchgehende Stoßstange, die von 14" bis 20" über den Boden reichen soll.	Docket 1-9 1-10		1.10.72	
Energieaufnahme Wagenbug Verkleinerung Innenraum, Türfunktion nach Aufprall Begrenzung Verzögerung Fixpunkt im Wageninnern.	Docket 2-7			1. 9.72
Lenkanlage Begrenzung Verschiebung Lenkrad bei Aufprall mit 30 mph	Docket 70-3		1. 1.72	
Energieaufnahme Fahrzeugheck Verkleinerung Innenraum bei Heckaufprall, Begrenzung Verzögerung Fixpunkt im Wageninnern	Docket 2-7		1. 1.73	
Dachfestigkeit Begrenzung der Dacheindrückung bei stat. Belastung der vorderen Dachecken	Docket 2-6		1. 1.73	
Seitentürfestigkeit Mindest-Widerstandswerte der Türen bei stat. Eindrückung	US-Norm 214	1. 1.73		

	Docket-Nr. US-Norm	Gesetz	ausgearb. Vorschlag	Ankündigung
Seitenaufprall Seitliche Knautschzone	Docket 2-6			1. 9.74
Kraftstoffsystem Absolute Dichtheit des gesamten Systems bei Frontalaufprall mit 30 mph und Heckaufprall mit 20 mph	Docket 70-20		1. 1.72	
Absolute Dichtheit bei Heckaufprall mit 30 mph und Frontal- oder Heckaufprall mit 30 mph und nachfolgendem Kippen des Fahrzeugs bei vollem Tank			1. 1.73	
Brandschutz Feuerwand zwischen Tank und Innenraum				1. 9.73
Haubensicherung Verankerungssystem so, daß Eindringen der vorderen Haube in Windschutzscheibe bei Aufprall vermieden wird. Verschlusskontrollanzeige	Docket 69-17		1. 1.73	
Passives Rückhaltesystem Passives Rückhaltesystem für Vordersitze, aktives Rückhaltesystem für Hintersitze	US-Norm 208	1. 7.73		
Passives Rückhaltesystem für alle Sitze			1. 1.74	

List of current and announced approval standards and regulations for the US market, compiled by Arno Jambor in May 1971

2. The ventilation of the cabin was absolutely insufficient. Larger air volumes must be realized here. We are aware that the front end will build taller for this.
3. Despite all the limitations, the location and temperature of the trunk still remain a makeshift solution; here, an improvement would be necessary as well.
4. At the given price, we cannot do without sales in the USA, but to do so the vehicle would also have to meet safety regulations, which would mean a complete redesign."

These recommendations, which, however, did not really contain any new findings, came too late to be considered in the decision paper for the board. On July 1, 1971, the paper titled "C 101—Preparation of a decision paper for the board paper on the further handling of the project in the development division" was submitted to its initiator, Hans Scherenberg. Based on the feedback collected from the specialist departments, some of which amounted to a new concept, it presented two different scenarios:

"Case A: Improving and making the current C 101 concept ready for series production," and

"Case B: Complete redesign of a C 101 successor."

The necessity for this had arisen from findings that had already been formulated very clearly in the introductory summary of the decision paper for the board:

"It has been shown that a series start-up is not possible before the second half of 1974. The development of the four-rotor Wankel engine and the automatic transmission are decisive for the schedule. By the aforementioned start-up date, the current

	Docket-Nr. US-Norm	Gesetz	ausgearb. Vorschlag	Ankündigung
Insassenschutz bei Seitenaufprall und Überschlag Festlegung Beschleunigungswerte für Kopf und Brust bei Seitenaufprall	Erg. zu US-Norm 208, Docket 69-7		1. 7.73	
Dito bei Überschlag			1. 7.74	
Aktives Rückhaltesystem Forderung nach verbesserten Gurtsystemen: 3-Punkt-Gurt, automat. Sperrung, Einhandbedienung, akustisches und optisches Warnsystem	Docket 69-7 (US-Norm 208)		1. 1.72	
Sicherheitsgurt-Verankerung Verschärfte Prüfbedingungen für die Verankerungspunkte	US-Norm 210	1. 1.72		
Integrierte Sitzsysteme Sitze sollen Schutz bieten bei Seitenaufprall				1. 1.74
Kopfstützen Erweiterung bestehender Forderungen, aufblasbare Kopfstützen, Verbesserung der Sicht nach hinten	Docket 1A/1B, (US-Norm 202)			1. 1.73
Aufschlagschutz im Wageninnern Polsterung Innenraum mit stoßabsorbierendem Material	Docket 2-1 (US-Norm 201)		1. 1.74	

	Docket-Nr. US-Norm	Gesetz	ausgearb. Vorschlag	Ankündigung
Forderung Mindestabstand Windschutzscheibe vom H-Punkt			1. 1.75	
Aufschlag auf Lenkung Begrenzung der auf den Körper einwirkenden Kraft, Kontaktfläche Lenkrad 258 cm^2, Lenkradpolsterung 1".	Docket 2-3, 2-4, (US-Norm 203)		1. 1.73	
Türrückhaltesystem Türe so auslegen, daß bei Aufprall Herausschleudern der Insassen nicht möglich	(US-Norm 206)			1. 1.74
Befestigung Windschutzscheibe Scheibe so einbetten, daß sie bei Frontalaufprall das herausgeschleudert werden der Insassen verhindern kann.	Docket 69-29, (US-Norm 212)			1. 7.72
Seiten- und Heckscheibenbefestigung Die Insassen sollen bei Aufprall im Wageninnern gehalten werden	US-Norm 212			1. 7.73
Betätigungseinrichtungen Verschärfung Standard 101, Beschriftung der Betätigungseinrichtungen	US-Norm 101	1. 1.72		

concept of the C 101 even with improvements must be considered outdated in terms of shape and chassis design, apart from the fact that the novelty effect has been lost in the public mind [with reference to the elaboration by Karl Wilfert]. If the C 101 idea were to be made ready for series production, it would require a complete redesign."

Regarding the capacity situation, the summary stated:

"Capacity constraints are expected in the areas of design engineering Sifi in both cases and Ut in case B. In Sifi, six or seven unbudgeted constructors would still be needed this year.

"In case B, the number of constructors at K1W in Ut [the chassis, axles, brakes construction unit] would have to be increased by eight or nine from the end of 1972.

"In the area of engine development—both in the design engineering and the testing department—the capacity requirements for the four-rotor development could only be met if the policy decision on the future of our passenger car engines planned for the second half of 1972 was in favor of the Wankel engine, and the development of a new series of reciprocating engines was thus dropped.

"Then the expected bottleneck at EV1 in the road testing department would also be eliminated.

"No additional investment is required to manufacture the necessary four-rotor engines for the development division alongside the two-rotor engines.

"However, if a facelift for the W 114 is seriously contemplated, development of the C 101 must be discouraged from a capacity point of view."

	Docket-Nr. US-Norm.	Gesetz	ausgearb. Vorschlag	Ankündigung
Beleuchtung der Betätigungseinrichtungen		1. 9.72		
Standardisieren der Lage der Betätigungen			1. 7.74	
Bremssystem Vorgeschriebene Verzögerungswerte, Zweikreisbremse, Warnleuchten für Fuss- und Feststellbremse	Docket 70-27 (US-Norm 105)		1.10.72	
Direktes Sichtfeld Mindest-Forderungen, Mindest-Sichtwinkel	Docket 70-7			1.7. 73
Indirektes Sichtfeld Verschärfung bestehender Forderungen, Forderung von 3 Spiegel	Docket 71-3a (US-Norm 111)		1. 1.74	
Noch größere indirekte Sichtwinkel, Wiedergabeeinrichtung			1. 1.76	
Wischfeld Forderung größerer Wischfelder	US-Norm 104			1. 7.73
Frontscheibenentfrostung u.Verhindern d.Beschlagens Verschärfung existierender Vorschriften	Docket 1-13 (US-Norm 103)			1. 7.73
Leuchten, Rückstrahl-Vorrichtungen Blinker Anforderungen der Klasse A, Leuchtfläche der Klasse B entsprechen, Farbe der Leuchten nach SAE Standard J 578 a, April 65, Forderungen an Plastic-Materialien, Bremsleuchten Anforderungen der Klasse A, Leuchtfläche muss der Klasse B entsprechen. Rückscheinwerfer nach SAE J 593 c, Februar 68, Kennzeichenbeleuchtung von oben und von der Seite	US-Norm 108	1. 1.72 1. 1.73		
Beleuchtungssystem Vergrößerung Lichtintensität, automat. Höhenverstellung der Scheinwerfer	Docket 69-19 (US-Norm 108)			1. 7.72
Reflektierende Oberflächen Die im Sichtfeld sich befindenden Fahrzeugteile dürfen einen gewissen Reflektanzwert nicht überschreiten	US-Norm 107			1. 7.73
Glatte Aussenkontur Forderung nach glatter Aussenkontur	Docket 2-5		1. 7.72	
Schmutzfänger Geforderet wirksame Raddeckung, Spritzwinkel ≦ 20°.	Docket 70-21		1. 1.72	

The estimated development costs including the engine were DM 43.6 million for case A and DM 50.9 million for case B.

Allocating these costs to the calculation of March 5, 1970, resulted in the following prime costs:

Case A: DM 164,300 for 500 units, DM 108,400 for 1,000 units, and DM 80,800 for 2,000 units.

Case B: DM 178,800 for 500 units, DM 115,700 for 1,000 units, and DM 84,400 for 2,000 units.

The investment and tooling costs for Sindelfingen in March 1970 were calculated at DM 2.8 to 2.9 million and for Untertürkheim DM 6.5 million. On the status of the cost estimates, it said, "Prime costs and manufacturing investment requirements are being revised and remain to be seen."

	Docket-Nr. US-Norm	Gesetz	ausgearb. Vorschlag	Ankündigung
Feuersicherheit im Fahrzeuginnern Verwendung von schwer entflammbaren Materialien	Docket 3-3 (US-Norm 303)	1. 9.72		
Begrenzung der ins Wageninnere dringenden Abgasmenge durch Heizung und geöffnetem Seitenfenster	–			1.10.72
Warndreieck Warndreieck im Innenraum, muss von Vordersitzen aus erreichbar sein.	Docket 4-2		1. 1.72	

In the meantime, Joachim Zahn had written a note to his colleague Hans Scherenberg on June 29 to address the issue of C 111 again. "Because of the question of a possible small series for the C 111, we also had in-depth deliberations on the board a few weeks ago. But I don't see that the matter has made any progress in the meantime. It should be noted that with the passage of time, topicality (and thus any conceivable success) becomes more and more affected, of course. In my opinion, we would therefore have to come to a conclusion relatively soon. Of course, the focus is on the concrete benefit (in relation to the effort) for our overall business. In terms of timing, there is also the fact that we will undoubtedly have to reckon on renewed queries on this matter in the near future (certainly on the occasion of the general meeting), the answer to which will of course depend to a large extent on what we actually want to do in the matter in concrete terms."

Vote without Alternative: No Chance for Series Production

At the board meeting of July 6, 1971, the C 111 was again brought up as an issue and discussed in detail. Langheck announced that the expected production costs were then being reviewed again, and independently of this, took the view that a positive opinion could only be justified "if a clear demarcation from the actual program tasks is ensured by forming special working groups in all areas involved— . . . development as well as production and sales." Staelin considered it "almost impossible to control the expected problems in the area of servicing" and saw "the danger that the matter could ultimately have a detrimental, rather than beneficial, effect on the general reputation of our company." Zahn pointed out that "the original promotional benefit envisaged has probably been largely achieved by now." On the other hand, he thought it would be "expedient if the development and public relations departments were given the opportunity to comment before a final opinion is formed—which, in his opinion, should preferably take place by this year's general meeting." As a result, the Board of Management maintained its earlier opinion that "series production of the C 111 model is not planned . . . unless the development and/or public relations departments present points of view that have not yet been taken into account," and clarified: "The official statements used externally must continue to be based on this being purely an experimental vehicle." The official decision to "discontinue further work on the C 111 model for good" was finally taken at the board meeting on November 23, 1971.

In the meantime, the business administration department had prepared a third cost estimate for the C 101 based on the new figures submitted by the plants and submitted it to Joachim Zahn on October 19. Compared with the previous cost estimates, an additional figure for a total production run of 250 units—an order of magnitude Zahn had mentioned to Flick—had also been calculated. The estimated cost price per vehicle was DM 296,100 for 250 units, DM 180,900 for a total of 500 units, DM 120,400 for 1,000 units, and DM 90,400 for 2,000 vehicles. Development costs, which accounted for 88% of the total increase, were cited as the main cause of the massive rise in prices compared to the March 1970 estimate. This statement attracted the attention of the head of development, who initially could not comprehend a cost pool of

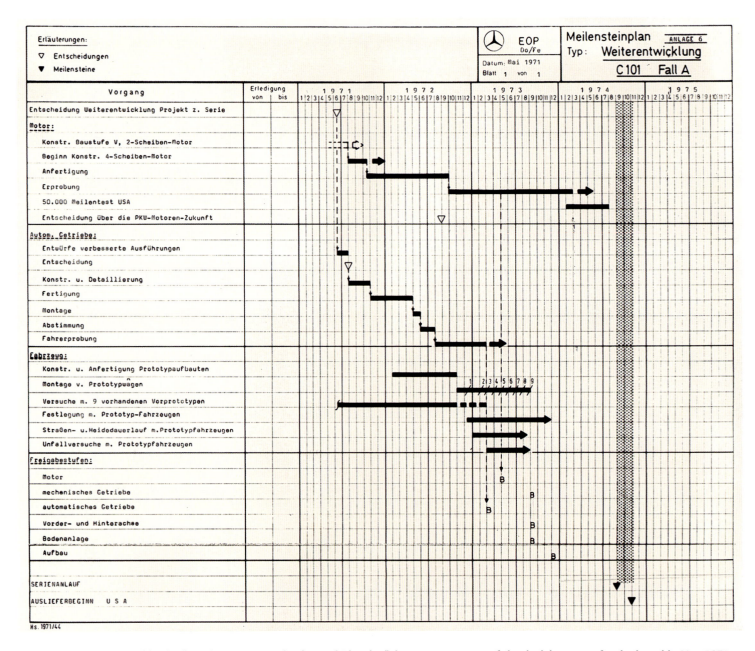

Milestone plans prepared by the "Development Organization and Planning" department as part of the decision paper for the board in May 1971 for the two cases of "further development" and "new concept." The results of the analysis were sobering and, in the end, led to the decision to refrain from series production of the C 111.

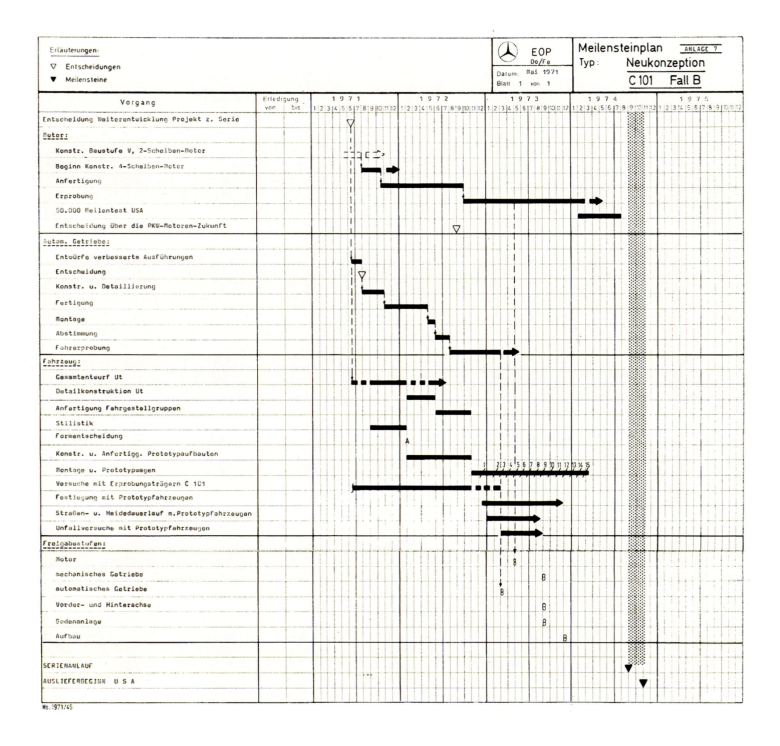

The C 111 was a star with a high media presence right from the start. *On the left*, in August 1969 during filming on the test track; *on the right*, with photographer and film actress Helga Anders during photo shoots for the magazine *Constanze*.

this magnitude. However, the development cost of DM 47.5 million estimated here was the average of the figures given in the decision paper for the board for Case A (preparing for series production) and Case B (new design).

The previous development costs for the C 101 project in the period from 1969 to March 1971 had been precisely determined by project manager Dr. Liebold and compiled in his note of May 11, 1971. According to it, DM 8.54 million had been incurred for the eleven vehicles built by then (i.e., about DM 776,400 per vehicle). Not even all that much compared to the SL Roadster of the R 107 model series, whose twenty prototypes cost DM 23.7 million (i.e., just under DM 1.14 million per vehicle). At the board meeting on November 9, 1971, however, total costs to date of around DM 15 million were mentioned for the C 111, which the board considered "justifiable in view of the advertising effect of this vehicle"—an assessment that also seems understandable from today's perspective.

Trade Fairs, Models, Majesties: The C 111 as the Object of Desire

The prospective buyers, who were of course unaware of the company's internal considerations, remained—despite clear statements by the company—in joyful anticipation. As early as April 17, 1969, Prince Sadruddin Aga Khan, art collector, car enthusiast, and United Nations High Commissioner for Refugees, had written to Joachim Zahn to express his interest in the new sports car, referring to the article published in *Automobil Revue* on April 10. Numerous other interested parties followed—partly, as mentioned, by submitting blank checks. At the end of November, Denis Jenkinson, car journalist and co-driver of Stirling Moss in the legendary Mille Miglia victory in 1955, let it be known to the press department that he would be happy to make himself available as a test driver if Daimler-Benz ever decided to make the C 111 available to a number of outsiders. Ernst Hutzenlaub, managing partner of Wankel GmbH, expressed a similar opinion in a letter to head of development Hans Scherenberg at the beginning of February 1970. In doing so, he offered not only himself, but also inventor and co-partner Felix Wankel as candidates for customer testing of the C 111. In the end, the company had to disappoint them all.

The fascinating design and the high attention the C 111 attracted inspired to stage the dream car together with attractive models. *Deutsche Auto Zeitung* for March 9, 1970, portrayed the C 111 in its series "Cars and Girls."

hobby magazine presented the C 111 on the front page with a sporty, dashing photo model and impressed with the depth of detail in the article itself. The photos published in the April 1, 1970, issue were taken on the test track in Untertürkheim.

In the first German issue of *Playboy*, the super sports car took over the automotive part in August 1972. Forty-seven years later, the November 2019 issue of *Playboy* was once again dedicated to the C 111 in its motor special "Playboy Cars" and focused on its fiftieth birthday.

Motor racing affinity: Even though the original ideas about possible motor racing—at least with regard to a factory commitment—were quickly shelved, the C 111 exuded pure sportiness, and the combination with world-class drivers like Juan Manuel Fangio (*left*) and Hans Herrmann (*right*) looked absolutely coherent.

Unique: Even rarer than the C 111, which served as a conceptual model, was the one-off that Daimler-Benz developed together with Porsche and Volkswagen for the heir to the Persian throne, Cyrus Reza Pahlevi, and delivered in October 1972.

This affected even loyal customers of the highest rank and name. After the Iranian ambassador had delivered the shah's wish to buy a C 111 during a visit in July 1970, he was able to experience the dream sports car at a presentation on the test track at the Untertürkheim plant but still received a negative response for his high-ranking employer—instead, Dr. Zahn, spokesman for the Board of Management, referred to the coming SL Roadster.

Even though the shah's wish could not be fulfilled in this case, the Persian ruling dynasty received an equally exclusive vehicle a good two years later, in October 1972. The single-seater, open-top sports car jointly developed by Daimler-Benz, Porsche, and Volkswagen, ordered as a birthday present for the twelfth birthday of the shah's son Cyrus Reza Pahlevi, was based on a Formula Super Vee racing car chassis from Fuchs in Rutesheim and resembled the C 111 due to its unusual color scheme and some design elements. So it is not surprising that both vehicles were

Not only was the C 111 the proverbial trump card of car-based card games, but it also played a central role in a marketing campaign by Shell mineral oil company in 1971. By filling up with at least 20 liters of fuel at a Shell filling station, motorists received a medal with one of sixteen "world-famous sports cars," including the C 111.

Public attraction: Even after its premieres in Frankfurt and Geneva, the C 111 continued to cause a sensation wherever it appeared. The snapshot from an exhibition in Hong Kong in November 1970 (*above right*) documents this more than clearly. The other photos show the C 111 in April 1970 at the New York Auto Show (*top left*) and in 1971 in Djakarta, Indonesia (*bottom left*), and Sydney, Australia (*bottom right*).

Even if no exhibition vehicle was available, the C 111 nevertheless remained a central theme at trade fair appearances of Mercedes-Benz, as here in 1970 in Brno, formerly ČSSR (*left*), and in 1971 in Kuwait (*right*).

Eagerly awaited: The C 111 traveled by airfreight to the industrial exhibition held in São Paulo, Brazil, in March–April 1971. *Auto Zeitung* picked up on this in its news and reported, "More kilometers in the air than on the road have been covered by the Mercedes C 111 prototype so far"—a statement that was undoubtedly true for car 32, which was only used as an exhibition vehicle.

In São Paulo, the C 111 was one of the attractions of the exhibition and stole the show from the 250 CE.

244 Dream Sports Car and Laboratory on Wheels: The C 111

At the Hanover Fair in April 1972, the C 111 could be admired on the IBM stand. The American hardware and software manufacturer used it to advertise computer-aided design using the finite element method. Car 31 was exhibited in the latest version with a widened front end.

In February–March 1973, three years after its premiere in Geneva, the C 111-II was presented in a very prominent position at the Mercedes-Benz special exhibition in Moscow. Car 34, which was used there, is pictured at right with the first visitors immediately after the opening.

captured together in a photo series on the test track in Sindelfingen.

Due to its great popularity, the C 111 continued to be used intensively in communication for a long time and served as an excellent flagship vehicle for the Stuttgart-based brand all over the world. In addition, the company, which was considered rather conservative at the time, also presented with the spectacular experimental vehicle the vivid proof that they were very intensively concerned with research and future topics. At the board meeting of September 4, 1973, board member Heinz Schmidt still referred "to the outstanding positive impact on our program that the C 111 had by being declared a 'mobile laboratory.'" Six months earlier, the C 111 had been the star of the Mercedes-Benz special exhibition in Moscow, which had taken place in February–March 1973 to great media response. Regardless of the development stop declared by the Board of Management, which referred to the further development into a production vehicle, a completely new variant was nearing completion at the same time, which, however, was to take another two and a half years: the C 111 with plastic floor assembly.

New Technologies: The C 111 with Plastic Floor Assembly

With this variant, which was developed from scratch, the C 111 once again lived up to its function as an experimental vehicle and played an important role in researching new technologies. It was about the use of plastics in automotive construction—not only for the bodywork, but also for the load-bearing floor assembly.

At the Hanover Fair in April 1967, the chemical company Bayer had presented a self-supporting vehicle floor assembly in modern sandwich construction made of plastic for the first time. It was built in "core composite design using chemical materials," as it was called at the time, and Bayer wanted to demonstrate the applicability of these materials for dynamically stressed vehicle structures. The technical components came from the BMW 2000.

The unusual vehicle concept, originally initiated in 1963 by designer Hans Gugelot and his staff at Gugelot Design-GmbH in Neu-Ulm, caused such a stir that even *Der Spiegel* reported on it. *Die Welt* newspaper called it "a small sensation," and *Welt am Sonntag* even called it "the most unusual car of the year."

After the trade fair presentation in Hanover, the floor assembly was built up into a complete vehicle in order to demonstrate the possibilities of chemical materials in automotive construction even more clearly. The resulting sports coupe was presented to the public again in October 1967—this time at the K'67 plastics fair in Düsseldorf—and was consequently given the designation K 67.

The core composite plastic floor assembly presented by Bayer was designed to be self-supporting, and the chassis, completed with BMW 2000 major assemblies, was subjected to thorough driving tests. The photos were taken in Sindelfingen in April 1969.

At the K'67 plastics trade fair in Düsseldorf, Bayer presented the plastic floor assembly built up into a complete vehicle. On the left in the picture is the floor assembly with attached cutaway body, and on the right, the likewise contemporaneous photo with the Bayer K 67 complete vehicle that still exists today.

New Technical Territory: The Plastic Floor Assembly for the C 111

A year and a half later, there were initial considerations also to design a variant of the C 101 along the same lines as the Bayer plastic car. As early as April 16, 1969—the decision for the GRP body of the C 101 had not yet been taken—a delegation from Farbenfabriken Bayer, on a visit to Sindelfingen, submitted the proposal to develop a sandwich floor system in conjunction with the ongoing construction of the Wankel sports car. On this basis, it was agreed that Bayer would use the design documents of the C 101 to examine the options and develop "fundamental proposals for a sandwich floor system and a non-structural body." An important goal was the development of an alternative to the previous sheet metal floor assembly that could also be produced inexpensively and easily for small series.

In conformity with the Bayer K 67, the new type of floor assembly was to be designed with two top layers of fiberglass-reinforced plastic (GRP) and hard polyurethane (PUR) foam for the support core. To enable a direct comparison between the core composite design made of chemical materials and the sheet steel floor assembly, a number of framework conditions had to be taken into account during the development. For example, the arrangement of the drive units and chassis components, the position of the fuel tanks laterally between the axles, the dimensions of the passenger compartment, and the appearance had to be adopted unchanged.

At the meeting on April 16, 1969, the experts from Farbenfabriken Bayer (FFB) suggested using the existing production facilities at Waggon- und Maschinenfabrik Donauwörth (WMD), which had also produced the Bayer car, to manufacture a test vehicle. With such a facility, three to ten raw frame floor assemblies could be produced with an investment of about DM 400,000. The weight of the Bayer car's floor assembly was said to be 170 kg, with the prospect of a possible reduction to 150 kg. The weight was thus in the order of magnitude of the sheet steel floor assembly of the C 111. As the skin-forming rigid foams used for the floor system were not yet suitable for a complete body, in the opinion of FFB, a "body made of fiberglass-reinforced polyester corresponding to Porsche racing cars" was proposed.

The conversation partners at Daimler-Benz AG noted that extensive laboratory and road tests would be necessary for a plastic floor assembly, since at that time no practical tests other than the two Bayer vehicles were known. In addition to the scheduling to be defined, they saw a need for clarification especially regarding the weight of the vehicle, the space requirements of the sandwich construction, and strength, rigidity, and temperatures in the engine compartment.

Just eight days later, another meeting was held in the presence of two FFB employees in Sindelfingen on the "development of a floor assembly in sandwich-fill construction." It was determined that a metal sandwich design, which would allow extreme lightweight construction with optimal rigidity values, "does not seem promising at the moment." In contrast, the feasibility of a sandwich floor assembly with GRP top layers was considered promising. The weight of such a floor assembly was now assumed to be as low as 130 kg.

Starting on June 18, 1969, the project was further developed in additional work sessions with FFB representatives as well as Messerschmitt-Bölkow-Blohm GmbH (MBB) as the parent company of WMD. The project manager at Daimler-Benz was Klaus Matthias, a member of the passenger car body design team in Sindelfingen. At the meeting on June 18, it was agreed that it was possible to develop a plastic floor assembly for the C 101 on the basis of the available research. It was also agreed that Farbenfabriken Bayer would provide a floor assembly with drive and chassis parts for the so-called "Heidedauerlauf" (heath endurance run, as rough road testing at Daimler-Benz was called) in order to be able to determine the dynamic load capacity of a plastic floor assembly. On July 25, the representatives of FFB and WMD confirmed that the documents submitted by design engineering in Sindelfingen corresponded to the ideas regarding concept and cross-section design, and that there were therefore no reservations about being able to construct a load-bearing floor system in plastic sandwich construction.

Because of the extensive specifications to be met, responsibility for the design of the floor assembly passed to Daimler-Benz, while FFB concentrated on extensive materials testing, and WMD on the manufacture and development of the necessary tools and fixtures.

For example, Farbenfabriken Bayer analyzed the material properties of the selected glass fabric types and resins in production conditions, optimized the edge zone reinforcements required for the connection between the support core and the GRP shells, and carried out bonding tests on flanges and crash tests on deformation bodies. Also discussed at the meeting on June 18

The chassis of the Bayer K 67 with plastic floor assembly in core composite construction during the crash test in Sindelfingen on September 19, 1969, after the collision

were considerations to integrate the front wings into the floor assembly to be able to absorb the collision energy in the best possible way in the event of rear-end collisions.

Things got loud at the next project meeting on September 19: A floor assembly of the Bayer car provided by Bayer and equipped with major assemblies was subjected to a crash test in the presence of the project partners in Sindelfingen. Propelled by the hot-water rocket common at the time, the vehicle collided head-on at 48 km/h in an outdoor area with a concrete block weighing several tons, which acted as a rigid obstacle. The test report of December 5, 1969, stated, "The behavior of the Bayer floor assembly on impact can be assessed positively for the plastic. The front end 'crumpled' (Bayer BMW approximately 160 mm, W 115 approximately 400–500 mm) back to the front axle, while the passenger compartment was not deformed. However, the decelerations were considerably higher than they occur in our vehicles. Furthermore, the deformation takes place over too short a period of time, so that decelerating—even belted—occupants with the front-end deformation is hardly possible."

With regard to the project goal of developing a sandwich floor assembly for the C 111, the test report stated, "In essence, it can be said that it is probably possible to produce a self-supporting plastic chassis that is equivalent to current sheet steel bodies in terms of deceleration time, max. deceleration, and deceleration distance. For this, the plastic chassis would have to be improved in the following respects:

a) Longer front end

b) No integration of the wheel arches into the front end in order to achieve more freedom with regard to the "side rail" design in terms of the possible deformation path.

c) Reduction of the amounts of glass and reduced density of the foam towards the impact-prone components in the front.

d) Improvement of the deep anchoring of the glass fabric in the core."

The decision not to integrate the front wings or front wheel arches into the floor assembly after all had already been made on the day of the crash test—also because the required joining method for the two GRP shells for the realization of a gapless body could not yet be expected to produce satisfactory results. In addition, the challenges of axle and steering mounting were discussed based on preliminary designs.

On the visit of a Bayer delegation to Sindelfingen, during which various fields of future cooperation were discussed on November 14, 1969, one of the topics was the sandwich floor assembly for the C 111. As the final body shape for the second series C 111, equipped with a sheet steel floor assembly, had been determined in the meantime, the construction of the plastic floor assembly and the creation of a 1:1 model could be tackled.

The progress of the project in the following months is documented in the minutes of the work sessions held in Sindelfingen and Donauwörth between the end of April and mid-June 1970. Problems arose from the fact that the existing major assemblies were to be used to a large extent for the floor assembly to be developed. Against this background, it seemed expedient to provide a separate support welded from formed aluminum sheets for the engine mount, the strut mount, and wishbone mount of the rear axle—the so-called rear support, which was to be bolted to the GRP/PUR floor system. The crossrail under the dashboard, the so-called component carrier, was also designed as a part to be manufactured separately and, like the majority of the floor system, was made of GRP/PUR.

New Challenges: Rigidity and Manufacture of the Floor Assembly

The basic structure and production of the plastic floor assembly for the C 111 were planned analogously to Bayer's concept vehicle. The floor assembly was also to consist of two synthetic resin shells with a number of fiberglass fabric layers—adapted to the loads—arranged in the top layers. The production of the floor assembly initially involved laminating the two shells in the molds developed for this purpose. After gluing the upper and lower shells together, the next step was to stabilize the space between them with foam to form an average 30 mm thick core composite.

In contrast to the polyester resin used for the bodywork, the more expensive epoxy resin had to be used for the floor assembly, which could be processed more accurately and was more resistant.

So-called edge zone reinforcements made of acrylic and polyamide fiber fleeces ensured that the polyurethane foam support core was firmly bonded to the shells. The inner shells in the side sills and in the ventilation system were supported in the production process by cores made of wood or gypsum, which were sheathed with a laminate of fiberglass fabric and resin and covered with edge zone reinforcement fleece that could be removed after filling them with foam.

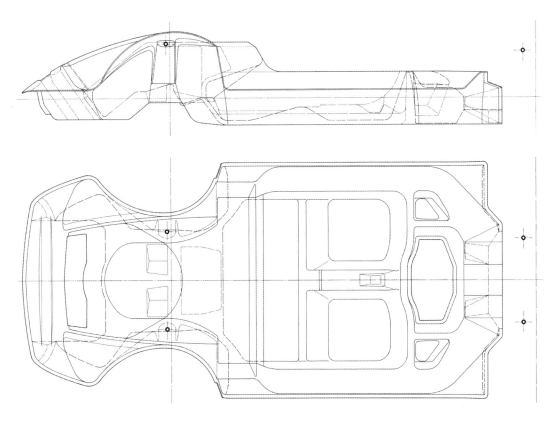

In the first draft of a GRP-PUR floor assembly for the C 111 drawn up by Klaus Matthias as early as 1969, the rear support was not yet integrated.

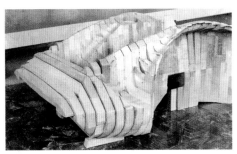  

The master model of the first design of a GRP-PUR floor assembly for the C 111 was painstakingly made from wooden ribs at Modellbau Apitz in Wullenstetten in September 1970.

  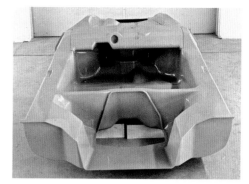

The now-completed master model of the first design of the GRP-PUR floor assembly, taken in October 1970 at Modellbau Apitz in Wullenstetten

 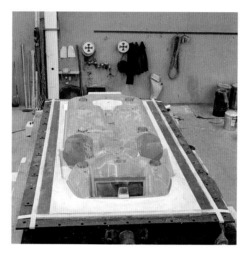 

The laminating and foaming equipment for the first design of the GRP-PUR floor assembly was developed in December 1970. The picture at the top left shows the mold making for the upper shell. In the picture at the top center, the finished form of the upper shell, rotated by 180° and with embedded master model, whose underside is now exposed. The following three photos (*top right to bottom center*) document the further phases of the mold construction for the bottom shell: the master model provided with release coating and the foam filling tubes, as well as the mold provided with the temporary outer supporting walls before and after filling with the mold material; finally, the illustration at the bottom right shows the finished laminating and foaming device for the upper shell. To the right of the mold, you can see the mold core for the inner shell of the outer side rail. The mold and support core are pulled out of the mold to the rear after the foaming process.

 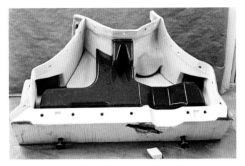 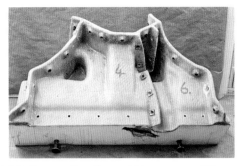

The component carrier was designed as a separate component. The pictures show the master model (*left*) as well as the mold in open condition with inserted core for the air duct (*center*) and in closed condition (*right*).

After the master model of the floor assembly was completed in its first version in October 1970, most of the laminating and foaming equipment was developed at Waggon- und Maschinenfabrik Donauwörth, while Bayer AG contributed the tooling for the component carrier. The more descriptive term "instrument carrier" was not used here to avoid misunderstandings and confusion with the dashboard, since this only made up a small part of the complex component.

The first foaming tests took place in Donauwörth in February 1971. The sandwich floor assembly created in the process weighed 149 kg, slightly less than the previous design made of sheet steel. The two GRP shells accounted for 60 kg, the bonding of the shell parts for 12 kg, and the polyurethane support core for 77 kg. Longitudinal and cross-sections were made of this initial foaming study to gain an impression of the foam distribution, the thickness of the foam within the floor assembly, and the effectiveness of the two-layer edge zone reinforcement fleece. For this purpose, the penetration of the outer layer of the fleece with foam and the anchoring of the inner layer with the GRP top layer were investigated.

Based on the knowledge gained from the analysis of the foaming studies, a floor assembly of the original design was finally created, with which torsional rigidity measurements were carried out in Sindelfingen. The results were less than satisfactory, mainly due to the very soft area connecting the aluminum stub of the rear support and the side rails.

Based on this finding, a weight- and rigidity-optimized variant was designed. A modification of the foaming mold should make it possible to insert the aluminum rear support into the mold before gluing the upper and lower shells, instead of having to glue it into a subsequently inserted pocket as before. This should result in a better connection between the rear

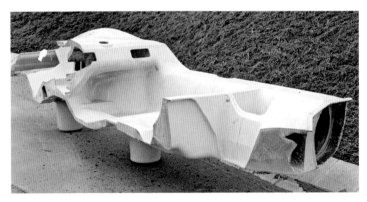
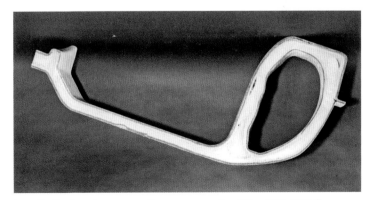

Longitudinal and cross-sections were made of the GRP-PUR floor assembly produced during the initial foaming tests and examined in detail. The picture on the bottom illustrates the profile of a side rail.

The GRP-PUR floor assembly of the first design, produced after the initial foaming tests, was tested for torsional rigidity in Sindelfingen in March 1971.

support and the GRP shells. The force application was also revised to achieve greater rigidity in the rear area. A redesign of the connections of the component carrier aimed at improving the previously unsatisfactory connection with the floor assembly. Finally, a further optimization consisted of adopting the widening of the front end, which had been carried out on car 31 in the meantime for the plastic floor group as well. The resulting modification of the ducts for the interior ventilation also enabled better integration into the floor assembly.

Well Thought-Out in Every Detail: The Design of the Further Developed GRP-PUR Floor Assembly

The details of the construction and the materials used were summarized by project manager Klaus Matthias in a very detailed essay in *Automobiltechnische Zeitschrift (ATZ)* of March 1983, from which the following information is taken.

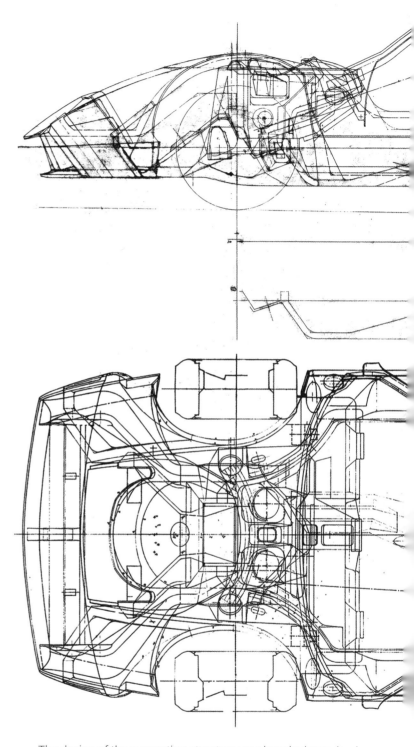

The design of the supporting structure was largely determined by the framework conditions already mentioned. Due to the unchanged arrangement of the drive units, chassis components, and fuel tanks; the defined dimensions of the passenger compartment; and the likewise unchanged appearance, the available space was largely dictated. A complete core composite

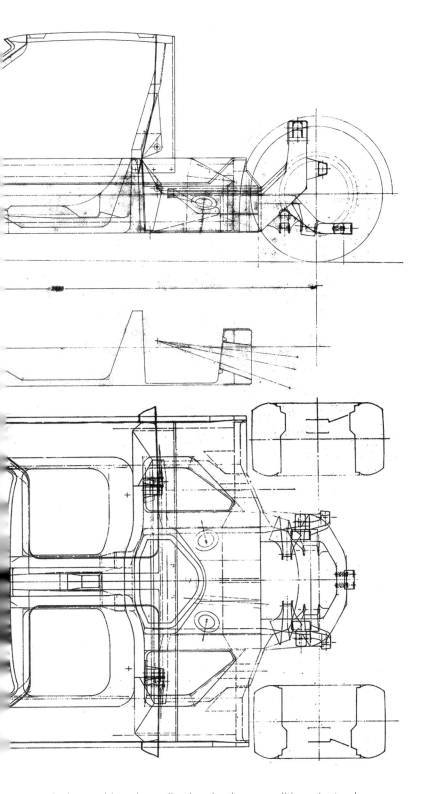

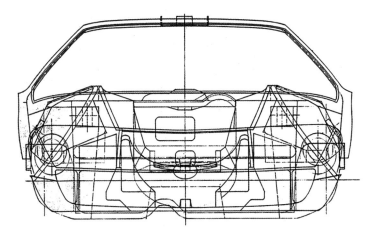

Section of the overall design of the GRP-PUR floor assembly for the C 111 in the weight- and rigidity-optimized variant prepared by Klaus Matthias. The GRP-PUR structure is shown complete with component carrier, rear support, and body structure and represents the development status in 1972.

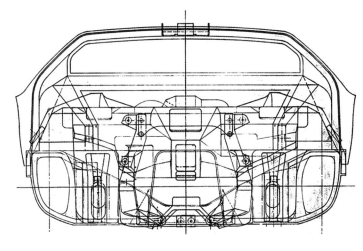

design could not be realized under these conditions. Instead, a mixed-design structure was developed, taking into account the specific design requirements on the different materials and their interaction.

The overall design was therefore quite similar to the floor system in sheet steel design. The core composite floor assembly, rear support, and front component carrier were connected in an integrating design to form a substructure on which the superstructure of the passenger compartment was placed.

In the area of the passenger compartment, the floor assembly was designed as a U-shaped shell, the lateral ribs of which were designed as hollow side rails. The required minimum thickness of the core composite resulted in a reduced internal cross-section, which could only be partially compensated for even by a greater height of the hollow side rails compared to the sheet steel floor system. Despite the associated deterioration in access conditions, the tank capacity was 15% lower.

Due to the position of the four-rotor Wankel engine and its low-lying side exhaust outlets as well as the rear-axle geometry, the shell in the area of the engine compartment was dissolved into a frame structure with stiffening surfaces. Toward the rear, the rear support was made of welded aluminum sheets, since no promising solution for the realization as a GRP-PUR core composite could be found due to the spatial conditions. Brackets for wishbone, suspension strut, torsion bar, and rear engine mounts were welded to this light-alloy frame construction. The supports for the front engine mounts were inserted through the side rails and integrated into the floor assembly during the foaming process. The rear support was bonded to the GRP-PUR floor assembly and additionally bolted at the transition points.

In order to be able to securely connect such vehicle components, via which forces are transmitted to the structure, to the floor assembly outside the rear support, special force transmission elements were developed. The task was to find a solution for a total of 106 fastening points (63 of which were in the upper shell and 43 in the lower shell) with direct transmission of the forces to the thin-walled top layers of the GRP-PUR core composite that was feasible in terms of production technology and weight-saving and was practicable for the installation of the add-on components. The new elements, specially designed by Klaus Matthias for this purpose, consisted of a round nut and a tooth lock washer bonded to it, and fulfilled a number of other requirements in addition to safe power transmission: They were easy and accurate to set in the top layer, minimized disturbances in the fiber composite of the top layers and in the core composite, and required no additional work on the demolded part in the production process. They were used for simple screw connections, but also in particular for highly stressed screw connections; for example, to connect the bearings of the lower thrust arms of the rear axle with the cross rail behind the driver's seat or to fasten the aluminum body structure, the seat rails (including the lower seat belt connection), and the strikers of the door locks to the GRP-PUR floor assembly.

The front cross bracing of the floor assembly was done by the glued-in component carrier. This was also a core composite construction with foamed-in ducts for the interior ventilation and

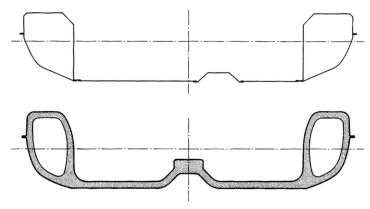

Cross-section comparison of the steel floor assembly and the GRP-PUR floor assembly in the seating area

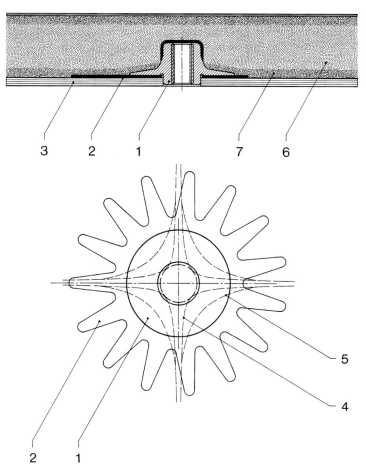

Graphic representation of the force transmission element specially designed for the GRP-PUR floor assembly in cross-section and as a top view. 1—Round nut with threaded insert, 2—Toothed washer, 3—Thickened top layer laminate, 4—Boundary lines of fabric displacement without fiber gating, 5—Boundary lines of fabric concentration as a result of fiber displacement, 6—Support core interior, 7—Edge zone reinforcement of the support core.

connected to the pedal floor panel in the lower area. By means of an upper plate that extended from the outer hollow side rails to the mounts for the front suspension struts, the U-shaped shell of the floor assembly, which was severely tightened in the area of the front axle, could be formed as a partially closed box.

This made it possible to compensate partially for the otherwise unavoidable loss of rigidity of the substructure. The forces from the front axle control arms and suspension struts were transmitted directly to the core composite component via welded aluminum mounting shells. The torsion bar bearings and the bracket for the

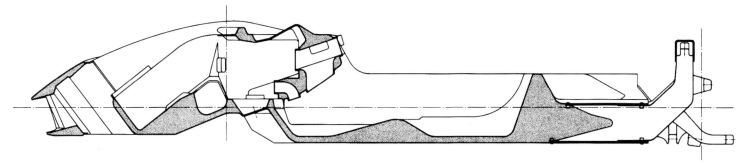

Longitudinal section through the GRP-PUR floor assembly (offset section). The GRP-PUR component carrier and the aluminum rear support are clearly visible.

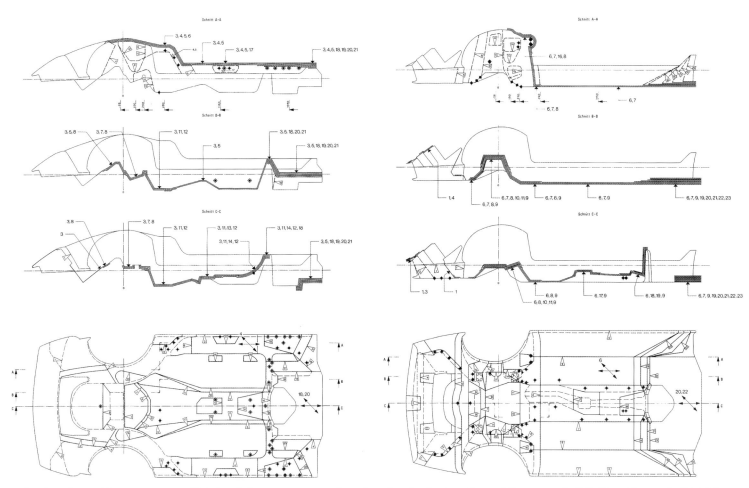

Laminating plans with arrangement of fabric reinforcements as well as three longitudinal sections of the upper shell (*left*) and lower shell (*right*); schematic representation in top view and various longitudinal sections. The black dots indicate the position of the 106 force transmission elements, the white circles those of the 16 bolt points; however, for reasons of clarity, only 58 of the 63 force transmission elements are marked for the upper shell.

steering damper mounts were attached to the bolted-on longitudinal supports.

While the recirculating ball steering system used in the vehicles with sheet steel floor assembly was bolted to the inside of the frame side rails, a new solution had to be found for the core composite floor assembly. The variant of a light-alloy subframe had to be avoided in order not to dilute the design of the core composite floor assembly and to allow for a material-compatible alternative. Klaus Matthias had already recognized the challenge at the start of the project and therefore suggested to the design engineering department in Untertürkheim as early as May 1970 that the installation of a rack-and-pinion steering gear, which promised advantages with regard to the transmission of force to the GRP-PUR floor assembly, should be worked out in terms of technical design. This request was rejected on June 4, 1970—on the one hand, because it did not correspond to "the steering system used in the company," and in-house production was out of the question given the expected low number of units, and on the other hand, because "a completely new design of the steering system at the expense of the W 116/W 123 development does not appear justifiable at the present time." Thus, after having to stick with the near-production steering system, a modification of the available recirculating ball steering system became necessary, which in some respects corresponded to a new design. Because of the forces expected to be transmitted via the steering gear, only mounting it to the bottom of the floor assembly with a bolt-on plane at right angles to the steering shaft came into question. This meant that the steering gear was largely only exposed to thrust forces instead of the otherwise predominant tensile and compressive forces—however, this resulted in the need for extensive modifications to the

The seat rails, previously attached to the cross rail and the floor panel, were attached to the side of the side rails and the center console in the GRP-PUR floor assembly. The increase in height of the side rails compared to the sheet steel version shown on the right is also clearly visible.

steering box to allow for a long steering shaft owing to the installation conditions. The core bond was also extensively modified in the area of the connecting point by bringing together the extensively thickened top layers and bonding them into one panel.

Due to the constructional framework conditions, the seat rails and door locks also had to be attached differently than on the vehicles with sheet steel floor assembly: The seat rails, previously anchored to the cross rail and the floor panel, were now attached to the side rails and the center console, and the strikers of the door locks were not screwed into a recess in the side rails but were freestanding on the vertical outer surface of the side rail. A recess for the strikers would have meant a disturbance in the flow of forces, to which a fiber composite design reacts more sensitively than a sheet steel design. In addition, the chosen arrangement reduces the risk of the strikers penetrating the side tanks in the event of a side impact.

The well for the spare wheel was left in front of the front axle, analogous to the previous overall concept. The spatial conditions resulting from the required thickness of the core composite construction, however, only allowed the use of a collapsible spare

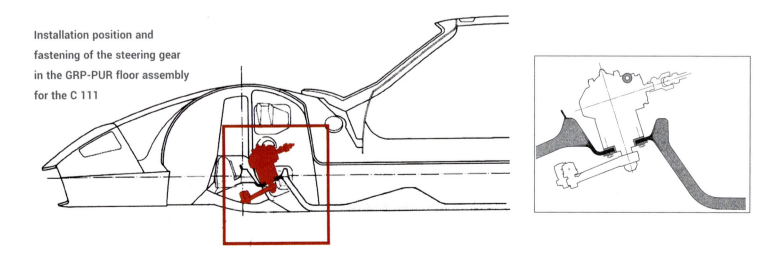

Installation position and fastening of the steering gear in the GRP-PUR floor assembly for the C 111

Mercedes-Benz C 111 with GRP-PUR floor assembly. The photo clearly shows the freestanding striker of the door lock mounted on the vertical outer surface of the side rail.

wheel due to the reduced width—a real breach of taboo at Daimler-Benz at the time. However, this made it possible to run the side ducts for the interior ventilation, which were foamed into the front end, from the front air intake to the open-top duct for the fan. Based on the knowledge gained from crash tests on individual deformation bodies, it was possible to design the front end of the vehicle in such a way that the behavior in a frontal impact could be expected to produce a positive result. With the aim of having sufficient deformation path available, the front area of the superstructure was integrated into the core composite floor assembly. In the original design, this had to be dispensed with, since there were no solutions available for connecting the two shells in accordance with the styling specifications. In order not to have to accept any additional gaps or visible flanges and to be able to keep the outer appearance of the vehicle unchanged, Klaus Matthias had in the meantime worked out a design in which the upper and lower shells of the floor assembly were connected in the front end area by an almost vertical adhesive flange running parallel to the outer skin and invisible from the outside. The remaining horizontally arranged flanges of the floor assembly were designed in such a way that they allowed the half-shells to be bonded securely and at the same time could be used to connect the GRP-PUR floor system to the GRP superstructure.

The body structure of the passenger compartment consisted of the roll bar, roof bar, front roof cross rail, and front wall pillars, which were constructed as closed profile beams made of aluminum. The superstructure and frame floor system were bolted together, and the force was transmitted to the upper top layer shell of the core composite component via the aforementioned specially designed force transmission elements.

Complex Implementation: Manufacture of the Further Developed Floor Assembly

The framework conditions that had to be taken into account in the development of the core composite floor assembly for the C 111 resulted in increased production effort compared to the Bayer demonstration floor assembly. Undercuts, for example, necessitated additional mold separations in the laminating and foaming equipment and made the laminating workflow more difficult. In addition, the hollow side beams and air ducts also required further laminating and supporting devices, and finally cores and especially the rear support had to be fixed in the laminating and foaming device.

Because of the high costs associated with the construction and testing of the further-developed plastic floor assembly, head of development Scherenberg had already expressed the wish at the beginning of February 1972 to discuss the further steps in one of the next development meetings. In a February 17 status report prepared for this occasion, Dr. Liebold named costs of DM 100,000 for the modification of the laminating and foaming device [which was de facto equivalent to making a new one] as well as DM 30,000 for the production of the plastic body in Rastatt. He pleaded for "this project to be completed now by all means after the long constructive preparation," "because—even apart from the still-undecided further development of the C 101—this is purely a development of fundamentals." However, Liebold's recommendation, while undoubtedly understandable, disregarded the fact that the board had decided three months earlier to "definitively stop further work on the C 111 model." Presumably Hans Liebold related this decision exclusively to the development for series production and not also to the use as a "mobile laboratory."

He went on to say about the possible prospects, "If proven, approximately 500 to 1,000 further floor assemblies can be produced in this form, the costs of which, including connecting parts, are estimated at DM 8–10,000/piece compared to approximately DM 35,000 for a small-series sheet metal floor assembly. The weight should be approximately the same as the steel floor group. In the above circumstances, we also consider it appropriate to mold two further floor groups for crash and fatigue tests."

Liebold raised the question of whether the side tanks should be retained in the plastic floor assembly or whether, for safety reasons, the rear tanks currently being tested in car 35 should be used. In terms of space, the plastic floor assembly is less suitable for this, as two 40-liter tanks would require an 80 mm body extension. On the other hand, the side tanks are presumably already much better protected against side impact by the sandwich shell, which is about 30 mm thick. The impact strength of the epoxy laminate could possibly be increased at this point by man-made fibers. However, a subsequent transition from side tanks to rear tanks is not possible without a new foaming mold.

In the passenger car technical meeting on March 27, 1972, the desired approval was given for the further development of the plastic floor assembly. In this context, Liebold raised the issue of tank location for discussion, as he had done in his February 17 paper. Scherenberg did not consider it necessary to take this aspect into account in the design, "since it is a plastic test and small-scale production of the C 101 is increasingly unlikely."

After the decision was made to complete the optimized floor assembly, a new master model first had to be created, since the original specimen had, as expected, been severely damaged during the production of the laminating and foaming device and was no longer available as a basis. A newly manufactured floor assembly of the first version served as an alternative, which was then adapted by Modellbau Apitz according to the new design status. The modified master model was handed over to WMD at a project meeting in Donauwörth on June 28, 1972. This was followed by the construction of the new laminating and foaming device.

To determine the uniform foam distribution and perfect formation of the anchorage zone, two test foamings were carried out in Donauwörth in November 1972, the results of which were, however, worse than had been expected, given the results of the first foaming tests in February 1971. For example, insufficient anchorage of the edge zone in the area of the floor plate was evident, and by taking several foam samples, large differences in the density of the foam were found.

The master model modified with the front end widening for the weight- and rigidity-optimized version of the GRP-PUR floor assembly, taken by Klaus Matthias at Modellbau Apitz in Wullenstetten in June 1972.

After WMD had promised to remedy the deficiencies in the foam distribution and the anchoring of the edge zone, the first complete substructure was finally finished in the spring of 1973. It weighed 171.5 kg, about 20 kg more than the steel floor assembly. To reduce this additional weight, various optimizations were worked out for the production of the following floor assemblies. One of these measures was aimed at saving the amount of resin used for bonding the edge reinforcement fleeces. By applying the fleeces to the not-yet-cured laminates of the upper and lower shells as well as pressing them on with vacuum support—specially manufactured, true-to-shape cover maskings made of rubber were used—it was finally possible to completely save the resin for the bonding—after all, almost 10 kg.

With the first complete floor assembly, both rigidity and strain measurements were carried out in the further course in Sindelfingen with the aid of innovative methods. The Stresscoat and PhotoStress processes used for this provided consistent results. In the Stresscoat test, the top of the floor assembly was painted on the

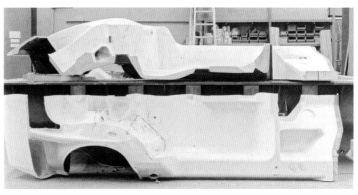

The GRP-PUR floor assemblies produced during the test foaming in November 1972 were examined in detail. After a total of seven cross-sections on the first foaming study, a longitudinal section was made on the second foaming study in order to analyze the foam distribution and the anchoring of the edge zone.

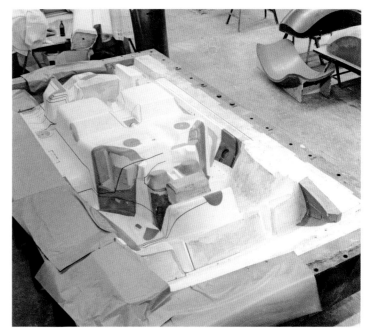

Based on the knowledge gained during the test foaming in November 1972, the laminating and foaming device was optimized. The picture, taken in February 1973, shows the laminating and foaming tools for the upper shell (*left*) and the lower shell (*right*). The cutting lines of the glass fabric layers are clearly visible.

Finally, in spring 1973, the first complete floor assembly was finished. The photos were taken by Klaus Matthias at Waggon- und Maschinenfabrik Donauwörth.

test fixture and fixed at the rear end, and the test load was applied at the front left via a lever arm. This measurement was first used to determine main stress zones and directions as a basis for the PhotoStress investigation. The latter makes use of the methods of photoelasticity. The 1.5- to 2.5-mm thick photoelastic layer of epoxy resin was applied to the floor assembly with a reflective binder. Under load, main strain directions, their signs and the main strain difference could then be determined with the reflection polariscope. With both measuring methods, a maximum strain of 1.0 per mile was determined for the floor assembly on the tension side, which was at the limit of the permissible value. For the body-in-white construction stage with roof structure and roll bar, however, lower elongations were to be expected. Based on the results of the measurements, the fabric plan was revised in the area of the rear support connection.

The rigidity measurements of the GRP-PUR floor system showed that the torsional rigidity was only 60% of the value of the sheet steel frame floor system but was still better than the target range, which was considered realistic considering the general conditions. The situation was similar for the values of the body shells. At this construction stage, the torsional rigidity of the body with GRP-PUR floor system reached 62% of the value of the body with steel sheet frame floor system.

After the decision in spring 1972, the development process had turned out to be more laborious than expected, as Dr. Hans Liebold found in an internal note dated August 10, 1973: "After lengthy tests, the first plastic floor assembly for road tests (C 101 W 36) is to be foamed today. Bodywork construction is scheduled to start on 27.8. in Rastatt, so that the bodywork can be completed in the second half of September in [Sindelfingen]." At the same time, Liebold asked that "the individual parts still missing for the steering linkage be given the necessary urgency." Ten days later, on August 20, 1973, Klaus Matthias specified Leguval W 35 polyester resin produced by Farbenfabriken Bayer as the material for

With the first complete floor assembly, measurements of bending strength and torsional rigidity as well as strain measurements were carried out in Sindelfingen in June and August 1973, in each case with the aid of innovative methods. The pictures show the floor assembly in the measurement setup (*left*), **during the examination with Stresscoat** (*center*), **and with optically active surfaces** (*right*).

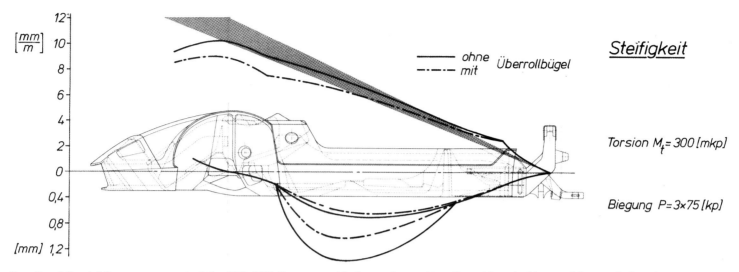

Results of the rigidity measurement of the GRP-PUR floor assembly for torsion and bending with and without roll bar carried out in June 1973. The gray shaded area marks the target area.

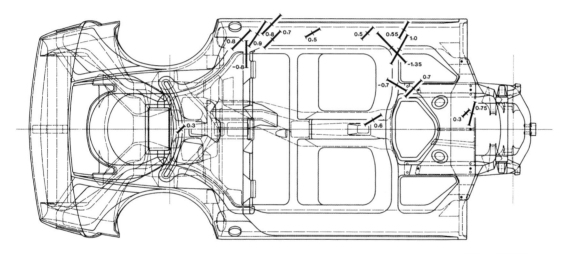

Graphical representation of the GRP-PUR floor assembly with plotted strains under torsional load (4,000 Nm) as determined during the measurements in August 1973

manufacturing the GRP body. The bodywork was to be manufactured as usual at Waggonfabrik Rastatt, which, following its takeover by Bauknecht, now operated as Bauknecht Werk Rastatt GmbH.

Despite the extensive preliminary work and the urgency formulated by Liebold, delays occurred again in the further course after the production of the second floor assembly—the first to be built up into the finished vehicle—had led to partly unexpected results.

Apart from defects in the top layers, which could be eliminated by reworking, there was an unexplained weight difference: With a total material input of 150.8 kg, the finished floor assembly weighed only 141.8 kg. WMD was unable to provide an explanation for the lower weight of this second floor assembly (the first for road tests).

Since it was to be feared that the edge zone reinforcement did not meet the requirements, the planned use for rough road testing did not seem possible, and so the acceptance of this floor assembly was initially refused by the client.

On the other hand, on October 2, 1973, the third floor assembly now planned for car 36 was accepted, for which the specified design weight of 150 kg had been reached. No defects were found in the visual inspection of the top layers either, so that the floor assembly could be handed over to body testing in Sindelfingen for completion with the superstructure (roll bar-windshield frame-roof bar construction) and the control arm bearings for the front and rear axles.

Project with Obstacles: The Vehicle Build

However, the rest of the process stalled again. Messerschmitt-Bölkow-Blohm GmbH, as the parent company of WMD, was not prepared to accept that Daimler-Benz had refused to accept the second floor assembly. In a letter dated February 26, 1974, it presented an explanation for the protested underweight of the floor assembly. According to this, the weight difference was only due to a reduced use of laminating resin in the production of the top layers. Based on this explanation, this floor assembly was also finally accepted by Daimler-Benz—a decision that was to turn out to be not very fortuitous in retrospect. At least the project was now moving forward again, and on June 19, 1974, the third sandwich floor assembly, completed in the Sindelfingen body test department, was finally delivered to Rastatt. A good month later, the production and assembly of the body were completed, and the unit consisting of the floor assembly and body could be transferred to Sindelfingen on July 26.

For capacity reasons, however, the completion of car 36 was then delayed again—especially because the floor assembly showed strong deviations from the constructionally specified dimensions in some cases. Therefore, many installation parts that had been made according to the drawing had to be modified or adapted. Some major assemblies could not be installed according to the drawing even after adjustment work. In a development report dated September 23, 1975, Joachim Kaden, an engineer in the advance engineering department at Untertürkheim, summarized the special features of the vehicle build.

The KE 419, with variable-length intake manifold, was fitted as the engine. For reasons of space, it was equipped with dry sump lubrication, the oil tank of which was fitted at the front left of the engine compartment. The air filter with tangential air intake made it

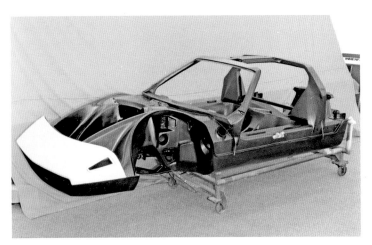

The GRP-PUR floor assembly was built up in the next production step with the aluminum body structure and the front longitudinal supports to form the floor system. Pictured is the floor system of car 37, taken in June 1975.

The third GRP-PUR floor assembly used for car 36 was fitted with the body in June–July 1974 at Waggonfabrik Rastatt.

Like car 31, which was provided for reference purposes, car 36 also received the widened front end for optimized cooling air supply.

necessary to cut out the support plate on the right wing, since the upper trailing arm did not allow installation closer to the engine. In the meantime, the latest four-speed automatic was planned as the power transmission, but in the end the five-speed manual transmission from ZF was used again, which had already been planned during the construction of the floor assembly. However, the part intended for attaching the gearshift bracket to the frame floor system deviated so far from the drawing that the shift lever had to be extended downward by 10 mm, and the counter plates attached under the vehicle floor had to be newly made and adapted to the vehicle. Such subsequent changes to a GRP-PUR floor assembly were always detrimental to the core composite and should therefore actually be avoided in general.

The installation of the pedal assembly also showed that there was not enough space both in height and to the side. No adjustment was made in the lateral direction to avoid weakening the load-bearing wall. This meant that the pedal assembly sat 15 mm too far to the right, necessitating changes to the center console and throttle linkage.

The radiator arrangement had been designed according to the latest status of car 31. This was made possible because the new vehicle had also received the wider front end realized on car 31. Because of the spare wheel well, however, the cooling air outlet was only 190 mm high (instead of the 210 mm provided for in the design, or 240 mm in car 31), which is why an additional oil cooler was fitted. During assembly, the radiator support on the left and right had to be milled out by 10 mm each. Extensive changes were also required for fitting the front and rear axles. The slightly shorter thrust arms compared to vehicles 31 to 35 had already been designed in the early phase of the plastic frame floor project in September 1970.

Car 36, the first C 111 with GRP-PUR floor assembly, photographed in August 1982, seven years after its completion

The steering was derived from the production W 115 sedan, and the steering gear had already been provided by the Untertürkheim test department in March 1972 in a variant with light-alloy housing and long steering shaft. Although already considered in the design, the mounting holes had to be reworked due to the confined space, and the distance to the steering column lever was also so small that the steering mounting screws had to be turned off.

As in the cars with sheet steel floor assembly, the fuel system consisted of two foam-lined, rubber-encased side tanks made of soft aluminum, which were housed in the side sills but only had a capacity of 50 liters each due to the greater wall thickness of the sills. The maximum permissible speed of the collapsible spare wheel, which was carried as a spare, was 210 km/h, and it was inflated using a compressed air cylinder, since the 12 V compressor that was actually intended would have taken about fifteen minutes to do so.

The narrower headlight housings with rectangular headlights, which differed from the other cars, lacked a little design elegance—and not only in Joachim Kaden's opinion. In contrast to cars 32 to 35, the pop-up headlights were not directly connected to the front hood but were separated from it by a bridge—as already realized on car 31 as part of the widening of the front end. On car 31, this had a width of 35 mm, on car 36 of 125 mm. On the one hand, this made it possible to support the crash element in the front area and, on the other hand, still offered enough space for a rectangular headlight under the headlight cover—a practical example of the old designer maxim "form follows function." As with cars 31 to 35, the headlights were operated via a crank mechanism with a reversible electric motor. The wheel cutouts on the front wheels had to be enlarged in the front area to prevent the wheels from rubbing.

The constrictions resulting from the double-shell construction of the floor assembly affected not only the pedal system, the gearshift, the steering, and the reduced tank capacity, but—contrary to the original planning—also the interior. By reducing the width of the center tunnel to that absolutely required by the air-conditioning system, moving the brake and clutch pedals to the side, and bulging out the rear wall behind the driver's seat, it was possible to improve the driver's position at least to such an extent that the first driving tests could be carried out. Despite this rework, the space conditions in the passenger compartment were considerably less favorable than in the other cars. The distance between the center of the steering wheel and the seat backrest was 20 mm less, between the lower edge of the steering wheel and the driver's seat 40 mm less, and between the brake pedal and the lower edge of the steering wheel 30 mm less, and the driver's headroom was also 30 mm less. The GRP-PUR floor assembly weighed 150 kg, the floor system (GRP-PUR floor assembly with aluminum superstructure and brackets) 181 kg, and the entire body shell 330 kg, and the kerb weight of the car was 1,316 kg. This meant that the total weight of car 36 was slightly less than that of cars 31 to 35, not least due to the use of light metal for the bolted-on roof assembly and the integral rear support. The integration of the front end section and the ventilation ducts into the floor assembly and the component carrier certainly played a role here as well.

The GRP-PUR floor assembly, which was more voluminous than the sheet steel version, only allowed the accommodation of a collapsible spare wheel. The hydraulic unit and the control unit of the first-generation anti-lock braking system are also clearly visible.

Practical Test: Start of Road Testing

Car 36 received its road approval at the beginning of September 1975 with the official registration number S—CL 1668, and the first driving tests were immediately carried out with racing tires in Hockenheim. Apart from minor irregularities in straight-line running, the car made a stable impression and immediately achieved the lap times of the cars with the same engine and steel floor assembly. More surprisingly,

Comparison of the front design of car 35 with sheet steel floor assembly (*top*) and car 36 with GRP-PUR floor assembly (*bottom*). Clearly visible are the widened front with rectangular auxiliary headlights on car 36, as car 31 had also received in the summer of 1971, the wide bridges between the hood and the headlights, and the narrower headlight housings with rectangular headlights.

after changing to street tires, the car proved to be extremely unstable, especially when turning, which even the optimization of all toe and camber values was unable to change. According to Dr. Liebold, the "rubbery steering feel" that occurred when weaving at medium speed was possibly due to the more indirect steering with longer spindle and light-alloy housing. The rest of the behavior, however, was clearly attributed by Liebold to the lower torsional rigidity compared to the vehicles with steel floor assembly. This influenced the wheel load distribution within the axles to such an extent that the self-steering behavior was subject to major changes, while the racing tires responded little to this, and the alternating springing of the rear axle was in any case more closely adapted to that of the front axle by a torsion bar. To improve the rigidity, the bearing of the front stabilizer torsion bar was moved back from the body structure to the bulkhead floor after the test runs and the modification was carried out on car 36. The resulting significantly reduced deformation length of the floor assembly led to much-improved handling during the last tests at Hockenheim, even with street tires.

The noise characteristics of the vehicle were also found to be disappointing and "rather worse" than cars 31 to 35 during the first test runs. The four-rotor engine equipped with a variable-length intake manifold with its reduced maximum power allowed significantly less remarkable driving performance: For example, compared to earlier light barrier measurements up to 274 km/h, the car reached "only"

Car 36, the first C 111 with GRP-PUR floor assembly, at the K`75 plastics fair in Düsseldorf in October 1975

about 230 km/h ahead of the east curve in Hockenheim, but the cars seemed "much more elastic from low revs." The emergency wheel, intended as a spare, was run on car 35 on a trial basis, alternately replacing the front and rear right street tire. With normal street tire pressure (3.3 or 3.7 bar), the vehicle, as Dr. Liebold put it in his development report dated September 23, "lost a lot of precision in the permissible speed range (up to 200 km) and tended to push over the axle in question but was still quite drivable on the small circuit in Hockenheim even with forced driving, so that careful use in the event of a breakdown also seems possible on the road."

According to Liebold, difficulties initially arose with regard to heating, especially on the large Hockenheim circuit, where, despite the wider front end opening, the oil temperature already reached 140°C (284°F) in the course of one lap at an outside temperature of 25°C (77°F). The installation of the additional oil cooler in front of the main cooler did not bring any improvement in this respect but increased the water temperature up to 120°C (248°F). After enlarging the outflow cross-section by omitting the bottom front cover plate in the car floor, the temperatures could be significantly reduced, although Liebold still diagnosed poorer flow conditions due to the spare wheel well, which protruded about 30 mm farther into the outflow than car 31. Despite their large cross-section, Liebold had apparently not taken the exhaust air shafts into account in his assessment, which extend almost to the floor of the vehicle on both sides of the spare wheel well. By installing an additional oil cooler in the rear, as was also fitted to cars 33 to 35, the maximum oil and water temperatures could finally be reduced to 130°C (266°F) and 95°C (203°F), respectively (i.e., still below the values of cars 34 and 35).

Liebold summarized the results of the road tests in the development report already cited: Thus, "the significantly reduced torsional rigidity compared to the previous cars, especially . . . with street tires, was very negatively noticeable, while there were hardly any disadvantages with racing tires. The somewhat cramped seating conditions can probably still be improved to some extent, while the noise behavior, which is rather worse offhand, is currently still being investigated. However, an appreciable improvement over the vehicles with steel floor assembly can hardly be expected here either, so that the use of this construction method, according to the first impression, should at best lead to cost advantages for corresponding small series."

Regardless of this assessment, the C 111 was still a spectacular vehicle that attracted attention. Bayer AG also took advantage of this when they presented the brand-new car 36 as an eye-catcher for their stand at the K`75 plastics trade fair in Düsseldorf in October 1975.

New Goals: A Second Test Car with GRP-PUR Floor Assembly

The second plastic floor assembly, which had initially not been accepted due to unexplained weight deficiency, was also built up into another test car, which was then consequently designated as car 37. The vehicle, which was originally intended for rough road testing and subsequently for a frontal impact test, was given a new purpose while still in the assembly phase. In a note to head of development Scherenberg on May 22, 1975, Liebold suggested using the vehicle "in between for the record-setting attempts," in which a C 111 was to be equipped with a supercharged five-cylinder diesel of the model OM 617 in order to beat the existing speed records over various distances.

To this end, Liebold suggested that only the load-bearing parts of the body be produced in the previous form and connected to the floor assembly, while the doors as well as the front and rear hatches were to be produced in a lightened version. The interior equipment could also be "minimized from the outset"—and thus optimized in terms of weight—"since it will not be needed in the usual form later on either." The background to the targeted weight savings was a plan to set new acceleration records in addition to the speed records. In mid-June 1975, the Sindelfingen body development department defined the necessary modifications, and in Johann Tomforde and Joseph Gallitzendörfer the styling department compiled "measures for weight reduction that are formally acceptable." In doing so, they determined a savings potential of 14 to 20.7 kg for the outer skin "apart from interior appointments and other material savings."

On October 16, 1975, the first driving tests were carried out at the Hockenheimring with car 37, which had been fitted with a five-cylinder turbodiesel engine as proposed by Hans Liebold. The results are documented in a development note from the following day.

Despite limitations regarding the realized boost pressure and the available final-drive ratio, the previously calculated acceleration values had been achieved at the first attempt, and a top speed of 227 km/h had been measured "with a slight headwind and very slight incline."

However, the test drive also revealed unsatisfactory torsional rigidity, which Dr. Liebold commented on: "However, the greater torsional elasticity of the plastic floor assembly had an even less favorable effect on driving stability during the tests. On the undulating track in front of the east bend in Hockenheim, the car with 205 VR 14 tires could only be kept on course at the speed reached with great concentration despite changes to the tire pressure and toe-in. Due to the much better behavior of the first sandwich car (car 36) with racing tires, it can also be concluded that car 37 will behave less problematically with this. However, the car has an approximately 8% higher c_d x F, whose influence on the driving performance is currently being calculated."

Regarding the planned record-setting attempts, he continued, "We should . . . briefly clarify on the track definitively intended for the long-distance tests whether the handling there is not sufficient with the 205/70 VR 15 street tires at least, which were last used on the C 101. Otherwise, there is still the possibility of converting one of the parked C 101s with a steel floor assembly." Further acceleration measurements were carried out in Hockenheim with both racing tires and the 15-inch street tires, but in the end the alternative outlined by Liebold of converting a C 111 with a sheet steel floor assembly for the record-breaking tests was realized.

The reduced torsional rigidity compared to car 36 was attributed to three causes: the ultimately unresolved weight deficiency of the floor assembly, the modifications carried out in the transition area from the rear support to the outer side rail, which were primarily due to the installation of a rapid refueling system, and finally the lightened GRP body.

According to project manager Klaus Matthias, in order to be able to use the vehicle as a test vehicle for further driving tests with the diesel engine, modifications to the core composite floor assembly would have been necessary, but these could not be satisfactorily carried out on the finished component for various reasons. Conceivable measures to increase the torsional rigidity were

- an extension of the lateral box-type outriggers of the rear support up to the outer shells of the outer side rail and a positive and non-positive connection with the GRP shells,
- an extension of the fork-shaped longitudinal bars of the rear support and a direct connection of their upper branch with the crossrail behind the seats and the aluminum body structure,
- a retrofitting of additional diagonal struts from the suspension strut mount of the rear axle to the roof structure and to the outer side rail,
- a straightening of the connection of the bolt-on flanges for the suspension struts of the front axle to increase the transverse stability and stiffen the design in the area of the steering gear, and
- a use of the weight saving achieved compared to the sheet steel variant to optimize the rigidity.

Car 37, the second C 111 with GRP-PUR floor assembly, photographed in December 1981, six years after its completion. In its external appearance, car 37 corresponds exactly to the successful record-setting car from the world record run in June 1976. Clearly visible are the missing pop-up headlights, the rim covers, and the weight-reduced rear trim.

After car 37 had already been planned for record-setting attempts in its construction phase, a receptacle for the rapid refueling system was installed at the rear end of each of the outer side rails, which had not been provided for in the original design. The resulting weakening of the structure in the transition to the rear support was diagnosed as one of several causes for the reduced torsional rigidity after the driving tests.

According to a development note of December 8, 1975, prepared by Dr. Liebold, car 37 was to be equipped with a 2.3-liter four-cylinder M 115 engine as well as the regular doors and hoods and thus prepared for the originally planned rough road test, the so-called "Heidedauerlauf" (heathland endurance test—a special test cycle originally carried out on rough roads in heathland). However, no archival sources can be found for this conversion and the aforementioned testing, and neither seems very plausible: On the one hand, the further development of the C 111 was officially ended anyway, and on the other hand, after the spectacular record-setting run in June 1976, car 37, like the actual record-setting car it resembled in every detail, was shown at trade fairs and exhibitions all over the world.

Conclusion: Valuable New Insight

Klaus Matthias's conclusion on the tests with the sandwich floor assembly, published in his already cited article in *Automobiltechnische Zeitschrift*, was rather sobering overall: "An independent core composite design—with a component concept adapted to the requirements of the construction method—would certainly have produced a more favorable result. However, the comparison of the lightweight construction key figures for the average cross-section shows that advantages—in terms of rigidity and weight—are not to be expected for the GRP/PU core composite construction compared to a sheet steel construction. When the project was brought to an end in 1975, no statement could be made about the costs of a small-series version in GRP/PU core composite design, since the series technology was still imperfect."

Despite this cautious assessment by the project manager and the partly disappointing results, the development of the C 111 with GRP-PUR core composite floor assembly can certainly be considered a success. The design, manufacture, and measurement of such a floor assembly; its assembly into a complete vehicle; and its testing had led to fundamental and valuable findings in every phase of development due to the need to devise solutions for constantly new problems—even if these were ultimately not applied in series production.

The development of the C 111 as an experimental vehicle and high-performance sports car came to an end in 1975 with cars 36 and 37, the two examples with GRP-PUR floor assemblies, and the "mobile laboratory" was subsequently to mutate into a record hunter.

Aiming for Maximum Performance:
The C 111 as a Record-Setting Car

Please note: A breakdown of the departmental abbreviations used in the cited reports and minutes can be found in the appendix.

Even before the last C 111 with a Wankel engine was completed with car 36, the second phase of the development history began in the spring of 1975, in which the mid-engined coupé caused a sensation as a record-setting car. The starting point for these activities was considerations at Daimler-Benz to make greater use of the better efficiency of the diesel engine in view of the energy and oil price crisis. This led to the OM 617 3-liter five-cylinder engine—at that time the world's most powerful diesel engine for passenger cars with 80 hp/59 kW, which was launched in the Mercedes-Benz 240 D 3.0 in October 1974. In view of the corporate average fuel economy (CAFE) regulations for passenger cars sold in the US market, which were introduced in 1975 and came into force in 1978, the idea was even considered of offering this engine in the S-Class as well and achieving the necessary increase in power through turbocharging.

From Mobile Laboratory to Record Hunter: The C 111-II D

The actual starting signal for the record-breaking car development was given in May 1975. At the press trial drive of the new S-Class top model 450 SEL 6.9 in Le Hohwald, Alsace, Hans Liebold and Prof. Scherenberg, the member of the board responsible for development, talked about the possibilities of "undercutting the records set by Opel in Dudenhofen . . . with a supercharged OM 617 in the C 101." The talk was about a record drive at the Opel test center in Dudenhofen, which had taken place almost exactly three years earlier at the market launch of the Opel Rekord Diesel. Equipped with a forced-induction version of the 2.1-liter production diesel, the record-breaking car, based on the Opel GT and extensively reworked aerodynamically, had set 18 international class records and two world records during the three-day drive in June 1972, including the 10,000 km at 190.88 km/h.

With the C 111, Daimler-Benz had a very suitable starting point for the record-setting attempts. In a note to Hans Scherenberg dated May 22, 1975, Dr. Liebold summarized his assessment: A weight-reduced vehicle with a fully fueled kerb weight of 1,000 kg should be able to reach a speed of 218 km/h when using a 150 hp/110 kW diesel engine, and even 225 km/h with 170 hp/125 kW.

Less than two weeks later, on June 3, 1975, project manager Hans Liebold gave the test department an official assignment under the subject "Preparation of a C 101 with OM 617 ATL for record drives." The scope of the assignment was defined as follows:

"With an OM 617 ATL [exhaust gas turbocharger] the C 101 is to attack the speed records currently held by Opel from 1 km flying start to 10,000 km as well as the acceleration records for diesel vehicles class 8 (2,000 to 3,000 cc).

"For this purpose, to begin with:
1. Prepare two engines with a displacement reduced by approximately 5 cc for a test bench run (50 h, 150 hp, 4,500 rpm) and subsequent vehicle installation.
2. Finish the sandwich floor assembly of the C 101 car 37 intended for rough road testing and subsequent crash tests with the main body components as normal and then equip it with doors, front end, and adapted hatch in a very light version as well as with minimal equipment.
3. Complete the car with lightened major assemblies and calibrate it."

The Opel diesel record car during its record drive at the Opel test center in Dudenhofen in June 1972

Ernst Haug, an employee of the body construction department in Sindelfingen, and his boss Theodor Reinhard immediately took up the subject and, in a memo dated June 12, 1975, defined the body and the deviating features of the car 37 intended for the record drive in a thirty-point list with all the details:

Substructure

Sandwich plastic floor assembly
Integrated aluminum engine-transmission carrier
Steering knuckle brackets f./r. axle "steel"
Windshield profile frame with tubular reinforcement and "steel" pillars
Roof center bar profile frame "steel"
Roll bar profile frame "steel"

Bodywork

1. Body large mold with front-end widening GRP 2.5–3 mm thickness
   Polyester resin Leguval W 35 Bayer Leverkusen
   Material structure:
   Gelcoat
   2 x 225 g/m² glass mat
   1 x 163 g/m² fabric
   1 x 225 g/m² glass mat
2. Front hood GRP 1–1.2 mm
   Material structure:
   Gelcoat minimal
   1 x 225 g/m² mat
   1 x 163 g/m² fabric
3. Rear trunk material structure as in item 2, GRP
   Protruding bulge in the center area for cylinder head and intake manifold. The shape should be established on a vehicle from ST1, and a negative mold should be created. Side openings to the outside with recessed support flange for inserting Plexiglas windows. New opening for rear refueling.
4. Rear window cover, outside rear GRP
   Material structure as item 2
   Extension to the front corresponding to 20 mm shifted rear window and protruding bulge for cylinder head cover. The view to the rear is thus somewhat impaired.
5. Rear bumper GRP
   Material structure as in item 2, removable for tank installation or removal. No passageway for exhaust pipes and no ventilation slots.
6. Trunk is omitted; crossrail in new design; material structure as in item 1, GRP.
7. Doors, outer skin and inner frame
   Material structure as item 2 GRP. Inner frame in modified version for special locking mechanisms and without hinged window
8. Switch panel and glove box, material composition as item 2 GRP. All other interior trim parts are omitted.
9. Locking mechanisms for flaps with quick-release fasteners without Bowden cables. Door lock and retaining ring are omitted.
10. Pop-up headlights are omitted. The two passing lights already intended in the front end air intake are supplemented with two main beams.
11. Carrier for taillights, material construction as pos. 2 GRP.
12. Front left and right indicators like car 12 [this and the following mentions do not explicitly refer to car 12, but the C 111-II as a whole]
13. Taillights left and right like car 12
14. Windshield wiper system like car 12
15. Front air intake grille wire mesh
16. Rear grille above bumper wire mesh
17. Air intake grille rear wing wire mesh
18. Glass windows, windshield 4.8 mm thick (previously 5.6) without antenna, door windows Plexiglas with small sliding windows, rear window glass like car 12.
19. Exhaust heat and sound-insulating mats or sheets are all omitted.
20. Heating and cooling system omitted, fresh air supply with flap or vent regulation required.
21. Exterior mirror is omitted, interior mirror like car 12.
22. Driver's seat like car 12, passenger's seat without mechanism fixed in minimum weight version
23. Fuel filler necks front left and right enlarged from 60 to 100 mm.

24. Rear fuel filler necks left and right through side rail in engine compartment 100 mm Ø new.
25. Side rail openings (for tank pipe left and right) reinforced at the bottom with rail rear wall, additional support plates and brackets on the wheel arch panel or roll bar
26. Rear window moved forward by 20 mm
27. Crossrail under rear window new
28. Rear wall behind seat backrest with opening for V-belt pulley alternator
29. Gas-pressured springs for lightened doors with low extension force
30. Rear trunk stay is replaced by support rod; rear lock is omitted.

A large part of the deviations from the previous design listed in this paper resulted from the weight saving required by Liebold, which was particularly important regarding short distance and acceleration records. To ensure that the design aspects did not fall by the wayside here, Joseph Gallitzendörfer, designer of the first hour in the C 101 project, and project newcomer Johann Tomforde formulated "measures to reduce the weight of the outer form that are formally acceptable" in a note to Hans Liebold and Theodor Reinhard dated June 16. In it, they proposed the following modifications:

- Reduction of the profile cross-section of the louver grille in the rear: 0.850 kg
- Replacement of the taillights with a smaller version: 0.900 kg
- Omission of reversing lights: 0.820 kg
- Omission of number plate and number plate illumination: 0.560 kg
- Omission of exterior mirrors: 1.450 kg
- Reduction of the aluminum grille inserts on the engine compartment cover and radiator grille and omission of the grilles on the air intake in front of the wheels: 1.276 kg
- Use of an 80 mm shorter and 0.8 mm thinner windshield: 3.700 kg
- Omission of windshield wipers (without drive): 0.613 kg
- Omission of the pop-up headlights: 3.600 kg
- Replacement of the Mercedes star with a lighter version: 0.150 kg

In this way, the two stylists defined a savings potential of 14 kg on the outer skin alone; they held out the prospect of a further reduction by 6.7 kg if the windshield was made of 4 mm thick Plexiglas.

Official Kick-Off: Board of Management Mission for Record-Setting Attempts

On 15 July 1975, the record-setting attempts came up for the first time in a board meeting. Dr. Hans Scherenberg reported that the familiar motor journalist Fritz B. Busch "intended to set speed records [class records for vehicles with diesel engines] over 1 mile or 1 km and . . . asked for the provision of an appropriate engine." In addition, the Daimler-Benz head of development proposed "to attack the long-distance endurance speed records for diesel vehicles in their own right with an OM 617 diesel engine with exhaust gas turbocharging installed in a C 111 body." This would "benefit the image of the five-cylinder diesel vehicles, which had been received extremely positively by the press, and at the same time would once again underline the experimental character of the C 111 model." A series of tests lasting about six months would be necessary for preparation, the costs of which he estimated at about DM 650,000.

After in-depth discussion, the Board of Management agreed to the provision of a diesel engine for the record-setting attempts planned by Fritz B. Busch, and recommended "to continue to consider to what extent own record-breaking attempts with corresponding diesel engines appear appropriate from an image point of view."

Following the decision of the Board of Management, the diesel engine development department headed by Dr. Manfred Fortnagel built two more examples for Fritz B. Busch's record-setting attempt in addition to the two high-performance diesel engines planned for the C 111. The engines were ready for installation in the first days of October 1975. Compared to the standard engines without turbocharging, the bore had been reduced by 0.1 mm to 90.9 mm to keep the total displacement below the 3,000 cc mark and to be able to compete in the 2,000 to

3,000 cc class. The turbocharger used was the T 04 B model from the US manufacturer Garrett AiResearch; the boost pressure was 2.8 bar at charger speeds of 130,000 rpm, with the peak pressure in the main combustion chamber reaching 135 bar, the temperature upstream of the turbine almost 800°C (1,472°F), and the maximum charge air temperature 200°C (392°F). The acceptance diagram for the first engine handed over to Fritz B. Busch, with the individual designation EA 25-015, showed a maximum output of 188 hp/138 kW at 4,350 rpm and a maximum torque of 33.5 mkp/329 Nm at 3,600 rpm.

The EA 25-013 engine intended for the C 111, car 37, produced an output of 191.6 hp/140.9 kW at 4,200 rpm on the test bench. At the beginning of October, it was installed in the just-completed test car with GRP-PUR floor assembly and lightened body. The first driving tests took place on October 16, 1975, at the Hockenheimring and were documented by Hans Liebold in a memo dated the next day. Although a boost pressure of only 2.5 bar (with intercooler 2.2 bar)—0.3 bar less than on the test bench—was measured, the calculated acceleration values were achieved straightaway. With the advised kerb weight of approximately 1,070 kg for the long-distance tests, the quarter mile was covered in 13.8 seconds and the kilometer in 26.0 seconds, in each case with a standing start, corresponding to an average speed of 104.9 and 138.5 km/h, respectively. The final speeds were 156.6 and 197.9 km/h.

Since the intended final-drive ratio of 3.23 was not yet available, the calculated top speed could not be achieved, and "227 km/h were measured for car 37 with light barriers in a slight headwind and on a very slight incline, with the engine at 4,600 rpm already at the start of the governor range." Liebold wrote about the acceleration attempts, "If [these] are still of any interest to us at all, the car can be slimmed down by about 170 kg for this purpose, which should still improve the stated acceleration values by about 3%."

Referring to the further-increased torsional elasticity compared to car 36, the first C 111 with GRP-PUR floor assembly, Liebold recommended to clarify whether the driving behavior on the track definitively intended for the record-setting attempts was not sufficient, at least with the street tires used lately, and suggested the conversion of an existing C 111 with steel floor assembly as an alternative. The measures required for this were recorded by body constructor Ernst Haug and Theodor Reinhard in a memo dated November 12, 1975:

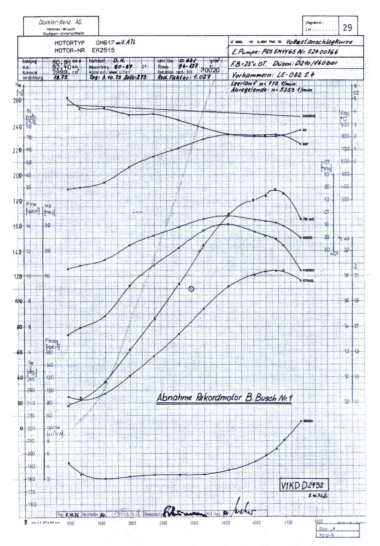

Performance diagram of the turbocharged 3-liter five-cylinder diesel engine OM 617 A with the number EA 25-015, taken on October 3, 1975, at the acceptance test prior to delivery to Fritz B. Busch

New components:	
Front hood	GRP
Doors	GRP
Rear hood	GRP
Rear crossrail	GRP
Switch panel	GRP
Interior trim	GRP
Hinge for front hood	Aluminum
Hinge for bearing plates	Aluminum

Lock for front hood	Aluminum
Door hinges	Aluminum
Door hinges counter bearing	Aluminum
Lock case	Aluminum
Bearing plates for door handle	Aluminum
Quick release for rear hood front and rear	Aluminum
Protective grille, front and rear	Aluminum
Side rail shells, outer	Aluminum
Crossrail over suspension strut Front axle	Aluminum
Crossrail over rear axle	Aluminum
Windshield 5 thick (previously 5.6) [dimensions in mm]	
Rear window	Plexiglas
Door windows	Plexiglas
Driver's seat with GRP backrest without backrest adjustment	
Crossrail on rear wall, top	Steel
Cover opening in rear wall	Aluminum
Gas-pressured spring with low operating force	

First Test: The "Diesel Star"

While preparations for the record drive of the C 111 Diesel were underway in Untertürkheim and Sindelfingen under the project management of Hans Liebold and Joachim Kaden, Fritz B. Busch was completing and testing his special design called "Diesel Star." The renowned journalist and classic car enthusiast had developed the idea for his record-setting attempt when he made a stopover at the Bonneville Salt Flats on his 94-day long-distance endurance test of a VW Golf over 30,514 km from Alaska to Tierra del Fuego, which he started in October 1974. In the process, he learned of the

The "Diesel Star," built by Fritz B. Busch and equipped with a Mercedes-Benz five-cylinder turbodiesel engine, with which Busch reached a top speed of 253.705 km/h in November 1975

records that the American Virgil William Snyder had set in various displacement classes with diesel-powered record cars, and saw an opportunity to beat some of these records.

Busch had built the "Diesel Star" with a small team of supporters in the workshop of his classic car museum in Wolfegg based on a Formula 2 chassis from the British manufacturer GRD. The self-designed streamlined body had a c_d value of 0.29. The five-speed manual transmission came from a De Tomaso Pantera; this was the 5 DS-25 from ZF, which had also been used in modified form in the C 111 since 1969. At the VW proving ground in Ehra-Lessien, Busch initially set three international class records on October 28, 1975, when he covered the quarter mile at 103.650 km/h, the half kilometer at 112.247 km/h, and the kilometer at 138.116 km/h—in each case with a standing start.

In doing so, he surpassed two records set by British racing driver Patsy Burt in a 130 hp/95 kW turbocharged Mercedes-Benz 220 D in October 1970, as well as a record set by the Opel GT team in June 1972 by a margin of around 25 km/h. However, the Diesel Star lacked any directional stability at more than 220 km/h and was practically undrivable in this speed range. Measurements in the VW wind tunnel revealed the cause to be a front-axle downforce of 350 kg, which was far too high. A correction of the front section lowered the downforce to 60 kg without worsening the c_d value, and on November 16, 1975 Busch was also able to tackle the flying kilometer and the flying mile in Ehra-Lessien. With 249.324 km/h and 249.188 km/h, respectively, he improved the records of the 2,000 to 3,000 cc displacement class, which V. W. Snyder had achieved on the Bonneville Salt Flats in August 1974, by almost 20 km/h. The top speed of Busch's "Diesel Star" was measured at 253.705 km/h. The supercharged OM 617 provided by Daimler-Benz had given a first taste of its performance there.

However, the records achieved by Busch—at least those with a flying start—did not last long, and this was not even related to the activities of Daimler-Benz. On this side of the Atlantic, it had apparently gone unnoticed that Snyder had already improved his records, set a year earlier, to 306.083 and 305.846 km/h in August 1975. His record-breaking car was powered by a boosted Isuzu diesel engine with a displacement of 2.4 liters. With the recognition by the FIA, which did not take place until November 1975, the records achieved by Fritz B. Busch were immediately obsolete again.

Circular Track and Wind Tunnel: The Record Preparations

Independently of this, preparations for the record-setting attempts planned with the C 111 went ahead in Untertürkheim. It was obvious that the records achieved by Snyder were out of reach, but Daimler-Benz did not have any acceleration records over short distances in mind but instead aimed for best performances over very long distances. A central question was the choice of the route on which the record run was to take place. So it was a good thing that the "Società Autopiste Sperimentali Nardò" (SASN), founded on July 1, 1975, as a subsidiary of the FIAT Group, put into operation a high-speed test track that had just been completed in the southeastern Italian region of Puglia.

The 12.55 km long circular track known as the "Pista di Nardò," "Anello di Nardò," or "Circuito di Nardò," located about 20 km northwest of the town of the same name, was built at the beginning of the 1970s with public funds to promote the structurally weak Italian south. It was originally planned as a site for a particle accelerator, and the FIAT Group took over the site after the initially intended use no longer seemed opportune. It was designed as a high-speed track with a maximum banking of 13°, and speeds of up to 240 km/h were achievable without lateral forces. The test area comprised four car lanes each 4m wide, one car hard shoulder, two truck lanes, one truck hard shoulder, and

The high-speed test track near Nardò in southern Italy, photographed in November 2006 from aboard the International Space Station (ISS)

separated by a crash barrier, a lane for checking the test lanes. In order to keep the forces acting on the test vehicles within limits, the direction was changed on a daily basis: clockwise one day, then counterclockwise the next.

On February 25, 1976, two employees of the Daimler-Benz test department visited the still very little frequented test track to check its suitability for high-speed tests, for radiator measurements, and for handling tests. With a 450 SEL 6.9, they made sure that driving free of lateral forces was possible at speeds between 210 and 250 km/h. In view of the record drive, the test department employees stated in a report on March 4: "For the planned endurance run (30–50 h at V_{max}), the circular track is excellently suited. Mr. Mininanni gave his consent for us to set up a depot on the car hard shoulder for refueling and changing tires. Electricity is not available at the track. An emergency generator would have to be taken along. Equipping the vehicle with the automatic speed measuring device should make sense. This allows the average speed of each lap to be registered automatically."

On February 19, 1976, the C 111 no. 31, now equipped with a diesel engine, was examined in the large wind tunnel in

Untertürkheim to determine the extent to which detachable parts such as front end spoilers, wheel spats, etc. could improve the drag coefficient. This showed that an 11.6% reduction in the c_d value from 0.345 to 0.305 was possible through the following measures:

- Fitting a 50 mm high front spoiler
- Removing the exterior mirrors
- Masking of the door, hood, and hood vents
- Masking of the additional air intakes at the front end
- Covering of the rims with wheel discs
- Crowned (outward curved) lateral front end extension in the area of the headlights

After the wind tunnel measurements, the car received a rapid refueling system similar to the one used in Formula 1. For the two side tanks, a filler neck with a diameter of 10 cm was installed directly in front of the rear wheel arches. This closed automatically when the refueling hose was disconnected after the refueling process was complete. Since diesel fuel foams heavily during filling, an additional vent was installed in the two tanks in addition to the filling opening, through which the air and diesel foam could escape quickly without hindering the filling process. The two air

In the spring of 1976, for the upcoming record drive, car 31 was fitted with a rapid refueling system whose vents were housed in the vehicle's front end.

Car 31 during wind tunnel testing in February 1976. At this time, the car already had the turbodiesel engine, the openings for the pop-up headlamps were sealed, and the new headlights were mounted in the front. The ventilation openings in the front end and the gaps of the hood were provisionally taped off for the measurement.

vents were each located under a flap on the air outlet ducts of the front hood. As soon as straight diesel fuel instead of foam could be seen in the attached transparent vent hose, the refueling process was complete and the tank hose could be removed—always before the vent hose. With the constant circling on the record track, it was to be expected that the fuel would always be pushed into the tank on the outside of the curve by the centrifugal force. Therefore, additional pumps were installed to counteract this centrifugal effect.

Field Test: Testing of the Record-Setting Car

In the period from March 30 to April 2, 1976, setup and test runs were carried out on the test track in Nardò with car 31, which had only been completed twenty-four hours before loading. Even during the first test run on the test track in Untertürkheim, the car appeared, as Hans Liebold noted in a memo dated April 5, "surprisingly very unstable, which, apart from errors in the wheel alignment, is probably mainly due to the change in the weight distribution of the heavily lightened car with diesel engine. . . . After correcting the wheel alignment, changing the tire pressure, and reinforcing the front torsion bar, it appeared fine enough to be loaded."

In Nardò, the vehicle proved to be unacceptable even in this form, so that, as Liebold noted, "first tests were carried out with increased tire pressure difference front/rear and a further reinforced torsion bar at the front. As the car still yawed too much, especially in the incoming, relatively strong crosswind, a 65 mm high spoiler running across the entire width of the car was provisionally attached to the front end of the car, which had been tested earlier at Hockenheim. After this, the vehicle only required slightly increased concentration when driving and behaved absolutely smoothly in light crosswinds and broken-in tires."

Liebold was of the opinion that "tests in the wind tunnel led to an improvement in crosswind sensitivity" and that "optimizing the angular position and height of the vehicle would still promise an

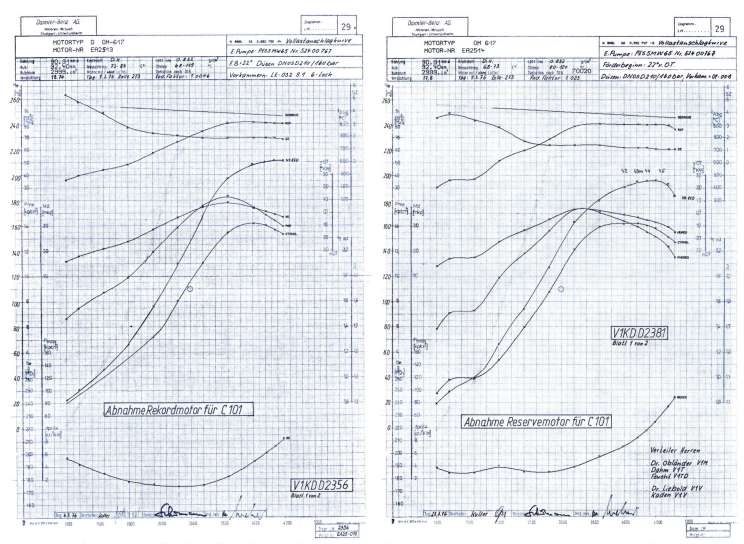

Performance curves of the 3-liter five-cylinder diesel engines OM 617 A with the numbers EA 25-013 and EA 25-014, recorded during acceptance as record engine and reserve engine on February 9 and March 9, 1976, respectively

increase in speed." The latter he concluded from the fact that "the lap times were regularly about two seconds better with a full tank than with an empty one." Tire temperatures and wear were so even that, in Liebold's estimation, "you can expect about twelve hours of lifetime for the rear tire."

The engine presented an inconsistent picture during testing, as Liebold noted: "With the originally installed EA 25-013 engine, which had already run for 6½ hours in the car on Behr's radiator test bench, thermal problems occurred in Nardò right from the start. . . . During the first attempts, a reasonably even water temperature of 93° was initially established, which rose to about 120° after fifteen laps. During the subsequent drive to the depot, the engine overheated so badly that it had to be switched off." After various measures failed to remedy the situation, the engine was prophylactically exchanged for the replacement EA 25-014 engine on the morning of the third day of testing, whereupon—as Liebold put it—"no more problems occurred at all. During the rest of that day's rides and the entire ten-hour drive the next, the temperatures remained absolutely constant. At an outside temperature of approximately 20°C (68°F), the coolant temperature was a constant 88°C (190°F), the oil temperature 110°C (230°F). Both the charge air and transmission oil temperature were 120°C (248°F). The boost pressure, which had fluctuated between 1.8 and 2.1 bar on the first engine, was now constant at 1.9 bar despite the same turbocharger. . . . Because of the approximately 20 hp lower output (190 hp against 210), the lap averages hereby dropped from max. 252 to max. 246 km/h, with a ten-hour average of 241.6 km/h. With the necessary refueling stops every 2½ hours, during which the drivers were changed at the same time, the average speed was 238 km/h over ten hours. Since most of the refueling stops can be shortened to about 1 min, among other things, by the planned conversion to oil level check without hood removal, . . . and the speed can probably be increased noticeably by aerodynamic measures, a continuous speed of more than 240 km/h should also be achieved with 190 hp." In addition, a "somewhat longer final-drive ratio seemed expedient" to Liebold, with which the ZF 5-speed transmissions newly ordered for the record drive were then to be equipped.

On the bodywork, Liebold noted, "Now that no more acceleration tests are planned, the extreme weight reduction of the body can be scaled back somewhat. In particular, for conditions like those in Nardò, it is imperative to improve ventilation and provide protection against the strong sunlight. The position and illumination of the display instruments, which are now partially covered by the steering wheel rim, should also be improved. The radio system must also be improved, since the voice communication was only faultless in the vicinity of the paddock. . . . For this purpose, tests should be carried out with different car antennas and a modified earphone."

Fine Tuning: Aerodynamic Optimization

On April 29, 1976, car 31 again went to the large wind tunnel in Untertürkheim, where further measurements were taken to improve the c_d value on the basis of the configuration determined and implemented in March. With a 50 mm high front spoiler, covered wheel rims, removed exterior mirrors, an externally lined and cambered front section in the headlight area, and negative attitude of the bodywork (−10 mm at the front, +20 mm at the rear compared to the original state), a drag coefficient of 0.294 was determined. Previously, numerous variants with different widths and heights of front spoilers, tail fins, and covered wheel arches at the front and rear had been tested, but without achieving a better overall result. In the end, the car was lowered by 45 mm at the front in favor of the lowest possible c_d value.

Things were also progressing on the engine side: On June 1, Fritz Clauß and Dr. Manfred Fortnagel of the diesel engine testing department summarized in a development report the results of an endurance run over eighty hours to which they had subjected the EA 25-013 high-performance engine on the test bench. The five-cylinder engine with an output of 195 hp/143 kW was operated alternately for 1.5 minutes at 4,200 rpm and 1.5 minutes at 4,600 rpm; after each two-and-a-half-hour period, there was a half-minute idling phase to simulate the refueling stop. After running for twenty-nine hours, two camshaft bearings broke due to a lack of valve clearance of the exhaust valves, after no check of the valve clearance had taken place up to this point.

After replacement of all camshaft bearings in polished finish and in conjunction with a copper-plated camshaft, the run was continued to eighty hours, with valve clearance checked at thirty-five, forty-two, fifty-four, and sixty-five hours and adjusted at fifty-four hours on three intake valves. The oil consumption was 143 g/h, so in two and a half hours—the time interval between two refueling stops—it was 357.5 g or 0.44 liters. As the endurance run had not revealed any further complaints, the final assessment of

When the wind tunnel test was carried out in April 1976, car 31 was already equipped with the rapid refueling system. Differently dimensioned and positioned front spoilers were examined, as were various detachable parts. The front end section, which was extended and cambered in the area of the headlights, was initially only carried out provisionally during the measurement.

the engine test was "It is reasonable to assume that if the valve clearance is checked and readjusted, the record-setting attempt can be made."

Meanwhile, the record-breaking 10,000-mile (16,093.4 km) drive planned for the second week of June was being prepared in general staff fashion in all the specialist departments involved. Project management was in the hands of test engineer Joachim Kaden and his boss, Dr. Hans Liebold. A meeting on May 15, 1976, dealt with the points that still needed to be clarified. It was decided, for example, that the left fuel tank would be enlarged by 9 liters to allow for a more favorable arrangement of the pit stops. In addition, the car was to receive a new intercooler, the installation of which, however, had to be carried out very carefully and was to be assessed during the final wind tunnel test on May 28. The valve clearance adjustment should also be practiced on this occasion.

On May 26, the two new five-speed transmissions that had been ordered were collected from ZF in Schwäbisch Gmünd; one of them was installed in the record-breaking car and the other in car 34, where it was first gently broken in for 1,000 km and then tested in a 1,000 km full-throttle run under operating conditions on the Hockenheimring and the Heilbronn-Würzburg motorway. To reduce transmission oil temperatures and minimize the risk of transmission failure, an oil cooling system was installed.

Also on May 26, the spare parts to be carried in the car during the record run were also determined. This was an important decision because during the record-setting attempt, necessary repairs were only permitted with these spare parts. The list included the following items:

As a result of the wind tunnel measurements, car 31 received the extended and cambered front end section, which had only been provisional until then.

1 cylinder head complete (with jets, prechambers, glow plugs, slide rail, camshaft, bearings, chain tensioner, exhaust gasket, and contingent necessary screws— without exhaust manifold, intake manifold, and turbocharger parts) 43.00 kg
1 set of injection lines (adapted to engine EA 25-007, individually marked with cylinder 1–5) 0.60 kg
2 V-belts Polyflex II 9.5 x 940 0.10 kg
2 head gaskets 0.52 kg
1 alternator 35 amps, pulley Dw 61 Ø with standard fan 4.05 kg
1 oil filter element 0.39 kg
1 charger lubricating oil line 0.25 kg
1 valve cover gasket 0.13 kg
1 set of drive plates (clutch) 2 pieces 1.10 kg
2 windshield wiper blades
1 windshield wiper arm 0.60 kg
4 spare bulbs
10 fuses

In the end, the spare parts resulted in an additional weight of around 51 kg.

The richly instrumented cockpit of the C 111-II record-setting diesel car. Additionally installed instruments show, among other things, the charge air temperature, the exhaust gas temperature, the transmission oil temperature, and the outside temperature.

The C 111-II diesel, photographed on the site of the test track at the Mercedes-Benz Werk Untertürkheim in May 1976

The engine compartment of the C 111 test car 31 was filled by a five-cylinder diesel with exhaust gas turbocharger and intercooler instead of the four-rotor Wankel engine.

Difficult Start: The Way to the Record

At the board meeting on May 25, 1976, Hans Scherenberg had informed his colleagues about the state of preparations and suggested that "these record drives should be carried out as soon as possible," which the board noted with approval. In addition to the two project managers, Liebold and Kaden, Erich Waxenberger, responsible for sporty vehicles in the test car construction department, and Guido Moch, head of the operational test department, were assigned as drivers, who would take turns after every two and a half hours of driving time. In addition, the team comprised five engineers, three technicians, two foremen, and fourteen mechanics. The caravan from Untertürkheim to Nardò consisted of a total of thirteen vehicles: ten passenger cars from the test department, which also completed corresponding test programs on the 1,670 km journey, two trucks, and an additional tanker truck with the fuel required for the record-setting drive. It was decided to bring 7,000 liters of diesel from Germany in order not to take any risks regarding the quality and composition of the fuel. Seven vehicles of the first column—four test cars and the three commercial vehicles—left for Italy on June 3; the remaining passenger cars followed four days later.

After the preliminary tests had started in Nardò on June 8 at 1 p.m., the record drive was started on June 10 at 8:00 in the morning, with Erich Waxenberger at the wheel. After forty-nine laps or 619.373 km, the first pit stop was made, and Hans Liebold took over the wheel. The stop lasted one minute and six seconds; as the engine died at the start, the car was pushed back and started again. After lap 97, Dr. Liebold came into the pits and handed the car over to Joachim Kaden. However, the next regular pit stop was not to happen. On the 127th lap, after a total driving time of six hours and eighteen minutes, the car touched the crash barrier at top speed, and the record-setting attempt was abandoned.

The record-breaking drivers of 1976 (*left to right*) **Dr. Hans Liebold, Joachim Kaden, Guido Moch, and Erich Waxenberger**

What had happened? Kaden, who as a test engineer and active autocross driver was very familiar with the behavior of cars at the limit, later recalled, "After I had taken over the vehicle from Dr. Liebold and had driven it for some time, the self-aligning torque noticeable in the steering wheel became smaller and smaller, despite constant cornering, and then finally disappeared completely. For the test engineer, an unmistakable sign that something out of the ordinary is happening—really not a pleasant feeling. I remember exactly how all the hairs stood up under my helmet and on the back of my neck. Very shortly after the self-aligning torque disappeared completely, there was quite a thump. The car swerved to the left and collided with the crash barrier quite roughly. As I initially suspected that I had lost the left front wheel, I didn't want to brake but tried to keep the car on course as best I could and let it coast to a stop. I didn't feel any

Start of the record-setting attempts in Nardò on June 8, 1976. The clearly relaxed mood shows that the actual record drive has not yet begun.

Car 31 after contact with the crash barrier. The unnaturally protruding left front wheel and the damage to the front wing show that something is wrong here. Despite the high speed, the damage was kept within limits thanks to Joachim Kaden's level-headed reaction, and the record-breaking attempt could be restarted the next day.

After the spectacular but minor accident, the damage is carefully examined on the lifting platform.

fear—it only came when I had come to a stop and smoke was billowing from the front left. Since the driver's door was blocked by the crash barrier, I thought, now the car will burn down and you'll be stuck in it. But then I remembered that the car also has a passenger door, and I got out of the car quite frantically."

The example shows once again how small causes can have a big effect. The actual cause of the accident was probably the loss of a balancing weight on the left front wheel. The resulting imbalance led to a permanent load at the high driving speed, which resulted in the fastening of the lower wishbone being torn out of the floor assembly. Upon inspection, it turned out to be a fatigue fracture. On the vehicle, which was now a good six years old and had covered around 35,000 km in extreme operating conditions, an approximately 20 mm long old crack appeared on the wishbone mount, which had not been discovered before the drive despite thorough examination.

The problem was solved by inserting a new crossbar and reinforcing it on both sides. During the repair, however, further defects were discovered: The support strut for the exhaust bracket between the exhaust pipe and the transmission had broken off in one place and cracked in a second place. The air deflector for the intercooler air duct was also torn off at one lug and torn at the second. In addition, the nuts for fastening the turbocharger to the exhaust manifold had come loose and the gasket was damaged. The clutch lining of the dual-disc clutch was also damaged.

Not only could the above points be remedied, but the accelerator pedal was also modified: Because of the poor metering, the return spring was reinforced, whereby a somewhat stiffer accelerator pedal had to be accepted. For safety reasons, a second throttle cable was laid in parallel.

After repairs, which fortunately could be carried out on-site, the car started again on June 11 at 8:00 a.m. Erich Waxenberger was at the wheel, just like the first time. After one hour and fifty-nine minutes, even before the first pit stop, the second record-setting attempt also had to be aborted. This time the cause was a defect in the right front wheel bearing, where the clearance was found to be 0.

Sixteen and a half hours later, at 12:30 a.m. on June 12, the C 111 was at the start for the third time. This time everything went smoothly. After 1,273 laps, 26 pit stops, 5 wheel changes at the rear and 2 at the front, and 5 valve clearance checks, the C 111 passed the 10,000-mile mark at 4:25 p.m. on June 14, to the cheers of the record-breaking team after a total driving time of almost sixty-four hours. During the drive, which lasted almost three days, the Mercedes-Benz team with the C 111 set a total of sixteen international class records in Class 8 (diesel engines from 2,000 to 3,000 cc displacement) as well as three world records.

10 km	220.619 km/h	
10 miles	251.353 km/h	
100 km	251.148 km/h	
100 miles	252.875 km/h	
500 km	254.086 km/h	
500 miles	252.930 km/h	
1,000 km	253.307 km/h	
1,000 miles	252.737 km/h	
5,000 km	252.903 km/h	
5,000 miles	252.540 km/h	World record
10,000 km	252.249 km/h	World record
10,000 miles	251.798 km/h	World record
1 hour	253.770 km/h	
6 hours	252.578 km/h	
12 hours	253.616 km/h	
24 hours	253.616 km/h	

The development report by Erich Waxenberger, dated June 24, which summarized the course of the record drive, shows a whole series of interesting details. The longest pit stop, including deceleration and loss due to acceleration, had taken 4 minutes and 3.2 seconds; the shortest was 62.4 seconds. Between twenty-six and forty-two seconds, respectively, were required for deceleration and acceleration before and after the pit stop.

After completion of the drive, the cylinder head had to be dismantled under supervision in accordance with the FIA regulations, so that the displacement could be checked by the technical commissioner. When the cylinder head was dismantled, it was found that the lower nuts securing the turbocharger to the exhaust manifold were loose, and the tightening torque of the cylinder head bolts on the left row had reduced to one-third of the specified value. The valve clearance check had shown no changes after the first twenty-four hours of driving, then only on the second exhaust valve: after thirty-six hours by 0.08 mm, after forty-eight hours by approximately 0.2 mm, and after fifty-four hours by a further approximately 0.3 mm.

The total fuel consumption was 19.68 l/100 km, with a consumption of 19.35 l/100 km measured during the first twenty-four hours, a consumption of 19.85 l/100 km for the second twenty-four hours, and a consumption of 20.05 l/100 km for the last sixteen hours. During the record drive, it was noticed that the

The pit crew shows the driver the number of laps.

Every second counts during the pit stop. The refueling is clearly visible with the fuel supply at the rear and the tank vent at the front of the vehicle.

Toward the world record: the C 111-II diesel during its record drive in Nardò in June 1976

Relieved and satisfied faces at the group photo session in Nardò after the C 111 set the world record over 10,000 miles.

The staff of the testing department (Heinz Bäuchle, Werner Borgward, and Lothar Frenzel) with a record trophy they prepared on-site—a cover of the right rear wing of the C 111 on which they recorded the international class records and world records achieved. Originally intended to improve the air supply to the turbocharger installed on the right side, the cover plate was not used in the record drive and could therefore be rededicated as a trophy.

side tanks emptied unevenly, with the difference being up to half a tank. By switching the respective feed pump on and off, this effect had to be corrected by the driver while driving. With a full tank, lap times shorter by up to 2.7 seconds than with an empty tank were clocked. The oil consumption was 0.7 l/1,000 km. The time difference between day and night averaged only about one second per lap, with the fastest lap time recorded during the hottest part of the day at 1:00 p.m. The interior ventilation proved to need improvement, since an interior temperature of up to 50°C (122°F) was measured at outside temperatures of around 30°C (85°F). The soiling of the windshield by insects was found to be a nuisance, especially when the sun was low.

"Faster Than Porsche": The Response from the Press and the Public

At the board meeting on June 15, 1976, Hans Scherenberg was able to inform his colleagues about the successful completion of the record drive. The head of development reported that the project had "proved to be a special incentive for the employees involved" and suggested that "this group of people should be congratulated and awarded in an appropriate way at an internal celebration," which was welcomed by Joachim Zahn, Chairman of the Board of Management, and Richard Osswald, head of human resources. In addition, the Board of Management decided to brief the press at an event on June 21 in Untertürkheim, whereby the program should be "largely technical in nature." After a corresponding interjection by Heinz Schmidt, Zahn and Scherenberg stressed that "the impression must be avoided at all costs that DB is thinking of a return to motorsport in any form."

On the day of the board meeting, the company issued a press release, which, as expected, was quickly picked up by the media. For example, as early as June 16, a report appeared in *Bild-Zeitung* with the headline "Mercedes set three diesel world records." Numerous other newspapers joined in. *Cannstatter Zeitung* and *Untertürkheimer Zeitung* carried the somewhat sensational headline "Faster than Porsche." They were referring to the record over 10,000 miles that the Swiss team Jo Siffert/Rico Steinemann/Charles Vögele/Dieter Spoerry had achieved in October–November 1967 with a Porsche 911 R at the Autodromo in Monza. The C 111 had surpassed the record speed at the time of 210.293 km/h by more than 41.5 km/h.

The successful record-breaking drivers and the top management of passenger car development, photographed on June 21, 1976, at the press presentation of the record-breaking car on the test track at the Untertürkheim plant. *From left to right*: **Joachim Kaden, Hans Werner (head of overall vehicle test department), Erich Waxenberger, Dr. Hans Liebold, Guido Moch, Karl-Heinz Göschel (head of passenger car test department), Dr. Kurt Obländer (head of passenger car engine test department), Dr. Hans Scherenberg (head of development), Friedrich van Winsen (head of passenger car development).**

At the press event on June 21, 1976, on the test track of the Untertürkheim plant, Head of Development Hans Scherenberg and the record-breaking driver team explain the technical features of the record-setting car to media representatives.

The record-breaking car made a guest appearance at the special exhibition *Das Auto—90 Jahre jung* (*The Car—90 Years Young*), which opened at the Deutsche Museum in Munich on July 1, 1976, before appearing at the product presentation at the Daimler-Benz General Meeting on July 16.

In February 1977, the C 111 record-breaking car was exhibited at the Envitec '77 environmental protection technology trade fair in Düsseldorf, and in October 1977, it was one of the highlights at a special exhibition to mark the seventy-fifth anniversary of the Berlin-Marienfelde plant.

At the end of February 1977, the C 111 record-breaking car travelled to Sydney on board a Lufthansa Boeing 747 cargo plane, where it was first presented to the press and Mercedes-Benz dealers before being on display at the Melbourne International Motor Show and then in the showrooms of a number of Mercedes-Benz branches.

On June 21, representatives of the national and international press turned up for the presentation of the record-breaking vehicle in Untertürkheim. After the welcoming address by Prof. Scherenberg and the screening of a film about the record-breaking drive, the participants went to the test track where the record-breaking car was demonstrated to the media. Another sensation there was the presentation of an S-Class test car with a turbocharged five-cylinder diesel engine, which was immediately picked up by the press. *Bild-Zeitung* wrote on June 22 under the headline "Mercedes builds the fastest production diesel in the world": "In two years at the latest, Mercedes will build a large diesel passenger car." *Handelsblatt* formulated the question "Soon diesel engines for the Daimler-Benz S-Class?," and *Stuttgarter Zeitung* reported "Powerful diesel before the end of this decade. 110 hp engine intended for S-Class."

With this announcement and the demonstration of the diesel engine's performance through the record drive, the fuel-efficient compression-ignition engine picked up considerable momentum. The successful record-setting car was then also used consistently in communication. It made its first appearance at the special exhibition "*Das Auto—90 Jahre jung*" (*The Car—90 Years Young*), which opened on July 1 at the Deutsche Museum in Munich, before becoming a highlight of the product presentation on July 16 at the Daimler-Benz General Meeting held at the Museum in Untertürkheim. Joachim Zahn had previously highlighted the records of the C 111 and the resulting press response in his speech at the shareholders' meeting. This was followed in February 1977 by appearances at the environmental protection technology trade fair "Envitec '77" in Düsseldorf and at various exhibitions and trade fairs in Australia. In October 1977, the record-breaking car was one of the highlights of a special exhibition at the Berlin-Marienfelde plant to mark its seventy-fifth anniversary. At the end of November 1976, Daimler-Benz AG was even presented with a trophy donated by the ONS, the highest national sports commission at the time in recognition of the world records achieved.

With a trophy, the ONS, the highest national sports commission, honored the world records achieved five months earlier in November 1976.

The record-breaking diesel car also made an appearance in advertisements. While German-language newspapers ran an advertisement with the rather sober headline "Mercedes diesel sets world records," the British sales company Mercedes-Benz UK Ltd. advertised under the headline "Is this your idea of a taxi?" with a picture of the record-breaking car promoting the current 200 D, 240 D and 300 D diesel models. Information about the background to the record drive was provided by an advertisement with the headline "Why is this Mercedes setting diesel world records?," which appeared in 1977 as part of the advertising campaign "Mercedes initiatives—research for the better car." What the public could not suspect at the time was that the records set by the C 111-II were just the beginning, and more spectacular record-breaking drives in Nardò were to follow.

With advertisements at home and abroad, Mercedes-Benz used the successful record drive to improve the image of diesel passenger cars, which were considered to be ponderous.

293

With Aerodynamics to Success: The C 111-III

During the successful record drive of the C 111-II D, the project team had come to two conclusions: The turbocharged five-cylinder diesel had not yet reached its performance limit, and a vehicle designed from the ground up specifically for record-breaking runs with a significantly lower c_d value would enable considerably higher speeds even with the same power output. In addition, new record-breaking drives could once again demonstrate the performance potential of the turbodiesel—and this at a time when the S-Class with diesel engine, already announced in June 1976, was to be presented and launched on the market. The fact that a new record-breaking vehicle was actually developed on the basis of these findings is largely thanks to an impetus from stylistics.

Birth of a Record-Breaking Car: The Aerodynamics Study from 1977

As part of the press trial drive of the Mercedes-Benz coupes of the 123 model series presented at the Geneva Motor Show in March 1977, the media representatives were to be given an interesting look behind the scenes. Since the technology had already been presented in detail at the debut of the underlying sedans a good year earlier, head of styling Bruno Sacco suggested illustrating the complex design development at Mercedes-Benz under the heading "From Idea to Form" at the press event. For this purpose, the Mercedes-Benz stylists were to present their respective contributions to shape development at realistic workplaces in the "Kuppelbau" (domed building), the presentation room of the stylistics department in Sindelfingen.

Since a future production vehicle under development was out of the question for this purpose, for understandable reasons, and the original design models from the development process of the C 123 coupes were no longer available, the obvious alternative from Sacco's point of view was to illustrate the shape development with a design study. In a project meeting with the designated head of development, Werner Breitschwerdt, with the future head of development for passenger car bodies, Guntram Huber, and two representatives of the press department on December 10, 1976, Sacco stated, "This process could be most impressively accomplished by means of a pure fantasy product à la C 111 further development." The choice of a particularly sophisticated vehicle in terms of aerodynamics also provided an opportunity to present the conflicting areas of a concept with daily practicality and optimal aerodynamic design—a particularly important aspect of development in the future.

Sacco's proposal for this unusual item on the program of the press trial drive was officially presented at the passenger cars technical meeting in Sindelfingen on January 17, 1977, where, as the minutes for agenda item "C 123: Press presentation at the end of March 1977 in Sifi" document, it was given the green light: "The proposal prepared by STL for holding this event was accepted in all essential points. The C 123 as the focus in the cupola building, parallel lectures as well as presentation of the design development history. Under the motto 'How a shape is created,' information on car body styling is to be conveyed to the trade press at pavilion-like stands in the domed building. To this end, a 1:1 model study of a body with optimal F x c_d is to be shown in particular; built on the C 111 chassis concept, record-setting attempts are to be carried out with it in due course."

Irrespective of the approval in the technical meeting, the project also came up in the board meeting on March 3, 1977. Under the agenda item "Presentation on the occasion of the presentation of the C 123 in Sindelfingen," the minutes of the meeting record a course of events that is reminiscent of earlier controversial discussions about the role of the C 111 as well as of the fears, expressed time and again, of fueling speculation about a possible return to motorsport with pertinent signals. "Schmidt [explains] the proposal to present the C 123 to motor journalists once more in a special way on the occasion of an event in Sindelfingen from March 28 to April 1, 1977, following the official presentation at the Geneva Motor Show. . . . This event is to be complemented—as Breitschwerdt then explains using a model—by presentations and lectures on the possibilities of further improving automotive design. This is to be demonstrated, among other things, by the design development of a vehicle, but also—as an example of functional and progressive styling—by a 1:1 model of a C 111 successor.

"These considerations are welcomed by Zahn. On the other hand, he points out that the exhibition of a C 111 successor model could also be understood as an announcement of a return to motor racing, especially if Breitschwerdt is presented as Scherenberg's designated successor. The question remains whether the public will once again accept that it is only a 'mobile laboratory.'

"After Schmidt points out that the presentation will be made by Scherenberg, Hoppe also asks whether this would not raise expectations that could not be fulfilled as with the C 111. On the other hand, every company has a 'dream car.' In his view, it therefore depended on whether the knowledge contained in this 'dream car' has already been realized, at least in part, in our production vehicles.

"This bridge is a given, as Breitschwerdt and Reuter note. The C 111 successor models above all demonstrate the extremely favorable c_d value. . . . In Zahn's opinion, the use of true-to-scale models is suitable for a demonstration of the methodical development of car styling. This, too, could show what we are working on—which, as Schmidt once again emphasizes, is what this exhibition is all about. The later record drives would then be enough proof that we can also put these findings into practice.

Bruno Sacco (*left*) and Arno Jambor (*right*) discuss the dimensional concept of the aerodynamics study.

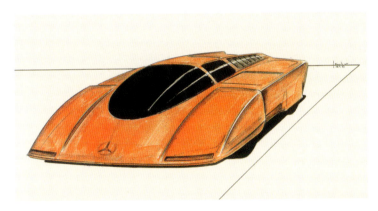

"Breitschwerdt and Schmidt agree with this view. As a result, there is agreement to exhibit a 1:5 scale model of the shape of a prototype sports car, emphasizing that it is merely a styling system study and not a concrete product consideration. A full-size model could then possibly be exhibited at the 1977 IAA to underline the development work in the passenger car sector here as well. However, a final opinion on this issue is deferred for the moment."

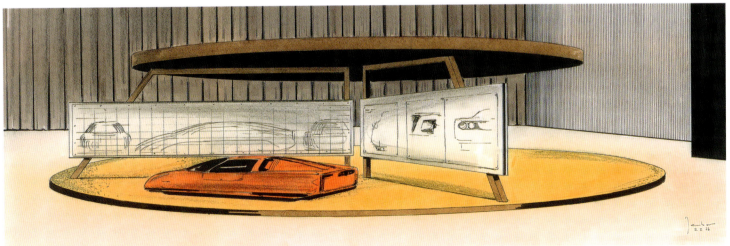

The design drawings by Arno Jambor, dated January 16 and February 2, 1977, give a first impression of the shape of the planned aerodynamics study (*top*) and of the spontaneously conceived—and actually realized—presentation concept.

Optimization in the Wind Tunnel: Development of the Streamlined Shape

At the time of the board meeting, the development of the C 111 S, as the project was now internally called, was already quite advanced. As early as January 1977, Arno Jambor—responsible in the stylistics department for the dimensional concept and as project manager for the C 111 S—had drawn up the specifications with a view to the press event scheduled for the end of March, which are reproduced verbatim below:

STYLING STUDY
2-seater, aerodynamic coupé

Assignment
A fully enclosed 2-seater coupé is to be conceived with a minimum vehicle cross-section and the lowest possible drag coefficient c_d.

Design concept
Shape optimization based purely on results obtained in the wind tunnel

In detail
Front end
Design the front end section as low as possible to avoid lift

Sides
Covers on the front and rear wheel arches. Ventilation of the front wheel wells may be necessary to dissipate the cooling air for tires and brakes.
Wheel covers must be quick and easy to remove.
Gullwing doors should have the largest possible opening width to allow easy entry.
Separation window between engine compartment and occupant compartment. Louvers in the bodywork allow indirect vision via the interior mirror.

Rear end
In the course of the aerodynamic investigations, variants with a long tail will be measured. Ventilation of the engine compartment across the entire width of the rear section.

Vehicle interior
Overall concept of the interior in forward-looking contemporary taste, with the driving position of the C 111 to be adopted largely unchanged.
High level of comfort in the interior.
Newly designed seats, soft look and feel with good lateral support. Adjustment hidden. Integral head restraint.
Review of possibly making it simpler and easier to read the instruments, analogous to international trends and developments in automotive engineering and other technical devices.
Use of valuable materials.

Design sketches of the vehicle and its interior had also been made in January 1977, and three 1:5 plasticine models had already been measured in the model wind tunnel in Sindelfingen in February. Responsible for the measurements was the budding engineer Rüdiger Faul, who had already specialized in vehicle aerodynamics during his studies at the University of Stuttgart and was hired on the spot by Daimler-Benz—even before he graduated—on January 1, 1977.

Faul was thus in the right place at the right time as a specialist in this increasingly important field. He was to accompany the aerodynamics development of the C 111 in all further project phases as the person responsible and also made a name for himself a few years later in the development of the Sauber-Mercedes Group C racing sports cars.

On January 17, Arno Jambor had documented an initial assessment of the aerodynamic characteristics of the new design study in a communication to Breitschwerdt and Sacco under the subject "Aerodynamic values for C 111/C 111—Study." The head of the department responsible for aerodynamics, Hans Götz, and his newly appointed colleague Rüdiger Faul had stated a c_d value of approximately 0.25 and a frontal area of approximately 1.2 m² to Jambor, resulting in a c_d x F of approximately 0.30 m².

Based on these values and the data for the record-breaking car of 1976, Götz considered it conceivable to increase the top speed to 300 km/h with the same output. A c_d value of 0.22 had already seemed possible to Faul in conversation with Jambor, for which he had only received a resolute head shake from Götz—but even this confident estimate was to be bested by the results of the

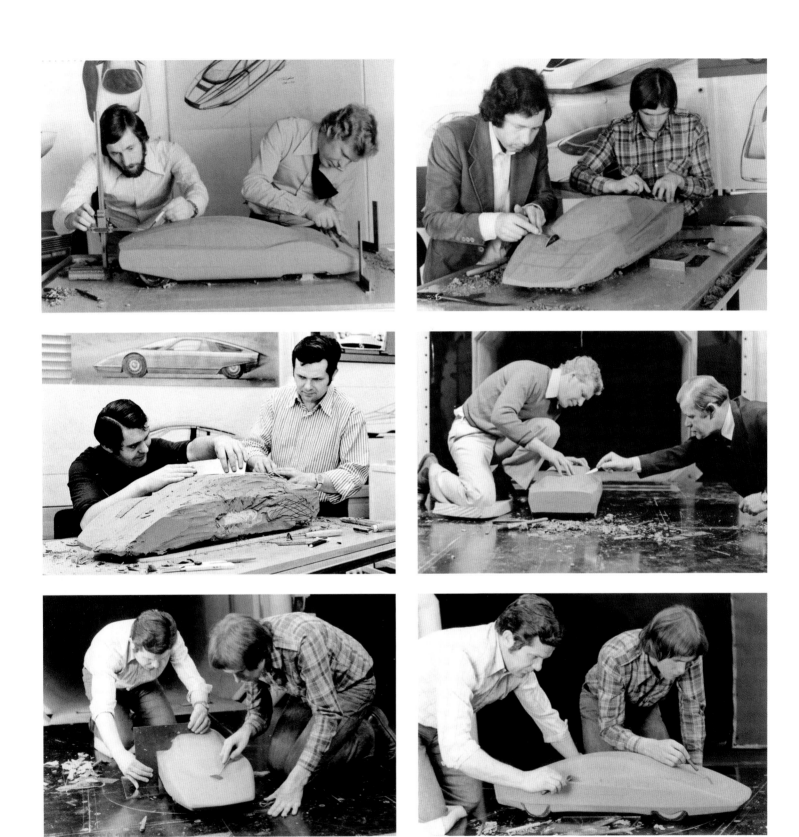

In January 1977, the development of the C 111 S began with the creation of 1:5 scale models. *Top row*: **Johann Tomforde and Peter Pfeiffer** (*photo on the left*) **as well as Stefan Heiliger and model maker Guler** (*photo on the right*) **fine-tuning plasticine models**; *center left*: **Gérard Cardiet and Georg Reule building a plasticine model**; *center right and bottom row*: **Peter Pfeiffer and Joseph Gallitzendörfer** (*center right*) **as well as Reule and Guler during optimization in the wind tunnel.**

wind tunnel measurements. Faul summarized his measurement results in a communication dated February 17: "Although the models already had very favorable drag coefficients in their initial state, these could be further reduced in the course of optimization. However, this required further measures that only seemed feasible on a record-breaking vehicle (smooth underbody, closed wheel arches, extreme rear length . . .). Further improvement of the drag coefficient of models of a vehicle is no longer possible." Faul also goes straight into the risks and side effects: "Such optimized vehicle bodies react very sensitively to disturbances in the flow around them. Therefore, an increase in the drag coefficient of $\Delta c_d = 0.07-0.08$ can be expected for the finished 1:1 vehicle. This increase is made up of radiator and surface resistances (panel gaps)."

The optimizations carried out in the course of the investigations reduced the c_d value for model I from 0.2104 to 0.1416, for model II from 0.1824 to 0.1388, and for model III from 0.1504 to 0.1329. Faul attributed the fact that the values already

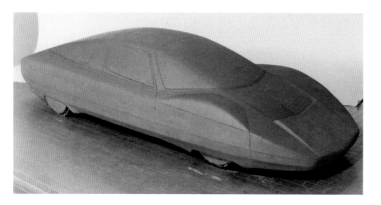
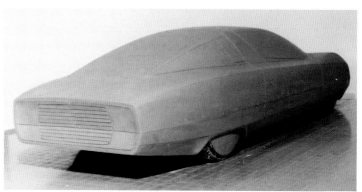
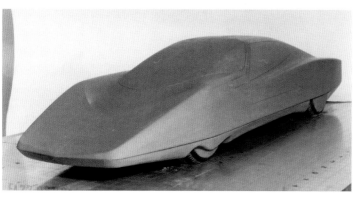
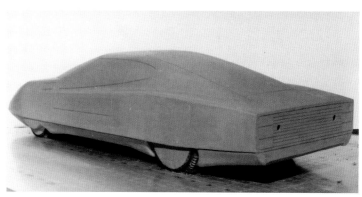

The completed 1:5 scale models according to the designs of Peter Pfeiffer (*top*), Stefan Heiliger (*middle*), and Gérard Cardiet (*bottom*). The fact that Cardiet's model was photographed with Heiliger's design drawings has no deeper significance.

Discussion of the finished 1:5 scale design models with the top management of the development department. At left (*left to right*) are Peter Pfeiffer, Joseph Gallitzendörfer, and Arno Jambor. At right (*left to right*) are Joachim-Hubertus Sorsche, Hans Scherenberg, Werner Breitschwerdt, Guntram Huber, Joseph Gallitzendörfer, Bruno Sacco, Friedrich van Winsen, and Arno Jambor.

The group photo shows the 1:5 scale models of the aerodynamics study by Stefan Heiliger (model II, *front*), Peter Pfeiffer (model I, *center*), and Gérard Cardiet (model III, *rear*), which were created in January 1977 and optimized during elaborate wind tunnel tests. As a result of the internal competition, the design by Peter Pfeiffer was realized in the end.

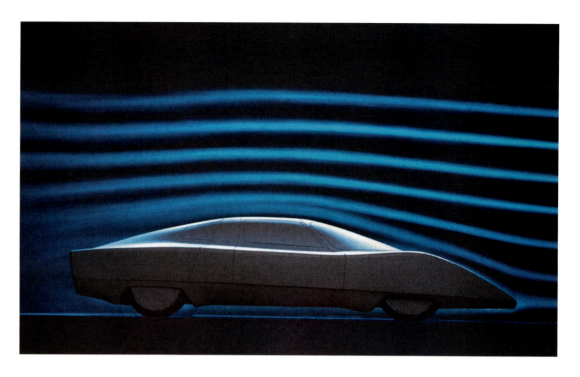

A 1:5 scale model of the C 111 S being examined in the model wind tunnel in Sindelfingen

improved from model to model in the initial state to the fact that "models II and III were already pre-optimized on the basis of the measurement results of model I or I and II" and continued: "The most significant drag reductions on all three models came from changes to the rear of the vehicle. In addition to the length of the tail, the tail inclination at the top and bottom as well as the lateral narrowing were of particular importance. . . . Changes to the vehicle floor and the front end area, on the other hand, had less influence on the drag."

The designers of the three 1:5 models were stylists Gérard Cardiet, Stefan Heiliger, and Peter Pfeiffer. All three had worked on the first C 101 eight years earlier. The variant designed by Pfeiffer had the lowest c_d value after aerodynamic optimization. Accordingly, it was built as a 1:1 plasticine model and measured in the large wind tunnel in Untertürkheim on February 24 and 25, 1977. In his report of March 16, Rüdiger Faul stated: The model had a smooth underbody, as is also intended for the roadworthy vehicle. The wheel arches were shown. The model was fitted with 205/70 HR 14 tires. The cooling air flow was not shown on the model. Due to the optimization work on the 1:5 model, the 1:1 model already had an exceptionally favorable drag coefficient (c_d = 0.174) when delivered."

Regarding the optimization achieved during the examination, Faul noted, "Detailed modifications have reduced the drag coefficient by 5.17% to c_d = 0.165. In combination with a rear extension of 500 mm and a frontal area reduction, an overall improvement of 16.09% was achieved. The drag coefficient c_d was 0.146. Due to time constraints, the measurements had to be stopped at this stage. Minor improvements still seem possible."

Regarding the aerodynamic force coefficients on the finished vehicle, Faul considered a prognosis to be "hardly possible, because apart from for the radiator, the position, type, number, and air routing of the other required coolers are not known. Their installation has a decisive influence on both the drag coefficient and the lift coefficients for the roadworthy vehicle. In doing so, it should be possible not to exceed a drag increase of Δc_d = 0.06." Against the background that "the model, like all aerodynamically highly efficient vehicles, proved to be very sensitive to crosswind influences" . . . and . . . "the vehicle's center of gravity is not in the middle of the wheelbase, but behind it . . . ," it seemed to Faul that "the use of two tail fins was indispensable for the variants of the C 111 S."

In accordance with the board resolution of March 3, the vehicle was presented at the press event in Sindelfingen from March 28 to April 1, 1977, on the basis of design drafts—including 1:1 drawings—and 1:5 plasticine models. The spectacular design study was in the public eye right from the end of March, when the first reports on the design development presented in Sindelfingen first appeared in the regional daily press. Four weeks later, the trade press published more detailed articles. While *Automobil Revue* of April 28 illustrated 1:5 models in its article on the "Visit to the Styling Department of Mercedes-Benz" and did not go into more detail about the unusual vehicle in the text, *Handelsblatt* ran a report on the same day under the headline "A Mercedes never built. Style study of a two-seater coupé demonstrates future trends in car construction" and referred at least indirectly to the C 111: "For the driving position, there was a requirement to make extensive use of the knowledge gained during the construction of the C-111."

One day earlier, *Bild-Zeitung* also had its say—as usual with a sensational headline: "Are the famous Silver Arrows coming back?" The text then read: "On the drawing boards at Mercedes, real 'Silver Arrows' are being created again, flat flounders with low-slung snouts and the famous gullwing doors of the first SL. They are sporty two-seaters of even more futuristic appearance

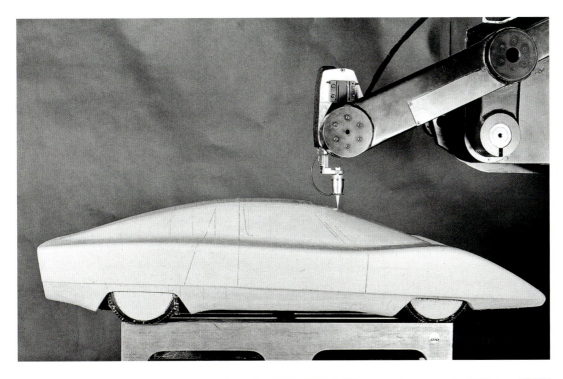

Scanning of the 1:5 scale model (*top*) **to generate a digital dataset, which was then plotted out in the form of a line drawing** (*bottom*)

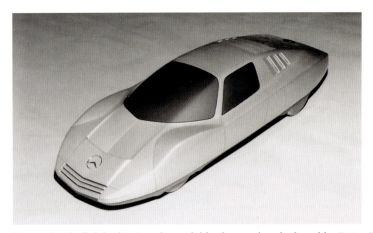 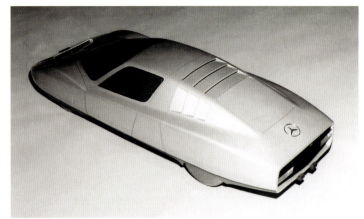

The perfectly finished 1:5 scale model in the version designed by Peter Pfeiffer was exhibited at the presentation in the Sindelfingen "Kuppelbau" ("domed building") and formed the basis for the 1:1 scale model.

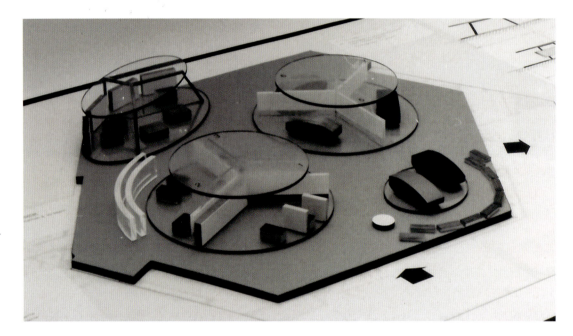

Model representation of the concept developed by Arno Jambor under deadline pressure for the presentation "From Idea to Form"

The design process was presented in the "Kuppelbau" under the heading "From Idea to Form" on the thematic display islands on conception and exterior design (*left*) as well as on interior design (*center*), while the actual reason for the event—the new 123 series coupe—was presented on its own thematic display island (*photo on the right*).

At the end of March 1977, the "Kuppelbau" in Sindelfingen presented itself as the ideal venue for the press presentation of the new Mercedes-Benz Coupe models. The images show the islands for the presentation of the exterior design (*above*) and the interior design of the new aerodynamics study.

"From Idea to Form": Claus Hieke, Peter Pfeiffer, Bernhard Elsner, Gérard Cardiet, and Ferdinand Hellhake present their work on the exterior design (*top*). At center, Arno Jambor (*second from left*) with Heinrich Drexel, Werner Heinz, and Gunther Ellenrieder to his right explains the dimensional concept (*middle*), while Gerhard Honer and Siegfried Greger (*first and second from left*) with their colleagues from the interior design provide an impression of their work (*bottom*).

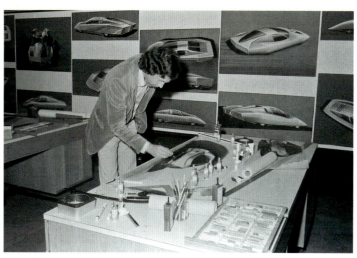

In the interior design area, Michael von Klein demonstrates the design development of the seat intended for the aerodynamics study (*top*); together with Franz Baglyas, he works on the interior mockup of the new vehicle (*center left*), while Gerhard Honer puts the finishing touches to the dashboard (*center right*). The pictures below show Honer creating design sketches for the interior (*left*) and Stefan Heiliger with his exterior design draft (*right*).

Design sketches of the C 111 S by Stefan Heiliger (*bright red vehicle*), **Gérard Cardiet** (*light blue vehicle and silver vehicle, bottom left*), **Klaus Kallenbach** (*silver vehicle, center right*), **and Theodor Schott** (*gray-blue vehicle, bottom center and right*)

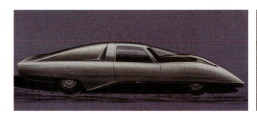

The futuristic interior designs are by Gerhard Honer (*top*), Michael von Klein (*center*), and Theodor Schott (*bottom*). In contrast to the exterior, however, the interior design that was actually realized was based less on these designs and more on the design of production vehicles that was common at the time.

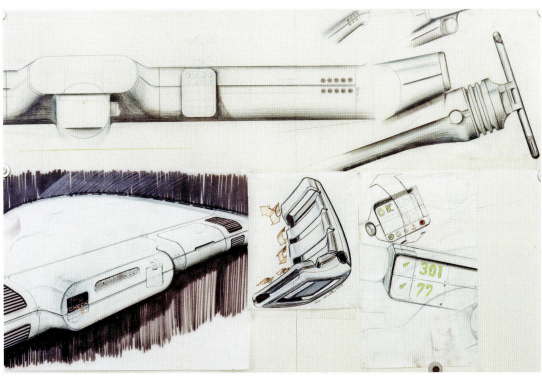

than the legendary SL. Cautious as ever, the member of the Mercedes Board of Management explained: 'All just studies. . .' But at least the models are also tested in the factory's own wind tunnel in order to find out the least air resistance. The sleek racers are probably not just a gimmick for the stylists after all."

auto, motor und sport did not mention the unusual vehicle until its issue of June 8, 1977, but featured the 1:5 model in perfect finish on the cover. Under the headline "Mercedes: The car of tomorrow," a richly illustrated fourteen-page article reported in detail on current research priorities—including aerodynamics—and also presented the design development, using the latest sports car study as an example, but without making a connection to the C 111 and possible high-speed applications: "The Mercedes bodies of the eighties and nineties should not only be safer, but also more streamlined. For tests in the wind tunnel, the designers in the state-of-the-art Sindelfingen styling center also develop extreme sports car shapes, which, although they have no prospect of series production, can provide important insights into the best possible aerodynamic design of various body details."

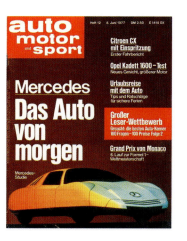

The design process and the diverse research activities of Mercedes-Benz as well as the aerodynamics study were covered by *auto, motor und sport* in its issue of June 8, 1977, with a detailed article under the headline "The car of tomorrow."

From the Aerodynamics Study to the Driving Car: The Technical Conception

In the meantime, the realization phase had already begun in Untertürkheim and Sindelfingen. On April 12, 1977, only eleven days after the press event in the Sindelfingen "Kuppelbau" had ended, Hans Liebold had drawn up an official assignment for the test department under the subject "New construction of 2 improved C 101 with diesel engine (C 101/3)" and sent it on its way for approval. The scope of the assignment was defined as follows:

"In aerodynamically heavily revised form,
2 units C 101 with OM 617 ATL
are to be built. This should create a basis for possible further diesel records.

"The floor assemblies and major components are adopted from the previous C 101 in a slightly modified form.

"Strongly lightened bodies made of GRP with optimized $c_d \times F$ are mounted over space frames.

"The flow conditions are still to be determined in the wind tunnel."

In the aforementioned assignment for the test department, the designation C 101/3 is found for the first time, which from then on was used in addition to C 111 S. For the "testing and setup in [Untertürkheim and Sindelfingen], the procurement of test and spare parts and the preparation of the record-setting drive, etc.," a separate assignment for the test department followed on May 4, 1977, and on May 7, Hans Feucht of the diesel engine test department drew up a further assignment for the test department with the following scope under the subject "Construction of OM 617 A engines for record-setting drives with C 101/3":

"Engines are to be built for carrying out record-setting drives in the C 101/3.

"As preliminary tests to develop the durability of pistons, connecting rod bearings, valve seats, and camshaft bearings, among other things, 80 h endurance runs are conducted on the test bench."

At the beginning of April 1977, a project group with representatives from the advance engineering test department, the chassis design department, the body design department, and the stylistics department had begun with the detailed technical conception of the vehicle. In favor of a smaller frontal area, the width and track width of the vehicle were to be reduced compared to the C 111-II. Joachim Kaden, who coordinated the activities of the advance engineering department as he had done with the C 111-II Diesel, documented the results of the first meeting on April 4 in a memo with the subject "Construction of 2 C 101 vehicles for future record-setting attempts."

The initially intended track width of 1,260 mm was to be achieved on the front axle by shorter shock absorbers and on the rear axle by changing the offset of the rims. A reduction of the rear axle track width by changing the suspension points was rejected for construction reasons. The decision on whether to use an aluminum or GRP body was deferred for the time being. Production capacities at Waggonfabrik Rastatt for two GRP bodies would be available at short notice. The covers for the wheel arches should be designed so that they can be folded up for wheel changes, and the front end of the car should be designed so that the radiator already used in Nardò could be installed. The spring travel of front and rear axle should be limited to 50 mm in the interest of a small c_d x F.

The proposal to use rack-and-pinion steering because of its light weight and space requirements was rejected with reference to the schedule. Instead, the installation of a recirculating ball steering system with a double-buckled steering column was investigated. For a quick wheel change, one jacking point was provided on the rear axle and two jacking points on the front axle, whereby the rear jacking point was to be approached from the rear, similar to car 31, so as not to interfere with refueling. Arno Jambor's wish to use smaller 13-inch wheels on the front axle could not be realized because of the double wishbone axle, according to the chassis design department. The tires were Dunlop 230/600-15 racing tires, for which the manufacturer had specified a mileage of at least 6,000 km on the outside of the track and at least 12,000 km on the inside of the track. The floor assembly was not to be made of riveted aluminum profiles as originally intended, but of steel because of its greater stability.

At the project meeting on April 21, the track width at the rear axle was specified at 1,370 mm, and the wheelbase was increased from 2,620 mm to 2,720 mm. For the wheelbase extension, a whole series of positive effects are noted in the minutes:

1. The articulation angles of the half-shafts are reduced to a permissible level.

The construction of the 1:1 plasticine model began as early as January 1977. The substructure consisted of a steel profile frame, which was initially clad with wood. Then the plasticine was applied, which was then used to develop the vehicle shape analogous to the final 1:5 model.

2. The installation of a single-disc clutch with flat flywheel, as on the M 110, is possible.
3. Modifications to the transmission input shaft, engine flywheel, and mounting bolts are not necessary as the clutch flange length can be increased from 29 mm to 60 mm.
4. The engine, which is now 12 mm longer due to necessary modifications to the components, can be accommodated.
5. The crossrail under the rear window does not need to be cut out so much, if at all.
6. The engine can be lowered by 30 mm at the front; this eliminates the bulge provided on the hood and improves visibility to the rear. In addition, the return flow of the engine oil to the oil pan is improved in favor of a lower engine oil temperature.
7. The transmission can be lowered by 10 mm, which benefits the articulation angle of the half-shafts.
8. The capacity of the fuel tanks is increased by about 6.5%.
9. The stability of the vehicle (straight-line stability, crosswind sensitivity) is improved.
10. The rear wall of the passenger compartment no longer needs to be bulged out toward the front.

The minutes also include two additions that were discussed in Sindelfingen on April 25. To avoid a body modification in the rear area necessitated by the increase in wheelbase, the track at the rear axle was set at 1,350 mm. The change from the initially defined 1,370 mm was to be achieved by increasing the offset of the rims from −40 mm to −50 mm.

The finished 1:1 plasticine model was scanned in the so-called DEA machine (Digital Electronic Automation) at the beginning of March 1977 and thus documented as a digital construction dataset.

It was also decided to lengthen the trailing arms of the rear axle by 100 mm to be able to avoid modifications in the rear wall area.

The 1:1 plasticine model of the C 111 S, finished with a perfect paint job, photographed on the factory premises in Sindelfingen

In mid-March 1977, the so-called mockup model was built in the model workshop of the styling department—a design model with opening doors and elaborate interior.

The finished mockup model in its final finish, photographed in the "Kuppelbau" in Sindelfingen

For transporting the mockup model, sturdy tie-down eyes could be attached to the wheels for securing after removing the wheel covers (*photos top and center*), **and by removing the taillights and the rear grille, the rear end was also easily accessible.**

The mockup model of the C 111-3 was photographed in 2008 especially for the press release for the exhibition *Milestones in Automobile Design*, which presented seven vehicle exhibits at the Pinakothek der Moderne in Munich from June 25 to September 14, 2008.

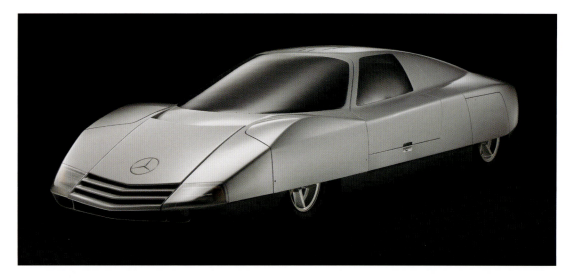

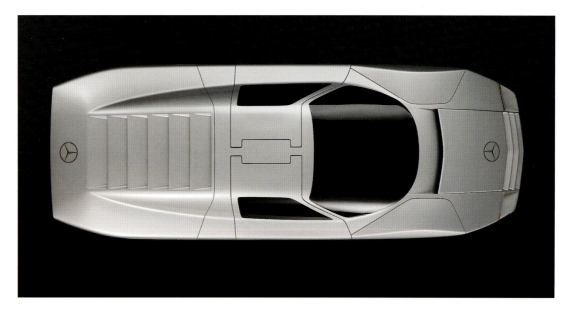

If the C 111-3 were not sitting on a table, the observer would hardly get the idea that it is a 1:5 scale model. The model, created with the greatest attention to detail, was presented to Prof. Hans Scherenberg upon his retirement at the end of 1977.

Project Planning: The Scheduling of the Production Steps

Also on April 25, Hans Liebold documented that the schedule agreed with all those involved, after the decision had apparently been made in the meantime in favor of a plastic body to be manufactured in Rastatt. With additions of April 27, the following milestones were defined:

1. Wind tunnel tests in Untertürkheim to determine the air flow rate for the radiator, charge air, ventilation, and determination of the inlet and outlet openings — 18th week
2. Transport of the interior mockup to Rastatt for molding of the outer skin — end of 19th week
3. K1V submits sketches and drawings of the chassis parts modified compared to C 101 II to A1KS — 17th week by mid-May
4. A1KS submits drawings for the complete floor assembly to A1VB — from end of April to end of May
5. Delivery of the floor assemblies from A1VB to Rastatt — 26th week and 31st week respectively
6. Completion of the vehicles in Rastatt — 33rd week (1st vehicle)
7. Equipment installation and bodywork finish at A1VB — end of September
8. Installation of engine and axles at V1V and start of testing — beginning of October
9. Possible record runs — mid- to late October at the earliest or from March 1978

In a high-level project meeting on May 11, 1977, the effects on the schedule of the changes to wheelbase and track width determined at the end of April were discussed. The minutes prepared by Liebold on the same day summarize the updated scheduling:

"In order not to completely upset the planning in Rastatt, which especially in view of the factory holidays there would certainly have ruled out driving tests this year, the following compromise was reached between all those involved:

1. The mockup model will be completed on one side and simultaneously scanned this week.
2. After provisional completion on both sides, the mockup model will be brought to Rastatt on 18.5.
3. After molding the outer skin in GRP, the model will be returned to ST1M by 20.6.
4. From the end of VI [June], the final optimization of the $c_d \times F$ and the design of the cooling air flow is carried out in the large wind tunnel. The Rastatt bodies are completed by re-molding possibly modified sections.

The frame floor system of the C 111 S was built in the body development workshop in Sindelfingen. The photos were taken at the beginning of August 1977.

Also at the beginning of August, the mockup model of the C 111 S was molded at Waggonfabrik Rastatt, and production of the plastic bodywork began on this basis (*photos top and bottom left*). At about the same time, with hardly less production effort, another example was made (*photo on bottom right*): a detailed 1:5 scale model.

5. In week 26, the first floor assembly will be delivered to Rastatt by A1VB. The second floor assembly follows in the 31st week.
6. In week 33, the first body will be completed in Rastatt and taken to Sindelfingen (A1VB) for equipment installation and body finishing.

"In week 39, the first car will be delivered to V1V in Ut. for installation of the engine and axles, so that testing can begin at the beginning of October as planned."

The compromise solution described by Liebold, which made the need for rework seem very likely, met with little understanding from the aerodynamicists—especially since aerodynamics played a decisive role in the success of the project, and some issues were still far from being resolved.

High-Tech Shell: The Body of the Record-Setting Car

The design and characteristics of the body are described in a technical article published by Hans Liebold, Manfred Fortnagel (head of the diesel engine test department), Hans Götz (head of the body shell test department, which also included aerodynamics development), and Theodor Reinhard (head of special passenger car body designs) in the February 1979 issue of the trade journal *Automobil-Industrie*. The corresponding text passages are quoted here—for the most part verbatim:

"When designing an appropriate body, attention had to be paid above all to the highest possible rigidity and . . . fatigue strength with regard to the speeds to be expected. With low weight, the body had to be largely insensitive to expected vibrational excitations.
In order to accomplish these tasks,
the following reinforcements:
one layer of chopped strand mat . . . [225 g/m²],
one layer of carbon fiber fabric . . . [190 g/m²]
and another layer of chopped strand mat . . . [225 g/m²] [embedded in a chemically and thermally particularly resistant unsaturated polyester resin] were used on all major body surfaces. With this laminate construction it was possible to achieve the desired strength with a wall thickness of only 1.8 mm. Particularly heavily stressed or vulnerable parts were partially reinforced with 19 mm wide tapes made of boron fibers, as previously only used in aeronautical engineering on particularly stressed components. The total body weight was approximately . . . [200 kg].

After the optimization in the wind tunnel had led to a substantial lengthening of the rear end, the corresponding moldings could no longer be attached directly to the steel floor assembly. For this purpose, an aluminum tubular lattice body was built, which inherently stiffened the tail section and transmitted all forces to the actual floor assembly. At the same time, additional components, such as the rear radiators, pumps, etc., could be attached to this.

Since all maintenance and possibly repair times are counted in the endurance records and lower the average speed accordingly, quick accessibility to the components was absolutely necessary. On the other hand, the aerodynamic shape demanded as perfect a cladding as possible, so that securely closing and quickly opening flaps had to be fitted to all body openings. For example, the cover flaps above the wheel arches were to be able to be pushed open by themselves for steering corrections in the event of a possibly necessary larger wheel angle, which required corresponding hinges and latches.

On the engine cowling, a large lid in the hood for major work on the engine was fitted with another small lid, which is sufficient for checking the oil level, for example. Smaller flaps with quick-release fasteners for the four refueling openings were also required. A particular problem here was the connection of steel and aluminum parts to the GRP laminate body. The large-area, partly spiderlike design of the detachable parts made it possible to achieve an appropriate level of strength. The large single-arm windshield wiper, for example, which still rested perfectly on the windshield even at top speed and was normally carried in the car for reasons of drag, also required a strong mounting console, for which an aluminum design was used."

Detail Modifications and Wind Tunnel Studies: The Optimization of the Record-Setting Car

On June 7, a number of details were determined in a meeting in Rastatt. By routing the front tank vent lines under the upper wishbones, space was to be created for the fresh air ducts to the passenger compartment. The two rear tank valves were to be placed at the front end of the hood and not, as originally intended, between the door and the hood, to allow fuel to be introduced with an enhanced flow. Finally, the position of the driver's seat was also changed, with its center moving from 315 mm to 235 mm off to the side of the center of the vehicle. In this position, there was more space for the driver's head, the pedals could be designed more ergonomically, the steering column did not need to be cranked so much, and the point where the driver looked through the windshield was now in the less curved area.

On July 1, 1977, Helmut Weller from the wheels and tires test department spoke up after Michelin had expressed its interest in providing racing tires for the record-setting attempts in Nardò. The French tire pioneer had already offered to carry out corresponding investigations regarding a demanded top speed of 325 km/h in the earliest project phase at the end of January.

On August 8, the advance design engineering department presented its research results on another diesel record project. A development engineer from the US aerospace company Rockwell International had approached the Mercedes-Benz of North America sales company in April to ask for support for a record-breaking project on the Bonneville Salt Flats. The plan was to

The 1:1 wooden model of the C 111 S created from the digital data is examined in the large wind tunnel in Untertürkheim. The glued-on wool threads illustrate the flow pattern. Clearly visible is the rear extension of 508 mm, which has significantly lowered the c_d value. On the left of the vehicle is Rüdiger Faul.

equip a record-breaking vehicle he had designed, which had won the flying kilometer and flying mile records in the 2,000 to 3,000 cc class with Fred Larsen in October 1967, with a Mercedes-Benz turbodiesel and take the displacement-independent record for diesel vehicles at Bonneville.

In Stuttgart, this request was received with mixed feelings. Head of development Scherenberg signaled agreement in principle, while head of testing Göschel had reservations above all because of the development capacity this would tie up, and made it clear that "we only can realize either the new Nardò car . . . or the record-setting drive on the salt lake." He added that "a great deal of effort will have to be made on the engine side for this record run, since the Nardò equipment isn't going to win anything." The dilemma was solved by calculations by design advance engineering. For the existing vehicle, with a c_d x F value of 0.21, calculation engineer Jutta Beifuß, assuming an output of 300 hp/220 kW, determined a maximum possible record speed of 385.98 km/h as an average of the runs in both directions. The targeted top speed of 400 km/h could not be achieved under the given conditions because at 2 miles, the acceleration distance on the return journey was too short due to the position of the timing system. Thus, although a speed of 399.93 km/h was calculated in one direction with an acceleration distance of 4 miles, a value of only 372.02 km/h was calculated for the drive in the other direction.

On August 19, 1977, Rüdiger Faul documented the results of the latest wind tunnel tests, which he had carried out in the large wind tunnel in Untertürkheim on a 1:1 wooden model that had been completed in the meantime. In the as-delivered condition with smooth wheel discs and without cooling air flow, the c_d value was only 0.216. Faul attributed the significant deterioration compared to the value of 0.165 measured on the 1:1 clay model to a stylistic revision of the model, which had not been tested in the

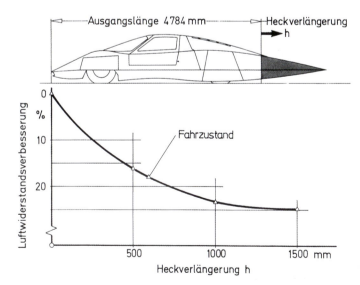

Influence of the rear extension on the percentage improvement of the drag coefficient. The implemented extension of 508 mm was the best compromise in terms of low wind resistance and high practicability.

wind tunnel due to time constraints. This meant that drastic changes to the delivered wooden model were no longer possible, and optimization had to be limited to the use of detachable parts, which were examined in numerous variations.

For example, a drag coefficient of 0.180 was achieved through a rear extension of 508 mm, as well as changes to the lateral body narrowing and the upward-sloping vehicle floor in the rear area. With faithful cooling air flow, a value of 0.198 was measured, whereby the cooling air proportion with $\Delta c_d = 0.018$ was extremely low. Due to the previously diagnosed strong crosswind sensitivity, the vehicle was equipped with two tail fins, resulting in a c_d value of 0.208 in the final state. Very detailed pressure measurements, especially in the area of the cooling air inlet for the radiator as well as possible air inlets and outlets for the intercooler and the intake air for the engine, yielded important findings: While nearly dynamic pressure was measured in the area of the cooling air inlet, the possible positions for the other inlets resulted in lower pressures than in the area of the outlets. The air intake openings for the intercooler and intake air were therefore placed at the front of the vehicle, to the right of the cooling air opening for the radiator.

Putting the Concept on Wheels: Building the Driving Cars

Meanwhile, the first vehicle was gradually taking shape. On August 25, the project team clarified further details, and five days later, the measurement of the first floor assembly fitted with a body was completed. From August 31 to September 3, the vehicle, which had been given the designation "car 41" in accordance with the system used for numbering individual vehicles on the C 111, was pre-assembled in Untertürkheim and handed over to the body development department in Sindelfingen for interior fitting and finishing. Considering the framework conditions to be taken into account for high-speed testing, Hans Liebold documented the coordinated schedule in a communication dated September 5:

"According to preliminary information from Nardò, a two-lane closure will only be considered for testing in the intended speed range if the initial tests with complete closure are positive. As this is currently only possible over Saturday/Sunday, the testing still planned at the beginning of October presupposes a start of driving on 8.10. Under these circumstances, the following schedule, already discussed with all stakeholders, must be observed:

Completion at A1VB	by Friday 23.9.
Measurement of the frontal area (A1VB)	Saturday 24.9.
Verification of the aerodynamic parameters and the flow conditions in the large wind tunnel Ut. (A1R)	Monday 26.9.
Final assembly in Ut. and pre-testing on the test track (V1V)	until Monday 3.10.
Verification in Hockenheim	Tuesday 4.10.
Customs clearance and departure to Nardò	Saturday and Sunday 8./9.10.

This schedule assumes a one-week reduction in the turnaround time scheduled for A1VB Sifi this spring. In addition, V1V still has to carry out assembly work in Sifi on parts that have only just been delivered. Consideration for the work going on there is a matter of course."

In the minutes, Liebold also addressed a technical change, noting that "with the D 42 [the second C 101/3], which is currently being molded in Rastatt, the tank ventilation is relocated to the outer ends of the windshield. At the same time, this allows for a more favorable routing of the radiator lines. Both measures make the air ducts to the engine and into the interior usable again without hindrance and prevent weakening of the front-end assembly of the body. D 41 will be modified accordingly after the drives in Nardò."

On September 24, the rear wheels intended for the new car were tested with the record-breaking car of 1976 on the test track in Untertürkheim. These were 9½ J x 15 H 2 BBS rims, which were fitted with 230/600-15 Dunlop slicks. A total of 600 laps were completed in a clockwise direction on the second outer concrete ring of the 85 m skid pad. After every five laps, where the speed was between 73.9 and 76.9 km/h, the drive was interrupted to cool down the tires. The front left tire was changed after 370 laps and then again after 120 laps, the rear left tire after 370 laps, while the two right-hand tires did not need to be replaced. After completion of the tests, which lasted over 41 hours, the following tire pressures were measured: 2.50 bar at the front left and 2.65 bar at the rear left (2.70 and 3.00 bar at the start of the test respectively).

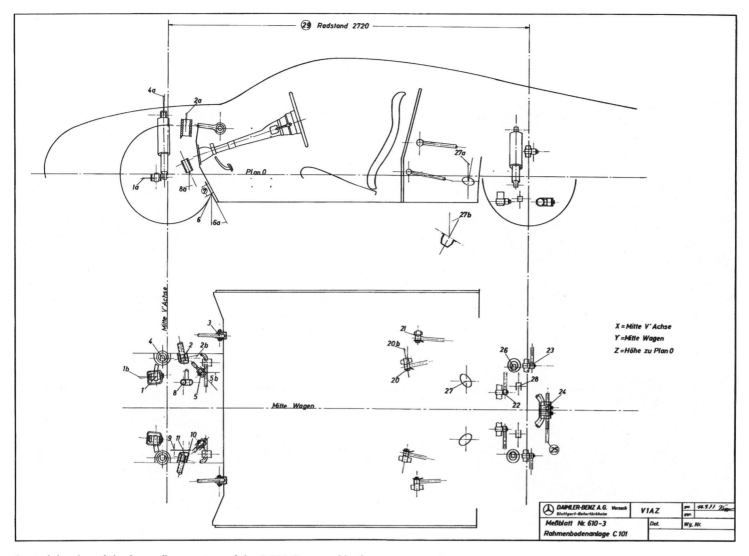

Control drawing of the frame floor system of the C 111 S as used in the measurement

Subsequently, the left rear wheel, which was crack-free after the tests, was further tested on the fatigue test bench. As with the C 111-II Diesel, 8 J x 15 H2 Kloth-Senking wheels were to be used as front wheels, which had already been tested.

A few days earlier, the acceptance of the engine with the internal number EA 25-122, intended for car 41, had taken place in the diesel engine test department. The results are summarized in a communication by Werner Kolter and Manfred Fortnagel dated September 30. With a modified cam shape and larger diameter injectors compared to last year, as well as a larger turbocharger compressor wheel, a peak output of 218–220 hp/ 160–162 kW at 4,200–4,500 rpm and maximum torque of 40 mkp/392 Nm at 3,600 rpm were measured. The turbocharger with the larger compressor wheel was, as the press release stated, "at the upper limit of a single-stage turbocharger in terms of pressure ratio and speed."

On September 26 and 27 and October 3, the roadworthy car 41 was examined in the large wind tunnel in Untertürkheim. As usual, Rüdiger Faul documented the results in a development memo. As delivered, the vehicle fitted with Dunlop 230/600-15 slicks with cooling air flow achieved a c_d value of 0.259. Through a series of optimization measures (smooth underbody, crowned wheel discs, 40 mm high rear spoiler, body widening in front of and behind the wheels, rear widening and negative stance of the vehicle), the drag coefficient could be reduced to 0.230 in the end, whereby the cooling air component with $\Delta c_d = 0.019$ was very low, as was already the case with the 1:1 wooden model. With regard to the cooling air flow, Faul found that the air flow

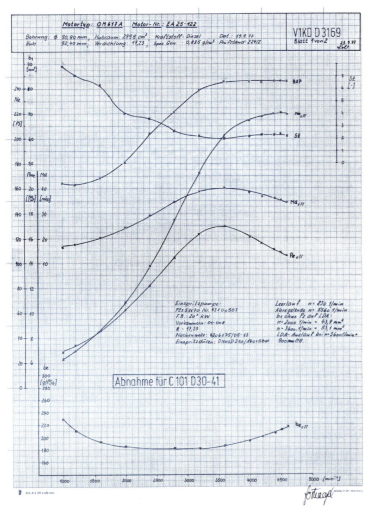

Performance diagram of the 3-liter, five-cylinder diesel engine OM 617 A with the number EA 25-122, taken during the acceptance on September 19, 1977

rates at the radiator, the oil coolers, and—despite improvements to the cooling air routing—also at the intercooler did not quite reach the required values. In his report, which was only completed after the driving tests, he points out that, for driving, the water cooling system proved to be oversized, the oil cooling system undersized, and the transmission oil cooling system and the charge air cooling system sufficient.

Departure for Nardò: The High-Speed Testing

Finally, on the morning of October 6, the time had come. A fleet of five cars, one panel van, and two trucks set off for southern Italy to test the record-breaking car. After an overnight stay at the Agip motel in Pescara, the caravan arrived in Nardò on October 7, and the test runs began on October 8. Project managers Liebold and Kaden, as well as the key disciplines involved—aerodynamics, engine testing, and transmission testing—summarized the course and results of the testing in development reports and file notes. Hans Liebold started with a report dated October 19. This is reproduced below in unabridged form, since it not only very well documents the development of the vehicle, which is fundamentally new in many respects, but also authentically summarizes the complex interrelationships and ever-new challenges firsthand.

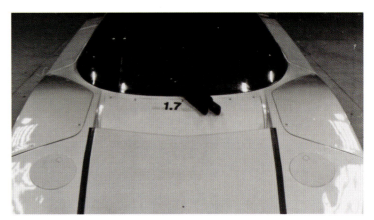

At the end of September, car 41 was examined in the large wind tunnel in Untertürkheim. The picture shows the initial state of the vehicle equipped with two tail fins. The BBS wheels on the rear axle, which were later replaced by Kloth-Senking wheels, are also clearly visible. The picture on the right shows the original design of the front wheel spats, which were accepted as a whole, as well as the flaps for fuel tank ventilation initially placed in the front end area, and the removable windshield wipers.

"The first of the two newly built diesel record-breaking cars was tested on the Nardò circular track immediately after completion. After preliminary optimization of the chassis and engine settings as well as the cooling and the most important bodywork details, a consistent lap speed of 314 km/h could be achieved. After the implementation of further identified measures, in particular a further lengthening of the gearing, as the result of which the governor of the injection pump kicking in now limits the speed to approximately 320 km/h even on downhill and tailwind stretches, the envisaged endurance record speed of 300 km/h seems achievable next spring. However, the vehicle already makes extreme demands on driving concentration in this speed range, especially in crosswinds, darkness, and rain, so that a significantly higher speed yet can probably no longer be realized here.

The C 101 D 30-41 was driven on the shortened test track on Saturday evening (1.10.) after completion as scheduled and again on Tuesday after being checked in the wind tunnel, whereby 200 km/h could not be significantly exceeded. The driving impression was extremely favorable, however, so that the vehicle was cleared through customs on the same day and set in motion for Nardò, where a complete closure of the course had been agreed for the weekend, since joint use of the track during the week was made dependent on the agreement of all the other test teams, which was to be decided after the first test runs.

During these first drives, the car seemed very unsteady under full load and became increasingly unstable above 250 km/h. Apart from the still-too-soft roll stiffness and damping, the main cause for this was obviously the slick racing tires used for the first time on this car, since the behavior could already be improved quite considerably by adjusting the wheel alignment. With the current values (tire pressure 2.7/3.0 bar; front −10', rear −45' camber; 20' total toe-in each) a very even tire wear pattern could be achieved with completely uniform, low temperatures across the tread width and quite low wear. Lengthening the suspension struts on the outside of each curve to achieve almost complete freedom of roll at the approximately 0.3 g that occurred at over 300 km/h in the outer lane of the elevated track, which was designed to be free of lateral forces at 250 km/h. This also largely prevented the stop buffers from coming into play on those parts of the track where more pronounced bumps have since developed. Larger rolling movements with a corresponding yaw reaction now still occur in stronger crosswinds, which is probably due to the increased roll moment caused by the attached crosswind fins.

The fact that at the speeds of over 300 km/h achieved right away, considerable accelerations from the road still act on the car was shown by a number of unexpected damages to various components (cracks on the body, frame, and transmission housing; break of a camber strut; etc.). At least the vehicle could still be kept under control even in the case of the latter damage, which resulted in the slashing of the outer rear tire, as well as in the case of the break of a drive shaft bearing at the transmission end, the complete ripping open of the driver's door, and the subsequent detachment of the rear floor panel, all of which occurred at top speed.

Additional difficulties were caused by the seasonal wind, which was quite strong at times, and occasional rain showers, so that the winter time is hardly suitable for actual endurance record-setting attempts, especially as the illumination of the track appears to be much too low at speeds of up to 320 km/h due to the 50% reduction in light intensity. The installation of 50 W bulbs as opposed to the 100 W bulbs used on the old car was introduced for thermal reasons due to the full encapsulation of the actual headlamps.

For further tests, however, additional cooling should be aimed for when switching back to stronger bulbs. In contrast, the attachable windshield wipers proved to be fully functional even above 300 km/h, just as it was still possible to drive flat out in the rain with the hand-profiled slicks on the spot and used as intermediate tires. Under these circumstances, however, the otherwise quite quiet car is said to have been audible around the entire track. With the full rain tires, which are probably only needed in extreme conditions on the banked track, the car definitely seemed too unstable above 250 km/h for longer operation.

In addition to the handling, the engine oil cooling proved to be the most critical during the first tests, as the intended engine and transmission oil cooler at the rear of the car was completely inadequate. Even with an enlargement of the NACA inlet [a streamlined air inlet named after the US National Advisory Committee for Aeronautics (NACA), the NASA predecessor organization that developed and communicated this air inlet in 1945] and the installation of two additional oil coolers on the car floor and on the rear wheel arch, cooling was only just sufficient under the given outside temperatures. Only the relocation of the second oil cooler into the front end (in front of the radiator) resulted in a constant temperature level of approximately 125°C, which should be able to be kept in check even at higher outside temperatures when the transmission cooler section is engaged or possibly enlarged. The water temperature of 82°C has so far remained almost unaffected. The transmission oil temperature is approximately 100°C.

The cooling of the charge air, on the other hand, proved not to be as critical as had been assumed after the wind tunnel tests. The constant end temperature was initially 120°C and could be reduced to 100°C in each case both by blading the two intake openings [meaning the attachment of additional air scoops to the two air intakes in the front end of the car] as well as by separating the engine intake air. Since taking the intake air directly from the side of the car tended to raise the boost pressure slightly, the scoops were omitted again during the further tests, with the exception of a short front spoiler test. An influence of the air resistance was not determined in either case. The level of boost pressure behind the radiator was last between 1.9 and 2.1 bar.

The maximum lap speed was initially always achieved on the second lap. As the engine warmed up further, the boost pressure usually dropped a little, and the engine speed dropped by about 200 revs. A change of the injection pump settings increased the pulling power on the headwind and uphill sections but did not yet significantly change the temperature behavior. In any case, the maximum speed of 4,800 rpm (corresponding to about 320 km/h) was also determined on the downhill and tailwind sections by the governor of the injection pump kicking in. In order to increase the average speed and to protect the engine (at 4,800 rpm, the turbine shaft of the first turbocharger broke), a further lengthening of the overall gearing has now become unavoidable. ZF has already been contacted from Nardò via V1AG to negotiate the special production of a longer fifth gear, as the current final-drive ratio can supposedly not be lengthened further (currently final drive 2.58, fifth gear 0.705).

In addition to a number of major body modifications to improve drag and the air intakes to the various major assemblies, various changes had to be made to the interior to improve ventilation and visibility. In both cases, the presence of a body designer skilled in working with GRP contributed quite significantly to the great agility that laminating GRP parts in itself allows. In addition, to facilitate smooth steering of the car at the high speeds, the 380 Ø steering wheel was exchanged for a standard one from the W 123. This also improved the still-far-too-poor visibility of the instruments and control buttons. In addition to the absolutely necessary modifications to these components, a steering wheel with 400 mm Ø and not too thick a rim should be provided for further drives. ST1's seat with transverse divisions in the seat surfaces was also tested but proved to be too high and too hard and offered poor lateral support. The backrest in particular gives the impression of a trellis. In addition to the aforementioned shading of the instruments by the steering wheel rim, the reading range is also too narrow in many cases, while the lighting is perfect. However, this does not apply to the push buttons, whose position can only be recognized in daylight by feeling them. As the comparison of the boost pressure indicators with a second instrument carried along showed, the accuracy of individual indicators is also still completely inadequate.

After carrying out all the essential detailed tests, the car was prepared for the scheduled ten-hour run on Friday evening. Among other things, a crack about 400 mm long was found in the bell housing, which made the planned implementation on Saturday impossible. As the replacement transmission had already been used due to the bearing fracture of one of the driveshafts, which was caused by a deviation in the drawings of the shaft or the transmission for as-yet-unknown reasons, the remaining two of the four newly manufactured transmissions, which had arrived in Ut. in the meantime, were brought from there to Pescara during the night, where they were collected by us while the car was being prepared for the modification. After installation of the new transmission the following night, the designated sets of tires were briefly broken in on Sunday morning. The gearshift already locked up at this point, so that only the gate 4/5 could be engaged from the outside. For the endurance run, it was therefore necessary to start in fourth gear. Then the left tank was emptied separately first, which after the initial drop resulted in a constant lap speed of about 307 km/h. After switching to the right tank, this speed dropped to a constant 295 km/h, which confirmed the suspicion of fuel heating. The driving time with one tank of fuel was about 2 h 25 min as before, but the driving distance was correspondingly farther. After refueling, the transmission had completely locked up and the car could no longer be moved.

The fourth transmission was therefore also still installed on Sunday and broken in briefly in the evening. Here, the same damage as with the third transmission occurred after only one lap. In order to be able to assess the effect of the measures for the thermal insulation of the fuel system (pumps, collecting tank, and filter, as well as the additional injection of fresh air into the engine compartment) taken in the meantime, the car was started on Sunday night again in fourth gear. A constant lap speed of 314.0 km/h was then achieved on the left tank, which only dropped to a constant 312.5 km/h when driving on the right tank. (Incidentally, the highest speed ever reached on this track is said to have been achieved by Niki Lauda in a Formula 1 Ferrari at 312 km/h.)

After the car is returned to Ut., in addition to the changes already described and a larger number of recorded detailed changes, the planned changes to the charge air duct and tank ventilation will be made in particular. To speed up engine checks and wheel changes, extensive body modifications still need to be realized. Detailed changes concerning the drag, which could not be clearly assessed due to the engine speed limitation by the injection pump, should be checked again in the wind tunnel. This also applies to a possible change of the crosswind fins. After delivery of the new transmissions, another short preliminary test will probably be necessary before the actual record-setting attempt. Although the transmissions used now do not differ in principle from those used since 1969, it should be considered whether a ZF expert should not be consulted, since the presence of the Dunlop racing manager during the first two days of the last test proved to be very useful. If necessary, a Bosch engineer should also be called in again.

A detailed assembly report is issued on the measured values and detailed tests. The same applies to the measures carried out by V1FR and V1M as well as EMZ, whose laser light barrier with the newly developed calculator for the immediate determination of the individual lap and overall average speed has generally proved itself well. According to the administration people in Nardò, a complete closure for record purposes can probably be done with about a month's notice."

During initial testing of the C 111-III in Nardò, various configurations were examined and tested in detail. Car 41, shown in the photos, is initially still equipped with scoops on the front air intakes and a rear section with a Plexiglas window and two stabilizer fins.

The vehicle received a new slatted engine compartment cover, and the NACA air intake between the tail fins had been reduced in size by taping it off. On the right of the vehicle is body constructor Ernst Haug.

Joachim Kaden and Hans Liebold have a technical exchange shortly before the start of the next round of testing.

Detailed Analysis: Findings from the Tests

Further interesting details were contained in the report by Joachim Kaden, dated November 2, 1977, which is also quoted here unabridged for the reasons already given:

"In the period from 8.10. to 16.10.77, test runs were carried out with the C 101 D 30-41 car in Nardò. The damage that occurred and the work that was carried out are summarized below. In addition, the work and modifications still to be carried out on the vehicle are listed.

1.) Transmission and half-shafts

After the first 3 laps, the left half-shaft had slipped out of the diametral pitch gearing on the transmission (no. 0 10 811). During dismantling, it became apparent that the deep groove ball bearing on the half-shaft, which serves to secure the shaft axially, had burst at the recess for the outer circlip. The right half-shaft could not be removed in Nardò. Disassembly is done in Ut. with appropriate tools.

As the left half-shaft had damaged both a bearing seat (fretting marks) and the diametral pitch gearing when it slipped out of the transmission, the transmission could not be used any further. The driving tests were therefore continued with the transmission no. 0 10 812. Shifting difficulties occurred on this transmission after a short driving time. During an inspection, it was found that the circlip on the shift shaft's centering spring had popped out of its groove. In addition, the shift shaft runs very tightly in its guides. After another 4 hours of trial runs, a visual inspection of the transmission housing revealed a crack between the two bearings of the clutch release shaft. Removing the transmission also revealed that the transmission input shaft is pressing on the thrust bearing cover plate in the flywheel and the ball bearing of the left half-shaft is damaged again. The bearing was destroyed during dismantling attempts. Old cracks were visible on the fracture surface. The tests were continued with a new transmission (no. 010 814).

On this transmission, after 6 laps, the gear shift could no longer be operated properly. Changing the different gears was now only possible with the help of hammer blows on the transverse shift shaft. Starting for the further tests therefore was done in 4th gear. When trying to start after 2 ½ hours of continuous operation, the two gears of the transmission were simultaneously engaged.*

After 2 laps, the gates of transmission no. 0 10 813 then installed could no longer be selected. Therefore, as in the case of transmission no. 0 10 814, starting was done in 4th gear. With the gear ratios used so far—5th gear 0.705, final drive 2.58—engine speeds up to 4800 rpm were reached. After consultation with the relevant departments (V1TD, V1KD, V1AG), it was decided to design the gear ratios in such a way that at 4500 rpm are not exceeded 325 km/h. According to preliminary information from ZF, this is only possible by means of the 5th gear. This would then have to be geared at 0.64

*) Disassembly in the meantime showed that the shift shafts had seized on the guide due to manufacturing defects.

**) In the meantime, a 5th gear of 0.643 was agreed with ZF. In addition, 4th gear was changed to 0.846, which again achieves a reasonable gear spread.

2.) Engine cooling

As the engine oil temperature had already risen to 140°C after 2 laps of full throttle without having reached constant end, the height of the NACA inlet at the rear was increased from 55 mm to 75 mm. This measure had no effect. Therefore, the reserve oil cooler including the transmission cooling section was mounted in the floor of the rear. After several laps, the engine oil temperature was 135°C with no constant end. A further additional oil cooler (220 x 260 mm) in the area of the left rear wheel arch brought about a constant end temperature of 132°C. The outdoor temperatures were between 22°C and 23.5°C.

As a final measure, the radiator mounted in the floor of the rear was installed in the front end, in front of the radiator (flow pipe 18 x 1, return 20 Ø x 1). This measure limited the engine oil temperature to 126°C at 22°C outside air temperature. The water temperature was not noticeably affected by this (82°C–85°C). The cooling effect of the individual engine oil coolers should be examined more closely on the Behr test stand or in the DB wind tunnel.

The charge air temperature could be reduced from 110°C to 100°C by fitting 2 scoops to the two intakes at the front of the vehicle. After the intake air for the engine was no longer branched off from the air coming from the front, but was drawn in on the right side behind the driver's door, 100°C charge air temperature could be maintained even without these scoops.

Adding an 'ear' to the engine air intake point did not improve the situation. Due to the higher wind resistance, the average engine speed even dropped by about 500 rpm.

3.) Clutch/clutch actuation

When cold, the clutch throw-out travel was sufficient and the clutch disengaged perfectly. When the clutch was warm, it was no longer possible to engage reverse gear (unsynchronized). During further attempts, so much air collected in the line to the slave cylinder in the course of 2 laps that it was no longer possible to operate the clutch. The clutch pedal fell to the floor without resistance. Since a more favorable routing of the hydraulic line is not possible on the C 101, this behavior should be prevented according to V1AG by using a clutch slave cylinder with two sealing collars.

4.) Engine compartment temperature

Since the entire engine compartment heated up a lot when driving with the plexiglass cover, it was replaced with the scaled grille after just a few laps. Even with this, the engine compartment temperatures were still very high, especially on the right side of the engine. This is essentially due to heating by the turbocharger and the exhaust as well as by the warm cooling air of the intercooler, which is about 150°C.

The right tank pumps, the right tank valve and the rear area of the right tank were therefore insulated with an aluminum asbestos mat. To further reduce the engine compartment temperatures, the turbocharger and part of the exhaust pipe are to be sheathed. The air, which then heats up very strongly in this jacket tube, is routed directly via a pipe elbow to the scaled grille and the outside. If these measures are not yet sufficient to keep the temperature of the fuel, which also heats up strongly, within tolerable limits, the effect of a fuel cooler plumbed into the return line of the injection pump will also be investigated.

5.) Wheel suspension

After installing harder shock absorbers, a significant improvement in handling was achieved by raising the car on the outside of the turn. The springs were preloaded in such a way that the car was parallel to the road at speeds of approximately 310 km/h. Toe and camber values of the wheels were adjusted before raising. To avoid damage to the caster struts by pipe wrenches and similar tools needed to adjust the caster, the center pieces of these struts should be fitted with a hexagon. The front torsion bar must be cranked down by a further 10 mm approximately so that there is enough space for the tie rods when turning the wheels.

6.) Instruments, dashboard, interior

Some of the instruments made by VDO are not correct and, apart from the rev counter, are not very easy to read either.* Part of the instruments was also covered by the 380 Ø mm steering wheel. A steering wheel with 400 Ø mm and a slightly thinner rim should be provided. A W 123 stock steering wheel used on a trial basis already proved to be better.

The recognizability of the switching status of the various push-button switches is completely insufficient. While the varying degrees of illumination of the push buttons can still be roughly recognized at night, this is completely impossible during the day. The use of pull switches with clearly visible travel or rocker switches with soft actuating levers would be desirable here. The 'cruise control switch' used as contactor for the VHF radio is located too awkwardly. In future, the radio system is to be operated via the passing light contact of the combination switch.

The radio system itself or the accessories (throat microphone, earphones) are not yet reliable enough. This resulted in intermittent disruptions, but also in the total loss of the connection to the car. We therefore ask the department V1E to procure more reliable parts in sufficient numbers and on a trial basis to replace the throat microphone with a microphone attached to the helmet and placed close to the driver's mouth, such as is often used in flight operations.

The large fuel reserve lamp must be placed higher, as it is out of field of vision in its current position. Visibility of the roadway is good. However, a sun visor cannot be dispensed with. A temporary visor was installed in Nardò. To suppress sunlight through the side windows, they should be tinted at the top edge. However, it should be noted that only toughened safety glass and not laminated glass is used (emergency exit). The rear window of laminated safety glass showed two small cracks at the beginning of the drives, which have now increased in length to 40 and 110 mm respectively. The installed fresh air nozzle for the driver brings a sufficient amount of air into the passenger compartment, but the jet of air blows too directly onto the driver's wrist. To avoid this, this air should in future escape through a flat, wide vent between the instrument panel and the upper edge of the dashboard.

The lack of a suitable place for the driver's left foot to rest was particularly unpleasant when driving, as the left thigh was used to steady the left hand on the steering wheel. A temporary support was therefore installed in Nardò. The accelerator was put in a steeper position to relieve the right foot. When [one is] driving in the rain, large amounts of water penetrated into the vehicle interior through the very poorly sealing door rebate on both sides of the vehicle.

*The instruments are currently being calibrated. The calibration of the rev counter already carried out showed max. errors of 50 rpm.

7.) Body

The plexiglass covers in front of the headlamps should be better adjusted. The seal between the front wings and the body still needs to be improved. Dirty rainwater flowing between the wing and the body partly runs over the windshield and side windows and also penetrates into the interior, as already described under point 6. It still takes too much time to remove and especially to install the tail section. A possibility to flip up the tail around a rear pivot point should be investigated. In this case, the wheel arches, which are now firmly laminated to the vehicle, could be attached to the rear and contribute to its reinforcement. The tail lamps installed for the test drives must be thermally insulated from the oil cooler located close to them.

The opening angle of the rear fuel filler flaps must be increased to maintain sufficient distance from the retaining ring of the tank valves. The fastening of the individual cover plates to the underside of the wagon must be improved in order to prevent individual parts from detaching, as happened in Nardò.

8.) Other incidents or measures

Two more grooves than intended by the design are required on the rear shock absorbers to adjust the level upwards. . . . . The jack levers are extended by 300 mm to ensure safe lifting of the car.

Dept. V1FR is investigating the possibility of replacing the 5 stud bolts of the wheel fastening with a center-lock mechanism. The wheel change times are increased too much by the stud bolts.

As there were other vehicles on the track, a rear-view mirror was installed for the test runs in Nardò. It is not absolutely necessary for the actual record-breaking run.

During an inspection, a crack was discovered at a node of the tail boom, which was welded together from aluminum tubes. Reinforcement was provided by an additional gusset plate on the right and left side of the vehicle. In addition, when the engine was dismantled, a stress crack was found on the bell housing, next to an aluminum rib welded on to hold the clutch master cylinder. In future, therefore, the mount for the clutch slave cylinder should also be cast on."

The serious deficiencies in the transmissions, which had largely influenced the testing, were discussed in a meeting with representatives of ZF on November 2, 1977, and the results were documented on November 11 in an internal memo by Werner Walter, a staff member in the major assembly testing department. The bearing damage on the first transmission was attributed to a defect in the half-shaft manufactured by Daimler-Benz, while the crack that occurred on the second transmission, which ran in a transverse direction over the entire clutch housing component, was apparently caused by a material defect. However, no reliable explanation was found for the blocking of the gate in the third and fourth transmissions, so that further analyses were commissioned from ZF. At the same time, all four transmissions were to be repaired—one with the same gear set and the remaining three with the modified ratios for fourth and fifth gears.

Fine-Tuning: Optimization of the Record-Breaking Cars

Also dated November 11 was a memo by Ernst Haug summarizing the results of a meeting in Sindelfingen on the completion of the bodies for cars I (41) and II (42). The background of the meeting on November 8 was the revision of the rear section, which was to enable an improvement of the c_d value and the handling in crosswinds as well as an easing of the necessary installation and monitoring work in the engine compartment. In addition, the front and rear wheel spats were to be changed in favor of shorter installation times. Independently of this, a revision of the front-end assembly had already been carried out on car 42. The ducts for the water and oil coolers, charge air, engine compartment, and interior ventilation in the front end area were modified in favor of improved flow. The valves of the tank ventilation were accordingly moved back to the area of the front wall pillar, and the coolant lines were removed from the ducting areas. These changes should now also be subsequently incorporated in car 41.

In a supplementary meeting on November 10, it was decided that a second tail variant would be produced, which instead of the two steeply and extensively projecting stabilizers (tail fins) would have a lower design that was continuously elongated from the mold. A alternating mounting of these two rear variants that could be realized quickly should open up the possibility of determining the different handling. In order to complete the development as quickly as possible, car 41 was intended as a model carrier for a rear section to be newly designed. For this purpose, it was to be fitted with a GRP tail section with a reduced outer contour, to which the corresponding molds of the modified tail variants could be applied during the tests. This new tail section base should be manufactured in the forty-sixth and until the forty-seventh week (November 14–December 11, 1977) in Rastatt and at the end of the forty-seventh week installed on car 41. The modeling work in the styling department was then planned for afterward.

The building of car 42 with the modified design of the front-end assembly could therefore continue until the rear hood was attached starting in the forty-eighth week (November 28–December 2) in Rastatt. After completion of the modeling work for the shape design of the new rear section in the styling department, the necessary wind tunnel measurements were to be carried out in the forty-ninth week (December 5–December 9). Assuming positive test results, the new rear section should be used on both cars. For this purpose, car 41 with the new plasticine rear-end model was to be delivered to Rastatt in the middle of the fiftieth week (December 12–December 16). Car 42, built with the modified front-end assembly, was then to be fitted with the new rear section and shipped in the fourth week (January 23–January 27) of 1978 to the body development department in Sindelfingen. Subsequently, car 41 was fitted with the modified front-end assembly and the new rear section in Rastatt and was delivered to Sindelfingen in the seventh week (February 13–February 17) There, the completion of car 42 and car 41 should take place in weeks 5 to 7 (January 30–February 17) and 8 to 9 (February 20–March 3).

Progress was also made with the engine. On November 15, Werner Kolter, Manfred Fortnagel, and Fritz Clauß documented the results of an eighty-hour endurance run to which they had subjected the EA 25-121 engine. In the so-called two-point program, the engine, with about 220 hp, was operated alternately for 1.5 minutes each at a speed of 4,200 rpm and 4,600 rpm. The following damage was found: After twenty-one hours, the alternator tensioning yoke was cracked; after forty-three hours and then another four times, the charge air hose from the compressor to the intercooler was cracked; after fifty-two hours, the cylinder head showed cracks in the pre-chamber and exhaust valve seat at cylinders 3 and 4; and after sixty-five hours, there was a blow-by of the cylinder head gasket at the wide web areas. The appropriate remedial measures were taken immediately and tested in further trials.

On November 10, 1977, the above-mentioned employees of the diesel engine test department had again measured the EA 25 122 engine used in the Nardò test and summarized the results in a communication dated December 23. After the original acceptance on September 19 with an output of 218–220 hp/160–162 kW, the output had increased to 221–223 hp/163–164 kW after an increase of the injection quantity by approximately 4 mm³ carried out in Nardò. A second measurement with the injection quantity reset to the original value showed a slight drop in output to 214–218 hp/157–160 kW. The original governor kick-in at 4,650 rpm was to be increased to 4,800 rpm before starting the next test drives.

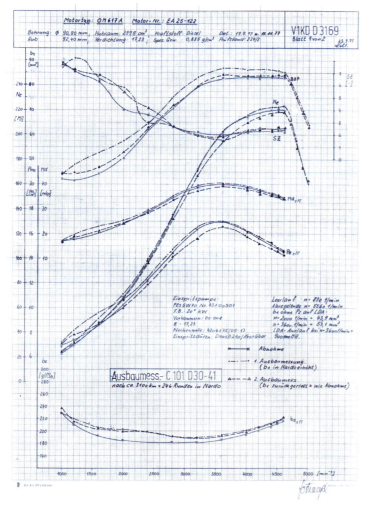

Performance diagram of the 3-liter, five-cylinder diesel engine OM 617 A with the number EA 25-122, taken on November 10, 1977, after testing in Nardò. In addition to the original acceptance curves, the diagram contains the measured values with the injection quantity increased in Nardò and subsequently reduced to the initial value.

In a communication dated December 2, Bernd Göckeritz from the wheel and tire test department also contributed his results of the test drive in Nardò. Regarding the wheels, he notes that the cast magnesium wheels from Kloth-Senking used at the front had proven themselves and should "be left as they are." The two-piece BBS wheels mounted on the rear axle were, as the report states, "okay in terms of durability, but manufacturing is still inadequate." Accordingly, Göckeritz recommended that Kloth-Senking wheels also be developed for the rear axle. The bolt fastening of the wheels had not proved successful due to tilting of the wheels during installation and removal, as well as scraping off of rim material at the bolt thread, and the development of a center lock mechanism was recommended. The wheel spats used so far were to be modified and given such a strong curvature that they "protrude about 20 mm over the widest part of the tire in the center section." The handling characteristics of the 230/600-15 slicks at 2.7/3.0 bar were rated as good, and the expected mileages when driving clockwise were calculated as follows: front left 2,800 km or 9.5 hours, front right 10,600 km or 35.5 hours, rear left 8,200 km or 30.5 hours, and rear right 4,600 km or 15.5 hours. The intermediate tires of the same dimension, intended for a wet track, were also "okay," while the 215/600-15 rain tires were found to be "too spongy" and "could not be used in this form." In a meeting of the tire test department with Michelin on December 20, it was decided that Michelin would also check "which tires could be made available for the tests in Nardò in March 1978."

From December 2 to 8, car 41, equipped with a new rear-end model, was examined in the large wind tunnel and aerodynamically optimized. Rüdiger Faul summarized the results in a report dated December 27, 1977. As delivered, the car had a drag coefficient of 0.242, which Faul estimated to be in good agreement with the c_d value of the car driven in Nardò, as the car deviated in some respects from the configuration optimized in the wind tunnel measurement of September–October 1977. Once again, the delivery condition was modified in many ways, and on December 7, a c_d value of 0.180 was measured for the variant, optimized after long trials with two 80 mm long partial front end spoilers mounted on the left and right, and a 15 mm high spoiler mounted in the center of the front end, a 40 mm high rear spoiler, a rear center fin, rear wheel spats extended downward, and a NACA inlet for the engine intake air in the right

Car 41, equipped with the new rear-end model, was examined and aerodynamically optimized in the large wind tunnel at the beginning of December 1977. The photos show the initial state with the two stabilizer fins and the final state of optimization with a centrally positioned single tail fin and a rear wheel spat extended downward.

After the wind tunnel measurements at the beginning of December 1977, the tail section with the centrally positioned stabilizer fin was revised and "symmetrized" in the model workshop of the styling department (*left*), and the result was then measured again in the wind tunnel (*right*).

door. Afterward, the rear-end model was revised in the design area and "symmetrized" (i.e., revised with regard to perfect and symmetrical lines) and examined again in the wind tunnel before delivery to Rastatt on December 13. Starting from a minimally worse value of 0.182, a final state with a c_d value of 0.175 could be realized by changes to the position and dimension of the partial front end spoilers and the center spoiler. Faul calculated a value of 0.185 for the roadworthy condition.

On February 25, 1978, the meanwhile completed car 42 was also examined in the large wind tunnel in Untertürkheim. Faul documented the results in a development report dated April 5.

In January 1978, car 41 received the modified front section and the revised rear section, which had already been realized on car 42 at Waggonfabrik Rastatt.

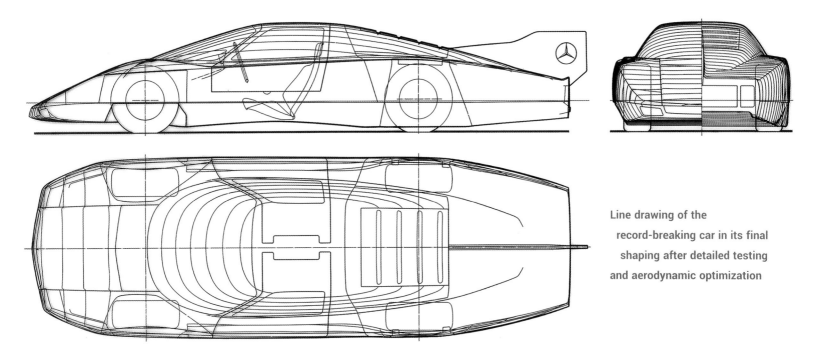

Line drawing of the record-breaking car in its final shaping after detailed testing and aerodynamic optimization

The car, fitted with 17/63-15 Michelin X racing tires, was in design position and freely sprung. The tanks were filled, the driver's seat was loaded with 75 kg, and 50 kg was added on the passenger side to simulate the spare parts box. During the measurement, air flowed through the following coolers: the radiator and one engine oil cooler in the front end, a combined engine oil-transmission oil cooler in the rear end, and a cross-flow intercooler on the passenger side of the bulkhead between the cockpit and the engine compartment. The cockpit ventilation was open, and the NACA inlet for primary air supply to the engine was functioning. The engine compartment cover was fitted with ventilation slots. In the front end area, two 80 mm high 90° partial front end spoilers were fitted 160 mm behind the leading edge of the front end, extending to the wheel arches. The clear span between the two spoilers was 450 mm.

With a frontal area of 1.4782 m², a drag coefficient of 0.191 was measured, and a value of 0.282 m² was produced for $c_d \times F$. The resistance component for radiator and cockpit flow as well as for primary air supply and engine compartment ventilation was very low at $\Delta c_d = 0.023$—especially considering that the air flowed through three oil coolers, one radiator, and one intercooler. Compared to car 41, status October 1977, the front-axle downforce coefficient could be increased, and the rear-axle lift coefficient could be reduced. The lateral force coefficients were slightly smaller overall, but the distribution between front and rear axle was more uneven. This left the answer as to whether

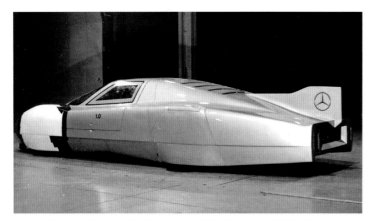
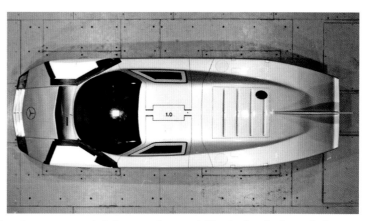

During the wind tunnel testing of car 42 in February 1978, the front wheel spats were extended downward on a trial basis, but in the end, they were not implemented. In the top view (*right*), the modified exhaust outlet in the engine compartment cover is clearly visible.

the measures taken against crosswinds were sufficient to the driving tests in Nardò.

At the beginning of February 1978, Goodyear was the thirdtire manufacturer to supply sample tires for the record-breaking project, and on February 9, Dunlop, Michelin, and Goodyear were scheduled to carry out tire tests in operating conditions in Nardò between March 11 and 19. On February 24 and 25, exactly five months to the day after the last such tests, the record-breaking car from 1976 was again used on the skid plate in Untertürkheim to test the new Kloth-Senking center-lock wheels. The aim of the tests was to achieve 600 laps on the second outer concrete ring of the 85 m diameter skid plate at the maximum possible speed without the wheels breaking or showing cracks. This was done in a clockwise direction, so that the left wheels were constantly stressed. Mounted were the new Goodyear tires, and the speed achieved was between 75.10 and 78.16 km/h. The front left tire was changed after 320 laps and then again after 280 laps, while the other three tires did not need to be replaced.

In addition to the wheels themselves, their new center-lock mechanism was also examined. It was noted that the nuts did not twist relative to the wheel; during the first change of the front left wheel after 320 laps, the nut loosening torque was at the upper limit. After the nut was removed, the wheel was stuck on the gearing and could only be loosened with greater force after several kicks against the tire. In contrast, all four wheels were easy to remove at the end of the tests. The testing of the wheel bolting was continued on the small circuit of the Hockenheimring on February 28. However, Wankel-engined car 34 was used, since the record-breaking car from 1976 was being prepared for its trade fair appearance in Geneva. The tests at Hockenheim, which were again run on Goodyear tires, confirmed the results obtained earlier: the nuts had not twisted during the tests and were easy to loosen.

One day earlier, on February 27, the diesel engine test department had documented the acceptance of three high-performance OM 617 A engines for testing in Nardò in a development note from Werner Kolter and Manfred Fortnagel. The engines EA 25-124 for car 41, EA 25-122 for car 42, and EA 25-125 as reserve engine were accepted. Compared to the previous acceptances, the following changes had been made. The speed governor restriction was increased to 4,700 rpm, and the larger turbine housing was used with an A/R ratio of 0.96

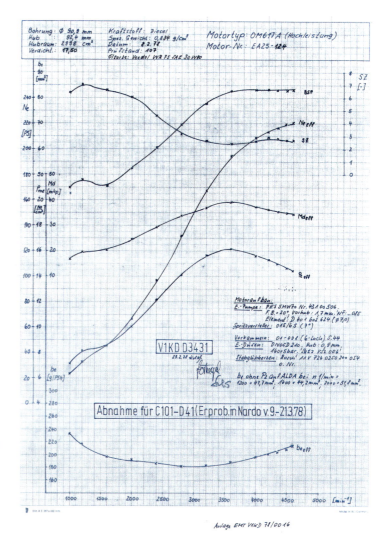

Performance diagram of the 3-liter, five-cylinder diesel engine OM 617 A with the number EA 25-124, taken on February 8, 1978, during acceptance for testing in March 1978.

instead of 0.81 before. This ratio of turbine inlet cross-section A and angle of incidence R of the gases on the turbine wheel determines the response behavior and performance of the turbocharger, whereby a larger A/R value generally stands for slower spool-up but higher performance. This change caused a reduction in the pressure ratio and speed and thus a slight drop in the maximum combustion chamber pressure. The slightly lower boost pressure resulted in a slight increase in temperature upstream of the turbine, but no loss of power. The measured outputs were 220–228 hp/162–168 kW at 4,600 rpm.

Dress Rehearsal: The Record-Breaking Cars in Nardò

On March 7 and 8, 1978, almost exactly five months after the first trial of the C 101/3 in Nardò, the two cars left for southern Italy. The trucks with the record-breaking cars left first on March 7, and the engineers and technicians set off one day later. Testing began one day after arrival on March 10. An important item on the program, which was examined from March 11 to 19, was the testing of the tires provided by Dunlop, Goodyear, and Michelin, with experts from the respective suppliers on-site. The results of the test drives were documented by Dr. Liebold as usual in an exemplary manner in a development report dated 28 March. This very interesting and detailed report is also reproduced here unabridged:

"In continuation of the tests carried out in October 1977 in preparation for new diesel records, runs were again carried out on the test track near Nardò with the C 101 D 30-41 and the D 42, which had been completed in the meantime.

In addition to testing the bodywork, which had been significantly modified since then, two newly manufactured transmission variants, and the prepared chassis modifications, a final tire selection was to be made during these tests.

Although the c_d improvement expected after the wind tunnel tests was obviously not achieved, lap averages of over 320 km/h were subsequently attained. In the final ten-hour run, all the world records on the current FIA list were surpassed, so that, if continued appropriately, all the records, except the flying km and flying mile [the standard disciplines for the land speed record, a good 1000 km/h at the time with rocket propulsion, the author] should be in our hands after 24 hours. The average achieved over the 10 hours, including refueling, driver changes etc., was over 312 km/h.

The car's handling is now almost as unproblematic with the Dunlop tires as it was with the D 31 from 1976, which was approximately 60 km/h slower. The vehicle is also satisfactory in the dark and in moderate rain or crosswind.

Compared to the last tests in October 1977 . . . the achievable speed was initially very disappointing, since despite the c_d improvement of approximately 23% measured in the wind tunnel, the lap speeds achieved with the same tires and almost the same engine output (removal status 1977: 223 hp, installation status 1978: 220 hp) were not the expected approximately 20 km/h higher, but rather almost 10 km/h lower in both cars, even with an optimal gear ratio.

On the other hand, the extensive shape changes in the rear area resulted in a significant improvement in crosswind sensitivity despite measured larger yaw moments, especially after the provisional fitting of an enlarged tail fin. A major contribution to this was made by the front spoilers that had been omitted in October due to the wind tunnel measurements, which now only had to be removed for trips to the workshop because of the ground clearance, which immediately had a very negative effect every time.

While the improvement proposed by A1RA no longer had any noticeable effect on the c_d value, it could eventually be brought back to roughly the old value by reworking it by hand, especially the floor paneling. Planned further work, especially on the lower sides of the cars and the shoulders between the wheels, promises further improvement here. Together with a slight increase in engine power through changes to the turbine and the injection pump, this has in the meantime enabled lap times to be raised at least to the targeted 320 km/h, for which the lengthening of the ratios of 4th and 5th gear was set in motion last year while still in Nardò. With the Dunlop tires, 320 km/h was achieved almost exactly at the desired 4400 rpm. On the other hand, the transmissions with further lengthened 3rd, 4th and 5th gear, which were ordered in the meantime after the optimistic c_d expectations and the anticipated smaller diameters of the Goodyear and Michelin tires and had only been delivered the evening before departure, proved to be too long under the given circumstances. As expected, the shifting problems observed in October were no longer found. Instead, the crack in the bell housing, which back then occurred for the first time, developed this time on both cars uniformly after a few hours of running and led to the complete breakage of the housings. Since the transmission suspension has not been changed since 1970 and D 31 was also driven for about 100 hours in Nardò in 1976, the current overstressing can really only be explained by the strong shocks that occur at the high driving speeds on the track, which is slightly sagging in some places. Even massive provisional reinforcements using tubes bolted to the side of the housing showed cracks on the strong connecting plates after only a few hours and had to be reinforced further. The new transmission housings used remained undamaged—but these reinforcements should be revised again before the next runs.

Vibration fractures, which were also partly stimulated by the heat radiation of the exhaust pipe, also occurred on the thin-walled plastic paneling parts, especially in the floor area. As with the last tests, all immediately necessary improvements and repairs (e.g. after a collision with one of the dogs occasionally roaming around the track) could be carried out at short notice by laminating appropriate reinforcements or making new ones in a modified form. Until the next deadline, however, the fairing parts will be reinforced throughout with carbon fiber mats and boron strips and attached more closely spaced to tubular frame stiffeners.

The quick-release and snap fasteners required for the almost total covering of all chassis parts have generally proved their worth. However, the floor paneling is now fastened with through bolts after all. For better accessibility of the cylinder head, the actual hood is separated from the rear fairing over an even larger area. This should also improve the practically non-existent view to the rear with the current slots.

Even after the turbine modification (conversion to the downsized 0.81 in. housing), which raised the boost pressure to approximately 2.3/2.1 bar, the engines did not exhibit any significant problems. Despite relatively effective fuel cooling, however, the lap speed achieved with decreasing tank content still dropped from max. 321.7 to approximately 314 km/h. Since an automatic temperature adjustment of the injection pump can apparently not be realized, it should be considered whether the delivery rate should not at least be calibrated to a medium fuel temperature and a somewhat richer setting should be accepted in cold condition. We will also improve the fuel cooling and insulation. The average fuel consumption in its current form is 16 l/100 km. The quick-fill system still needs to be improved, as difficulties were encountered here, probably due to the modified tank vent lines. In contrast, because of the problems with uneven emptying of the tanks that occurred in some cases in 1976, both can now be switched separately from the driver's seat. The spare pumps for fuel and transmission oil cooling can also be operated directly from the instrument panel.

The instruments themselves are much clearer than in D 31. The view through the steering wheel, which still needs considerable stiffening, is also satisfactory. To further relieve the driver, telemetric transmission of the most important measured values to the pit was tested for the first time, which generally worked flawlessly, as did the improved system for immediate processing of the light barrier measurements for lap time, integrated average speed, etc. In contrast, the new two-way radio with a fixed 100 watt transmitter in the pit was completely disappointing. For the 10-hour run, therefore, the old system from 1976 had to be used again.

The greatly changed design of all coolers, which only had to be altered a little during this year's tests, means that no more thermal problems can be expected, even at outside temperatures that are considerably higher than the 15° C that were rarely exceeded this time. The internal ventilation still needs to be modified.

To improve the handling, an even larger number of shock absorbers and torsion bars had been prepared this time, with the help of which it was possible to find a set-up without too much bumpiness that almost completely suppressed roll oscillations, even in crosswinds, while at the same time a powerful steering shock absorber largely calmed the steering. With the Dunlop 230/600-15 racing tires already used in October, it was thus possible for the first time to achieve almost problem-free handling again, allowing the driver largely fatigue-free, relaxed driving in this speed range.

At the same time, the slicks with the new 204 tread compound allow about twice the previously calculated running distance on the uppermost (most banked) lane, so that the first tire change (on the outer rear wheel of the turn) will not be necessary before 12 hours. Running times of up to 83 hours were calculated for the remaining wheels. The final 10-hour run was also completed without changing tires.

For the intermediates, the old 484 compound was retained. Wear should be lower on a damp or wet track anyway. When it started to rain, the handling again remained virtually unchanged (max. 316.6 km/h), while the outright rain tires even with a slightly stiffened tread still seemed too unstable. We have therefore asked Dunlop to also provide intermediates with even larger grooves. An outright water layer on the banked track can be ruled out anyway.

In contrast, the tests with the Goodyear tires (9.3/23.5-15 front / 10.5/24.0-15 rear) were very disappointing. The exterior of these tires is slightly wider, which makes attaching wheel spats slightly more difficult, but they proved to be equal to the Dunlop in rolling circumference, despite the previous diameter information (which contributed to the abandonment of the longer gear ratios). With basically the same construction (diagonal nylon carcass), they obviously have much less lateral rigidity, which led to strong yaw oscillations in the upper speed range. In addition, they heat up much more strongly (max. 88° C) and unevenly than the Dunlops (on average approximately 50° C, with completely even distribution over the tread width), which presumably also contributed to the significantly higher rolling resistance, which made the car approximately 4 km/h slower in otherwise identical conditions. Finally, unlike the Dunlops, they require quite high holding forces for the steering on the circular track. The Michelin mixed radials in the delivered size 17/63 15 X were also not satisfactory in terms of stability and again required extreme driving concentration due to their high sensitivity to crosswinds. In this case, the holding forces of the steering were very low, but the steering itself, in contrast to the other tires, only responded after a noticeable free travel, which was not significantly improved even by reducing the steering column friction. The dynamic rolling circumference was about 2% less than that of the Dunlops. Since the rolling resistance was probably also slightly lower, the lap speed (always in direct comparison and in comparison with the Dunlops) was on average about 1 km/h higher. Although Michelin showed up with the largest staff and more than 100 tires, only last attempts (after the 10-hour run) with wider rear tires (20/63-15 X) that had been flown in showed a clear improvement. In contrast to the recent excellent "straight-line running" of the Dunlops, however, the car still had to be steered constantly with these Michelins, as it tended to pull to the side even in very slight crosswinds (at this time it was almost calm for the first time) or presumed deviations in the track slope. Further tests could not be carried out due to time constraints, but it seems unlikely that the properties of the Dunlop tires (same size front and rear!) can be surpassed significantly in the foreseeable future for the special circumstance of this circular track. The Michelin representatives initially also hoped for a service life in the range of a double tank filling, whereas with the Dunlops can now be driven over 5 to 6 tank fillings.

During the tests, as is customary in Nardò, the direction of travel was changed every day. In view of the relatively high speed along the edge of the uppermost lane, a counter-clockwise direction of travel seems more advisable this time for new record-breaking attempts, as there is considerably more crumple zone available for the driver in the event of a possible brush with the crash barrier.

As the track is now heavily used by several companies (for this year's attempts we had to make arrangements with BMW and British Leyland, among others), we could only be offered the weekends for the actual record-breaking attempt. The track can be reserved for 3 consecutive days only from 29.4. to 1.5., so that this date has already been bindingly agreed. Detailed assembly reports on measured values and test details will still be prepared by all departments involved."

The C 111-III, photographed on the test track in Untertürkheim on April 18 shortly after its completion and a few days before its transport to Nardò

Rear view of the record-breaking car, taken on May 2, 1978, under the southern sun after successfully completing the record-breaking drive

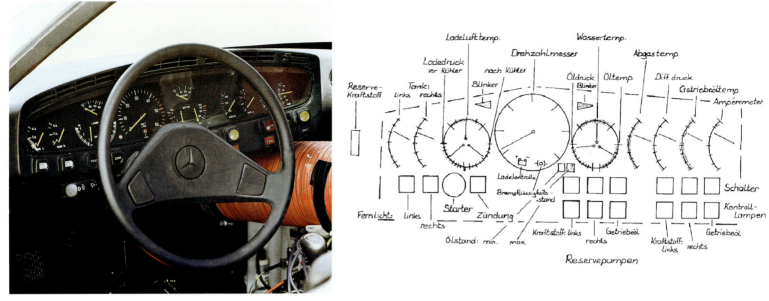
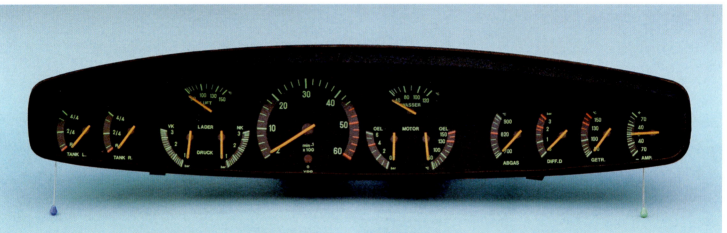

Cockpit and instrument panel of the C 111-III with explanation of the instruments, switches, and indicator lights

The rear end, which was extended for aerodynamic reasons, was supported by a space frame in which the transmission oil cooler and the fuel cooler were also mounted.

The well-filled engine compartment of the C 111-III with the 230 hp/ 169 kW 3-liter, five-cylinder turbodiesel, photographed in April 1978 on the test track at the Untertürkheim plant

The OM 617 A 3-liter, five-cylinder turbodiesel as a production engine with automatic transmission (*top*) and as a record-breaking car engine with the ZF 5-speed transmission and its integrated rear-axle drive (*bottom*)

Project manager and record-setting driver Hans Liebold at the wheel of the C 111-III, photographed on the test track at the Untertürkheim plant on April 18, 1978, a few days before departure for Nardò

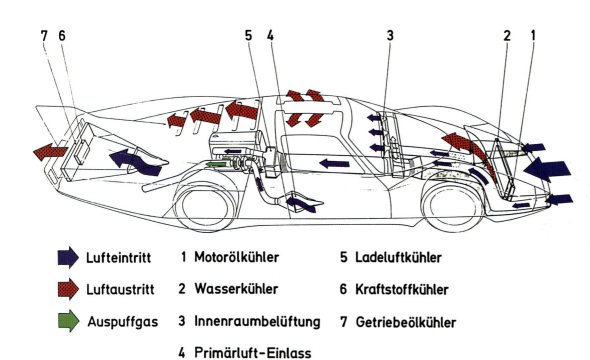

The diagram illustrates the air flow and the complex cooling system of the C 111-III.

➡️ Lufteintritt
➡️ Luftaustritt
➡️ Auspuffgas

1. Motorölkühler
2. Wasserkühler
3. Innenraumbelüftung
4. Primärluft-Einlass
5. Ladeluftkühler
6. Kraftstoffkühler
7. Getriebeölkühler

In a report dated April 6, Werner Kolter and Manfred Fortnagel summarized the results of the test drive from the perspective of the diesel engine test department. Car 41, with engine EA 25-124, had run a total of 427 laps or 5,397 km, of which ten hours, corresponding to 247 laps or 3,122 km, were endurance runs. Car 42 completed 169 laps or 2,176 km with engine EA 25-122 and another 28 laps or 354 km with engine EA 25-125. During the ten-hour endurance run, the engine had not shown any functional faults, but the following damage had occurred during the preceding testing. After sixty-four laps, the boost pressure had dropped as a result of a defective line from the charge air manifold to the boost pressure enrichment unit; the silicone line that was subsequently installed and insulated by rubber tubing showed no defects. After 124 laps, the cylinder head gasket had blown at the wide web areas between cylinders 2 and 3 and 4 and 5; the defect was later remedied by a widened cooling slot and an improved cylinder head gasket.

At outside temperatures of 13°C–18°C (55°F–64°F), the oil temperature in the sump was 108°C–112°C (226°F–234°F) during the ten-hour run due to the installation of an enlarged oil cooler in front of the radiator. In order to achieve the oil sump temperature of 130°C (266°F) recommended with regard to friction loss, it was suggested not to connect the rear auxiliary oil cooler during the next test run. The water temperatures were 82°C–85°C (180°F–185°F). The fuel temperature upstream of the injection pump was generally approximately 7°C (45°F) above the temperature in the supplying tank. Due to the heating of the rear end of the tank in the engine compartment, the fuel temperature rose from the filling value of 20°C (68°F) by almost another 20°C (68°F)—especially on the warmer, right side.

The turbine inlet temperature of the exhaust gas was initially 680°C (1,256°F) at engine speeds of 4,000–4,400 rpm, then 725°C (1,337°F) after changing the turbocharger housing. The temperature of the charge air after the outlet of the intercooler was a maximum of 85°C (185°F) at outside temperatures of 15°C–18°C (59°F–64°F). In car 41, the boost pressures before and after the intercooler were 2.1 and 1.9 bar, respectively. After changing the turbocharger housing, the boost pressures were then a constant 2.2 and 2.1 bar, respectively, at engine speeds of 4,200–4,400 rpm.

The engine speeds with a final-drive ratio of 2.58 and a fifth gear ratio of 0.64 were between 4,000 and 4,400 rpm in both vehicles, with a gear ratio of 0.60 even only between 3,800 and 4,100 rpm, while maximum engine output is reached at 4,600 rpm. In the ten-hour endurance run, the engine speed was between 4,300 and 4,500 rpm. An April 17 memo, also prepared by Kolter and Fortnagel, documents the results of the measurements carried out on the EA 25-124 engine removed from car 41. According to this, the increase in injection volume by approximately 5 mm³ carried out in Nardò, as well as the use of the smaller turbine housing, resulted in a power increase of 7 hp/5 kW and 12 hp/9 kW at a charge air temperature of 135°C (275°F) and 105°C (221°F), respectively. Since a charge air temperature of 85°C (185°F) was measured in Nardò, it could be assumed that an output of 235 hp/ 173 kW at 4,500 rpm was achieved. However, this could not be verified on the test bench, since these low temperature curves could not be reproduced there. On April 7 and 14, the diesel engine test department had subjected the high-performance EA 25-121 engine with about 230 hp/169 kW to a sixty-hour endurance run in a two-point program (alternating between 1 minute 15 seconds at 4,400 rpm and at 4,600 rpm). Apart from a leak in an injection line, the endurance run was completed without damage, and the valve clearance remained constant throughout the run.

Puzzlement and irritation arose in answering the question as to which factors were responsible for the speed level achieved during the test runs, which Hans Liebold found disappointing. After intensive discussions between the aerodynamics development department and the advance engineering test department, the most likely explanation in the end was a simple calculation error in estimating the achievable speed.

Busy Weeks: The Final Preparations

Regardless of this, the preparation of the record-breaking drive went ahead with military precision. In a communication from Joachim Kaden dated April 6, the schedule was set. April 17 was defined as the last date for the completion of cars 41 and 42 in Rastatt and their transport to Untertürkheim. One day later, measurements and test drives were to take place there, followed by loading and customs clearance on April 19.

The truck convoy for the expedition to Nardò included:
- 2 trucks with the two record-breaking cars
- 2 small trucks with workshop, refueling system and spare parts
- 1 small truck with tires, tire mounting equipment and balancing machine
- 1 support car with caravan
- 1 estate car with caravan

The convoy was scheduled to depart on April 20 and arrive on April 22, while the car convoy, consisting of fourteen vehicles, was scheduled to depart on April 24 and arrive at the track around noon the following day. Test drives were scheduled for the afternoon and the following day. On April 26, the three engines prepared for the

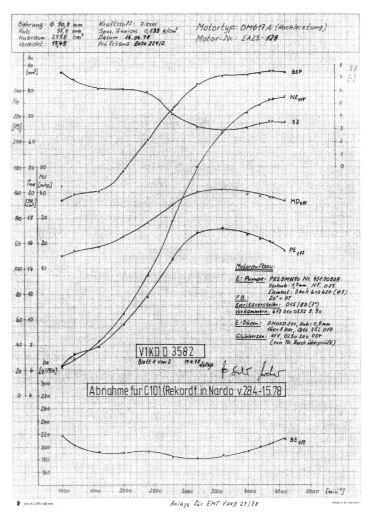

Performance diagram of the 3-liter, five-cylinder diesel engine OM 617 A with the number EA 25-129, taken on April 16, 1978, during acceptance for the record-breaking drive in April/May 1978

record-breaking attempt were to start their journey from Untertürkheim in order to arrive in Nardò on April 27. The three newly built high-performance engines EA 25-129, EA 25-130, and EA 25-131 were tested on the test bench from April 14 to 17. To achieve the specified 230 hp/169 kW, as the report by Kolter and Fortnagel dated April 20 shows, the injection quantity had been increased further compared to the previous acceptances, and the turbine housing had been changed back from A/R 0.96 to A/R 0.81. Maximum power was now 233–234 hp/171–172 kW at 4,600 rpm, and maximum torque 41–42 mkg/402–412 Nm at 3,600 rpm.

The drivers' briefing was also scheduled for the same day that the engines were due to arrive in Nardò. In contrast to the record-breaking team of 1976, this time not only Mercedes-Benz employees were involved. While Hans Liebold and Guido Moch

The plans for the pit stops, meticulously drawn up by Joachim Kaden, contained the work to be carried out for each stop and the staff assigned to it—here, as an example, two plans for cleaning the headlights and changing the right rear wheel.

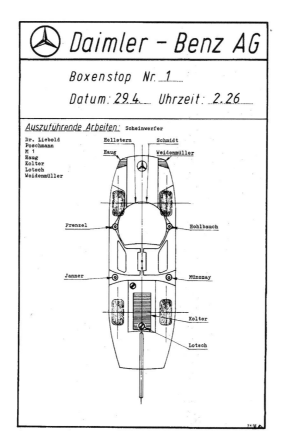
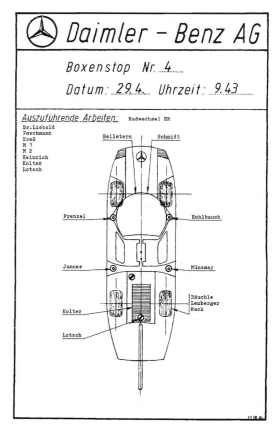

were back, two ex-racing drivers and motor journalists—Belgian Paul Frère and Swiss Rico Steinemann—took the place of Erich Waxenberger and Joachim Kaden. By his own admission, project coordinator Kaden was not very comfortable with the speed level of the new record-breaking car and was thus able to show off his organizational talent and technical expertise to greater effect, since he was now able from the pit to monitor and control the overall process, which he himself had meticulously planned. Not only had he planned each pit stop in detail with all the work involved, but he had also noted the staff assigned to each stop on a chart with a vehicle plan view.

On April 28, the new engines were to be installed and the cars made ready for the start so that the record-breaking attempt could start punctually at midnight on April 29. The official list of tools and spare parts carried on April 28, 1978, showed the following items, which added up to a total weight of 60.34 kg:

1. Tools

    Open-end spanner 10/11, 12/13, 14/15, 17/19

    Water pump pliers, combination pliers, hammer

    2 Phillips head screwdrivers

    2 flathead screwdrivers

    1 handsaw   1.92 kg

2. Spare parts and material

1 cylinder head complete	43.00 kg
1 set of injection lines	0.60 kg
2 V-belts 9.5 x 1,030	0.10 kg
2 head gaskets	0.52 kg
1 alternator, 55 amps, with pulley and bracket	5.10 kg
1 oil filter element	0.39 kg
1 turbocharger lubricating oil line	0.25 kg
1 valve cover gasket	0.13 kg
1 roll of lasso tape	0.28 kg
2 windshield wipers with arm	3.70 kg
4 headlamp lenses	1.24 kg
4 bulbs	0.05 kg
1 tube of adhesive	0.10 kg
1 oil return line	0.20 kg
1 injection line, straight	0.12 kg
2 spoilers, front	1.22 kg
1 steering damper	0.80 kg
1 pressure line to the injection pump	0.10 kg
1 return line for turbocharger oil	0.20 kg
2 torsion bars	0.32 kg

This collection of miscellaneous things, any one of which could have put an end to the high-speed run, was picked up by Mercedes-Benz employees on the track for the record-breaking attempt before the start.

Interesting details on conducting the record drive are published in the essay in the February 1979 issue of *Automobil-Industrie*: "Already during the test drives . . . strong attention was paid to the ergonomic conditions. For example, a precisely fitting steering wheel and a suitable resting surface for the left foot proved to be absolutely necessary in order to be able to immediately intercept any incipient course deviation with firmly supported hands; for example, under the influence of a crosswind. Correctly positioned two-way radio buttons, clearly readable instruments, and sufficient ventilation were also important. . . . Two-way radios were installed for communication with the pit crew. Because of the relatively high sound level in the outwardly rather quiet vehicle, throat microphones were used. In order to relieve the driver, in contrast to the previous drives, the most important measured engine values were recorded by means of telemetric transmission at the box by point recorders, for which the measured values were automatically retrieved as the car drove by. The respective speed of the passing car was also measured automatically by using a light barrier (independently of the official timekeeping), and the last lap speed and average speed since the start of the drive were immediately determined by a computer. All these devices were made and tested in-house. Since, as mentioned, all pit stop times for driver changes, refueling, and maintenance of the vehicle are fully included in the record time, all possibilities were also exhausted here through rehearsed pit plans. For example, refueling with 140 l of diesel oil took only 20 seconds, in the end, with simultaneous checking of the oil level and tire condition as well as cleaning of the windshield. A change of wheels on one axle, now fitted with center-locks, was completed in 16 seconds, and a valve adjustment took just over 3 minutes.

Under these circumstances, the drivers also had to practice switching with re-buckling and plugging into the two-way radio, just as driving at night and in the rain were tested beforehand. Finally, an unforeseen problem was caused by the fog, which suddenly appeared on the record-breaking night and was quite thick in places. Driving close to the crash barrier, the speed could be maintained unchanged."

Triumph Despite Breakdowns, Night, and Fog: The Record-Breaking Drive in Nardò

Before the record run, the entire track was searched for foreign objects, and a rich assortment of the most diverse objects was found, each of which could have caused a puncture. The start took place as planned on April 29 at midnight, and the drive was very successful in the end, despite several unforeseen incidents. It proved to be a fortunate circumstance that two record-breaking cars were available. Hans Liebold summarized the records achieved and how the drive went in a development report, which is also reproduced here in unabridged form.

On 29. and 30.4.1978, nine world records and two class records were set with cars C 101 D 41 and C 101 D 42 respectively. These and the previous records are compiled below. How the record runs went is also described.

1. Compilation of the previous and new records

1.1 Class records of the class diesel vehicles up to 3 l engine capacity (Group III, Class 8)

	C 101 D 31 1976	C 101 D 41 April 1978	Improvement in %
10 km		260.347 km/h	
10 M		272.052 km/h	

1.2 World records (without cubic capacity limitation)

		C 101 D 41 April 1978	Improvement in %
10 km	283.10 km/h		
10 M	282.06 km/h		
100 km	302.01 km/h	316.48 km/h	5
100 M	306.85 km/h	319.84 km/h	4
500 km	294.58 km/h	321.86 km/h	9
500 M	285.22 km/h	320.79 km/h	12
1000 km	285.42 km/h	318.31 km/h	12
1000 M	278.10 km/h	319.09 km/h	15
1 h	306.87 km/h	321.84 km/h	5
6 h	277.42 km/h	317.80 km/h	14
12 h	273.93 km/h	314.46 km/h	15

The world records over 10 km and 10 M could not be achieved, as the acceleration phase still factors too strongly here. With a vehicle specially lightened for these short distances—dismantling of parts not necessary here—and an engine output also slightly increased for short distances, these records could also be improved.

2. Course of the record runs

Due to the low outside temperatures of max. 20–25° C on 28.4., the cooling systems for water and oil were changed on both vehicles before the start of the record runs. During the test runs in October 77 and March 78, these systems had been designed for max. outside temperatures of up to 40° C.

The following details were changed:
1. The three cooling air slots in the front end were laminated shut
2. The remaining opening was reduced by 5 mm from the bottom to 75 mm
3. The rear engine oil cooler was decommissioned

Measure no. 3 simultaneously lowered the transmission temperature, as the transmission oil cooler is attached to the rear engine oil cooler.

Water and engine oil temperatures were monitored via telemetry, while transmission oil and air temperatures were radioed to the pit by the driver. In addition, the exhaust gas temperature and the boost pressure were transmitted telemetrically to the box.

2.1 Drive with car C 101 D 42

The record runs were started with this vehicle, as almost all the test runs, including the 10 h endurance run, were carried out with car 41.

Direction of travel:	Counter-clockwise.
Start:	29.4. 12 midnight
Driver:	Paul Frère

1st fuel stop: 2:29:43 a.m.
Distance driven: 63 laps = 796.34 km
Average: 319.14 km/h

At the end of lap 62, the driver came into the pit area too fast and therefore continued for another lap.

Quantity refueled: 137 l
Consumption/100 km: 17.2 l
New driver: Rico Steinemann

Around 3:00 a.m. fog forming, therefore 3:50 a.m. driver change.

2nd fuel stop: 3:49:26 a.m.
Distance driven: 33 laps = 417.13 km
Average: 313.96 km/h
Quantity refueled: 70.5 l
Consumption/100 km: 16.9 l
New driver: Guido Moch

Around 4.30 a.m.: Daylight is sufficient for track illumination.

3rd fuel stop: 5:31:39 a.m.
Distance driven: 43 laps = 543.53 km
Average: 319.05 km/h
Quantity refueled: 95.7 l
Consumption/100 km: 17.6 l
New driver: Dr. Hans Liebold

4th fuel stop: 7:23:02 a.m.
Distance driven: 47 laps = 594.09 km
Average: 320.03 km/h
Quantity refueled: 81.1 l
New driver: Paul Frère

At this fuel stop, the two tanks did not fill up completely, so the average consumption is not given here
Front right tire change!
The front right tire was changed early as heavy wear on the outer shoulder became apparent during the individual stops.
By using center-locks, the wheel change on the front axle (18.4 s) is no longer decisive for the length of a pit stop (here 24 s).

5th fuel stop: 9:49:31 a.m.
Distance driven: 62 laps = 783.70 km
Average: 321.00 km/h
Quantity refueled: 131.5 l
Consumption/100 km: 16.8 l
New driver: Rico Steinemann

Scheduled right rear wheel change.
Wheel change time = pit stop time = 28 sec!
Due to the two Camlok fasteners used on the rear wheel spats, a wheel change here takes longer and affects the length of the pit stop. Improvements are planned here.

6th stop
End of the record-breaking drive with car 42. Puncture on the right rear tire on lap 17 at km marker 6. The bursting tire destroyed the bodywork in the area of the wheel. It was therefore not possible to continue the drive.

Summary of car 42
Total distance: 265 laps = 3349.67 km
Overall average: 316.97 km/h
Total distance by the
5th fuel stop: 248 laps = 3134.78 km
Overall average by the
5th fuel stop: 319.05 km/h
Total consumption by the
5th fuel stop: 16.45 l/100 km

2.2 Drive with car C 101 D 41
After car 42 failed, it was decided to restart the record-breaking attempts with car 41. As the telemetry system and the spare parts had to be taken over from car 42, the restart could not be carried out until 12:40 p.m.
Driver: Dr. Hans Liebold
During the first run of car 41, a disproportionately low fuel consumption was observed compared to car 42. It was therefore decided to increase the quantity at the injection pump during the first pit stop.

1st fuel stop: 3:21:03 p.m.
Distance driven: 68 laps = 859.54 km
Average: 320.23 km/h
Quantity refueled: 134.5 l
Consumption/100 km: 15.65 l
New driver: Guido Moch
E-pump readjusted

2nd fuel stop: 6:01:12 p.m.
Distance driven: 67 laps = 846.90 km
Average: 317.29 km/h
Quantity refueled: 132.5 l
Consumption/100 km: 15.65 l
New driver: Paul Frère

3rd fuel stop: 8:41:25 p.m.
Distance driven: 67 laps = 846.90 km
Average: 317.16 km/h
Quantity refueled: 139.5 l
Consumption/100 km: 16.47 l
New driver: Rico Steinemann

4th stop: 9:04:10 p.m.
Distance driven: 9 laps = 113.76 km
Average: 294.63 km/h
The driver reports running over a small animal (hedgehog)
Pit stop required to check the vehicle
Findings: Spoiler broken
Front right wheel full of spines in places
Measures: Spoiler and wheel changed

5th stop: 9:12:01 p.m.
Distance driven: 25.28 km
Average: 193.22 km/h
Driver reports: Burnt smell
Vehicle comes into the pits for a check.
Findings: Everything OK

6th stop: 9:37:26 p.m.
Distance driven: 126.40 km
Average: 298.39 km/h
Driver reports: Vibrations
Vehicle comes into the pits for driver change
New driver: Dr. Hans Liebold

7th fuel stop: 11:29:09 p.m.
Distance driven: 46 laps = 581.45 km
Average: 312.28 km/h
Distance travelled since
last fuel stop: 67 laps = 846.90 km

Average since last stop: 302.95 km/h
Quantity refueled: 139.5 l
Consumption/100 km: 16.47 l
New driver: Guido Moch

Due to the 3 unscheduled pit stops, the average between fuel stops 3 and 7 dropped by about 15 km/h!
The previously driven overall average was worsened by 4 km/h.

8th fuel stop: 2:09:14 a.m.
(Saturday 30.4.78)
Distance driven: 67 laps = 846.90 km
Average: 317.42 km/h
Quantity refueled: 132.0 l
Consumption/100 km: 15.58 l
New driver: Paul Frère
At this fuel stop, the right rear tire was changed as scheduled.

9th stop: 2:40:17 a.m.
Distance driven: 12 laps = 151.68 km
Average: 293.10 km/h

Failure of the vehicle on lap 12 by the half-shaft ripping off [meaning the driveshaft] at the right rear.
According to the responsible department, the failure is almost certainly due to overheating of the sleeves
caused by excessively high ambient temperatures. Various measures to reduce the engine compartment temperature are therefore currently being tested in the wind tunnel in Ut. The results will be reported separately.

The vehicle was refueled again to calculate the total fuel consumption.
Quantity refueled: 25 l
Consumption/100 km: 16.48 l
Total fuel quantity: 703 l
Total distance: 4398.81 km
Total consumption/100 km: 15.98 l

The comparatively relaxed mood expressed by the pictures suggests that these shots were taken during the trial runs.

A tire blowout with major damage to the streamlined bodywork was the end for the record-breaking run of car 42. The fact that Rico Steinemann managed to bring the car to the pits in one piece speaks well for the driver and the car.

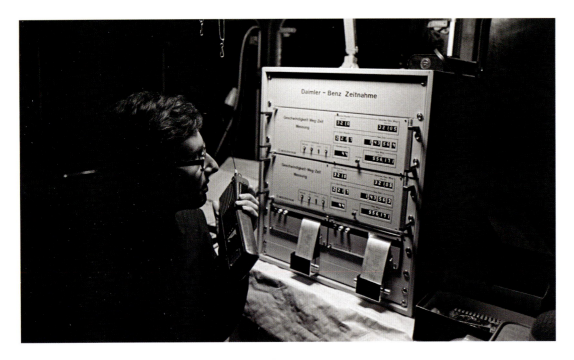

The timing system, housed in the hold of a van, was operated by dedicated light barriers and provided accurate data on lap times, speeds, and driven distances in real time.

The well-rehearsed and perfectly organized pit crew contributed to the success of the record-setting drive with short stops.

The C 111-III flat out on the track for the record-breaking attempt in Nardò

The team of drivers after successfully completing a record-breaking run (*left to right*): **Guido Moch, Paul Frère, Hans Liebold, and Rico Steinemann**

After the drive, the entire project team—at least those employees who were on-site in Nardò—also poses for the photographer: *in the foreground, to the left of the drivers*, **head of development Werner Breitschwerdt**; *to the right of the drivers*, **Friedrich van Winsen, head of passenger car development**; and, *to the right*, **Guntram Huber, head of passenger car body development**. Project manager Joachim Kaden stands behind the vehicle in the second row on the left below the speed display, which shows the highest lap speed achieved during the run.

"Mercedes Diesel Collects Records": The C 111-III in the Press and Public

The Daimler-Benz press department communicated the spectacular success with the publicity-grabbing speeds of around 320 km/h in a press release that chief press officer Günther Molter had sent out immediately on May 2, the Monday following the record-setting drive. In the text, the designation C 111-III was officially mentioned for the first time. The public was already aware of the futuristic-looking, record-breaking car through the press reports that appeared from the end of March, but a connection to the C 111 or to future record-breaking runs was not yet a subject of discussion.

The "New Mercedes Coupe," pictured on the front page of the July 13, 1977, issue of *Auto Zeitung*, was to make a huge splash in a different form in 1978.

Reporting by *Auto Zeitung* at the time stood in stark contrast as it explicitly mentioned the C 111 in its article "Die neuen deutschen Autos" ("The new German cars") on July 13, 1977. The front page featured a drawing dubbed the New Mercedes Coupe, reminiscent of the C 111-II in shape and color. In this regard, the article stated, "The C 111 is being revised stylistically and in terms of shape. . . . Connoisseurs speculate that this car will be used immediately if BMW becomes active with a twelve-cylinder. . . . The Mercedes study is used as another test mule for new diesel engines."

Automobil Revue put it more concretely two months later. In the IAA Novelty Preview of its September 8, 1977, issue, it published a photo of the 1:1 scale design model and pretended to be well informed in the caption "For coming diesel records? The Sindelfingen styling study for an ultra-streamlined sports coupe ("AR" 18/1977) is not to become a production model, but a one-off for even higher diesel records. In the picture, the clay model in natural size."

In fact, it was not this 1:1 model that was exhibited at the IAA in Frankfurt, which opened a week later, but the 1:5 design model that *auto, motor und sport* had already presented on the cover of its issue of June 8, 1977. In the exhibition, it was to illustrate the topic of "How a shape is created—the basics of design"—as it had been communicated in the press since the end of March. In contrast to the report in *Automobil Revue*, no reference of the streamlined coupe to record drives was apparent.

Instead, the record-breaking run of June 1976 was made the subject of discussion and showcased with an almost life-size color photo. This served as the backdrop for the 300 SD Turbodiesel, the first series-produced passenger car with a turbodiesel engine, which made its debut at the IAA and was equipped with a less highly developed variant of the five-cylinder used for the record-breaking drive.

In its issue of January 4, 1978, *auto, motor und sport* also made no reference to future record-setting drives—after all, four months after statements to that effect in the *Automobil Revue*. The article "New Cars 1978" read, "Even slightly faster [than the 260 km/h mentioned in the previous sentence] will probably be a car that the Daimler-Benz engineers are currently working on: the successor to the C 111, equipped with a particularly streamlined gullwing body and powered by a turbocharged five-cylinder diesel engine. Like its predecessor, however, this car has no chance of ever going into production." Under a drawing showing the 1:1 design model with an orange exterior, the vehicle was labeled "Mercedes C 111 successor."

World premiere of the 300 SD, the first production passenger car with a turbodiesel engine, at the IAA in September 1977. A large photo of the successful record-breaking run in June 1976 served as the background.

At the IAA in September 1977, Mercedes-Benz illustrated its design process with numerous photos under the heading "How a shape is created." Also on display was the 1:5 scale model of the aerodynamics study presented six months earlier.

No chance of production. In its issue of January 4, 1978, *auto, motor und sport* published a realistic illustration of the vehicle described as the "Mercedes C 111 successor."

At the AAA motor show in Berlin at the end of March 1978, a hard model of the C 111-3 was exhibited together with the W 196 R Silver Arrow on a replica part of the AVUS high-banked curve, but there was no hint of future record-breaking drives.

A photo taken on April 18, 1978, shows the Mercedes-Benz C 111-III that had just been completed together with the 300 SD Turbodiesel due to be launched on the market shortly; it vividly demonstrates the low height and very low frontal area of the high-performance coupe.

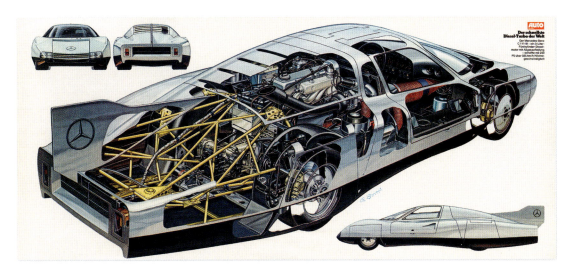

"Silver Flounder": Under this headline, *Auto Zeitung* published a detailed article on the C 111-III and the development of the C 111 since 1969 in its issue of July 11, 1979; it also included this attractive x-ray graphic of the vehicle.

With advertisements at home and abroad, Mercedes-Benz upgraded the image of diesel passenger cars, which were regarded as ponderous, and supported the market launch of the 300 SD Turbodiesel, which made history as the first S-Class with a diesel engine and the first series-produced passenger car with a turbodiesel engine.

Even at the Berlin motor show "AAA—Autos, AVUS, Attraktionen," where a 1:1 scale hard model of the C 111-3 was exhibited together with a W 196 Formula 1 Silver Arrow on a recreated high-banked curve of the Berlin racetrack AVUS from March 24 to April 2, 1978, any reference to an upcoming record-breaking drive was missing.

After the press release about the successful record-breaking run was published on May 2, 1978, numerous reports appeared in the national and international press, including a whole series with engaging headlines:
"The new Mercedes Diesel goes 325 km/h" (*Bild-Zeitung*, May 3)
"Taught the diesel to sprint" (*Mannheimer Morgen*, May 3)
"Diesel world record racer from Mercedes" (*Berliner Morgenpost*, May 4)
"Mercedes diesel collects records" (*Süddeutsche Zeitung*, May 5)
"The Thunder Diesel" (*Münchner Abendzeitung*, May 10)
"Mercedes world records only a 'by-product'" (*Sindelfinger Zeitung*, May 13)
"Turbodiesel as a rocket!" (*Neue Tiroler Zeitung*, May 13)
"Only fat Neubauer was missing" (*Kurier, Vienna*, May 19)
"Limits of the diesel engine still far from reached" (*Rhein-Zeitung*, May 20)
"Nine world records as a by-product" (*Kreiszeitung, Böblingen*, May 24)
"A diesel—faster than any racing car!" (*Bild am Sonntag*, June 4)

On May 5, *Stuttgarter Zeitung* reported in a commentary titled "More than just records!" about the record-breaking drive and its background and summed it up as follows: "More power from diesel engines—that would reduce numerous prejudices against this power unit and make diesel even more attractive, to the advantage and benefit of us all. For these reasons, the Nardò records are not only interesting for the drivers, because they are more than records, they are progress!"

Even *Der Spiegel* addressed the records in its May 8 issue in a full-page article under the headline "Gun to the head" and took them as an opportunity to report on turbocharging: "Can cars be made faster and more frugal with the help of turbochargers? Daimler-Benz set new world records with a turbodiesel. Last week, the clever minds behind the steep radiator foreheads once again showed the way forward for car shapes and engines: In order to save energy in series production, Daimler-Benz announced in Stuttgart that in future 'fuel-efficient and environmentally friendly engines as well as aerodynamically favorable body shapes will play an increasingly important role.' Actions speak louder than words. . . . The success was scored by . . . a streamlined plastic vehicle called 'C 111-III' with . . . a drag coefficient of only 0.195 and an average consumption of just under 16 liters of diesel fuel—just as it comes from the filling station." After some remarks about turbo engines, the article ended with the following sentences: "In America, where particularly economical, environmentally friendly engines are already required by law, a turbodiesel would meet with a more favorable buyer climate. And that's exactly where the Stuttgart turbodiesel world record holders intend to offer their first Mercedes-Benz 300 SD with turbocharger—as early as next month."

The record-breaking drive and the worldwide media response came at just the right time at the beginning of May 1978, since the market launch of the 300 SD Turbodiesel began just a few weeks later—the first S-Class with a diesel engine, aimed primarily at the North American markets and reserved for export to the USA and Canada. In the USA, advertisements appeared in 1978 and 1979 featuring the 300 SD Turbodiesel together with the C 111-III; for example, with the headline "These two Mercedes-Benz cars just rewrote Diesel history—by adding the word 'performance.'" In those countries where the S-Class with diesel engine was not offered, the C 111-III was used to spice up the image of diesel passenger cars. The advertisement headlines read, "With 9 new world records, the Mercedes diesel shows what it is capable of" or "The world record vehicle Mercedes C111-III proves what a production diesel engine is capable of." The English-language headlines put it more succinctly: "This Mercedes-Benz just ran 12 hours at 195.4 mph and set 9 new world records. This Mercedes-Benz is a Diesel" and "Some people take the future of the Diesel car more seriously than others." Still in 1981, a US advertisement related the newly introduced 300 D Turbodiesel to the C 111-III and proclaimed, "The Mercedes-Benz 300 D Turbodiesel Sedan—and the most successful engine transplant in automotive history."

In his speech at the general meeting on June 21, 1978, Joachim Zahn, Chairman of the Board of Management, also addressed the record-setting drive: "As a particularly pleasing result in the current year and one that is remarkable for the technical development work, I would like to mention the world speed records set in Nardò in Italy with a turbo version of the five-cylinder diesel engine in the new test vehicle C 111-III. All nine records so far have been held by petrol-engined vehicles. This gave a new technical dimension to this type of drive, which was criticized just a few years ago as being outmoded and poor in performance. We were and remain convinced that the diesel engine is by no means at the end of its technical possibilities, and see here a very significant contribution on our part to the improvement of energy saving and exhaust emission values."

Continuation in Autumn: More Records within Reach

The success of the record-breaking drive was discussed by the Board of Management at the meeting on May 9, 1978. Regarding item 4 of the agenda, "Report on the record-setting runs in Nardò," the minutes read, "After a short report by Breitschwerdt on the course and result of the record-setting runs in Nardò, there is agreement to repeat the record-breaking attempts over twenty-four hours and 10,000 miles in autumn this year, which had to be aborted this time."

In fact, the record-setting runs had achieved remarkable results, but for the reasons described in Liebold's development report, not all distances and times could be covered as planned. By telex dated April 6, 1978, Daimler-Benz AG had asked the Commissione Sportiva Automobilistica Italiana for permission to run record-setting attempts at the Autodromo Nardò. Speed records over 10, 100, 500, 1,000, 5,000, and 10,000 km, and 10, 100, 500, 1,000, 5,000, and 10,000 miles, as well as over 1, 6, 12, and 24 hours were mentioned. Due to the premature end of the record-setting run, the records over 5,000 and 10,000 km, over 5,000 and 10,000 miles, and over twenty-four hours could no longer be set and were to be made up for in another record-breaking drive. Hans Liebold and Joachim Kaden lost no time and immediately started with the preparation and planning.

On May 9, important points for the next drive were discussed in a project meeting documented by Kaden. Reflective pylons should be used to make it easier to enter the pit lane, "especially at night and in fog"; drivers should be given sufficient opportunity to practice entering at night. For starting after the pit stop, the possibility of using a shorter ratio first gear should be examined with ZF. In order to provide better acceleration for the record distances of 10 km and 10 miles, it was suggested that the gear ratios be reviewed overall. In future, the spoilers should be made of rubber or brushes to avoid damage. The operator of the test track should be asked to repair the track surface about 500 m after the box, renew the lane markings, and investigate what means could be used to prevent small animals such as snakes and hedgehogs from crossing the track.

For the next long-distance record-setting attempts and the previous practice, Hans Liebold and Joachim Kaden considered two alternative dates: the weekends of September 16–17 and 23–24 and September 30–October 1, with the start scheduled for midnight on Saturday in each case. In the spring of 1979, as the

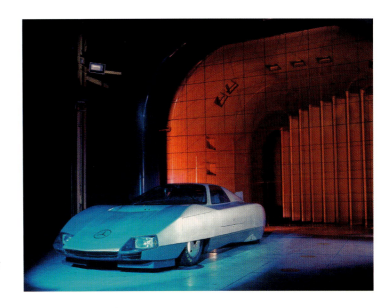

Car 42, which had been provisionally repaired after its major tire damage, was measured again in the large wind tunnel in Untertürkheim in May 1978. These beautiful color photographs were taken at the time.

minutes of the meeting dated May 10 indicate, "the short distance records over 10 km and 10 mi. as well as the 'fastest lap on a closed track' could be run with a petrol engine." At this point, Liebold and Kaden had already set their sights on achieving the unofficial lap record; at the same time, it was clear that a diesel engine could not be considered for the performance potential required for this.

Also on May 10, 1978, the engine test department asked the development measurement center to "prepare a ten-point channel with telemetry in digital display," measuring the following values: outside air temperature, engine speed, water temperature, oil temperature (engine inlet), exhaust gas temperature, boost pressure downstream of cooler, charge air temperature, transmission oil temperature, fuel temperature upstream of injection pump, and engine compartment temperature.

In a memo dated May 12, Hans Liebold summarized the measures to be taken on the vehicles themselves. Initially, it was suggested that a third car be built "for the most important PR purposes," since cars 41 and 42 could not be available for exhibitions in view of the next mission in September. The new exhibition vehicle to be built, a show car in today's terms, was to correspond as closely as possible in appearance to the two driving cars but did not need to be functional. For capacity reasons, Liebold suggested not to make a new floor assembly as a basis, but to use the first GRP-PUR floor assembly foamed only for measurements at the time. The two cars damaged in Nardò, which had been restored in the meantime for wind tunnel tests and short demonstration runs, were to be completely overhauled in Rastatt.

In the meantime, the wheel and tire test department, in coordination with Dunlop, had also analyzed the serious tire damage that had led to the abortion of the first record-setting attempt. Apparently, the tire had a bad bond between the tread and the rubber base, but this had not been noticeable during rolling in and only came loose after sixteen laps of use. The resulting cavities under the tread led to strong heat generation and vibrations, which, however, could not be recognized by the driver as tire damage. As the vehicle continued to drive, protector parts came loose, and the exposed carcass was worn through layer by layer until the tire burst and damaged the vehicle. A similar tire of identical manufacture had been run on the fast test bench at Dunlop in England. After thirty-five hours at 350 km/h and ten minutes each at a speed increased by 10 km/h, it was without findings up to 450 km/h, and only at 460 km/h small pieces came loose from the protector. No other tires with poor bonds were found in any of the tests.

On May 16 and 22, 1978, provisionally repaired car 42 was examined in the large wind tunnel in Untertürkheim. For the condition in the record-breaking attempt, the result was a c_d value of 0.184 with a frontal area of 1.50046 m², corresponding to a c_d x F of 0.276. Numerous improvement measures were also examined. Rüdiger Faul summarized the results in a technical report dated June 9. In it, he described two ways to further reduce drag. He considered a reduction of the c_d value by 15% to 0.156 by means of side skirts reaching almost to the ground to be feasible only if it should be possible "to reduce the lift occurring at the same time, or to regain the previous, relatively favorable downforce level necessary for driving stability in crosswinds." A "further and significant reduction in drag" would, as Faul wrote, "only be conceivable by exploiting the 'slipstream effect' when driving with two vehicles." Earlier measurements on 1:5 models had shown "c_d improvements of approximately 17% for both models" when they were "at a defined distance behind each other of approximately 0.6 x vehicle length." An interesting idea, but its implementation seems difficult to imagine under the conditions that apply during a record-setting run. In his report, Faul recommended the following further examinations in addition to measures to reduce lift, which could not be carried out on the dates mentioned due to time constraints: "Optimization of both the skirts and the front end spoilers in brush design; influence of the radiator covers in the air intake and outlet, likewise in the rear area if a smaller oil cooler can be used; influence of the modified exhaust gas discharge."

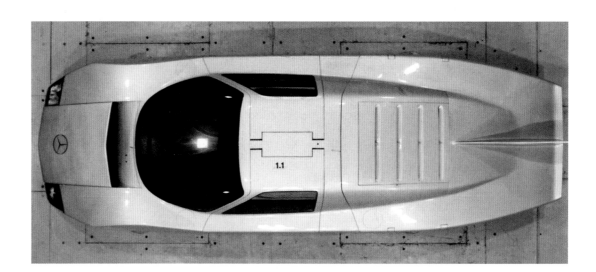

Car 42 from an unusual angle during wind tunnel testing in May 1978

Return to Nardò: Thermal Testing

Car 41 was in Nardò again in mid-July. This time the aim was to check the changes to remedy the overheating symptoms observed in May in mid-summer conditions. Hans Liebold documented the results of the test conducted from July 15–17 in a technical report dated July 20, large parts of which are quoted here:

1. Engine cooling

Even with outside temperatures of up to 38°, no unacceptable engine temperatures occurred with fully covered slits on the top of the hood (as during the record-setting runs in May). The water temperature indicated in the car never exceeded 100°. Also, the engine oil temperature only rose slightly above 130° when the Michelin tires increased the revs to max. 4800.

2. Component temperature

By leading the exhaust upwards and the exhaust duct behind the intercooler, the temperature at all previously critical components (propeller shaft tubes, wheel guide joints, oil pumps, etc.) was brought down to a harmless level. Only the alternator, which now protrudes slightly into the exhaust duct from below, overheated unacceptably and failed twice. A possible remedy is to drive the alternator from the transmission (a variant is said to be available at ZF) or from one of the half-shafts.

3. Transmission

To reduce the transmission temperature [which in April had reached 135°C after 7 ½ hours of running, the author], in addition to targeted cooling of the transmission oil pumps, a transmission with a rigid through-drive (without differential) and one transmission each with a 40% and 0% locking rate were prepared. With the transmission driven first without differential, the temperature did not rise above 110°, and the car was easy to drive with practically the same size tires. However, even a 1.5‰ difference in rolling circumference between the right and left rear wheel required unacceptably high steering forces in the long run. As a maximum difference of 5‰ can occur after a one-sided wheel change, this transmission variant was abandoned. Due to time constraints, only the transmission without lock-up could be installed, which at least on the dry track could be driven without any problems. The transmission oil temperature also did not rise above 110°.

4. Tires

The Dunlop tires also did not heat up above 80° C despite surface temperatures of up to 50° on the track. Surprisingly, however, after changing wheels within the first 5 to 10 laps, [according to the report of the wheel and tire test department after 16 laps, then after 12 more laps, in each case again on the right rear, presumably due to local overheating, the author] two tires again showed signs of delamination on the protector. Since these tires were previously driven for 1 hour on the roller test bench at 300 km/h and then holographed, the damage that occurred during the last record-setting drive can no longer be dismissed as an isolated case. Fortunately, during the scheduled set-up tests with Michelin racing tires, it was now also possible to achieve very stable handling when using the same size tires on the front and rear rims after optimizing the tire pressure. Since these tires are also very precise and roll quite well, they are rather preferable to the previous Dunlops in terms of handling. Although only the last night was available for endurance testing, a roughly equivalent service life can also be expected according to previous extrapolation. In addition, Dunlop intends to supply us with tires in the new extremely flat design for 19-inch rims, which are also made in radial design and may be an alternative.

5. Spoilers

The "flap spoilers" made in Rastatt worked well with the calculated spring preload of approximately 10 kg per flap section. By inserting test plates, it could be proven that the individual sections opened fully when fake hedgehogs were placed on the track and then immediately popped back into the initial position.

6 Animal collision

A bigger problem, at least in the current warm season, are animals […;] under these circumstances [one must] reckon on abandoning a possible record-breaking run every night. We are currently clarifying whether chemical spraying of the edges of the track or complete wire fencing on both sides of the track is the more favorable remedy. . . . Since the simultaneous failure of both headlamps must be expected at night in the event of a flock of birds, chemical light sticks were suspended lengthwise from the outer crash barrier on a trial basis, which, at a cost of DM 1.20 per stick, at least provide an indication of the track perimeter throughout the night.

7 <u>Driver comfort</u>

With the current daytime temperatures of 35 to 38° and little cooling at night, temperatures initially exceeded 50° at driver head height, rising to 58° in the midday hour. After changes to the fresh air supply, this level could be lowered by about 10°, but for this reason alone, record-breaking runs during the height of summer seem impractical. With the existing southern latitude, the length of the night is no longer appreciably different from spring and autumn anyway. Due to the inevitable interruptions (animal collisions, alternator overheating and driving ban during track use by the other vehicles on Monday), only 574 laps could be completed in the scheduled time from Saturday morning to Tuesday morning, representing an endurance test of about 22 ½ hours at an average speed of 322 km/h (max. lap speed 328.4 km/h). The planned 24 hours could therefore not quite be achieved."

Further interesting details of this test can be found in the technical report by the diesel engine test department of August 9 prepared by Fritz Clauß: "Due to overheating symptoms during the last record-setting run in Nardò, the modifications pre-tested in the wind tunnel such as exhaust and exhaust air duct behind intercooler upward, fuel cooler, [and] air flow to the half-shaft in car C 101 D 41 with the EA 25-129 engine were carried out over a total of 22 h 26'; i.e., 573 laps ≙ 7,242 km driven at max. outside temperatures of 38°C (100°F).

Damage related to the engine that has occurred:

1. Boost pressure too low and high exhaust gas temperature (hose strap burst downstream of intercooler).
2. Alternator no longer charges after 207 or a further 366 laps (max. determined temperature at housing was 142°C, also too many consumers as the result of measuring equipment—it is being investigated whether it is possible to drive the alternator from the transmission).

"In summary, it can be said that the measures taken have reduced the overall temperatures to a tolerable level."

As the report showed, the telemetry gave the following readings at an outside temperature of 20°C to 38°C:

Outside temperature	20 °C	38 °C
Water outlet	90 °C	112 °C
Oil temperature (engine inlet)	88 °C	104 °C
Charge air temperature	88 °C	102 °C
Transmission oil temperature (upstream of cooler)	94 °C	107 °C
Fuel temperature (upstream of pump)	36 °C	60 °C
Temperature right half shaft inside	40 °C	68 °C
Exhaust gas temperature	680 °C	780 °C

A twelve-point recorder was used to measure temperatures at numerous other spots. In conclusion, Clauß recommended: "Because of the water and/or oil temperatures, adjustment to the expected temperatures should be carried out under all circumstances immediately before record-breaking drive."

On August 31, Bernd Göckeritz from the wheel and tire test department commented on the tire defects that had occurred again in the minutes of a meeting. In the case of the two tires, after sixteen and twelve hours, respectively, there was a delamination of "a piece the size of about DM 5 coin as a result of overheating." Subsequently, one of the two tires was examined at Dunlop in England and one in Untertürkheim. While Dunlop attributed the overheating to a protector that was too thick and did not diagnose a faulty bond between the protector and the carcass, the Untertürkheim team found that the delamination occurred

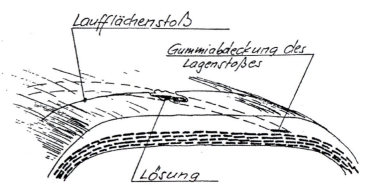

The sketch from Bernd Göckeritz's meeting minutes illustrates the position of the observed delamination, where the cover of the upper carcass layer coincided with the tread joint.

precisely at the point where the upper carcass layer was covered with a thin rubber strip and where the tread joint also ran. According to the minutes, "the existing 230/600-15 tire was to be upgraded" for the new date in spring 1979.

Record-Breaking Car for the Road: The C 111-III as a Two-Seater

On August 11, 1978, Hans Liebold had written to Werner Breitschwerdt, member of the Board of Management responsible for development, and commented in detail on the latter's wish to present "for demonstration purposes a road-going version of the diesel world record car," "in which guests could also get a ride."

"In addition to the required modification to the visibility and comfort, lighting, brake, exhaust, and refueling systems, this also requires major modifications to the drive (starting gear), suspension (ground clearance), steering (lock), and tires and wheel bolting. The installation of a passenger seat requires the relocation of the intercooler and a completely changed routing of the air to it and the intake air. For safety reasons, the tail fin, for example, must be made of flexible material. Since the two existing cars, which are currently being prepared and optimized (e.g., front end reinforcement, installation of air jacks, improved design of the hot air discharge system, etc.) for further diesel record-setting attempts in the spring [the original plan to run in September–October had thus apparently already been discarded], are still intended for testing with a more powerful engine for setting the absolute lap world record, building a new two-seater version is unavoidable."

Against this background, Liebold advocated for a completely new floor assembly. "Since A1VB does not have the capacity to build a new floor assembly in the foreseeable future, the suggestion investigated by K1V some time ago of a light-alloy floor assembly made of riveted, flat sheet metal, which can be adapted to the existing body shape and built in our workshop, is suitable for this case. According to preliminary calculations, the weight of such a floor assembly would even be reduced by approximately 100 kg. At the same time, the necessary space for a larger steering angle lock, spare wheel, possibly trunk, etc. could be created and experience gained with this construction method.

"Since the preparation work here and in Rastatt remains the same, it is expedient to build two cars, if necessary in different sheet thicknesses and in short and long tail versions. In terms of timing, the bodies in Rastatt can be built after the changes to the record-setting cars; i.e., from October 7-8. Building the floor assemblies also appears to be feasible during the winter with flexible cooperation with all the parties involved, so that the vehicles should be roadworthy in spring 79."

As a basis for Liebold's communication, Joachim Kaden had compiled a very detailed list of points "to be observed when building a C 101 III for use on the road" in a note dated August 10:

- Transmission with shorter first gear
- Headlamp with low beam and parking light
- Larger indicators and brake lights
- Hazard warning light system
- Rear number plate with lighting
- Steering wheel lock with ignition starter switch
- Tanks with baffled walls (possibly foam filling)
- Standard fuel filler necks
- Electrically adjustable exterior mirrors
- Interior mirror possibly periscope
- Larger wheel angle
- Greater ground clearance
- Tail fin made of hard rubber (regulation)
- Radio with Ari (motorist broadcast information)
- Brake booster
- Opening option for side windows
- Simple backrest adjustment (regulation)
- Handbrake
- Exhaust downward (possibly with silencer)
- Windshield wiper with intermittent setting
- Side doors lockable
- Interior heating (possibly with air conditioning)
- Jacks and jack points
- Rims without center-lock (40 mkg)
- Engine with vacuum pump and heavier flywheel
- Sprayed star on tail fin and front end, not glued on

A decision was made on August 14 at the passenger car technical meeting. Under agenda item "C 111/III passenger seat," the minutes noted, "It was to be investigated whether a passenger seat could be installed in this vehicle for demonstration purposes. This would require the relocation of the charge air duct and various lines, as well as a change in the floor. An undertaking with considerable effort, which would practically no longer allow a later conversion to original condition for record-breaking runs. Mr. Breitschwerdt stipulated: An existing C 111/III vehicle will not be converted to a passenger seat; additional new vehicles with passenger seat will not be built."

Le Mans and Once Again Nardò: Further Uses of the C 111-III

Another use of C 111-III was also investigated. Hans Liebold had commissioned construction advance engineering to calculate the "possible lap times of the C 101 on the 13.66 km circuit of Le Mans." In a communication dated August 28, 1978, Jutta Beifuß summarized the results:

"In the most recent specification in Nardò, the C 101 achieves a lap time of 4' 6.85," which corresponds to an average speed of 198.5 km/h. For a vehicle lightened by 100 kp, we calculated a time of 4' 4.52," corresponding to 200.4 km/h. With an optimal final-drive ratio of 2.73, this results in a time of 4' 3.97," equal to 200.9 km/h."

A comparison with the results achieved at Le Mans in June 1978 showed that "the average speed of the first four cars over 24 h (with fuel stops, driver and tire changes, and other pit stops) is still above the optimal average speed of the C 101. For this reason, we refrained from further calculations of fuel consumption and average speeds."

The C 111-III thus would have had no chance at the legendary "24 Hours of Le Mans," but in the end, it would not set any more records either. In its meeting on September 18, 1978, the model and product planning committee (AMP), consisting of the Board of Management members Werner Breitschwerdt (Development), Heinz C. Hoppe (Sales), Werner Niefer (Production), and Dr. Gerhard Prinz (Materials Management), as well as Karl Pater (Head of Finance) and Dr. Heinz Kiwitz (Corporate Planning), once again discussed the company's motorsport activities under the agenda item "Development expenditure for record-setting vehicles and rally participation." The minutes state, "With regard to further record-setting runs with the diesel record vehicle C 101-III, he [head of development Werner Breitschwerdt] could only suggest refraining from doing so in view of the effort required. Only three record times would still be missing in this class. However, achieving this would be associated with a certain risk, but above all, also with considerable capacity commitment in the relevant company test departments for the preparation of these drives. Therefore, nothing more should be done in this field for the time being, and one should wait until the established records would be bested by other vehicles. Then, if necessary, further procedural measures could be considered. He had also already discussed this topic with Prof. Zahn and Mr. H. Schmidt, who would also support this view. However, a discussion should take place again on this to determine the further course of action."

The rest is history. New diesel record runs were not on the agenda again for Mercedes-Benz until twenty-seven years later, when three E 320 CDI sedans, all standard except for a roll bar, covered 100,000 miles at an average speed of 224.823 km/h on the high-speed track in Laredo, Texas. Although the C 111-III did not achieve any further diesel records, it was used in communication for years—for example, in an advertisement with the witty headline "At some point we no longer saw that a diesel had to be lame, loud, and boring." When the advertisement for the launch of the E-Class W 210 series appeared in the summer of 1995, the successful record-breaking car had long been a museum piece. However, car 41 did not immediately receive its place of honor—instead, it was to make history again in the spring of 1979 after extensive conversion work with further spectacular records.

This advertisement by the Hamburg advertising agency Springer & Jacoby, which worked for Mercedes-Benz from 1990 to 2006 and made a name for itself with creative headlines, used the C 111-III for many years after its record-breaking drive as evidence of the changed image of diesel passenger cars. It appeared in June 1995 for the market launch of the E-Class 210 series.

New Power Unit, Optimized Aerodynamics: The C 111-IV

As early as May 1978, immediately after the successful record-breaking drive with the C 111-III, project managers Hans Liebold and Joachim Kaden developed the plan to achieve further records—not only the still-missing long-distance records over 5,000 and 10,000 km, over 5,000 and 10,000 miles, and over twenty-four hours, but also the short-distance records over 10 km and 10 miles as well as the "fastest lap on a closed track," which is not officially recognized by the FIA. The latter record was set by US racing driver Mark Donohue on August 9, 1975, when he drove a lap at 355.848 km/h in a Porsche 917/30 Turbo with over 1,000 hp/735 kW at the Alabama International Motor Speedway.

That the C 111-III with its diesel engine would not be able to break this record was undisputed from the beginning, which is why Hans Liebold had already considered a petrol engine as a power unit in May 1978. The calculation team of the advance design engineering department was given the task of calculating the necessary engine output for an initial speed of 360 or 380 km/h. The calculation was carried out by a team of engineers. The result was communicated by calculation engineer Jutta Beifuß in a technical report dated June 1, 1978. Depending on the c_d value, she had calculated a power requirement of 327–373 hp/240–274 kW, based on the key data of the C 111-III with half a tank of fuel.

Wind Resistance and Engine Power: The Focal Points of Development

In addition to the question of the power unit, the preparations also focused on further aerodynamic optimization of the record-breaking car and the procurement of suitable tires. From September 12 to 25, 1978, car 42 was examined in the large wind tunnel in Untertürkheim, and the results were summarized by Rüdiger Faul in his tried-and-tested manner in a technical report dated October 24. The aim of the measurements had been to test "with regard to a targeted top speed of approximately 400 km/h, measures to increase downforce on the front axle and to achieve downforce on the rear axle while maintaining or even improving yaw behavior as far as possible."

Faul went on to say: "A rough calculation by V1V showed that with an engine output of 500 hp and a frontal area of 1.5005 m², taking into account the . . . special conditions of the track in Nardò

In September 1978, car 42 was extensively tested in the large wind tunnel in Untertürkheim—with the aim of presenting a configuration with a low drag coefficient and the best possible downforce. Variants with a flat front spoiler, a cambered front-end section, cambered front wings, lateral spoilers, and two stabilizer fins with or without additional wings were measured.

for v_{max} = 400 km/h, a drag coefficient of c_d = 0.200 must not be exceeded. . . . After the overhaul of the vehicle in Rastatt, the new measurements determined a drag coefficient of c_d = 0.203 in the as-delivered condition, 10.9% higher with this c_d value, the 400 km/h are not quite achievable. Since downforce-generating measures create additional drag, measures to improve the drag coefficient were also necessary in addition to aerodynamic measures to keep the car planted on the ground. . . .. No consideration was given to stylistic concerns when modifying the vehicle."

In the course of the very extensive measurements, more than ninety variants were examined, with different features provisionally executed in clay, cardboard, and hard foam. These included lateral spoilers in front of the front and rear wheels, differently dimensioned front-end flat spoilers, partial front end spoiler boxes, front wings, rear wings, lateral tail fins, differently cambered versions of the center section of the front end, a rear end that was again significantly longer than the C 111-III, and differently designed spoilers at the rear. Faul wrote, "In variant 1.76, with slightly higher front-axle downforce compared to April 78 . . . , slightly lower rear-axle lift . . . and considerably improved yaw behavior due to two tail fins, the best c_d value of all ninety-three . . . measurements was achieved with c_d = 0.154. . . . Depending on the size of the downforce coefficients, c_d values between 0.164 and 0.190 are possible for the 500 hp vehicle. The prepared measures for generating downforce also allow asymmetrical downforce generation by aerodynamic forces, which is desirable to compensate for the asymmetrical axle load caused by the centrifugal force on the circular track in Nardò." Rüdiger Faul concluded his summary with a series of recommendations: "After the modification of car 41 in Rastatt, it was to be tested again in the wind tunnel to check the aerodynamic force and aerodynamic moment coefficients. In addition, it is necessary to investigate the lift behavior of the vehicle with the front axle at maximum extension. In order to avoid discussions about driving performance and measured values in the future, the C 101 vehicles should be examined in the wind tunnel after every rebuild, [after] every modification, and before new missions. A difference of 10.9% between the measurement before and after the revision of car 42, without any formal or functional changes having been made to the vehicle, should be reason enough."

In addition to the aerodynamics, the tire issue also proved to be essential: Here, not only was sufficient durability at speeds beyond the 400 km/h mark to be taken into account, the wheel loads to be expected in Nardò and the lateral forces to be assumed at this speed were decisive above all. As a result of comprehensive calculations submitted on September 25, the advance design engineering team recommended moving the vehicle's center of gravity as far forward as possible.

In a meeting on October 3, 1978, in which Hans Liebold, Joachim Kaden, and the Sindelfingen body developer Ernst Haug discussed the modification of car 41, a number of measures were decided that took this recommendation into account.

Instead of the two 70-liter fuel tanks in the sills, smaller tanks with a capacity of 25 to 30 liters were planned, which were to be placed as far forward as possible because of the center of gravity and encased in rubber for safety reasons.

The fast-fill tank valves at the front and rear should be removed and replaced with normal fuel filler caps at the front. The fuel pumps should be moved directly behind the tanks, also in favor of a more forward center of gravity.

The battery with 44 Ah should be placed at the front left, and the lead should be made of aluminum for weight reasons. The front lateral spoilers planned because of the wind tunnel tests were to be designed to be adjustable with an angle of attack of 15°–45°.

Finally, a halon fire extinguishing system was planned, with the extinguishing agent tank to be located in the front end, in the former area of the intercooler.

New Requirements: The Rebuild of the C 111-III

During October, car 41 was rebuilt at Waggonfabrik Rastatt based on the results of the wind tunnel testing of car 42 the previous month. In addition to a rear extension of 500 mm, this mainly involved a widened, more cambered front with a pronounced front-end spoiler, plus two stabilizer fins and lateral spoilers in the rear. As functional as the changes to the bodywork might have been—after all, they had been made on the basis of wind tunnel tests—they were unsatisfactory from a stylistic point of view. In agreement with Rüdiger Faul's statement "No consideration was given to stylistic concerns when modifying the vehicle," design chief Bruno Sacco noted his assessment "No design brief, wild cultivation of form" on a photo showing the modification of the C 111-III to the C 111-IV. Obviously spurred on by this criticism,

Based on the knowledge gained in the wind tunnel, car 41 was rebuilt in October–November 1978 at Waggonfabrik Rastatt. The lattice structure in the front end carried the very strong flat front spoiler, and for the extended rear, the space frame received an additional mounted latticework.

By the end of October 1978, the modified front-end section and the extended rear end had also been realized in terms of bodywork.

the stylistics department made efforts to develop an alternative that was satisfactory from a design point of view. In October and November 1978, three extremely elegant and sleek-looking 1:5 models were created, which, however, were not further developed into a 1:1 model, let alone a real vehicle. Even if the C 111-IV, which was already quite advanced at the time, did not exactly impress with its design elegance, it still had a head start that was almost impossible to catch up on in terms of time and, as the wind tunnel tests confirmed, was obviously suited to fulfilling the expectations placed on it—at least with regard to its performance.

By the end of November 1978, tires to meet the demands of the record run were in development not only at Dunlop but also at Michelin. At Dunlop, one of the new tires had successfully completed a bench test—starting with ten hours at 350 km/h, then increasing in increments of 10 km/h for ten minutes at a time up to the final speed of 500 km/h, where the test was stopped after ten minutes without complaint.

What may seem like a collection of sofa cushions actually shows a stress test for the wing between the tail fins, which in the end showed no weaknesses in stability despite being loaded with 400 kg.

Between the beginning of October and the end of November 1978, Peter Pfeiffer and Joseph Gallitzendörfer drew up different designs for the C 111-IV, which were characterized by design elegance and homogeneity and were realized as 1:5 models. In the end, they were not developed further because there was not enough capacity for this, and the conversion of the C 111-III had already progressed very far in the meantime.

Things were also progressing on the engine side. This time, the construction and testing of the necessary power unit was not carried out by the test department for near-series engines, but by the engine laboratory for piston engines (E6LK), which was part of the Daimler-Benz research department. On December 20, 1978, the engineer responsible for the project, Gert Withalm, was able to announce that a V8 engine based on the 4.5-liter standard M 117 unit, bored out to 4,820 cc and equipped with two turbochargers, had achieved an output of 492 hp/362 kW at 6,000 rpm without the use of an intercooler. With adjustments to the turbochargers, an increase in engine speed to 6,500 rpm, and the use of other fuels, Withalm held out the prospect of further output increases. The 5-liter light-alloy V8, which was in fact particularly suitable, could not be used because the installation space for the required mixture preparation system—two standard K-Jetronic units, as initially used in the preliminary tests—was not available in the vehicle. The solution was to use a mechanical injection pump from the standard 6.3-liter V8 M 100, housed in the V of the engine. For space reasons, however, this was only possible with the gray cast iron version of the M 117.

For aerodynamic reasons, the use of an intercooler had to be abandoned. Due to the very high exhaust gas temperature of almost 1,100°C (2,012°F), only turbochargers from Kühnle, Kopp & Kausch (KKK) were considered, since the Garrett AiResearch

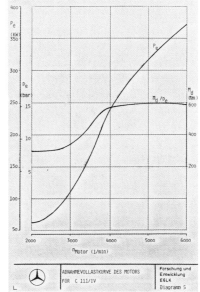

The power unit of the C 111-IV was a version of the M 117 passenger car V8 engine with biturbo charging, which was bored out to 4.8 liters. The full-load power curve shows an output of 503 hp/370 kW at 6,000 rpm.

turbochargers suitable for this engine power used turbines made of less heat-resistant material, which also had about 30% higher centrifugal forces due to the speeds, which were approximately 20,000 rpm higher. The lower part of the oil pan has been extended by 56 mm to accommodate a larger quantity of oil and prevent oil foaming due to splashing. This was important in view of the extreme operating conditions in which the oil level is constantly tilted due to the effect of centrifugal force. Using premium fuel and a boost pressure of 2.2 bar, a power output of 380 kW/517 hp at 6,000 rpm or 408 kW/555 hp at 6,500 rpm was achieved. For the record-breaking drive, the engine was set to 370 kW/503 hp at 6,000 rpm.

Mammoth Measurement in the Wind Tunnel: The Detailed Optimization of the C 111-IV

From January 11 to 18, 1979, car 41, which had been rebuilt at Waggonfabrik Rastatt on the basis of the last measurement, was examined in the large wind tunnel for aerodynamic testing and optimization. Rüdiger Faul documented the results in a technical report dated March 9. In the meantime, not only had the modifications made provisionally during the previous investigation been carried out in GRP, but a number of other detachable parts had also been prepared in Rastatt, with which possible optimization measures could now be evaluated. As delivered, a drag coefficient of 0.159 was measured, which was within the expected range.

This photo from early December 1978 shows the almost completed C 111-IV. After extensive wind tunnel tests, far-reaching changes were made. The wings above the roof and between the two fins were omitted, and the front spoiler was optimized, as were the lateral spoilers in the rear.

This photo, also taken in early December 1978, shows the vehicle with the canopy wing removed and the flaps open. The different rims at the front and rear and the modified fuel filler necks, which were accessible via the former air vents, are clearly visible.

However, neither the downforce at the front axle nor at the rear axle corresponded to the expected values. With sixty-six variants, the measurement again examined a large number of different designs. For the vehicle equipped with a flat front spoiler and partial front end spoiler boxes, a c_d value of 0.150 resulted without downforce-enhancing measures at the rear. Operational variants optimized with regard to front-axle and rear-axle downforce achieved c_d values between 0.174 and 0.186. The cooling air proportion could be reduced from $\Delta c_d = 0.022$ to $\Delta c_d = 0.014$ by omitting the intercooler as well as the transmission oil and fuel coolers. A definitive variant was not determined during the examination. Instead, the measurements had the aim, formulated in the aforementioned technical report by Faul, "to investigate a wide range of possible measures to increase driving stability with the lowest possible increase in drag, in order to be able to draw on them when setting up the vehicle on the track in Nardò."

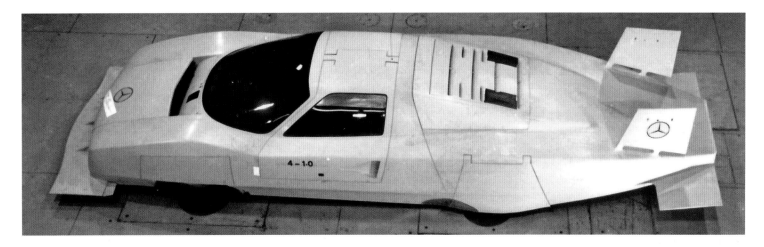

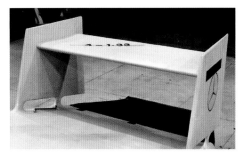

During the wind tunnel test in January 1979, numerous variants with different detachable parts were again examined, including canopy wings, rear wings and spoilers with end plates. The large photo shows the initial state with the canopy wing and the wing between the tail fins removed. The vehicle, primed in matte gray, was internally given the nickname "Gray Monster" in allusion to the US record-breaking cars known as "Green Monsters."

Some variants—for example, with a wing above the roof of the vehicle—were "not considered as driving versions due to the unfavorable relationship between drag coefficient and lift coefficients" but nevertheless went into practical testing in some cases. Different rear wings between the two vertical stabilizer fins were also investigated in the wind tunnel. In principle, however, these had, as Faul noted, "the disadvantage that the generated downforce acts on both rear wheels. Since the outside rear wheel is already highly loaded by the centrifugal force acting on the vehicle, further loading by the downforce . . . is not desirable for tire load reasons." Lateral spoilers at the rear proved to be an alternative to rear wings. According to Faul, these detachable components, jokingly and lovingly referred to as lobster tails, enabled "an even more favorable ratio between drag and downforce increase . . . than with the rear wings" and also allowed asymmetrical downforce forces to be generated at the rear axle. As Faul explained, asymmetrical downforce was also possible on the front axle "with the help of differently set trailing edge flaps and the end plates on the flat front spoiler." The trailing edge flaps were also "connected to the front axle in such a way that they are more negatively inclined during rebound, thus counteracting the rebound." According to Faul, "Which of the examined variants should actually be used in the record-breaking attempt had to be determined during the driving tests."

While the wind tunnel measurements were still running, the question of the record distance was discussed. Leo Levine, head of communications at Mercedes-Benz of North America, replied to an inquiry from the Untertürkheim sports department in a telex dated January 16: "At present, the fastest track available for use in the United States is the Transportation Research Center in Ohio, which is 12 kilometers per lap. We do not believe this track is as fast as Nardò, since it has straights and turns, rather than just being a circle. Renault was there in 1978 but ran into weather and mechanical problems." So the Pista di Nardò it was. At the end of February, the dates for the driving tests and the actual record-breaking drive were defined: The trial runs were to take place from March 24 to April 1, after which further tests were scheduled for the weekend of April 28–29, preparatory work for April 30, and the record-breaking run for May 1, 1979. The driving tests at the end of March were also intended to gain practical experience with the new tires developed by Michelin and Dunlop and to determine the tires to be used for the record.

On March 19, Bernd Göckeritz from the wheel and tire development department in Untertürkheim shared positive results from the test bench trials underway at Michelin. The tires intended for driving tests were already to be mounted on the provided rims at Michelin, briefly tested on the test bench at levels of 350 km/h and 400 km/h, and then examined by x-ray and ultrasound. The idea was to fill them with nitrogen, as this cannot diffuse as quickly as air. It was also explicitly pointed out by Michelin that "it is essential to carefully scan the track for foreign objects before starting the runs."

On March 15 and 16, car 41 was measured again in the large wind tunnel in Untertürkheim. As Rüdiger Faul noted in the technical report of April 3, the tests were "primarily used to design the downforce distribution asymmetrically in order to take account of the conditions specific to the track in Nardò. In addition, the aerodynamic drag of probable vehicle states should be determined in order to be able to infer the expected driving performance." On the results, Faul continued, "The drag coefficients of the examined vehicle variants that are suitable for the driving tests were between 0.190 and 0.200. . . . Compared to the measurements in January, the cooling air ratio increased from $\Delta c_d = 0.014$ to $\Delta c_d = 0.017$ due to the re-commissioned transmission oil cooler in the rear and a targeted engine compartment ventilation, whose cooling air

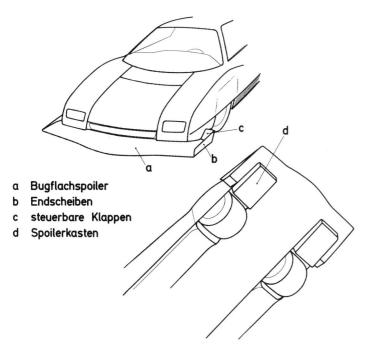

a Bugflachspoiler
b Endscheiben
c steuerbare Klappen
d Spoilerkasten

The flat front spoiler of the C 111-IV was perfectly adapted to the track conditions in Nardò with an ingenious system of different-sized end plates, controllable flaps ("trailing edge flaps"), and spoiler boxes.

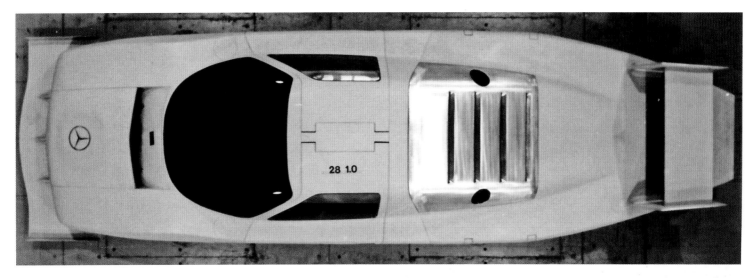

In March 1979, car 41 was examined in the wind tunnel for the last time in the run-up to the record-breaking drive—in particular to optimize the asymmetrical downforce distribution. The large photo shows the initial state with symmetrical end plates at the front and a large rear wing, but without lateral spoilers at the rear. The optimized hood immediately catches the eye due to its lack of paint

intake is located in the area of the headlamps. . . . With the downforce coefficients achieved, the drag coefficient could not be lowered below the value of the diesel world record vehicle. Lower c_d values . . . can be achieved on the modified vehicle, but only by foregoing part of the downforce."

Dress Rehearsal: Test Drives in Nardò

On March 21 and 22, 1979, a convoy of trucks and cars set off from Untertürkheim for southern Italy to test the new record-breaking car in operational conditions as planned from March 24. After returning to Untertürkheim, Hans Liebold wrote a management summary of the results in a note to Werner Breitschwerdt, head of development, dated April 2: "In the car used for the last world record runs, a 4.8 l M 117 with two turbochargers and a dyno power of 504 hp was installed. The shape of the front end was changed and an extended rear end was added to the body. A flat spoiler at the front and two lateral downforce plates at the rear increased the contact pressure of the wheels. After a provisional increase of the boost pressure, the following driving performances were achieved in Nardò:

Fastest lap	404.4 km/h
10 km with standing start	approximately 325 km/h
10 miles with standing start	approximately 340 km/h

"By installing the reserve engine with max. 5% more power and better controllability as well as a planned modified intake manifold, all these values should still be slightly improved.

"For the records over 100 km and 100 miles, the maximum permissible speed as regards the tire will still be determined by Michelin after test bench trials. So far, it has been driven at 380 km/h, which corresponded to an average of 374 km/h with a standing start. A final value of approximately 380 km should be expected. The current world records (316.4 and 319.8 km/h,

During testing of the new record-breaking car in operational conditions, the canopy wing was also used at the instigation of Hans Liebold despite the aerodynamically unfavorable prognosis. The vehicle then completed the record-breaking drive in May without the mighty detachable part.

respectively) are held by our C 101 D 30-41. A record-setting date of 5.5. is being considered."

Breitschwerdt introduced the subject as the agenda item "Record runs" at the board meeting of April 3, 1979, and as the minutes record, "reached agreement to carry out record-breaking attempts over 10 km and 10 miles on the Nardò track on 5.5.1979 with a C 111/3 vehicle with turbocharged 4.8 l petrol engine, subject to a particularly negative development in the energy sector." With the concluding remark, the board made the realization of the record-setting drive conditional on no day-to-day political events occurring that would make such a run inopportune.

Bernd Göckeritz summarized the results of the test in late March pertaining to wheels and tires in a technical report dated April 5. As with the record-breaking C 111-III, Kloth-Senking wheels of sizes 8 J x 15 H2 (front) and 9½ J x 15 H2 (rear) were used. Michelin had provided two different versions of each of the two dimensions 20/63-15 and 23/67-15, which were thoroughly tested in different combinations. The tire design was based on the following dynamic wheel loads: 329 kg (front left), 524 kg (front right), 427 kg (rear left), and 520 kg (rear right). The best results were achieved with a combination of four different tires and a tire pressure of 3.4 bar. The 20/63-15 was mounted at the front and the 23/67-15 at the rear—in each case on the left on the inside of the curve as a type 1 and on the right on the outside of the curve as a type 2, which was less temperature sensitive compared to the type 1 but had less lateral stability. The speed of 404.4 km/h mentioned by Hans Liebold was achieved with this combination.

There was also an endurance run of thirteen laps (equivalent to 164.3 km or 102.1 miles) at 380 km/h. The track, the report notes, "was searched daily for foreign objects before the start, and many iron and sheet metal parts, as well as stones and glass, were found." At an outside temperature of 20°C (68°F), tire temperatures between 46°C and 60°C (115°F and 140°F) were

The C 111-IV in its final configuration as it was used for the record-breaking run in early May. The photos were taken in April 1979 on the test track of the Untertürkheim plant and show very well the asymmetrically designed end plates of the front end spoiler and the lateral downforce plates at the rear.

The cockpit of the record-breaking car shows the instrumentation familiar from the C 111-III and the new larger steering wheel. The two red hoses that supply the engine with air are clearly visible (*left*). The 4.8-liter V8 fills the engine compartment of the C 111-IV very well (*right*).

measured at the end of the endurance run. Runs with different camber values between −45 and −15 angular minutes showed a high camber insensitivity in this range, without significant influence on the temperature distribution. For the upcoming record run, Michelin was to provide the tires in the tested combination, with nitrogen filling as in the previous trials. Michelin was also to check what speed could be permitted for the 100-mile record. The promise was "380 km/h, possibly 390 km/h."

For Dunlop tires, the report noted that they were "not used for various reasons."

Success Despite Obstacles: The World Record Run of the C 111-IV

The actual record-breaking drive then took place on May 5–6, 1979, with Hans Liebold at the wheel. The record-setting driver documented the course and the results in a technical report of May 15, which is reproduced here largely unabridged:

"The C 101 D 30—41, initially intended as a practice car for the previous year's diesel records and used as the actual car after the failure of the D 42, was revised again in the wind tunnel to achieve the absolute lap world record, with the focus on an optimized c_d with significantly increased downforce . . . . Subsequently, a 4.8 l M 116 [in fact, as described, it was a bored-out M 117 from the same engine family, i.e., an M 117 with a larger engine capacity, the author] with 2 KKK turbochargers from E6LK . . . was adapted and installed.

The selection of the prepared spoilers and tires was carried out with the general chassis optimization and engine tuning in March in Nardò. After checking all components in Ut. and installing the former backup engine, the actual record-breaking attempts were undertaken there again on 5 and 6 May. During these drives, a number of partly unexpected difficulties arose again, which indicated the limit load of major assemblies or components. In addition to improving the lap world record by 48 km/h, the FIA world records over 10 km to 100 miles were also beaten by 37 to 60 km/h respectively.

For later tests, aerodynamic lateral force and roll moment compensation is planned to relieve the tires which are subjected to unacceptable stress due to the sideslip (maximum lateral force load on the right rear wheel 300 kg). According to our information, corresponding attempts have only been made by Daimler-Benz in 1938 [Here Liebold refers to a historical photo of a Silver Arrow with side wings mounted vertically on both sides next to the cockpit. However, these could not—as now envisaged—counteract the lateral force, but only the yawing moment, the author]. Now that such measures are unavoidable for tire reasons, it is imperative that they be treated confidentially so as not to give any clues to a possibly interested competitor. For economic policy reasons, alternative fuels should also be used in the future.

In the following, we briefly report on the course of the two series of trials in Nardò:

During the tests in March, in addition to the scheduled testing of a number of tires prepared by Michelin . . . the effect of the various downforce aids was first clarified. With 4 different tires at the 4 corners of the car, it was possible to achieve sufficiently stable handling to make it possible to drive with the front-end spoiler and the rear lateral tail fins alone. These "lobster tails" presumably come at the expense of hardly any additional drag due to their location in the vortex area, while delivering sufficient downforce values. The effect of the flaps on the flat front-end spoilers controlled by the front suspension and the yaw stabilization by the two fins also met the expectations from the wind tunnel, so that after a slight increase in the boost pressure a lap average of 404.4 km/h was achieved in very stormy winds.

The last set of tires was also used for a 100-mile pre-test, which allowed a provisional sustained speed of

380 km/h over this distance. Since v_{max} had not yet been driven at this time and intermediate stops were necessary for the temperature measurements anyway, the right-hand tank—on the side of the crash barrier—was not filled during these runs. The effect of the tank switch-over and the additional tank cross-feed pump was therefore only tested in Ut. at a standstill. During the drives themselves, the car, which is now set extremely low for aerodynamic reasons, reacted very sensitively to small level deviations on the sometimes quite bumpy track by spring settling or making changes to the downforce aids. As soon as the rubber buffers came more into play, the steering had to be held extremely tightly, which was even easier to achieve in the full-throttle position with two firmly supported legs on which to rest the arms than at partial load, although on the other hand any reduction in speed greatly contributed to unloading the car noticeably. (According to K1V's calculations, the speed for the tire load with sideslip partly factors to the fifth power)

Before the actual record-setting drive, the lunch break on 4.5. was only enough for a quick check of the tires, which had been changed again by Michelin (now only different at the front and rear), and a double check of the v_{max}. On the handling plate of the site, the engine was adjusted with rolling tires.

The first record-breaking attempt on 5 May, 8 a.m. was then aborted at full speed due to the lack of timekeeping [the timekeepers were present at the track, as Liebold informed separately, but one timekeeping system was the casualty of communication problems, the author]. During the repeat that started immediately afterwards, the clutch suddenly started to slip shortly after reaching full torque in 5th gear, so that this attempt also had to be aborted. After removal, the clutch plates themselves proved to be in full working order, but a small amount of grease residue was found from the throw-out bearing. However, it was probably the fact that for the first time the car was started again immediately after a stop from full speed and a corresponding transfer of heat to the transmission that was responsible for this behavior. Subsequent investigations showed a very strong dependence of the friction lining used on the temperature. [. . .]

Because of the known limit load (transmittable torque of the dual-disc clutch with Textar lining 538 max. 600 Nm, existing engine torque 600 Nm), V1A had ordered a three-disc clutch with sintered linings before the record-breaking run, which was delivered by Fichtel & Sachs two days before departure (transmittable torque approximately 900 Nm). As this clutch was still completely untested, one of the 2 spare clutches of the type previously used was initially installed again in Nardò, but for reasons that could not be clarified after the fact, it exhibited vibrations from the first to the last start that had never been observed before and slipped in all gears when full torque was applied. The second backup clutch had inadvertently been given two discs with lining resilience, so that a combination had to be fitted with the parts that had already been running, which again turned out negative.

Finally, the new three-disc clutch was installed, and although it slipped again on the approach to the track after an extremely cautious start when applying full torque, it seated itself far enough during a subsequent run-in lap with slowly increased torque that the two full-throttle laps could still be carried out right before nightfall. Due to the very careful start and early upshifting, the values for 10 km and 10 miles with a standing start were each about 5 km/h lower than in March, but are still considerably above the previous FIA world record (Gregg 1978 on Porsche 935). The fastest closed-track lap was improved from 355.7 km/h (Donohue on Porsche 917—Can Am, Talladega 1975) to 403.9.

For the longer distances the next morning, a speed of 385 km/h was agreed with Michelin, which, likewise with an extremely careful start, led to a 100 km/h average of 375 km/h [meaning the value for 100 km with a standing start, the author]. Afterwards, this run was aborted due to impermissible transmission oil temperature. (A finding from ZF is not yet available.) After fitting a replacement transmission and an improved transmission oil cooler air intake, the run was started again.

This time the car stopped on the last lap due to fuel starvation, although the right tank was still 1/4 full. Presumably, the additionally installed cross-feed pump, which was supposed to pump the rest of the right tank contents to the left after the automatic switch-over, did not manage to do this sufficiently against the centrifugal force of approximately 0.5 g. For the last attempt, therefore, they drove extremely "light-footed" and even coasted for 4 km on the penultimate lap with the clutch disengaged, which brought the engine to about 2 km past the finish line. However, this lowered the lap average for 100 miles by about 10 km/h.

For a possible attack on these records by outside companies* and the eventual use of alternative fuels, wind tunnel tests with pitched or profiled tail fins and corresponding front fins are planned after the IAA in order to at least partially compensate for the lateral force and unload the tires. Because of the strong dependence on any airflow impacting from an angle (virulent crosswind behavior) to be expected in any case, the driving tests must then be carried out when there is largely no wind. However, the confirmation of a lap world record improvement can be done at any time (as already prophylactically practiced on 4.5.) by an employee of the track in Nardò. For the possible confirmation of the 10-km/10-mile world records (which Porsche waived at Talladega), the arrival of the FIA commissioners from Milan at short notice could be attempted. The records over longer distances are probably out of the question, if only because of the much larger fuel quantities for ethanol or methanol operation due to the much lower calorific value. In addition to an engine agreed with E 6, we will work with V1A to find a suitable transmission, clutch and drive shafts with modified sleeves. The wind tunnel tests for the lateral force compensation and the subsequent body modification in Rastatt are planned for autumn/winter 79/80. Because the overlapping of the crash barriers requires driving in clockwise direction again in the future [due to the way the crash barrier elements were connected, unhindered "sliding along" the crash barrier in the event of a collision was only possible when driving clockwise, the author], a thicker wearing layer of silicone dust should be applied to the side sill on the driver's side then facing the crash barrier, as was now used under the front-end spoilers that regularly strike the ground at certain parts of the track. A substantial improvement of the track surface at the critical points was already promised to us for August of this year (during the factory holidays there) by the track manager in Nardò.**

Michelin is ready to develop new tires—probably with a larger diameter—on request . . .

*) According to a call from Luigi Colani, BMW intends to attack our lap record and the absolute road world record (432 km/h, Caracciola 1938) at Nardò with the 800 hp—M 1 and an exterior shape developed by him.

**) However, due to difficulties with prospective customers, we have been implored to stop publicly pointing out collected items from the track. In fact, track employees had already combed the track before us this time, so that the search hardly yielded anything."

Final preparations for the record-breaking run in May 1979

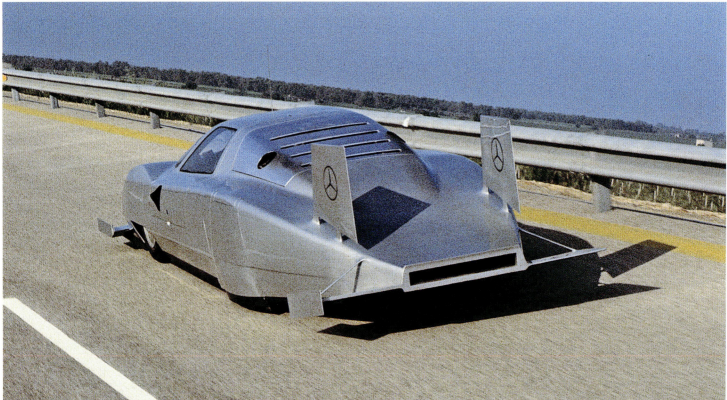

The C 111-IV on the track in Nardò

"Miraculous Car" or "Publicity Stunt": The Record-Breaking Drive in the Press and Public

At the board meeting on May 8, 1979, Werner Breitschwerdt, head of development, informed his board colleagues, as documented in the minutes, "about the record-breaking runs at the high-speed test track in Nardò/Southern Italy, during which, after technical difficulties had been solved and despite unfavorable wind conditions, existing world records over distances of 10 km, 10 miles, 100 km, and 100 miles were beaten, in some cases considerably." One day earlier, Breitschwerdt had also discussed the record at the technical meeting for passenger cars in Sindelfingen and, as the minutes show, emphasized the commitment of the employees. "Prof. Breitschwerdt was able to see for himself on-site how this success was achieved. He praised the enthusiasm of all those involved, which is rarely found today, and thanked everyone, including those at home, who contributed to this success."

While Breitschwerdt had still spoken of the "aerodynamically advanced C 111/III" in Sindelfingen, the designation "C 111-IV" is found for the first time in the minutes of the May 8 board meeting—as well as in a press release published on the same day by the Daimler-Benz press department. Under the title "Five absolute world records with the new Mercedes-Benz experimental vehicle C 111-IV, top speeds of over 400 km/h on the Nardò track," the research character of the test drive was highlighted in addition to the records achieved:

"Tests were carried out at the aerodynamic limits at speeds of over 400 km/h, and the influence of aerodynamic measures and spoilers was investigated. . . . The practical driving tests were carried out as part of the further development of aerodynamic measures and lightweight construction as well as of low rolling resistance tires, with the aim of improving vehicle efficiency and saving energy.

"In the course of the test drive, Dr. Hans Liebold, head of passenger car advance engineering at Daimler-Benz AG, set four new world records, achieving the following absolute averages with a standing start (subject to recognition by the FIA):

320.615 km/h over 10 kilometers	(283.101 km/h)
335.454 km/h over 10 miles	(282.673 km/h)
375.670 km/h over 100 kilometers	(316.484 km/h)
367.396 km/h over 100 miles	(319.835 km/h)

(previous figures in brackets)

"In addition, Dr. Liebold improved the absolute circuit world record of 355.9 km/h, which is not recognized in the FIA lists . . . to the new value of: 403.978 km/h."

The media quickly picked up the press release on a broad front and published reports with catchy headlines:

Even if the decoration was not completely coherent in every respect, the cake donated by the Cosimino Hotel-Restaurant in Porto Cesareo for the achieved circuit record put everyone in a good mood. The photo on the right shows the record-breaking driver in a relaxed mood as he cuts the masterpiece to the applause of those present.

"The miraculous Mercedes car set new world records" (*BZ Berlin*, May 8),
"Mercedes wonder flounder: With technology from the year 2000" (*Bild-Zeitung*, May 9),
"The super star bombs over the track at over 400" (*Express Cologne*, May 9),
"Virtually flying" (*Cannstatter Zeitung* and *Untertürkheimer Zeitung*, May 9),
"World records for safety" (*Münchner Abendzeitung*, May 12).

The article with probably the most sensational headline was published by *Bild am Sonntag* in its May 13 issue. Under the headline "One hedgehog—and I would have been dead! This is how a Mercedes test engineer got the world record," a news item appeared with statements by the record-breaking driver: "What a driver, what a car! Mercedes test engineer Dr. Hans Liebold (52) is a man with a pioneering spirit. . . . BILD am SONNTAG spoke to the daring driver. Dr. Liebold calmly, composedly, as if he was talking merely about a slice of buttered bread: I drove very close to the crash barriers, my elbows pressed firmly against my thighs. The ground temperature 38 degrees. That caused tire problems. We additionally cooled the particularly stressed right rear wheel with air through an opening in the wheel well.' Fear? No, only if the rev counter dropped a little. Then I knew: The world record is not going to happen. At a speed of 400 km/h, the many undulations on the track constantly create trouble and mean danger. One little hedgehog on the track—and I wouldn't have been able to give you the interview. The lateral forces in the curves pressed against the car like a powerhouse. We also wanted to test the resilience of a car. The C 111-IV passed the test.' The physical condition? 'I feel splendid. Not the slightest difficulty with the circulatory system.'"

In July 1979, a Michelin ad—which today would probably be called an "advertorial"—in *auto, motor und sport* described the successful record drive and the important role tires had played in the process.

While the tabloids and the trade press reported positively on the spectacular success, there were also dissenting voices with regard to design aspects—at least one: Designer Luigi Colani expressed his views in an article titled "Colani's style critique. Dubious publicity stunt" that was provocative as usual in *sport auto* magazine in September 1979. Colani, who had always been one of the most colorful personalities on the design scene, harshly criticized the aerodynamic shape of the record-breaking C 111-IV. Coincidentally, the article appeared just as Colani was presenting his own record-breaking GT 80 car study at the IAA. In the July 4,

In September 1979, Luigi Colani did not hold back on his criticism of the C 111-IV in *sport auto* magazine. A month later, an article appeared about Colani's "winged car," with which the master planned to start at Le Mans the following year and also break the records achieved by Rudolf Caracciola and Hans Liebold. However, the star designer was apparently once again too far ahead of his time.

1979 issue of *auto, motor und sport*, which showed sketches of Colani's miracle car, the master was quoted with the following statement: "To drive 400 km/h with an aerodynamically well-thought-out car is so safe today that one should actually let a woman take the wheel." The article reported Colani's ambitions to use his first winged cars at Le Mans in 1980 and break the records of the C 111, ending with the words "So we can only hope that his Le Mans outing will not prove to be a flop like many of his automotive design excursions. The new Lotus 80, which is based on Colani's ideas, has not yet made the breakthrough this season in any case." The GT 80 was not to be spared this fate either.

Untertürkheim and Orbassano: Wind Tunnel Comparison Measurements

The C 111-IV, on the other hand, did not belong on the scrap heap, even if it ultimately was not to run again: In June 1979, it was once again the subject of wind tunnel tests. As part of a comparative measurement between the large wind tunnel in Untertürkheim and the Fiat wind tunnel in Turin, the condition at the time of the record-breaking drive was first remeasured in Untertürkheim. In addition, some modified variants were investigated and measurements were carried out for oblique incidence flow. Rüdiger Faul summarized the results achieved in a technical report dated July 24. As delivered, a c_d value of 0.182 was measured with cooling air flow. Without cooling air flow and with covered NACA air intakes in the doors, the value was 0.158. Total downforce and downforce distribution deviated, as Faul explained, "in part considerably from the March 79 variant . . . used as a basis for the chassis setup." He blamed this on "above all, the rather massive supports for the lateral spoilers at the rear, which were added in Rastatt before the record-breaking drive."

According to Faul's report, the changed downforce distribution also revealed "that the vehicle level set during the record run did not lead to the desired vehicle position at 400 km/h, thus causing a drag deterioration." The results measured with oblique incidence flow were also very interesting. At an angle of attack of 5°, the downforce coefficient of the C 111-IV decreased by more than 50% due to significantly increased rear-axle lift coefficients. Remarkable in this context is Faul's remark that an angle of attack of 5°—which at first glance seems very low—can be classified as quite realistic, since at a speed of 400 km/h, even with a crosswind of force 6 (39 km/h) entering the runway at 90°, there is only an oblique angle of attack of 5.57°. Against this background, larger oblique angles of attack were not relevant in practice.

The measurements in the FIAT wind tunnel in Orbassano near Turin, also carried out in June, were aimed at determining the influence of boundary layer suction on the c_d value that can be realized there. This was of interest because Daimler-Benz was at the time considering installing a similar facility in the large wind tunnel in Untertürkheim. This allows reducing the bottom boundary layer—a layer of air in which the air flow velocity is reduced due to air friction at the floor of the wind tunnel. It continues to build up over the length of the measurement section and influences the measurement result, especially when measuring vehicles with very low ground clearance. Nowadays, it is possible to elegantly avoid the formation of a ground boundary layer—for example, by equipping the wind tunnel with a "rolling road" that moves at air flow velocity.

The influence of boundary layer suction could be easily determined in the FIAT wind tunnel by turning it on and off. Although the C 111-IV was explicitly chosen as a test object with particularly low ground clearance, the measured effect ultimately proved to be quite limited.

As a side effect, Rüdiger Faul, who followed the investigation on-site, came into unexpected possession of a case of Piedmont red wine. The FIAT aerodynamicists had bet that the bizarre-looking, shiny silver monster from Untertürkheim with its jagged bodywork would never achieve a c_d value of less than 0.2. The wind tunnel results proved them wrong, and in the evening the Daimler-Benz team could enjoy a tasty nightcap.

Even though the C 111-IV was no longer to be used for setting records, it still made a grand appearance: At the Berlin trade fair "AAA—Auto, AVUS, Attractions" in April 1980, visitors and media representatives had the opportunity to experience the record-breaking car in demonstration drives with the successful record-breaking driver Dr. Hans Liebold at the wheel.

With the C 111-IV and its records achieved in difficult conditions, the development of the C 111 record-breaking cars was not yet over. As already outlined by Hans Liebold in his report of May 15, on the basis of the knowledge gained with the C 111-IV, an attempt was to be made to raise the achievable speeds significantly once again with a newly developed record-breaking car.

In June 1979, the C 111-IV was in the FIAT wind tunnel in Orbassano near Turin for comparative measurements. The photos taken by Rüdiger Faul show the record-breaking car in this unusual environment for a Mercedes-Benz.

The C 111-IV poses for the photographer at the Berlin trade fair "AAA—Auto, AVUS, Attraktionen" in April 1980: together with five-time Formula 1 world champion Juan Manuel Fangio and a record-breaking car of a completely different kind—the Economobile from Untertürkheim, in which apprentice Frank Maier covered the record distance of the equivalent of 1,284 km on 1 liter of diesel in October 1979.

In addition to the photo session for the press, the C 111-IV also did some demonstration runs at the 1980 AAA with Dr. Hans Liebold at the wheel.

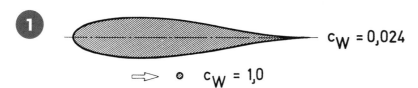

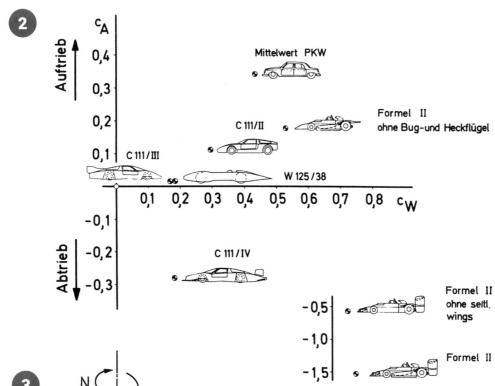

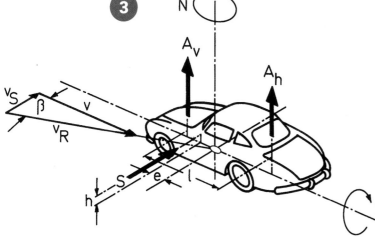

v: Air flow velocity
v_S: Crosswind velocity
v_R: Resulting air flow velocity
β: Oblique angle of attack
A_v: Front-axle lift
A_h: Rear-axle lift
S: Lateral force
N: Yaw moment
L: Roll moment
l: Wheelbase
e/h: Distance of the point of application of the lateral force from the point of pressure in longitudinal/vertical direction

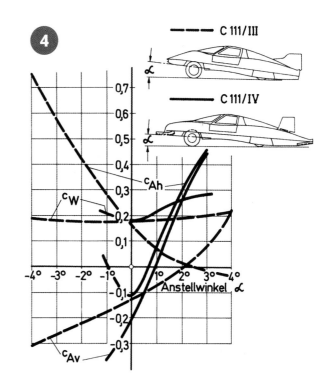

384   Aiming for Maximum Performance: The C 111 as a Record-Setting Car

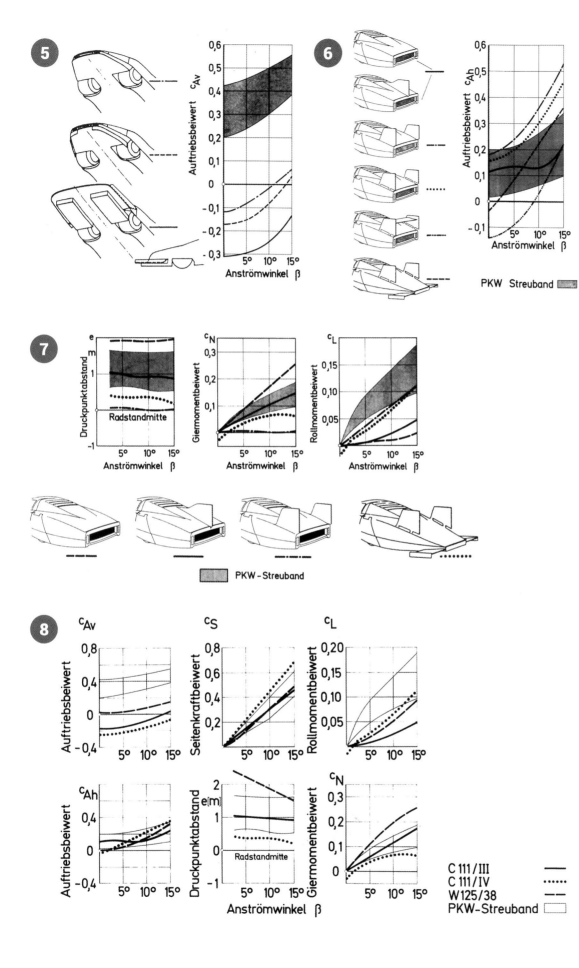

The basics of aerodynamics: The graphics drawn by technician Manfred Kürsten with the measurement results of Rüdiger Faul are largely taken from the lecture "Aus der aerodynamischen Entwicklung der Experimentalfahrzeuge C 111 I–IV," held by Hans Götz in June 1980 at the "4th Colloquium of Industrial Aerodynamics Aachen."

1. Streamlined profile and circular cylinder with equal air resistance
2. Relation of wind resistance and lift of different vehicles
3. Aerodynamic forces and moments on the vehicle
4. Influence of the angle of attack α on wind resistance and lift behavior
5. Influencing the front-axle lift through partial front spoilers and flat front spoilers
6. Rear-axle lift with oblique incidence flow with different rear variants
7. Influence of different tail fins on crosswind sensitivity
8. Aerodynamic coefficients of various Mercedes-Benz record-breaking cars in comparison with the passenger car scatter band

Unfinished Vision: The C 111-V

Even during the preparations for the record-breaking drive with the C 111-IV, the idea of testing an aerodynamic lateral force and roll moment compensation in later trials had manifested itself on the basis of the knowledge gained. This had been documented by Hans Liebold in his technical report on the record-breaking run of the C 111-IV, dated May 15, 1979. A few weeks earlier, at the request of Hans Liebold, calculation engineer Wolfgang Rüdt from the advance design engineering department had already made very extensive calculations, which he summarized in a paper dated April 26 titled "Use of aerodynamic aids to absorb lateral forces during cornering." The task was defined there as follows: "Since the limit for the load capacity of the tires already became apparent at speeds around 400 km/h on the Nardò track, it should be investigated whether either the tire loads can be reduced and/or the achievable speeds increased by absorbing lateral forces with the aid of wings."

New Miracle Cure? Aerodynamic Lateral Forces and Their Potential

In his report, Rüdt contrasted the advantages of aerodynamically generated lateral forces with the disadvantages:

<u>Advantages</u>
- The lateral forces generated by a profiled wing, like the lateral acceleration, also grow with the square of the speed (i.e., lateral force requirement and aerodynamic lateral force follow the same law).
- With the appropriate design, compensation of the roll moment of the centrifugal force is possible, thus avoiding the heavy wheel load on the outside of the curve.
- An increase in speed and thus in the necessary lateral tire forces causes a very sharp increase in the heat load on the tires. This part of the tire heating can be reduced by the wing.

<u>Disadvantages</u>
- The lateral force of the wing is normally highly dependent on the angle of attack. Even small crosswinds therefore already cause large changes in the wing lateral forces. . . . Without special design measures, extreme crosswind sensitivity is to be feared.
- The aerodynamic forces and moments generated by the wing can no longer be neglected when considering driving stability, whereby the demands for low crosswind sensitivity and [high] driving stability are partly in conflict with each other.

The conclusion after very complex calculations, partly carried out with the available vehicle dynamics software, was not quite as optimistic as hoped:

The sum of the lateral tire forces with wing reaches the level of the forces at 400 km/h without wing only at just under 500 km/h. The tire load is nevertheless greater at 500 km/h, and the stability of the vehicle more critical. . . . Despite lateral force of the wing, the heat load on the tires has increased. It would be conceivable to increase the proportion of the wing force. However, it must be taken into account that an aerodynamic lateral force of 496 kp is already applied at 500 km/h. Further enlargement would probably already pose strength problems.

All in all, a significant increase in speed in Nardò to us seems to be associated with great difficulties and risks as a result of the problems to be expected (tire load, crosswind sensitivity, stability)."

Aerodynamics and Powertrain: The Development Priorities of the C 111-V

Despite this rather cautious assessment, Hans Liebold did not allow himself to be discouraged, and on May 16, 1979, he gave the test department an assignment with the following scope under the title "Further development C 101 V":

"In continuation of the high-speed tests with the C 101 V, studies are to be carried out with

- M 117 engine with increased or identical power output and alternative alcohol-based fuel
- improved aerodynamics to relieve tire and chassis stress.
"The associated work on
    chassis components
    power units
    in particular the development of a suitable transmission and corresponding clutches
    bodywork (scope Rastatt & Sifi)
are to be charged to this test department assignment."

The transmission development department became active as early as June, and Werner Walter communicated the first results in a memo dated July 3: "In the world record vehicle C 101 with the M 117—ATL—engine [ATL = exhaust gas turbocharger], a ZF five-speed transmission of model 5 DS 25 was used during the record-setting runs, which is designed for a maximum of 400 Nm. In order to have a sufficiently dimensioned transmission available with regard to a further engine output increase to 800 hp (max. torque approximately 900 Nm), contact was established with Hewland in England, which builds special five-speed transmissions for racing and sports vehicles. On the occasion of a visit . . . the most important points regarding gear ratios, operating conditions, and connection dimensions were discussed."

In a memo dated August 7, 1979, Hans Liebold informed Director Friedrich van Winsen, who had succeeded Rudolf Uhlenhaut as head of passenger car development in 1972, about the concept of the vehicle:

"Engine

An 800 hp ethanol engine based on the M 116 is being prepared by E6LK. The mixture preparation . . . and the components to be used (housing, head, intercooler) are still being clarified.

Power transmission

A transmission designed for the intended Md and n [torques and engine speeds] was agreed with Hewland. The three-disc clutch from Fichtel & Sachs is adjusted to the existing conditions (should withstand > 100 mkg).

Chassis/suspension

According to the contours of the 24/67–415 TRX (f) and 28/70–415 TRX (r) under development at Michelin, a tire envelopment is currently being created, according to which A1KS will modify the drawings of the floor assembly in a way that one specimen can be produced at A1VB.

Bodywork

"Preliminary tests on the aerodynamic lateral force compensation necessary for tire relief are currently being carried out in the model wind tunnel in Sifi. Because of the extreme sensitivity to crosswinds in a symmetrical design (for full compensation, K1VB calculated a 600 N change in lateral force with a crosswind change of only 20 km/h), we will probably operate the front end sides in a stalled condition and, to avoid vortex impact on the slightly pitched and profiled tail fins . . . design them either centrally (one fin) or as end plates (possibly winglets) of the flat front spoiler. Both would also benefit visibility.

"In order to find an aesthetically satisfactory shape again, A1KS produces a sketch that takes the tire envelopment and the new requirements of the engine into account, after which A1STG draws up a proposal that is then agreed among it, A1R, A1KS, and V1V. A 1:1 clay model is then created, from which the plastic body can be immediately molded in Rastatt after the final wind tunnel tests.

"For all other parties involved, the priority of the other ongoing projects was explicitly acknowledged and taken into account during the scheduling process."

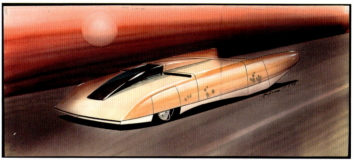
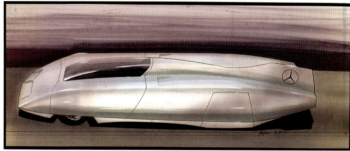
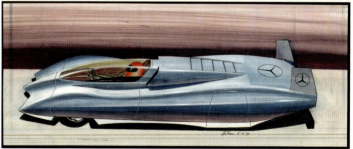
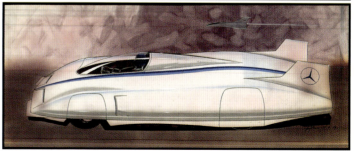

The first design drafts—here four variants by Jürgen Haußmann that date from August 1979

With his concluding remark, Dr. Liebold actively took up the problem of a lack of development capacities, which had been discussed again and again for a long time, especially since head of development Breitschwerdt had confirmed in the passenger car technical meeting in Sindelfingen on July 16, 1979, that "the current test department assignment for the C 111 further development is to be given lower priority than the work on the W 201 . . . and Auto 2000." To ensure that the result of the C 111-IV, which was not very satisfactory from the designers' point of view, would not be repeated, stylists Harald Leschke and Jürgen Haußmann immediately set to work and put the first drafts on paper as early as August.

The scheduling situation was discussed again at the passenger car technical meeting on August 27, 1979. Breitschwerdt again stipulated that the time-bound research vehicle "Auto 2000" should be given priority. The completion of C 111/5—the deviating spelling is found in this form in the minutes—was to take place by the end of 1980/beginning of 1981, as the minutes of the meeting state. The promise given by the design department to produce a 1:1 clay model by December 1979 was therefore moot.

The Special Problem of the C 111-V: Wind Resistance, Downforce, and Lateral Force Compensation

In October 1979, Rüdiger Faul carried out the first basic tests on the C 111-V in the small wind tunnel in Sindelfingen on a modified 1:5 model of the C 111-III. He documented the results in a technical report dated November 7. Faul examined a total of 21 variants, achieving a "max. total lateral force of 3,000 N at 450 km/h with still satisfactory yaw stability." In his conclusion, Faul stated, "The fitted asymmetrical tail fins worsened the product $c_d \times F$, which are factors in the driving resistance, by approximately 25% compared to a model variant with symmetrical tail fins (approximately like C 111/IV). When redesigning the C 111/V, we believe it is possible to keep the increase in resistance smaller by better integrating the detachable parts."

Faul also summarized the task of the project and recommendations for the new design that followed from the measurements in a section titled "The special problem of the C 111/V" in a concise and comprehensible way:

"The C 111/V to be newly conceived is to be designed in such a way that it can travel the circular track in Nardò at a speed of about 450 km/h. This is not possible with the C 111/IV, as the centrifugal forces that occur at 450 km/h, combined with the higher engine power required, can no longer be transmitted by the rear wheels.

"To partially compensate for the centrifugal forces, a force generated by the air is particularly suitable, as both forces with the square of the driving speed. However, the measures required for this are associated with a considerable increase in the vehicle's wind resistance due to detachable parts, which requires a higher engine output than in the C 111/IV for the same vehicle speed. The higher engine output reduces the transmittable lateral force on the rear axle.

"In order to break out of this dilemma, we would like to make some more far-reaching suggestions for the new conception—at the moment only a wheelbase extension of 100 mm and the reduction of the vehicle height by approximately 50 mm compared to the C 111/IV are planned: The envisaged central driver position would make it possible to place the pedal in front of the front axle and thus move the driver position forward. This would allow the engine to be moved forward by approximately 700 mm. The vehicle's center of gravity thus moves closer to the pressure point [the point at which no torque is generated when drag force and lift are applied at this point]. This reduces the yaw moment and the pressure point distance. In addition, the front axle, which is free of longitudinal forces, defrays more of the centrifugal force. The fins we use could be made smaller, which reduces the wind resistance and thus the required engine power, further increasing the transmittable lateral force at the rear axle.

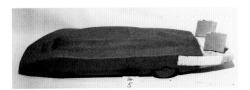 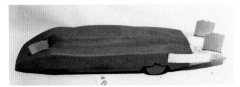 

Rüdiger Faul conducted the first wind tunnel tests as part of the C 111-V project with modified 1:5 models of the C 111-III. Shown are three of a total of twenty-one variants with different versions of the two rear fins and another fin in the front end.

"By redesigning the floor, the vehicle height could also be reduced by the height of the oil pan (approximately 120 mm) (dry sump lubrication). This reduces the vehicle's frontal area and aerodynamic drag, as well as the required engine power.

"Due to the lower vehicle height and moving the maximum cross-section forward (necessitated by the engine relocation), the overall vehicle length and thus the vehicle weight can be reduced with the same narrowing. In addition, there are more favorable conditions for c_d value optimization. The conditions are ideal when the maximum cross-section is ⅓ of the vehicle length.

"A variety of benefits can be achieved through the described measures. We therefore ask all those involved in the project to weigh the necessary additional expenditure—a steel floor assembly to be redesigned or perhaps even a monocoque that is about ¾ lighter and easier to manufacture—against the advantages described. Since a new, partially modified floor assembly is to be built anyway, the additional expense ought to be kept within limits.

"If the necessary increase in driving stability were to be achieved by aerodynamic measures alone—which is unquestionably possible—the c_d value of the C 111/V would fall well short of those of the C 111/III and C 111/IV. We also ask that this aspect be included in the considerations."

With regard to the measurement results, Faul asked the calculation team of the advance design engineering department "to take the aerodynamic test results into account in their stability calculations and, based on the calculations, to tell us the most usable variant for driving stability as well as further requirements."

Side Fins or Crabbing: The Lateral Force Generation in the C 111-V

Wolfgang Rüdt, who apparently knew Faul's findings before the report was completed, gave his assessment in a statement on October 31. In Rüdt's opinion, the effect that could be achieved by aerodynamic measures was still too small. "At the previous weight of the vehicle and an assumed track banking of 10°, the lateral force of 5,960 N still to be applied by the tires at 450 km/h would only be about 520 N less than for the C 111/IV at 400 km/h." In addition, with the variants equipped only with tail fins, the lateral tire force required at the front axle would be increased instead of reduced as desired due to the fin force acting far back. Rüdt and the calculation team then considered "how to generate a lateral aerodynamic force even without aerodynamic detachable parts." They concluded that "by tilting the entire vehicle against the flow . . . a considerable part of the total lateral aerodynamic force required could already be generated."

Rüdt went on to say, "This inclined position could be achieved, for example, through purposefully incorporated 'crabbing.' To this end, the following measures would have to be taken:
- Inclined installation of the entire rear axle or toe-in adjustment of the rear wheels so that they produce an equidirectional steering angle
- On the FA [front axle] only the steering wheel must be mounted in an off-center position
- If necessary, install the driver's seat turned in line with the steering angle of the rear wheels so that a view in the direction of travel is possible without turning the head
- Possibly measures to reduce the load change reaction

"Advantage:
"The aerodynamic lateral force is generated without having to accept the disadvantages of a large static yaw moment (increased load on the front axle) or increased crosswind sensitivity.
"The wind resistance in the direction of travel is no greater than in the model variants with fins that generate lateral forces.
"Since the crab angle cannot be enlarged at will, presumably for constructive reasons, additionally attached but much smaller fins can still increase the aerodynamic lateral force. Since the fins then only have to apply part of the total aerodynamic lateral force, yaw stability in crosswinds is no longer so strongly impaired.
"[At a crab angle of 5°,] "a speed of 450 km/h and a frontal area of the vehicle of 1.5 m² results in . . . an aerodynamic lateral force of 2,710 N. The drag coefficient c_d is still below the values of those variants that achieve similarly high lateral force coefficients by means of fins."

Design and Technology: The Concept of the C 111-V

At the end of September, even before Rüdiger Faul carried out his basic research on modified models of the C 111-III in the model wind tunnel, a first 1:5 model of the C 111-V was completed in Sindelfingen, which was very appealing in terms of design. By the end of October, it had been cautiously revised, and by mid-November further variants had emerged, whereby the unbiased observer could not be certain in all cases that it was actually

In autumn 1979, the first 1:5 scale model of the C 111-V was created. The photos show the work status at the end of September (*above*) and at the end of October 1979.

intended to be a record-breaking car. One of the designs could have been mistaken for a flying object that had materialized straight from the future, despite the clearly recognizable four wheels.

Another model, developed in mid-November 1979, was distinguished by its unusual cockpit: It was located relatively far back on the vehicle body, where it was placed off-center on the left side. With its slightly asymmetrical shape, which approximated a vertically positioned wing profile, it was designed—in interaction with likewise-profiled surfaces attached to the side of the vehicle body—to generate aerodynamic lateral forces. No less unusual was another variant whose cockpit was placed centrally and relatively far forward but had a distinctly asymmetrical profiled shape. As a result, it was also designed to generate aerodynamic lateral forces, with a front center fin and two tail fins to support this effect. The two seemingly exotic variants were examined in the wind tunnel in mid-December 1979, but in the meantime—not least due to Wolfgang Rüdt's explanations—the realization began to emerge that a vehicle with the lowest possible c_d value and the smallest possible frontal area, in which the lateral force compensation was essentially achieved via crabbing and not primarily through aerodynamic measures, would probably represent the most promising alternative. Hans Liebold even had a test sedan from the 123 model series converted to crabbing and found that driving it took some getting used to but was ultimately possible without any problems.

Irrespective of stylistic aspects and the aforementioned refinements to compensate for or reduce lateral forces, important cornerstones of the vehicle design were discussed in two project

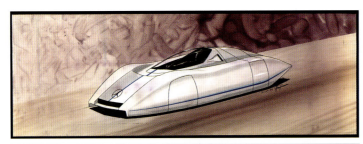

The drafts by Jürgen Haußmann, dating from the beginning of November 1979, correspond to the 1:5 model from the end of October 1979.

Car or spaceship? The photos of the 1:5 model from mid-November 1979 show a rather exotic-looking variant of the C 111-V.

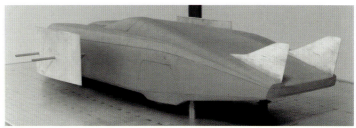

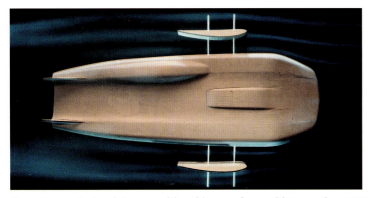
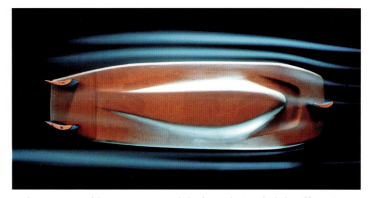

Two other variants of the record-breaking car from mid-November 1979, are also presented in a very unusual design. The cockpit is off-center on one side of the vehicle (*top and bottom left*) or in a conventional position but with an asymmetrical design (*bottom right*).

meetings on December 1979 and the results were documented in two memos by Joachim Kaden, excerpts of which are reproduced here, in part verbatim:

Transmission
A sample five-speed transmission with the ratios 2.33/1.675/1.343/1.146/1.0 was ordered from Getrag. The transmission is designed for a continuous load of 70 mkp and will soon be available for installation tests.

Final drive
With the gear ratio of 2.18 still to be manufactured, this results in a speed of 458.8 km/h at an engine speed of 7500 rpm. The current longest ratio of 2.24 results in a maximum speed of 446.5 km/h.

The rear-axle differential should be arranged in such a way that the joints of the half-shafts run in design position without articulation angle.

Engine

In order to be able to reduce the cross-sectional area of the vehicle even further, the engine is to be fitted with dry sump lubrication (overall height). In addition, also because of the cross-sectional area, the turbochargers are to be arranged behind the engine.

Floor system

The two frame side rails are to be moved more towards the center of the vehicle. This results in an increase in the rigidity of the floor system. In addition, to further increase rigidity, the engine is to be bolted firmly to the chassis without engine mounts. It is then also possible to connect the engine and the transmission firmly to the chassis at further points. The pedal system is not adopted from any production vehicle. The pedals are attached directly to the appropriately prepared chassis.

The position of the Getrag 5-speed transmission and the driver's seat position—shoulders below the upper edge of the wings—result in a wheelbase of 2800 mm. The propeller shaft required for this is then 170 mm long.

Track width FA = 1300 mm (steering wheel angle ± 17°)

Track width RA = 1270 mm

Scheduling

By mid-January, the conceptual work at STMK will be completed. End of January 1:5 model ready for wind tunnel tests. Duration 2 weeks. Mid-February start of work on 1:1 model until end of March. The work on the body, which will then begin, is estimated to take 7 months, including the production of an intermediate positive. The intermediate positive is to be checked again in the wind tunnel. The vehicle should be roadworthy at the end of 1980. The construction of the monocoque is expected to start at the beginning of May 80.

Radiator

Because of the very limited space available for the radiators and oil coolers, the surface area of these is to be reduced and the block depth increased. V1FZ will determine the expected required cooler sizes together with Behr. Since heat measurements will soon be carried out on a methanol engine at V1FZ, the special problems of methanol operation can then also be taken into account.

Body

. . . The spoilers at the front and rear shall be designed in such a way that the downforce can be changed without great effort during the test runs. The driver's viewing dome is made of polycarbonate—curved in two dimensions. As this "glass" is easily scratched when removing the insects, sufficient backup domes must be ordered. The front spoilers must be adjustable in order to avoid damage to the FA when the springs compress. A possibility of connecting the FA—as with the flaps of car IV—should be investigated constructively.

Tires

Since the current conception of the vehicle is based on an axle load distribution of 1:1 and the rear wheels still have to transmit the drive forces, tests with narrower tires on the RA are not carried out, even if this means that the narrowing of the body cannot be optimally executed.

Concretization: Design Development, Construction Details, and Scheduling

At the beginning of 1980, the project literally took shape. In the stylistics department, Gunther Ellenrieder completed the dimensional concept in January, and on this basis the designers Ferdinand Hellhake and Jürgen Haußmann worked out a series of designs in January and February. In contrast to the C 111-IV, which had been developed from the C 111-III with a high degree of improvisation according to the requirements of aerodynamics, the new vehicle now presented itself again as a consistent whole.

Unlike its predecessors, the C 111-V was strictly designed as a single-seater, with a minimal frontal area, a correspondingly very low seating position, and with a monocoque-like structure instead of the previous design with a classic frame-floor system.

Further construction details were set in a meeting on March 7, 1980. The results are quoted in excerpts below:

"According to the latest test bench results of dept. E6LK, the use of intercoolers can be dispensed with. The intake opening for the two turbochargers (NACA inlet) should be in the range 1,900–2,000 mm in the center of the vehicle. The two chargers are also installed in this area.

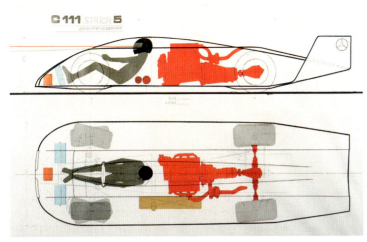

The dimensional concept drawn up by Gunther Ellenrieder in January 1980 formed the basis for the further development of the C 111-V. The crabbing position of the front and rear wheels is clearly visible.

In January 1980, Ferdinand Hellhake (*left*) and Jürgen Haußmann (*right*) work on the 1:5 model of the C 111-V. In the middle is their boss Joseph Gallitzendörfer, designer of the first hour of the C 101 project.

The design drawings by Jürgen Haußmann (*above*) and Ferdinand Hellhake (*below*), dated from the beginning of February 1980, show two variants of the same basic concept, once with "crayfish tails" and fins and once with a rear center fin.

The injection quantity of the injectors mounted upstream of the compressor inlet is not to be regulated by a linkage, but by the boost pressure by means of a pressure cell. The control will probably be carried out by two KA flow distributors.

"In order to be able to determine the installation position of exhaust pipes and turbochargers, a monocoque mockup is made by V1V. The steering wheel becomes removable. Fastening mechanism like our old racing cars . . .

"Location of various major components:

"Battery:

"At the front left accessible from the wheel arch. The battery should be as far away from the tank as possible for safety reasons.

"Tank:

"On the right, as far forward as possible. Height to lower edge of body. Normal filler neck directly on the tank.

"Telemetry . . . and two-way radio on the right front next to the tank, accessible from the outside.

"The master brake cylinder must be installed transversely for reasons of space. Actuation by angled lever.

"Dept. E6LK wants to try to reach the max. power of the engine at approximately 7,200 instead of 7,500 rpm. This takes into account the change in the final-drive ratio from 2.18 to 2.07."

On March 25, 1980, Ernst Haug drew up a schedule for the "development and construction of the C 111-V":

Model delivery 1:1	week 19 [05.05.–09.05.1980]
Mold templates model	weeks 20/21 [12.05.-24.05.1980]
1st Negative molds from 1:1 clay model	weeks 22-24 [26.05.-13.06.1980]
1st Demold and assemble negative mold	week 25 [16.06.-20.06.1980]
Creation of 1:1 positive hard model	weeks 26-28 [23.06.-11.07.1980]
Finish positive model 1:1	week 29 [14.07.-18.07.1980]
Delivery 1:1 positive model to wind tunnel UT	week 30 [21.07.-25.07.1980]
Company holidays in Rastatt / wind tunnel measurements	weeks 31-33 [28.07.-01.08.1980]
Working mold set	weeks 34-36 [18.08.-05.09.1980]
Parts production / floor assembly delivery	weeks 37/38 [08.09.-19.09.1980]
Models for interior	weeks 39/40 [22.09.-03.10.1980]
Assembly of driving car	weeks 41-46 [06.10.-14.11.1980]
Finish driving car	week 47 [17.10.-21.11.1980]

Ride comfort at 450 km/h. In order to provide the record-breaking driver with the best possible comfort during his drive and thus promote his concentration, this draft of the driver's seat of the C 111-V was created in the design division.

Wind Tunnel and Calculation Skills: The Development of the C 111-V

In a technical report dated June 10, Rüdiger Faul documented the results of very extensive wind tunnel tests on the 1:5 model of the C 111-V. He examined a total of 82 variants in the Sindelfingen model wind tunnel, with the main focus on driving stability considerations. The most striking result, according to Faul's report, was "the increase in the downforce coefficients determined for some variants as the angle of attack increased."

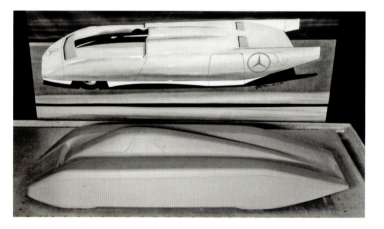

During the wind tunnel tests, the initial condition of mid-January 1980 (*above*) was further developed into the variant with flat front spoiler, front center fin, and "crayfish tails" with fins.

 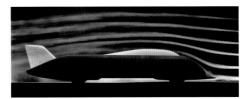 

In the end, further development took place on the basis of the 1:5 model shown, which was equipped with a flat front spoiler, a reduced front center fin, and a rear center fin instead of the "crayfish tails" with lateral fins. The photos were taken at the end of March (*left*) and in mid-April 1980 (*center and right*).

In conclusion, Faul stated, "With aerodynamic lateral forces of up to 2,300 N at a vehicle speed of 450 km/h, the centrifugal force compensation, related to the vehicle weight of the C 111-IV, could not yet be achieved at the desired level. Assuming a track banking of 10° and a vehicle weight of 1,467 kg, the increase in lateral force from 400 km/h to 450 km/h can be compensated for, but there is no further relief of the tires from lateral force (lateral acceleration occurring at 10° track bank angle: 400 km/h: 0.442 g; 450 km/h: 0.606 g). Higher aerodynamic lateral forces could be realized at the expense of the c_d value and the driving stability. We do not consider this desirable. It would seem much more sensible to us to reduce the need for aerodynamic lateral force by reducing the vehicle mass. Therefore, we ask all those involved in the project to continue their efforts to reduce the weight of the vehicle in order to keep the centrifugal forces small."

In May 1980, the stylistics department completed a 1:1 plasticine model of the C 111-V, which was examined in the wind tunnel starting

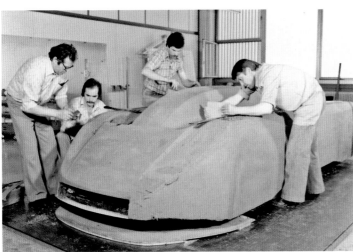 

In the period from mid-March to early May 1980, the 1:1 plasticine model of the C 111-V was created in Sindelfingen.

Stylist Jürgen Haußmann at the 1:1 design drawing of the C 111-V he created, taken in mid-May 1980

The 1:5 model of the C 111-V with perfect finish corresponds to the state shown on the 1:1 design drawing, which formed the basis for further development.

on May 28. However, the measurement results obtained, documented by Rüdiger Faul, were significantly worse than had been expected after the measurements on the 1:5 model. Based on a c_d value of 0.241 with a frontal area of 1.3074 m², the best drag coefficient achieved after four days was 0.212 with cooling air flow. However, this resulted in an unacceptably high lift coefficient. The measurements were then discontinued and resumed in July after major modifications to the model were carried out over several weeks.

The as-delivered condition on July 21 showed a c_d value of 0.203 with a frontal area of 1.2777 m²—still significantly more than the 1:5 models. After extensive modifications, it could finally be lowered to 0.101. That was the lowest drag coefficient that had been measured on a 1:1 model in the large wind tunnel up to that point. This had only become possible by converting it into a half-body—a model without ground flow—but this variant was out of the question as a record-breaking vehicle, as the lift forces generated at the targeted top speed would be higher than the normal force caused by the vehicle's weight. An extractor fan could have provided a remedy, as it had been used in the Chaparral 2 J racing car of 1970 or in the Brabham BT46B

The two photos from May 28, 1980, document the original condition of the C 111-V at the beginning of the wind tunnel tests. The not-yet-perfectly-executed joints of the wheel spats were taped off during the measurements.

In mid-July, the 1:1 plasticine model of the C 111-V was scanned after extensive modifications to create a digital dataset of the exterior shape.

Formula 1 racing car of 1978 and had ensured considerable downforce. Faul, however, did not consider this solution safe enough, since—as he wrote—"in the event of a fan failure, the vehicle turns into an aircraft." The c_d value for a possible driving variant, which could only be realized with attached side skirts, was 0.16. Another series of measurements was used, as Faul explained, "primarily to generate sufficient downforce on the model without allowing the c_d value to increase too much. In some cases, solutions were tested that were known from the C 111/IV (crayfish tails). In addition, the model was equipped with a trailing edge flap whose angle of attack can be varied. This component is to be controlled on the driving car by the rear axle. In combination with a [likewise tested] center wing on the front end, which is to be controlled by the front axle, the aim is to maintain ideally constant downforce values during compression and rebound movements of the vehicle." The model reacted very sensitively to changes to the side skirts, especially in the area of the wheel arches, so that "final coefficients for the vehicle with skirts can only be determined when functional skirts are available from design engineering." Special detachable parts—two profiled fins in the area in front of the rear wheel arches and an unprofiled, front center fin with 10° pitch—were used in an attempt to "achieve aerodynamic lateral forces of the desired magnitude when driving straight ahead without crabbing."

Faul wrote, "The increase in resistance due to these detachable parts was more than 20% and is thus significantly greater than the increase in resistance due to crabbing with the same lateral force in each case. In addition, these detachable

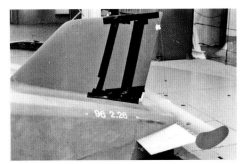

The two photos above, taken during the wind tunnel tests that were carried out again over several days at the end of July 1980, show the as-delivered state on July 21, and the three pictures below document some of the numerous variants examined: with front center fin and two side fins in the rear, with "crayfish tails" and trailing edge flap and as a half-body without underbody flow.

parts proved to be disadvantageous in the case of an oblique angle of attack. Therefore, we once again propose to dispense with such detachable parts altogether and to limit ourselves exclusively to crabbing variants on the driving car."

The calculation team of the advance design engineering department had also not remained idle with regard to the record-breaking car project. In a communication dated August 12, 1980, Wolfgang Rüdt presented detailed results of his complex calculations, which were intended to determine the downforce values to be aimed for in the C 111-V at the front and rear axles, as well as the forces acting at the wheel contact points when driving on a circular track at 450 km/h, which were needed as a starting point for strength calculations at both axles. The calculations were based on the following vehicle data:

Weight	1,150 kp
Static front-axle load	612 kp
Static rear-axle load	538 kp
Wheelbase	2,800 mm
Track width front	1,300 mm
Track width rear	1,270 mm
Center of gravity height	350 mm
Cross-sectional area	1.3 m²
Target c_d value	0.16
Speed	450 km/h
Bank angle of the track	10°

As a result of the calculations, it was determined that the lateral force on the rear axle is significantly lower than on the C 111-IV under the assumptions made. Rüdt recommended clarifying in discussions with the tire manufacturer whether lowering the rear axle downforce, which would reduce aerodynamic drag, is possible and advantageous with increased slip and crab angle. Based on the assumed values, Rüdt determined the same load at the outside wheel with slightly lower lateral forces on the front axle, but a higher load at the inside wheel than on the C 111-IV.

New Framework Conditions? Dark Clouds over the C 111-V

Three weeks earlier, on July 21, 1980, the C 111-V had been discussed again in the passenger car technical meeting. Under agenda item "C 111/5: Progress of the work on the body," the construction of two vehicles or two bodies was discussed. The minutes of the meeting noted, "Production of the first C 111/5 in Rastatt with similar manufacturing technology as for the predecessor vehicles (body mass approximately 220 kg); construction of the second body at MBB in lightweight construction (first mass forecast by MBB): 75 kg." Unfortunately, the authors have no further archival sources on a lightweight body that was apparently to be manufactured by MBB. According to the minutes, the further procedure was as follows. "It was decided to postpone the realization of the second phase (MBB body); the aerodynamic optimizations are to be completed on the first vehicle; the [also not documented by other sources] booking of the Nardò circuit for record-breaking runs is to be canceled; the installation of a suitable power unit with reduced output that more clearly incorporates today's energy situation and the c_d x F reduction of the C 111/5 and a continuation of the project in modified form will have to be decided separately."

Apparently, the first dark clouds had appeared in the sky above the record-car project. However, at the next meeting on July 28, information was first provided on the aerodynamics development, and then the resulting impact on the project was discussed. Under agenda item "C 111/5: Current status of the c_d measurements (clay model)," the meeting minutes note, the current c_d value of 0.101 (with cooling air flow) is sensationally favorable. The measurements are being continued; the lift values are still considerably too high. The current results confirm the view that high speeds can be achieved even with less powerful propulsion units than previously envisaged for version 5."

The conclusion of the "E1-EA1 meeting" on August 14, 1980—a regular meeting that was named after the "Passenger Car Development" and "Passenger Car Body Development" directorates involved—was quite similar. Regarding agenda item "C 111/5: Speed targets/engine performance," the minutes stated, "The latest, extraordinarily favorable c_d results on the 1:1 clay model require information on the target speed for further setup (lift and lateral force optimization). Consideration seems appropriate as to whether the intended publicity effect of an aerodynamic test vehicle can be achieved with a turbocharged V8 engine (approximately 800 hp), whose consumption can certainly not be as effective in terms of advertising as, for example, the 16 l/100 km for the modified D 30 ATL in the C 111/3. Taking into account today's c_d predictions, required engine outputs as a function of target speeds shall be determined and submitted."

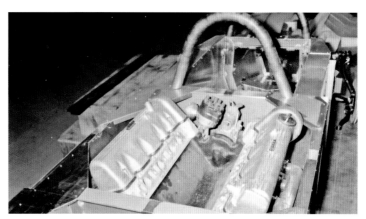

The photos taken in mid-September 1980 document the work status on the chassis of the C 111-V at that time. The very narrow monocoque structure in favor of the smallest possible frontal area is clearly visible. And the V8 engine is located directly behind the cockpit. The rear axle was not yet installed at the time the photo was taken.

Nevertheless, the further-revised 1:1 plasticine model was again tested in the large wind tunnel from September 16 to 18, 1980. In the initial state without side skirts, the c_d value was 0.171. The lift coefficients were, as Faul put it in his report, "again not satisfactory but could be brought to the order of magnitude suggested by K1V with prepared detachable parts." Once again, numerous variants were examined with different detachable parts. In addition to a rear wing, crayfish tails mounted at the rear, and an additional vertically mounted panel on the leading edge of the flat front spoiler, side skirts mounted on the inside of the body were also used. In his technical report of October 22, which summarizes all the wind tunnel tests carried out on the 1:1 model from May to September, Faul remarked in summary on the measurement results:

The 1:1 plasticine model of the C 111-V is revised again in the design studio in Sindelfingen. The photo was taken in mid-September, shortly before completion for the next wind tunnel tests.

"During the development of the C 111/V, all aerodynamic force and aerodynamic moment coefficients are relevant due to the limits of physics when driving on the track in Nardò at the targeted driving speed. Therefore, the necessary aerodynamic development effort is greater than on other vehicles. The measurements so far were mainly intended to bring all coefficients to orders of magnitude that K1VB described as usable. This was mainly done by varying detachable parts such as flat front spoilers, side skirts,

 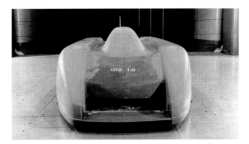 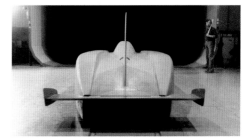

The 1:1 design model of the C 111-V in the large wind tunnel in Untertürkheim, taken on September 16, 1980, in its initial state for renewed wind tunnel tests

'crayfish tails,' rear wings, and tail fins. Shape optimization in the usual way has not yet taken place."

Faul also pointed out the complex relationships among aerodynamics, engine performance, and driving stability: "Thus, despite the high engine power available, the c_d value of the vehicle is of considerable relevance, since the necessary longitudinal force (engine power) at the rear axle and thus also the remaining lateral force essentially depend on it. The tires, which have proven to be a critical component on the C 111/IV, are also subjected to higher loads with poorer c_d values."

His summary emphasized further, imperative measurements: "For driving tests in the intended speed range (approximately 450 km/h), it is still urgent to investigate and minimize the changes in aerodynamic force and aerodynamic moment during compression

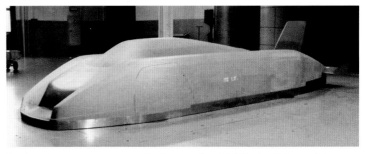

During the measurements in September 1980, the 1:1 model was equipped with side skirts in sections, whose drag-reducing influence again became apparent. Extending the skirts to the rear edge of the vehicle resulted in a significant reduction in the c_d value but also reduced the downforce compared to the variant that was only equipped with side skirts up to the front edge of the rear wheel arches.

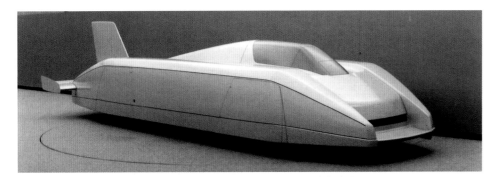 

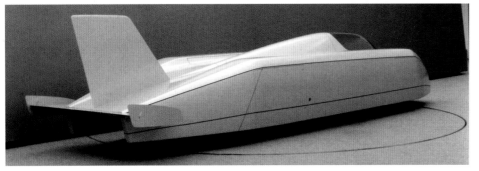 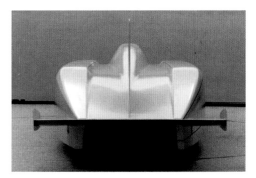

The 1:1 design model in its final state with a perfect finish, taken on October 2, 1980, in the "Kuppelbau" domed building in Sindelfingen

and rebound movements of the vehicle as well as simultaneously occurring crosswinds. Before that, we don't think driving tests are acceptable."

Discontinued and Unfinished: The End of the C 111-V

However, none of this was to come to pass. In the E1-EA1 meeting on September 25, despite promising wind tunnel results, the future of the project darkened further, as the minutes for agenda item "C 111/5: Aerodynamics" documented:

"The c_d investigations on the 1:1 clay model of the C 111/5 indicate significantly better results for the roadworthy vehicle than for the C 111/4 only with side skirts.

"The developed downforce measures for a target speed of 450 km/h appear to be sufficient for steady-state driving conditions; transient driving conditions could not be measured due to time constraints.

"The continuation of the planned project with approximately 800 hp engine power was considered dangerous; the imponderables at such speeds appear too high.

"A final decision will have to be made by Prof. Breitschwerdt."

Against this background, the concluding sentence of the minutes seems difficult to understand: "The further construction (molding) of the driving car will be started immediately in Rastatt."

The decision taken by head of development Breitschwerdt regarding the ambitious record-breaking project should hardly have come as a surprise. In view of the current efforts at the time to reduce the costs of the development division, to focus the existing development capacities on upcoming production vehicles such as the 201 and 124 series, and, in this context, also to end the current rally sport commitment, the C 111-V, whose development still held a whole series of technical challenges and communications-related imponderables, was not a project that was likely to maintain its place on the list of priorities, despite its innovative character and the investment already made.

The official end of the ambitious project was decided at the passenger car technical meeting on September 29 and October 13, 1980. Under agenda item "C 111/5: Project completion," the minutes of September 30 first state, "Due to the increased risks and due to the lack of promotionally effective claims, Prof. Breitschwerdt determined that record-breaking attempts should be abandoned after completion of the vehicle." In this scenario, the C 111-V could have found its place in the Mercedes-Benz Museum—right next to the spectacular T 80, a record-breaking car that had also never been used. However, the decision of October 13 then also ruled out this possibility, as the minutes on "C 111/5: Project stop" recorded: "Contrary to earlier determinations, the completion of the vehicle is now also rejected; the project is to be stopped with immediate effect."

Thus, Rüdiger Faul concluded the summary of the results of his wind tunnel tests with a sobering conclusion: "The C 111/V project was stopped effective 13.10.80. Therefore, all recommendations contained in the following text created earlier [prior to the project stop] that still refer to a roadworthy vehicle are to be seen as hypothetical." Even though some activities that had already been started continued for a few weeks, the decision to discontinue the project that had been made earlier was ultimately upheld.

This marked the end, after almost exactly twelve years and in a completely unspectacular manner, of the development of a vehicle series that combined extraordinary dream sports cars and record chasers under the magical designation C 111. Not only did each of these vehicles represent the highest level of what was technically possible at its time, they also stand for innovation and fascination to this day.

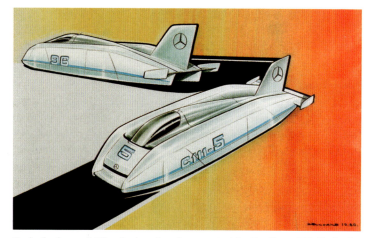

End of a legend: The design drawing created by Ferdinand Hellhake in October 1980 illustrates the final state of the C 111-V and at the same time stands for the end of the development—not only of an ambitious record-breaking car project, but of the C 111 as a whole.

Lifelines:
Biographies of All C 111s Ever Built

This chapter describes the curriculum vitae of each C 111 built, in the order of the car numbers. Much of the individual information has already been presented in the previous chapters but is summarized here once again in a clear manner and in relation to the respective vehicle. With a few exceptions, the photographic material essentially relates to the current condition of the vehicles preserved to the present day, since almost all relevant historical photographs have already been presented in chapters 2 and 3 of this book. Thus, all vehicles still in existence and available at the time of the photographs are documented here with a set of four current studio photos, consisting of the front view, the semiprofile views from the front and from at an angle, and a photograph of the interior.

The naming of the individual vehicles also requires a note at this point. As already described in chapter 2, two different systems were used. The first, immediately comprehensible principle corresponded to a consecutive numbering of the test cars beginning with number 1. In autumn 1969, a new system was introduced that distinguished between the two series of the C 111. Thus, the five cars of the first series were now designated with the numbers 22 to 26, and the car numbers of the second series presented in March 1970 started with 31. The classification of the Sledge as car no. 21 does not appear to be entirely stringent, since it occupies a special position and is not—as the car number suggests—to be assigned to the series of cars 22 to 26. One of the numbers was assigned twice. In April 1970, a new vehicle was built to replace the crashed car 24. It was given the internal number 24 a, but—contrary to what the car number would lead one to expect—it had a body of the second series.

Instead of just the car number, internal company sources sometimes use more comprehensive designations that correspond to the system generally used for Mercedes-Benz test vehicles at the time. The individual car number is appended to the internal construction designation of the company; for example, W 114 V 23–132 designates test car no. 132 within the W 114 series, equipped with a 2.3-liter carburetor engine and thus corresponding to the 230/8 model.

Consequently, C 101 W 36–22 stands for car 22 with a three-rotor Wankel engine (and 3.6-liter capacity equivalent), C 101 W 48–33 for car 33 powered by a four-rotor Wankel, C 101 E 45–25 for car 25 with a 4.5-liter V8, and C 101 D 30–31 for the record-breaking car 31 with a 3-liter diesel engine.

Car 1 or 21

The first test car was built in March 1969 in the advance engineering test department in Untertürkheim. The floor assembly of the first version, completed on March 26, still had a wheelbase of 2,500 mm and was equipped with a semi-trailing arm rear axle adopted from the W 114. In order not to lose any time, the car was only given a makeshift body made of sheet metal, whose angular appearance earned it the internal nickname "Sledge." The first test run of the vehicle, which had not yet been fitted with a roof and side parts and was only provisionally completed, took place on the afternoon of April 1, 1969, on the test track. After completion with fixed side parts and a roof with gullwing doors, the first drive on public roads took place on April 16. The test car had the red number plate S–04214.

On May 2, 1969, it went to the Hockenheimring for the first time, and on May 13 the first test of the car, which by then had been equipped with a flatter front hood, took place there. At the beginning of June, the front hood was modified again, and the vehicle was tested in the large wind tunnel of the Forschungsinstitut für Kraftfahrwesen und Fahrzeugmotoren Stuttgart (FKFS—Research Institute for Automotive Engineering and Vehicle Engines Stuttgart). The results obtained led to an optimized rear end design. In this configuration, car 1 was thoroughly tested at the Hockenheimring, and from July 15 onward together with car 2, which had been completed in the meantime. The Sledge was operated mainly with the KE 308 three-rotor motor, but in the meantime also with the KE 305, KE 312, KE 301, and KE 315.

Car 1 being hauled away after its accident on the test track on August 8, 1969

On August 5, there was an accident on the test track in which car 1 was severely damaged by contact with a crash barrier. However, the Sledge was repaired and testing continued at the end of November. Car 1 made a high-profile appearance at the end of February 1970 during a photo shoot on the test track, where the first C 111 was photographed together with the last car of the first series and the first of the second series. For this purpose, it had been painted in fluorescent orange. In May 1970, car 1 was scrapped—certainly also because it could be used only for testing the engine due to its technical status, and the four-rotor engine could not be mounted due to the insufficient space.

Car 2 or 22

The first "real" C 111, with a 2,620 mm wheelbase, five-link "racing rear axle," and plastic body, was built in June–July 1969. On June 10, the floor assembly was delivered from Sindelfingen to the test department in Untertürkheim; from there it was transferred to Rastatt as a finished chassis on June 25 after being measured and completed with major assemblies. The GRP body was manufactured and installed there, and then the vehicle went to Sindelfingen for painting and interior finishing. On July 7, the styling department had specified the paintwork in pearl-white effect paint, the upholstery in gray-black patterned houndstooth fabric, and the upholstery of the seat shells in black man-made leather; seven days later, the body development department delivered the car to the test department in Untertürkheim with a perfect finish. Here, the dummy engine was replaced by the KE 309 three-rotor engine, so that testing at Hockenheim could start on time on July 15, the 63rd birthday of Rudolf Uhlenhaut. The bodywork did not yet correspond to the final design in some points. The laminate thickness of 3 mm was significantly higher than originally intended, and the front grille, which was actually intended as an air intake, was positioned lower than on the subsequent cars. Immediately after the first test drives in Hockenheim, car 2 was measured in the wind tunnel of the FKFS in Untertürkheim on July 16 and 17, and the air routing was changed for the subsequent cars on the basis of the knowledge gained.

This was followed by further test runs at the Hockenheimring, where the KE 309 was replaced by the KE 305, taken from car 1 due

Car 2, fitted with racing tires on light-alloy wheels, at the Motor Presse Club (MPC) test day at the Hockenheimring on September 10, 1969

to loss of compression. On August 13, 1969, the car went to the Nürburgring. The vehicle had the red number plate S–04243. Car 2 was then transferred to Rastatt and received an optimized body made of thinner-walled laminate, with the front grille and headlamp actuation also being modified. In addition, by modifying the exhaust system and lengthening the rear section by 65 mm (instead of the 60 mm initially envisaged by design engineering), an enlarged trunk of 224 liters was made possible, which was even directly accessible without opening the hood. The latter was also to have windows in the side parts, which would allow improved visibility.

The schedule for the changes was very ambitious in that car 2 was firmly scheduled for the press trial drive from September 1 to 5 at the Hockenheimring. The modifications were carried out in Rastatt until August 27, and from August 28 to 30 the paintwork and an overhaul of the interior took place in Sindelfingen. The upholstery of the seats was changed to dark gray-cognac check fabric. At the press launch, car 2 covered a total of 1,450 km, with a fuel consumption of 38.6 l/100 km and an oil consumption of 6.5 l/1,000 km measured with street tires. Due to its optimized bodywork, which distinguished it from all the other vehicles in the test fleet, car 2, with number plate S–P 8316, was to a certain extent the showpiece vehicle within the series. It also had this role at the IAA in Frankfurt, where it was available for test rides (in the passenger seat) on the outdoor exhibition grounds.

After the IAA, the test drives were continued—initially still with a three-rotor engine, with the KE 309, KE 308, and KE 301 engines serving as power units. Car 2 was also used for the opening of the Salzburgring on September 20–21 and for Udo Jürgens's visit to the Untertürkheim plant on September 25. On July 22, 1970, with a mileage of 15,961 km, the four-rotor KE 408 engine was installed. The car was painted in the color weissherbst and went to the endurance testing department for engine and major assembly testing. After a mileage of 12,615 km, the engine was replaced with KE 406 at the end of August 1970 because of a knocking noise. At the same time, the decision was made to move the exhaust pipe and the pre-silencer, which had been relocated next to the transmission underneath the trunk when the four-rotor engine was installed, back to the right wheel arch because of the strong heat development. After a further 21,905 km, which had already been reached on November 10, 1970, the KE 406 was also removed due to poor compression of the fourth rotor. Since no other four-rotor Wankel was available and a "hard endurance run" had to be suspended anyway due to the season, the test runs were not resumed until April 1971 with the 322 hp/236 kW KE 406, which had been repaired in the meantime. The top speed was limited to 220 km/h in order to protect the engine; the only exception was a road performance test on July 13, 1971, when the car achieved a sprint time of 6.2 seconds for 0–100 km/h. For 1 kilometer with a standing start, a value of 25.2 seconds was measured, with a final speed of 252 km/h being reached. Testing finally ended with an odometer reading of 62,819 km—not due to engine failure, but as a result of an accident on the motorway on April 17, 1972, in which the vehicle collided with the crash barrier. Car 2 was then cannibalized and scrapped on May 8, 1972. It ended up being the C 111 with the highest mileage. Fuel consumption over the entire distance was 26.9 l/100 km, oil consumption 2.5 l/1,000 km.

Car 3 or 23

The second "real" C 111, also the first in the final body design of the first series, was completed on August 2, 1969. The test department in Untertürkheim had received the floor assembly on June 26, and the chassis, completed with major assemblies, was delivered to Rastatt on July 5. The delivery to Sindelfingen for painting and interior finishing took place on July 30. Twelve days earlier, the styling department specified white effect paint for the exterior and seat covers in check cognac, with seat shells in cognac-colored man-made leather. The first test runs took place on August 4 at the Hockenheimring, with the KE 315 engine mounted. Before the start of testing, the car had been extensively photographed on the test track, and this was also when the first pictures of the C 111 were taken for the press department.

After the test drives in Hockenheim and even before the testing, which took place together with car 2 at the Nürburgring on August 13, car 3 was painted in fluorescent orange at the request of the body development department in Sindelfingen. More photos were taken of car 3 on the test track and on the Hockenheimring in this outfit, and spectacular and very dynamic film footage was also shot. The new livery was changed back to pearl-white effect paint before the end of August in favor of a uniform appearance of the test fleet. In this context, the upholstery was also renewed after press officer Artur Keser had expressed to Friedrich Geiger after a presentation for selected media representatives that the brown interior "was generally disliked." The new upholstery combined light gray and black patterned houndstooth fabric with side bolsters in black man-made leather. On August 21, the vehicle was registered and received number plate S–P 3436. During the press driving demonstration at the Hockenheimring, car 3, fitted with racing tires, covered a total of 1,815 km, consuming 37.7 l of fuel and 2.75 l of oil per 100 and 1,000 km, respectively.

On September 23, test engineer Guido Moch carried out a road performance measurement on the motorway near Riegel, where the top speed of the car equipped with racing tires was determined to be 263 km/h. At that time, the KE 312 engine had been installed, replacing the originally mounted KE 315 immediately after the press demonstration. On October 11, 1969, car 3 was presented to the public together with the Mercedes-Benz passenger car model range during a Bundesliga football match in Stuttgart's Neckar Stadium, and two days later it was handed over to the body development department in Sindelfingen with an odometer reading of 5,183. Still in October, the vehicle received a modified rear section in Rastatt, which—as with car 6 four weeks earlier—was extended by 100 mm to accommodate an enlarged trunk. In this context, the vehicle was painted in the color weissherbst and also received a new interior in cognac-colored check fabric; the seat shells continued to be upholstered in black man-made leather. In April 1970, car 3 underwent initial trials with air conditioning in Sindelfingen and was then transferred back to the test department in Untertürkheim. On June 15, 1970, the vehicle received the new number plate S–V 8944 and the four-rotor engine KE 404, which was removed again after two months and 1,100 km and used for car 33. At the end of October 1970, KE 403 was installed, which was also used in the early summer of 1971 to carry out investigations into exhaust gas detoxification by afterburning. In September 1971, car 23 received an automatic transmission, which remained installed until the end of its active career. In the course of its withdrawal from test operations at the beginning of 1973, the vehicle was finally re-equipped with a manual transmission and a dummy engine.

Car 3 then became part of the factory's own vehicle collection and was initially exhibited for many years in the German Automobile Museum at Langenburg Castle. This was followed by numerous

Car 3, studio photos from 2016

appearances at exhibitions and events; for example, in 2007 at the Europapark Rust, in 2007–2008 at the "Mercedes House" in Brussels, and in late 2010–early 2011 at the traditional *Advent Calendar* of the Munich branch, where twenty-four vehicles from the Mercedes-Benz history are staged every year in the multi-story shop window facade at the Donnersberger Brücke during Advent. In 2015, the vehicle was exhibited at the special exhibition, *C 111—Timeless and Visionary,* at the Mercedes-Benz Museum and in 2019 at the Techno-Classica Essen to mark the "50 years of the C 111" anniversary.

Car 4 after the accident in Hockenheim on January 29, 1970

Car 4 or 24

Car 4 was completed on August 16, 1969, after the floor assembly had been completed on July 9. On August 6, the Sindelfingen stylists had specified the paintwork in white effect paint and the upholstery in blue and black patterned houndstooth fabric but changed the latter seven days later in favor of houndstooth beige and black. Testing began on August 19 at the Hockenheimring and continued at the Nürburgring, using the KE 306 engine. At the press trial drive in Hockenheim, the car, registered on August 21 with number plate S–P 3437, covered 1,605 km. The oil consumption of 6.25 l per 1,000 km was as high as in car 2; the fuel consumption is not documented. At an odometer reading of 3,352 km, the three-rotor engine was removed on October 6, 1969, and the 4.5-liter V8 engine with number U 9 was fitted in its place on October 14. With this, car 4 ran until January 15, 1970, and had 4,537 km on the clock. One day later, the KE 315 Wankel engine was installed and endurance testing continued in Hockenheim. On January 29, car 4, with an odometer reading of 5,170 km, was severely damaged in a collision with the north gate of the Hockenheimring circuit.

After makeshift repairs to the bodywork, the car was used for two crash tests in June 1970, where the safety of the fuel tanks housed in the sills was examined in side impact tests. The vehicle was then cannibalized and scrapped.

Car 5 or 25

The floor assembly of car no. 5, which was planned as an exhibition car for the IAA, was delivered to Untertürkheim on July 25, 1969, and completely measured there on August 1. Then the major assemblies were installed, including the mockup of a three-rotor engine. After the body was built in Rastatt, the vehicle received its paintwork and interior in Sindelfingen and was transported to Untertürkheim on August 22. Completion in the advance engineering department there took place on August 28, and the car was again transferred to Sindelfingen for preparation for use at the trade fair. On the same day, the decision was made there to paint the exhibition car as the first and initially only   C 111 not in pearl white like the other examples—and as decided ten days earlier—but with an eye-catching effect paint in the color weissherbst and to cover the seats with houndstooth fabric in cognac/black. This contributed greatly to the spectacular appearance of the show car, and the C 111 was one of the most admired vehicles at the exhibition. After the IAA, the car was used at other trade fairs and exhibitions: until the end of the year in Paris, Turin, and London; at the Jochen Rindt shows in Vienna, Essen, and Munich; and at the beginning of 1970 at trade fairs in Brussels, Leiden, Stuttgart, and finally in Chicago. Between its appearances at the "Motor–Sport–Freizeit" trade fair in Stuttgart at the beginning of February and the Chicago Auto Show at the end of February, the car was still being photographed in the Mercedes-Benz Museum for the "Autos und Mädchen" (Cars and Girls) series of *Deutsche Auto Zeitung*.

After returning from its exhibition tour, this C 111 was also integrated into the test fleet. This compensated for the accident-related loss of car 4, and for exhibitions, the focus was now on the revised version presented in Geneva in the meantime anyway. In July 1970, car 5, by now consistently designated as car 25, received the 4.5-liter V8 engine with number U 18 and was registered with number plate S–W 1484. Since the eight-cylinder engine was built

Car 5 in exhibition use, here at the Stuttgart trade fair "Motor—Sport—Freizeit" ("Motor-Sport-Leisure") in January–February 1970

taller than the Wankel engine, the hood had to be modified. The air ducting in the front area was also revised and designed in a similar way to the cars of the second series. Beginning on October 15, 1970, with an odometer reading of 2,439 km, car 25 completed an endurance program for chassis testing on the small circuit of the Hockenheimring, for which it was fitted with street tires. At the beginning of November 1971, the V8 engine U 82 was installed and was replaced by the four-rotor engine KE 406 from the crashed car 22 on April 18, 1972, at an odometer reading of 21,446 km. Due to loud engine noise, it was removed again on July 27. From October 5, KE 414 was used instead and remained fitted until January 17, 1974, with an odometer reading of 25,607 km. Subsequently, the usable parts were removed, and the car was scrapped.

Car 6 or 26

Car 26 plays a special role in the history of the C 111 in several respects: It was the first example of the Wankel sports car to be built with a four-rotor engine. This contradicts the common belief that the cars of the first series were basically equipped with a three-rotor engine and the cars of the second series with a four-rotor engine.

The floor system was provided by Sindelfingen on August 8, 1969, and the measurements in Untertürkheim were completed four days later. After assembly in Rastatt, where the car was given a body that was 35 kg lighter than those of its predecessors, the paintwork and interior were done in Sindelfingen. The stylists had specified a paint finish in white effect paint on August 19, and the upholstery was in dark gray-and-red patterned check fabric with seat bolsters in black man-made leather. On September 8, 1969, car 26 was delivered to the advance engineering department in Untertürkheim and completed with the first installable four-rotor KE 402 engine. The first test drive of the vehicle, registered with number plate S–P 2288, took place on September 10 on the test day organized by the Motor Presse Club (MPC) at the Hockenheimring, where the four-rotor engine was not a topic in the communication. Car 6 was transferred again to Rastatt on September 17, where it received an enlarged trunk in the same way as car 22, although it was not accessible without opening the hood—in contrast to the solution implemented for car 22. For this purpose, the rear section and the hatch were extended by 100 mm. In this context, car 26 also received a new paint job in the color weissherbst in Sindelfingen.

By November 17, KE 402 had been removed and reinstalled twice due to various defects. It was removed again on January 22, 1970, with an odometer reading of 2,837 km, and the KE 407, KE 405, and KE 406 engines used thereafter did not remain in service for long either. At the end of February 1970, the vehicle was photographed together with car 1 and car 31 for PR purposes on the test track in Untertürkheim. On March 5, at an odometer reading of 3,833 km, car 26 received its first KE 402 engine again, with which it also completed the press driving demonstration in Monthoux on March 10, together with car 31. From March 31 to September 17, car 26 covered a total of 4,901 km; KE 405 was installed again but was removed and reinstalled four times during this period. On September 21, 1970, at an odometer reading of 8,734 km, KE 408 was installed, which had made its debut in car 31.

In April 1970, car 26 was used at the Untertürkheim plant for the demonstration for "Monsieur 100,000 Volt," the French chansonnier Gilbert Bécaud. On June 2, 1970, it entered the annals of C 111 history for a second time. During performance measurements on the Karlsruhe-Freiburg motorway, the car reached a stopped top speed of 299 km/h, making it the fastest C 111 with a Wankel engine to this day.

In late autumn 1970, as requested by Rudolf Uhlenhaut, the vehicle was equipped with the "anti-blocking device"—the first version of the ABS anti-lock braking system developed jointly with Teldix. During testing, it became apparent that the front brakes were not powerful enough when the innovative system was used.

In March 1981, car 26 was transferred from the test department to the factory's own vehicle collection. After that, it was used at numerous exhibitions, including from August 1983 to February 1986 and from November 2002 to April 2007 at the

Car 26, studio photos from 2016

Auto- und Technikmuseum Sinsheim. In 2010, it was exhibited as part of the super sports car presentation at the Techno-Classica Essen and in the Mercedes-Benz Museum as well as at the Essen Motor Show. Five years later, it made another high-profile appearance at the IAA in Frankfurt, where it was part of the stage set for the impressive live presentation of the current Mercedes-Benz model range.

Car 24 a

Car 24 a also occupies a special position in the C 111 test car fleet—and not only because of its unusual numbering. It was built at the end of April 1970 as a replacement for the crashed car 24, which was to be transferred to the body development department in Sindelfingen in exchange for car 23 and was no longer available after its accident at the end of January. This also explains the different designation 24 a. Since the C 111 had made its debut in March 1970 with an optimized body design, it made sense—especially in view of the intended use—to equip the replacement vehicle with a body of the new design as well. On April 27, the Sindelfingen stylists specified the paintwork in the weissherbst and the upholstery in houndstooth fabric of the color "cognac light," with the seat bolsters—as on the other vehicles—in black man-made leather. Since four-rotor engines were not available in sufficient quantities, car 24 a received the three-rotor unit KE 308, which had previously been used in the Sledge. Exhaust pipe and presilencer were placed next to the transmission underneath the trunk, analogous to the solution first used on car 32. The vehicle was registered on July 23, 1970, with number plate BB–K 390.

In January 1971, the Sindelfingen-based "bodywork test car" was the first C 111 to have the top of the hatch and the air outlet ducts on the hood painted in matte black. Karl Wilfert had already suggested this in August–September 1970 to avoid the reflections

Car 24 a, studio photos from 2016

he complained about, especially on the concave upper side of the engine compartment cover.

In autumn 1973, at an odometer reading of 10,546 kilometers, car 24 a received the KE 410 four-rotor version, which was equipped with the innovative variable-length intake manifold, instead of the three-rotor KE 308 engine used until then. Within this context, the exhaust system was changed back to the original configuration, and the vehicle was equipped with air conditioning. However, initial start-up with the new engine proved to be very laborious, and so at an odometer reading of 10,818 km—after not even 300 km—the KE 412, likewise equipped with a variable-length intake manifold, was finally installed in April 1974.

After that, the vehicle was used in Sindelfingen for a few more years before it was handed over to the factory's own vehicle collection in October 1984. It was subsequently used for numerous exhibitions—for example, it was on display for many years in the EFA Museum in Amerang. Further high-profile assignments followed in 2012–2013 at the Autoworld Museum in Brussels, in 2014–2015 at the *Andy Warhol. CARS* exhibition at the MAC Museum in Singen, in 2018 at Retro Classics in Stuttgart, in 2018–2019 in the exhibition *Cars. Driven by design* at the Kunstpalast Düsseldorf, and in 2020–2021 in the special exhibition *Badisch-Schwäbischer Erfindergeist* at the Auto- und Uhrenmuseum Schramberg.

Car 31 or 7

The first C 111 of the second series was built between December 1969 and February 1970. On January 14, the advance engineering test department in Untertürkheim received the floor system from Sindelfingen, where production had begun on December 10. After extensive finishing work and the installation of the major assemblies, the completed chassis was shipped to Rastatt nine days later, where it was fitted with the body and transferred to Sindelfingen for painting and interior fitting on February 9. On January 20, the styling department had specified the equipment. The paint finish in weissherbst was no surprise, and fabric in a gray and white houndstooth pattern was specified for the upholstery. On February 16, car 31 arrived back in Untertürkheim and received the KE 408 engine. With that, the car immediately went into testing, which, given the very tight schedule, took place on the small circuit of the Hockenheimring. In addition, the new car was extensively photographed on the test track in Untertürkheim. On March 10 and 11, car 31, which had been registered on February 25 with number plate S–U 21, did duty at the press trial drive at the Circuit de Monthoux as part of the Geneva Motor Show.

In April, the vehicle was measured in the large wind tunnel of the FKFS; the black mesh on the top of the air outlet ducts, with which car 31 was the only C 111 to be equipped, had already been removed by this time. As the only roadworthy example of the second version at the time, the first C 111 of this design was in great demand for experimental testing as well as for driving demonstrations. Car 31 had been operated with the KE 402 engine since the end of March 1970, which had been replaced by KE 406 from the end of May to the end of July. With this engine, it reached a top speed of 280 km/h on June 3, 1970, in the road performance measurements carried out together with car 26, and a few days later it was presented in Berlin—not only to the West Berlin public at the AVUS, but also to a delegation from the vehicle industry of the GDR. Another remarkable demonstration followed in August, when the Wankel sports car was demonstrated on the test track to those US astronauts who were to land on the moon with Apollo 14.

From the end of October to the beginning of December 1970, cooling air measurements were carried out in the wind tunnel of the FKFS in two comprehensive series of measurements, the results of which were to enable an improved thermal balance. The solution was to widen the front end of the car by a total of 140 mm, which allowed the radiator and oil coolers to be placed next to each other. The car also received additional air intake openings below the pop-up headlamps. After the shape approval in April 1971, the changes were carried out in the summer. The first driving test with the modified body took place at the Hockenheimring in August 1971. Even in its revised form, car 31 still made a trade fair appearance. At the Hanover Fair in April 1972, it was on display on the IBM stand promoting computer-aided design using the finite element method.

In 1976, six years after its debut in Geneva, car 31 once again caused a sensation when it successfully completed the record-setting run on the test track in Nardò in southern Italy. The conversion to a record-breaking diesel car was suggested by Dr. Hans Liebold in November 1975, after the originally planned car 37, with a GRP-PUR sandwich floor assembly, had shown unsatisfactory torsional rigidity during test runs. In March and May 1976, the car was measured in the large wind tunnel of the FKFS and used in preliminary tests in Nardò from March 30 to April 3.

Car 31 was then back in Nardò from June 8 to 16 to finally successfully complete the spectacular record-breaking attempts.

On June 21, the record-breaking car was presented to the media at a press conference in Stuttgart. Even after that, it was a popular exhibit at numerous exhibitions and events around the world for many years; one of its first uses was on July 16, 1976, at the Daimler-Benz AG General Meeting held at the company museum, where it was one of the highlights of the product presentation.

In September 1977, car 31 was also once again in real test use, when it completed a test program on the skid plate of the test track to test the wheels intended for the C 111-III record car. In February 1978, tests were again carried out on the skid plate with car 31 in the same context, which were aimed at testing the fatigue strength of new center-lock wheels.

Even after it had come into the care of the company's own vehicle collection, car 31 was one of the most frequently requested exhibits. At the IAA 2007, for example, it made a highly publicized appearance in the special exhibition *Cars and Personalities*. In the spring and summer of 2010, the vehicle was presented at a number of driving events as the only roadworthy C 111 at the time, as part of a communication campaign to mark the market launch of the Mercedes-Benz SLS AMG super sports car—starting in April at a press event on the test track at the Untertürkheim plant and the ADAC Eifelrennen to the "Goodwood Festival of Speed," the "Le Mans Classic," the "Classic Days Schloss Dyck," and the "AvD Oldtimer Grand Prix Nürburgring" in August. In the summer of 2011, it was in front of the camera together with the SLK 250 CDI—the first SLK with a diesel engine—which had just been presented, in order to strikingly showcase the performance

Car 31 on the test track in Untertürkheim, taken in spring 1970. Characteristic of the first vehicle of the second series are the black meshes on the top of the air outlet ducts, which were, however, removed again as early as April 1970.

Car 31 after conversion to a record-breaking car, studio shots from 2014

potential of the compression-ignition engine. Car 31 also had high-profile exhibition appearances in 2015 at the special exhibition *C 111—timeless and visionary* in the Mercedes-Benz Museum, in 2016 and 2018 at the "Auto e Moto d'Epoca" classic car fair in Padua, and in 2019 at the Techno-Classica Essen on the occasion of the "50 years of the C 111" anniversary.

Car 32 or 8

The second C 111 of the revised version was built in early 1970, shortly after car 31. The test department in Sindelfingen produced the floor assembly from January 15 to 27, and the completion with major assemblies took place until February 5 in the advance engineering test department in Untertürkheim. After the body was installed at Waggonfabrik Rastatt, the vehicle arrived back in Untertürkheim on February 23. On February 26, it was transferred from there to Sindelfingen, where—as specified in the equipment assignment of January 20—the paintwork was in weissherbst and the interior with seats in light cognac houndstooth pattern. On March 9, delivery was made to Untertürkheim, from where the vehicle was transported to the Geneva Motor Show. The exhibition vehicle equipped with the mockup of a four-rotor engine was the first C 111 on which the relocation of the exhaust pipe and the pre-silencer to under the trunk, as proposed by Rudolf Uhlenhaut, was realized.

Since the C 111 of the latest design was in great demand as an exhibit for shows all over the world, and four-rotor Wankel engines were only available to a limited extent anyway, car 32 remained a pure exhibition piece and was not integrated into the test fleet. After returning from an exhibition tour lasting almost two years and appropriate conditioning, the vehicle was transferred from the department responsible for the organization of industrial fairs to the museum in June 1972 and taken over into the stock of the company's own vehicle collection.

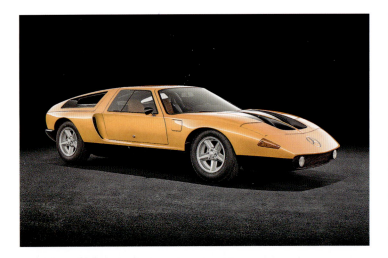

Car 32, studio photos from 2016

This has been followed to this day by numerous appearances at exhibitions and events all over the world, including in 2009 and 2012 at the "Classic Days Schloss Dyck," in 2010 at the super sports car presentation as part of the Paris Motor Show, in 2011 at the Mercedes-Benz Gallery Unter den Linden in Berlin, in 2014 at the Concours d'Élegance in Chantilly, and at the exhibition *L'Automobile & la mode* as part of the Paris Motor Show, in 2015 at the special exhibition *C 111—timeless and visionary* at the Mercedes-Benz Museum, in 2017 at the Rétromobile classic car fair in Paris, and from November 2019 to July 2020 at the exhibition *Concept Car. Beauté pure* in the palace of Compiègne, about 70 km north of Paris.

In January 2024, car 32, which had been used purely as a show car from the outset, was transferred to the *Fascination of Design* section of the Mercedes-Benz Museum, where it replaced car 33 after about eighteen years.

Car 33 or 9

At the beginning of March 1970, even before the debut of the new version of the C 111 in Geneva, production of the third example of this version began in Sindelfingen. By the end of the month, the floor assembly was built in Sindelfingen and the drivetrain was fitted in Untertürkheim in April. From April 28 to May 22, 1970, the body was installed in Rastatt, and on May 25 the vehicle was transferred back to Untertürkheim. To carry out the painting and interior fitting, the car went to Sindelfingen on June 2. As specified in the equipment assignment on April 27, the paintwork was in weissherbst and the upholstery in gray and white houndstooth pattern, as on car 31. Back in the test department in Untertürkheim, the vehicle could not be completed with a four-rotor Wankel engine before August—the KE 404, which had been taken from car 23 for this purpose. Car 33, registered with number plate S—Y 6200, thus joined the test fleet. Right at the beginning of its active duty, it was used for testing the fluidic element, which enabled the two side tanks to be emptied evenly and was successful at the first attempt.

In December 1970 it completed a test program to measure the trunk temperature, and in August 1971 it took part in a test at the Hockenheimring together with car 25, car 31—which had just been rebuilt with a widened front end, and car 34. A few months earlier, in April 1971, car 33 had been used in a demonstration for the automotive enthusiast and star conductor Herbert von Karajan. In August 1972, it appeared in a story by journalist and automotive historian Halwart Schrader, which was published in the first German edition of *Playboy*.

In September 1975, the vehicle was handed over to the company's own vehicle collection and was initially exhibited at the museum for a few years. It was then used at various events and exhibitions and has been one of the exhibits in the *Fascination of Design* section since the opening of the new Mercedes-Benz Museum in May 2006.

In January 2024, it was replaced there by car 32 and subsequently restored to running order. Car 33 was the first C 111 to be put back into operation with an original four-rotor Wankel engine after a break of more than twenty years and was demonstrated to the media and the public at Pebble Beach in August 2024.

Car 34 or 10

The floor assembly of the fourth C 111 of the second series was built in Sindelfingen from April 16 to May 15, 1970. In June, the frame floor system completed the rigidity measurements suggested by Klaus Matthias, which had already been planned for car 33, with which the torsional rigidity of the C 111 could actually be examined for the first time and compared with the calculated values. In October, the rigidity was measured again, this time in combination with the riveted and bonded plastic body. The vehicle was then

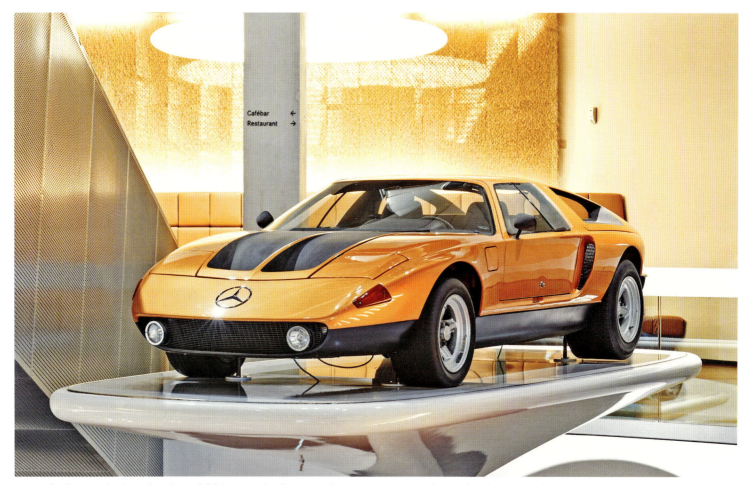

Car 33 in the *Fascination of Design* exhibition area in the Mercedes-Benz Museum, photo taken in 2017 before it was replaced by car 32

completed and registered with the number plate S–Z 4170. According to the equipment assignment of September 4, 1970, the paintwork was in weissherbst and the upholstery in gray and white check fabric. At the front, the body had additional air intake openings below the pop-up headlamps to improve the supply of fresh air to the interior.

It was not only in this respect that car 34 took on a pioneering role: It was the first C 111 to be equipped with the anti-lock braking system developed together with Teldix, and the only vehicle in the test fleet to be fitted with a trunk that was accessible from the outside without opening the hood, similar to the solution implemented on car 22. In February 1971, an automatic transmission specially developed for the combination with a mid-engine was also fitted, based on the unit for the 600 model. Originally, car 34, with automatic transmission, air conditioning, and ABS, was to be presented at the Geneva Motor Show in March 1971, but for a number of reasons this did not materialize. The completion of the KE 412 engine planned for the vehicle was delayed, and so car 34 could not be completed until February 15, 1971. In February–March 1973, it made a high-profile appearance when it was presented in a very prominent position at the Mercedes-Benz exhibition in Moscow.

Car 34, like car 35, was one of the two C 111s that remained in the test department's fleet the longest. In May 1976, it was still being used in preparation for the world record attempts when it was broken in in operating conditions at the Hockenheimring and on the Heilbronn-Würzburg motorway with one of the two new ZF five-speed transmissions for the record-breaking diesel car. In February 1978 it was used again to test the wheel bolting system intended for the record-breaking C 111-III car on the small Hockenheimring circuit. It was only in August 1991 that it was transferred to the company's own vehicle collection. Numerous appearances at

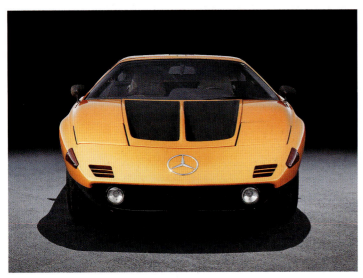

Car 34, studio photos from 2014

On the engine compartment cover of car 34, the contour of the trunk lid that can be opened from the outside is clearly visible.

exhibitions and events followed, including at the German Automobile Museum in Langenburg and in summer 2001 at the exhibition to mark the presentation of the 230 series SL at the Deichtorhallen in Hamburg.

Particularly popular were its appearances in the summer of 2010 at the "Monterey Car Week" in California, which also includes the Pebble Beach Concours d'Élegance, in 2011 at the super sports car exhibition in Paris, and in 2012 at the Epoqu'Auto classic car show in Lyon. In May–June 2013, car 34 was exhibited together with a 300 SL "Gullwing" and a 1937 Silver Arrow in the outdoor area of the Museo Mille Miglia in Brescia, where the three classics, presented in glass showcases, promoted a special exhibition of the Daimler Art Collection in the neighboring Museo di Santa Giulia. Immediately afterward, car 34 made an appearance at the Goodwood Festival of Speed in the south of England, then in 2015 it was part of the special exhibition *C 111–timeless and visionary* at the Mercedes-Benz Museum, followed two years later by highly acclaimed exhibition appearances at the Concours d'Élegance in Apeldoorn/Netherlands and at the IAA in Frankfurt.

Car 35 or 11

Production of the fifth and initially last C 111 of the second series began on May 19, 1970, four days after the frame floor system of car 34 was completed. On June 22, one day after its completion, the floor assembly was sent to the advance engineering test department in Untertürkheim. The installation of the major assemblies took place there as usual, and Waggonfabrik Rastatt then built the body before the body development department in Sindelfingen took over the painting and interior finishing. As with car 34, the equipment assignment of September 4 defined a paint finish in weissherbst and upholstery in gray-and-white check fabric combined with black

"Duels among Friends" on May 18, 2003, in Fellbach. Car 35 with Dr. Hans Liebold in friendly competition with an NSU Wankel Spider from 1966.

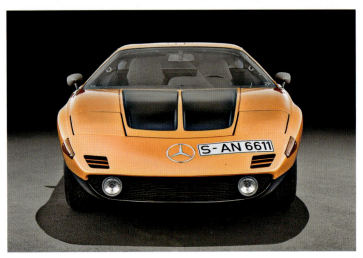

Car 35, studio photos from 2014. The fuel filler flap was relocated in front of the rear right wheel arch when the rear tanks were installed.

man-made leather. Since functional four-rotor engines were still not available in sufficient numbers, car 35 initially received a 3.5-liter V8 engine from the M 116 series, with which it could be used for testing the body and chassis. In the spring of 1972, the vehicle was equipped with two rear tanks, and in May 1972, car 35 received the KE 416 engine, which was the first four-rotor engine to be equipped with the innovative variable-length intake manifold, thus offering significantly improved torque. On August 29, 1972, the vehicle was registered with number plate S–AN 6611.

In October 1974, Walter Scheel, German President at the time, took the passenger seat of car 35 as part of his visit to Untertürkheim to experience a demonstration drive on the test track, with head of development Dr. Hans Scherenberg at the wheel. Together with car 34, the vehicle remained in the fleet of the test department for a long time, and the handover to the company's own vehicle collection did not take place until August 1991. After that, car 35—like the other C 111s of both series—was used at numerous exhibitions and events. Car 35 made a spectacular appearance on May 18, 2003, when it was driven by Dr. Hans Liebold on a course around the Classic Centre as part of the "Duels among Friends" event to mark the tenth anniversary of the Fellbach Classic Centre. At the same time, this demonstration marked the last time that a C 111 with a Wankel engine was driven for the next twenty-one years.

Between November 2013 and June 2014, car 35 was again fitted with a 3.5-liter V8 engine from the M 116 series in the prototype workshop of the passenger car development department in Sindelfingen. This meant that the Mercedes-Benz Classic vehicle collection once again had a roadworthy C 111 of the second series, which was subsequently used at numerous classic car events and once again attracted maximum attention forty-five years after the debut of the first C 111.

Car 36 or 12

More than five years after the presentation of the first C 111 of the second series, another example of the Wankel sports car was completed in July 1975 in car 36. Apart from the outwardly almost unchanged appearance and the largely identical chassis and drivetrain, car 36 was a completely newly designed vehicle. In contrast to all C 111s of the first and second series built up to that time, the frame floor system was not made of steel but was designed as a GRP-PUR floor assembly in core composite construction. Against this background, a classification as an independent series would probably have been justified.

After a long development phase and elaborate preliminary tests, which were due to the innovative design and production principle, the floor assemblies for two test cars were built at Waggon- und Maschinenfabrik Donauwörth in August and September 1973. On June 19, 1974, one of these sandwich floor assemblies was initially delivered to Waggonfabrik Rastatt after completion in the Sindelfingen body test department, where—as with cars 22 to 35—production and installation of the body took place. After the return delivery of the unit consisting of body and frame floor system on July 16, 1974, there were delays in the completion of the vehicle, since numerous installation parts had to be modified due to dimensional deviations of the floor assembly.

More than a year later, the time had finally come. On September 1, 1975, car 36 was registered with number plate S–CL 1668, and shortly afterward the first test runs were carried out at the Hockenheimring. The KE 419 engine with the now-tried-and-tested variable-length intake manifold was used. Shortly after the first driving tests, the brand-new vehicle was on display at the stand of Farbenfabriken Bayer AG at the K'75 Düsseldorf plastics trade fair from October 7 to 14.

Further test programs from the time after that are not documented—apparently mainly because work on the C 111 had meanwhile concentrated on its use as a record-breaking car.

Car 36, studio photos from 2014

However, car 36, as well as the remaining cars 34 and 35 in the test vehicle pool, were repeatedly used for demonstration runs on the test track. After being handed over to the company's own vehicle collection in March 1981, car 36 was also used at numerous exhibitions and classic car events.

From 2005 to 2008, for example, it was exhibited for almost three years at the then newly opened Mercedes-Benz Classic Centre in Irvine, California, taking part in the "Amelia Island Concours d'Élegance" in Florida in March 2006 and the "Classy Chassis Concours d'Élegance" in Houston, Texas, in August 2006. From September 2011 to November 2012, it was one of the exhibits in the *125 Years of the Inventor of the Automobile* exhibition series, with numerous stops throughout Germany, and in early 2013, it had a stint in the Mercedes-Benz Gallery on the Champs-Elysées in Paris. In 2015, it was on display at the Rétromobile in Paris, Retro Classics in Stuttgart, and the *C 111 —timeless and visionary* special exhibition at the Mercedes-Benz Museum, among other events. In 2016, it made an appearance at the Bremen Classic Motorshow, and at the "50 years of the C 111" anniversary, it was also one of the cars on display at the Techno-Classica Essen in March 2019.

Car 37 or 13

The second vehicle with the innovative sandwich floor assembly was also built in 1975, whereby the unit actually intended for car 36 was used. Daimler-Benz had initially not accepted this floor assembly, which was manufactured in August 1973, because of its unexplained weight deficiency. Originally intended for rough road testing and a subsequent frontal collision, car 37 was scheduled for a new purpose while still in the construction phase. It was to be fitted with a turbocharged five-cylinder OM 617 diesel engine and a modified body with lightened doors and hatches and was to be used in this configuration in the diesel record-breaking drive in Nardò.

The first driving tests were carried out on October 16, 1975, at the Hockenheimring. Car 37 achieved the desired acceleration and speed figures right away but showed unsatisfactory torsional rigidity, which was considered a hindrance for the planned record-breaking run. Against this background, it was decided to convert car 31, which was built on the classic sheet steel floor assembly, for the record-breaking attempt. Car 37 was now to be

Car 37, photo taken in 1981. The record-breaking car configuration analogous to car 31 is clearly recognizable.

used again, according to the original plan, for rough road testing. For this purpose, it was delivered to Rastatt on December 3, 1975, where the record car configuration was to be changed to the standard version. However, this apparently did not happen, and the vehicle remained in the variant of the record-setting car.

After the spectacular records achieved by car 31 in June 1976 and the resulting great demand to present the record-breaking car at exhibitions, not only car 31 but also the outwardly identical car 37 was used as a show car all over the world. In November 1980, it was handed over to the care of the company's own vehicle collection and subsequently went on numerous other assignments at exhibitions and events. For many years, it was on display at Mercedes-Benz Belgium and at the Museo Juan Manuel Fangio in Balcarce, Argentina.

Car 41

The first example of the C 111-III, the first C 111 record-setting car consistently developed for optimal aerodynamics, was built in the summer of 1977. The floor assembly was built in Sindelfingen in June and delivered to Waggonfabrik Rastatt in early July. The GRP body was installed there, and the equipment installation and body finish followed in Sindelfingen. After the measurement of the body was completed on August 30, the engine and axles were assembled in the advance engineering test department by September 3, and final assembly took place in Sindelfingen within three weeks. After checking the aerodynamic characteristics in the large wind tunnel in Untertürkheim, it was off to final

Car 41 in its first version with two stabilizer fins during testing in Nardò in October 1977

assembly in the advance engineering test department and, on October 4, to pre-testing on the test track.

The next day, the vehicle was loaded and transported by truck to Nardò, where it was subjected to extensive trial runs from October 8 to 16. At that time, the vehicle still had two stabilizer fins on the rear section. It was measured again in the large wind tunnel at the beginning of December to optimize the rear section in particular. The revision of the front and rear sections took place at the beginning of 1978, and from March 11 to 19, car 41 was tested in Nardò again together with car 42, which had been completed in the meantime.

In the last week of April, both vehicles were there again to conduct the record-breaking attempt immediately after further testing. When car 42 had to stop the run at 10:30 a.m. on April 29 due to a tire blowout, the record-setting attempt was restarted at 12:40 p.m. with car 41, after taking over spare parts and telemetry equipment from car 42. After a total distance of 4,398.81 km, the vehicle failed due to the right driveshaft ripping off, but at this point it had already achieved nine world records and two class records and had thus achieved its objective.

But this was not to be the end of its record-breaking career. In mid-July, car 41 was tested again in Nardò; the test run over a total of 7,242 km served primarily as a thermal check. Although further long-distance record runs, initially planned for September

Car 41 in its specification as C 111-IV, studio shots from 2014

1978, did not materialize, the idea of beating the unofficial circuit speed record set by Mark Donohue in 1975 had still come up in May 1978. The extensive bodywork modifications required for the targeted speed range of around 400 km/h were investigated in September 1978 during wind tunnel measurements of car 42 with provisional detachable parts, then implemented on car 41 and tested again in the large wind tunnel in mid-January 1979 and mid-March 1979. From March 24 to 28, the car—which in the meantime had been fitted with a 4.8-liter V8 with biturbo charging and was consequently designated the C 111-IV—underwent extensive driving tests in Nardò. The actual record-setting attempts finally took place on May 5 and 6 and were concluded with four absolute world records and the unofficial circuit record of 403.978 km/h. In mid-June, car 41 was examined in the configuration of the record-breaking run in the large wind tunnel in Untertürkheim and for comparative measurements in the FIAT wind tunnel in Orbassano.

In July 1985, the successful record-breaking car was transferred to the company's own vehicle collection and was subsequently used at numerous exhibitions and classic car events. For example, it was exhibited for two years from the end of 1996 at the US Mercedes-Benz plant in Tuscaloosa, Alabama. The C 111-IV had to be part of the *C 111—timeless and visionary* special exhibition of the Mercedes-Benz Museum in 2015 and of the Techno-Classica Essen at the "50 years of the C 111" anniversary.

Car 42

Production of car 42 began at the end of June 1977 with the manufacture of the floor assembly in Sindelfingen. At the beginning of August, the frame floor system was delivered to Rastatt, where the body was installed by the beginning of September. Based on the knowledge gained in the meantime, among other things with car 41, the vehicle was given a modified front end section with improved flow. The rear section, optimized according to the role model of car 41, was realized in January, and the vehicle was transferred to the advance engineering test department at the end of the month. Final assembly in Sindelfingen took place in February 1978, and on February 25 the finished vehicle was measured in the large wind tunnel in Untertürkheim. The first test in operational conditions took place together with car 41 from March 11 to 19 in Nardò.

Car 42 has been on display in Legends Room 7, "Races and Records," since the opening of the new Mercedes-Benz Museum in 2006.

In the last week of April, both vehicles went to Italy again to chance the record-breaking attempt after further testing. Car 42, which was less stressed at the time, was chosen as the record hunter and started punctually at midnight on April 29. After a total of 3,349 km and ten and a half hours, the run ended when the right rear tire burst and severely damaged the bodywork at the rear. Car 42 was thus out of the running, but the record-breaking attempt was restarted two hours later with car 41. In mid-May, car 42, which had been provisionally repaired in the meantime, was measured again in the wind tunnel—not least because the possibility of further record-breaking attempts in autumn was in the offing.

When it became clear that these runs would probably not take place, car 42 was nevertheless not ready for the museum. As part of the plans to break the unofficial circuit speed record held by Mark Donohue since 1975, the car played an important role in the aerodynamic optimization of the record-setting car intended for this purpose. Thus, in September 1978, it was measured in the large wind tunnel in numerous variants, which differed by provisional body modifications executed in clay, cardboard, and hard foam. The optimal configuration determined in the process was then implemented on car 41.

After that, car 42 had had its day after all—apart from the fact that it was used for PR purposes alongside the specially built show car ("car 43"). In July 1985, together with car 41, it was transferred to the company's own vehicle collection and was used at numerous exhibitions in 1986, and at the "100 Years of the Automobile" anniversary, as well as in the following years. From 1996 to 2000, it was on display at the Museum of Transport in Lucerne. Since the opening of the new Mercedes-Benz Museum in May 2006, it has been one of the exhibits in the Legends Room 7, "Races and Records," where—together with the other record-breaking cars on display—it captivates visitors with its spectacular staging in the banked turn.

"Car 43"

After the successful completion of the record-breaking attempts, a third example was built as a show car in addition to the two driving cars 41 and 42 used in Nardò, in order to be available for the most important PR tasks. For the externally identical but non-functional vehicle, which is referred to in individual sources as car 43, the first GRP-PUR floor system set up for measuring purposes was used, which was brought to Rastatt for this purpose on May 16, 1978. Completion took place by the end of July, and in October 1978 the car was exhibited at the International Motor Show in Paris and the International Motor Show in Birmingham. In April 1981, the exhibit was transferred from the department responsible for the organization of industrial fairs to the company's own vehicle collection. From 1982 to 1984, it was first exhibited in the "Hall of Fame Museum" of the Indianapolis Motor Speedway and from 1986 to 2005 in the then newly designed Daimler-Benz Museum. Numerous other assignments followed; e.g. in spring 2009 at the exhibition series *Time Travel of Innovations*, in 2015 at the Techno-Classica Essen and the special exhibition *C 111—timeless and visionary* at the Mercedes-Benz Museum, in 2016–2017 at the exhibition *Strom-Linien-Form* at the Zeppelin Museum Friedrichshafen, and again in 2019 at the Techno-Classica Essen.

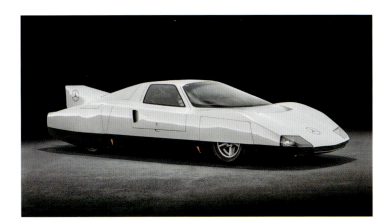

"Car 43," the show car of the C 111-III built for PR purposes, studio shots from 2014

Unbroken Fascination:
The C 111 Today

Many years after its active phase as a mobile laboratory and record hunter, the C 111 has lost none of its fascination and is still one of the most sought-after exhibits in the Mercedes-Benz Classic vehicle collection. The C 111 also played an important role in the communication campaign that demonstrated the unique tradition of Mercedes-Benz super sports cars in 2010 at the presentation of the Mercedes-Benz SLS AMG. During the planning phase, the realization that a roadworthy example brings history to life far more impressively than a mere exhibition piece was once again confirmed.

Track test: Car 31, the C 111 record-breaking diesel car from 1976, at a press event on the tradition of super sports cars on the test track at the Untertürkheim plant in April 2010. The wheel spats used in the record-breaking run are not fitted here.

"Festival of Speed": the C 111 record-breaking diesel car at the eponymous event in Goodwood, southern England, in July 2010

Pole position: the C 111 record-breaking diesel car at the head of a starting field of top-class super sports cars at the Le Mans Classic event in July 2010

Diesel power. At the launch of the SLK 250 CDI, the first Mercedes-Benz SLK with a diesel engine, the C 111 record-breaking diesel car showcased the performance and sportiness of the compression-ignition engine. The picture was published in a press release in November 2011.

In the case of the C 111, with its unusual Wankel engine, this resulted in a special challenge. As early as September 1974, head of testing Karl-Heinz Göschel and project manager Dr. Hans Liebold had pointed out in an internal correspondence that during the examination of the Sindelfingen body test car 24 a, they had "refrained from dismantling the engine, since almost no spare parts are available and it seems doubtful whether the engine could be rebuilt," and added, "A replacement engine is also no longer available."

Against this background, the C 111 was only very rarely used for driving events, especially after it had been placed in the care of the company's own vehicle collection. The last such use of a C 111 with a Wankel engine had taken place in May 2003 as part of the "10 Years of the Mercedes-Benz Classic Centre" anniversary. The first C 111 record-breaking car was used in the super sports car activities in 2010. In addition to the classic sports car body, it had a diesel engine that was near production in many respects and for which sufficient spare parts were available if required.

Despite the extremely positive echo in the media and the public, however, this could not be considered the last word on the subject. Thus, three years after the very successful campaign of 2010, in which the C 111 had received a very high level of media presence, the decision was made to restore an example of the second series presented in 1970 to roadworthy, operational condition and thus put it back on the road.

Dream car: the C 111, staged in December 2012 during the photo shoot for a communication campaign launched in May 2013 for the dream cars of the then-current Mercedes-Benz portfolio

Since the availability of suitable Wankel engines and corresponding spare parts had not improved since 1974, the decision-makers at Mercedes-Benz Classic decided to use a historically authentic V8 engine instead of the Wankel engine for pragmatic but, above all, also conservation reasons: This not only made it possible to expect a manageable start-up effort and uncomplicated driving operations but also allowed the few remaining Wankel engines and original parts to be spared and preserved for posterity without further adverse effects. Car 35, which had already been equipped with a 3.5-liter V8 from the M 116 series at the end of 1970, was ideally suited for the conversion.

The prototype workshop of the passenger car development division in Sindelfingen—with the successors of those Mercedes-Benz engineers and technicians who had built the spectacular test cars forty-five years earlier—took on the task of converting car 35 to the M 116 reciprocating piston engine in cooperation with the Mercedes-Benz Classic workshop. In one respect, the otherwise authentic V8 engine was optimized: Instead of the original electronically controlled Bosch D-Jetronic petrol injection system, the classic was given a modern electronic injection system that is easier to control in terms of performance and exhaust emissions.

The dream sports car, which is now roadworthy again, had its first outing in June 2014 at the Silvretta Classic Rally Montafon. This was the prelude to a whole series of other events at which the C 111 appeared, which received a strong response from the public and the media worldwide. The articles with driving impressions published in the trade press after the coveted test drives also made an important contribution. Car 35 made high-profile appearances in August 2014 at the Classic Days Schloss Dyck and at the end of November at "Stars & Cars," the traditional end-of-season motorsport event organized by Mercedes-Benz.

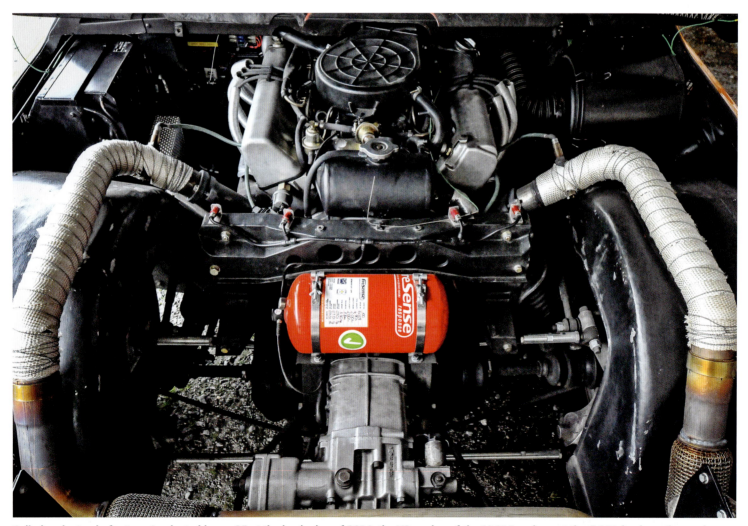

Cylinders instead of rotors: Implanted in car 35 at the beginning of 2014, the V8 engine of the M 116 series put the C 111 back on the road.

Power station with powerful car: the C 111 at the historic Vermuntwerk hydroelectric power station during the Silvretta Classic Rally Montafon 2014

Demo run on Schlossallee: The C 111 also made a high-profile appearance at the Classic Days Schloss Dyck in August 2014.

Elegance in the palace gardens: Car 32 poses in front of Chantilly Castle as part of the Chantilly Arts et Élegance Richard Mille in September 2014.

"Stars & Cars": The C 111 was also one of the stars at Mercedes-Benz's traditional end-of-season motorsport event in November 2014.

A few days after "Stars & Cars," the C 111 became a star when it was presented together with the latest high-performance sports car from Mercedes-AMG, model Dree Hemingway, and Formula 1 drivers Nico Rosberg and Lewis Hamilton at the key visual of the Mercedes-Benz Fashion Weeks 2015. The photo by renowned photographer Collier Schorr was taken in August 2014 in the new wind tunnel of Mercedes-Benz passenger car development in Sindelfingen. The year 2015 started in mid-January with an

Fashion, models, champion drivers: What at first glance may appear to be a marketing photo for a James Bond film is in fact the key visual of the Mercedes-Benz fashion engagement at the 2015 Fashion Week.

Unique specimens among themselves: At the Retro Classics vintage car show in Stuttgart in March 2015, car 36, the one-off with plastic floor assembly, stands next to a 300 SL "Gullwing," which is also unique due to its unusual Bavarian blue paintwork.

appearance at the Mercedes-Benz Fashion Week Berlin; the C 111 also garnered publicity at the "Fashion Week Warsaw" in May and at the "London Collection Men" in June.

The remarkable popularity that the C 111 had gained, not least through the activities with car 35, was further enhanced when the Mercedes-Benz Museum opened a special exhibition on April 28, 2015, dedicated entirely to the C 111 in all its variants. Nine vehicle exhibits and four engines brought the development of this brand icon to life, and around 200,000 interested visitors came to see the exhibition *C 111—timeless and visionary* until November 15.

Four years earlier, the C 111 had already played a role—albeit a more reserved one overall—in a special exhibition at the Mercedes-

"Timeless and visionary": Under this heading, the Mercedes-Benz Museum dedicated a comprehensive special exhibition with nine vehicle exhibits and four engines to the C 111 from April 28 to November 15, 2015.

Benz Museum. The Daimler Art Collection showed more than 250 exhibits in its most extensive presentation to date under the title *Art & Cars & Stars*. One of the highlights was the legendary Cars series by Andy Warhol, which was created in 1986 on the occasion of the "100 Years of the Automobile" anniversary. The C 111 was present not only in this series, but also in the eponymous sculpture by the Berlin sculptor Michael Sailstorfer. For this real-life collage, the artist had painstakingly converted a Mercedes-Benz 190 E sedan into his very own version of the C 111 by hand, his dream car from childhood days.

In spring 2013, the Daimler Art Collection, on its world tour with around 200 works, reached the Museo di Santa Giulia in Brescia in

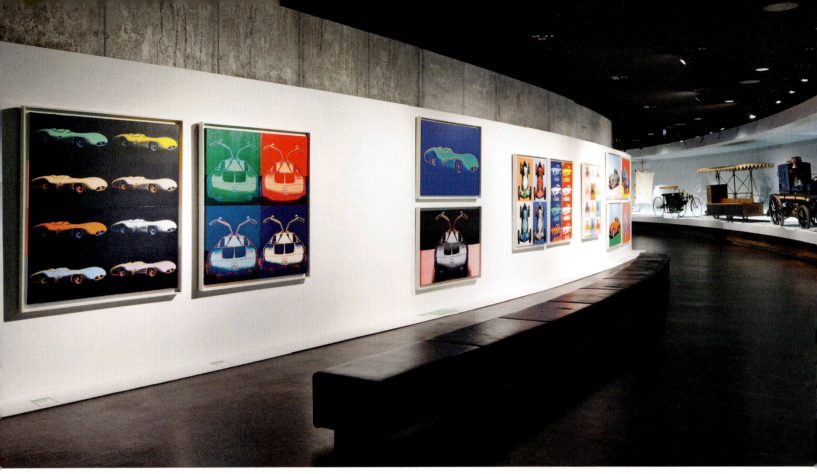

Art & Cars & Stars: **One of the highlights of the special exhibition of the same name was the legendary Cars series by Andy Warhol, which was created in 1986 for the "100 Years of the Automobile" anniversary. From May to November 2011, the Daimler Art Collection displayed about 250 further exhibits at the Mercedes-Benz Museum in addition to parts of the Cars series.**

DIY dream car: The C 111 was even more present in the sculpture by the Berlin sculptor Michael Sailstorfer. The artist had painstakingly created his very own version of the C 111 out of a Mercedes-Benz 190 E sedan by hand.

northern Italy, the starting and finishing point of the legendary Mille Miglia. Together with a 300 SL "Gullwing" and a 1937 Silver Arrow, the C 111 also made an appearance in May–June. The three vehicles, which were presented in glass showcases with a large-scale reproduction of the associated work from Andy Warhol's Cars series, drew attention to the exhibition at the Museo di Santa Giulia in the outdoor area of the Museo Mille Miglia.

At the beginning of May 2015, ten days after the opening of the C 111 special exhibition at the Mercedes-Benz Museum, car 35 competed in the Rallye Bodensee Klassik with Ellen Lohr at the

Warhol in Brescia: In May–June 2013, the C 111 (car 34), together with a 300 SL "Gullwing" and a 1937 Silver Arrow, brightened up the outdoor area of the Museo Mille Miglia and drew attention to the art exhibition of the Daimler Art Collection at the Museo di Santa Giulia with a large-scale reproduction of the respective Warhol work.

Group picture with C 111: The unusual sports car has made several appearances in the traditional *Advent Calendar* of the Mercedes-Benz Munich branch, which has been attracting attention every year since 2004—here, car 34 (*second row, third from the left*) in December 2019.

wheel, and on the last weekend in June it was on display at the Goodwood Moving Motor Show in southern England, which was held as part of the Festival of Speed.

Shortly afterward, it was off to the USA, where it took part in the Monterey Car Week with the prestigious Pebble Beach Concours d'Élegance in August and the no-less-renowned Colorado Grand outing in September. After a test drive with US TV star Jay Leno, the C 111 also made a high-profile appearance on *Jay Leno's Garage*, an extremely popular TV show and YouTube channel about exceptional cars and motorbikes.

Back in the Old World, car 35 was used in October 2015 at the Zoute Grand Prix, a top-class classic car event in Knokke-Heist, Belgium.

Lake Constance paradise: the C 111 in front of a picturesque backdrop in Lindau at the "Rallye Bodensee Klassik" in May 2015

Spring, sun, flowery meadows: the C 111 at the "Rallye Bodensee Klassik" in May 2015 with motorsport all-rounder Ellen Lohr at the wheel

The sound of the sea and the Pacific expanse: the C 111 at the Concours d'Élegance in Pebble Beach, California, in August 2015

"Tour d'Élegance": the C 111 as one of around 200 high-caliber vehicles at the excursion with start and finish in Pebble Beach

Vast land: In September 2015, the C 111 was one of the stars of the renowned Colorado Grand, a five-day drive for racing and sports cars through the Rocky Mountains of around 1,000 miles, starting and finishing in Vail, Colorado, which has been held since 1989 to benefit charitable causes.

The high-profile driving appearances of car 35 and the special exhibition in the Mercedes-Benz Museum also attracted the attention of some former employees from the development and testing departments who had worked on the spectacular project forty-five years earlier. The result was not only a renewed networking of the contemporary witnesses, but also the initiative to create a documentation, from which, in cooperation with Mercedes-Benz Classic, this book finally emerged.

Even after the very intensive activities in 2014 and 2015, during which the C 111 was featured in all trade magazines and in the public eye to the highest degree, things did not go quiet around the dream sports car. In addition to car 35, cars 32, 34, 24 a, and 31 were also used—as in previous years—at numerous exhibitions and classic car events.

In July 2017, car 35, with racing legend Klaus Ludwig at the wheel, took part in the Schloss Bensberg Supersports Classics, a classic rally through the Bergisches Land region, followed by a Concours d'Élegance, where current super sports cars complement the field of vintage cars and late-model classics.

The year 2019 was marked by a milestone birthday for the C 111—fifty years earlier, the mid-engined sports car had caused a sensation at the IAA Frankfurt. For Mercedes-Benz Classic, the

Primus inter pares: The C 111 and three other high-performance sports cars with the star in the courtyard of Schloss Bensberg in Bergisch Gladbach, the starting and finishing point of the Schloss Bensberg Supersports Classics (SBSC) in July 2017. Lined up next to the C 111 are a 300 SL Roadster, a Mercedes-AMG GT R, and a Mercedes-AMG GT C Roadster.

Cloudy day and good mood: Despite less-than-ideal weather conditions, the C 111 driven by racing legend Klaus Ludwig raised the spirits of participants and spectators at the classic outing through the Bergisches Land region in July 2017.

Snapshot: This photo of car 34, taken in November 2018, documents one of the rather rare occasions when the C 111 can be found in the "hallowed halls."

anniversary of the brand icon was reason enough to pep up the stand at Techno-Classica Essen in April 2019 with six original exhibits covering the entire range of the C 111's development history. The two evolutionary stages of the Wankel sports car were covered by car 23 as well as car 36, the first vehicle with plastic floor assembly. The second stage of the C 111's life was illustrated by the three successful record-breaking car variants, and the 1:1 design model of the unrealized predecessor SLX rounded off the presentation. On the way back to Stuttgart, the first stop was the Mercedes-Benz Museum. There, the vehicles were posed for a family photo before taking their place again in the "hallowed halls."

Two and a half months later, five years after its premiere drive, car 35 took to the starting line again in July 2019 at the Silvretta Classic Rally Montafon. And the vehicle also had a spectacular appearance in the extraordinary year 2020 with its numerous

Round birthday: To mark the fiftieth anniversary of the C 111, Mercedes-Benz Classic presented the entire development of the iconic coupe with six vehicle exhibits at the Techno-Classica Essen in April 2019.

Welcome home. After returning from the Techno-Classica Essen in April 2019, the birthday cars were unloaded at the Mercedes-Benz Museum to pose for a group photo before returning home to the "hallowed halls."

Anniversary photo: For the family photo for the fiftieth birthday, five variants of the C 111 as well as one predecessor lined up in front of the Mercedes-Benz Museum.

challenges: The C 111 had to be part of the Classic Insight press event Dream Cars by Mercedes-Benz, a driving event with almost two dozen dream cars from more than 130 years, which was held on the grounds of the Mercedes-Benz Test and Technology Centre in Immendingen.

At the press launch for the first edition of this book in November 2021, all variants of the C 111, including the SLX, were presented at the Mercedes-Benz Classic Center in Fellbach. Also present were protagonists from the development of the vehicle, who had contributed valuable information.

Dream cars in front of dream sceneries: the C 111 at the Silvretta Classic Rally Montafon in July 2019, five years after it celebrated its road debut at the same event

In April 2022, the C 111 came together with the VISION EQXX technology vehicle at the Mercedes-Benz Advanced Design Center in Sophia Antipolis, between Nice and Cannes, having covered over 1,000 kilometers in real everyday traffic on a single battery charge during the journey from Sindelfingen to Cassis on the Côte d'Azur.

Three months later, the C 111 was one of five vehicle exhibits to be admired at the special Warhol exhibition at the Petersen Automotive Museum in Los Angeles, together with forty Warhol originals from the Mercedes-Benz Art Collection. This was not the only time museum visitors too very long journeys upon themselves—in some cases even on transcontinental flights—just to see the original C 111. For Monterey Car Week in August, the C 111 left the Petersen Automotive Museum to lead the traditional Pebble Beach Tour d'Élégance after a short detour to the Mercedes-Benz Classic Center in Long Beach. For the weekend, it then took its place in the Mercedes-Benz Star Lounge at the Concours site in Pebble Beach, along with matching art by Andy Warhol and current dream cars, before returning to the museum in Los Angeles until the end of January 2023.

In February 2023, the C 111 shone at the International Concours of Elegance (I.C.E.) with a highly dynamic demonstration on the frozen and snow-covered Lake St. Moritz. And in mid-June 2023, it made perhaps its most spectacular appearance in recent years: During the *Design No. 5* event at the Mercedes-Benz International Design Center in Carlsbad, California, the C 111 accompanied the world premiere of the new Mercedes-Benz Vision One-Eleven show car, whose development it had itself inspired and which is featured in detail in the following chapter.

Just over a year later, the C 111 was once again the focus of public attention. In August 2024, it was presented as a running model equipped with the original four-rotor Wankel engine of 1970 for the first time after a break of over 21 years. The hopes of enthusiasts and media representatives who had hoped since 2014 to experience a C 111 with an original Wankel engine on the road had come true. The venue was Pebble Beach Automotive Week in Monterey County, California/USA, in which the experimental car of 1970 took part in the Pebble Beach Tour d'Élégance, in the media tour organized by Mercedes-Benz USA as part of their Classic Driving Experience and—out of competition, as usual for the Mercedes-Benz cars from the company's own collection—in the Pebble Beach Concours d'Élégance. Once again, the response in the media and public was enormous.

Gullwings approaching: The brand icons C 111, 300 SL, and SLS AMG on the fast track of the Mercedes-Benz Test and Technology Centre Immendingen, taken in September 2020 at the Classic Insight press event Dream Cars by Mercedes-Benz.

Premiere: At the press launch of the German edition of this book on November 4, 2021, all variants of the C 111, including its predecessor SLX, were gathered at the Mercedes-Benz Classic Center in Fellbach.

Archive treasures: The documents and photos from the Mercedes-Benz Corporate Archives shown at the premiere gave an impression of the scope and range of content of the archive holdings used for the book.

Eyewitnesses: Important contributions were also made by the protagonists from the development of the C 111: Prof. Peter Pfeiffer, Prof. Klaus Matthias, Rolf Kreß, Rüdiger Faul, Joachim Kaden, Karl Lemberger, and Wolfgang Kalbhenn (*from left*).

Game changer: In April 2022, the VISION EQXX technology vehicle covered more than 1,000 km in real everyday traffic on a single battery charge on a drive from Sindelfingen to Cassis on the Côte d'Azur, thus proving its outstanding efficiency. At the Mercedes-Benz Advanced Design Center in Sophia Antipolis between Nice and Cannes, the record-breaking car encountered the C 111 at a press event.

Art object: From July 23, 2022 to January 22, 2023, the C 111 made a guest appearance at the renowned Petersen Automotive Museum in Los Angeles. For the special exhibition *Andy Warhol: Cars—Works from the Mercedes-Benz Art Collection* it was exhibited together with four other classics as well as forty Warhol originals and attracted numerous visitors, some of whom came especially for the C 111.

Art break: To participate in the "Monterey Car Week" in August 2022, the C 111 took time out from the Warhol exhibition. In the workshop of the Petersen Automotive Museum, it was prepared for the trip to Long Beach and for use in Pebble Beach (*top*).

Marcus Breitschwerdt, CEO of Mercedes-Benz Heritage GmbH, did not miss the opportunity to get behind the wheel himself and drive the sensational sports car on the trip from Los Angeles to Long Beach and then as the lead vehicle of the Pebble Beach Tour d'Élegance.

Dream car and work of art: The presentation of top-class vehicles in the Mercedes-Benz Star Lounge at the Monterey Car Week in August 2022 was officially opened by Dimitris Psillakis, CEO of Mercedes-Benz USA. In addition to the very latest models and studies, the C 111 and the matching original artwork by Andy Warhol once again attracted attention.

Icon with an ocean view: The C 111 poses on 17-Mile Drive in Pebble Beach in the afternoon before its appearance at the Pebble Beach Tour d'Élegance in August 2022 in front of an extremely attractive backdrop despite the fog.

Classic on ice: At the event The I.C.E. St. Moritz (International Concours of Elegance) in February 2023, the C 111 presents itself to the public and the jury of the Concours of Elegance on the frozen and snow-covered Lake St. Moritz.

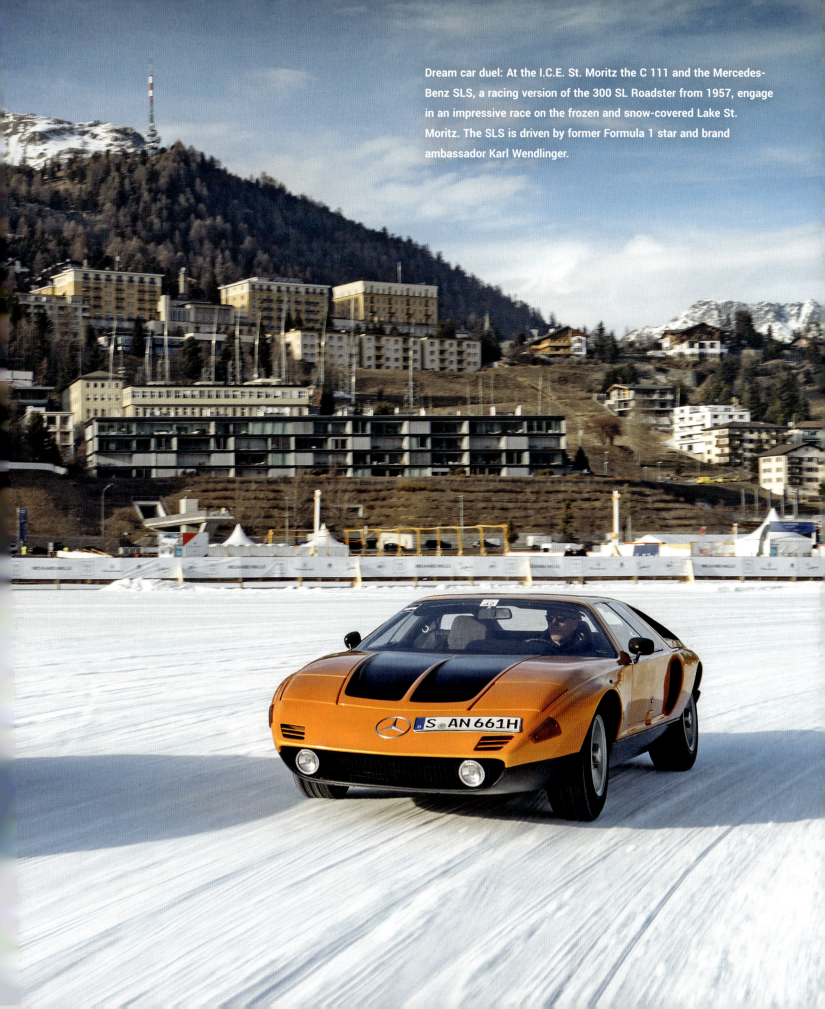

Dream car duel: At the I.C.E. St. Moritz the C 111 and the Mercedes-Benz SLS, a racing version of the 300 SL Roadster from 1957, engage in an impressive race on the frozen and snow-covered Lake St. Moritz. The SLS is driven by former Formula 1 star and brand ambassador Karl Wendlinger.

Back to the future: At the world première of the Mercedes-Benz Vision One-Eleven inspired by the C 111 at the event *Design No. 5* in Carlsbad, California, in June 2023, the 1970 role model could not be missing.

In January 2024, car 33, which had been on display at the Mercedes-Benz Museum since 2006, was removed from the *Fascination of Design* exhibition area and replaced by car 32, which was the second C 111-II vehicle built and had been in use as a show car from the very beginning.

In the Mercedes-Benz Classic workshop in Heimerdingen, car 33 underwent a thorough technical inspection. The main focus was the original four-rotor Wankel engine from 1970, which was to be restarted for the first time after a break of more than twenty years.

At the traditional Pebble Beach Tour d'Élégance from Pebble Beach to Big Sur, two classic cars with the star led the field: the original, perfectly restored Mercedes 2-liter supercharged racing car from 1924 . . .

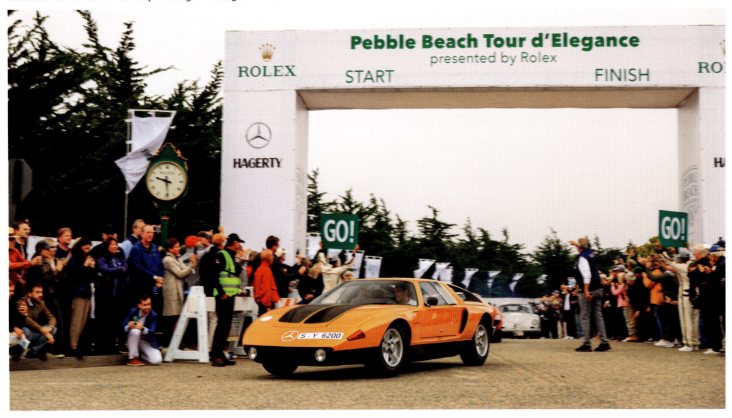

. . . and the Mercedes-Benz C 111 from 1970, which, after a break of more than 21 years, was back on the road with an original four-rotor Wankel engine, thus making the dream of numerous Wankel enthusiasts come true.

On a media tour organized by Mercedes-Benz USA as part of its Classic Driving Experience, starting from the Mercedes-Benz Star Lounge in Pebble Beach and covering around 50 kilometers . . .

. . . on Highway 1 towards Big Sur and back, the C 111 was one of the much-noticed stars among the assembled classic cars and Young Classics with the three-pointed star.

Dawn Patrol: At the traditional start of the Pebble Beach Concours d'Élegance, as one of around 200 participants, the C 111 with its original four-rotor Wankel engine drove onto the Pebble Beach golf course at dawn . . .

. . . where the judges' assessment took place on the lawn near the 18th hole. The C 111 took part in the "Wedge Shaped Concept Cars & Prototypes" class—out of competition, as usual for the Mercedes-Benz cars from the company's own collection.

Future and Tradition:
The Vision One-Eleven

VISION ONE-ELEVEN

For generations of car enthusiasts of all ages, the Mercedes-Benz C 111 not only was the proverbial trump card in a car top trumps deck but also became the ultimate dream sports car, for which those willing to buy even sent in blank checks. Marcus Breitschwerdt, Chairman of the Management Board of Mercedes-Benz Heritage GmbH, was able to experience the excitement firsthand in August 2022. During his drive from the Petersen Automotive Museum in Los Angeles to the newly opened Mercedes-Benz Classic Center in Long Beach—and also during the subsequent Pebble Beach Tour d'Élegance—the C 111 was surrounded by interested people wherever it came to a stop, and more than once, Breitschwerdt was asked when the fascinating sports car would go into production.

It is therefore not surprising that the C 111 remained present in the minds of Mercedes-Benz designers as one of the brand's best-known design icons. Stefan Lamm, at that time Head of the Advanced Design Studio in Carlsbad, California, and Steffen Köhl, Head of Advanced Exterior Design, first came up with the idea of creating a sports car study as an avant-garde interpretation of the future of the C 111 for the design icon's fiftieth birthday. Just like the role model, it was to combine a dynamic design idiom with innovative drive technology.

Reinterpreting a long-established icon is always a daring endeavor. At the same time, however, it also offers the opportunity to create a new icon, and this is the declared aim of Mercedes-Benz Design. So it wasn't just the Advanced Design Team in Carlsbad that was full of unbridled enthusiasm. Design Chief Gorden Wagener and the Mercedes-Benz Board of Management also gave the green light for the ambitious project, and the design teams in Carlsbad and Sindelfingen set to work.

First, a specimen of the dream sports car from 1970 swapped its place in the vehicle collection of Mercedes-Benz Classic with the design studio in Sindelfingen, where it was subjected to a careful analysis by the creative minds of Mercedes-Benz Advanced Design. Based on the findings, the first design sketches and a digital model of the new vehicle study were created. After its further development and detail optimization, this three-dimensional digital data model was brought to life in clay models: first on a scale of 1:4 and finally on a scale of 1:1.

This first life-size clay model merely reproduces the shape of the vehicle; it is equipped neither with windows nor with opening doors, so that a look into the interior, which had not even been conceived at that time, would not be possible anyway. After further fine-tuning, the so-called transparent model was created, which at least has a transparent roof and thus also allows views of the interior.

The transparent model finally formed the basis for the final shape of the show car. In this vehicle, which was built from scratch, not only was the complete interior realized in every detail, but also the powertrain, which is what makes it a functional car in the first place.

The development of the interior design was once again a special challenge, which at the same time also offered great opportunities—after all, the aim was to make the best possible use of the potential opened up by the compact, innovative electric powertrain and thus to develop a completely new interior concept for sports cars.

The final steps of the development process consisted of the implementation of the electric drive with its new battery technology as well as innovative axial flux motors and the development of an equally future-oriented user interface that enabled visionary user experiences by merging the analogue and digital worlds.

Finally, in June 2023, the time had come: at *Design No. 5– Creating Iconic Luxury*—an exclusive event at which the Mercedes-Benz design division presented its latest creations and strategies to the relevant media—the Mercedes-Benz Vision One-Eleven saw the light of day. The location of the world premiere could not have been better chosen: the Advanced Design Center in Carlsbad, California, where the idea for the development of this extraordinary study was born.

The details on the conception, design, and technology of the spectacular vehicle reproduced on the following pages are largely taken from the Mercedes-Benz press release, which has been supplemented and enriched with valuable explanations from important project participants.

Stocktaking: Steffen Köhl (Head of Advanced Exterior Design, *top*), Stefan Lamm (Head of Advanced Design & Strategy), and Matthias Schenker (*bottom, from left*) **analyze the exterior and interior design of the 1970 dream sports car.**

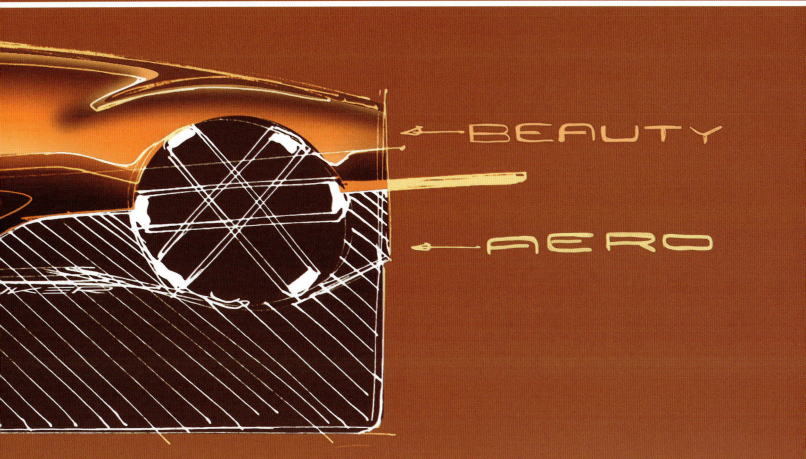

Creative teamwork: Steffen Köhl and Stefan Lamm (*standing, from right*) as well as Matthias Schenker and Maxim Kimmerle *(seated, from right)* with the design sketches that emerged after the first brainstorming phase (*top photo*). In the bottom photo, Steffen Köhl with the 3-D data model created in the next step.

A vision becomes reality: The 1:1 scale model sculpted by Veli Cetin represents the ideas of the exterior designers in real size and brings the sketches and data model of the show car to life.

The Exterior:
One-Bow Design in Its Most Athletic Form

The body design of the Mercedes-Benz Vision One-Eleven consistently follows the so-called one-bow design, which the Stuttgart brand implemented for the first time in the F015 Luxury in Motion show car presented in 2015, and which illustrates the Mercedes-Benz design philosophy of Sensual Purity. With an arch stretched tightly over the greenhouse, it also shapes the design language of the all-electric sedans EQS and EQE. The Vision One-Eleven's uniform bow line stretches from the low-slung front end to the muscular rear, giving the vehicle's silhouette, which is only 1,170 mm high, a sculptural appearance.

This harmonizes perfectly with the copper-orange alubeam paintwork. It provides an unmistakable reference to the distinctive color of the C 111 without just adopting it. The color of the Mercedes-Benz Vision One-Eleven is considerably more powerful than that of the C 111 and also changes with the light, thus conveying not only a sense of quality but also a certain extravagance.

Further notable features of the side view include the flush-fit gullwing doors—a distinctive attribute that, in addition to the C 111, also characterized the 300 SL und SLS AMG high-performance sports cars—and the side windows, which are opaque from the outside and camouflaged by a pixelated pattern. Yet another is the large-diameter wheels inserted seamlessly into the wheel arches beneath voluminous flared wings. This reinforces the impression of an uncompromisingly sporty and aerodynamically refined driving machine. The wheel design incorporates powerfully structured elements evocative of electric motor windings—a clear indicator of the state-of-the-art, all-electric powertrain underpinning the Mercedes-Benz Vision One-Eleven. They stand in spirited contrast to the vehicle's iconic, minimalist, and smooth surface design, which is more akin to a sculptural art piece. This contrast is typical of the special features the brand applies to its design thinking and an unmistakable characteristic of the Vision One-Eleven.

Another striking contrast arises through the very low-slung front and rear skirts finished in matte black. The two deeply scooped aerodynamic elements are visually connected by two blade profiles in the same color running along the flanks beneath the sills. These profiles feature piercings that are backlit in blue. The functional aerodynamic elements also serve as a further design reference to the C 111, which is painted black on the lower portion of its bodyshell. The dark "keel line" of the Mercedes-Benz Vision One-Eleven generates an impression of seamless transition between the vehicle and the ground beneath it that is even more powerful than that of the 1970 dream sports car that served as an inspiration. The form of the car appears fused with the road surface.

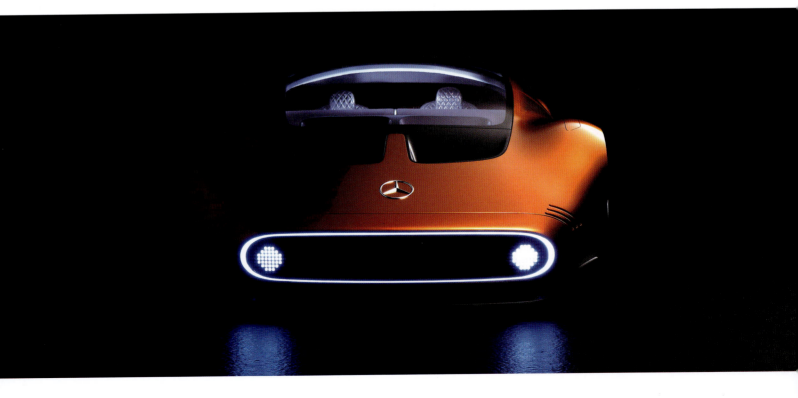

483

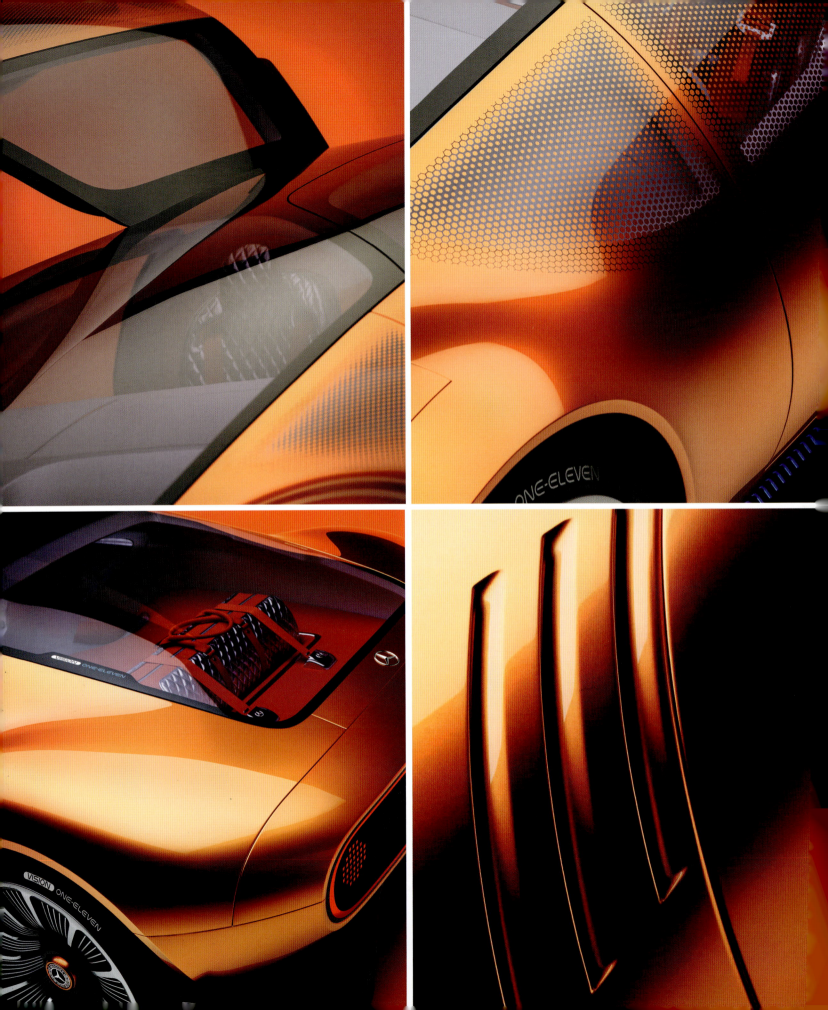

The Front-End Design:
Iconic High-Tech Look with Historical Reference

From the frontal aspect, too, the Mercedes-Benz Vision One-Eleven is powerfully evocative of the C 111. In detail, however, there are striking differences: One standout example is the distinctive front end, which on both vehicles consists of a low-lying rectangular element with rounded ends left and right. On the C 111, this is a closed plastic element with a honeycomb structure, fitted with round foglamps complementing the folding headlights above. The corresponding part on the Vision One-Eleven appears very similar at first glance. However, upon closer inspection, it reveals itself as a high-tech feature. The panel is a flexible external display with a 3-D pixelated look. It interprets the C 111's characteristic round lights in digitized form and can also convey messages to other road users.

In contrast to the C 111, the Mercedes-Benz Vision One-Eleven bears a U-shaped and strongly profiled front apron. Above the slender light band, both forefather and descendant show further similarities, most notably the black air ducts on the hood.

The Rear-End Design:
Aerodynamic Features and Digital Elements

The rear-end of the Mercedes-Benz Vision One-Eleven is likewise dominated by a powerfully profiled diffuser. Spanning the breadth above it is a display that echoes the shape of its counterpart at the front end and features the same pixelated structure in the red taillights. Similar to the blade profiles along the sides, blue lighting effects are also visible at the rear. The inner face of the wheels is fitted with circular lighting elements, which are clearly perceptible in the rear view.

The front of the Vision One-Eleven is characterized by the U-shaped, strongly profiled apron and a display with 3-D pixel optics, which interprets the round lights of the C 111 in digitized form (*top right photo*). The black cooling air ducts are also iconic.

The display in the rear end shows a pixel graphic that is structurally the same as the front with red illuminated taillights. Circular light elements on the inner sides of the rear rims create blue light effects in the rear end as well, just like the wing profiles on the sides.

The Interior Design:
First Sports Car Interior with a Lounge Concept

The visionary character of the Mercedes-Benz Vision One-Eleven and the aspiration to combine maximum sportiness with luxurious spaciousness is consistently implemented in the interior. Here, for the first time, we see the combination of elements that at first sight seem incompatible: a sports car interior with a lounge concept.

It reflects the paradigm shift from self-driven sports car to autonomous electric vehicle within the super sportscar segment and unites two completely different states of being. In race mode with the backrest upright and the compact driver-oriented touchscreen, the interior becomes that of a minimalist driving machine. Conversely, in lounge mode, the seats are fully integrated into the interior sculpture, which merges sills, center tunnel, and luggage compartment into a single unit.

This creates a whole new, exceptionally airy spatial concept. In contrast to previous mid-engine sports cars, it takes advantage of the compact proportions of electric motors to extend the interior rearward. Consequently, the lounge-like interior invites occupants to take their time and relax—a completely new approach for the sports car of the future.

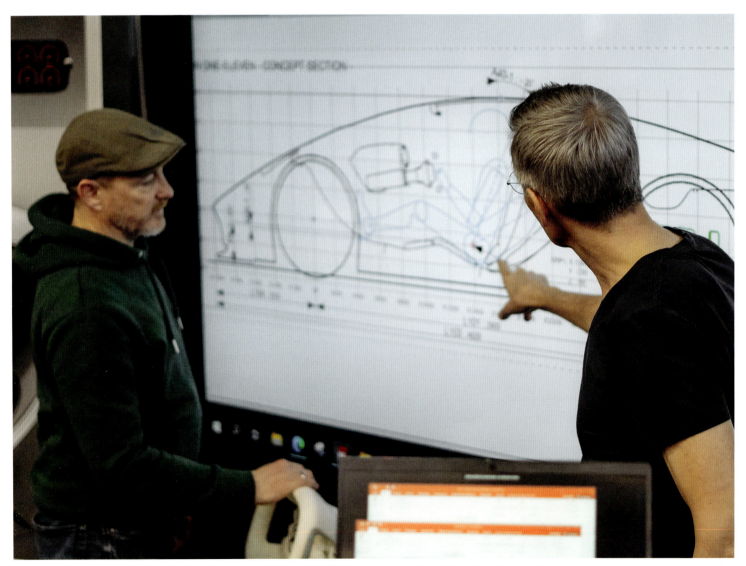

Hartmut Sinkwitz (Head of Interior Design, *on the right*) and Kai Goldbeck discuss the Vision One-Eleven's lounge concept, which is innovative for a sports car interior.

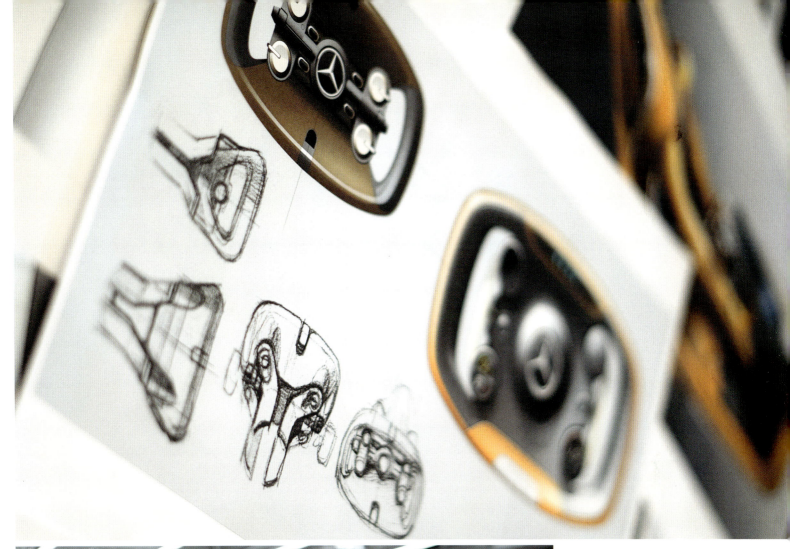

Digitally generated design sketches also play an important role in the interior design process (*top photo*). Hartmut Sinkwitz and Alexander Hoffart discuss the innovative interior concept of the sports car study. In the background is the C 111 from 1970, which served as a source of inspiration not only for the exterior design.

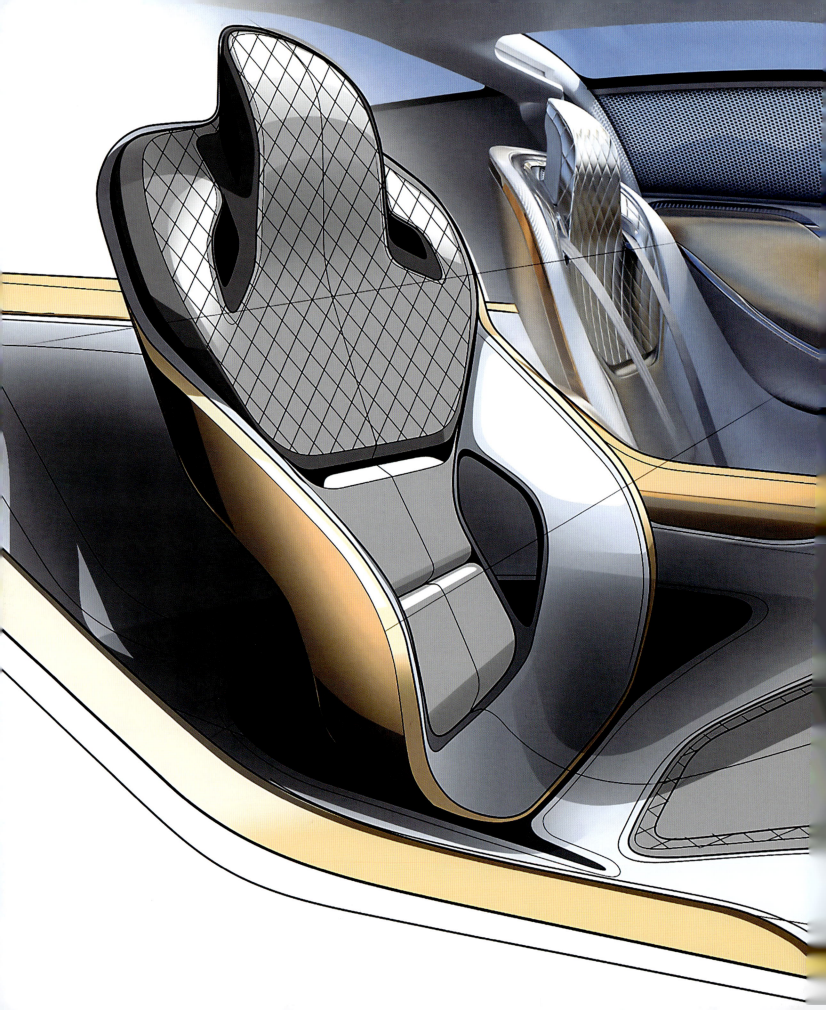

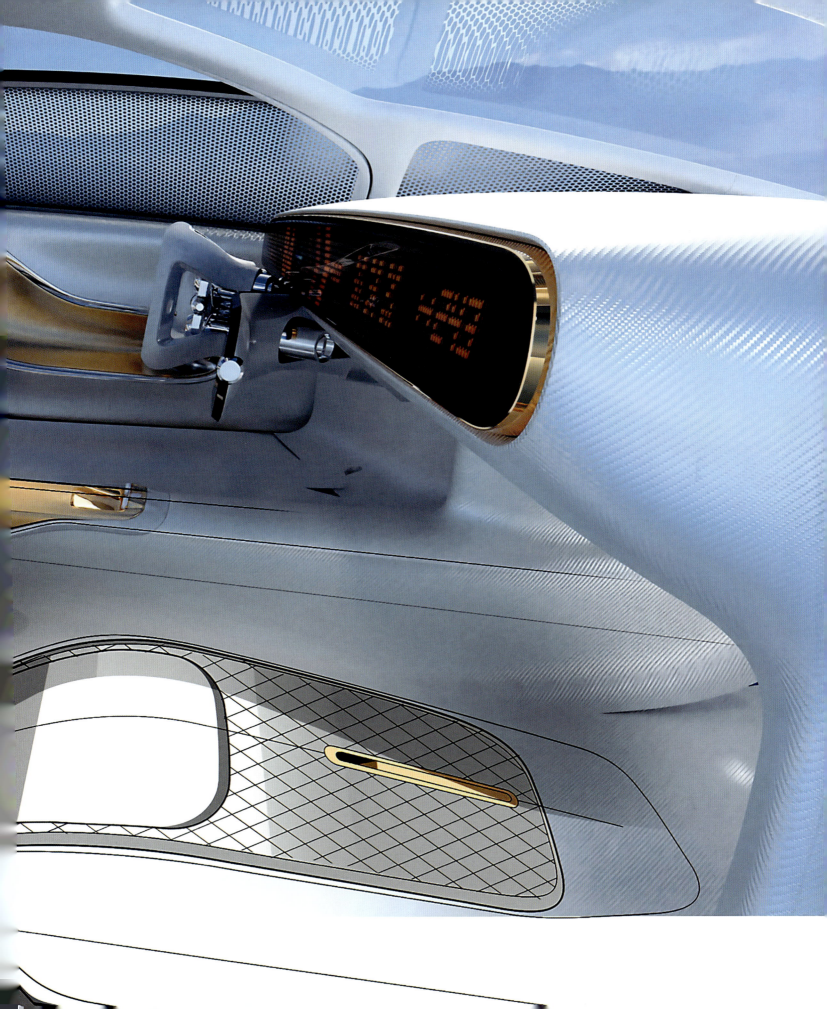

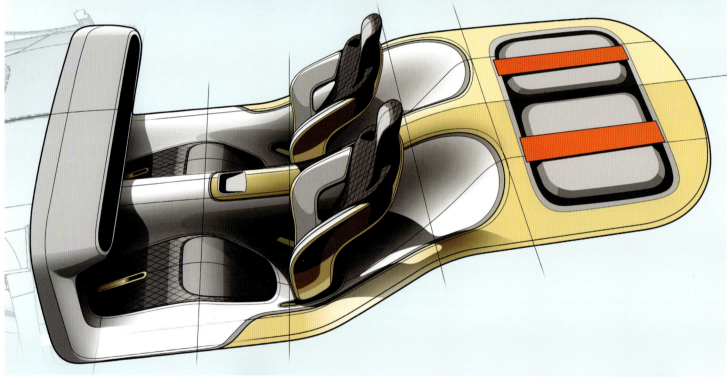

The design sketches by Peter Balko and Michael Plessing visualize the innovative lounge concept of the Vision One-Eleven and the purist controls in the gullwing door, an iconic design element of the extraordinary sports car.

494   Future and Tradition: The Vision One-Eleven

Futuristic and Luxurious Ambience with Contrasting Colors

The interior design of the Vision One-Eleven reflects future luxury based on a progressive color concept and extraordinary material combinations. The richly contrasting colors and materials attract attention at first glance. Large surfaces such as the dashboard are upholstered in white fabric displaying a tech-look honeycomb structure. The material is made from 100% recycled polyester. Other elements such as the armrests on the sills and center console, as well as the rear parcel shelf beneath the expansive rear windshield, are clad in bright orange leather. This creates a smooth transition from interior to luggage compartment. The sustainably processed leather was tanned by using coffee bean husks. Polished aluminum in the steering-wheel spokes and inlaid as straps across the armrests underscore the tech look and feel. The same applies to the brake and accelerator pedals, both of which are made from polished aluminum and floor mounted.

Otherwise, the interior equipment in the Mercedes-Benz Vision One-Eleven has been reduced to a minimum. Like the exterior, the task here too was to keep the number of add-on features to a bare minimum. The seats are good examples since they don't follow the classic format. Instead, the seat cushions are integrated flush-fit into the floor. This creates the initial impression of the bucket seat in a Formula 1 race car. The orange four-point harness and its high-gloss polished buckle further reinforce the sporting character.

Nevertheless, the innovative seats combine this sporting feel with luxurious comfort because, unlike in a Formula 1 race car, the angle of the backrest can be adjusted. The silver shimmer of their diamond-quilted upholstery is another eyecatcher that underscores the first-class interior ambience. Between the seats is a compact center console, freestanding in space like a work of art. As with the side sills, the top is a rich orange, which also covers the load compartment floor and thus reaches forward in the form of three fingers. This clear color accent enlivens and reinforces the subtle contrast of the technoid silver and precious pure white interior. This clear color concept in the interior has a soothing effect and makes a strong statement. The orange tone of the side sills, center console, and

The development process for the exclusive paintwork of the Vision One-Eleven was a much more complex challenge than that of the C 111 a good fifty years earlier—after all, the design specification of an iridescent depth effect in the light had to be implemented perfectly.

load compartment floor is also found on the steering wheel and seatbelts, and in the screen design.

The only highly complex feature in the interior is the leather-clad steering wheel, which is fitted with various functional controls and state-of-the-art touch elements. With its analogue three-dimensional controls and lovingly designed details, it forms a deliberate contrast to the clean-technoid design of the two-dimensional display. To give the driver an unobstructed view of the display, the steering wheel is deliberately kept low.

This is complemented by a compact touchscreen with high-resolution display mounted to the side of the steering wheel and angled toward the driver. It shows all relevant vehicle information as required. It also makes easy and quick operation possible for the driver.

The color-graded yarn rolls, which illustrate the development of the color and material concept in the interior during the design process, convey an aesthetic of their own.

The design team of the "Color & Trim" department inspecting the selected colors and materials. In the top photo, *from left to right*: Belinda Günther, Hartmut Sinkwitz, Anna Greif, and Silke Noack. Also pictured below is Marcelo Sordi, responsible for the making of the show car.

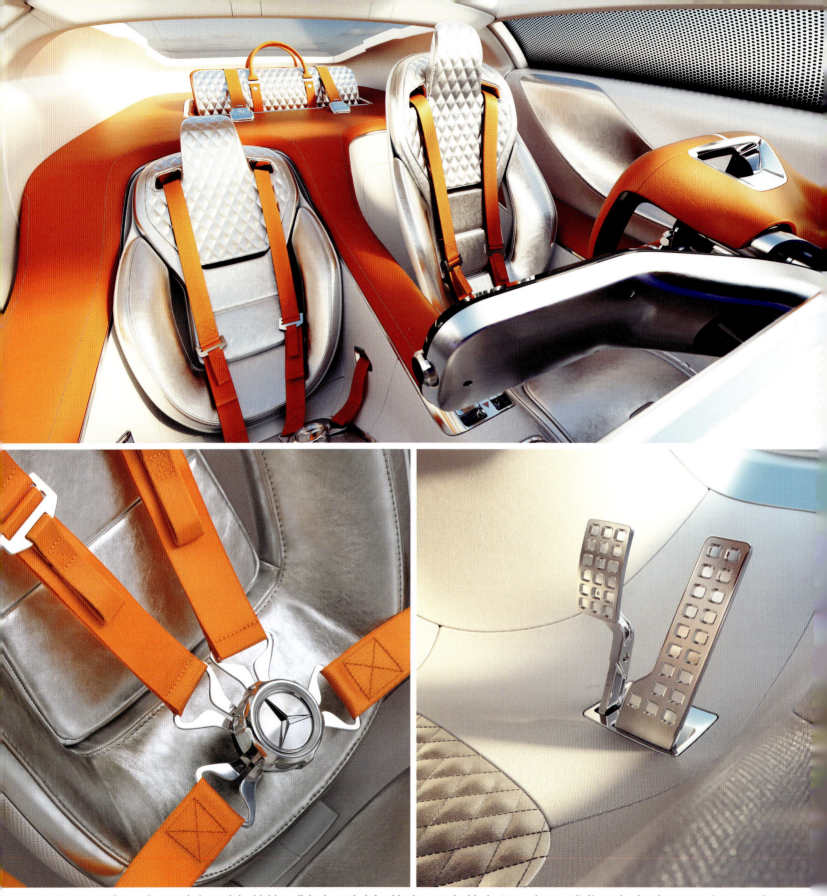

The orange four-point seat belts and the highly polished seat belt buckle decorated with the Mercedes star (*left*) emphasize the sporty character of the vehicle. The brake and accelerator pedals are made of polished aluminum and installed in the floor-mounted position typical of a sports car.

Fusion of Analog and Digital: UI/UX with Retro-Futuristic Pixel Look

The contrast to the modern interior is provided by the slender pixel display spanning the entire breadth of the dashboard, picking up on the form of the front and rear light bands. Here too, the pixel structure is intentionally coarse, which gives the information displayed—such as the current speed—a strikingly bold appearance. Moreover, the 3-D pixel display shows digital art pieces as a coarsely rasterized stream of QR codes in the style of "early digital" news tickers. This is done with the help of 3-D glass pixels—so-called voxels—that show a changing color gradient depending on the viewing angle. The corresponding real image then appears razor sharp on the high-resolution screen next to the steering wheel.

This combination of vastly differing representations of the same image embodies a further interpretation of the MBUX Hyperscreen with a focus on flexible interfaces. The retro-futuristic, 8-bit look thus creates an additional X-factor. The development in the Mercedes-Benz Vision One-Eleven reinforces the increasing fusion of physical and digital.

The 3-D pixel display, which runs across the entire width of the dashboard with its retro-futuristic look, takes up the shape of the two luminescent bands at the front and rear and emphasizes the generous width of the interior. The high-resolution touchscreen next to the steering wheel provides the corresponding information as a razor-sharp real image.

Creating an Experimental Spatial User Interface: Augmented Reality Takes the User Experience to a New Level

For the premiere of the Vision One-Eleven, Mercedes-Benz designers have created a visionary user experience with the aid of augmented reality (AR), setting it inside a virtual prototype of the Vision One-Eleven interior. As soon as the driver dons the Magic Leap 2 augmented reality headset, their experience is enriched with high-definition digital content that is contextually integrated into their surroundings. It creates a seamless spatial blend of physical interior and digital user interface beyond the screen. In effect, the entire car becomes the user interface.

Mercedes-Benz has been exploring the benefits of AR since the launch of the F015 concept car in 2015. The AR UI in this new car presents a vision of the future that works on two levels: the information attached to the dashboard and information placed in the environment inside and outside the car. This marks the next step from screen-based UI with Mercedes-Benz intuitive zero-layer technology to an AR UI that arranges zero-layer elements around the user in space. Elements include modules, 3-D icons, and the navigation map. The control interface around the dashboard and steering wheel is also augmented with additional contextualized information attached to actual objects such as buttons or switches.

The 180° AR view incorporates the world outside the virtual prototype—fusing the car effortlessly with its surroundings and placing the driver at the center. Map elements are projected into the environment, which is enriched with further information such as places of interest or hidden hazards such as roadworks beyond a bend. With this x-ray view, the system enhances situational awareness by blending out unimportant details to create an uncluttered image of relevant input. Elements that obstruct the driver's line of sight—such as the A-pillar, doors, or even the hood—then appear "transparent." Mercedes-Benz designers and experts worked with the technical specialists at Magic Leap to develop and refine the AR experience showcased in the Vision One-Eleven, using the highly advanced Magic Leap 2 AR glasses. The spatial user interface is a beacon for a Mercedes-Benz user experience that is unencumbered by technology. It is part of a

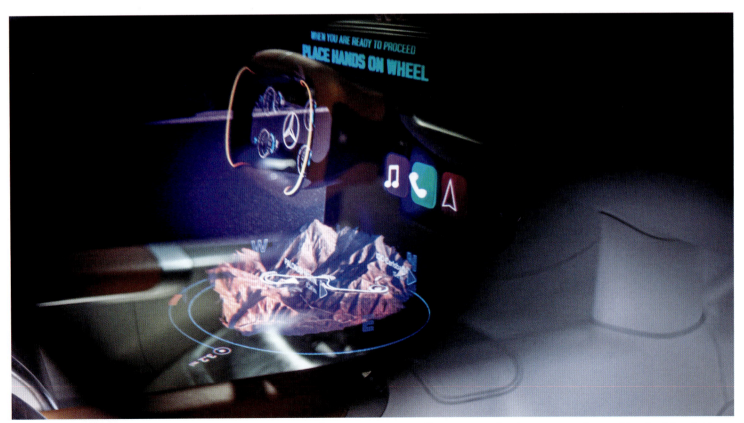

A three-dimensional user interface around the dashboard and steering wheel, as well as a 3-D navigation map, can be used by the driver in the Vision One-Eleven with the aid of state-of-the-art augmented-reality goggles developed together with Magic Leap.

At the world premiere in Carlsbad, Benjamin Kuhn (Head of Advanced UX/UI Design) presents the augmented reality-based user interface, which summarizes all situations currently relevant to the driver in a clearly structured overview (*top photo*). In a high-tech interior mockup modeled on the Vision One-Eleven, Tom Schillinger demonstrates the augmented reality experience by using Magic Leap 2 AR goggles (*bottom photos*).

wider vision that looks toward extended reality, whereby technology and hardware cease to be the focal point, instead becoming fully integrated and seamless facilitators of user needs and wishes.

Exclusive Products from the Mercedes-Benz Collection: The "LIMITED EDITION 1 OF 111"

Together with the presentation of the sports car study, Mercedes-Benz launched the "LIMITED EDITION 1 OF 111" collection. For the first time, a design study was accompanied by an exclusive lifestyle collection. This translates the zeitgeist of the 1970s into the here and now and combines casual sportiness with lavish attention to detail. In addition to the distinctive coloring of the Vision One-Eleven, the individual accessories also invoke the vehicle's hallmark design elements. The five articles are each limited to 111 pieces and thus offer admirers of this fascinating study an exclusive opportunity to take its style home with them. All products bear "LIMITED EDITION 1 OF 111" lettering—either embossed, printed, or engraved. The high-quality packaging, also in orange, is embossed on the top with the Mercedes star and "LIMITED EDITION 1 OF 111" lettering.

The weekender bag in silver, orange, and black is a luxurious carry-all made of high-quality cowhide with a striking diamond pattern. The two embossed leather badges on the left and right show the Mercedes-Benz logo on one side and the Limited Edition labeling on the other. In addition, there is a pendant made of black leather embossed with "Vision One-Eleven." In addition to the two leather carrying handles, the travel bag has a shoulder strap with leather shoulder padding. The weekender bag can carry approximately 40 liters.

The modern-fit sweat hoody in orange and gray has a pocket and drawstring with black flat-belt cord, printed in white with the label "LIMITED EDITION 1 OF 111." The back features an embossed 3-D star with a diameter of approximately 20 cm, and the raglan sleeves have a gray insert with a tonal diamond pattern.

In addition to the Carl Zeiss Vision N2020 lenses in orange, eye-catching design features of the sunglasses include the striking, slightly upward offset double bridge. The 19-gram classic aviator sunglasses with retro flair are "made by ic! berlin for Mercedes-Benz." "Limited Edition" is engraved on the inside of the

side piece, the Star Pattern on the outside. Another highlight of the frame, made of highly polished stainless steel, is the familiar screwless joint system from ic! berlin.

The orange cotton cap with a metal buckle has a tonal embroidered star at front center, and the "Limited Edition" label is printed in white on the left side. The Mercedes-Benz lettering can be found on the inner straps, which are also orange.

The cover for the iPhone 14 Pro, orange on the outside, lining in gray microfiber on the inside, is made of liquid silicone with rubber soft-touch finish. The "LIMITED EDITION 1 OF 111" lettering is printed in white on the front, tonal gray on the inside, and the Mercedes-Benz star is printed in tonal orange on the front and tonal gray on the inside.

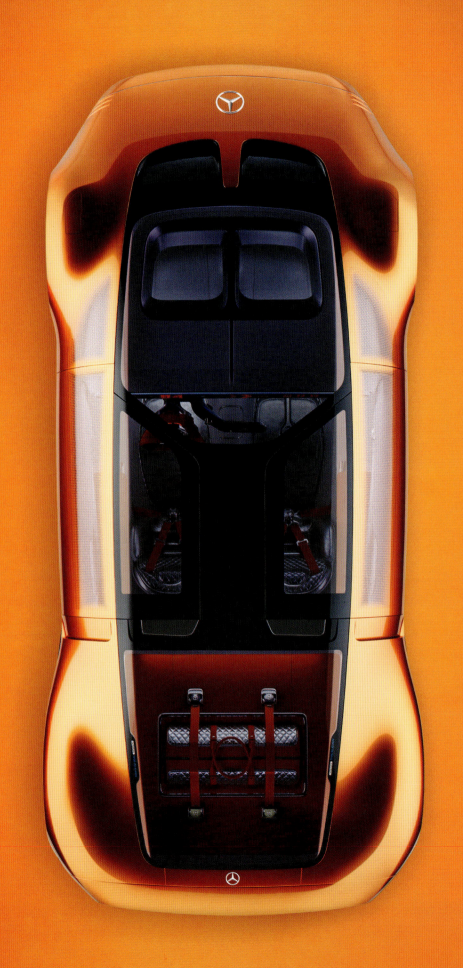

Innovative Electric Powertrain:
High-Performance Axial-Flux Motor and All-New Battery Technology

Technology highlights include a new battery concept featuring high-performance liquid-cooled cylindrical cells with a novel cell chemistry. Once more, the extensive knowledge of the motorsport experts from Mercedes-AMG High Performance Powertrain in Brixworth found its way into this promising concept for future performance-oriented batteries. Aside from that, the Vision One-Eleven features two exceptionally powerful and advanced axial-flux motors from YASA. Mercedes-Benz is developing this technology together with YASA to large-scale production maturity for its next-generation electric drives. YASA is a British electric-motor specialist based in Oxford and has been a 100% subsidiary of Mercedes-Benz AG since July 2021. The company has thus secured access to a unique future technology that has the potential to take electric mobility to a new level of performance.

Tim Woolmer, Founder and Chief Technology Officer of YASA, summarizes the advantages of the new drive technology: "Axial-flux motors are significantly lighter and more compact, yet more powerful than comparable radial-flux motors currently used in 99% of all electric cars. In an axial-flux motor, the electromagnetic flow runs parallel to the motor's rotational axis, which is highly efficient. In a radial-flux motor, the flow runs perpendicular to the rotational axis. Compared to radial-flux motors, they have considerably higher and more enduring power reserves, which delivers a whole new level of performance."

Alongside its power and torque density, another major benefit is the narrow package, which reduces both its weight and dimensions. The weight of an axial-flux motor is just one-third of that of current electric motors with the same power output. At the same time, it requires just one-third of the space occupied by a radial-flux motor.

The innovative electric powertrain of the Vision One-Eleven includes a novel battery concept made of liquid-cooled round cells and two advanced and powerful YASA axial flux motors at the rear wheels.

This opens up completely new options for engineers as well as new freedoms in the design of an electric vehicle as demonstrated by the Vision One-Eleven. The future generation of YASA axial-flux motors will be produced at the Mercedes-Benz Berlin-Marienfelde plant. The motors manufactured there will be at the heart of the forthcoming powertrain for the performance segment.

Markus Schäfer, Chief Technology Officer and Member of the Board of Management of Mercedes-Benz Group AG, sums up the innovative character of the new show car: "The Mercedes-Benz Vision One-Eleven combines breathtaking design with groundbreaking powertrain technology. Like its historical namesake, it explores new paths for the future of sporting performance. At the

Demonstration model of the YASA axial flux motor. *From left to right*: **housing, rotor including magnets, stator, rotor including magnets, housing cover.**

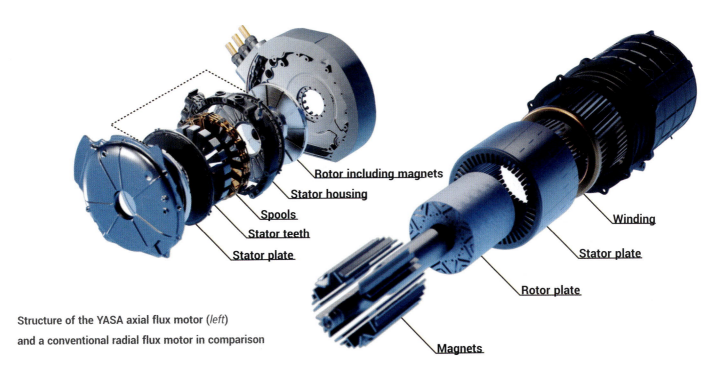

Structure of the YASA axial flux motor (*left*) **and a conventional radial flux motor in comparison**

heart of the compact and extremely efficient powertrain is the innovative YASA axial-flux high-tech electric motor. It offers a motorsport-like power output from a considerably smaller package. This makes the YASA axial-flux motor ideal for electric high-performance vehicles. Combined with the liquid-cooled, cylindrical-cell battery with Formula-1-inspired cell chemistry, the Mercedes-Benz Vision One-Eleven is yet another proof point for the broad performance spectrum encompassed by our four-pronged development strategy for electric drive." There is no better way to summarize the potential of the Vision One-Eleven, and we can look forward to seeing how Mercedes-Benz will continue to advance the development of electric mobility in the future.

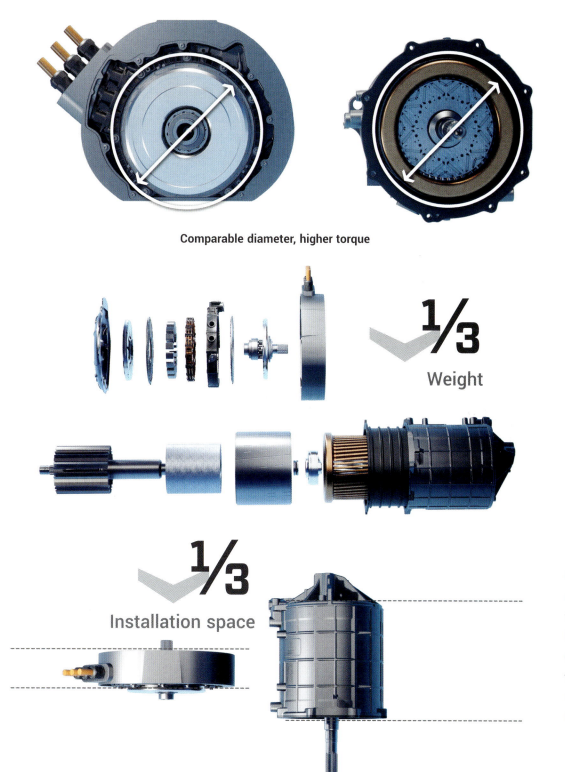

Comparable diameter, higher torque

Compared to conventional radial flux motors, YASA axial flux motors impress with a higher torque at a comparable diameter; they weigh only one-third at comparable power and require only one-third of the installation space.

In the Spotlight:
World Premiere in Carlsbad, California

After the spectacular presentation of the Vision One-Eleven at the Mercedes-Benz International Design Center in Carlsbad, California, the worldwide media response was overwhelming, with numerous reports from all over the world. An article published by Simon Ostler on the website goodwood.com on June 16, 2023, stated:

"As concept cars go, this latest one from Mercedes is one of the more eye-catching we've seen so far this year, and there have been some pretty good ones. . . . Mercedes has no doubt taken this opportunity to shout about its heritage, but rather than sit on its laurels and live in the past, this new Vision One-Eleven is a forward-thinking and progressive investigation into where the company might turn next. . . . Mercedes has gone all out with its latest design showcase, but the looks of this retro-inspired One-Eleven concept are simply the draw for what lies underneath. We won't complain should a new Mercedes sportscar that looks like this ever arrive, but what we can be certain of is that car manufacturers have barely scratched the surface of what's possible for the future of EVs. Is the issue of bloated and overweight electric models soon to be an issue of the past?"

The message of the Vision One-Eleven seems to have been received.

The extremely positive response that both the C 111 and the Vision One-Eleven have received from the public and the media shows that the fascination with the iconic sportscar remains unbroken more than fifty years after its creation—and there can be little doubt that this will continue to be the case in the future.

Gorden Wagener (Chief Design Officer of Mercedes-Benz Group AG) and Markus Schäfer (Member of the Board of Management and Chief Technology Officer of Mercedes-Benz Group AG) at the world premiere of the Vision One-Eleven in Carlsbad

The Mercedes-Benz C 111 from 1970 and the sports car study inspired by it at the world premiere of the Vision One-Eleven in June 2023 in Carlsbad, California; in the foreground, the demonstration models of a conventional radial flux electric motor and the innovative YASA axial flux motor

Appendix:
Data, Codes, and Sources

Deciphering the Departmental Abbreviations Used in the Cited Sources

A1KS	Construction: passenger car bodies, special designs	**V1AG**	Test department: passenger car major assemblies, transmissions
A1R	Test department: passenger car bodies, body shell	**V1E**	Passenger car test department: electrics and electronics
A1RA	Test department: passenger car bodies, body shell, measurement technology (including the wind tunnel)	**V1FA**	Passenger car test department: chassis development, driving operations
A1VB	Test department: passenger car bodies, test department workshop	**V1FR**	Passenger car test department: wheels and tires
A1STG	Development passenger car bodies, stylistic design	**V1FZ**	Passenger car test department: overall vehicle, vehicle accessories
E1	Development: passenger cars	**V1GR**	Passenger car test department: overall vehicle, wheels and tires
E1V	Test department: passenger cars		
E6	Research	**V1KD**	Passenger car test department: engines, combustion, diesel engines
E6LK	Research: engine laboratory, piston engines		
EA1	Development: passenger car bodies	**V1M**	Passenger car test department: engines
EMZ	Electronics, measurement center	**V1MD**	Passenger car test department: engines, diesel engines
K1V	Passenger car construction, advance engineering	**V1TD**	Passenger car test department: engines, diesel engines
K1VB	Passenger car construction, advance engineering, calculations	**V1RE**	Passenger car test department: wheel and tire development
ST1	Stylistics: passenger cars		
ST1M	Stylistics: dimensional concept	**V1V**	Passenger car advance engineering
STG	Stylistics: design	**V1VO**	Passenger car test department: advance engineering
STL	Stylistics: management		
STMK	Stylistics: dimensional concept/construction		
V1A	Test department: passenger car major assemblies		

Note on the original German-language documents shown in the book: A link to the translations can be found at https://schifferbooks.com/products/mercedes-benz-c-111.

Technical Data

Variant	C 111 "Sledge"	C 111-I	C 111-I	C 111-I
Year	1969	1969	1970	1969
Car	Car 1	Cars 22-24	Car 25	Car 26
Engine	three-rotor Wankel	three-rotor Wankel	V8 gas	four-rotor Wankel
Engine model	M 950/3	M 950/3	M 117 E 45	M 950/4
Fuel type	Premium gas	Premium gas	Premium gas	Premium gas
Displacement (cc)	3600 (displacement equivalent)	3600 (displacement equivalent)	4520	4800 (displacement equivalent)
Output (hp/kW) at engine speed (rpm) according to press release	258/190 at 7000 –	289/212 at 7050 approx. 280/206 at 7000	330/242 at 6100 –	367/270 at 6500 –
Torque (mkg/Nm) at engine speed (rpm) according to press release	30/294 at 5000 –	30/294 at 6550 ca. 30/294	41/402 at 5000 –	41,4/406 at 5500-6000 –
Compression ratio	9.3	9.3	11.1	9.3
Engine weight (kg)	152.7	157.6	272	183
Clutch	Single-disc clutch Fichtel & Sachs MF 240	Single-disc clutch Fichtel & Sachs MF 240	Dual-disc clutch Fichtel & Sachs MF 215/2	Dual-disc clutch Fichtel & Sachs MF 215/2
Transmission	ZF 5-speed 5 DS-25/1	ZF 5-speed 5 DS-25/1	ZF 5-speed 5 DS-25/1	ZF 5-speed 5 DS-25/1
Gear ratios I./II./III./IV./V./R	2.42/1.47/1.09/0.958/0.846/3.75	2.58/1.61/1.21/1.0/0.846/2.86	n. d.	2.58/1.61/1.21/1.0/0.846/2.86
Final-drive ratio	4.22	3.77	n. d.	3.77
Overall ratio in 5th gear	3.57	3.19	n. d.	3.19
Rims (street tires)	6 ½ J x 14 H 2	7 ½ J x 14 H 2	7 ½ J x 15 H 2	7 ½ J x 14 H 2
Rims front/rear (racing tires)	7 J x 15 H 2 / 9 J x 15 H 2	10 K x 15 H 2 / 13 K x 15 H 2	10 K x 15 H 2 / 13 K x 15 H 2	10 K x 15 H 2 / 13 K x 15 H 2
Tires (street tires)	Fulda 195 VR 14	Michelin X 205 VR 14	Michelin XWX 205/70 VR 15	Michelin X 205 VR 14
Tires front/rear (racing tires)	Dunlop Racing 4.75/10.00-15// 5.75/12.00-15	Dunlop Racing 4.50/11.60-15// 5.50/13.60-15	Dunlop Racing 4.50/11.60-15// 5.50/13.60-15	Dunlop Racing 4.50/11.60-15// 5.50/13.60-15
Tank capacity (l)	116	116	116	116
Top speed (km/h) according to press release	238 –	263 ca. 260	n. d. –	299 –
Acceleration 0-100 km/h (s) according to press release	5.2 –	5.5 ca. 5	n. d. –	5.3 –
Fuel consumption (l/100 km)	approx. 33	37.7–38.2	46.7	26.9 (Car 22, M 950/4)
Wheelbase (mm)	2500	2620	2620	2620
Track width front/rear (mm) with street tires	1380/1370	1380/1390	1380/1390	1380/1390
Track width front/rear (mm) with racing tires	n. d.	1440/1390	1440/1390	1440/1390
Length (mm)	3970	4250	4250	4350
Width (mm)	1775	1820	1820	1820
Height (mm)	1150	1125	1125	1120
Empty weight (kg)	n. d.	n. d.	n. d.	n. d.
Kerb weight (kg) *without tools, with street tires and spare wheel	1048	Car 22: 1218* Car 23: 1217* Car 24: 1200*	1411	1217*

n. d.: Data not documented; – : Information not relevant/not available

Variant	C 111-II	C 111-II	C 111-II	C 111-II
Year	1970	1970	1975	1975
Car	Cars 31, 33, 34	Car 35	Car 36	Car 37
Engine	four-rotor Wankel	V8 gas	four-rotor Wankel	5-cylinder turbodiesel
Engine model	M 950/4	M 116 E 35	M 950/4	OM 617 A
Fuel type	Premium gas	Premium gas	Premium gas	Diesel
Displacement (cc)	4800 (displacement equivalent)	3499	4800 (displacement equivalent)	2999
Output (hp/kW) at engine speed (rpm) according to press release	365 at 6500 approx. 350/257 at 7000	n. d. –	n. d. –	191/141 at 4200 –
Torque (mkg/Nm) at engine speed (rpm) according to press release	41.4/406 at 5500-6000 approx. 40/392 at 4000-5500	n. d. –	n. d. –	n. d. –
Compression ratio	9.3	n. d.	9.3	17.5
Engine weight (kg)	217 (construction stage III: 230)	273	n. d.	244
Clutch	Dual-disc clutch Fichtel & Sachs MF 215/2	Dual-disc clutch Fichtel & Sachs MF 215/2	Dual-disc clutch Fichtel & Sachs MF 215/2	Dual-disc clutch Fichtel & Sachs MF 215/2
Transmission	ZF 5-speed 5 DS-25/1	ZF 5-speed 5 DS-25/1	ZF 5-speed 5 DS-25/1	ZF 5-speed 5 DS-25/1
Gear ratios I./II./III./IV./V./R	2.857/1.72/1.21/0.92/0.705/2.86	2.857/1.72/1.21/0.92/0.705/2.86	2.857/1.72/1.21/0.92/0.705/2.86	2.857/1.72/1.21/0.92/0.705/2.86
Final-drive ratio	4.22	4.22	4.22	3.56
Overall ratio in 5th gear	2.975	2.975	2.975	2.51
Rims (street tires)	7 ½ J x 14 H 2	7 ½ J x 14 H 2	7 ½ J x 15 H 2	7 ½ J x 14 H 2
Rims front/rear (racing tires)	10 K x 15 H 2 / 13 K x 15 H 2	10 K x 15 H 2 / 13 K x 15 H 2	10 K x 15 H 2 / 13 K x 15 H 2	10 K x 15 H 2 / 13 K x 15 H 2
Tires (street tires)	Michelin X 205 VR 14	Michelin X 205 VR 14	Michelin XWX 205/70 VR 15	Michelin X 205 VR 14
Tires front/rear (racing tires)	Dunlop Racing 4.50/11.60-15// 5.50/13.60-15	Dunlop Racing 4.50/11.60-15// 5.50/13.60-15	Dunlop Racing 4.50/11.60-15// 5.50/13.60-15	Dunlop Racing 4.50/11.60-15// 5.50/13.60-15
Tank capacity (l)	116	116 (with rear tanks 70)	100	100
Top speed (km/h) according to press release	n. d. approx. 300	n. d. –	n. d. –	227 –
Acceleration 0-100 km/h (s) according to press release	n. d. approx. 4.8	n. d. –	n. d. –	n. d. –
Fuel consumption (l/100 km)	n. d.	n. d.	n. d.	n. d.
Wheelbase (mm)	2620	2620	2620	2620
Track width front/rear (mm) with street tires	1410/1405	1410/1405	1410/1405	1410/1405
Track width front/rear (mm) with racing tires	1445/1390	1445/1390	1445/1390	1445/1390
Length (mm)	4440	4440	4440	4440
Width (mm)	1825	1825	1825	1825
Height (mm)	1120	1120	1120	1120
Empty weight (kg)	n. d.	n. d.	n. d.	n. d.
Kerb weight (kg)	Car 31: 1303 (with light-alloy wheels) Car 34: 1424 (with automatic transmission)	n. d.	1316	n. d.

n. d.: Data not documented; – : Information not relevant/not available

Variant	C 111-II Diesel	C 111-III	C 111-IV	C 111-V
Year	1976	1978	1979	1980
Car	Car 31	Cars 41, 42	Car 41	(Planning status)
Engine	5-cylinder turbodiesel	5-cylinder turbodiesel	V8 gas with biturbo charging	V8 gas with biturbo charging
Engine model	OM 617 A	OM 617 A	M 117 E 48	M 117
Fuel type	Diesel	Diesel	Premium gas	Methanol
Displacement (cc)	2999	2999	4820	n. d.
Output (hp/kW) at engine speed (rpm) according to press release	196/144 at 4500 ca. 190/140	233-234/171-172 at 4600 230/170 at 4400-4600	503/370 at 6000 500/368	800/588 –
Torque (mkg/Nm) at engine speed (rpm) according to press release	38/373 at 3600 38/373 at 3600	41-42/402-412 at 3600 41/402 at 3600	61/600 at 5100-5600 –	n. d. –
Compression ratio	17.5	17.5	6.0	n. d.
Engine weight (kg)	244	244	240	n. d.
Clutch	Dual-disc clutch Fichtel & Sachs MF 215/2	Dual-disc clutch Fichtel & Sachs MF 215/2	Dual-disc clutch Fichtel & Sachs MF 215/2 or triple-disc clutch Fichtel & Sachs MFX 184	Triple-disc clutch Fichtel & Sachs
Transmission	ZF 5-speed 5 DS-25/1	ZF 5-speed 5 DS-25/2	ZF 5-speed 5 DS-25/2	Getrag 5-speed
Gear ratios I./II./III./IV./V./R	2.857/1.72/1.21/0.92/0.705/2.86	2.857/1.72/1.21/0.846/0.643	n. d.	2.33/1.675/1.343/1.146/1.0
Final-drive ratio	3.07	2.58	n. d.	2,18
Overall ratio in 5th gear	2.17	1.65	1.82	2.18
Rims (street tires)	8 J x 15 H 2	–	–	–
Rims front/rear (racing tires)	–	8 J x 15 H 2 / 9 ½ J x 15 H 2	8 J x 15 H 2 / 9 ½ J x 15 H 2	n. d.
Tires (street tires)	Michelin XWX 215/70 VR 15	–	–	–
Tires front/rear (racing tires)	–	Dunlop Racing 230/600-15	Michelin 20/63-15 X// 23/67-15 X	n. d.
Tank capacity (l)	116	140	60	n. d.
Top speed (km/h) according to press release	260 > 250	327.3 –	404.4 > 400	450 –
Acceleration 0-100 km/h (s) according to press release	n. d. 6.5	n. d. –	n. d. –	n. d. –
Fuel consumption (l/100 km)	19.68	15,98	n. d.	–
Wheelbase (mm)	2620	2720	2720	2840
Track width front/rear (mm) with street tires	1410/1405	–	–	–
Track width front/rear (mm) with racing tires	–	1260/1320	1260/1320	1300/1270
Length (mm)	4440	5380	6200	n. d.
Width (mm)	1825	1715	1715	n. d.
Height (mm)	1120	1045	1045	n. d.
Empty weight (kg)	1106	1284	1393	n. d.
Kerb weight (kg)	1247 (tanks full, with spare parts)	1531 (tanks full, with spare parts and driver)	1484 (with 20 l in left-hand tank, with driver)	1150

n. d.: Data not documented; – : Information not relevant/not available

Weight by Construction Groups

Construction group	Weight (kg) Car 1		Weight (kg) Cars 22-26		Weight (kg) Cars 31-35	
Engine complete	152.7		157.6 ... 183.0	[12]	217.0	[17]
Clutch	15.4	[1]	15.4		15.0	
Transmission	58.6		58.6		65.3	[18]
Pedal system	4.1	[2]	5.0		3.5	
Control	1.1		1.0		1.5	
Front axle	69.8	[3]	70.0		86.0	
Rear axle	85.6	[4]	57.2		67.5	
Wheels and tires	88.2	[5]	110.0 ... 137.4	[13]	127.0	[19]
Brake system	7.3	[6]	8.5		43.2	
Steering and gear shift	23.7	[7]	20.5		26.2	
Fuel system	14.4		19.5		21.0	
Exhaust system	35.3		38.2 ... 52.4	[14]	27.0	[20]
Radiator	20.3	[8]	23.0		36.0	[21]
Electrical equipment	39.8		40.2		41.5	
Tools, first aid kit, and fire extinguisher					15.0	
Floor system	143.0	[9]	154.5 ... 167.3	[15]		
Fluids	108.0	[10]	115.0		121.0	[22]
Chassis total					1042.0	
Body (and equipment)	115.0	[11]	ca. 240 ... 280	[16]	245.0	
Screws and bolts, connecting hoses, and small parts			ca. 29			
Car's kerb weight	990.0		1218 (Wagen 22) 1217 (Wagen 23) 1200 (Wagen 24) 1217 (Wagen 26)		1303.0	
Front axle load			549.0 ... 554.0		610.0	[23]
Rear axle load			647.0 ... 668.0		693.0	[24]

[1] With light-alloy bell housing and pressure plate approx. 3.9 kg lighter
[2] With intermediate plate made of light alloy approx. 1.4 kg lighter
[3] Estimated weight reduction with light-alloy lower wishbones and brake callipers 13 kg
[4] Light-alloy brake callipers approx. 2.6 kg lighter, double wishbone axle approx. 15-20 kg lighter
[5] 4 x 195 VR 14 on light-alloy wheels, spare wheel made of steel (weight reduction with 5 light-alloy wheels 6.0 kg). With 5 racing tires of the projected sizes 4.50/11.60-15 or 5.50/13.60-15 (tubeless) probably also approx. 88 kg
[6] Without brake booster approx. 6 kg less
[7] With wooden steering wheel approx. 1.2 kg lighter
[8] With plastic fan approx. 0.6 kg lighter
[9] Painted, with water pipes and seat rails, without windscreen. Aluminum version approx. 30 kg lighter
[10] With oil pan as per drawing approx. 2 kg more
[11] Hood, front end panel, wings, spare wheel well, seats, headlights (makeshift body). Final light-alloy body expected to be significantly lighter
[12] 3- or 4-rotor engine
[13] Street or racing tires
[14] Various versions
[15] Various sheet thicknesses
[16] Various versions
[17] Construction stage III: 230 kg; M 117: 272 kg
[18] ZF transmission with aluminum cover: 59.8 kg; automatic transmission with clutch: 102.7 kg
[19] Rear wheel with racing tires 19 kg, front wheel with racing tires 16 kg, light-alloy wheel 20 kg, steel wheel 25 kg
[20] M 117: 32 kg
[21] Aluminum radiator with oil cooler/fan: 16.5 kg, brass radiator with oil cooler/fan: 24.5 kg
[22] Fuel 116 liters, engine oil 10 liters, transmission oil 13 liters, brake fluid 0.4 liters, coolant 16.5 liters
[23] Unsprung masses per wheel 49.9 kg
[24] Unsprung masses per wheel 39.8 kg

Please note: Remarks 1 to 11 refer to the savings potentials expected in April 1969 compared to car 1

Sources and Further Reading

Holdings of the Mercedes-Benz Classic Archives and Archive Library

Personal communications from

Dipl.-Ing. Rüdiger Faul (July and August 2021, January 2023)
Prof. Stefan Heiliger (May 2020)
Dipl.-Ing. Arno Jambor (January to July 2023)
Dipl.-Ing. Joachim Kaden (May 2020 and July 2021)
Karl Lemberger, Manfred Dierks, Hans-Peter Hiller, Rolf Kreß, and **Robert Münzmay** (May 2020)
Prof. Klaus Matthias (July 2019 to October 2020, March 2021)
Prof. Peter Pfeiffer (September 2020, August 2021, January and June 2023)
Dr.-Ing. h. c. Bruno Sacco (September and November 2019)
Gert Straub (March 2020, March and July 2021)
Steffen Köhl and Stefan Lamm (March 2023)
Hartmut Sinkwitz and Belinda Günther (March 2023)
Benjamin Kuhn (March 2023)

Books

Ansdale, Richard F. *The Wankel RC Engine: Design and Performance.* London, 1970.
Becker, Sascha, Fried Meysen, Kurt Möser, and Marcus Popplow. *Felix Wankel: Leben und Werk in Bildern.* Gudensberg, Germany, 2002.
Bensinger, Wolf-Dieter. *Rotationskolben – Verbrennungsmotoren.* Berlin, Heidelberg, and New York, 1973.
Frère, Paul, and Julius Weitmann. *Mercedes-Benz C 111: Experimental Cars.* Lausanne, Switzerland, 1981.
Hack, Gert. *Alles über Diesel-Autos. Diesel-Personenwagen – Entwicklung, Technik, Typologie.* Stuttgart, Germany, 1981.
Hildebrandt, Roland. "Gescheiterte Innovation? – Der Wankelmotor und die Erfinderpersönlichkeit Felix Wankel aus technik- und wirtschaftsgeschichtlicher Sicht." Master's thesis, Martin Luther University Halle-Wittenberg, Halle/Saale, Germany, 2006.
Klauke, Dieter. *Der Wankelmotor – da war doch mal was?* Norderstedt, Germany, 2019.
Knapp, Ulrich Christoph. *Wankel auf dem Prüfstand: Ursprung, Entwicklung und Niedergang eines innovativen Motorenkonzeptes Cottbuser Studien zur Geschichte von Technik, Arbeit und Umwelt*; Vol. 28. Münster, Germany, 2006.
Korp, Dieter. *Protokoll einer Erfindung: Der Wankelmotor.* Stuttgart, Germany, 1975.
Kurze, Peter. *Wankel im Blick. Paul Botzenhardt fotografiert NSU Spider – Ro 80 – Mercedes C 111.* Bremen, Germany, 2003.
Ludvigsen, Karl E. *Mercedes-Benz Renn- und Sportwagen: Vom Blitzen-Benz zum McLaren-Mercedes; Die Geschichte der Silberpfeile.* Stuttgart, Germany, 1999.
Möser, Kurt. *Der Wankelmotor – Faszination einer Erfindung. Begleitheft zur Sonderausstellung 23.6.1995 – 1.10.1995.* Mannheim, Germany, 1995.
Naumann, Fritz. *Blick aus der Grube: Erinnerungen eines Automobilingenieurs.* 2nd ed. Schönaich, Germany, 2001.
Popplow, Marcus. *Motor ohne Lobby? Medienereignis Wankelmotor 1959–1989.* Technik + Arbeit 11. Schriften des TECHNOSEUM Landesmuseum für Technik und Arbeit in Mannheim. Ubstadt-Weiher, Germany, 2003.
Popplow, Marcus. *Felix Wankel: Mehr als ein Erfinderleben.* Erfurt, Germany, 2011.
Schultz, Horst. *Das große Wankelbuch:. Chronologie einer Entwicklung.* Altlußheim, Germany, 2022.
Schulz, Eberhard. *Autobiographie: Von Schulz zu Isdera.* Wendhausen, Germany, 2021.
Vieweg, Christof. *Holy Halls: The Secret Car Collection of Mercedes-Benz.* Bielefeld, Germany, 2019.

Manuscripts

Götz, Hans. "From the aerodynamic development of the experimental vehicles C 111 I-IV." Manuscript of the lecture at the 4th Colloquium on Industrial Aerodynamics, Aachen, Germany, June 18, 1980.
Jundt, Hartmut, and Wolfgang Kalbhenn. "Einblicke in die Kreiskolben-Entwicklung bei Daimler-Benz." Unpublished manuscript, Rottweil/Breuberg, Germany, 2018.
Naumann, Fritz. "Historie zum Mercedes-Benz C 111." Unpublished manuscript, Stammham, Germany, 2009.

Magazine articles

Bensinger, Wolf-Dieter. "Der heutige Entwicklungsstand des Wankelmotors." *Motortechnische Zeitschrift* 31, no. 1 (1970): 1–7.

Eisele, Erwin, Hermann Hiereth, and Gert Withalm. "Der Motor des Mercedes-Benz-Rekordfahrzeugs C 111/IV." *Motortechnische Zeitschrift* 41, no. 2 (1980): 49–50.

Engelen, Günter, and Jürgen Zerha. "Wankel-Mut: Report mit zwei Mercedes-Benz C 111 in Hockenheim." *Motor Klassik* 6, no. 9 (1989): 9–17.

Enke, Kurt, and Erwin Löffler. "Der Versuchswagen C 111 von Daimler-Benz." *Automobiltechnische Zeitschrift* 72, no. 3 (1970): 200–206.

Groth, Peter. "Alfred Zimmer – Pionier der FEM-Anwendung." *Automobiltechnische Zeitschrift* 102, no. 5 (2000): 338–341.

Koch, Michl, Malte Jürgens, and Jürgen Zerha. "Angriff über den Flügel: Der C 111 und sein Nachfolger." *sport auto* 18, no. 9 (1986): 5–15.

Liebold, Hans, Manfred Fortnagel, Hans Götz, and Theodor Reinhard. "Aus der Entwicklung des C 111 III." *Automobil-Industrie* 25, no. 2 (1979): 29–35.

Ludvigsen, Karl E. "The Development of the C 111: Mercedes' Brilliant New Wankel-Engined Sports Car." *Automobile Quarterly* 8, no. 3 (1970): 326–335.

Ludvigsen, Karl E. "C 111 Impressions." *Automobile Quarterly* 8, no. 3 (1970): 336–339.

Matthias, Klaus. "Aus der Entwicklung des C 111 III: Experimentierfahrzeug mit tragender Bodengruppe in Kernverbund-Bauweise aus Chemiewerkstoffen." *mobiles* 8, no. 8 (1982): 70–85.

Matthias, Klaus. "Experimentierfahrzeug mit tragender Bodengruppe in Kernverbund-Bauweise aus Chemiewerkstoffen." *Automobiltechnische Zeitschrift* 85, no. 3 (1983): 107–115.

Scherenberg, Hans. "Abgasturboaufladung für Personenwagen-Dieselmotoren." *Automobiltechnische Zeitschrift* 79, no. 11 (1977): 479–486.

Web specials and video

mb4.me/MBVision111

Web special mercedes-benz.com: Vision One Eleven, June 2023

sensualpurity.com/design5

Web special Mercedes-Benz Design: Vision One Eleven, June 2023

mb4.me/C111Book

Video: Driving scenes of the Vision One-Eleven on the test track in Immendingen, June 2023

The publisher, editor, and authors do not guarantee the permanent availability of the linked material.